NEW OXFORD HISTORY OF MUSIC

VOLUME III

THE VOLUMES OF THE
NEW OXFORD HISTORY OF MUSIC

FLEMISH (?) INSTRUMENTALISTS OF THE LATER FIFTEENTH CENTURY

The standing figures are playing (left to right) pipe (*galoubet*) and tabor, triangle, shawm (?), buzine, harp, two lutes, three shawms, psaltery, and alto or tenor soft shawm; the seated figure in the right foreground is playing a portative organ. The manuscript from which this picture is taken is Spanish, but the illustrations are by Flemish artists

(British Museum Add. 18851, fo. 184v)

ARS NOVA
AND THE
RENAISSANCE
1300–1540

EDITED BY

DOM ANSELM HUGHES

AND

GERALD ABRAHAM

LONDON
OXFORD UNIVERSITY PRESS
NEW YORK   TORONTO

Oxford University Press, Amen House, London E.C.4

GLASGOW NEW YORK TORONTO MELBOURNE WELLINGTON
BOMBAY CALCUTTA MADRAS KARACHI LAHORE DACCA
CAPE TOWN SALISBURY NAIROBI IBADAN ACCRA
KUALA LUMPUR HONG KONG

———

© *Oxford University Press 1960*

First published 1960
Reprinted 1964

PRINTED IN GREAT BRITAIN

GENERAL INTRODUCTION

THE present work is designed to replace the *Oxford History of Music*, first published in six volumes under the general editorship of Sir Henry Hadow between 1901 and 1905. Five authors contributed to that ambitious publication—the first of its kind to appear in English. The first two volumes, dealing with the Middle Ages and the sixteenth century, were the work of H. E. Wooldridge. In the third Sir Hubert Parry examined the music of the seventeenth century. The fourth, by J. A. Fuller-Maitland, was devoted to the age of Bach and Handel; the fifth, by Hadow himself, to the period bounded by C. P. E. Bach and Schubert. In the final volume Edward Dannreuther discussed the Romantic period, with which, in the editor's words, it was 'thought advisable to stop'. The importance of the work—particularly of the first two volumes—was widely recognized, and it became an indispensable part of a musician's library. The scheme was further extended in the new edition issued under the editorship of Sir Percy Buck between 1929 and 1938. An introductory volume, the work of several hands, was designed to supplement the story of music in the ancient world and the Middle Ages. New material, including two complete chapters, was added to volumes i and ii, while the third volume was reissued with minor corrections and a number of supplementary notes by Edward J. Dent. The history was also brought nearer to the twentieth century by the addition of a seventh volume, by H. C. Colles, entitled *Symphony and Drama, 1850–1900*.

Revision of an historical work is always difficult. It it is to be fully effective, it may well involve changes so comprehensive that very little of the original remains. Such radical revision was not the purpose of the second edition of the *Oxford History of Music*. To have attempted it in a third edition would have been impossible. During the first half of the present century an enormous amount of detailed work has been done on every period covered by the original volumes. New materials have been discovered, new relationships revealed, new interpretations made possible. Perhaps the most valuable achievement has been the publication in reliable modern editions of a mass of music which was previously available only in manuscript or in rare printed copies. These developments have immeasurably increased the historian's opportunities, but they have also added heavily to his responsibilities. To attempt a detailed survey of the whole history of music is no longer within the power of a single writer. It may even be doubted whether the burden can be adequately shouldered by a team of five.

The *New Oxford History of Music* is therefore not a revision of the older work, nor is it the product of a small group of writers. It has been planned as an entirely new survey of music from the earliest times down to comparatively recent years, including not only the achievements of the Western world but also the contributions made by eastern civilizations and primitive societies. The examination of this immense field is the work of a large number of contributors, English and foreign. The attempt has been made to achieve uniformity without any loss of individuality. If this attempt has been successful, the result is due largely to the patience and co-operation shown by the contributors themselves. Overlapping has to some extent been avoided by the use of frequent cross-references; but we have not thought it proper to prevent different authors from expressing different views about the same subject, where it could legitimately be regarded as falling into more than one category.

The scope of the work is sufficiently indicated by the titles of the several volumes. Our object throughout has been to present music not as an isolated phenomenon or the work of a few outstanding composers but as an art developing in constant association with every form of human culture and activity. The biographies of individuals are therefore merely incidental to the main plan of the history, and those who want detailed information of this kind must seek it elsewhere. No hard and fast system of division into chapters has been attempted. The treatment is sometimes by forms, sometimes by periods, sometimes also by countries, according to the importance which one element or another may assume. The division into volumes has to some extent been determined by practical considerations; but pains have been taken to ensure that the breaks occur at points which are logically and historically justifiable. The result may be that the work of a single composer who lived to a ripe age is divided between two volumes. The later operas of Monteverdi, for example, belong to the history of Venetian opera and hence find their natural place in volume v, not with the discussion of his earlier operas to be found in volume iv. On the other hand, we have not insisted on a rigid chronological division where the result would be illogical or confusing. If a subject finds its natural conclusion some ten years after the date assigned for the end of a period, it is obviously preferable to complete it within the limits of one volume rather than to allow it to overflow into a second. An exception to the general scheme of continuous chronology is to be found in volumes v and vi, which deal with different aspects of the same period and so are complementary to each other.

The history as a whole is intended to be useful to the professed student of music, for whom the documentation of sources and the bibliographies are particularly designed. But the growing interest in the music of all periods shown by music-lovers in general has encouraged us to bear their interests also in mind. It is inevitable that a work of this kind should employ a large number of technical terms and deal with highly specialized matters. We have, however, tried to ensure that the technical terms are intelligible to the ordinary reader and that what is specialized is not necessarily wrapped in obscurity. Finally, since music must be heard to be fully appreciated, we have given references throughout to the records issued by His Master's Voice (R. C. A. Victor) under the general title *The History of Music in Sound*. These records are collected in a series of albums which correspond to the volumes of the present work, and have been designed to be used with it.

J. A. WESTRUP
GERALD ABRAHAM
ANSELM HUGHES
EGON WELLESZ

CONTENTS

ILLUSTRATIONS

INTRODUCTION TO VOLUME III

THE title and scope of the third volume of the *New Oxford History of Music* enable us to bypass all barren controversy concerning the dividing line between the Middle Ages and the Renaissance. Despite the marked change of style initiated by Dunstable, Dufay, and their English and Burgundian colleagues, it would be a gross over-simplification to suggest that in music the Renaissance began during the second quarter of the fifteenth century. Historical development is a seamless web: ways of thought and technical devices make themselves unobtrusively apparent long before they become general and fashionable, and tend to linger on long afterwards. History abhors firmly drawn lines. In determining the arbitrary *terminus ad quem* of the present volume, it was actually found convenient to adopt different dates for different subjects—as early as 1520 or as late as 1540. Such limits unquestionably include that great flowering of the human spirit and intellect in Europe which we call the Renaissance, and the volume begins at the opening of the fourteenth century with an account of the typically medieval developments which are conveniently known—after Philippe de Vitry's treatise of *c.* 1325—as *ars nova*. Yet certain medieval forms and techniques and habits of thought persisted almost to the end of the period: and *ars nova*, though in some respects an end rather than a beginning, contains the germ of much that we regard as typical of the Renaissance. Ockeghem still employed the musical and poetical form of the thirteenth-century *rondeau*: the theoretical and mystical relationships between mathematics and music, so typical of medieval thought, still occupied Tinctoris in the late fifteenth century and reached their final decadent exaggeration in the mensuration canons of Josquin des Prez. On the other hand, Besseler[1] has rightly pointed out that *ars nova* is the first full manifestation of pure musical art, freed from the service of religion or poetry and constructed according to its own laws: and as the first of the Avignon Popes, John XXII, bitterly complained in his Bull 'Docta Sanctorum', words were now treated as mere pretexts for music.

This new attitude to music is reflected also by the writers of the fourteenth century, particularly Johannes de Grocheo,[2] with his un-

---

[1] *Die Musik des Mittelalters und der Renaissance* (Potsdam, 1931), p. 129.

[2] His treatise was published, with German translation, by Johannes Wolf in

precedented emphasis on practical music, and the anonymous author
of the didactic poem *Les Échecs amoureux*.[1] The influence of Aristo-
telian thought, the growth of empiricism, the need for 'imitation of
nature', make themselves felt in music as in the other arts and fields
of European thought. Giotto points the new way in painting, and the
musicians imitate nature most vividly in the *chaces* and *cacce* that are
the musical counterparts of characteristic pages of Chaucer and
Boccaccio.

> Et musique est une science
> Qui vuet qu'on rie et chant et dence,

wrote Machaut himself.

Yet Machaut himself was also, in a sense, the last of the trouvères, as
Oswald von Wolkenstein, two generations later, was the last of the
Minnesinger. The music of chivalry was dying but not dead, just as
chivalry itself may be said to have died in the century between Crécy
—where Machaut's old master John of Luxembourg, 'last of the
knights errant', fell—and Malory's *Morte d'Arthur*. It died beautifully
and picturesquely, nowhere more so than at the Burgundian Court
of which Binchois was the chief musical ornament and in Philip the
Good's last, futile, Crusading gesture, the *Vœu du Faisan* in 1454, for
which Dufay wrote music. The realities of chivalry were blown away
by cannon and gunpowder, and the knightly class was elbowed aside
by the rising wealthy bourgeoisie. The typical princes of the fifteenth
century were sometimes merchant princes like the Medici in Florence
and the rulers of the Venetian republic; and this coming ascendancy
of the middle classes is reflected in the emergence of a corpus of
recorded popular song quite as much as in the work of the Flemish
painters. Finally, the most powerful of all the agents of the 're-birth'
of learning and of its swift advance among the middle classes also
came to the help of music, at first tentatively in missals and theoretical
works, then with growing effect as *chansons* and *frottole*, Masses and
motets, began to pour from the Venetian press of Ottaviano de
Petrucci at the outset of the sixteenth century.

The growing autonomy of music is reflected even in that of the
Church. The medieval musician had gradually ceased to regard the
plainsong tenor as something sacred to be adorned with counterpoints: it had become a technical device, a mere basis for composition.
But the choice of secular *canti fermi* for cyclic Masses by Dufay and

Sammelbände der internationalen Musikgesellschaft, i (1899–1900), pp. 69–130; new
edition by E. F. Rohloff (Leipzig, 1943).
[1] Published by Hermann Abert in *Romanische Forschungen*, xv (1904), pp. 884–925.

his contemporaries is profoundly significant. At the same time pre-monitions of the Reformation were already making themselves heard in the Hussite songs of Bohemia.

One further point must be made: the picture of European music from 1300 to 1530 or thereabouts has to take in a wider scene. European musical culture was still at first centred in north-west France and Flanders, with important native schools in England and northern Italy. Political events helped to unify European music: the Avignon exile promoted Franco-Italian intercourse; and Agincourt brought the English Court musicians (and English euphony) to Paris and into contact with their Franco-Flemish colleagues whom, as we know, they immediately influenced. Another political event, the marriage of Mary, the heiress of Burgundy, to Maximilian of Austria (afterwards Emperor as Maximilian I) planted a chapel of Netherlanders at Innsbruck and brought Germany also, hitherto unremarkable for anything but *Minnesang*, into the Franco-Flemish sphere of musical influence. Towards the end of the period covered by the present volume, that influence dominated Europe from the Iberian peninsula to Poland.

The editors gratefully acknowledge the help of Professor Kurt von Fischer, Dr. F. Ll. Harrison, and Mr. Gilbert Reaney, who have read various chapters and suggested valuable emendations. The bibliography has been largely, though not solely, compiled by Dr. Harrison, the index by Miss Margaret Dean-Smith. The editors are responsible for the section on Italian lute music in Chapter XII. Chapter V has been translated by Mr. T. Evans, Chapter VIII by Mr. Norman Suckling, and Chapter X by Mr. Stanley Godman.

I

ARS NOVA IN FRANCE

By GILBERT REANEY

THE SOCIAL BACKGROUND

IN France the fourteenth century in many ways simply continued to develop tendencies already present in the thirteenth, whether in the political or the artistic field. Yet this continuation represented at the same time a decline, if only in the sense of a descent from a peak, in the arts. For the thirteenth century *was* a peak, a classic epoch of medieval music, art, sculpture, and architecture. The building of the great cathedrals, the production of the towering organa in three or four parts, the development of the motet as the principal form of polyphonic music—all these belong to the achievements of the thirteenth century. Yet the disintegration which becomes manifest in the fourteenth century already sets in in the thirteenth. Bourgeois criticism of upper-class morals, so evident in the later *Roman de Fauvel*, finds its way into the second half of the *Roman de la Rose*, and the secularization of the motet is no doubt evidence of the dissatisfaction with Church and Papacy which again finds full expression in *Fauvel*. This work exists in twelve manuscripts, one of which contains a large collection of musical interpolations, whose vitriolic texts link up very fittingly with the principal text of the *Roman*. The bitter satire of *Fauvel* is sufficient to show to what extent corruption was rife among both nobility and clergy at the very beginning of the fourteenth century, when the semi-exile of the Popes at Avignon (1305–78) had only just begun. Later came far worse things, the Hundred Years War (1337–1453), the Schism (1378–1417) when two Popes ruled, one at Avignon, the other at Rome, the débâcle of chivalric ideals under John II of France (1350–64); and these brought in their train famine, excessive taxation, and the ex-soldier banditry of the *Grandes Compagnies*. In spite of all this, art and music flourished, though often in *fin-de-siècle* forms which reveal an excessive preoccupation with detail. In art and architecture we find an interest in miniature work which manifests itself in skilful carving in wood, stone, ivory, gold, and silver. Gothic arches and columns become slender, and interest in the whole gives way to interest in the part. Even in music the same tendencies come to light, since we are presented with extensive melismas, brittle hockets, and exact reproductions of minute rhythmic details. The centre of music had shifted northwards from Paris, with the music of *Fauvel* to Picardy, with Philippe de Vitry and Guillaume de Machaut to Champagne. We have little information about the musicians of this period, with the exception of Vitry and Machaut, but such names as Thomas of Douai, Vauquier of Valenciennes, Garinus of Soissons, Guisard of Cambrai, and Reginald of Bayeux confirm that polyphonic music was moving out of Paris.[1] Jehannot de l'Escurel, who apparently died in 1303, seems to have been a Parisian, though his thirty-four extant works are with one exception monodies.[2] The exception is a three-part *rondeau*, evidently modelled after the works of Adam de la Hale in this form.[3] It is perhaps no coincidence that the period of what is known as *ars nova* begins about the time when the Popes moved to Avignon; it also happens that the death of Machaut exactly coincides with the start of the Papal schism. During the following period, dealt with in Chapter V, the artifices of Machaut's compositions were developed to an extreme which, to quote one of the very musicians who employed these extreme methods, 'would not have pleased Philippe [de Vitry] who is now dead'.[4]

THE NOTATION

Ars nova is the title of a musical treatise written by Philippe de Vitry about the year 1320 in Paris.[5] It is not the only sign of a conscious feeling that new things are in the air, since both the progressive theorist Johannes de Muris and the conservative Jacobus de Liège speak of a new art and modern performers and composers. It is significant that all the new activity was to be seen around the years 1320–30, and probably earlier since the *Roman de Fauvel*, which was concluded in 1316, contains signs of it. The treatise *Ars novae musicae*

[1] These names occur in the important motets 'Musicalis scientia—Scientie laudabili' and 'Apollinis—Zodiacum'. Cf. Richard H. Hoppin, 'Notes biographiques sur quelques musiciens du XIVe siècle', *Compte-rendu du Colloque International d'Ars Nova, Liège, 1955* (1959).
[2] Printed in Friedrich Gennrich, *Rondeaux, Virelais und Balladen*, i (Dresden, 1921), pp. 307–72.
[3] Cf. Jacques Chailley, *Adam de la Halle: Rondeaux* (Paris, 1942). L'Escurel's three-part *rondeau* and Adam's 'Tant con je vivrai' are recorded in *The History of Music in Sound* (H.M.V.), iii.
[4] Cf. Gilbert Reaney, 'The Manuscript Chantilly, Musée Condé 1047', *Musica Disciplina*, viii (1954), p. 70.
[5] Text, ed. Gilbert Reaney, André Gilles, and Jean Maillard, in Musica Disciplina, x (1956), p. 13; translation, ibid. xi (1957), p. 12.

of de Muris is dated 1319,[1] the Papal Bull which condemns the members of the new school 1324–5,[2] and the treatise of Jacobus c. 1330.[3] The use of the term *ars nova* to define a period is therefore not unjustified, though the fact that the new art is less novel than it appeared in 1320 makes one doubtful on this point. One cannot indeed deny the ripe wisdom of Jacobus, when he says that the art of Franco was more perfect than that of the moderns, though he is playing on the word perfection a little too much. He says:

Fundatur autem ars musicae mensurabilis in perfectione, ut dicunt non modo veteres, sed moderni; . . . sic autem est de arte antiqua, de arte magistri Franconis. Ars enim nova, sicut visum est, multiplicibus et variis utitur imperfectionibus in notulis, in modis, in mensuris, quasi ubique imperfectio se ingerit (Coussemaker, *Scriptorum*, ii, p. 427*b*).

(The art of measured music is founded on perfection, as not only the ancients but also the moderns declare; and such is the *ars antiqua*, the art of Master Franco. For the new art, as we have seen, makes use of many and varied imperfections in notes, modes, measures, in fact almost everywhere.)

In condemning the moderns Jacobus tells us quite a lot about their methods. The main aim seems to have been subtlety, achieved by greater variety of notes and notational usage. The imperfect measures, i.e. duple rhythms, as against the normal perfect or triple rhythms, were evidently new and extremely popular, whether applied to the shortest or the longest notes. Imperfection was undoubtedly one of the watchwords of the new school, for it was applied in the sense of reducing the value of a preceding note in triple rhythm as well as in that of duple rhythm.[4] It was normal for a breve to imperfect a long in the thirteenth century, e.g. perfect long ▌ = ♩ ., long imperfected by breve ▌ ▪ = ♩ ♩. In this case the larger value was imperfected by the next smaller one, but the *ars nova* introduced the system of imperfection by more remote values, e.g. the imperfection of the long by the semibreve and the breve by the minim. Guillaume de Machaut even put a minim in front as well as one behind the breve, e.g. ♦▪♦ = ♪♩♩♪, as Ugolino of Orvieto still laments in the mid-fifteenth

---

[1] This work is printed, though under various titles, in Gerbert, *Scriptores ecclesiastici de musica* (St. Blaise, 1784), iii, pp. 312–15, 256–7 (after 312*b*, second line from bottom), 292–301. Extracts in Oliver Strunk, *Source Readings in Music History* (London, 1952), pp. 172–9.

[2] Latin text and translation in *Oxford History of Music*, i (2nd ed., Oxford, 1929), pp. 294 ff.

[3] Coussemaker, *Scriptorum de musica medii aevi nova series*, ii (Paris, 1867), pp. 185 ff. Complete edition in eight volumes by Roger Bragard, *Corpus scriptorum de musica*, iii.

[4] Coussemaker, op. cit. ii, p. 428*b*.

century.[1] Jacobus also dislikes the coupling together of very long notes in ligatures, necessitated by the new isorhythmic motet-tenors.[2]

All these points are very interesting, but we are dependent on the two leaders of the *ars nova* movement, Philippe de Vitry and Johannes de Muris, for a succinct statement of the principal innovations. These seem to be restricted to the codification of the four prolations and the introduction of the minim ↓ as a note-form. Johannes de Muris said the same rules must apply in practice to all note-forms, so that either two or three notes of the smaller species should equal one of the next larger species, according to whether duple or triple rhythm is in use.[3] The four prolations were thus

(a)

(b)

(c)

(d)

The word 'prolation' strictly refers only to the relation of minim to semibreve, the relation of semibreve to breve being known as 'time'. The old relation of breve to long of course retained the name 'mode', though the long was rarely used outside the tenors of isorhythmic motets. The semibreve now became the unit by which music was measured, the long of *c.* 1200 being approximately equal to the semibreve *c.* 1320. Both can in fact be accurately transcribed by the modern dotted crotchet, even though the long of the Notre Dame School is a little slower than the semibreve of Johannes de Muris and Philippe de Vitry. Between 1320 and 1420 there was only a slight slowing-down in the speed of the measure, which equals M.M. 60–70. It is interesting to note how widespread is the use of triple prolation in the fourteenth-century motet, from the *Roman de Fauvel* to the MS. Chantilly 1047. And it is the trochaic form of triple prolation,

[1] U. Kornmüller, 'Musiklehre des Ugolino von Orvieto', *Kirchenmusikalisches Jahrbuch*, xx (1895), p. 33.

[2] Coussemaker, op. cit., ii, p. 428*b*.

[3] Gerbert, op. cit., iii, pp. 293*a*–295*b*. English translation in Strunk, *Source Readings in Music History*, pp. 174–8.

popularized by Philippe de Vitry, which predominates. In the *ballades*, *rondeaux*, and *virelais*, however, duple prolation is very common, though rare in combination with duple time.

THE ROMAN DE FAUVEL

The music in the *Roman de Fauvel*[1] reveals the transition between the *ars antiqua* and the *ars nova* very clearly. It is an anthology of music ranging from 1189 to 1316, for although most of the three-part motets are new, the collection of conductus for instance includes many works composed by the Notre Dame school. The *lais* again seem to be new in many cases, though it is not easy to distinguish between old and new works in this type of piece. The *lai* at all events seems to have been the oldest musical form cultivated by Guillaume de Machaut. A collection like that to be found in the *Roman de Fauvel* is unique, though musical interpolations in the form of secular songs had been common since the *Roman de Guillaume de Dole*.[2] Never before or since, however, has there been an interpolation on such a scale as *Fauvel*, which contains not only a small selection of secular songs but also *lais*, motets, conductus, and many forms of Gregorian chant: some 160 pieces in all. The manuscript which contains these works also contains the previously mentioned *ballades*, *rondeaux*, and *refrains* of Jehannot de l'Escurel. These thirty-four pieces are obviously only part of a collection, since they stop at the letter G; but they are very closely paralleled by the fourteen similar works interpolated in the *Roman de Fauvel* itself.[3] The interpolator of the music seems to have been one Chaillou de Pesstain,[4] and if he was not a composer in the modern sense of the word, he certainly seems to have cleverly adapted many of the pieces both musically and textually. He was not the author of the *Roman*, since this was written by Gervais du Bus, whose name is given in an anagram.[5] Moreover, it would appear that Philippe de Vitry had a hand in the composition of certain pieces, at least in the three motets which form a supplement to the collection. The attribution is, however, by no means certain, and depends on the fact that two of the three works are quoted by Vitry in his treatise *Ars nova*, while stylistically all three are very like his known works. They

---

[1] Paris, Bibl. Nat., fr. 146. Facsimile of the music in Pierre Aubry, *Le Roman de Fauvel* (Paris, 1907); transcription of the polyphonic pieces in Leo Schrade, *Polyphonic Music of the Fourteenth Century*, i (Monaco, 1956). Cf. vol. II, pp. 246, 380, 391–2.
[2] Cf. vol. II, p. 243.
[3] Transcriptions in Gennrich, op. cit., i, pp. 307–72.
[4] A. Långfors, *Le Roman de Fauvel* (Paris, 1914–19), pp. lxxi–lxxii.
[5] Ibid., pp. 137–8.

are indeed the first clearly defined examples of isorhythm,[1] and one of them uses red notes, an innovation attributed to Vitry. The other Fauvel piece which uses red notes, 'Quomodo cantabimus—Thalamus', might just as well be without them, since they seem to serve no real purpose.[2]

Fortunately we can date the *Roman de Fauvel* with accuracy: part I, 1310, part II, 1314, and the interpolations 1316. The three-voice motets are undoubtedly the most up-to-date works, but the monodic secular songs are not far behind. Since the last three motets could hardly be earlier than 1316, and as they incorporate the feature of isorhythm in its typical *ars nova* form, we may perhaps date the *ars nova* period from 1316. If, however, we consider the use of the minim as a characteristic of the notation of the period, and the minim tails were certainly added a little later than 1316 in *Fauvel*, we shall doubtless date the *ars nova* from *c.* 1320, the approximate date of Vitry's treatise. Marchettus of Padua, in his *Pomerium* of 1318,[3] still considers the French notation without the distinctive note-shape of the minim.[4] His authority is most valuable in permitting us to decide how to transcribe the groups of semibreves without tails which we find in most of the *Fauvel* motets *à* 3. Undoubtedly at the time of Chaillou de Pesstain this would be done in the trochaic manner typical of the *ars nova* motet. Thus ♦ ♦ ♦ (= *ars nova* ♦ ♦ ♩) = ♩. ♩ ♪; ♦ ♦ ♦ ♦ (= *ars nova* ♦ ♩ ♦ ♩) = ♩ ♩ ♩ ♪; ♦ ♦ ♦ ♦ ♦ (= *ars nova* ♩ ♩ ♩ ♦ ♩) = ♫♫ ♩ ♪.

PHILIPPE DE VITRY

This renowned poet, musician, statesman, and ecclesiastic was born on 31 October 1291, according to his own words, though to which Vitry he belonged—there are six of them in Champagne alone —is uncertain. He was a friend of Petrarch, and Bishop of Meaux from 1351 till his death in 1361. It must be assumed that his life as an officer of the Royal Household, a position he held from the time of Charles the Handsome (1322–8) till 1351, left him time to write and compose, though some of his works, as we have noted, seem to date from as early as 1316, when he was undoubtedly already in minor

[1] Cf. vol. II, pp. 391–2.
[2] For a new attempt to decide what extant compositions can be attributed to de Vitry, see Schrade, 'Philippe de Vitry: Some New Discoveries', *Musical Quarterly*, xlii (1956), p. 330, and the separately printed commentary to his *Polyphonic Music*, i, p. 30.
[3] Strunk, 'Intorno a Marchetto da Padova', *Rassegna musicale*, xx (1950), p. 314.
[4] Gerbert, op. cit., iii, pp. 175*b*–178*b*. Translation in Strunk, *Source Readings in Music History*, pp. 167 ff.

orders.[1] Only one treatise attributed to him in the sources seems to be really his: the *Ars nova*. The *Ars contrapunctus*,[2] *Ars perfecta*,[3] and *Liber musicalium*[4] are all later works based on his principles, and sometimes merely on his authority. A glance at the several chapters of the concise but forthright treatise *Ars nova* reveals the most important features of the new doctrines: (*a*) the codification of the different species of measure (the four prolations), (*b*) the use of mensuration signs, (*c*) the introduction of red coloration (dealt with in special detail). The brief mentions of the semiminim ♪[5] must be considered purely theoretical at this period, since this note-form does not appear in his motets, as the authors of the *Quatuor principalia musicae* point out.[6] The anonymous author of a treatise of second rhetoric (rules of fourteenth-century versification and poetic style) was not far wrong when he said that Vitry 'trouva la manière des notes, les quatre prolations, les notes rouges et la nouveleté des proportions'.[7] If de Vitry did introduce the use of mensuration signs, it was some time before there was any standardization in usage. In the *Ars nova* treatise he indicates mode by ▤ or ▤, according to whether it is perfect or imperfect. A circle indicates perfect time, a semicircle imperfect. Prolation, later shown by putting three dots inside the circle if perfect, two if imperfect, is not indicated in the *Ars nova*.[8] Only the use of circle and semicircle gained popularity, and these were rare before the last quarter of the century. The greater use of imperfect or duple rhythms, achieved by employing not only the four prolations but also red notes, was undoubtedly one of Vitry's major accomplishments. In one work which he quotes in his treatise, and which is generally held to be one of his compositions, 'Garrit gallus / In nova fert animus', the tenor contains groups of notes now black, now red, as follows:

Ex.1

(Notes within the bracket are red)

---

[1] For full biographical details, cf. A. Coville, 'Philippe de Vitri', *Romania*, lix (1933), and Armand Machabey, 'Notice sur Philippe de Vitry', *Revue musicale*, x (1929), pp. 20–32.   [2] Coussemaker, op. cit., iii, pp. 23–27.

[3] Ibid., pp. 28–35.   [4] Ibid., pp. 35–46.   [5] *Musica Disciplina*, x, pp. 23 and 30.

[6] Coussemaker, op. cit., iv, p. 257*a*; iii, p. 337*a*.

[7] E. Langlois, *Recueil d'Arts de seconde rhétorique* (Paris, 1903), p. 12.

[8] Coussemaker, op. cit., iii, pp. 19*b*–21*a*.

As the upper voices are measured in conformity with the tenor, a transcription in score gives the following irregular pattern of $\frac{3}{4}$ and $\frac{2}{4}$ bars.[1]

Ex. 2

(*Triplum*: The cock crows, weeping sorrowfully, and the assembly of cocks [the French nation] mourns, for it is handed over to the cunning satrap.

Motetus: One is minded to tell of forms changed into something new.)

This late *Fauvel* motet is an excellent example of Vitry's use of isorhythm, a technical feature of fourteenth-century motet composition which was to become almost universal. Philippe de Vitry was undoubtedly the person who introduced isorhythm, as it is called

[1] Paris, Bibl. Nat., fr. 146, f. 48; facsimile in Aubry, *Le Roman de Fauvel*, and Willi Apel, *The Notation of Polyphonic Music* (Cambridge, Mass., 4th ed., 1949), p. 331. Full transcriptions in *Denkmäler der Tonkunst in Österreich*, xl (1933), pp. 2–3, and Schrade, *Polyphonic Music*, i, p. 68.

nowadays, or *color*, as it was rather ambiguously named in the Middle Ages. The anonymous authors of the *Quatuor principalia musicae* almost admit as much when they say:

In motetis vero ponuntur diversi colores, non rubei vel nigri, sed perfectionum, ut cantus magis elucidatur. Sed quia longum esset circa ista insistere, motetis Philippi de Vitriaco remitto, qui diversis coloribus compositi sunt, ut patet intuenti (Coussemaker, *Scriptorum*, iv, p. 272*b*; iii, p. 350*b*).

Various colours are used in motets, not red and black but colours of perfections, so that the *cantus* [*firmus*] stands out more clearly. To avoid tediousness, I refer you to the motets of Philippe de Vitry, which are manifestly composed in isorhythm.

Isorhythm has been explained provisionally in volume II.[1] It developed naturally from the rhythmic *ordines* of thirteenth-century modal notation, as used in the motet. As soon as these become more than two or three notes, e.g. ♩. | ♩. ♪. ‖ ♩. ♩. | ♩. ♪. ‖ or more than a simple group *ordo* (the obvious starting-point of isorhythm) such as ♩. ♩ ♪ ♪♩ ♪ ‖, we have what is commonly called isorhythm, the division of a voice or voices into identically repeated rhythmic groups. The word *color* was taken from rhetoric, and in the Middle Ages meant quite simply a repetition of any kind. Nowadays it is common to speak of *color* as referring to a melodic repetition and *talea* to a rhythmic one, but strictly speaking this should only apply to the type of composition where melodic and rhythmic repetitions differ in length. It was naturally the tenor *canto fermo* which first made use of isorhythm in the motet, but later the principle tended to invade all parts. Vitry never wrote a completely isorhythmic motet so far as we are aware, though his 'Vos quid admiramini/Gratissima'[2] approaches this type of composition at times:

Ex. 3(a)

[1] Cf. pp. 390–1.   [2] Transcription in *Polyphonic Music*, i, p. 56.

Hocketing sections such as this seem to be the point of departure for complete isorhythm, and undoubtedly these sections form the climax in the fourteenth-century isorhythmic motet.

A feature already evident in the motets of Vitry and developed by Guillaume de Machaut is the use of diminution in the isorhythmic tenor and later in the other voices also. Usually the first half of the piece is in the greater rhythm, while the second half is in some form of diminution, usually duple or triple. A good example is Vitry's 'Douce playsence/Garison',[1] of which the first tenor-repetition is given here in its normal and diminished forms.

Ex. 4

[1] Facsimile, *Die Musik in Geschichte und Gegenwart*, i (Kassel and Basle, 1949), pl. xxvii; transcriptions, *Archiv für Musikwissenschaft*, vii (1925), pp. 249–51, and *Polyphonic Music*, i, p. 72.

The motets known or at all likely to be by Vitry add up to no more than twelve,[1] even including such unlikely cases as 'Orbis orbatus', no. 6 of the three-part motets of the *Roman de Fauvel*. Of these twelve, three are cited as works of Vitry by diverse theorists, four are in *Fauvel*, two more are cited in the *Ars nova*, one is attributed to Vitry in the lost Strasbourg manuscript, another in Paris, Bibl. Nat., lat. 3343. An additional set of texts belonging to a lost four-part motet is also to be found in this last manuscript. The following list gives the relation of *color* to *talea* and shows where hocket and diminution are used.[2] (V = vocal introitus, I = instrumental introitus, ° = hocket section, > = diminution, C = *color*, T = *talea*.)

		Tenor periods	
'Douce playsence / Garison'	3v	$4 > 4$	$C = 4T$
'Vos quid / Gratissima'	4v	$6 + °7\frac{1}{2}$	$C = 6\ (7\frac{1}{2})\ T$
'Cum statua / Hugo'	3v	$9(= 7 + °2)$	$C = 3T$
'Colla jugo / Bona condit'	3v	$7\frac{1}{2} > 7$	$2C = 6\frac{1}{2}T$
'Tuba sacra / In arboris'	3v	$I + 3 > °3$	$C = 3T$
'Orbis orbatus / Vos'	3v		
'Firmissime / Adesto'	3v	$8\ (>)\ 8$	$C = 8T$
'Garrit gallus / In nova'	3v	6	$C = 3T$
'Tribum quem / Quoniam'	3v	$V + 12$	$C = 6T$
'Impudenter / Virtutibus'	4v	$V + 5 > °5$	$C = 5T$
'Petre clemens / Lugentium'	3v	$V + °7$	melodically free
'O canenda / Rex quem'	4v	$8 > °4$	$C = 4T$

According to the anonymous author of the second rhetoric quoted earlier, Vitry also 'found the manner of the *lais* and simple *rondeaux*'. These forms have been generally explained in volume II of this history,[3] but once again there is a difference between thirteenth- and fourteenth-century usage in the direction of discipline and regularity. It would be silly to say Vitry invented these song forms, but it may be that he fixed the poetic forms, and introduced *ars nova* innovations into the music. The simple *rondeaux* are of course the triolets, the eight-line works which predominated in the fourteenth and usually

[1] Cf. the list of 13 ('Dantur officia/Quid' is very doubtful) in G. Zwick, 'Deux motets in dits de Philippe de Vitry et de Guillaume de Machaut', *Revue de musicologie*, xxx (1948), pp. 31–5.

[2] Based on Besseler's list in *Archiv für Musikwissenschaft*, viii (1926–7), pp. 222–4. Schrade adds 'Aman novi probatur/Heu Fortuna' (*Polyphonic Music*, i, p. 48) to the list.   [3] Pp. 243–6, 247–50.

in the thirteenth century. In poetry there is little difference between, say, the *rondeaux* of Adam de la Hale and the five in *Fauvel*. The characteristic seven-syllable line is still there, but the fluctuating line-length of the thirteenth-century forms is far less apparent. In fact four out of the five works are isometric, i.e. they have lines of the same length and metre throughout. The music is very like that of l'Escurel, if not more elaborate. It is interesting to see the same melody set twice, first with what is doubtless the original text, and secondly with a typical *Fauvel* text, spoken in this case by Fortune.[1]

Ex.5

1.4.7. A touz jours sanz re - ma - noir 2.8. weil du
3. qui pris m'a par un vë - oir
5. Je ne de - sir au-trea - voir 6. qu'a - voir

cuer ser - vir ma da - - - me,
son gent cors sanz bla - - - sme.

(For ever and unceasingly I will serve my lady from my heart, for she has taken me for her own truly; I desire no other possession than that of her sweet person.)

Second text: Fauvel est mal assegné   de venir a son desir,
                 trop a son bobant mené,   Fauvel est mal assegné.
                 Tant a graté que ordonné   est de son mauvès gesir:
                 Fauvel est mal assegné   de venir a son desir.

(Fauvel made a bad choice [when he sought Fortune] to assuage his passion; he has boasted too much. He has flattered so much that he must cease from his evil doings.)

The *lais* of *Fauvel* are not so markedly different from their thir-teenth-century counterparts, though even Machaut has at least seven *lais* that cannot be considered real *ars nova* works.[2] Poetically the *Fauvel lais* have the same form as Machaut's, namely twelve strophes, of which the last has the same poetic form and music as the first.[3] The influence of the sequence is visible in the double versicles of each strophe, which are occasionally subdivided to make four sections identical in music as well as in metre and rhyme. The modal rhythms

[1] Paris, Bibl. Nat., fr. 146, f. 19*a* (19ᵛ*c*, 20*a*). Facsimile in Aubry, *Le Roman de Fauvel*.
[2] Friedrich Ludwig, *Guillaume de Machaut: Musikalische Werke*, iv (Wiesbaden, 1954), nos. 1, 2, 5, 12, 15, 19; i (Leipzig, 1926), *lai* from the *Remède de Fortune*.
[3] One *lai* with only nine stanzas seems incomplete. Another *lai* has fourteen strophes.

of the *ars antiqua* continue to reign in the music, though the possibility of greater notational nuance is clearly felt. As must have been the case in the conductus, we find change of mode for the different sections, modes 1, 2, and 3 being as popular as in the thirteenth century. Here is the opening of one of the most charming *Fauvel lais*, which is noteworthy in the later stanzas for its frequent use of repeated notes on one syllable, suggesting instrumental accompaniment.[1]

Ex.6

1a.	Pour	re - cou -	vrer a -	le - gian - ce	des	maux
b.	en	tant que	fais el -	loin - gnan - ce	de	cel -
c. A -	mours m'a	fait des		m'en - fan - ce	son	a -
d. et	par sa	dou - ce		ple - san - ce	plus	que

que   je   trai
-le en   qui j'ai mis mon de-sir de cuer ·vrai,
- mant   tres   gay,
moi   l'a - mai; tou-te au-tre a-mour en les - 'sai,

, fe - rai en   sa   re - mem - bran - ce pi - teus lay.

las de moi   fait, de ten - ran - ce j'en mou - rai.

(To ease the pains I feel after leaving the one who has my heart, I shall compose in her remembrance a sad *lai*. Amours has made me her very gay lover since my childhood, and by her sweet pleasure I loved her more than myself; all other loves I abandoned, and now, weary of myself, I shall die of love.)

THE BALLADE AND VIRELAI

The anonymous *rhétorique* also mentions that Vitry 'found the manner of the *ballades*' as well as the *lais* and simple *rondeaux*, but apart from the six *ballades* from *Fauvel* which are musically like the *rondeaux* and may have connexions with Vitry, we know only the text of a curious *ballade* by this composer replete with mythological references in the fashion of the time.[2] This poem is one of six *ballades* all concerned with Jean de le Mote, who is the author not

---

[1] Paris, Bibl. Nat., fr. 146, f. 28 *bis*. Facsimile in Aubry, *Le Roman de Fauvel*. See also Reaney, 'The Lais of Guillaume de Machaut and their Background', *Proceedings of the Royal Musical Association*, lxxxii (1955–6).

[2] E. Pognon, 'Ballades mythologiques', *Humanisme et Renaissance*, v (1938), p. 409.

only of four of these *ballades*, but also of a whole series of *chansons* and *ballades* (actually all *ballades*) interpolated in the rather tedious poem *Li Regret Guillaume*,[1] written on the death of Guillaume of Hainaut presumably for his daughter Philippa, Queen of England, in which country Jean de le Mote seems to have resided for some time. Although we know of no music by le Mote, he was evidently both poet and musician, since Gilles li Muisis mentions him as one of the poet-musicians still living in 1350.[2] In any case le Mote was evidently a prime mover in the development of the fourteenth-century *ballade*, and some works of Machaut seem to owe quite a lot to him.[3] If the *Fauvel* and l'*Escurel ballades*, and even those of Jehan Acart's *La Prise amoureuse* (1332),[4] seem less mature than those of Machaut, Jean de le Mote (writing *c*. 1340) seems even more regularized formally than the master himself, for instance in the use of a refrain which is not independent of the strophe throughout his poems.[5]

The fourteenth-century *ballade* in its usual fixed form is evidently a standardization of the troubadour-trouvère *chanson* as described on pp. 237–40 of volume II. It normally has the two *pedes* and *cauda*, *AAB* form, defined by Dante, with the additional refinement of a refrain. It invariably has three stanzas, while its companion form, the *chanson royal*, differs from it only in having five stanzas. A less popular form than *AAB* is *AABB*, which however occurs five times among Machaut's *ballades*.[6] In this type there is an *overt* and a *clos* ending for both first and second half, *B* as well as *A*. Such a work is the mature and charming *ballade* no. 40, 'Ma chiere dame',[7] which, however, has an unusual poetic form, *aaabaaab bbbabbba*, that of the *complainte* interpolated in the *Remède de Fortune*.[8] This long verse *dit* contains examples of both types of *ballade* as well as *rondeau, virelai, lai*, and the *chanson royal* and *complainte* unique in Machaut's musical output. The normal verse-form of the fourteenth-century ballade is *ababbcC*, with decasyllabic lines throughout, or the very common eight-line variant with a short line of seven syllables as line 5. Longer

---

[1] Ed. Auguste Scheler (Louvain, 1882).

[2] 'Or y rest Jehans de Le Mote‖ qui bien le lettre et le notte‖ trouve'. Kervyn de Lettenhove, *Œuvres de Gilles Le Muisit*, i (Louvain, 1882), p. 89.

[3] E. Hoepffner, 'Die Balladen des Dichters Jehan de le Mote', *Zeitschrift für romanische Philologie*, xxxv (1911), pp. 163 ff.

[4] Hoepffner, *La Prise amoureuse von Jehan Acart de Hesdin* (Dresden, 1910).

[5] Hoepffner, *Zeitschrift für romanische Philologie*, xxxv (1911), pp. 158 ff.

[6] Ludwig, *Guillaume de Machaut: Musikalische Werke*, i (Leipzig, 1926), and Schrade, *Polyphonic Music*, iii, *ballades* 6, 19, 38, 40, and *baladelle* from the *Remède de Fortune*.

[7] Easily available in Arnold Schering, *Geschichte der Musik in Beispielen* (Leipzig, 1931), p. 17, as well as in Ludwig's and Schrade's editions of Machaut.

[8] Hoepffner, *Œuvres de Machaut*, ii (Paris, 1911), pp. 1–157.

stanzas were used, but not often where musical notation is found. In the *ballades* set to music, Machaut has one case of a nine-line stanza,[1] one of twelve,[2] one of fourteen,[3] and the above-mentioned example of a sixteen-line strophe, but none of these are isometric, and all but the last use shorter lines than the decasyllable throughout.

The decasyllabic line was in fact a coming thing, and whoever gave the decisive impulse to its use, Vitry, Acart, Jean de le Mote, or Machaut who made it famous—Chaucer in fact imitated Machaut in this respect in *The Canterbury Tales*—it became the favourite line in fourteenth-century lyric poetry, whether *ballade*, *rondeau*, or *virelai*, though in the *virelai* Machaut still follows the thirteenth-century ideal of variety, perhaps owing to his long stanzas. His followers, however, restricted the *virelai* to one stanza as a rule, and very often used the decasyllabic line throughout.[4] In spite of the variety in the verse-forms of Machaut's *virelais*, they have certain features in common, which are emphasized particularly in the music: a refrain which occurs at the beginning of the piece and then at the end of each stanza, two *pedes* which follow the opening refrain and form a double versicle with *overt* and *clos*, and a *cauda* which has the same verse-form as the refrain and is immediately followed by it. Briefly this gives the form *AbbaA*.

GUILLAUME DE MACHAUT

Guillaume de Machaut (*c.* 1300–77), another Champenois, was like Vitry highly esteemed as a musician, and served a number of royal masters. As secretary to John of Luxembourg, King of Bohemia, who obtained important benefices for him, he travelled as far north as Poland and Lithuania and east to the court of Prague. After the death of John at Crécy he found favour with such men as the Duke of Berry, Charles of Navarre, and even Charles V himself, and eventually settled down as canon of Rheims.[5] Traces of his travels are to be found in his highly conventional poetry, which has little interest for the modern reader apart from the beauty of sound which makes it ideal for musical settings. The complete works of Machaut are copied

[1] *Ballade* 12.
[2] *Ballade* 19 and the *baladelle* from the *Remède*.
[3] *Ballade* 6.
[4] Cf. exs. 5–11, 38, 39, 64, 69 in Apel, *French Secular Music of the Late Fourteenth Century* (Cambridge, Mass., 1950).
[5] Full biographical details in Machabey, 'Guillaume de Machault', *Revue musicale*, xi (1930), pp. 426–47, and *Guillaume de Machault*, i (Paris, 1955), pp. 13–83.

in seven great manuscripts, apparently under his own supervision, and six contain musical notation. They appear to be written in approximately chronological order, with the *lais* first, followed by the motets, the Mass, the *double hoquet* ('Hoquetus David'), and the *ballades*, *rondeaux*, and *virelais* last.

According to Froissart it took six months to write a *lai*,[1] and certainly these are very long compositions, though all but two are monodic throughout. As in the *virelais*, one finds two types of melody, one pure and folksong-like, the other synthetic and similar to the melismatic, decorated lines of the *ballades*.[2] The typical trochaic major prolation of the Vitry and Machaut motets occurs notably in two works,[3] while three are three-part canons at the unison.[4]

The kind of canon at the unison called *chace* in the manuscripts is indeed a popular form of early fourteenth-century polyphony. Such works occur in the Picard roll (Paris, Bibl. Nat., Coll. de Pic. 67) and particularly in the Ivrea manuscript, which was apparently used at the Papal court at Avignon.[5] The well-known 'Se je chant' is remarkably complex, but is undoubtedly for three voices, as Nino Pirrotta discovered.[6] The following extract is from the most exciting part of the piece, where the hunt, suggested in the music by rapid hocketing, is in full swing:[7]

Ex.7

---

[1] Cf. J. Froissart, *Poésies*, ed. Scheler, i (Brussels, 1870), p. 285, lines 2202–3.

[2] Cf. exs. 13 and 14.

[3] Ludwig, *Guillaume de Machaut: Musikalische Werke*, iv, *lais* 17 and 18; Schrade, *Polyphonic Music*, ii, *lais* 12 and 13.

[4] Ludwig, op. cit., *lais* 16 and 17; Schrade, op. cit., *lais* 11 and 12. See also Reaney, 'The Lais of Guillaume de Machaut and their Background'.

[5] Cf. *Archiv für Musikwissenschaft*, vii (1925), p. 194.

[6] 'Per l'origine e la storia della "caccia" e del "madrigale" trecentesco', *Rivista musicale italiana*, xlviii (1946), p. 305.

[7] Full transcription à 2 in *Archiv für Musikwissenschaft*, vii (1925), pp. 251–2; recorded in *The History of Music in Sound*, iii; facsimile in *Die Musik in Geschichte und Gegenwart*, i, cols. 715–16.

(Ho, quiet there; ho, I see them; ho, throw, throw, or you lose them. Huo, huo, houp; huo, huo, houp; hareu, he's got away. Hau, hahau, &c; he's on the wrong scent, thank God. Hou, &c., pick him up. Hau, hahau, hahau; ha-ha, he's dead, let's go and feed our hawks.)

Incidentally, the first line of this *chace* is reproduced as the refrain of Machaut's *ballade* no. 12.

One of the problems of fourteenth-century music, and indeed of medieval music in general, can be studied in the *lais* of both Machaut and *Fauvel*. This is *musica ficta*.[1] The system is a little more regularized in the fourteenth century, and we recognize that all scales, except perhaps the Mixolydian and the Phrygian modes, which are built on G and E respectively, are forms of the D mode and the C mode. Each of these may be transposed by one or two flats, but very rarely the opposite way, by one or two sharps. The fact that *musica ficta* is primarily a matter of melodic or harmonic propriety is revealed by

its inconsistent notation in the manuscripts. Thus 🎼 needs an

F♯, to avoid a diminished fifth, but 🎼 does not. A process of attraction seems to be at work in both melody and the combination of melodies that forms the harmony of the medieval period. The longer the note-values, the more important that accidentals should be used when called for. Thus in these two examples the pull of the first F is upwards, hence F♯ is called for, while in the second case the downward attraction to E does not necessitate a ♯. (The principal accidentals used at the time of Machaut are F♯, C♯, G♯, B♭, and E♭.) Hard and fast rules, however, cannot be laid down, and only careful study of the various circumstances in which *ficta* is reproduced in the manuscripts will reveal when it is necessary if it is not indicated by sharp or flat symbol. Unfortunately there is no sign for the natural in most medieval manuscripts, though an exception occurs in the *Fauvel lai* 'Talant que j'ai d'obeïr',[2] where the flat is employed as a natural. Usually the transposing flat or flats are inserted as a key-signature, and in polyphonic music this often results in the so-called 'partial signatures'. These occur in particular where the upper part or parts are a fifth away from the lower part or parts. Thus the *triplum* and *motetus* of a motet with a compass of about a ninth above middle C will usually have no signature, while tenor (and contratenor, if there is one) with a similar compass above F a fifth below middle C will have a signature of one flat. This is the case, for instance, in Machaut's earliest datable motet, 'Bone pastor', written

¹ Cf. vol. II, pp. 231, 367–93. See also Reaney, 'Musica Ficta in the Music of Guillaume de Machaut', *Compte-rendu du Colloque International d'Ars Nova, Liège, 1955* (1959).
² Paris, Bibl. Nat., fr. 146, ff. 17–18v.

for the election of Guillaume of Trie as archbishop of Rheims in 1324.[1]

Tenor: BONE PASTOR

(*Triplum*: Good pastor Guillermus, thy breast is not defenceless. *Motetus*: Good pastor, who excellest all other pastors in morals.)

MACHAUT'S MOTETS

Most of Machaut's motets are French ones, only six being in Latin. It would seem that Machaut started with this traditional form of polyphony, only to realize that it was unnecessary to have more than one voice singing text in love-songs, which these French motets are, in spite of their traditional Latin tenors.[2] To this natural development we seem to owe the *ballades*, *rondeaux*, and *virelais* with solo *cantus* and accompanying tenors and contratenors without text. The motet 'Bone pastor' is in Latin, it is true, but this merely conforms to the necessity of using the official language of church and state in works written for special occasions of public interest. The same would seem to apply to the later Latin motets, which are singularly unified in their demands for peace.[3]

[1] Ludwig, *Guillaume de Machaut: Musikalische Werke*, iii (Leipzig, 1929), and Schrade, *Polyphonic Music*, iii, no. 18.

[2] French tenors are used in the three non-isorhythmic motets, nos. 11, 16, 20. The first two are *virelais*, and the third is a *rondeau*.

[3] Motets 19, 21, 22, 23.

Only motet no. 4, 'De bon espoir/Puis que la douce', is isorhythmic in all parts, though no. 13 is virtually so. Machaut was not the first musician to write completely isorhythmic motets. Indeed some anonymous works from the Ivrea manuscript are evidently very early examples of this form, which became so popular after Machaut; the following is an example:[1]

(*Triplum*: Rachel weeps for her sons, the messengers of Christ, who are in chains . . . seeing great rulers, kings, dukes, presidents . . . trusting in Mammon, piling on burdens, creating vain things.)

Overlapping between *colores* and *taleae* occurs in seven works, of which motet no. 4 may again be cited. It has two repetitions of the

[1] Full transcription in *Denkmäler der Tonkunst in Österreich*, xl (Vienna, 1933), pp. 5–6.

color to three of the *talea*, after which the same repetitions are given in duple diminution, i.e. the values are halved. It comes as no surprise, therefore, to find that a motet missing from the great manuscripts, but attributed to Machaut in the Freiburg fragment, is completely isorhythmic and has overlapping *color* and *talea*.[1]

The introitus already favoured by Philippe de Vitry—a separate free section preceding the isorhythmic tenor—occurs as a monody in the three-part motets 9 and 19, and as a duet in motets 21–23, which are four-part works. The introitus to motet 23, 'Felix virgo/Inviolata', is one of the most moving passages in fourteenth-century music.

CYCLIC MASSES

The Machaut Mass,[2] which follows the motets in the great manuscripts, is a very important work, though only one short movement is to be found in a manuscript other than those devoted solely to Machaut. It is the first polyphonic Mass written entirely by one man, though the less unified and anonymous Tournai Mass is possibly earlier.[3] Both works contain not only *Kyrie*, *Gloria*, *Credo*, *Sanctus*, and *Agnus Dei*, but also the *Ite missa est*, set in motet style. The so-called Toulouse Mass[4] also contains an *Ite*, though it lacks a *Gloria*. This *Ite* is called *Motetus super ite missa est*, but is actually in the usual three-voice song style, though all Ites in cyclic masses are called motets.[5] Another fourteenth-century Mass cycle, the Barcelona Mass,[6] is like Toulouse a composite work, consisting of *Kyrie*, troped *Gloria*, *Credo*, troped *Sanctus*, and *Agnus Dei*. All are in different styles, and one movement is by the composer Sert. The Tournai Mass appears to have been composed in two parts, since the strict note-against-note style of the *Kyrie*, *Sanctus*, and *Agnus Dei* is very archaic. The *Gloria* and *Credo*, on the other hand, are very similar to those of Machaut, and were either modelled after them or formed the model for them.

---

[1] G. Zwick, 'Deux motets inédits de Philippe de Vitry et de Guillaume de Machaut', *Revue de musicologie*, xxx (1948), pp. 50 ff.; transcription, pp. 53–57.

[2] Jacques Chailley, *Guillaume de Machaut: Messe Notre-Dame* (Paris, 1948); Machabey, *Guillaume de Machault: Messe Notre-Dame* (Liège, 1948); G. de Van, *Guglielmi de Mascaudio Opera*, i. *La Messe de Nostre Dame* (Rome, 1949); H. Hübsch, *Guillaume de Machault: La Messe de Notre Dame* (Heidelberg, 1953); Ludwig and Besseler, *Guillaume de Machaut: Musikalische Werke*, iv, p. 1; Schrade, *Polyphonic Music*, iii, p. 37.

[3] Coussemaker, *Messe du XIIIᵉ siècle* (Paris, 1861); Schrade, *Polyphonic Music*, i, p. 110; Van den Borren, *Missa Tornacensis* (American Institute of Musicology, 1957).

[4] Published by Schrade, *Polyphonic Music*, i, p. 132; see also H. Harder, 'Die Messe von Toulouse', *Musica Disciplina*, vii (1953), p. 119. The same manuscript contains ten monophonic Mass cycles: cf. Schrade, Commentary to *Polyphonic Music*, i, p. 135.

[5] Schrade, 'The Mass of Toulouse', *Revue belge de musicologie*, viii (1954), p. 91.

[6] Barcelona, Bibl. de Catalunya, MS. 946, ff. 1–8; published by Schrade in *Polyphonic Music*, i, p. 139.

Machaut's composition is, however, far superior and is for four
voices, while Tournai is for three. Machaut binds his Mass together in
several ways, not least important of which is the use of a plainsong
canto fermo in *Kyrie* (Gregorian Mass IV), *Sanctus*[1] (Mass XVII),
Agnus Dei (Mass XVII), and *Ite missa est* (Mass VIII). These movements are in isorhythmic style. The *Gloria* is in what may be called
ballade form, i.e. it is formally divided into sections corresponding to
the *pedes* and *cauda* of the *ballade*.[2] The *Credo* also has a sectional
structure of variation type, which is somewhat more complex than
that of the *Gloria*.[3] The general texture of both movements, however,
is a note-against-note one reminiscent of the conductus.

(And I look for the resurrection of the dead, and the life of the world to come.)

The use of the motif certainly gives unity to the work

---

[1] The *Benedictus* is recorded in *The History of Music in Sound*, iii.
[2] Gombosi, 'Machaut's Messe Notre-Dame', *Musical Quarterly*, xxxvi (1950), pp.
208–9.   [3] Ibid., pp. 211–12.

as a whole, and is indeed a hallmark of Machaut's mature style; but it is by no means restricted to the Mass. Duple prolation, often in conjunction with duple time, prevails throughout the Mass, and is characteristic of late fourteenth-century Mass composition.

'HOQUETUS DAVID'

In the motets Machaut was directly inspired by Philippe de Vitry, but the Hoquetus is a very individual work. A textless piece, it is set in three parts to the isorhythmic tenor 'David' taken from the Alleluia 'Nativitas' (now 'Solemnitas').[1] This fascinating work is doubtless meant to be performed on instruments, a very likely combination being the popular shawm, bagpipe, and slide trumpet.[2]

Ex. 11

David Triplum
David Hoquetus
David Tenor

MACHAUT'S SECULAR POLYPHONY

In spite of the intrinsic worth of these different musical forms, Machaut's chief claim to fame lies in the polyphonic *ballades, rondeaux,* and *virelais*[3] which, unlike his other works, were frequently copied outside his own complete manuscripts. *Ballade* 31, 'De toutes

[1] *Liber Usualis* (1947), p. 1676. For lay-out of *color* and *talea* in the 'Hoquetus David', cf. article 'Color' in *Die Musik in Geschichte und Gegenwart*, ii, col. 1577 (the last minim should be a semibreve).

[2] Guillaume de Van, *Guillaume de Machaut: Double Hoquet* (Paris, 1938); Ludwig and Besseler, *Guillaume de Machaut: Musikalische Werke*, iv, pp. 21–23; Schrade, *Polyphonic Music*, iii, p. 65.

[3] Ludwig, *Guillaume de Machaut: Musikalische Werke*, i; Schrade, *Polyphonic Music*, iii.

flours', appears for instance in the four Italian manuscripts Paris, Bibl. Nat., fonds italien 568, Paris, Bibl. Nat., nouv. acq. fr. 6771, Florence, Bibl. nazionale, Panciatichiano 26, and Modena, Bibl. Estense, M. 5. 24 (*olim* lat. 568). *Ballade* 18, 'De petit po', occurs in six different sources, not counting five of the complete manuscripts. For the anonymous author of second rhetoric, Machaut is 'le grand rhetorique de nouvelle forme, qui commencha toutes tailles nouvelles, et les parfais lays d'amour'.[1] If this is a little exaggerated, nevertheless he seems to have been responsible for popularizing the new, more or less fixed forms of *ballade* and *rondeau*, and introducing the three-part *chanson* with solo *cantus* and two or sometimes three accompanying voices without text. Indeed he gave what may be considered as models for the composition of the principal song forms in the interpolations of the *Remède de Fortune* (*c.* 1342).[2] More interesting still from the modern student's viewpoint is the so-called *Veoir Dit*, or true story in verse.[3] This remarkable 9037-line poem tells in verse, letter, and song the story of the sexagenarian poet's love for a girl called Péronne. Written *c.* 1365, the *Veoir Dit* not only contains four *ballades* and three *rondeaux* with music,[4] but also gives some very interesting information about fourteenth-century composition. For instance, we learn that it was customary to embellish or simplify a melody in the fourteenth century, since Machaut tells Péronne to learn his *ballade* 33, 'Nes que on porroit', without adding or taking away.[5] Again, he tells us that he wrote the text of an unspecified *rondeau* a long time ago, though he has only just composed music for it.[6]

The earlier three-part *ballades* and *rondeaux* often have a very instrumental-looking *triplum* for the third part, but this tends to be replaced by a contratenor later.[7] Indeed, even the large four-part works give way eventually before the three-part work with solo *cantus*

[1] Langlois, *Recueil d'Arts de seconde rhétorique* (Paris, 1903), p. 12.

[2] Cf. above, p. 14.

[3] Paulin Paris, *Guillaume de Machaut: Le Livre du Voir Dit* (Paris, 1875).

[4] In all the complete manuscripts, with the exception of the beautiful but very faulty codex written for the Duke of Berry, these pieces are placed with the other *ballades* and *rondeaux* and not in the *Veoir Dit* itself.

[5] Paris, *Le Livre du Voir Dit*, p. 69, letter 10; Ludwig, *Guillaume de Machaut: Musikalische Werke*, ii (Leipzig, 1928), p. 55*.

[6] *Le Livre du Voir Dit*, p. 242, letter 31; *Guillaume de Machaut: Musikalische Werke*, ii, p. 56*.

[7] Of the earlier type are *ballades* 18, 19, 23 and *rondeau* 1. *Ballades* 17 and 29 have different texts in each voice, the first piece being also a *chace*. The four-part *ballades* and *rondeaux* usually have a *triplum* and a contratenor, though *ballade* 34 has a second *cantus* instead of a *triplum*. The three-part *rondeau* 'Ma fin est mon commencement' is recorded in *The History of Music in Sound*, iii.

and accompanying tenor and contratenor, which dominates the field
for over a hundred years. How these works were performed is not
clear. The usual view is that the *cantus*, the only part with text, was
sung, while the other parts were played on instruments. This may well
be true, though it seems likely that the *cantus* was often doubled or
replaced by an instrument.[1] In some cases the instrumental setting of
the *cantus* would have been even more complex than the part which
lies before us in the great manuscripts, if we are to judge from the
arrangement of 'De toutes flours' in the Faenza tablature, which
could equally well be for keyboard instrument, harp, or lute.[2]
Machaut indeed tells his beloved in the *Veoir Dit* that his 'Nes que
on porroit' can be played on organ, bagpipes, or other instruments,
for it is in the very nature of the piece that it should be so performed.[3]
Here he is evidently referring to the *cantus*, for these instruments were
mainly melody instruments in the Middle Ages. Tenors are mainly
harmonic supports for the *cantus*, while the contratenors either combine with the tenors, as in the *ballades* from the *Remède de Fortune*,
or form more lively, decorative parts, as in this *rondeau* from the *Veoir
Dit*, of which the text is a number anagram giving the name Péronne.[4]

Ex.12

---

[1] Cf. Reaney, 'Voices and Instruments in the Music of Guillaume de Machaut',
Kongress-Bericht Bamberg 1953 (Kassel and Basle, 1954), pp. 245 ff.

[2] Transcription in Dragan Plamenac, 'Keyboard Music of the 14th Century in Codex
Faenza 117', *Journal of the American Musicological Society*, iv (1951), pp. 189–90.

[3] Paris, *Le Livre du Voir Dit*, p. 69, letter 10; *Guillaume de Machaut: Musikalische
Werke*, ii, p. 55*.   [4] *Rondeau* 17.

(Seventeen, five, thirteen, fourteen, and fifteen.)

Many of the *virelais* are monodic; indeed only seven have the
addition of a textless tenor,[1] and a further one contratenor as well,[2]
out of thirty-three works in this form. Even more than in the *lais*, the
syllabic, folksong-like type of melody comes to the fore, and in these
works *musica ficta* is rarely needed. It has been noticed in volume II[3]
that secular song often makes use of the major modes, though the
D mode has its fair share of opportunities as well. Here is one of
Machaut's liveliest melodies, which appears to be in C major till the
very end, when it falls to A. This would appear to be a condescension
to modal theory, which applies only to the end of a piece. Thus if the
piece ended on A, the whole of it would be considered as being in the
mode whose dominant was A, namely the D mode.[4]

(I. When I've been to see my lady, I feel neither pain nor sorrow, by my soul.
Refrain: Heavens, it's only right that I should love her blamelessly and in good

---

[1] Nos. 27, 29, 31, 32, 36, 37, 38 in Ludwig; Nos. 24, 26, 28, 29, 30, 31, 32 in Schrade.
[2] No. 26 (Ludwig); No. 23 (Schrade).
[3] Cf. pp. 231 ff.
[4] *Virelai* 13.

faith. II. The memory of her beauty and great charm excites and inflames me
night and day with passion. *Refrain.* III. And if in her great mercy she should
deign to accept my sincere love, I will serve her without an evil or slanderous
thought. *Refrain.*)

If we contrast this simple melody with the florid one of Ex. 12, with
its melodic-rhythmic motives which unify the piece in a successful, if
somewhat artificial manner, we may be forgiven for preferring the
former. Not all the *virelais* are so straightforward as this one, however.
Their melody too is often synthetic, usually without the complexity
common in the *ballade*. For instance a number of motives, one to each
bar, may be joined together in different ways, as in 'Plus dure'.[1] The
most common motive, to be found in all four prolations, is ♩♪♩♪.
In a *ballade* like no. 34, one motive may be part of a larger motive,
which may be part of a still larger motive, as in bars 10–14 of the
contratenor.

Particularly instructive is *ballade* 38, 'Phyton, le mervilleus serpent',
which was taken as a model by the Machaut disciple Magister
Franciscus,[2] who followed it very closely in his 'Phiton, Phiton,
beste tres venimeuse',[3] dedicated to Gaston Phébus, Count of
Foix.[4] The first three bars of both pieces are identical, but it is
fascinating to see how both composers, for instance, write the entire
tenor on the material of the first three bars.[5] Franciscus is doubtless
the same man as the F. Andrieu, also named in MS. Chantilly,
Musée Condé 1047, who wrote the four-part *ballade*, 'Armes, Amours',
with two *cantus* to the poet Deschamps's lament on Machaut's
death.[6]

---

[1] Conveniently available in Davison and Apel, *Historical Anthology of Music*, i
(Cambridge, Mass., 2nd ed. 1949), p. 49. See further Reaney, 'The Ballades, Rondeaux
and Virelais of Guillaume de Machaut: Melody, Rhythm and Form', *Acta Musicologica*,
xxvii (1955), p. 53.

[2] Cf. article 'Franciscus', *Die Musik in Geschichte und Gegenwart*, iv, cols. 634–6.

[3] Facsimile in *Die Musik in Geschichte und Gegenwart*, iv, pl. 28; transcription in
Musica Disciplina, viii (1954), pp. 98–99.

[4] Cf. article 'Gaston Phebus', *Die Musik in Geschichte und Gegenwart*, iv, cols.
1441–4.

[5] Partial analysis of Franciscus's tenor in *Die Musik in Geschichte und Gegenwart*, iv,
col. 636.

[6] Transcription in *Guillaume de Machaut: Musikalische Werke*, i, *ballade* 41.

MACHAUT'S HARMONY

Harmonically Machaut's works are eminently worthy of study, and here again the *ballades, rondeaux,* and *virelais* are in the forefront of interest. They are in a more note-against-note style than the motets, which retain features of the thirteenth-century organa, owing to the long notes in the isorhythmic tenors. In spite of numerous thirds and sixths in unstressed positions, fifth and octave are still the mainstays of fourteenth-century harmony, though consecutives are not allowed in strict note-against-note work, *unless they are unavoidable,* as often in four-part cadences. Counterpoint is successive, i.e. the *cantus* will be composed first, the tenor second, *triplum* or contratenor third in three-part songs, and *triplum* or second *cantus* last in four-part works. Contratenor and *triplum* are harmonized with the tenor rather than with the *cantus,* though in the best four-part works, such as *ballade* 34 and *rondeau* 10, all parts blend together. Machaut's perfect cadence is $^6_3\ ^8_5\ \binom{7\text{-}8}{4\text{-}5}_{2\text{-}1}$, usually with leading-note to fifth as well as final. In four-part cadences the middle voice is usually doubled at the octave. Pure note-against-note writing is, however, very unusual in Machaut, and the use of different types of ornament produces a dissonance technique of great complexity. Appoggiaturas, passing-notes, escape-notes, and the like may clash with each other, though one cannot deny that when they are avoided the resulting harmonies may be superb, as at the beginning of the second half of *rondeau* 10:

Ex. 15

In bar 1 the A of the top part harmonized against the B of the two middle ones was not thought of as a dissonance by the medieval composer, because he harmonized the upper parts separately with the lowest one. In this case, A and B against D form a fifth and sixth respectively, two consonant intervals. The *cantus* B in bar 2 is of course intentional, and the dissonance resolves on to C. Moreover its potency is reduced by its short duration.[1]

MINOR COMPOSERS

Though we know few composers of this period apart from Machaut and Vitry, it seems possible to attribute a few works to Egidius de Murino, whose name is quoted in both motets mentioned on p. 2, note 1,[2] but whose nationality is uncertain. He is best known today for his very practical treatise on note-forms and motet composition.[3] He significantly points out that in motets the music should be composed before the words, which should then be laid out under the various (undoubtedly isorhythmic) sections.[4] Jean Vaillant apparently kept a school at Paris, and a piece by him in the Chantilly MS. 1047 is dated 1369.[5] Of the five pieces by Vaillant, all in this codex, only one is a *ballade*, and this apparently a late one, but the three-part *rondeau* with a different text in each voice is an admirable example of how fourteenth-century musicians unified their compositions by the use of melodic-rhythmic motives, here as much as fourteen bars in length.[6]

Pierre des Molins is represented in the Chantilly manuscript by only one piece but that a famous one, 'De ce que foul pense', one of the most frequently copied compositions of the late fourteenth century;[7] his only other known work is 'Amis tout dous vis',[8] which is also found in two decorated, presumably instrumental versions as 'Die molen van Pariis'.[9]

Solage, the most prolific composer of the Chantilly codex with ten compositions,[10] obviously modelled his works on the polyphonic

---

[1] For a fuller discussion of fourteenth-century harmony, see Reaney, 'Fourteenth Century Harmony and the Ballades, Rondeaux and Virelais of Guillaume de Machaut', *Musica Disciplina*, vii (1953), pp. 129–46; T. Georgiades, *Englische Diskanttraktate aus der ersten Hälfte des XV. Jahrhunderts* (Munich, 1937), pp. 55–66, &c.

[2] Cf. article 'Egidius de Murino', *Die Musik in Geschichte und Gegenwart*, iii, cols. 1169–72.

[3] Coussemaker, *Scriptorum*, iii, p. 118.

[4] Ibid., p. 125*a*.

[5] Cf. Reaney, 'The Manuscript Chantilly, Musée Condé 1047', *Musica Disciplina*, viii (1954), p. 79.

[6] Transcription in Apel, *French Secular Music of the Late Fourteenth Century* (Cambridge, Mass., 1950), no. 76.

[7] Original notation and transcription of two versions in Wolf, *Handbuch der Notationskunde*, i (Leipzig, 1913), pp. 354–60.

[8] Transcription in Friedrich Kammerer, *Die Musikstücke des Prager Kodex XI E 9* (Brno, 1931), p. 145.

[9] Transcription of one in Schering, *Studien zur Musikgeschichte der Frührenaissance* (Leipzig, 1914), p. 66, the other recorded in *The History of Music in Sound*, iii. Both transcriptions in Kammerer, pp. 145 ff.

[10] Transcriptions in Apel, *French Secular Music*, nos. 31–40.

songs of Machaut, though a late piece like the *ballade* 'S'aincy estoit'[1] shows him complete master of the subtleties of the late *ars nova*. It was in the direction of rhythmic variety and extreme syncopation that the late fourteenth-century followers of Machaut exhausted his methods, while the North French *chanson* composers, Cordier,[2] Cesaris,[2] and their successors, prepared the way for Dufay and Binchois by ridding the polyphonic song of the rhythmic and notational complexities that were destroying it.

[1] Transcriptions in Apel, *French Secular Music*, no. 34.

[2] Complete editions in Reaney, *Early Fifteenth-Century Music*, i (American Institute of Musicology, 1956).

II

THE FOURTEENTH CENTURY IN ITALY

By LEONARD ELLINWOOD

THE SOCIAL BACKGROUND

THE previous volume made little mention of musical developments in Italy after the flowering of the plainsong repertory. This is not strange, for conditions on the peninsula prior to the thirteenth century were not conducive to the arts. During that century, however, the factional strife between Guelfs and Ghibellines did much to dissolve the vestiges of the feudal society, so that during the fourteenth century there was a rising national or state consciousness. At the end of the century this was expressed in such works as the motet 'Viva San Marco glorioso' by Johannes Ciconia and the following madrigal by Paolo da Firenze on the occasion of the conquest of Pisa by Florence, 1406:[1]

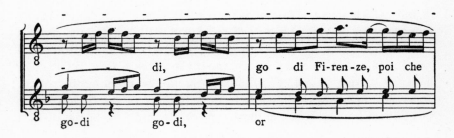

[1] After H. Besseler, *Die Musik des Mittelalters und der Renaissance* (Potsdam, 1931), p. 164.

(Rejoice, rejoice, Florence, since you are so great.)

This was accompanied by a growing insistence on genuine democratic powers on the part of the rising industrial and mercantile classes, a movement which was strongest in the independent cities of the northern areas, Padua, Bologna, Perugia, and particularly Florence. Anglès[1] lists chronologically the *jongleurs*, minstrels, singers, and organists in service at the Catalonian court during the century. Their names bespeak English, French, and Italian origins and a wide variety of instruments played. We know from the lives of Adam de la Hale (whose *Jeu de Robin et de Marion* received its first performance at the court of Charles d'Anjou in Naples, 1283) and Guillaume de Machaut that musicians frequently travelled widely. There is no record, however, of any travel outside the Italian peninsula by the composers discussed below.

Valentino Osterman[2] cites the municipal records of Cividale in Friuli, which show payment of four gold ducats to bagpipe players (*pivadori*) for playing at a festival on 18 August 1396, and the records of Udine showing payment of one gold ducat to 'Giovan Francesco trombetta e tre suonatori' to accompany an ambassador to Cividale. Festival music was used for all occasions: a new painting, betrothal, marriage, ordinations, first Mass, the assembly of the Signoria, the election of magistrates, the departure or return of an army, or of a

---

[1] 'Cantors und Ministrers in den Diensten der Könige von Katalonien-Aragonien im 14. Jahrhundert', *Bericht über den Musikwissenschaftlichen Kongress in Basel*, 1924.
[2] *La vita in Friuli* (Udine, 1940).

distinguished visitor. Luigia Cellisi[1] has surveyed the various municipal documents of Florence, and listed all matters pertaining to the
music of this period. They show uniforms and instruments purchased,
with salaries paid to the municipal trumpeters (*trombetti*) and fifers
(*pifferi*). From the names cited, it is apparent that the 'town band'
consisted of only two or three such musicians during this period.
At Venice[2] in 1322 three singers of the Doge's chapel, Lorenzo ab
organo, Marcantonio Aloiso, and Antonio Fatolario, had their pay
raised from 30 to 50 ducats per year, while another, Giambattista del
Friuli, was to receive 20 ducats per year. The only payment to a composer which has been observed is in an account book of Andrea dei
Servi[3] which records 9 *solidi* paid to Francesco Landini on 29 September 1379 'pro quinque moctectis'. If these were sacred motets, no
further trace of them has survived.

Manuscripts of the trecento abound with illuminations showing the
role of music in the daily life of the times. One of the best is a medical
miscellany which belonged to the Cerruti family of Verona c. 1405[4]
containing a number of miniatures from the second half of the fourteenth century. They include scenes such as the following, each named
as indicated:

fo. 71. *Animalia castrata*: a pastoral scene with two shepherds, one playing
on a shawm.

fo. 100. *Sompnus*: a man lying in bed, while a servant stands nearby playing him to sleep with a viol.

fo. 104. *Cantus*: an altar with a large antiphonary on a lectern, from which
two boy choristers and two tonsured men are singing, standing.

fo. 104ᵛ. *Organare cantum vel sonare*: a singer accompanied by a viol and
organetto.

fo. 105. *Sonare et balare*: a hall with two dancers and, standing to one side,
two musicians with shawms and one with a bagpipe.

Here is music from every facet of the community. Painters did not
depict many musical scenes until the following century, possibly
because of the fact that their demand came almost entirely from the
needs for church decoration. Giotto and Pietro Lorenzetti both portrayed the Dance of Salome, the former with a viol and a harp in the

---

[1] 'Documenti per la storia musicale di Firenze', *Rivista musicale italiana*, xxxiv
(1927), pp. 579–602; xxxv (1928), pp. 553–82.

[2] Fr. Caffi, *Storia della musica sacra nella già cappella ducale di San Marco in Venezia
dal 1318 al 1797* (Venice, 1855; facsimile reprint, Milan, 1931).

[3] Cf. Taucci, 'Fra Andrea dei Servi', *Rivista di studi storici sull' ordine dei Servi di
Maria*, ii (1935), p. 32.

[4] Described and reproduced in part by Julius von Schlosser, 'Ein veronesisches
Bilderbuch und die höfische Kunst des XIV Jahrhunderts', *Jahrbuch der kunsthistorischen
Sammlungen des allerhöchsten Kaiserhauses*, xvi (Vienna, 1895), pp. 144–214.

background, the latter with a single viol. Pietro Cavallini painted St. Agnes being led to the torture, accompanied by the two municipal trumpeters and cymbals. Two paintings show angels with the popular *organetto*: Andrea Buonaiuti's The Liberal Arts, from the fresco of the Triumph of St. Thomas, and Andrea Orcagna's polyptych in S. Maria Novella, Florence.[1]

EXTENT OF MUSICAL CULTURE

While Florence was unquestionably the most active centre music-ally, as well as in the other arts, it was not alone in their cultivation. Little is known about most of the composers, but their seats of activity, if not places of birth, are almost universally indicated in their surnames. From Padua we know of the theorists Marchettus and Prosdocimus de Beldemandis; the author Antonio da Tempo, whose treatise describes the verse forms used during the century; and the composers Bartolino, Grazioso, Domenico Datalo, and Johannes Ciconia.[2] From Bologna, there were Jacopo and Bartolomeo. From Perugia, Niccolò and Matteo[3] are known. Both Giovanni and Donato were originally from Cascia in Umbria, and other individuals were from Genoa, Rimini, Caserta, and Pistoia.[4] Rome was quiet musically until after the return of the papacy from Avignon. Milan was the scene of Sacchetti's tale which is cited below, but no composers were active there until after the erection of its cathedral.

No composers of the fourteenth century are known to have come from Venice, although at the end of the period it was one of the most active centres. According to Marin Sanudo, the elder,[5] the first large organ at San Marco was built by a German *c*. 1312, and we have the names of the organists for the next hundred years. Another index of the extent of the musical culture of the trecento is afforded by the roster of professions and skills of its composers. Giovanni da Cascia, Francesco Landini, and Andrea dei Servi were organists, both in churches and in secular functions, the latter being a member of the order of the Servi di Maria, as were several of the Venetian organists. Vincenzo da Rimini and Bartolomeo da Bologna were abbots of monasteries. Donato da Cascia was a Benedictine monk, as Bartolo-

---

[1] Pietro Toesca, *Florentine Painting of the Trecento* (Florence, 1929).

[2] The last-named was born at Liège. See p. 147.

[3] Appointed organist in the newly erected cathedral at Milan, 1402. Cf. Cesari and Fano, *La cappella musicale del duomo di Milano*, i (Milan, 1956).

[4] F. Ghisi, 'Un frammento musicale della "ars nova italiana"', *Rivista musicale italiana*, xlii (1938), pp. 162–8, describes the musical activity here.

[5] C. von Winterfeld, *Johannes Gabrieli und sein Zeitalter*, i (Berlin, 1834), p. 20.

meo da Padova may also have been. Among the Augustinians were the Venetian organist Giacomo Eremitano and the composers Egidio (presumably Egidius de Murino), Guglielmo, and Corrado da Pistoia. Antonio da Cividale was a Dominican. Francesco Landini, whose arguments in Latin verse for the nominalism of William of Ockham have been preserved,[1] was respected as a philosopher.

MUSIC IN CONTEMPORARY LITERATURE

The authors of trecento *novelle* have given us several references to music. One of the best from Boccaccio's *Decameron* (1353) comes at the end of the first day:

Dopo la qual cena, fatti venir gli strumenti, comandò la Reina che una danza fosse presa, e quella menando la Lauretta, Emilia cantasse una canzone, dal leùto di Dioneo ajutata.

(Supper ended, instruments being fetched, the queen ordered a dance, which Lauretta was to lead, while Emilia was to sing a song to the accompaniment of Dioneo's lute.)

In his *novella 74* Sacchetti describes a prank which Bernabò of Milan played on a notary named Bartolomeo Giraldi who had come to him on an embassy. Bernabò had an unruly horse brought for the notary with the stirrups so badly adjusted that he could not reach them:

Costui s'andava con le gambucce spenzolate a mezzo le barde, combattendo e diguazzando; e quello cotanto che diceva, lo dicea con molte note, come se dicesse uno madriale, secondo le scosse che avea, che non erano poche.

(The man was dangling his short legs in the middle of his saddle-blankets while fighting and [as it were] splashing [with his arms in the attempt to retain his seat]; and what he spoke was uttered with many broken syllables, as though he were singing a madrigal in time with the jerks [of the horse], which were by no means few.)

In *novella 111* Sacchetti complains that although he has composed 'a thousand madrigals and *ballate*' he can hardly win a mere greeting from a girl.

Like Sacchetti, Giovanni da Prato used real rather than fictitious characters in his *Il Paradiso degli Alberti* (1389). Among them was the foremost composer of the century, Francesco Landini. In Book III:

Much to the pleasure of all, and especially Francesco, two young maidens danced and sang 'Orsu, gentili spiriti'[2] so sweetly that not only were the people standing by affected but even the birds in the cypress trees began to sing more sweetly.

[1] Wesselofsky, *Il Paradiso degli Alberti* (Bologna, 1867).
[2] No. 138 in Ellinwood, *The Works of Francesco Landini* (Cambridge, Mass., 1939).

In Book IV:

After this story, the sun was coming up and beginning to get warm; a thousand birds were singing. Francesco was ordered to play on his *organetto* to see if the singing of the birds would lessen or increase with his playing. As soon as he began to play, many birds at first became silent, then they redoubled their singing and, strange to say, one nightingale came and perched on a branch over his head. When he had finished playing, the question was raised whether one animal had the power of listening more than any other, in view of the fact that the nightingale appeared to hear the sweetness and harmony of Francesco more than any other bird which happened to be there.

The intermezzo before Sercambi's *novella 97* (1374–c. 1390) recounts that the singers presented Francesco's 'Vita non è più miser'.[1]

The sonnets from Simone Prodenzani's (b. c. 1355) *Saporetto*[2] have been frequently cited for their references to specific compositions of the trecento and the description of their performance with instruments by his hero, 'Il Sollazzo'. No. 47 from the section entitled 'Mundus Placitus' mentions several of our composers by name:

> Quella sera cantaro ei madriali,
> Cançon del Cieco[3] a modo perugino
> Rondel franceschi de fra Bartolino,
> Strambotti de Sicilia a la reale.
>
> D'ogni cosa Sollazzo è principale,
> Comme quel che de musica era pino;
> El tenor gli tenea frate Agustino
> E'l contra maestro Pier de Giuvenale.
>
> Del Zaccaria suoi caccie et suoi cançone,
> De frate Biascio ancor ne disse alcuna,
> Ch'eran melodiose, dolce et buone . . .
>
> (That evening they sang madrigals,
> Songs of the blind [Francesco] in the Perugian manner,
> French rondels of Fra Bartolino,
> And strambotti of Sicily, right royally.
>
> In each Solazzo was the leader,
> As one who was full of music;
> The tenor was borne by Fra Agustino,
> And the contratenor by Master Pier de Giuvenale.
>
> From Zaccaria *cacce* and songs,
> From Fra Biagio other works were sung
> Which were melodious, sweet, and good. . . .)

---

[1] No. 100 in Ellinwood, *The Works of Francesco Landini* (Cambridge, Mass., 1939).
[2] Edited by Debenedetti in *Giornale storica della letteratura italiana*, Suppl. 15 (1913).
[3] Francesco Landini.

THIRTEENTH-CENTURY INFLUENCE

One of the effects of the Albigensian Crusade (1209–29) had been to scatter the troubadours, *jongleurs*, and other musicians, a large number of whom settled at the Hohenstaufen courts in southern Italy and Sicily, and in the palaces of various Ghibelline princes in the north. But even prior to the Albigensian Crusade, most of the best known of the Provençal troubadours had visited Italy. Salimbene, in his *Cronicon parmense* (1247), cites a Cardinal who, when asked for alms by a *jongleur*, replied:

If thou art fain to get food, I will give to thee right willingly for love of God; but for thy singing and playing naught will I give, for I know how to sing and play the viol as well as thou.

The earliest native Italian troubadours had used the language and verse forms of Provence, but soon came to develop their own vernacular idiom, while retaining many of the older verse forms. There is definite evidence that the principal poets and poet-composers of the trecento were all directly familiar with this literature of the previous century, so that its influence cannot be over-estimated in its effect on their own styles.[1] Contemporary with these Italian troubadours were the followers of St. Francis of Assisi, whose Canticle of the Sun set a pattern for the *laudi spirituali* of the fraternities of penitents, organized since the eleventh century throughout northern Italy (see vol. II, p. 266).

Monody by no means ceased at the end of the thirteenth century, with the rise of polyphony in Italy. True, the verse forms concentrated more and more on the madrigals and *ballate*, but a few of these are known in one part only. The Rossi codex has four, including the following sonnet:[2]

(a) Ex. 17

A - mor mi fa can - - -tar a la fran - ce - - scha. *Fine*

(b) Per - che que - sto m'a - - - -

[1] Cf. Gidel, *Les Troubadours et Pétrarque* (Angers, 1857); Giulio Bertoni, *I trovatori in Italia* (Modena, 1915); and H. J. Chaytor, *The Troubadours of Dante* (Oxford, 1902).
[2] After J. Wolf, *Jahrbuch der Musikbibliothek Peters*, xlv (1938), pp. 53–69.

-ven   no   nol'   so   di - - re.

b.   Che quella donna che me fa languire
a.   Temo che non vedrebbe la mia tresca;
b.   Ne y son fermo ce far el mio core
b.   E consumarmi sanzi perso amore,
a.   Ch'almen moro per cosa gentilesca.
b.   Donne, di vero dirve posso tanto,
b.   Che questa donna per cui piango e canto
a.   E, come io sa, in sum morbida e frescha.

(Love causes me to sing in the French manner. Why this happens to me I cannot explain. Because that lady who causes me to languish I fear would not see my dancing; my heart is set on her and I am glad to be consumed with love, because at least I die for a lovely creature. Ladies, truly I may tell you this much: that this woman, for whom I weep and sing, is, as I well know, very soft and fresh.)

The Squarcialupi codex has eleven monodies,[1] *ballate* and madrigals, five by Gherardello da Firenze, five by Lorenzo Masini, and one by Niccolò da Perugia. Among these is the following setting of a Boccaccio *ballata* by Lorenzo Masini:[2]

Ex. 18

___

[1] Described by S. A. Luciani, 'Le ballate a una voce del codice Squarcialupi', *Archivi a'Italia*, Serie II, vol. iii (1936), pp. 60–66.

[2] Wolf, op. cit.

-vo - - so Veg - - gen-do
-sa - - to Più non ve-

me per al - tri es - ser lasc- ia - - to.
-dre'l bel vi - so a - mo - ro - - - so.

(I do not know which I prefer, to live or to die, to have less grief. I would like
to die, since life is a burden to me, seeing that I am forsaken for other men.
On the other hand, I would not die, since being dead I would no longer see her
lovely, amorous face. Therefore I am weeping, envious of him who has made her
his own, and has deprived me of her.)

Both the above examples are in the *ballata* form, which will be discussed below. Lorenzo's work has the *da capo* written out.

The only other monodies in the principal manuscripts of the Italian
ars nova are the instrumental *istampite* and *saltarelli* in the British
Museum MS. Add. 29987, which are discussed in Chapter XII. *Laudi*
continued to be written during the century, e.g. the poems of Bianco
da Siena, but none appear to have been set polyphonically until the
fifteenth century.

INFLUENCE OF THE POETS

When the music of the trecento first came to the attention of
modern scholars it was considered strange that such a florid art should
have emerged so suddenly, with so little to precede it. Polyphony in
northern Europe had evolved during the two previous centuries at a
steady pace, but even in the fourteenth century Machaut had achieved
nothing so free and expressive as the work of these Italian masters.
Furthermore, it was a new practice to give personal credit so carefully, thereby forsaking medieval anonymity even in sacred compositions. We now suspect that this was due to the continued cultivation
of the troubadour art in the south during the thirteenth century,
with its resultant effect on Italian verse. Trecento polyphony is
greatly beholden to the achievements of Italian poets of the period.
The *dolce stil nuovo* of Dante's sonnets was essentially a style intended to be sung. Indeed two poets contemporary with him were
known by musical cognomens: Benedict of Umbria, known as the
frater della cornetta, and Cenne della Chitarra. Consequently, it was
only natural that after a century or more of singing their lyrics, both
secular *lais* and sacred *laudi*, as monodies, musicians familiar with

the conductus of the church music should adapt that style as polyphonic accompaniments of their own songs, while still preserving the old style of the monody by keeping it as melody in the upper parts.

Dante's influence in this field was in his lyrics, rather than in the Divine Comedy. Whereas in the latter he provides a climax to the entire medieval literary concept, in his verses he is very much the forward-looking creator of a new literary medium. Unfortunately, if any of his verses were set by trecento composers the music has not survived. Boccaccio[1] attests that 'in his youth Dante was exceedingly fond of music and singing, and was friend and companion to all the best singers and players of his time. Because of this fondness, he often composed poems which he then had set to pleasant and skilful music'. In his *De vulgari eloquentia*, II, 4, Dante states that poetry 'nihil aliud est quam fictio *rethorica* in musica posita'. Allusions to music are plentiful in his other works; those in the Divine Comedy are more often to sacred music, as the following from Canto IX of the *Purgatorio*:

> Io mi rivolsi attento al primo tuono,
>   e *Te Deum laudamus* mi parea
>   udire in voce mista al dolce suono.
> Tale imagine appunto mi rendea
>   ciò ch'io udiva, qual prender si suole
>   quando a cantar con organi si stea;
> Ch'or sì, or no s'intendon le parole.

> (At the first thunder-peal I turned attentive,
> And *Te Deum laudamus* seemed to hear
> In voices mingled with sweet melody.
> Exactly such an image rendered me
> That which I heard, as we are wont to catch,
> When people singing with the organ stand;
> For now we hear, and now hear not, the words.
>   H. W. LONGFELLOW)

Allusions to music in the minor works speak of many aspects of secular music,[2] but describe the monodies of the previous century. Apart from the above quotation, there are no references which might refer to the new polyphony described by succeeding authors. In discussing Dante's relations with the music of the times, we should not overlook his classic reference to the singer Pietro Casella, long but

---

[1] *Vita di Dante*, chap. 8.
[2] Cf. Arnoldo Bonaventura, *Dante e la musica* (Leghorn, 1904).

incorrectly hailed as the first Italian madrigalist.[1] None of Casella's compositions are known.

Boccaccio's works abound with musical references.[2] Some from the *Decameron* have been cited above. The music to Emilia's *ballata* is not known but his 'Non so quali mi voglia' was set by Lorenzo Masini.[3] Two of Boccaccio's other poems were set as madrigals: 'Come in sul fonte fu preso Narciso' by Lorenzo Masini, and 'O giustizia regina, al mondo freno' by Niccolò da Perugia. Others were set in the sixteenth century.

Petrarch's relation with the music of his times was even more intimate, although still not as intimate as in the case of Franco Sacchetti. These two men furnish a contrast which must be borne clearly in mind. Petrarch, like Dante and Boccaccio, came from the older, noble level of Italian society, and hence was never intimate with even the most talented of the rising bourgeois poets and musicians, except from the viewpoint of a patron. Culcasi[4] states that Petrarch was quite musical himself and could set his own verses to music; but no example of such setting is known. His madrigal, 'La fiera testa che d'uman si ciba', was set by both Bartolino da Padua and Niccolò da Perugia, while his madrigal 'Non al suo amante più Diana piacque' was set by Jacopo da Bologna. Two letters survive which Petrarch wrote to Philippe de Vitry,[5] and there is a eulogy on the latter's death noted in the margin of Petrarch's manuscript copy of Vergil, now in the Ambrosian library at Milan.

Franco Sacchetti (*c.* 1330–*c.* 1400) is the poet most intimately associated with the music of the trecento. The collection of his poems in the Ashburnham MS. 574 of the Biblioteca Medicea Laurenziana of Florence gives the name of a number of composers who set particular texts to music. Twelve of these compositions have been located.[6] Seven were set by Niccolò da Perugia, while three others were set by Francesco Landini. The latter exchanged rhymed letters, after the manner of the times,[7] with Sacchetti. A lament on the death

[1] *Purgatorio*, ii. 101–7. Cf. the discussion by Ellinwood, 'Origins of the Italian Ars Nova', *Papers of the American Musicological Society*, 1937.

[2] Cf. Bonaventura, 'Boccaccio e la musica', *Rivista musicale italiana*, xxi (1914), p. 405; and Gutman, 'Der Decameron des Boccaccio als musikgeschichtliche Quelle', *Zeitschrift für Musikwissenschaft*, xi (1929), p. 397.

[3] Cf. p. 38 above.

[4] *Il Petrarca e la musica* (Florence, 1911). Cf. also L. Frati, 'Il Petrarca e la musica', *Rivista musicale italiana*, xxxi (1924), p. 60.

[5] Cf. Corille, 'Philippe de Vitri', *Romania*, lix (1933), pp. 520 ff.

[6] Cf. Ettore Li Gotti and Nino Pirrotta, *Il Sacchetti e la tecnica musicale del trecento italiano* (Florence, 1935).

[7] Cf. Natalino Sapegna, *Il trecento* (*Storia letteraria d'Italia*, Milan, 1934).

of Gherardello by Sacchetti is mentioned on p. 77. Additional references in his works to music and musicians have already been made.

Other poets, whose lines have been identified with the extant music,
are Giannozzo Sacchetti, a brother of Franco who was beheaded
15 October 1379 for conspiracy against the Florentine state, Bindo
d'Alessio Donati, Niccolò Soldanieri, Vannozzo, Malatesta, Antonio
degli Alberti, Rigo Belondi, and Stefano di Cino. We know that
Francesco Landini wrote at least nine of his own texts, and it may be
safely assumed that many other verses were likewise the work of the
composers who set them.

POLYPHONIC BEGINNINGS

We turn now to a study of the polyphonic music which flourished
so remarkably during the trecento. But first the reader should return
to volume II, chapter X, and re-read the section on the conductus, for
it is in that repertory that the sources of the new Italian style lie. The
present writer has discussed the details of the interrelation of the two
styles elsewhere;[1] the similarities may be noted here by comparing the
examples quoted below with those of the conductus. British Museum,
Egerton 274 contains examples of some of the links. It is one of the leading collections of the troubadour-trouvère art, and contains some music
in conductus style which is also found in the *Roman de Fauvel* displaying one of the earliest uses of the *via artis*,[2] a device we shall find to be
a peculiar characteristic of the Italian *ars nova* notation. The fact that
compositions in the conductus style have been noted in sources as late
as the fifteenth century[3] strengthens the likelihood of such a connexion.

Concrete evidence was produced by Johannes Wolf in 1937, when
he was able to publish the following two-part sequence by Bonaiutus
de Casentino from the Vatican manuscript lat. 2854:[4]

Ex. 19
REFRAIN

Hæc me - de-la cor-po-ra - lis Fructum det spi-

---

[1] Ellinwood, 'Origins of the Italian Ars Nova', *Papers of the American Musicological Society*, 1937.

[2] See p. 49 for an explanation of this term.

[3] Such as the Berlin, Preußische Staatsbibl. 40580, discussed by Johannes Wolf in the *Festschrift Peter Wagner* (Leipzig, 1926).

[4] *Acta Musicologica*, ix (1937), p. 1.

-cti - va | Vi - get | spes | so-la - | ti - | r.

(Let this bodily remedy yield fruit of spiritual love and joy. Let the bowels so be cleansed that the dregs of the mind are purged of every sin. Care for the body is worthy when it brings the gift of health to body and soul as well. When virtue of both body and mind is preserved, then thrives the hope of relief.)

Here is a strophic composition in sequence form from *c*. 1300 which gives definite proof of the application of the conductus style in the Florentine area at a time exactly midway between the compilation of the Florence manuscript (see vol. II, p. 313) and the Rossi manuscript to be discussed on the next page.

The *laudi* manuscripts, whose Italian monodies have been edited by Liuzzi (see vol. II, p. 266), also contain a few two-part Latin hymns and sequences.[1] Wolf[2] has published the original notation and a transcription of the trope 'Nato nobis hodie', from the parallel manuscript Florence, Bibl. naz., Magl. II, I, 212, showing an early use of the dot of perfection:

Ex.20

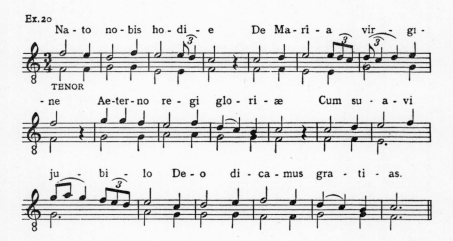

Na - to no - bis ho - di - e De Ma - ri - a vir - gi -
TENOR
- ne Ae-ter-no re - gi glo - ri - æ Cum su - a - vi
ju - bi - lo De - o di - ca - mus gra - ti - as.

(With pleasing songs of praise let us give thanks to God, the everlasting King of glory, born for us today of the Virgin Mary.)

[1] Listed by F. Ludwig, *Archiv für Musikwissenschaft*, v (1923), pp. 298 ff.
[2] *Handbuch der Notationskunde* (Leipzig, 1913–19), i, pp. 267–8.

MANUSCRIPT SOURCES

The manuscript sources for the music of this period were sur-veyed by Johannes Wolf in his *Geschichte der Mensural-Notation von 1250–1460* (Leipzig, 1904). In addition to his thorough study of the problems of notation Wolf listed in detail the contents of all the known manuscripts containing music of the period. Later Heinrich Besseler in two extended articles, 'Studien zur Musik des Mittelalters',[1] con-tinued this survey of manuscript sources by listing the contents of a number of smaller monuments which had since come to light.

The earliest of these manuscript sources is the Rossi MS. 215, deposited since 1922 in the Vatican library. During the first part of the nineteenth century it had been in the private collection of the bibliophile Giovanni Francesco de Rossi. Upon his death in 1854 it was handed over by his widow to the Jesuits at Lainz, Austria. Its contents were first called to the attention of the scholarly world by Monsignor Gino Borghezio of the Vatican library at the Archaeo-logical Congress in Brussels, 1925. Its music has since been described by Johannes Wolf in the *Jahrbuch der Musikbibliothek Peters*, xlv (1938), 53–69, while its texts have been discussed by Fernando Liuzzi in the *Atti della pontifica accademia romana di archeologia, Rendi-conti*, xiii (1937), pp. 59–71. At present the manuscript consists of but eight doubled leaves, folios 1–8ᵛ and 18–23ᵛ, with the middle section missing, so that out of twenty-nine compositions which it still con-tains, five are incomplete owing to the missing section. Four are monodies, one is a three-part *caccia*, and the rest are in two parts each. There are twenty madrigals, six *ballate*, one *rondello*, and one *canzonetta*. Two have mixed Italian and French texts. The others are purely Italian. Liuzzi dates the manuscript as compiled between 1370 and 1380. From the dialect spellings and the geographical names which occur in the text, he infers that the source was in the Venetian territories, possibly near Verona or Padua. All the works are anony-mous, but comparison with works in the manuscripts listed below show that three are by Giovanni da Cascia and two by Piero. Since these were both active in the second quarter of the century, and since the notation practices are not as fully developed as in the other manuscripts, it is likely that the music in this Rossi codex dates from two to four decades earlier than the manuscript itself.

The main body of trecento music is contained in five principal

---

[1] *Archiv für Musikwissenschaft*, vii (1925), pp. 167 ff., and viii (1926), pp. 137 ff.

manuscripts which will now be considered in relatively chronological order.[1]

British Museum Add. 29987 is one of the earliest manuscript sources, dating from the last years of the fourteenth century. It bears the arms of the Medici family and in 1670 was known to have belonged to Carlo di Tommaso Strozzi. Both text and music are taken down in a manner which would indicate dictation rather than copy work. This is the only manuscript in which the form of the composition is stated; *madrialle*, *ballata*, or *chaccia* is either written out or indicated by initial at the head of each work, together with the name of the composer, e.g. 'Madrialle di francescho degli orghanni' (madrigal of Francesco the organist). In several works in both this and the next manuscript the vowel is repeated during a melismatic passage, giving clear indication that the voice continued throughout the entire passage, long as it might seem. The texts are in varying hands and spellings, even the names of the composers appearing in several forms. That this manuscript is contemporaneous with its contents is also suggested by the fact that several composers not included elsewhere are represented here by a few works each. All the earlier composers are well represented here, but of the final generation, coming at the turn of the century, Paolo and Andrea have but one work each, and Zaccaria has none in this collection.

Paris, Bibl. Nat. ital. 568 dates from the end of the fourteenth century, with a more modern binding which bears the three French lilies and the monogram of Charles X. It contains 163 Italian, 35 French, and 9 sacred Latin works. It appears to be one of the sources from which the Squarcialupi codex (see below) was compiled, to judge by internal evidences. In 1827 Fétis transcribed from this manuscript Landini's 'Non arà ma' pietà'—the first transcription of trecento music to be noted since the organ transcription of the latter's works in the early fifteenth century. It is the principal source for Paolo's works and the earlier composers are well represented, but it has none of Zaccaria's works.

Florence, Bibl. naz. pan. 26 contains 151 Italian and 24 French compositions. It is noteworthy in that here the form of the madrigal is more carefully indicated than elsewhere.

The Reina codex, so named after a former owner (Paris, Bibl. Nat. n.a. fr. 6771), contains 117 French, 104 Italian, and 2 Flemish works.[2]

[1] For more detailed discussion cf. Wolf, *Geschichte der Mensural-Notation*, or Ellinwood, *The Works of Francesco Landini*.
[2] For detailed discussion and list of contents, see Kurt von Fischer's study in *Musica Disciplina*, xi (1957), p. 38.

The composers are indicated here less frequently than in the other four manuscripts. It was completed not later than the first half of the fifteenth century. It is discussed in Chapter V.

The most famous monument of trecento music is the Squarcialupi codex (Florence, Biblioteca Medicea-Laurenziana, pal. 87). It has every appearance of having been compiled more as a museum piece than for actual use, in marked contrast to the other manuscripts. Each composer's works are in a section by themselves, with his portrait in the illuminated initial at the beginning of the section. Borders are elaborately floriated, and the whole copied on fine vellum with an eye for appearance, but without sufficient care against copyist's errors in the music. It contains what may have been an attempt to collect all the works of the twelve principal composers of the era; in this the compiler was nearly successful, with the exception of Giovanni da Cascia, who was probably the earliest of the group and had been living his last years away from Florence. Only two important composers are not represented, Piero and Don Paolo. The manuscript was compiled by or for Antonio Squarcialupi (d. 1470), organist at S. Maria del Fiore, whose nephew later gave it to Giuliano de' Medici.[1]

Three manuscripts which contain a small number of compositions from the end of the period are Chantilly, Musée-Condé 1047, Bologna, G. B. Martini, MS. Q 15, and Modena, Biblioteca Estense M. 5. 24. These collections from the mid-fifteenth century show the last stages of the transition into the blended Flemish style which succeeded the distinctive Italian and French practices. The Chantilly manuscript represents only a few Italian composers, and their texts are either French or Latin. The Bologna and Modena manuscripts are the principal sources for the last group of Italian trecento composers, and are also principal sources for the relatively few sacred compositions of the period. In all three manuscripts red notation of coloration is used side by side with white.

A newly discovered codex in the state archives of Lucca was announced at a congress of the sciences, held at Pisa in 1939, by Professor Augusto Mancini. Its contents have been described by Federico Ghisi.[2] A final manuscript of interest for the closing years of this epoch in Italian musical history is Oxford, Bodleian, Canonici

[1] Complete transcription by Johannes Wolf (Lippstadt, 1955).

[2] 'Italian Ars-Nova Music', *Journal of Renaissance and Baroque Music*, i (1946), pp. 173–91. See also Nino Pirrotta and Ettore Li Gotti, 'Il codice di Lucca', in *Musica Disciplina*, iii (1949), pp. 119–38 (with contents and concordances); iv (1950), pp. 111–52; v (1951), pp. 115–42.

misc. 213.[1] This is a miscellaneous collection of 140 folios from northern Italy, containing compositions by Flemish and Italian composers written between *c.* 1380 and 1436, with several dated at Venice during that period.

THE ITALIAN NOTATION

The common beginnings of *ars nova* notation have been discussed in the previous chapter. The distinctive Italian practices of the fourteenth century grew out of the use of the dot, or point, of division. According to Robertus de Handlo (*Regulae*) and Jacobus of Liège (*Speculum Musicae*) this usage was first established by Petrus de Cruce near the end of the thirteenth century. Nothing is known of the life of this important musician. Apel,[2] however, makes the interesting suggestion:

> One is almost tempted to reverse the usual assumption, by venturing the conjecture that Petrus was not a Frenchman whose ideas spread to Italy, but an Italian who came to Paris and introduced into the French motet certain features of a native thirteenth-century music.

His theoretical writings do not refer to this practice, but it may be observed in the few of his compositions which are known today.[3] By setting off a group of semibreves with this dot of division, any number, from the normal two or three up to seven, would have the total value of a single breve.

This changeable content of the breve forms the characteristic basis of the Italian notation of the period under discussion. Its use caused Marchettus de Padua, in his *Pomerium*[4] written between 1309 and 1343, to list eight different *divisiones* (in effect nothing more than modern time signatures) which during the first half of the century were frequently indicated by initials at the beginning of a com-

---

[1] This has been studied and about two-thirds of its contents transcribed in J. Stainer, *Dufay and his Contemporaries* (London, 1898), and Charles van den Borren, *Polyphonia Sacra* (Plainsong and Mediaeval Music Society, 1932). For a complete annotated inventory, with concordances, see Gilbert Reaney's study in *Musica Disciplina*, ix (1955), p. 73.

[2] *The Notation of Polyphonic Music* (Cambridge, Mass., 1942), p. 369.

[3] Transcribed in Y. Rokseth, *Polyphonies du XIIIe siècle*, iii (Paris, 1936), pp. 77–84; the motet 'Aucun / Lonc tans / Annuntiantes' is also published in Davison and Apel, *Historical Anthology of Music*, i (Cambridge, Mass., 1946), no. 34.

[4] M. Gerbert, *Scriptores ecclesiastici de musica* (Graz, 1784), iii, pp. 121 ff.

position. The breve, ■, equals in

This means that the breve would make three divisions on either a binary or ternary basis:

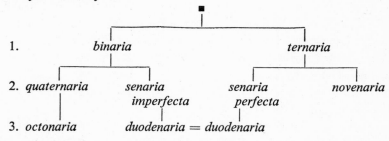

Towards the end of the period, the French mensuration signs of *tempus* and *prolatio* began to come into use, *tempus* corresponding to the second division above, and *prolatio* to the third. In addition to the breve signatures, *quaternaria*, &c., the signs ⊏⊤⊤⊐ and ⊏⊤⊐ are occasionally used, as in the madrigal transcribed below. These mean either *modus longarum perfectus* or *modus longarum imperfectus*, and indicate a ternary or binary division of the long.

Where the normal number of semibreves in a breve is present, they have tails added above, or in other words become minims, e.g. in *quaternaria*, ■ = ♩ ♩ ♩ ♩. Where this number is divided by two, three, or even four (as the case may be), the ordinary form of the semibreve is used, e.g. in *quaternaria*, ■ = ♦ ♦. The value of the ♩ remains constant within any *divisio*, e.g. in *quaternaria*, ■ = ♦ ♩♩ or ♩♩ ♦. Where the number of semibreves is fewer than the normal number of the *divisio*, those at the beginning have their usual value, while those at the end are lengthened, e.g. in *octonaria* ♦ ♦ ♦ means that the first two semibreves are normal, while the last is doubled (♩ ♩ ♩). This was known as *via naturae*. To vary it, the trecento composers developed what was known as *via artis*, by placing a tail under whichever semibreve in the group they wished to prolong, e.g. in *quaternaria*, ♦ ♦̧ ♦ means that the second note is double the length of a normal semibreve (♩ ♩ ♩), while ♩ ♦ means that the first note is three times as long as the second (♩. ♩). Where *via artis* is used, the dot of division must be used liberally to avoid confusion.

Returning to the subject of time values, we should point out that *binaria* results in binary or duple time (2/4); *ternaria* is triple time (3/4), and *quaternaria* is doubled duple or simple quadruple time (4/4). *Senaria imperfecta* is compound duple time (6/8), while *senaria perfecta* is simple triple time (3/2), little different metrically from *ternaria*. *Octonaria* is a combination of two *quaternariae* (8/4) while *novenaria* is compound triple time (9/8). *Duodenaria*, seldom met, is either compound quadruple (12/8) or simple triple (3/1) time. Of these metrical values, the longer ones occur in the madrigals and *cacce*, and are correspondingly more frequently noted on the manuscript. The shorter values occur more in the *ballate*, and are seldom indicated in the manuscript except in cases where the metre might be obscure. Since these latter compositions were possibly dance music, relatively simple, duple, or triple values are to be expected.

Where a composer might wish to shift for a brief passage from duple to triple time, as for instance from *ternaria* to *novenaria*, white or red notes are used. In practice the white notes are used most commonly in the divisions of the semibreve, although at times, even in the same composition, white breves, semibreves, and minims may be employed. This may be observed in the tenor part of the *pedes* to Francesco Landini's *ballata*, 'Se pronto non sara':[1]

Ex. 21

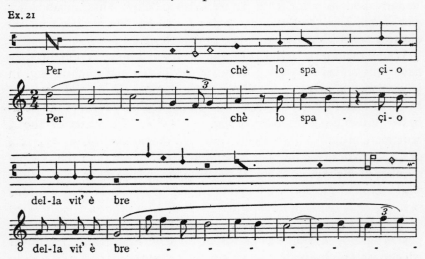

[1] Cf. the complete facsimile in Apel, op. cit., p. 391, and the transcription in Ellinwood, op. cit., no. 93.

ve,   Nes   sun 'deb - be tar -

ve,   ` Nes   -   -   -   -   -   sun deb - be tar -

(Since the span of life is short, no one ought to delay.)

When the semibreve is to contain three minims, instead of white notes the group ♩ ♩ ♩ is used, with the flags on the left side. They must not be confused with the semiminim, which has its flag on the right side. Other special signs are the ♦ and ♦, which equal the first two minims in the above group. The sign ♦ is the equivalent of the semibreve with a dot of augmentation.

Dots in the Italian notation differ little in their use from those employed throughout the history of mensural notation. We have stressed the use of the dot of division, *punctus divisionis*, above, as one of the principal characteristics of the notation. The dot of perfection, *punctus perfectionis*, which is ordinarily used to make certain the musician understands that a given note is to have its perfect or triple value, takes on the character of the dot of division when used with a breve. With the semibreve, it also takes on the character of the dot of augmentation, *punctus additionis*, which is our modern use of the dot, to increase the value of a given note by half. The fourth type of dot, *punctus demonstrationis*, is actually a dot of syncopation. It is always placed either before or after the first note of a syncopated passage. When used after the note it can be confusing if not recognized as the dot of syncopation; when used before its note, it can often pass as a dot of division. Towards the end of the trecento this dot of syncopation was indicated ⁝, which was much clearer.

The use of ligatures, like the shape of notes and rests, did not differ in this notation from those in use throughout the entire mensural era. All transcriptions in this chapter have had their note values reduced to one-quarter the original value, so that:

$$\blacksquare = o$$
$$\blacksquare = d$$
$$\blacklozenge = \rfloor$$
$$\blacklozenge = \rfloor$$
$$\blacklozenge = \flat$$

It may be added that the Italian *ars nova* manuscripts alone are consistent in the use of a six-lined staff, though this is not strictly a characteristic of the notation. The practices of the Italian notation were summarized by Prosdocimus de Beldemandis in his *Tractatus practice cantus mensurabilis ad modum Italicorum* (1422).[1] His caustic remarks about the French practices are but a reflection of other writers towards the end of the trecento, who are consistently scornful of things French, e.g. the Dante commentator, Benevenuto de' Rambaldi da Imola: 'Nam lingua gallica est bastarda linguae latinae.'[2]

THE FORMS

The musical forms employed in this music have already been mentioned in various connexions. In each instance they derive from, or are based on, verse forms which are described by two contemporary texts, the *Trattato delle rime volgari* written in 1332 by Antonio da Tempo, a magistrate of Padua, and the *Trattato de li rithimi volgari* written in 1381–4 by the poet Ghidino da Sommacampagna. The Venice, Biblioteca Marciana manuscript Lat. cl. 12, no. 97, a copy of the first work, also contains an anonymous *Capitulum de vocibus applicatis verbis*, discussing the trecento forms, which has been edited by Santorre Debenedetti.[3] This gives more instruction about the music than the others, but in general terms. In the discussion of motets there is a good description of hocket. These writers describe five forms of the madrigal, based on the arrangement of lines containing either eleven or seven syllables, with three lines to each stanza, and with two to four stanzas. There are two additional forms which have a ritornello of one or two lines. Li Gotti[4] has listed 222 madrigal texts with their sources, authors, approximate date, and metrical scheme, showing which ones conform with each of the various forms.

The madrigal has no immediate counterpart in any other medieval literature. Its verses are serious and expressive, in keeping with the fundamental concept of art-song which they represent, in contrast with the more frivolous texts of the other forms. There is frequent use of the incidents of Greek mythology in their lines. Fellowes[5] and

---

[1] Published by Coussemaker, but better in Claudio Sartori, *La notazione italiana del trecento* (Florence, 1938), where it begins: 'Ars scilicet Ytalica qua soli Ytalici ad presens utuntur.'

[2] For further details of Italian notation see Johannes Wolf, *Geschichte der Mensural-Notation von 1250–1460* (Leipzig, 1904), and Willi Apel, *The Notation of Polyphonic Music, 900–1600* (Cambridge, Mass., 1942). Cf. also the little anonymous treatise, *Notitia del valore delle note del canto misurato*, ed. Carapetyan as *Corpus Scriptorum de Musica*, v.

[3] *Studi Medievali*, ii (1906–7), pp. 59–82.

[4] 'L' "ars nova" e il madrigale', in *Atti della Reale Accademia di scienze, lettere e arti di Palermo*, Serie iv, vol. iv, parte ii (1945).

[5] *English Madrigal Composers* (Oxford, 1921).

Biadene[1] have both studied the etymology of the term madrigal, but
its exact origin and significance is still obscure. The form *madrialle* is
used in all the texts we have cited above, and in the captions of
British Museum Add. 29987. Antonio da Tempo uses the term *mandrialis* (*marigalis*), which Biadene holds to be another type of verse
entirely. Antonio's specifications, however, exactly fit the texts of the
music marked *madrialle*. We quote from his discussion:

Et circa hoc notandum, quod mandrialis est rithimus ille, qui vul-
gariter appellatur marigalis. Dicitur autem mandrialis a mandra pecudum
et pastorum, quia primo modum illum rithimandi et cantandi habuimus
ab ovium pastoribus. . . . Sonus vero marigalis secundum modernum cantum debet esse pulcher et in cantu habere aliquas partes rusticales sive
mandriales ut cantus consonet cum verbis. Et ad hoc ut habeat pulchram
sonoritatem expedit ipsum cantari per duos ad minus in diversis vocibus
concordantibus. Potest etiam per plures cantari secundum quod quotidie
videmus, et per unum etiam; sed non ita bene sonat auribus audientium
quando per unum cantatur, sicut quando per plures. Et quantum ad
sonum sive cantum, musici et cantores melius sciunt praedicta; et sic
audivi a pluribus musicis et magistris in cantu, quod etiam auribus meis et
intellectui meo parvo satis bene consonat, licet non sim magister in cantu.
In modo autem formandi sive compilandi verba mandrialis duo sunt
potissime genera: quidam enim sunt mandriales communes, quidam cum
retornellis sive voltis.

(And in this connexion it should be noted that the *mandrialis* is the
type of song which is commonly called *marigalis*. The term *mandrialis*
comes from *mandra*, a flock of sheep attended by shepherds, since we first
had this manner of singing songs from shepherds. . . . The music of the
marigalis according to modern practice should be beautiful, and should
contain certain rustic or *mandriales* parts, so that the music agrees with
the words. In order to have a pleasant sonority, it should be sung by at
least two persons in diverse blending parts. It is possible for it to be sung
by several, as we see daily, or by one person alone; but it does not sound
as well on the listeners' ears when sung by one as when sung by several.
As regards the music, the musicians and singers know best. I have heard
this from many musicians and masters of song—and indeed it sounds
well enough to my own ears and poor intellect, though I am no master of
song. Furthermore, in the matter of form or arranging the words of the
madrigal, there are two principal types: the common madrigals, and those
with ritornelli or *volte*.)

Debenedetti's anonymous *Capitulum* states:

Mandrigalia . . . volunt etiam esse de tempore perfecto et aere italico;
siquis aliquando miscetur aliquod tempus aeris gallici, bonum esset; si vero
in fine partium, esset melius.

[1] *Rassegna bibliografica della letteratura italiana*, vi (1898), p. 329; translated by E. J.
Dent, *Music and Letters*, xxix (1948), p. 121.

(The madrigals . . . should be in perfect [i.e. triple] time and the Italian style; and if at any point they should change into the time of the French style, that would be good, but would be even better if it came at the end of the sections.)

If any examples of the five forms of madrigal without ritornelli have survived, they have not been recognized as such. All the madrigals in these trecento collections have ritornelli of either one or two lines. In some of the earlier works the three phrases of music for the first stanza are repeated for the additional stanzas, and the one phrase of ritornello is repeated where the poem has a two-line ritornello. In other works the entire madrigal is set throughout with no repetitions. In those works which have the ritornello composed throughout, but repeat the first section for every additional stanza, there has been considerable uncertainty as to whether or not the ritornello is sung after each stanza. Tommaseo[1] gives as one definition of the term ritornello: 'Per coda di sonetto', and states that it was first used thus by Guittone d'Arezzo, a thirteenth-century Tuscan poet who was one of the most eminent forerunners of the *dolce stil nuovo*. Such is undoubtedly its significance in the madrigal, as coda rather than as refrain. In both Antonio and Ghidino the term *represa* is used for the repetition in the *ballata*, so that it is unlikely they would use the term ritornello in the same sense. Furthermore their examples of madrigals with ritornelli place the latter at the end of the poem, with not the slightest indication that it could be a refrain. The sense of the ritornello text is invariably one of apposition to the rest of the poem, a summing up in the form of a coda. This use of the ritornello is confirmed in Florence, Bibl. naz. pan. 26, where the additional stanzas are placed in advance of the music of the ritornello, and even have the incipit of the latter indicated, in some instances, at the end of the final stanza, even though it follows immediately in the next line of music on the page. The use of the incipit of the next lines to follow is consistent with the practice used in all the manuscripts to show the *represa* in the *ballate*. There are several instances where the ritornello is included as part of the stanza, a separate one being given for each successive stanza.[2]

Of the three principal forms of this period the madrigal most closely resembles the musical style of the earlier conductus, with its long florid melismatic passages. There is usually one at the beginning and end of each line of text, forming an extended musical phrase with

---

[1] *Dizionario della lingua italiana* (Turin, 1861).
[2] Cf. Landini's 'Musica son', Piero's 'Segugi a corte'.

the melismas on the initial and penultimate syllables. These phrases
are in multiples of three, corresponding to the number of stanzas set
by the composer. At the ritornello the metre frequently changes with
the appropriate time signature indicated, the section then consisting
of two phrases, or a single phrase repeated. There are frequent
examples of alternating fifths and octaves, brief parallel passages, and
hocket—traces of the improvised descant described by Anonymus III.[1]

Most of these madrigals appear to have been written about the
middle of the century. They employ the purer forms of the Italian
style of notation; the time signatures and changeable breve values
are used much more consistently than in the *ballate*. The earlier composers, Giovanni da Cascia, Jacopo da Bologna, and Piero, left only
madrigals and *cacce*, but no *ballate*. Others a little later left a few
ballate; while at the end of the century composers such as Andrea dei
Servi and Zaccaria left no madrigals whatever. The direct manner of
their performance was seriously questioned by Riemann,[2] whose line
of reasoning was carried still further by Schering.[3] Their thesis was
that the melismas were instrumental passages which were played
against an underlying, simpler, vocal part. Their position was not
maintained by any other scholar, and Schering himself later modified
his viewpoint.[4] It is now generally accepted that all the trecento music
was sung by solo voices wherever there is text, supported *ad lib.*
by instruments, and that parts without text were played on instruments alone. The one possible exception is in the case of the poly-
textual works discussed below.

The majority of the madrigals are in two-part polyphony. There is
always text with each part, so that there is no independent instrumental part as there is in the other forms. The following madrigal
by Giovanni da Cascia[5] is typical:

Ex. 22

[1] Coussemaker, *Scriptorum*, i, pp. 325 ff.
[2] 'Das Kunstlied im 14.–15. Jahrhundert', *Sammelbände der internationalen Musikgesellschaft*, vii (1906), p. 529.
[3] 'Das kolorierte Orgelmadrigal des Trecento', ibid. xiii (1911), p. 172.
[4] In later editions of Arrey von Dommer, *Handbuch der Musikgeschichte* (Leipzig.
3rd edn., 1914).   [5] For the source see p. 58.

(I no longer care for your reproaches, Love, who have scorned me for long; and I weep for the lost love I have shown you. One can trust love no more than a monk; believe me, who every day experiences this truth.)

Facsimiles of the original notation of this madrigal will be found in Wolf, *Handbuch der Notationskunde*, i, pp. 305 ff., from the two Florence manuscripts. They afford an interesting comparison between earlier and later styles of notation used for this music. This madrigal is typical in many ways, both in its melodic and rhythmic patterns and in its tonality, centring as it does on progressions leading to a tonality on A. Even more common is the tonality on D, as demonstrated in Francesco Landini's 'Per l'anfluença di Saturn' e Marte',[1] of which we give the beginning and ending of each phrase:

Ex. 23

[1] Ellinwood, op. cit., no. 6.

Less common are those with tonality based on C, while F and G are met but seldom.

The few which were written in three parts each have special features which tend to mark them apart from the regular madrigals. Six have two parts in canon with an independent third part;[1] two of these, Francesco Landini's 'De'! dinmi tu',[2] and Giovanni da Cascia's 'Nel boscho senza foglie', have their ritornelli in triple canon. We quote the latter, from the transcription by Marrocco:

Ex. 24

[1] Transcriptions of five of these have been published in Marrocco, *Fourteenth-century Italian cacce* (Cambridge, Mass., 1942).

[2] Ellinwood, op. cit., no. 10. In this the canon, contrary to the usual practice, is between the tenor and contratenor; cf. also the *ballata*, 'Amours par qui', transcribed in Wolf, *Geschichte der Mensural-Notation*, iii, p. 75.

1) This second deployment of the canon in the ritornello is unique

(I gathered her in my arms and kissed her. Never did I pursue a sweeter chase.)

Two of the madrigals, Landini's 'Musica son' and Jacopo's 'Aquila altera', are tritextual, having a different text under each of the three parts. These could not have been sung simultaneously as might appear from their position in the Squarcialupi codex, but rather were sung consecutively, possibly with voice and instruments alternating between the parts. Such performance becomes apparent when one notices the consecutive nature of the separate stanzas, each with its own ritornello, as in the following translation of Landini's famous lament:

> I am Music, who weeping regret to see
> Intelligent people desert my sweet
> And perfect effects for popular songs;
> Because ignorance and vice abound
> Good is deserted, and the worst is seized.

> Everyone wants to arrange musical notes,
> Compose madrigals, catches, and ballads,
> Each holding his own to be perfect;
> He who would be praised for a virtue
> Must first come down to earth.

> Formerly my sweetnesses were prized
> By knights, barons, and great lords.
> Now gentle hearts are corrupted.
> But I, Music, do not lament alone,
> For I see even the other virtues deserted.

There is no reflection of these madrigals in the musical style of those of the sixteenth century. However, Einstein[1] has pointed out a number of textual affinities between the two periods. Especially significant is the fact that the earliest madrigalists of the later period chose trecento texts for their treatment.

The *cacce*[2] are referred to in the sonnet by Prodenzani quoted on page 36, and in the tritextual madrigal of Francesco Landini just quoted, but they are not discussed by any of the contemporary treatises except Debenedetti's anonymous *Capitulum*. This states that

Cacie sive Incalci, a simili per omnia formantur ut motteti [which have just been discussed in some detail], salvo quod verba caciarum volunt esse aut omnes de septem, aut omnes de quinque sillabis.

(The *cacce*, or 'incalci', are in all respects formed like the motets, save that the lines of verse in the *cacce* should all be made up of either seven or five syllables.)

It goes on to speak of from one to five parts, with as many singers, in a manner more characteristic of the sixteenth than the fourteenth century. It does not refer to the canonic element at all, so that one questions whether the anonymous author had these *cacce* in mind. In contrast to the considerable number of madrigals and *ballate*, there are only twenty known *cacce*, but these are distributed over the

---

[1] 'Eine Caccia im cinquecento', *Liliencron Festschrift* (Leipzig, 1910).
[2] Cf. the contemporary French *chace* (see pp. 16 and 136).

entire trecento, with only a few examples from any one composer.[1] Rather the setting of a *caccia* appears to have been a composer's *tour de force*, which he achieved on but few occasions. The sole exception is Piero, from whom we have three *cacce*[2] and two canon-madrigals out of a total of nine extant works. Other composers who left more than a single specimen are Giovanni da Cascia, two; Vincenzo da Rimini, two; and Niccolò da Perugia, three.

The musical form of the *caccia* follows that of the madrigal, with florid melismas. The characteristic canon begins after the end of the first melisma; it is always between the two upper parts, cantus and contratenor, the tenor being an independent instrumental part in most instances. The conventional form comes to a full stop and begins the canon anew at the ritornello, which otherwise corresponds to the ritornello of the madrigal. This is true in seven of the works for which we have music. In three other instances the ritornello is in madrigal style without the canon; one of these drops the canonic part entirely, and continues with only cantus and tenor. The only two-part *caccia*, Lorenzo's 'A poste messe', likewise drops the canonic part at the ritornello, concluding instead with an extended monody. This reduction in the number of parts at the ritornello is just the reverse of the practice in the English carols of the next century, where an additional part frequently enters at the refrain. Four *cacce* lack a separate ritornello entirely.

The poetic form of the *caccia* is even more distinctive than its musical form. While not adhering to a strict pattern, it usually contains alternating blank verse and rhyme, with the eleven- and seven-syllable lines of the madrigals. Each one opens with a quiet introduction which soon breaks into an exciting dialogue as the hunting, fishing, or market scene is portrayed; at the ritornello, there is a return to the quiet mien of the beginning. Great stress is laid on vividness of description, to which end considerable onomatopoeia is used. The following is a close translation of Francesco Landini's 'Così pensoso com' amor':[3]

> Thus, thoughtful, as love guides me
> Along the green shore slowly,
> I hear: 'Lift that rock!'

[1] The texts have been edited by Carducci, *Cacce in rime dei secoli xiv e xv* (Bologna, 1896). Not all have extant music. The music has been published in Marrocco, op. cit. This edition also includes the five canon-madrigals, which should not be confused with the *cacce*.

[2] His 'Cavalcando' is recorded in *The History of Music in Sound*, iii.

[3] Translations of two other *cacce* will be found in Dante Gabriel Rossetti, *The Early Italian Poets* (London, 1861), with translations of a number of madrigals and *ballate*.

'Look at the crayfish, look! Look at the fish!
Catch him! Catch him!'
'This is marvellous!'
Isabella began screaming,
'Oh! oh!' 'What's the matter? What's the matter?'
'I've been bitten in the toe!'
'O Lisa, the fish is swimming away!'
'I've got him! I've got him!' 'Ermellina's caught him!'
'Hold on to him!' 'This is a fine fishing hole!'
Meanwhile I reached the troop of lovers
Where I found fair ladies and their swains
Who welcomed me with kindly looks.

An extract from the music (beginning with line 3 in the cantus) will
give an idea of the characteristically lively style of these pieces:

Ex. 25

In those instances where the musical ritornello is omitted, that of the text is accommodated in the closing phrases of music without coming to the customary full pause. Four of the *cacce* are strophic, with a second or third stanza sung to a repetition of the original music. Here, even more than in the case of the madrigal, the text to the ritornello is such that it could be sung only once, at the end of the entire work.

Marrocco is of the opinion that the *caccia* derives musically from the canon-madrigal. Unquestionably it derives from the madrigal, because of the similarities noted above, but from the two-part madrigal. Canon, particularly in the two-part *cacce*, is a logical development. In the three-part canon-madrigals, however, it is much farther advanced technically than in any of the three-part *cacce*. We find one canon at the fifth, between tenor and contratenor (Landini's 'De'! dinmi tu'), and two ritornelli with three-part canons —features which are found in none of the *cacce*. The *caccia* appears to have died out much as did the madrigal, almost before the end of the century. We have one work, however, by Niccolò Zaccaria, the last of the trecento composers. His 'Cacciando per gustar' shows more affinity between various sections and the accompanying tenor part than the earlier works did, with repeated figures and a closer imitation with less melisma. Here the tenor is provided with a text, independent of that of the two canonic voices, which constantly interjects ribald asides, closely akin to the street cries of Paris and London exploited by composers of a later age. The setting is a market-place, but not necessarily in Venice, as some writers would have it.

The *ballata* is the Italian counterpart of the French *virelai*, presenting in every respect a distinct contrast to the madrigal. As described by Antonio da Tempo and Ghidino da Sommacampagna, it may be in one of five forms, depending on the number of lines in the text. Each form varies within itself as to the use of lines with eleven or seven syllables. In each of these cases, as with the madrigals, definite models of each type are cited in full. The music in each instance has the same overall structure, two sections with a full stop between them. In all the manuscripts except one the second section of the music is labelled *secunda pars*: Florence, Bibl. naz. pan. 26 uses the term *andare*. Antonio da Tempo refers to the second part as the *pedes* or *mutatio*; the first part he calls the *volta*. The *pedes* is repeated each time, and then the performers return to the *volta* in a *represa*, giving the music the form *A B B A*. The poetic form may be extended so as to have two or three additional sets of text for further repetitions of the music. Where such is the case, the lines of the *volta* are repeated for each set of lines, giving an extended form as follows:[1]

Music: *A B B A   A B B A   A B B A*
Poetry: *A B C D   A E F G   A H I J*

Mario Apollonio[2] has drawn attention to the twelfth-century origins of the *ballata*; it was then frequently in dialogue form, but still with an *A B B A* sequence which was sung—perhaps partly while standing[3]—and danced. Antonio says, 'Et tales ballatae cantantur et coreizantur'. Both da Prato and Boccaccio explicitly describe the singing and dancing of a *ballata* with instrumental accompaniment. It is, however, an art dance as contrasted with such social dances as the monodic *istampite* and *saltarelli*.

Most of the two-part *ballate* have texts given with both parts, as in the case of the madrigals. There is a much higher proportion of three-part *ballate* than of madrigals, however, and in these the instrumental parts are common. In a considerable number the text is only furnished with the cantus part, leaving both tenor and contratenor parts to be played on instruments. That they were so intended is shown by the changes made between different manuscripts when the text is given in one but omitted in the other manuscript for the tenor or contratenor of the same composition. The part without text employs fewer repeated notes, and many more ligatures in its notation. Parts in all works given without text not only show more use of ligatures, but also employ wider and more frequent intervals, abandoning

[1] Cf. Ellinwood, op. cit., pp. xxviii ff., for a detailed analysis of the arrangement of the text in the 141 *ballate* by Francesco Landini.
[2] *Uomi e forme nella cultura italiana delle origini* (Florence, 1943).
[3] See p. 119.

the diatonic style of writing employed for the purely vocal parts. This
use of instruments is described in the 33rd sonnet of 'Mundus Placitus'
in Prodenzani's *Saporetto*:[1]

> Con la chitarra fe' suoni a tenore
> Con tanta melodia, che a ciaschuno
> Per la dolceça gli alegrava 'l core.
>
> Con la cetera ancor ne fece alcuno,
> Puoi venner pifar sordi cum tenore:
> Solaço incontenente ne prese uno.
>
> (With the lute he played the tenor
> With such melody, that everyone's heart
> Was cheered through its sweetness.
>
> With the cither he also made some [music],
> Then came the muted shawm with the tenor:
> Sollazzo immediately picked one up.)

The *ballate* vary in length. The monodic ones, cited above, frequently have but one phrase of text in the *volta*, as do some polyphonic settings. A few, such as Landini's three-part 'Partesi con
dolori', have some of the customary repetitions set throughout. In
none are there the extended melismas which are encountered in the
madrigals. Another characteristic, seldom found in the other Italian
forms of the period, is the use of a first and second ending, *verto* and
chiuso, most commonly with the *pedes* but occasionally also in the
volta. These endings are used to permit a wider range of harmonic
interest without destroying the tonality of the work. The following
show such use in Landini's 'Donna per farmi':[2]

Ex. 26

-re   Er - ran - do   gi - va   fuor   d'og - ni   sa -
-re   Che frut - to   di - ven - tai   per   tua   vir -

-lu-
-tu-

1   2   D.C.

- te.

- te.

Verto   *Chiuso*

2. Donna per farmi guerra o per mal dire,
        La fè non mi torrai,
   Ch'i'diedi a tte quando m'innamorai.
   Questo valor tien seco la mia fede
   Et fammi d'ogni pena trar diletto.
   Se l'occhio fer' aver di me ti vede,
   Ricorre la memoria al primo effetto
   Mostrandoti pietos' all' inteletto
        Tal che gli amari guay
   Da mme discaccio e fo cio che tu sai.

3. Donna per farmi guerra o per mal dire,
        La fè non mi torrai,
   Ch'i' diedi a tte quando m'innamorai.
   Fa', credi, pensa et di' puro a tuo posta
   C'ongni mal quanto in me pace mi fià.
   È ver che tua vergongni' assai mi costa,
   Chè biasmo segue a donna usar follia.
   Duolmi che la tua colpa vuo' far mia;
        Ma quanto più dirai,
   Tacendo mosterrò ch'i' non fallai.

   Donna per farmi . . .

(1. Lady, although you war on me and speak ill of me, you shall not turn away
that loyalty which I pledged when I fell in love with you.
   I am thinking of the time when, like a youthful flower, I was wandering far

from any bliss. And I am thinking of the time when love gave me to you so that through your power I became fruit.

Although killed in the shadows by strong wounds, I came back to the light, looking at which I shall never die.

2. Lady, . . .

My faith has such a power; and it causes me to draw pleasure from every sorrow. If my eye sees you, my memory goes back to your first effect,

When you showed yourself compassionate to my mood, so that I drive out my bitter woes and do what you know.

3. Lady, . . .

Act, believe, think, and speak, as you wish; every evil, in so far as it concerns me, will be peace to me. It is true that your shameful behaviour costs me a great deal, because blame follows the foolish acting of a woman.

And I regret that you want to burden me with your guilt; but the more you talk, the more I will show by my silence that I was not at fault.

Lady, . . .)

This is typical of the fully developed *ballata* towards the end of the century. Notice the remarkably modern half cadence at the *verto* of the *pedes*. More characteristic is a *pedes* ending on the supertonic, particularly in the most common tonality on D or the related one on G, as in Landini's 'Donna 'l tuo partimento':[1]

Ex. 27

¹ Ellinwood, op. cit., no. 116.

In the case of a tonality on C or its relative F the *verto* of the *pedes* frequently concludes on the mediant instead of the supertonic.[1]

In very few instances is there a change of rhythm in the course of a *ballata*, and then it does not come at the end of a section as in the madrigals. On the other hand, all forms of duple and triple rhythm are used for entire works. There is less use of the devices typical of the Italian notation, and more reliance on the use of white notation for brief metrical changes. Debenedetti's anonymous *Capitulum* states:

Volunt etiam esse de tempore perfecto et de aere ytallico, et in aliquibus locis vel punctis de gallico, sed non in principio nec in fine. Si quis vult quod trottetur faciat in simili aere, sed de tempore imperfecto; volta autem pedis vel pedum vult esse trium et non diverse.

(Moreover they should be in perfect time and in the Italian style [i.e. in duple prolation], and, at certain points, in the French style, but not at the very beginning or the end. If anyone wishes to make a *trotto*,[2] he may do it in the same style but in imperfect time; but the second section or its repetition should be triple and not the opposite.)

There are some *ballate* in the earlier Rossi manuscript but there are relatively few by composers prior to Francesco Landini. At the end of the century, they constitute almost the entire known output of Andrea dei Servi and Zaccaria.

Other forms described by Antonio da Tempo and the other writers are:

1. The sonnet, of which there are sixteen species. It has many elements in common with the *ballata*. Cf. the example given above under monodies, or Paolo's 'Lasso greve 'l partir'.

2. The *rotundellus*, or *rondello*, a round dance which has the first line repeated several times in the text but is otherwise much like the *ballata*. This is also represented by a single, two-part example in the Rossi manuscript: cf. the earlier monodies in this form found in Florence, Bibl. Laurenziana, plut. xxix, 1 (cf. vol. II, p. 243). Ghidino states:

Item nota che li rotondelli sono usitati in Franza, et oltra li monti, più che non sono in questa nostra Lombardia.

(Likewise note that rondels are used in France and beyond the Alps more than they are in this Lombardy of ours.)

3. The *cantus extensa* appears to be an extended *ballata* such as Landini's 'I' fu tuo serv', amore'.

---

[1] Cf. Ellinwood, op. cit., pp. xxxvi ff., for a detailed study of trecento tonalities.
[2] The *trotto* appears to have been a dance form: cf. Wolf in *Archiv für Musikwissenschaft*, i (1918–19), pp. 16 and 39.

4. The *serventesius* or *sermontesius*, the troubadour *sirventes*.

5. The *motus confectus*, possibly the motet.

SACRED WORKS

The trecento was on the whole a secular age. Its interests and activities were either personal or municipal, not centred around the church as so much of medieval life had been. The very fact that a French Pope, Clement V, had removed the seat of the papacy from Italy diminished the incentive for professional musicians to write new compositions for church festivals. The Bull of Pope John XXII in 1324–5 was also discouraging.[1] Consequently, even though a number of the more distinguished composers were church organists or singers, most of their works were written for occasions outside the church.

There are no motets by Italians of this period which employ a plainsong or other pre-existent tenor, as do the French motets of the thirteenth century. The few motets which were composed follow rather the secular forms and styles which have just been discussed: the madrigal, *caccia*, and *ballata*. The last-named form was more commonly used by the composers of the period immediately after 1400. In a work like the three-part 'Veri almi pastoris' by Corrado da Pistoia there is text in the *cantus* only with an instrumental tenor and contratenor, performed with a *verto* and *chiuso* at the end of the *volta*. Nor are there any examples of the mixed Latin and vernacular texts found in the earlier French works. Where a different text is provided for a second part, either *cantus* II or contratenor, it is always Latin as for the first part. In all the works examined, as in the polytexual secular works mentioned above, this second text takes on the semblance of a second stanza. Thus the homage intended to Francesco Zabarella in Johannes Ciconia's 'Ut te per omnes' would not be clear unless the listener heard the two stanzas consecutively.

Few of these motets, except a few of those of the early quattrocento, have any isorhythmic features.[2] This is consistent with the almost total absence of this technique from the secular works of the trecento. But a number of the motets use canonic devices, at times in imitation between the parts, and at times taking the form of the *caccia* for a portion of the work. Such is Ciconia's 'O felix templum'[3] which ends as follows:

[1] See pp. xvii and 3.
[2] Cf. C. van den Borren, *Polyphonia Sacra* (London, 1936).
[3] Ibid., p. 243.

Ex. 28

An earlier motet, 'Lux purpurata radiis' by Jacopo da Bologna,[1] ends with an interesting bit of hocket:

Ex. 29

Notice the interesting, and not uncommon, harmonic progression at the end. Contrast this with the ending of Ciconia's 'Ut te per omnes'[2] composed forty or more years later:

Ex. 30

[1] Cf. G. de Van, *Les Monuments de l'ars nova* (Paris, 1939).
[2] Van den Borren, op. cit., p. 180.

Portions of the Ordinary of the Mass had been troped polyphonically in the Notre Dame repertory in conductus style, but prior to the
fourteenth century no complete polyphonic movements on the texts
of the Mass itself were known. There are a number of settings by
various fourteenth-century composers,[1] for whom the *Credo* and
Gloria were the most popular sections, although a few settings of the
Sanctus and *Agnus* are known (perhaps less popular because their
texts were so short). The earlier settings are in two or three parts in
a close madrigal style, as in this *Gloria* by Gherardello:[2]

Ex. 31

(And on earth peace to men of good will. We praise thee.)

By the end of the trecento these Mass settings were, like the motets,
also in the *ballata* and *caccia* styles. An interesting feature, used in
both *Gloria* and *Credo* movements by a number of composers, was
the alternation between two and three parts for successive phrases of
text. In a *Gloria* setting by Ciconia,[3] the two-part phrases are marked
'dui' while the three-part phrases are marked 'chorus' although there
are still but two parts with text. A *Credo* setting by Bartolomeo da
Bologna[4] set in the same manner has the text in the cantus part only
in the three-part sections, while it is given with both parts in the two-
part sections. This fashion is common to England, France, and Italy.
Another interesting setting of the *Gloria* by Ciconia[5] repeats at 'Qui
tollis peccata' the music used at 'Laudamus te', so that the musical
form is: *A* (nine bars) *B* (thirty-two) *B* (same thirty-two repeated)
C (fifteen). The music, in three parts, has text only in the cantus.
The end of *B* is as follows:

[1] Cf. *supra*, p. 21, and F. Ludwig, 'Die mehrstimmige Messe des 14. Jahrhunderts',
Archiv für Musikwissenschaft, vii (1925), pp. 417–35.
[2] G. de Van, op. cit., pp. 1–4; and Pirrotta, *The Music of Fourteenth Century Italy*, i
(*Corpus mensurabilis musicae*, viii; Amsterdam, 1954), p. 53.
[3] Van den Borren, op. cit., p. 82.
[4] Ibid., p. 44.
[5] Ibid., p. 88. Also in A. T. Davison and W. Apel, *Historical Anthology of Music*, i
(Cambridge, Mass., 1946), no. 55.

Ex. 32

All these sacred works are consistently pitched higher than most of the secular works of the trecento, with an upper limit of as much as a fifth more at times. While this might be explained in terms of organ pitch, a factor known to have influenced compositions during the late Renaissance, it may well be due to the acoustic properties of the cathedrals for which they were composed. Even today, organists frequently transpose hymns and anthems to a higher pitch in order that they may carry more clearly through the vaulted bays of a large cathedral. The secular music, sung in smaller halls or in gardens, would not need the same timbre in the voices. That transposition may have been a common practice is attested by the existence of at least two works, the conductus 'Quid tu vides, Jeremia?' and Landini's 'De'! pon quest' amor', which have been transposed down a fourth or fifth in different manuscripts.

THE COMPOSERS

Giovanni da Cascia (Johannes de Florentia[1]) was the first of the trecento composers to achieve widespread and permanent fame. Villani[2] writes of his skill at the organ, his reforms in the musical service at the church of Santa Maria del Fiore, and his later service under Mastino della Scala, tyrant of Verona from 1329 to 1351, mentioning his madrigals in particular. The fact that Villani speaks of him in the perfect tense, coupled with the position of his music in the several manuscripts, leads us to believe that his career lay largely in the second quarter of the century. Adolfo Morini[3] has demonstrated that he was an Umbrian by birth. Twenty-one of his compositions are known today, all madrigals apart from two *cacce* and one *ballata*. In the Squarcialupi codex 'Johannes de Florentia' is the name assigned to his compositions, which come in the first section of the manuscript. At the end of the manuscript there is a blank section with

[1] Complete works in Pirrotta, op. cit. There has been so much confusion, even within recent years by otherwise well-informed writers, between the Latin and Italian forms of the names of these trecento composers, that we give both here in an effort to end the confusion.

[2] *Liber de Civitatis Florentiae famosis civibus.* The entire music section of this contemporary historian is quoted in Ellinwood, op. cit., pp. 301–3.

[3] *Giovanni da Cascia e Donato da Cascia musicisti umbri* (Spoleto, 1937).

only the miniature filled in, designed for the work of another Johannes 'horganista de Florentia', about whom nothing is known.

It would be foolhardy to attempt to point out many individual style practices in this period. Almost any device which might be noted can readily be found in various composers of the century, so that it is more truly a device of the era than of the individual. Nevertheless, there are a few details which are used more frequently by one than by all composers of the trecento. One of these is the form of their cadence. Giovanni favoured a cadence such as the following from the ritornello of his 'Nel mezzo a sei paon':[1]

Ex. 33

[can]　-　-　-　to.

Jacopo da Bologna (Jacobus de Bononia)[2] was a contemporary of Giovanni, with whom he contended, according to Villani, before Mastino della Scala. Thus he is the only non-Florentine composer to be mentioned in that source-book. He is also the only composer of the group to have left a theoretical work, *L'arte del biscanto misurato*. This is a brief work which discusses and illustrates note and ligature values in terms of perfection and prolation. He was probably a teacher of Francesco Landini. His interests in music pedagogy are evinced in the following madrigal text:

> Uselletto selvaggio per stagione
> Dolci versetti canta con bel modo.
> Tale che grida forte chi non lodo:
> Per gridar forte non si canta bene
> Ma con soave et dolce melodia
> Si fa bel canto e ciò vuol maestria.
> Pochi l'hanno et tutti si fan maestri,
> Fan ballate madriali e motteti;
> Tutti infioran Filipi e Marchetti.
> Sì è piena la terra di maéstroli
> Che loco più non trovano discépoli.
>
> (A wild bird during the season
> Sings sweet lines in a fine style.
> I do not praise a singer who shouts loudly:

---

[1] Wolf, *Geschichte der Mensural-Notation*, iii, no. 38. Also in Davison and Apel, op. cit., no. 50. Recorded in *The History of Music in Sound*, iii.

[2] Complete works, with an English translation of *L'arte del biscanto misurato*, in W. Thomas Marrocco, *The Music of Jacopo da Bologna* (Berkeley, Cal., 1954). The treatise has also been edited, with a German translation, by Johannes Wolf in *Theodor Kroyer-Festschrift* (Regensburg, 1933).

Loud shouting does not make good singing,
But with smooth and sweet melody
Lovely singing is produced and this requires skill.
Few people possess it, but all set up as masters
And compose ballads, madrigals, and motets;
All try to outdo Philippe [de Vitry] and Marchettus [de Padua].
Thus the country is so full of petty masters
That there is no room left for pupils.)

Jacopo left thirty-four known works, all madrigals except for single examples each of the *caccia* and sacred motet, and a *lauda* in the form of a *ballata*. His favourite type of cadence was that of the madrigal cited above:

Ex. 34

[dis] - - ce - po - li.

Fra Bartolino da Padova (Frater Bartolinus de Padua) has been wrongly identified with the Bartholus de Florentia[1] mentioned by Villani. In the sonnet by Prodenzani quoted earlier in this chapter he is called Fra Bartolino, while his portrait in the Squarcialupi codex shows him tonsured and wearing a Benedictine habit. Forty of his works have been identified, of which ten are madrigals.

Ser Lorenzo Masini,[2] or Lorenzo da Firenze (Laurentius de Florentia), is the last of the earlier group of musicians mentioned by Villani. Seventeen of his works are known today: ten madrigals, five *ballate*, a *caccia*, and a *Sanctus*.

Piero (Petrus) would appear to be a skilled composer, although not prolific. We know nine of his works, of which five are in canonic form—more than those left by any other. All are in Florence, Bibl. naz., pan. 26, with a few also in some of the other collections, but he was apparently unknown to the compiler of the Squarcialupi codex. One wonders if he was the 'Maestro Pier de Giuvenale' mentioned by Prodenzani.

Ser Gherardello da Firenze left nineteen known compositions,[3] sixteen of which are secular works collected with his portrait in the Squarcialupi codex. From the names of the composers who set Sacchetti's texts, as indicated in the Florence, Bibl. Laurenziana, Ashburnham 574, it appears that he had a brother and son, Jacopo

---

[1] Composer of a *Credo* in Paris, Bibl. Nat., ital. 568, printed in Pirrotta, op. cit.
[2] Composers with the appellation 'Ser' had either professional or social standing in the community. All, whether monk, priest, or organist, were designated 'Magister', but only a few of the lay composers were called 'Ser'.   [3] Printed in Pirrotta, op. cit.

and Giovanni, but their music is not known. Wolf[1] quotes a pair of sonnets exchanged by Franco Sacchetti and Francesco de Messer Simone Peruzzi on the death of Gherardello.

Don Vincenzo da Rimini (Dominus Abbas Vincentius de Arimino) likewise has a few folios in the Squarcialupi codex, with his portrait. He was an abbot of either Rimini or Imola. There are six known works: four madrigals and two *cacce*.

Don Donato da Cascia (Dominus Donatus de Florentia) is another Umbrian musician who was a priest at the Benedictine abbey of Cascia near Florence.[2] Seventeen of his works are known, all madrigals except for a single *ballata*.

Ser Niccolò da Perugia (Nicolaus praepositus de Perugia) was provost of the cathedral chapter at Perugia, judging from his title. He left forty compositions, in all the forms discussed above. Niccolò is one of the first to use the syncopated cadence which Francesco Landini used so frequently. This example is from the former's 'Nel mezzo già del mar':

Ex.35

[volta'n] cià.

Don Paolo da Firenze (Dominus Paulus de Florentia) is also called Paolo tenorista, i.e. 'Paul the tenor'. A document dated 1404 (Vatican, lat. 2664, cc. 252) describes him as abbot of Pozzoli in the diocese of Arezzo.[3] His eleven madrigals, a 'Benedicamus Domino', and all save one of his twenty-four *ballate* are in Paris, Bibl. Nat., ital. 568. If his 'Godi Firenze' actually does commemorate the conquest of Pisa by Florence in 1406, as suggested by several writers, his work is later than the style implies.

LANDINI

Francesco Landini, the famous blind organist of Florence (Magister Franciscus caecus horganista de Florentia) is both the most prolific and the best known composer of the entire period.[4] He is

[1] *Sammelbände der internationalen Musikgesellschaft*, iii (1901–2), p. 611.
[2] Cf. Morini, op. cit., and S. Clercx in *Revue belge de musicologie*, x (1956), p. 155.
[3] '. . . domino Paulo de Florentia, abate Pozzoli Arentine diocesis'. This was the *Camaldolensian* abbey of Pozzoveri. At the time of this document, Paolo was in the service of Cardinal Acciaiuoli in Rome. Cf. N. Pirrotta and E. Li Gotti, 'Paulo tenorista', *Estudios dedicados a Menendez Pidal*, iii (Madrid, 1952).
[4] Complete works, ed. Ellinwood (Cambridge Mass., 1939). Cf. also 'Francesco Landini and his music', *Musical Quarterly*, xxii (1936), pp. 190–216. An additional

mentioned in a number of contemporary documents, which are quoted in detail in the edition of his works. We have already cited several contemporary references to Francesco and his music. Villani devotes a long section of his *Liber de civitatis Florentiae famosis civibus* to facts about his life and praise of his accomplishments.

He was born *c.* 1325 at Fiesole, near Florence. Villani states that he was the son of Jacopo the painter, presumably Jacopo del Casentino. Francesco became blind in early childhood as a result of the smallpox, an affliction which helped him to develop the prodigious memory and great skill in improvisation for which he was widely renowned. In spite of his blindness, he was well trained in fields other than music. His grandnephew, Cristoforo Landini, distinguished Dante commentator of the following century, wrote that he was 'non indotto in Filosofia, non indotto in Astrologia' and then adds 'ma in Musica dottissimo' (not ungifted in philosophy, not ungifted in astrology, but most gifted in music). Villani cites a long list of instruments which he was able to play, and a new one, called the *serena serenorum*, which he invented. He also goes into many details to show how greatly Francesco excelled all others on the complicated organs, a skill which won him the laurel wreath from the king of Cyprus. This event, which presumably took place in 1364 at Venice, is not referred to in Petrarch's description of the festivities held in honour of the subjugation of rebels in Crete, an omission which has led some to question the accuracy of Villani's biographical sketch. On the other hand, Venetian historians have held that Francesco de Pesaro, the organist at San Marco, was the victor in the contest for organ-playing and that Francesco Landini was crowned as a poet instead. In 1375 Coluccio Salutati petitioned the bishop of Florence on Francesco's behalf, referring to the skill 'ex quo et urbi nostrae gloriosum nomen et ecclesiae Florentinae ab isto caeco lumen accedit' (through which our city receives a glorious name, and the Florentine church light from this blind man).

Francesco died on 2 September 1397 and was buried two days later in the church of San Lorenzo, Florence, where he had long served as organist. His tombstone was removed during the following century, and the reverse side used for another person. It was discovered about the middle of the nineteenth century in the convent chapel of San Domenico at Prato and was restored to the Capella Ginori of San

---

work, in the Lucca codex, 'Io ti so stato e voglio esser fedele', is referred to by Ghisi, *Journal of Renaissance and Baroque Music*, i (1946), p. 179. His *ballata* ' Amar sì li alti tuo gentil costumi' is recorded in *The History of Music in Sound*, iii.

Lorenzo in 1890, through the efforts of the Royal Commission of Fine Arts. The tombstone shows a full-length, recumbent figure, holding an *organetto* in playing position, surmounted with the Landini coat of arms: a pyramid with six golden mounds on a field of azure, with three branches of laurel protruding from the mounds. On either side are two small angels playing the lute and viol, while round the stone are the lines:

> Luminibus captus Franciscus mente capaci
> Cantibus organicis, quem cunctis Musica solum
> Pretulit, hic cineres, animam super astra reliquit.

(Francesco, deprived of sight, but with a mind skilled in instrumental music, whom alone Music has set above all others, has left his ashes here, his soul above the stars.)

A eulogy from Cino Rinuccini refers to his knowledge of the liberal arts and states that, although blind in the body, Francesco had a brilliant spirit which knew the theoretical as well as the practical in music, and that no one of his time could modulate sweeter songs or play more skilfully on musical instruments, particularly the organ. The theorist known as Anonymus V[1] discusses the notation of Francesco's 'Donna, che d'amor'. His name has been associated with the following type of cadence which is used frequently by most of the composers of the latter half of the trecento and early quattrocento. The example is the *chiuso* from the *pedes* of his 'Po che partir':[2]

Ex.36

[ama] - - - - - ra.

Francesco's *ballata* 'Questa fanciull' amor' was later arranged as a *Kyrie* in Munich MS. 3232a, and in organ tablature.[3] One other work, the *ballata*, 'Non arà mà pietà',[4] is also known in an organ tablature.[5] We quote the first phrase of both the original and the tablature:

---

[1] Coussemaker, *Scriptorum*, iii, pp. 395–6.
[2] Ellinwood, op. cit., no. 143.
[3] Wolf, *Handbuch der Notationskunde*, ii, p. 254.
[4] Ellinwood, op. cit., no. 135.
[5] See p. 424.

Ex.37

Non ... a - rà mà pie- -tà, ques-ta mia don - - - - - na,

Ex.38

OTHER COMPOSERS OF THE LATER TRECENTO

Grazioso da Padova (Gratiosus de Padua) is known only for two settings from the Ordinary of the Mass, both in *ballata* style.[1]

Fra Andrea dei Servi (Frater Andreas organista dei Servi) was a member of the order of the Servi di Maria. He is first mentioned in the account books of the cathedral at Pistoia in connexion with fees for performers on the patronal feast of St. James in 1366.[2] He is again

---

[1] Cf. De Van, *Les Monuments de l'ars nova*, i.
[2] Cf. Taucci, 'Fra Andrea dei Servi', *Rivista di studi storici sull' Ordine dei Servi di Maria*, ii (1935), p. 32.

mentioned a number of times between 1380 and 1389. From his portrait and description in the Squarcialupi codex, one would infer that he was also active in Florence. Thirty *ballate* by him are extant; he is also probably the Andreas whose *Sanctus* is in the Trent codex 92. He may possibly be identified with Andrea Stefani.[1]

Thus ended a century in which a completely independent polyphonic art developed in Italy. A rhythmic freedom and melodic spirit were fostered which merged temporarily with the more sombre northern art, only to break out afresh into the new forms of the quattrocento.

[1] Cf. A. Bonaccorsi, 'Andrea Stefani, musicista dell' "Ars nova" ', *La Rassegna musicale*, xviii (1948), pp. 103–5.

III

ENGLISH CHURCH MUSIC IN THE FOURTEENTH CENTURY

By Frank Ll. Harrison

CHANGES IN LITURGICAL PRACTICE

COMPARED with the relative abundance of musical manuscripts on the Continent, the remains of English liturgical polyphony of the fourteenth century are sadly meagre. Not a single complete manuscript has survived and, apart from those pieces in the Old Hall manuscript of the early fifteenth century which belong in style to the late fourteenth century, all our material is preserved on leaves or groups of leaves, some used as fly-leaves and some so defaced or mutilated through use as binding material as to be illegible or reduced to mere fragments. Some attempt may be made, however, to deduce from these remnants the main outlines of the developments in musical style and the changes in the liturgical function of polyphony which were taking place during the century. The nature of the change in liturgical practice may be judged by comparing the repertory of motets, conductus, and ritual tropes of the Worcester music and the Reading index with the Mass settings, motets, and antiphons of the Old Hall collection. The motet held its position as a distinct musical genre until the mid-fifteenth century, though it submitted to significant changes in melodic and rhythmic style. Tropes of the Ordinary and Proper of the Mass gave way to settings of the ritual texts of the Ordinary, excluding the *Kyrie*, but including the only tropes of the other parts of the Ordinary, the 'Spiritus et alme orphanorum' of the *Gloria* and the 'Benedictus Mariae filius' of the *Sanctus*, which were permitted in English secular rites. By the later years of the century the conductus had disappeared and the votive antiphon had begun the history which was to come to such a splendid climax in the early Tudor period. In general these changes in the liturgical function of polyphony reflect a period when the musical leadership the monasteries had held in the thirteenth century was coming to an end. The initiative in liturgical and musical development was passing to the secular foundations, to the cathedrals and the new collegiate churches and colleges, and, at the turn of the century, to the Royal Household Chapel.

THE NEW COLLEGE MOTETS

Of the three most important sets of manuscript remains of the first half of the century, one is connected with the Abbey of Bury St. Edmunds, while the provenance of the others is unknown. They give some idea of the development of the motet and conductus in England and of the ways in which the practice of English composers diverged from that of their French contemporaries. The technique of iso-rhythm, for example, appears here in a form little more developed than the short repeated patterns of the thirteenth-century motet, in contrast to the French development of the isorhythmic tenor as the structural and formal basis of the motet. To judge from these sur-vivals, the characteristic features of English technique were variety in the treatment of the tenor of a motet, the extension of *rondellus*[1] technique to both motet and conductus, conservatism in rhythmic style and therefore in notation, and the use of parallel thirds and sixths on a parity with the perfect intervals.

The first of these groups of leaves (Oxford, New College 362)[2] contains one voice of the *rondellus*-motet 'Balaam inquit vaticinans/ Balaam', which occurs complete in the great French collection at Montpellier (Bibl. Univ. H 196), in the eighth fascicle, for which Yvonne Rokseth suggested a date in the early years of the fourteenth century.[3] The New College leaves also have one work, 'Fulget caelestis curia/O Petre flos apostolorum'[4] in common with the Worcester group of remains, and one, 'Triumphat hodie/Si que la nuit',[5] with the fly-leaves of British Museum Add. 24198, a Missal which apparently belonged to the Augustinian Abbey of St. Thomas the Martyr in Dublin. In the New College manuscript, originally a large collection since the folio numbers still to be seen go up to ninety, there survive all or parts of fourteen motets, four conductus, and two pieces in simple descant style.[6] Eight of the motets are complete, while 'Balaam' and 'Triumphat hodie' can be completed from the sources referred to.

In the choice and treatment of their tenors these ten motets, three

---

[1] See vol. II, p. 374.　　　　　　　　　　　　　　　[2] See also vol. II, p. 356.

[3] Rokseth, *Polyphonies du XIIIe siècle*, iv (Paris, 1939), p. 140.

[4] Transcription in Manfred Bukofzer, *Sumer is icumen in: a Revision* (Berkeley, California, 1944), p. 98.

[5] Recorded in *The History of Music in Sound* (H.M.V.), ii.

[6] The contents are listed by Higini Anglès in *El Còdex musical de Las Huelgas* (Barcelona, 1931), i, pp. 229–31. He gives twenty-four pieces; of these No. 17 belongs to No. 16, No. 18 to No. 1, No. 19 to No. 6, and No. 22 to No. 21. Rokseth (op. cit., iv, p. 90, n. 4), counting the 'Balaam' motet (No. 10) as two, as it is in the Montpellier MS., makes the total twenty-one.

for four voices and the rest for three, provide interestingly varied examples of English methods. The choice includes the *neuma* (plain-song melisma) of the traditional kind in two cases, a French secular song in four cases, a complete respond and a complete antiphon, and two verses from a sequence. The remaining motet has a tenor of plainsong character which has not been identified. The rhythmic treatment of the tenors is equally varied, the nearest to the classical thirteenth-century method (the short repeated pattern) being in 'Regali ex progenie',[1] the antiphon used complete as the tenor of 'Rosa delectabilis/Regalis exoritur'. The tenor 'Agmina'[2] of 'De spineto/Virgo sancta Katherina' begins in conventional fashion with a repeated *ordo* of three longs; before the end of the first statement, however, it assumes varied patterns of longs and breves, and in the third and fourth statements has varied rhythms containing longs, breves, and semibreves. The effect is one of diminution, though it is not exactly applied to the relationship of the statements. The four-part 'O homo de pulvere/O homo considerans' is based on the *neuma* 'Filiae Jerusalem', the first words of a respond for a Martyr or Confessor, sung thrice in a rhythmic scheme made up of five different *ordines*. In the incomplete motet 'Apello Caesarem' the tenor 'Omnes' has thirteen statements in constantly changing patterns of longs and breves. This may be compared with the planning of the same tenor in Adam de la Hale's motet 'De ma dame vient/Dieus! coument porroie',[3] where it has four statements in each of three different rhythms. On the other hand, the composer of the lengthy motet 'Januam quam clauserat/Jacinctus in saltibus/Jacet granum' used one statement only of the third respond at Matins of St. Thomas of Canterbury as his tenor, setting it out in varied rhythms in phrases of three to nine longs separated by a long rest, ending with a phrase of eleven longs. The four parts may be reduced to three by singing the part marked *Tenor per se de Jacet granum* in place of the tenor and *quartus cantus*. This must be one of the earliest instances of such a 'substitute' part:[4]

---

[1] *Antiphonale Sarisburiense*, ed. W. H. Frere (London, 1901–26), pl. 526; not identified in Anglès's list.

[2] Rokseth (op. cit., iv, p. 182), following Ludwig, gives as the source of 'Agmina' an Alleluia 'Corpus beate virginis', the music of which has not been found in a liturgical source. However, the tenor of the New College motet is identical with the *neuma* 'agmina' in the St. Katherine respond 'Virgo flagellatur' (*Processionale Monasticum* (Solesmes, 1893), p. 214).

[3] Rokseth, op. cit., iii, p. 138.

[4] Oxford, New Coll. 362, fos. 84ᵛ–85; plainsong from Bodleian Library, MS. E Mus. 2, p. 75.

Ex. 39

(*Plainsong*: The grain lies covered with chaff

I: The door which the enjoyment of food had closed is opened to holy Thomas
by dread martyrdom. Thomas subdued the flesh
II: In the woods the boy Hyacinthus is slain, from whose ashes arises a
crimson flower.)

The use of a secular *chanson* as the tenor of a motet was one of the
trends in the French repertory of the late thirteenth century. In the
St. Lawrence motet 'Triumphat hodie' the *chanson* 'Si que la nuit'
is sung in *rondellus* manner by the two lower parts, which treat it in

hocket fashion towards the end, while 'A definement deste lerray', the tenor of 'Adae finit perpete/Adae finit misere', is disposed in three complete statements. In this case the tenor is in a higher clef than the duplum and is often the middle part. The *chanson* 'Mariounette douche' is used in both of the other motets with secular tenor, as the lowest voice in the four-part 'Solaris ardor Romuli/Gregorius sol saeculi/Petre tua navicula'[1] and as the middle part,[2] set to a Latin text, in 'Caligo terrae scinditur/Virgo mater':[3]

Ex. 40

(*I*: Earth's gloom is cleft, pierced by the sun's dart, while the Sun is born of a Star at the dawn of the Faith.

II: The Virgin Mother who is also daughter of the King Most High becomes the remedy for those who mourn.)

In both pieces it has one complete statement in the *virelai* form *abbaa*. Other instances of the use of a *cantus prius factus* as a middle part occur in the motet in honour of St. Edward 'Civitas nusquam conditur/Cibus esurientum (*tenor*)/Tu es caelestis curiae' and in 'Rosa delectabilis'. This practice is of some interest in view of its regular adoption in English descant after *c.* 1350 for setting ritual plainsongs. Another noticeable tendency in English motets of this period, found also in conductus, is the setting of words in phrases of equal length with the parts overlapping at the cadences. The typical procedure may be seen in 'Januam quam clauserat', where after an initial syllable the

---

[1] Recorded in *The History of Music in Sound*, ii.
[2] The identity of the melodies was noted by Rokseth.
[3] New Coll. 362, fo. 88ᵛ.

entry of the second part is delayed for two longs. Thereafter the plan of the phrases of this part is $9+8\times11+11$ longs, while that of the highest part is $8\times13+7$ longs. There is no movement towards iso-rhythm in the internal patterns of the phrases; rather the reverse, for the note-values are so disposed as to achieve a variety of pattern which is certainly intentional.

The rhythmic character of 'Januam quam clauserat' is determined by the use of longs and breves, with occasional semibreves, sung in a smoothly flowing rhythm and in a slower tempo than the same values were sung in the early thirteenth century.[1] This seems to have been the kind of rhythm most favoured in English polyphony until *c.* 1350. There is also found in the New College motets a rhythmic style in which the breve is divided into three or more semibreves, marked off by a *punctus divisionis*. This method has been given the name 'Petro-nian' because it is associated with the late thirteenth-century motets of Petrus de Cruce.[2] Examples occur occasionally in the triplum 'De spineto' and constantly in the highest part of 'Caligo terrae', which has the kind of rhythmic contrast between the upper parts which was a characteristic of de Cruce's style. The outer parts of 'Rosa delecta-bilis' show the next stage in the use of smaller divisions of the breve:[3]

Ex. 41

[1] See Apel, *The Notation of Polyphonic Music 900–1600* (Cambridge, Mass., fourth edition, 1949), p. 343.

[2] See vol. II, p. 380 and *supra*, p. 48; also Rokseth, op. cit., iv, pp. 79–80; Apel, op. cit., pp. 318–19; and Robertus de Handlo's *Regulae* (1326): 'Securius tamen et verius in Motetis et in aliis cantibus, ubi semibreves sunt, addatur punctus ... ut ponit Petrus de Cruce' (Coussemaker, *Scriptorum*, i, p. 387). [3] New Coll. 362, fos. 90ᵛ–91.

(*Plainsong*: Mary of the royal line.

   I: A sweet rose without a thorn arises, a queen of highest birth, she without
stain, she who comes forth as a rod from the root of Jesse.

   II: A royal mother arises, a soul of beauty; affection for this world's honour
is done away, the good flesh is seen to rise up restored.)

Here the notes in the triplet groups which are transcribed as quavers
are *semibreves majores* in the form ⭡, and the semiquavers are *semibreves minores* in the form ◆. This method of writing uneven patterns
within the value of the breve was one of the developments of the early
ars nova in France.

THE NEW COLLEGE CONDUCTUS

The two complete conductus in this manuscript show how English
composers of the period used their traditional *rondellus* technique to
give new life to a form which had gone out of fashion in France by the
early fourteenth century. In 'Fulget caelestis curiae/O Petre flos
apostolorum' two poems are set for three voices in interchange, with
a short prelude in which two voices sing a sequential melody in canon,
while 'Excelsus in numine' is a setting of a single poem treated in
rondellus manner by two parts over a wordless tenor, also with an
independent prelude. From the two voices of 'Sanctorum gloria'
which remain it is possible to see that its form is an expansion of that
of the English conductus of the thirteenth century, for it has a lengthy
prelude and shorter interludes in which two parts sing in *rondellus*
over the tenor, all without words, and sections in which the text is set
in homorhythmic style, that is, with uniform rhythm and simultaneous
words.

Finally, the manuscript has two specimens of the particularly
English form of homorhythmic treatment which has become known
as 'English descant'. 'Spiritus procedens a patre' is a setting of a
short text which ends with the words 'orphanorum paraclite', which
is clearly a troping elaboration of the Marian trope of the *Gloria*
'Spiritus et alme orphanorum'.[1] It is in a triple rhythm of longs and
breves with occasional semibreves and semibreve triplets. The other
piece is a curious affair in a very simple rhythm of almost unvaried

---

[1] Transcription in *The Worcester Fragments*, ed. L. A. Dittmer (Rome, 1957), p. 70.

breves, with several groups of repeated notes. The text, very casually indicated, begins with 'Jube' and ends with 'bene . d . .', and is possibly a troped form of the formula 'Jube domne benedicere' with which a reader asked the blessing of the officiant before a lesson.

PARALLEL MOVEMENT

The distinctive features of these examples are rhythmic simplicity and parallel movement of the parts. There cannot be much doubt that the parallel movement is a survival of the earliest forms of parallel organum in fourths, fifths, and octaves. A descant setting of the end of the *Te Deum*[1] shows that parallel thirds and sixths were used in this style. However, the New College pieces make it clear that parallel perfect and imperfect intervals were used on an equal basis, and this remained the general practice until parallel perfect intervals were forbidden by the teachers of a new style of descant in the late fourteenth century. The linear uniformity of parallel descant was contrary to the ideal of independence of line which the thirteenth-century motet inherited from the two-part *clausula*. It seems likely that in England the continued practice of parallel descant accounts for the frequent use of parallel movement in the motets and conductus of the fourteenth century. In 'Rosa delectabilis' and 'Civitas nusquam', for example, the outer parts constantly move in parallel thirds, fifths, and sixths, though they make perfect intervals with the tenor at the beginning of each *perfectio*. Again, while the chief functions of a *quartus cantus* were to provide a lowest part when the tenor rested and occasionally to turn the tenor into a middle part, it also complemented the upper parts in passages in which the idiom of parallel descant was adapted to the purposes of the motet, as in the ninth bar of 'Januam quam clauserat'.

THE HATTON MANUSCRIPT

Our second main source of polyphony in this period is a set of leaves in the contemporary binding of a manuscript in the Bodleian Library (Hatton 81), containing statutes from the reigns of Henry IV, V, and VI. The five pieces they preserve comprise two complete conductus, 'Ovet mundus laetabundus' and 'Hostis Herodes impie', two complete motets, 'Fusa cum silentio/Labem lavat/Manere' and 'Salve cleri speculum' on the tenor 'Sospitati dedit aegros', and an upper part and tenor, not easily legible, of a *rondellus*-conductus, 'A solis

---

[1] Transcription in Manfred Bukofzer, *Geschichte des englischen Diskants* (Strasbourg, 1936), and Gustave Reese, *Music in the Middle Ages* (New York, 1940), p. 399.

ortus cardine', which probably had two other voices. The form of the last piece corresponds closely to that of 'Ovet mundus',[1] which shows *rondellus* technique in a more developed stage than that of the New College *rondellus*-conductus. Here each of the two verses of the poem is repeated with interchange of the two upper parts and simple repeat, marked *recita* in the manuscript, of the two lower parts, which are wordless. In the first verse the part with words is disposed in four phrases of nine longs each and in the second verse in four phrases of six longs each, with a link of two longs at the end to lead back to the repeat, making a total length of 122 longs with the repeats. 'Hostis Herodes impie',[2] also for four voices, is a setting of a poem of four verses in which the upper parts sing the words in alternate verses. Repeat of each verse with interchange is not expressly indicated, but seems to be implied by the sign $\substack{\circ\\\circ}$ at the end of each verse in the lower parts, and by a link at the end of the piece which corresponds to a similar link at the end of each verse:[3]

Ex. 42 ¦
(i) Last Verse

Hic prin-ceps u-bi na-sci-tur rex Ju - de - o-rum par-vu-lus.   *etc.*

Hic princeps.

(ii) End of Last Verse   (*Repeat with interchange?*)

Ne . quis He-ro-dem quae-re - ret ho-rum vox so-nat ho - di - e.

((i) Here where the infant prince is born King of the Jews; (ii) a voice [of warning] sounds this day that none of them should [re]visit Herod.)

---

[1] Opening quoted in vol. II, Ex. 217. Partial transcription in F. Ll.Harrison, *Music in Medieval Britain* (London, 1958), p. 147.   [2] Vol. II, Ex. 218.
[3] The four-line verses are set in phrases of the following lengths, in longs:
          (1) $12 \times 2 + 10 \times 2$; (2) $4 \times 2 + 6 \times 2$; (3) $8 + 9 + 8 + 9$; (4) 6×4.
The total length, without repeats, is the same as that of 'Ovet mundus'.

The adaptation of the plainsong of the Epiphany hymn 'Hostis Herodes impie' for the beginning of the first verse, though it is not pursued,[1] may be regarded as an earlier stage of the technique of ornamented plainsong used in some of the Mass movements of the Old Hall manuscript. 'A solis ortus cardine' is another instance of the same idea, the opening of the poem being set to a melody adapted from the Christmas-tide hymn with that first line. All three of these conductus have dropped the vocalized prelude and interludes which were still used in the four conductus in the New College manuscript.

The three-part motet 'Fusa cum silentio' is conservative in design, being based on two complete and one partial statements of the tenor 'Manere' disposed in an unvaried rhythmic pattern in the fourth mode (breve, imperfect long, breve, two breve-rests), while the phrases of the upper parts are perfectly regular and always overlap. The remaining complete piece, 'Salve cleri speculum', is a *rondellus*-motet of the same type as the 'Balaam' motet of the Montpellier and New College manuscripts, but in four parts and with a more developed design. In the 'Balaam' motet[2] the tenor is the plainsong of four verses of the Epiphany sequence 'Epiphaniam Domino canamus', and is therefore originally in the form *aabb*. Each of the melodies *a* and *b* is actually sung four times, to allow for vocalized sections as well as those with text. Hence the design incorporates two features of the conductus: vocalized prelude, interlude, and postlude, and a single text repeated in interchange. The plainsong basis of 'Salve cleri speculum' is the melody of the prose 'Sospitati dedit aegros' for the feast of St. Nicholas,[3] and is therefore, like the 'Balaam' tenor, originally in the form of paired verses with the same music. The first two verses are set independently of the plainsong, the second verse being a *rondellus* repeat of the first. Thereafter the tenors sing alternate verses of the plainsong, so that the complete melody is sung in its original form. Meanwhile the upper parts sing in *rondellus* the alternate verses of the poem, which has something of the nature of a trope, for the words of each verse are related to the words of the corresponding verse of the prose.[4] One of the two pages on which the piece was written is very worn through having been glued to the inside cover of

---

[1] The words of the first verse, however, are an expansion of the first verse of the hymn. Cf. the words of 'Deus tuorum militum' (see p. 94, n. 1) and of 'Salve cleri speculum' (see Ex. 43).

[2] Transcription in Rokseth, op. cit., iii, pp. 258–62.

[3] *Antiphonale Sarisburiense*, pl. 360.

[4] Except in verses 7 ('Vas quod absorbit') and 8 ('O quanta sonuit'), which seem to have been interchanged.

the boards in which the manuscript was bound, but the recognition of the design of the music makes a reliable transcription possible :[1]

Ex 43

1 So - spi - ta - ti de - dit æ - gros o - le - i per - fu - si - o.

2 Ni - cho - la - us nau - fra - gan - tum af - fu - it præ - si - di - o.

Sal - ve cle - ri spe - - cu - lum an - ti - stes in - cli - te,

Sa -

Sal - ve sa - nans sæ - - cu - lum plebs pi - a pan - gi - te.

Sal - ve

ju - bar præ - su - lum

3rd Verse

So - spes a tu - mu - lo tur -

etc.

[So - spi - ta - ti

ba lan - guen - ti - um Re - dit ᵛ cum ju - bi - lo ca - nens præ -

de - dit æ - gros o - le - i per -

[1] Oxford, Bodleian, Hatton 81, fos. 45ᵛ–2ʳ. The total length is $4 \times 13 + 6 \times 12$ (actually verse 6 has 11 longs and verse 7 has 13, due to an overlap) = 124 longs.

(Plainsong: 1. The oil's unction restored the sick to health.
2. Nicholas was at hand to save the shipwrecked.
1st Verse: Hail, famous bishop, mirror for the clergy; hail, healer of this sick age—good people extol him; hail, glory of prelates.
3rd Verse: The crowd of sick people, saved from the tomb, comes home with rejoicing singing his praises; the seamen by a miracle escape shipwreck.)

This work is a fortunate survival, for it provides a link between the 'Balaam' motet and 'Ave miles caelestis curiae' in the Bury St. Edmunds leaves, which will be discussed below, and thus represents a hitherto unknown stage in the evolution of the peculiarly English form of conductus-motet with rondellus technique.[1]

THE BURY ST. EDMUNDS MANUSCRIPT

The manuscript E Mus. 7 in the Bodleian Library, which is marked in a fourteenth-century hand *Liber de armario claustri Sancti Edmundi*, has leaves containing polyphonic music bound in at the beginning and end. Since there are two pieces in honour of St. Edmund, there is little doubt that the manuscript from which the leaves were taken belonged to the Abbey choir. The four works which are complete in the leaves at the beginning have some features in common with the music in the New College and Hatton manuscripts. The upper parts of the four-part motet 'Petrum cephas ecclesiae/ Petrus pastor potissimus/Petre'[2] are written in regular phrases of the same length, an overlap being effected by a delay in the beginning of the second voice. The tenor, which is the *neuma* on the word 'Petre' in

---

[1] It seems likely that in liturgical function all three pieces are conductus, that is, substitutes for the *Benedicamus* at an Office rather than motets for use at Mass. The 'Balaam' melody was sung to the *Benedicamus* on Epiphany (see *Missale Sarum*, ed. F. H. Dickinson, col. 85, note), the prose 'Sospitati' was sung at Matins on St. Nicholas's day, and the text of 'Ave miles' has 'Benedicamus devote Domino' at the end of the penultimate verse.

[2] Transcription in J. F. R. and C. Stainer, *Early Bodleian Music* (London, 1901), ii, pp. 25–31.

the respond 'Petre amas me', is sung four times in regular phrases separated by rests, also with a deferred entry. Matters are so arranged, in rather too obvious a way for the musical interest of the piece, that the three upper parts sing, always in the style of parallel descant, while the tenor rests. Both pieces for the feast of St. Edmund are based on the plainsong of the antiphon 'Ave rex gentis Anglorum', which has the same melody as the Marian antiphon 'Ave regina caelorum mater regis angelorum'. The upper parts of the three-part motet 'De flore martyrum/Deus tuorum militum'[1] are in the style of Petrus de Cruce, and the tenor is the music of the antiphon as far as the word 'angelorum', sung twice in a rhythmic scheme with the form *aab*. The disposition of the tenor, as Bukofzer observed, is 'noteworthy for the incipient isorhythmic structure'.[2] While the *duplum* is written in regular phrases, those of the *triplum* are quite irregular. The other St. Edmund piece, the four-part 'Ave miles caelestis curiae',[3] is a further instance of the fusion of the techniques of *rondellus*-conductus and motet. In this case the plainsong is not originally in the form of paired verses, and has been arbitrarily divided by the composer into five sections. Each section is repeated by the lower parts in interchange while the upper parts complete the double *rondellus* design in the same way as in 'Salve cleri speculum'.

The music in the leaves at the back of this manuscript has a different appearance from that at the beginning. One of the four complete motets which they contain, 'Domine quis habitabit/De veri cordis adipe/Concupisco', occurs with French words in the Ivrea manuscript and in the Cambrai Cathedral manuscript 1328.[4] 'Deus creator/ Rex genitor' has a French tenor 'Doucement mi reconforte', while 'Pura placens', on an unidentified tenor, has a French *duplum* 'Parfundement plure Absalon'. Moreover, French influence on the technique of this group of pieces is clearly shown by the fact that the tenor 'Concupisco' and the tenors of 'Omnis terra/Habenti dabitur'[5] and 'Pura placens' are disposed in isorhythm repeated in diminution. Further, 'Omnis terra' is isorhythmic in the upper parts also, and all four pieces have the characteristic French *ars nova* rhythm of perfect time and greater (or 'perfect') prolation.[6] While it

---

[1] Transcription in Bukofzer, *Studies in Medieval and Renaissance Music* (New York, 1950), pp. 29–30.

[2] Ibid., p. 22.   [3] Transcription in ibid., pp. 30–33.

[4] See Heinrich Besseler, 'Studien zur Musik des Mittelalters', *Archiv für Musikwissenschaft*, vii (1925), p. 222, n. 2.

[5] Partial transcription in Harrison, op. cit., p. 148.

[6] See p. 4.

is possible that the music of these motets was written in France, there seems no doubt that they belonged to an English repertory, probably also that of St. Edmundsbury, about the middle of the century. This is confirmed by the presence of a wordless English descant, following 'Omnis terra', in the style typical of such pieces in the second half of the century. The outer parts are written in longs and breves, the highest part having occasional groups of imperfect semibreve and minim in greater prolation. Both the form of the middle part, which is entirely in breves, and the disposition of its ligatures suggest that it may be a *Kyrie* chant. The treatment of intervals corresponds to the new principles of descant composition which became current after *c.* 1350, and were explained in a number of short treatises, some in Latin and some for the first time in English, written between *c.* 1350 and *c.* 1450.[1]

ENGLISH DESCANT

This new descant was a development of the tradition of simple composition in virtually note-against-note movement which has already been referred to in connexion with the examples in the New College manuscript. In the course of the fourteenth century the method of writing three-part descant for ritual use changed, at least so far as written composition was concerned, from continuously parallel movement to a technique in which more attention was paid to independence of line. However, parallel imperfect intervals remained a characteristic idiom, especially at the approach to a cadence, and parallel fifths still appear occasionally until *c.* 1430. A number of examples of parallel descant of about the middle of the century have survived, some only in part, on leaves bound in at the beginning and end of a manuscript in the British Museum (Sloane 1210). They include settings of a troped *Kyrie*, of the *Gloria* and *Credo*, of the hymn 'O lux beata Trinitas', and of extra-ritual poems. In 'O lux'[2] the plainsong is treated in the highest part, while the other pieces appear to be independent of plainsong. Several of the poems are set in two parts moving in continuous parallel sixths with the octave at the cadences,[3] a treatment which was continued in the carols of the early

---

[1] See Bukofzer, *Geschichte des englischen Diskants*, and T. Georgiades, *Englische Diskanttraktate aus der ersten Hälfte des XV. Jahrhunderts* (Munich, 1937). The only writers named are Richard Cotell, who was at St. Paul's in 1394–5 (see Harrison, op. cit., p. 12), and Leonel Power, who spent the last years of his life (1441–5) at Christ Church, Canterbury (ibid., p. 42).

[2] Transcription in Harrison, op. cit., p. 150.

[3] See the opening of 'Virgo salvavit hominem', printed by Bukofzer, s.v. 'Gymel' in *Die Musik in Geschichte und Gegenwart*, v, col. 1143.

fifteenth century.[1] Elsewhere parallel movement in both perfect and imperfect intervals is used, and the rhythmic style ranges from smooth triple time to florid ornamental groups in which subdivision of the breve is shown by *semibreves maiores, minores*, and *minimae* (♩), and occasionally by the small circle discussed by Robert de Handlo in his *Regulae* of 1326.[2] The circle has been kept in this transcription to show its function of defining the rhythm of a group of *semibreves minores*:[3]

Ex 44
(i)

Et in ter - ra   pax ho-mi - ni - bus   bo-næ vo-lun - ta   -   tis,

(ii)

ri - tus   in - ta -   -   - cta   quo fe-   - cun-da-
du - ce   con - fra- -   - cta   par con- - fir-ma-
-ra   sunt   per - a -   -   - cta   ser-pens cal-ca-

tur e -   -   -   -   -   (ley - son).
tur e -   -   -   -   -   ley - son.
tur e -   -   -   -   -   (ley - son).

As conveniently brief examples of the new stage in the history of English descant which began in the second half of the century we may

---

[1] See *Musica Britannica*, iv (London, 1952), pp. 2–32, *passim*.

[2] Coussemaker, *Scriptorum*, i, pp. 389–90.

[3] (i) Brit. Mus. Sloane 1210, fo. 138; (ii) ibid., fo. 139ᵛ. This is the third section of the *Kyrie*; the opening is transcribed in Johannes Wolf, *Handbuch der Notationskunde*, i (Leipzig, 1913), p. 270.

cite two settings of the 'Deo gratias' response to the celebrant's *Ite missa est* at the end of Mass:[1]

Ex.45
(i)

Such functional treatments of ritual plainsong as these were composed by setting a 'counter', the term used in the treatises on descant, below the monorhythmic tenor[2] and a mean (*medius*) above it. This mean-tenor-counter technique was the almost invariable basis of three-part descant from this time onwards,[3] including virtually all the descant Mass settings and antiphons in the Old Hall manuscript. Momentary crossing of the tenor and counter parts was quite frequent, and should be distinguished from a fully 'migrant' treatment of the plainsong, in which whole phrases were transferred to the mean or

[1] Cambridge, Univ. Libr. Kk.i. 6, fo. 246; facsimile in Friedrich Gennrich, *Abriss der frankonischen Mensuralnotation* (Nieder-Modau, 1946), pl. 1.

[2] The writer has coined the term monorhythmic for a part written in a constant note-value. In (i) the tenor appears to be a simplified form of the fourth Sarum *Benedicamus Domino—Ite missa est* in *Missale Sarum* (ed. Dickinson, col. 635) which also appears as the tenth *Benedicamus* in *Graduale Sarisburiense*, ed. W. H. Frere (London, 1894), pl. 19*. In (ii) it is the fourth *Ite missa est* in *Missale Sarum* and the third in *Graduale Sarisburiense*.

[3] For examples see the *Kyrie* from Brit. Mus. Arundel 14, printed in Bukofzer, 'The Gymel', *Music and Letters*, xvi (1935), p. 83, and the settings of the *Sanctus* and *Agnus Dei* in a Public Record Office document, printed in Denis Stevens, 'A Recently Discovered English Source of the Fourteenth Century', *The Musical Quarterly*, xli (1955), pp. 37–40.

H

counter. In the present examples the tenor and counter move without parallel fifths, but the tenor and mean do not. The rhythm is typical of descant writing in this period, greater prolation being regularly assumed.

Descant settings with two parts written above the tenor, though rare, are not unknown. In a setting of the beginning and verse of the Alleluia 'Hic est vere martyr', for example, the plainsong is in the lowest part, but goes above the middle part when it has the upper notes of its octave:[1]

Ex. 46

This piece has an extraordinary concentration of the chromatic accidentals which occur in a mild form in the second of the 'Deo gratias' settings quoted above, and which were a marked feature of

---

[1] Oxford, Bodleian, Mus. d. 143, fo. 2ᵛ. E. W. B. Nicholson dated the writing c. 1380. The text and plainsong, which are not in the Sarum rite, may be seen in the Gradual of St. Yrieux (*Paléographie musicale*, xiii, Tournai, 1925, pl. 229) for the feast of St. Saturninus.

some French compositions of the late fourteenth century.[1] The leaves in which this Alleluia is found also contain, in various states of incompleteness, a descant setting of 'O benigne redemptor', also well supplied with accidentals, and of the fourth Sarum *Agnus Dei* with the plainsong in the middle part, and two fragmentary motets, one with an isorhythmic tenor.

ISORHYTHM IN ENGLISH MUSIC

The late appearance of the true isorhythmic motet in England tends to confirm the relatively independent development of English polyphony in the first half of the century, with its special treatment and partial synthesis of the motet and conductus. We have only fragmentary evidence for the early history of the isorhythmic motet in England, while one of the earliest pieces to show its adoption by English musicians has survived only in continental manuscripts. This is 'Sub Arturo plebs/Fons citharizantium/In omnem terram',[2] a motet in praise of English music and musicians by Johannes Alanus, a member of the Chapel Royal; it may have been written to commemorate a meeting of the Knights of the Garter at Windsor on St. George's Day, 1358.[3] Among the early surviving instances of the adoption of isorhythm in England are a fragmentary motet[4] in the same leaves as 'Hic est vere martyr', and a fragmentary *Gloria* in leaves in the binding of a Bodleian Library manuscript (Bodley 384). Enough remains of the *primus tenor* of the former piece to show that it is isorhythmic, the second *color* being in diminution by half, written out in the shorter values. This was the normal method in the motets of Guillaume de Machaut (1300–77), but not in those of the late fourteenth century, when the performer was expected to deduce the diminution from the first statement.[5]

Bodley 384 is a collection of homilies written in the thirteenth century contained in an English fifteenth-century binding, which was presented to the Bodleian by the Dean and Canons of St. George's,

[1] See Apel, *French Secular Music of the late Fourteenth Century* (Cambridge, Mass., 1950), Introduction, p. 13.

[2] In Chantilly, Mus. Condé, 1047 and Bologna, Bibl. G. B. Martini, MS. Q 15 (formerly Lic. Mus. 37). The former has pieces dated 1369 and 1389; see G. Reaney, 'The Manuscript Chantilly, Musée Condé 1047', *Musica Disciplina*, viii (1954), p. 85. The piece is transcribed in *Denkmäler der Tonkunst in Österreich*, Jg. xl, p. 9.

[3] See Brian Trowell, 'A Fourteenth-century Ceremonial Motet and its Composer', *Acta Musicologica*, xxix (1957), p. 65.

[4] With the text '. . . nec Herodis ferocitas errore plena . . .'.

[5] Sometimes with the help of a 'canon', or prescription, as in 'Sub Arthuro plebs': see the facsimile in Gennrich, *Abriss der Mensuralnotation des XIV. Jahrhunderts und der ersten Hälfte des XV. Jahrhunderts* (Nieder-Modau, 1948), pl. 18b.

Windsor, in 1612. The music may have belonged to Windsor, for the choir of St. George's had in 1384 a roll of polyphonic music bequeathed by John Aleyn (probably the composer of the motet mentioned above), who became a Canon in 1362 and died in 1373.[1] The remains of the *Gloria* in question are an upper part in lively greater prolation with some hocket in the final *Amen* section, and two tenor parts, one with the cue 'Exaudi me pater'. Both tenors are isorhythmic, with three *taleae* to one *color* and a second statement in diminution by half, written out in the manuscript. Since there must originally have been two upper parts with alternating text, the plan of the setting is very similar to that of an anonymous four-part *Gloria* in the Fountains Fragment.[2] The disposition of the words of the surviving part differs only slightly from the text of the upper part of the Fountains setting, which may be by Pennard,[3] an Old Hall composer, and is identical with that of the upper part of J. Tyes's *Gloria* in Old Hall.[4] The other contents of these leaves include two settings of the *Gloria* with the 'Spiritus et alme' trope, both independent of the plainsong. One is in parallel descant style, while the other follows the trend of the new descant style in its independence of line and ornamented melody in greater prolation:[5]

Ex. 47

¹ 'Unus rotulus de cantu music' ex legato Johannis Aleyn', in the inventories of 1384 and 1409–10; see M. F. Bond, *Inventories of St. George's Chapel, Windsor Castle 1384–1667* (Windsor, 1947), pp. 34 and 103.

² See Bukofzer, *Studies in Medieval and Renaissance Music*, pp. 88, 106–7. Each statement of the lower parts is sung twice. A similar treatment of a tenor occurs earlier in 'Domine quis habitabit', referred to above, p. 94.   ³ Ibid., p. 107.

⁴ Printed in A. Ramsbotham, H. B. Collins, and Dom A. Hughes, *The Old Hall Manuscript*, i (London, 1933), p. 50. Facsimile in Apel, *The Notation of Polyphonic Music*, p. 365.

⁵ Oxford, Bodley 384, fo. 1. Though the leaf is in a poor state of preservation, transcription of some passages is possible with the help of the reversed image on the binding, to which the leaf must formerly have been glued.

THE OLD HALL MANUSCRIPT

With the famous manuscript preserved in the Library of St. Edmund's College, Old Hall, Ware, we at last come to a collection of polyphony which, though not complete, is near enough to completeness to be studied as a whole. Written for the Royal Household Chapel, it is in the main a repertory of music for the Ordinary of the Mass, but includes in the original corpus some antiphons and motets. The pieces include a *Gloria* and a *Sanctus* by Roy Henry, who was for some time considered to be Henry VI. More recently stylistic analysis and research into the membership of the Household Chapel have shown that this was too late a date, and it has been generally agreed that the manuscript originated in the reign of Henry V (1413–22).[1] However, there are good grounds, both musical and historical, for believing that the original and largest layer of the manuscript was written in the previous reign, that Roy Henry was Henry IV (1399–1413), and that the pieces in later hands were added between 1413 and *c.* 1430.[2] In any event, the style of the descant pieces in the first layer suggests a date of *c.* 1400 or earlier.

The Mass settings in Old Hall, which provided for both festal and ferial masses, were set down in four groups according to text: *Gloria*, *Credo*, *Sanctus*, and *Agnus Dei*. In England the *Kyrie* of the Mass of the day was always sung in plainsong, with tropes assigned to the various kinds of double feast. Consequently English polyphonic Masses do not contain a *Kyrie*, except in the case of the Votive Mass of the Virgin, or 'Lady-Mass', which was celebrated once a week, and in some places daily. Virtually all the descant settings of the *Sanctus* and *Agnus Dei* in Old Hall are based on the plainsong,[3] and they are written down in liturgical order according to the rank of the day for which the chant was prescribed. The plainsong is almost always adapted as the middle part,[4] for the passages in which it

---

[1] See Bukofzer, *Studies in Medieval and Renaissance Music*, pp. 73–80.

[2] See Harrison, op. cit., pp. 220–1.

[3] The exceptions are Roy Henry's *Sanctus* (transcription in *The Old Hall Manuscript*, iii, p. 1) and a setting of each text by Chirbury (ibid., pp. 22, 116).

[4] The only exception is Typp's setting with 'migrant' treatment of the chant; see *infra*, Chap. VI, p. 179.

appears to 'migrate' momentarily to the counter are written-out cross-ings of the lower parts, and do not involve a significant change in the method of setting. More often than not the plainsong is transposed, examples of transposition by all intervals from the second to the fifth being met with. The most frequent interval of transposition is the fifth, as in Lambe's *Sanctus*:[1]

Ex. 48

The cadence at bars 10–11 was not exceptional in descant style when the plainsong fell one note, since it was an invariable practice that the counter should fall one step at every cadence.

In contrast to the *Sanctus* and *Agnus* settings, most of the Glorias and Credos in descant style are independent compositions. However, one *Gloria*,[2] anonymous and incomplete, has the chant of the fifth Sarum *Gloria* in the middle part, while two anonymous Creeds,[3] both in the rhythmic style of the late fourteenth century, are based on the Sarum *Credo* chant, also used in the middle part. Another anonymous *Credo*[4] has the chant in the highest part, and Typp's setting[5] uses it intermittently in all three parts. The two latter settings show the trend of the change in rhythmic style, for Typp's piece is in imperfect time and lesser prolation throughout, and the anonymous setting has a

---

[1] Old Hall, fo. 82 (cf. pl. I); complete transcription in *The Old Hall Manuscript*, iii, p. 9.
[2] Ibid., p. [8].
[3] Ibid., ii, pp. 1, 15; the first *Credo* is recorded in *The History of Music in Sound*, iii.
[4] Ibid., p. 8.
[5] Ibid., p. 44.

PLATE I

THE OLD HALL MANUSCRIPT
The page (fo. 82) shows the greater part of Lambe's *Sanctus* (see Ex. 48) in score

middle section in perfect time with the lesser prolation and a third section in imperfect time.

The Mass movements of the original layer written in *chanson* style, isorhythm and canon will be discussed in a later chapter. One further canonic piece which involves a remarkable use of plainsong may, however, be referred to here, since its special feature has not previously been noticed. This is a *Sanctus* by Pycard, one of the most adventurous minds among the Old Hall composers. W. Barclay Squire[1] noted the incipits of the two parts, upper voice and tenor, which the manuscript has, and added the comment that the other parts, presumably two, were missing. The editors of the modern edition followed suit, and did not print a transcription. The upper voice has the figure 3 under the fifth note from the beginning and again under the fourth note from the beginning of the *Benedictus*. The number can have no rhythmic meaning in either place, and is in fact the only indication that this part, which is a measured form of the third Sarum *Sanctus* with the trope 'Benedictus Mariae filius', is to be sung by three voices in canon, the following voices entering at the figure. To devise a canon on a pre-existing melody is a technical feat which may well be unique in this period. It is accomplished with the help of some free treatment of dissonance, which is not excessive in the circumstances and is equally characteristic of Pycard's other canonic pieces:[2]

Ex. 49

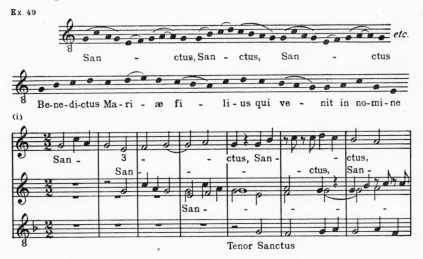

---

[1] 'Notes on an undescribed Collection of English 15th-Century Music', *Sammelbände der internationalen Musikgesellschaft*, ii (1900–1), p. 370.

[2] Old Hall, fo. 100ᵛ. On Pycard's love of canon see also below, p. 168.

(Holy, holy, holy. . . . Blessed is the son of Mary who cometh in the name [of the Lord].)

The antiphons in the original corpus use the same techniques as the descant Mass settings, and include free compositions, those with the ritual plainsong in the middle part, and one example of 'migrant' treatment of the plainsong.[1] Motets in the first hand which survive comprise five pieces, of which only two are complete. All four tenors which remain are isorhythmic, each with one statement marked thus

[1] Byttering's 'Nesciens Mater'; see below, Chap. VI, p. 179.

: ‖ : or thus : ‖‖ : to indicate the actual number of statements, the singer being expected to apply diminution. The texts of 'Arae post libamina/Nunc surgunt in populo' by Mayshuet,[1] who is almost certainly the French composer Mayhuet de Joan of the Chantilly manuscript, and the incomplete 'Post missarum solemnia' show that these pieces were written as motet-substitutes for the *Deo gratias* at the end of Mass.

A parallel case[2] is the motet 'Humanae linguae organis/Supplicum voces percipe/Deo gratias' in the leaves known as the Fountains Fragment, which contain six Mass settings in common with the original corpus of Old Hall.[3] That the motet was sung in place of *Deo gratias* is clear from the ending of both texts as well as from the source of the tenor, which is the third Sarum melody for *Ite missa est*, disposed in two isorhythmic statements, each with two *taleae*, the second statement being written out in diminution. The four voices are reducible to three by replacing the tenor and contratenor by the *solus tenor*. The beginning may be quoted as an illustration of the style of the motet in England about the turn of the century:[4]

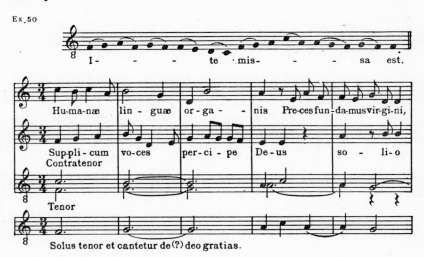

Ex. 50

<hr />

[1] Transcription in *The Old Hall Manuscript*, iii, p. 150.

[2] For yet other instances of motet substitution, see Chap. VI, p. 170.

[3] Thematic index and discussion in Bukofzer, *Studies in Medieval and Renaissance Music*, chap. iii. Another small collection of music from Fountains Abbey is listed and discussed in H. K. Andrews and Thurston Dart, 'Fourteenth-Century Polyphony in a Fountains Abbey MS Book', *Music and Letters*, xxxix (1958), p. 1, and Denis Stevens 'The Second Fountains Fragment: a Postscript', ibid., p. 148.

[4] Brit. Mus. Add 40011 B, fo. 14.

(*I*: With music of our human tongues let us pour forth prayers to the Virgin
whom the Holy Father by his divinity. . . .

II: Hear the voices of thy suppliants O God, on thy throne of glory . . . ? . . .,
because (we make?) memorial.)

The lively rhythm and active melodic lines of this style were soon to
give way to a more sophisticated rhythm and a more graceful and
flowing melody modelled on the French *chanson* of the early fifteenth
century. Byttering's 'En Katherinae solemnia'[1] and one of his settings
of the *Gloria*[2] in the first layer of the Old Hall collection show the
transition to the new style, which was to be fully realized in the compositions of Damett and Sturgeon, members of a later group of Royal
Household musicians, and in the later music of Cooke and Power,
both of whom lived through the period of transition to the new
'contenance angloise'.

[1] *The Old Hall Manuscript*, iii, p. 145.   [2] Ibid. i, p. 39.

IV

POPULAR AND SECULAR MUSIC IN ENGLAND
(to *c.* 1470)

By MANFRED F. BUKOFZER

SACRED AND SECULAR

MOST of the information about musical composition and a large part
of the music that has survived from medieval times comes from
ecclesiastical sources. This is natural because the art of reading and
writing and of musical notation was a pursuit of the learned and was
practised mainly in monastic centres and cathedral choirs. As the
written documents deal mainly with matters directly concerning the
church and worth being written down, it is inevitable that the preserved musical sources should give the impression that the church
dominated all aspects of music. But this is not true of the musical
life outside the church. Though very few pieces of popular and
secular music have survived, we know of its existence from many
casual and incidental references in chronicles and other non-musical
documents. Some of these remarks are highly picturesque denuncia-
tions of secular songs and dance music, which by their strong wording
prove that this kind of music was considered a formidable enemy,
whose power over the laity and even the clergy should not be
underestimated.

On the other hand it must be emphasized that the sacred and
secular spheres overlapped to a considerable degree, and that the
contrast between secular and sacred music was not as absolute as
has often been claimed. It is extremely difficult if not impossible to
give an *a priori* definition of sacred and secular style in music and to
determine on this basis in what way the one may have affected the
other. The distinction of secular and sacred is essentially one of
musical function, not of musical style. If we were to say, for example,
that preference for the major mode is proof of secular origin we
should be confronted at once with a great deal of sacred music in the
major mode which contradicts such an assertion. It is, of course,
always possible and indeed convenient to reason away such evidence
to the contrary by claiming 'popular influence', but such influence

should be assumed only if there is historical reason to do so and not for the sake of a preconceived theory. The use of the major mode is at best a clue and an attendant factor, but not in itself conclusive. Characteristics of style alone cannot tell us to which domain the music belongs; in fact the ideas of what constitutes 'sacred' or 'secular' style have changed in the course of time. The very attempt to define them in technical terms is modern and not in keeping with medieval thought, because it presupposes a definite contrast of spheres which did not exist in the Middle Ages.

The absence of such contrast can be shown simply by the observation that a secular song, if given a set of sacred words, could serve as sacred music, and vice versa. Only recently has it been recognized how frequently such interchange took place, and the more we learn about medieval music the more important it becomes. The practice of borrowing a song from one sphere and making it suitable for use in the other by the substitution of words is known as 'parody' or *contrafactum*. The full extent of these borrowings can only be known when the entire repertory of secular and sacred music has been closely compared.

POPULAR AND LEARNED

In the discussion of medieval music it has been too easily and too frequently assumed that everything secular was at the same time also popular, and everything sacred also learned. The courtly art of troubadour and trouvère song and the learned secular motet contradict this assumption, as do also 'popular' sacred compositions. The distinction between popular and learned does not necessarily coincide with that between secular and sacred, though it may sometimes do so. Each pair of terms is relevant only to certain aspects of music. While the latter is concerned with its function, the former considers its sociological aspects—its social origin and destination, for whom and by whom it was composed. The case may be complicated by the fact that popular music may emanate from a learned centre for popular consumption.

Although popular and learned are sociological categories they have nevertheless some bearing on musical style. Only that music will be recognized as popular which has a direct appeal and is composed in a relatively simple style. Again, it must be emphasized that the idea of 'simplicity' is a variable historical concept which changes as the musical resources change in any given period. For example, polyphony as such belonged in the Middle Ages essentially to learned or art music, so that 'popular polyphony' would be strictly speaking a contradiction in terms.[1] Yet we know from a report of Giraldus Cambrensis that part-singing, not of the learned kind, was already an old tradition in the latter half of the twelfth century.[2] While the nature of this part-singing is far from clear there are a few polyphonic compositions of the thirteenth century in which popular influence is clearly manifest. Of these the *rota* 'Sumer is icumen in'[3] is perhaps the best-known example. Increasing use of the 'imperfect concords', the third and sixth, has often been ascribed to popular influence. However, the presence or absence of such intervals is no infallible criterion. Other features of the music—the character of the melody and the rhythm, the declamation, and also the verse form and subject-matter of the lyrics—must be considered in conjunction with the origin and destination of verse and music if one wants to decide the question of popular *versus* learned.

MUSIC SET TO ENGLISH WORDS

Because of the preponderance of ecclesiastical sources it is not surprising that Latin is by far the most common language in musical manuscripts. All the more important, therefore, are the few and scattered compositions with English words, both sacred and secular. Several of these English lyrics are translations or free paraphrases of known Latin models, and there are also examples where the reverse is true. It is clear that translations from Latin were made for popular consumption, namely for the common folk who did not understand Latin. The presence of sacred lyrics in the vulgar tongue indicates a trend toward popularization of religious ideas by means of music. The foremost exponents of this trend were the Franciscan friars, whose activities in England will be discussed below.

The extant English lyrics with music are mostly sacred or moralizing, but not liturgical. It is characteristic that the popularization hardly touched strictly liturgical forms, such as the Mass, and seized on lesser forms of the liturgy or on forms not strictly liturgical, such as the hymn and the sequence, which were inherently close to simple

[1] Cf. M. Bukofzer, 'Popular Polyphony in the Middle Ages', *The Musical Quarterly*, xxvi (1940), p. 31.
[2] See vol. II, p. 315.
[3] Ibid., p. 402.

syllabic melodies with popular appeal. The manuscripts containing compositions with English words do not antedate the thirteenth century. Of the monophonic songs only 'Mirie it is while sumer ilast' (no. 2163)[1] is purely secular in nature. This fragment, the first secular song in English with music, is clearly indebted to the trouvère tradition and is preserved among other trouvère songs. The polyphonic compositions all date from the second half of the century. Of these only 'Foweles in þe frith' (no. 864)[2] and 'Sumer is icumen in' (no. 3223)[3] are secular. 'Foweles in þe frith' cannot really be called a popular composition, whereas the Reading *rota* displays popular as well as learned features. The *rota* appears with the *contrafactum* 'Perspice Christicola', which may take its cue from the stanza 'Perspice Christicolas' of the sequence 'Fulgens praeclara'.[4]

All other compositions with English words before 1300 are religious or moralizing. A few of these are popular only because they use the vernacular, not because of their music. Others, however, are written in what appears to be a popular musical style—which does not mean that they are necessarily of popular or secular origin. The hymn 'Edi beo þu hevene quene' (no. 708)[5] and the sequence 'Jesu Christes milde moder' (no. 1697),[6] both gymels of the late thirteenth century, display a smooth melodic style and a marked preference for thirds. The latter piece is a paraphrase of the sequence 'Stabat juxta Christi crucem'[7] though it is musically independent of the Latin model. Two monophonic sequences, 'Stond wel moder under rode' (no. 3211)[8] and the fragmentary '. . . stod ho there' (no. *52)[9] likewise paraphrase the Latin sequence just mentioned, each one differently; both also borrow its melody with only slight variants.

Another composition with English words, unpublished so far, is the two-part fragment '. . . in lyde' (no. *41):[10]

---

[1] Facsimile in J. F. R. Stainer, *Early Bodleian Music*, i, pl. 3. The English lyrics are designated by the numbers in C. Brown and R. H. Robbins, *The Index of Middle English Verse* (New York, 1943), where each item appears with a bibliography.

[2] Facsimile in *Early Bodleian Music*, i, pl. 6; transcription, ibid. ii. 10, and in Handbook to *The History of Music in Sound*, ii (London, 1953), p. 49. See also vol. II, p. 343.

[3] Facsimile and transcription in Grove's *Dictionary*, and many other publications.

[4] According to J. Handschin in *Musica Disciplina*, iii (1949), p. 66.

[5] See vol. II, p. 342.

[6] Facsimile in H. E. Wooldridge, *Early English Harmony* i (London, 1897), pls. 35 and 36; excerpts in G. Reese, *Music in the Middle Ages* (New York, 1940), p. 389. See also vol. II, p. 343.

[7] U. Chevalier, *Repertorium hymnologicum*, no. 19411; Latin text in *Analecta Hymnica*, viii, p. 55.

[8] Facsimile in *Early Bodleian Music*, i, pl. 5.

[9] Brit. Mus., Royal 12 E 1, fol. 193–4ᵛ.

[10] Cambridge, Corpus Christi College, MS. 8, fly-leaf.

Ex. 51

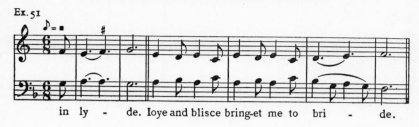

in ly - de. Ioye and blisce bring-et me to bri - de.

In spite of its brevity the example is worth publishing because it
illustrates the manner in which thirds and sixths gradually supplanted
the perfect intervals. It will be observed that the imperfect intervals
appear chiefly in passing on weak beats while the fifth is still the main
interval for the strong beats. In other popular compositions the third
appears freely also on strong beats.

MOTETS WITH ENGLISH WORDS

The transformation of the motet from a strictly liturgical form to
a purely secular composition which took place in France during the
latter half of the thirteenth century has no exact parallel in English
music. But at least the first step in this direction was taken when one
voice was supplied with sacred words in the vernacular. The first and
so far only motet with English words in the upper voice is 'Worldes
blisce have god day' (no. 4221)[1] which is set to the tenor *Domino*.
It shows that even so learned and sophisticated a form as the motet
did not escape popularization. Recently a fragment from the end of
the thirteenth century has come to light containing the English phrase
'Dou way Robin, the child wile wepe', which appears with music
amidst fragmentary Latin motet parts.[2] It had been suggested that the
short section in English might form the tenor of a motet, but too
little of the upper voice remained to prove this. Fortunately, however,
the suggestion was later confirmed by the discovery that the same
piece exists in a more complete though still mutilated form in another
fragment.[3] In this version the tenor is left undesignated, but the upper
voice carries the same Latin words, including also the beginning
'Veni mater gracie'. Taken together the two fragments allow a
tentative transcription[4] of the last section:

[1] Transcription in M. Bukofzer, 'The First Motet with English Words', *Music and
Letters*, xvii (1936), pp. 8–9; see also vol. II, p. 374.
[2] Princeton Univ. Library, Garrett MS. 119; cf. K. Levy, 'New Material on the Early
Motet in England', *Journal of the American Musicological Society*, iv (1951), p. 220.
[3] Brit. Mus., Cotton Fragm. xxix, fo. 36.
[4] The transcription is tentative because the fragment in the British Museum is hardly
legible in several places, and because the English mensural notation of both fragments,

Ex. 52

This piece is the first and so far the only known motet with English words in the tenor, and, what is more, the tenor is secular and may conceivably preserve a popular refrain not otherwise known. Tenors of secular origin were employed in the French motet together with secular words in the upper voices. That this type was not unknown in England is proved by a manuscript of English origin[1] in which a secular French motet has been copied in English mensural notation.

POPULAR MUSIC IN FOURTEENTH-CENTURY ENGLAND

Popular music in the fourteenth century is a direct outgrowth of the preceding period. That it developed rapidly and was widely practised can be inferred from the great number of references in secondary sources, such as sermons, chronicles, and archives. But the hazards of destruction must have been great because the number of extant compositions with English words is actually smaller than in the thirteenth century, although the number of lyrics destined for music is considerably larger.

though strongly suggestive of duple metre, is ambiguous. The music could be transcribed also in triple metre (third mode).

[1] Oxford, Bodleian, Douce 139; facsimile in *Early Bodleian Music*, i, pl. 8.

The first example to be mentioned here is the love song 'Bryd one brere' (Bird on briar, no. 521),[1] which is probably not much later than *c.* 1300. In the form in which it is preserved it is monophonic with two extra stanzas of words added at the bottom. However, the manuscript contains an empty staff under the first line of music and an empty space below the second. This seems to indicate, as does also the placing of the words under the empty staff, that the music was originally intended to be in two parts. The melody moves easily and gracefully in triple time:[2]

Ex. 53[1]

Bryd on-e bre-re, bríd, brid on-e bre-re, Kynd is co-me of
lov-e lov-e to cra-ve. Blith-ful bi-ryd, on me thu
re - we, Or greyth, lef, greith thu me my gra-ve.

(Bird on briar, bird on briar, our nature comes from love, love to crave. Blissful bird, have pity on me, or, my love, prepare thou my grave.)

The verse form of the song is a simple four-line stanza of eight syllables to each line, like the most common form of the Latin hymn, but certain words are repeated for musical reasons and thus make for some irregularity. This is only one of many examples in which music and verse do not exactly correspond, although in this case the general parallelism is quite clear. Such parallelism, however, does not always exist, and it would be rash to assume that the musical form can always be deduced from the verse form.

Even in English monasteries secular music was not necessarily frowned upon but actually welcomed on certain occasions. The Account Books of the monastery in Durham show that in the fourteenth century minstrels were almost regularly employed to play on the day of the Translation of St. Cuthbert, or privately before the

---

[1] Facsimile in J. Saltmarsh, 'Two Mediaeval Love-Songs set to Music', the *Antiquaries Journal*, xv (1935), facing p. 3, with transcription by F. McD. C. Turner, p. 20.

[2] The notation is not quite accurate and not consistently mensural. Bar 10, first note is a breve; the last five bars stand in the manuscript a third higher.

Prior.[1] The records of Durham for the year 1331 have preserved by chance a stanza of an English lament which was sung of old on Holy-Rood Day in memory of Lord Neville (no. 3894). It deserves to be printed here because it is one of the earliest authentic examples of what became known later as the 'traditional ballad metre':

> Wel qwa sal thir hornes blau
> Haly Rod thi day?
> Nou is he dede and lies law
> Was wont to blaw thaim ay.[2]

We would give much to have the tune of this lament. The reference in a secular song to Holy-Rood Day is of special interest because many hymns and sequences were composed for this feast.

The music for another English lyric may possibly have been preserved, though the case is not clear. A musical manuscript of the early fourteenth century[3] contains at the bottom of one folio the sacred poem 'Lytel wotyt onyman' (no. 1922) which is known to be an exact parody of a secular English lyric (no. 1921). The main part of the folio is taken up by the sequence 'Salomonis inclita' which is set as a three-part conductus. It has always been assumed that there is no relation between the music and the English words (which were added by a different, though not much later, hand). Since the music has sequence form and the poem is in stanzas the entire music would evidently not fit. Yet it is noteworthy that the second stanza of the sequence and the English lyric agree in many points of metre and verse form, and it is precisely the second stanza under which the English words appear. Possibly the scribe wanted to have the English words sung to that particular stanza. This would indeed be feasible, but only if an adjustment were made. Whatever may have been intended, the music of the sequence is written in a difficult rhythmic style and would certainly not represent the original melody of the secular song.

POPULAR HYMNS

Of all the liturgical forms the hymn could most easily enter the realm of popular music because its verse structure is simple and its melody is repeated for all verses as in a folk-song. It is no coincidence

---

[1] *Publications of the Surtees Society*, ciii, p. 582.
[2] Ibid., ix, p. 112.
[3] Cambridge, Caius College, MS. 512, fol. 260ᵛ.

that the Latin quotations and refrain lines of the fifteenth-century English carol are drawn more often than not from hymns.[1] 'Angelus ad virginem', a hymn on the Annunciation, held a position of unrivalled popularity in England. The majority of manuscripts in which it is transmitted are of English origin, and as early as the thirteenth century it was translated into English. The translation 'Gabriel fram evene king' (no. 888), which imitates the rather intricate verse form of the original in every particular, appears in a manuscript that gives the melody with its Latin text and the English version directly underneath.[2] The hymn was sung also as a pleasant pastime, as we learn from Chaucer, who puts it into the mouth of the 'poor scholar' Nicholas, Clerk of Oxenford:

> And al above ther lay a gay sautrye
> On which he made a nightes melodye
> So swetely, that al the chambre rong;
> And *Angelus ad virginem* he song.[3]

Two polyphonic settings of the hymn are known to exist, both of English origin. The first, dating from the second half of the thirteenth century, is a fragmentary two-part conductus setting in a rather primitive style, which assigns the melody to the upper voice.[4] The other appears as a late fourteenth-century addition to an Irish troper of the thirteenth century which includes in its original contents the tune of the same hymn in plainchant notation. The added polyphonic composition is for three parts with the melody in the middle voice, and it appears in two slightly different versions.[5] The following example gives the first three-part arrangement, which apart from its intrinsic musical merits has the advantage of being contemporary with Chaucer. The Latin words apply to all three voices and are written in the manuscript only once under the lowest voice, as was common in conductus settings. The words of the earlier English version have been added not only for the sake of comparison but also for practical reasons. The anachronism of singing a fourteenth-century composition to words perhaps a hundred years older need not disturb us because the hymn was certainly still sung in either language:

[1] Cf. the table in R. L. Greene, *The Early English Carols* (Oxford, 1935), p. lxv.
[2] Brit. Mus., Arundel 248; facsimile in *Early English Harmony*, i, pl. 34.
[3] *The Miller's Tale*, 3213.
[4] Brit. Mus., Cotton Fragm. xxix, fol. 36ᵛ.
[5] Cambridge, Univ. Lib., Add. MS. 710; facsimile in *Early English Harmony*, i, pls. 46 and 47. Recorded in *The History of Music in Sound* (H.M.V.), iii.

Ex.54[1]

An-ge-lus ad vir-gi-nem sub-in-trans in con-cla- ve,
[C.F.]
Ga-bri-el fram ev-ene king sent to the mai-de swe- te,

Vir-gi-nis for- mi-di-nem de-mul-cens,in-quit: 'A- ve, A-
Brou-te hire blis-ful ti-ding and faire he gan hire gre-ten: 'Heil

ve, re-gi-na vir- gi- num, Coe- li ter-ræ-que do-mi- num Con-
be thu-ful of grace a-rith, for go-des sone this ev-ene lith for

-ci-pi-es Et pa-ri-es In-ta- cta Sa-lu-tem ho-mi-
ma-nes loven wile man bi-comen and ta- ken fles of the mai-den

-num: Tu por-ta coe-li fa- cta, Me-de-la cri-mi-num.'
brith, man-ken fre for to ma- ken of senne and deu-les mith'.

* 𝄐 in original MS.   † third lower in MS.

[1] The variant setting of the music is given in Gleason, *Examples of Music before 1400*, p. 53. The unorthodox rhythmic interpretation of the ligature marked by an asterisk is suggested by the context and by the middle voice at 'tu porta'. Glossary: evene king = the king of heaven; a-rith = aright; lith = light; for manes loven = for love of

It should be noted how well the dance-like triple metre agrees with the metre of the words. Of this characteristic lilt the plainchant notation of the monophonic versions gives no indication. Another point of interest is the curious clash between the harmonic implication of the melody, which at the beginning clearly suggests C major to modern ears, and its actual harmonization by unexpected triads on G and F.

Popular hymns found their way even into liturgical books. A fifteenth-century processional of Benedictine nuns in Chester includes a hymn on the Nativity 'Qui creavit coelum'.[1] Its popular character is evident not only in the innocent simplicity of its tune but also in the alternating refrain-lines 'lully lu' and 'by by by'. Such onomatopoeic syllables have their parallels in many lullabies and carols of same period:

Ex. 55

Qui cre-a-vit coe-lum, lul-ly lul-ly lu,
Nas-ci-tur in sta-bu-lo, by-by by-by by,
Rex qui re-git sæ-cu-lum, lul-ly lu-ly lu.

(He who created heaven is born in a stable, the King who rules the world.)

THE FRANCISCAN FRIARS

It has been pointed out above that the Franciscans were more closely associated with popular sacred music than any other religious order. They gained influence over the populace by employing popular songs as a means of religious propaganda. It was their established policy to substitute sacred words, usually in the vernacular, for the original secular ones. This policy betrays not only a realistic attitude but also great trust in the powers of music, for they were sure that a well-known and catching tune would automatically give wide currency to the spiritualized version. The Franciscans wrote many new sequences and hymns, the two existing forms of sacred music which they found most suitable for their purposes, but their best

man; bicomen = become; brith = bright; manken = mankind; of senne and deules mith = of sin and devil's might.

[1] Huntington Library, San Marino, California, MS. EL 34, B 7, published with facsimile of the hymn by the *Henry Bradshaw Society*, xviii (1899). The melody is written in plainsong notation and could be sung accordingly. The rhythmic interpretation of our example is by Edgar T. Cook.

known contribution is the *lauda*, which was either newly composed
in the style of popular models or a plain *contrafactum* or parody of
a secular song. Although the Franciscans favoured popular models
they did not shun learned music, either monophonic or polyphonic,
as may be learned from the Italian Friar Salimbene (*c.* 1280) whose
chronicle gives a lively account of their musical activities in Italy.[1]

After establishing themselves in the British Isles the Franciscans
began to exert great influence on the growth of popular sacred music.
This can be gathered from the *Red Book of Ossory*, which gives us
unusually precise information about their methods, though it contains
no music. The relevant section of the *Red Book* consists of a series
of Latin cantilenas which are expressly described as parodies of
secular songs.[2] The author of the Latin lyrics, the Franciscan Richard
de Ledrede, was Bishop of Ossory, Ireland, from 1317 to 1360. A
rubric tells us not only the name of the author, but also the purpose
of the collection: it was written in order that the clerics would not
'pollute their throats by popular, immoral, and secular songs'.[3]
The *contrafacta* are in Latin and not, as usual, in the vernacular,
because they were destined for the clergy. But the method of substitution is the same as in other parodies. Evidently the Bishop of Ossory
would not have taken the trouble to 'protect' his clergy from secular
songs if they had not been under their spell themselves.

A further point of musical interest is the circumstance that some of
the poems indicate the tunes by a reference to the opening line or
stanza of the model. These quotations or *timbres* are most valuable
as they acquaint us with English secular songs (and also with a few
in French) of which there is no other record. Since the Latin adaptation was made to a ready-made tune and lyric it must follow the
metrical pattern of the original, though it will be seen presently that
an extra syllable here or there does not disturb the general parallelism.
It has been shown above that this holds true also of the parallelism
between verse and music. The following example from the *Red Book*
gives a very good idea of how these parodies were made. The cantilena
'Peperit virgo' carries at the top the inscription 'Mayde yn the moore
lay'. The complete lyric of this secular song happens to be known
and the two versions can therefore be compared:[4]

[1] Cf. F. Ludwig, *Repertorium organorum* (Halle, 1910), p. 247.
[2] The importance of this document, especially with regard to the carol, was pointed
out by R. L. Greene, op. cit., p. cxviii; for further literature see the same author's 'The
Maid of the Moor in the Red Book of Ossory', *Speculum*, xxvii (1952), p. 504.
[3] 'Ne guttura eorum . . . polluantur cantilenis teatralibus, turpibus et secularibus.'
[4] The correspondence was discovered by Greene; see his article in *Speculum*, xxvii
(1952), p. 505, where the Latin words are printed. The English words (no. 3891) are

Maiden in the mor lay,	Peperit virgo,
In the mor lay	Virgo regia,
Sevenyst[es] fulle,	Mater orphanorum,
Sevenist[es] fulle.	Mater orphanorum.
Maiden in the mor lay,	Peperit virgo,
In the mor lay	Virgo regia,
Sevenistes fulle,	Mater orphanorum,
[Sevenistes fulle]	Mater orphanorum,
Ant a day.	Plena gracia.

It will be seen at a glance how closely model and *contrafactum* agree, slight variants in the number of syllables notwithstanding, and there is no doubt that both could easily be sung to the same tune. This is true also of the other poems of the collection. They always imitate the metrical pattern of the model, sometimes even to the point of taking over the same rhyme.

The cantilenas of the *Red Book* are important in still another respect. Many of them are written strictly in carol form, as is, for example, the first cantilena of the collection. This Latin song on the Nativity has the burden 'Verbum caro factum est de Virgine Maria' which was to play an important role in the polyphonic cantilena of the fifteenth century.[1] The *Red Book of Ossory* is only one of several sources[2] showing that the Franciscans were directly associated with the development of the carol in England.

EARLY CAROLS

The origins of the English carol are not fully known,[3] but it seems certain that it was originally a dance song of fixed form, consisting of a recurring burden, sung and danced in a round by the entire group, and a variable stanza, sung standing by the leader or possibly a few soloists. The association of dance movement with the burden and standing with the stanza has its parallel in the performance of the Italian *ballata*. Indeed it is likely that the term 'stanza' owes its origin to the fact that it was performed standing, with the singers marking time in place.[4] The alternate cessation and resumption of dancing has survived to the present day in the performance of certain carols and folk-songs.[5] No musical examples of early English dance songs have

most easily accessible in K. Sisam, *Fourteenth Century Verse and Prose* (Oxford, 1921), p. 167. I owe a transcript of the *Red Book* collection to the courtesy of Dr. Greene.

[1] Cf. M. Bukofzer, *Studies in Medieval and Renaissance Music* (New York, 1950), p. 149, n. 59. The cantilena has been published by R. H. Robbins in *Modern Language Notes*, liii (1938), p. 241.

[2] Greene, op. cit., p. cxxv.   [3] Ibid., pp. xxix ff.

[4] Cf. N. Pirrotta, 'Ballata', in *Die Musik in Geschichte und Gegenwart*, i (Kassel, 1949–51), col. 1157.   [5] See Greene, op. cit., pp. lviii and xxxiii.

been preserved. The extant examples of English dance music from the thirteenth century belong to a more elevated type. They are related to the *estampie*, and the fact that they are in part polyphonic is further proof of their stylized character.[1]

The early carol was doubtless a monophonic song. The earliest extant examples of carol texts date from the middle or second half of the fourteenth century and their number is very small. It is interesting to observe that the Latin cantilenas which display the same form are older and known in much greater number. But this does not mean that they were the prototype of the carol because those of the *Red Book of Ossory* were admittedly imitations of secular models. The cantilenas of the *Red Book* do not all observe the carol form, nor do other English lyrics of the fourteenth century which later became associated with the carol. Certain poems stood originally outside the carol tradition and were only later turned into carols by the addition of a burden.[2] This interesting modification is indirect testimony to the increasing popularity of the carol form. But the opposite process is also known—the transformation of a carol into a stanzaic hymn. In one case, for example, the burden is omitted and replaced by alternating stanzas of the hymn 'Christe qui lux es', which may have provided at the same time the melody for the English song.[3]

Not a single carol known to date from the fourteenth century has been preserved in musical manuscripts of the period. However, one of them survives in a musical source of the early fifteenth century. This is the monophonic carol 'Lullay, lullay'[4] in Cambridge, University Library, Add. 5943. Its melody moves in the simple $\frac{6}{8}$ rhythm of major prolation and there is nothing in the music to contradict the assumption that it is the original tune. It is not surprising that this carol is still monophonic. The carol changed from a monophonic dance song into a stylized polyphonic composition about or shortly after the turn of the century. Those of the fourteenth century must have been predominantly if not exclusively monophonic, and it seems logical that the 'Lullay' carol should represent the primitive stage of the development. Survivals of the same stage may be seen in some of the earliest polyphonic carols which in their unison sections retain what may be described as monophonic relics.[5] It may also be

---

[1] See vol. II, p. 337.

[2] Cf. Greene, op. cit., p. cxxiv.

[3] Cf. Greene, op. cit., no. 152, and his comment in 'The Traditional Survival of two Medieval Carols', *English Literary History*, vii (1940), p. 231.

[4] Published in *Mediaeval Carols*, ed. by J. Stevens, *Musica Britannica*, iv (London, 1952), no. 1a; Greene, op. cit., no. 149d.

[5] Cf. Bukofzer, *Studies in Medieval and Renaissance Music*, p. 166.

noted that in one of the later carols[1] the burden is designated as 'foot'.[2] This brings to mind the term *pes* so frequently found in early English polyphony.

POLYPHONIC CAROLS: THEIR FORM AND STYLE

It is no exaggeration to say that the carol was the popular musical form *par excellence* in fifteenth-century England. The wealth of its literary sources[3] is matched only insufficiently by a relatively small number of musical sources, but they amply show what kind of music was sung to these charmingly ingenuous lyrics. By the early fifteenth century the carol had ceased to be a monophonic dance song and had become a polyphonic part-song which was no longer danced to. The parallel Latin form, the cantilena, also followed this trend toward polyphony. In common parlance 'carol' refers loosely to any religious song for Christmas; but in the fifteenth century it was a well-defined form in English, Latin, or macaronic verse consisting of a burden, always sung first, and a number of uniform verses or stanzas between which the burden was repeated. Although the carol developed concurrently and probably in connexion with such continental strophic forms as the *virelai* and the *lauda*, it must be regarded as specifically English, even if several continental cantilenas have the same form and the same musical style. The musical repertory of the carol is contained chiefly in four sources, the Selden[4] and Egerton[5] manuscripts, the Trinity Roll,[6] and the old layer of Add. MS. 5665 of the British Museum, which are complemented by several smaller collections and fragments.[7] The Trinity Roll represents the earliest stage of the polyphonic carol, and Add. MS. 5665 the latest.

Although the subject-matter of the carol may deal with every topic —sacred, political, or amorous—the majority are religious, though not liturgical. That the carols were sung as optional parts of the service can be inferred from rubrics in Add. 5665 which specify

[1] Greene, op. cit., p. cxxiv.

[2] Cf. also the *pedes* of the Italian *ballata* (see p. 65).

[3] A complete edition of the texts is found in Greene, op. cit.

[4] Oxford, Bodleian, Selden B 26. Facsimile in Stainer, *Early Bodleian Music*, i, pl. 37–97.

[5] Brit. Mus. Egerton 3307. Thematic catalogue by B. Schofield in *The Musical Quarterly*, xxxii (1946), p. 509. For its origin see p. 181.

[6] Cambridge, Trinity College O 3.58. Facsimile reprint in J. A. Fuller Maitland, *English Carols of the Fifteenth Century* (London, 1891).

[7] The entire body of carols is now available in transcription in *Mediaeval Carols*, edited by J. Stevens, in *Musica Britannica*, iv (London, 1952). The volume supersedes all former (and often very faulty) transcriptions. For a fuller discussion of the carol see Bukofzer, op. cit., p. 148, and the review of *Mediaeval Carols* in *Journal of the American Musicological Society*, vii (1954), p. 63.

various occasions of the liturgical year.[1] They served as processional music, and it is significant that the form of the carol is the same as that of the processional hymn, even with regard to certain points of performance. In comparison with the motets of the period the carol stands out for the popular appeal of its melody and the adaptation of a simple $\frac{6}{3}$-chord style to its harmony. Rhythmic complexities are gradually discarded and replaced by vigorous, if at times uncouth, rhythms which in their mixture of $\frac{6}{8}$ and $\frac{3}{4}$ time remind us of the Burgundian *chanson*. Repeated notes, simple and often angular melodic lines, and harmonic simplicity account for its uniform style, which at times still reminds one that the carol was once a dance. The characteristics of the dance disappear in the latest stage of the carol and certain metrical irregularities take their place.

In spite of its stereotyped literary structure the carol could be set to music in various ways. Burden and stanza are generally composed in a contrasting manner, but just as the last words of the verse often reiterate a phrase from the burden, so the music may show a corresponding likeness in musical rhyme. The settings vary from one to three voices[2] and if there are monophonic sections they are often repeated in harmony with melodic variation. The burden and certain sections of the verse, or even the entire verse, are frequently composed twice in related but different settings. The second of these (never the first) is sometimes marked 'chorus', thus providing a highly important piece of information, not only that the carols were performed by soloists and chorus in alternation, but also that the chorus began to sing polyphonic music, which was up to this time reserved for soloists.[3] It follows from the direction of the manuscripts that in the polyphonic carol 'burden' must not be confused with 'chorus'. The first was sung by soloists, as were the verses, and only the repeats were assigned to the chorus. The chorus sections often differ from the others by a larger number of voices. Thus a two-voice burden may be answered by a three-voice chorus. The carol 'Hail Mary full of grace'[4] is set for a three-voice burden and the verse for two soloists. This is one of the most common ways of alternating the voices; in other carols the scheme is more complex as, for example, in the now famous Agincourt carol 'Owre Kynge went forth to Normandy' with the burden 'Deo gratias Anglia'.[5] In this carol, more widely known than any

---

[1] On the suggestion that some carols were used as 'Benedicamus' substitutes, see F. Ll. Harrison, *Music in Medieval Britain* (London, 1958), pp. 416–17.—*Ed.*

[2] Occasionally four.   [3] Bukofzer, 'The Beginnings of Choral Polyphony', in *Studies*, p. 176.   [4] *Mediaeval Carols*, no. 2.

[5] Facsimile in J. A. Fuller Maitland, *English Carols of the Fifteenth Century* (London,

other because of its reference to the battle of Agincourt,[1] the two-part burden begins in unison and turns to two-part writing only in its second phrase. The entire burden is then repeated with variation by a three-part chorus. Similarly, 'Abyde Y hope'[2] begins with a burden for one solo voice which is repeated as the middle voice of a three-part chorus. Here also the entire verse is repeated by a chorus. Even more refined are certain carols of the Egerton manuscript, in which chorus sections are interspersed in both burden and verse, for example in the charming 'Ivy is good'.[3]

The musical settings of the carols are not arrangements of pre-existing folksong, as it has sometimes been assumed, but bear the mark of composed art-music in a popular vein. They are, in the words of Greene,[4] 'popular by destination' and not 'popular by origin'. Their style is so homogeneous that it is not always possible to decide which voice should be regarded as bearing the chief melody. On the whole the lowest voice seems to have the predominance as a rule, but sometimes the middle or the highest voice leads. An example of the latter is the macaronic 'Te Deum laudamus'[5] or the graceful 'Glad and blithe',[6] which, though it appears in a carol manuscript, is not a carol but an English paraphrase of the sequence 'Laetabundus', in which the end of each strophe retains the original Latin text. What is more, the upper voice distinctly paraphrases the melody of the sequence, so that the musical structure of the composition is also that of a sequence. The use of musical rhyme can be seen in the macaronic carol 'Ave Rex angelorum'.[7] The verse given in Ex. 56 repeats at the end the first words of the Latin burden: furthermore the music merely restates the last seven bars of the burden in the variant of the chorus. The carol is provided with two related settings of the burden for soloists and chorus respectively. It is set for three voices throughout—an unusual feature. It will be noticed that the outermost voices are the essential ones and always form a complete setting, while the middle voice could possibly be omitted:

1891), and Stainer, op. cit., i, pl. lxvi. Transcription in *Mediaeval Carols*, no. 8. Recorded in *The History of Music in Sound*, iii.

[1] The carol 'Enfors we us' with the verse 'Worship of vertu' (*Mediaeval Carols*, no. 60) also mentions Agincourt.

[2] *Mediaeval Carols*, no. 10.   [3] Ibid., no. 55.   [4] Greene, op. cit., p. xciii.

[5] *Mediaeval Carols*, no. 95. This carol and 'Salve sancta parens' make use of the plainsong melodies.   [6] Stainer, op. cit., ii, p. 134.

[7] *Mediaeval Carols*, no. 52. A chronicler records that a composition entitled 'Ave rex Anglorum', was sung when Henry V entered London after the battle of Agincourt (see *Gesta Henrici V*, ed. B. Williams, 1850, p. 63), but it would be hazardous to suggest that it was identical with this carol. More probably the incipit refers to an antiphon in honour of St. Edmund.

It is unfortunate that nearly all the carols in these collections are anonymous. In the Selden manuscript one carol is ascribed to Childe, and in the carols of British Museum, Add. 5665, Smert and Trouluffe are named as composers or authors. 'I pray ȝou all' in the Selden manuscript bears the signature 'quod J. D.', which has been taken as a possible reference to John Dunstable. But from the style of the music Dunstable's authorship seems unlikely: moreover the inscription seems to concern the words rather than the music.

Though most of the carols relate to Christmas or to Our Lady there are others with political or moral subjects. In addition to the carols on the battle of Agincourt mentioned above (pp. 122–3) we have references, in the Egerton manuscript, to Henry V in 'Pro divino auxilio', with burden 'Exsultavit cor', and to the Wars of the Roses in 'Jurandi jam nequitia', with burden 'Anglia tibi turbidas'.

The Egerton manuscript also includes in its collection of carols the drinking-song 'O potores exquisiti'.[1] It is the first known musical setting of an old Goliard poem which occurs as early as the *Carmina Burana*. The music is composed pretentiously as a strict isorhythmic motet, probably with parodistic intent. The opening of the piece is given below. The underlaying of the text in the lower voices is a matter of conjecture; and words not given in the original are enclosed in square brackets. Some instrumental treatment is clearly needed in the two lowest voices:

Ex. 57

(O rare drinkers, even though you have no thirst, drink without stint . . .)

Another drinking-song, which is simpler than 'O potores' but no less effective, is 'Tappster, dryngker', from the Selden manuscript.[2] It is a humorous composition which in its quick alternation of voices anticipates the spirit of the later catch:

Ex. 58

[1] Brit. Mus., Egerton 3307, fo. 72ᵛ–73; facsimile in Bukofzer, op. cit., facing p. 129.
[2] Stainer, op. cit., ii, p. 177. Recorded in *The History of Music in Sound*, iii.

SONGS IN ENGLISH MANUSCRIPTS

Secular song in England was fashioned after continental models, and it is therefore not surprising to find French songs in English collections: moreover French was still the 'polite' language of many in England. The paucity of English sources is especially deplorable in this branch of music. There is not much more than the contents of four fragmentary manuscripts containing various pieces: the Bodleian manuscripts Douce 381 (four English and two French songs), Ashmole 1393 (one in English), and Ashmole 191 (seven in English), with Cambridge, University Library, Add. 5943.[1] The first

[1] The first three manuscripts have been edited in Stainer, *Early Bodleian Music*; the

of these is mostly in the white or void notation which is usually taken to indicate a date after 1450. Wooldridge, Stainer, and Nicholson dated it earlier, and there is no reason to doubt their judgement in the matter.[1] The song 'I rede that thou be joly and glad'[2] occurs both in the Cambridge manuscript and in Bodleian, Douce 381. The repertory is almost completely anonymous; only the song 'Thys 3ol the beste' is ascribed in the Cambridge manuscript to one Edmund. The rest must be gathered from even more fragmentary sources and from the great number of continental manuscripts in which songs by English composers are widely scattered.

The earliest stage of fifteenth-century English song is represented by the Douce and Cambridge manuscripts just mentioned, which preserve a motley repertory of songs in two and three parts, in an extremely archaic style. 'Ie have so long kepe schepe',[3] for example, not only moves in the old-fashioned rhythm of major prolation, but contains barely concealed parallel octaves which show that this primitive type of two-part polyphony was at that time still practised in England, as it was also in Germany. Several songs are cast in a curtailed *virelai* form *ABB*, in which both parts are connected by musical rhyme and the repeats differentiated by the typical *ouvert* and *clos*[4] ending of the French form. A simple *ABB* form obtains also in the two-part 'I rede that thou be joly and glad', in which the composer is little concerned about the preparation of dissonances. That the two manuscripts cited transmit the same setting of this song confirms the close relationship of the two sources as to repertory (both contain French songs) and notation.

Ashmole 191 presents a much more mature stage of English songwriting. It is written in full black notation, but it cannot be earlier than the second half of the century because it includes a fragment of a *ballade* by Frye, which, like all the other compositions in this source, is anonymous here. In their blending consonant style and studiously melancholy tone the songs correspond very closely to the *chansons* by English composers in continental manuscripts. The three-voiced 'Go hert hurt with adversite',[5] one of the finest examples of the group, is not written in the customary *ballade* form but

last was published (in a limited edition of 100 copies) under the title *Music, Cantelenas, Songs &c. from an early Fifteenth Century Manuscript*, ed. L. S. M[yers] (1906).

[1] Concerning this question see Bukofzer, *Studies*, p. 92.

[2] *Oxford History of Music* (1st ed., 1901), ii, p. 129.

[3] Stainer, op. cit., ii, p. 54.

[4] The *ouvert* and *clos* endings have not always been joined correctly to the preceding music in Stainer's transcriptions.

[5] Ibid., p. 68. See also J. H. Harvey, *Gothic England* (London, 1947), p. 85.

otherwise displays all the characteristic features of English song: melismatic, or perhaps instrumental, passages at the end of major sections, sudden pauses with the third placed conspicuously at the top, and a marked preference for the Dorian mode.

CHANSONS BY ENGLISH COMPOSERS

English masters contributed to the great flowering of the fifteenth-century *chanson* on the Continent, writing in Italian, French, and English. To Dunstable are attributed a setting of 'O rosa bella'[1] (words by Giustiniani) and two French *chansons*, 'Puisque m'amour' and 'Durer ne puis'.[2] Untrustworthy or careless copyists have made the ascriptions in the manuscripts singularly inconsistent. Although 'O rosa bella' occurs in more than a dozen different manuscripts and a quotation in Tinctoris, only one of them names Dunstable; another ascribes the piece to Bedingham, while all the other sources are anonymous. The same ambiguity occurs in the case of 'Durer ne puis'. The music of 'O rosa bella' does not show pronounced English characteristics; neither do the other two *chansons* under Dunstable's name. The use of close imitation in three voices at the beginning of 'O rosa bella' reflects an Italian *chanson* style which may have been deliberately adopted because of the Italian words. Dunstable's French *chansons*, on the other hand, have only occasional imitative duets and a non-imitative contratenor, such as is typical of the Burgundian *chanson*.

In the Trent Codices 'O rosa bella' is supplied with a set of three complementary *concordantiae* by Bedingham. The fact that he is expressly mentioned here as the author of the additional parts may possibly imply that he was not the author of the original setting and thus indirectly supports Dunstable's claim to authorship. However this may be, the *concordantiae* are apparently so composed as to sound simultaneously with the *chanson* in six-part harmony, a very unusual occurrence at the time, and one which bears out once more the English fondness of sonority for its own sake. The two lower com-

---

[1] Recorded, together with Ciconia's setting, in *The History of Music in Sound*, iii. *

[2] See John Dunstable: *Complete Works*, ed. M. F. Bukofzer, *Musica Britannica*, viii (1953), pp. 133, 136, and 156. For 'O rosa bella' see also *Denkmäler der Tonkunst in Österreich*, vii, p. 229, and V. Lederer, *Über Heimat und Ursprung der mehrstimmigen Tonkunst* (Leipzig, 1906). Both works give the six complementary voices. The three-part version is also reprinted in A. T. Davison and W. Apel, *Historical Anthology of Music*, i (Cambridge, Mass., 1946), no. 61. For 'Puisque m'amour' see also *Denkmäler der Tonkunst in Österreich*, vii, p. 254, and A. Schering, *Geschichte der Musik in Beispielen* (Leipzig, 1931), p. 30.

plementary parts are purely instrumental, as the extreme leaps, the lacerated design, and the rests prove: but the extra *superius* can be sung by a treble voice.

We find in the same manuscript three other additional voices by an anonymous composer, called *gymel, alius gymel,* and *secundus contratenor* respectively. The function of these has been misunderstood.[1] Unlike Bedingham's *concordantiae* they do not belong together as a set but can only be added singly in various combinations. The *secundus contratenor* changes the three original voices into four-part harmony. Either the first or the second gymel may be combined with the treble of 'O rosa bella' and with this part only, to form two slightly differing two-voice settings or gymels, as the very designation of these two voices implies. Single voices of Dunstable's *chanson* were borrowed time and again by other composers for a great variety of derived compositions, secular arrangements, quodlibets, and Mass settings. 'O rosa bella' can in this respect vie with the even more famous 'L'homme armé' melody. Hert, who may be English on the evidence of his name,[2] and Ockeghem both appropriated Dunstable's treble, the former adding two new voices, the latter only one. The two settings have been edited erroneously as variants of one and the same composition, but they actually form a three-voice version and a gymel respectively, which use the borrowed voice in a different fashion.[3]

The *chansons* of John Bedingham, Robert Morton, and Walter Frye enjoyed great popularity at the Burgundian court, as we can infer from several Burgundian sources. Bedingham is known by three very melodious French *chansons,* 'Le serviteur', 'Grant temps',[4] and 'Mon seul plaisir',[5] which occur in several *chansonniers.* A fourth *chanson* by Bedingham appears in the sources, sometimes with Italian words and sometimes with French text as 'Gentil madonna' or

---

[1] Lederer corrects some of the mistakes in *Denkmäler der Tonkunst in Österreich*, loc. cit., but makes some arbitrary emendations prompted by his belief that all three voices should be played simultaneously.

[2] The name of Alan Hert occurs between 1413 and 1422 among those of the chaplains and clerks of the Chapel Royal, in lists which contain several names of composers found in the Old Hall manuscript (see Chaps. III and VI).

[3] *Denkmäler der Tonkunst in Österreich*, vii, p. 233. Hert introduces the borrowed voice after several bars' rest; Ockeghem starts his gymel without them (the rests that have been editorially supplied in Ockeghem's *discantus* must be deleted).

[4] Printed in *Denkmäler der Tonkunst in Österreich*, vii, p. 239 and xi (1), p. 70. 'Le serviteur' has the text incipit only and it is doubtful whether these are the original words. For 'Grant temps' see below, p. 131.

[5] Oporto, Laborde, and in a textless version also in Munich, MS. mus. 3232. Facsimile of 'Mon seul plaisir' (incorrectly described as 'Monsieur') in Apel, *The Notation of Polyphonic Music, 900–1600,* p. 137. Concordance in *The Musical Quarterly,* xxxviii (1952), p. 114.

'Fortune helas' and has been used as the basis for a cyclic Mass.[1]
Robert Morton (d. 1475) is the only composer of the group whose
connexion with the Burgundian court is well established. He instructed
Charles the Bold in counterpoint and was probably acquainted
personally with Binchois, Dufay, and Busnois. Although he died only
a year after Dufay his style belongs to a somewhat later generation.
Only secular compositions of Morton have survived, six *chansons*
and three textless pieces (probably *chansons* also).[2] One of the latter[3]
is written in a very pronounced English idiom, which is much less
marked in his other works. This piece occurs with Spanish words
in the *Cancionero de Palacio*.[4] Another textless piece, described as
motectus[5] in an Italian source, appears in a German manuscript,
Munich mus. 3232, as the German song 'Elend du hast umfangen',
and we can only guess as to the original language of the words. A
piece which from its title, 'La Perontina', has the appearance of an
Italian composition[6] can be identified from the Mellon Chansonnier
as the French *rondeau* 'Parachève ton entreprise', which we find
quoted as late as Fabri's *Le grand et vrai Art de pleine Rhétorique*
(1521). Morton also made a four-part arrangement of the 'L'homme
armé' *chanson*[7] which is closely related to an earlier version of the
same composition in the Mellon Chansonnier.[8] It is not certain
whether Morton merely added a bass and made the necessary changes
at the cadence, or whether he was also the author of the older version,
the first known setting of 'L'homme armé'.

ENGLISH SONGS IN CONTINENTAL MANUSCRIPTS

Of particular interest are the songs with English words that have
been preserved in various continental manuscripts. Five such have
come to light so far: 'Alas, alas is my chief song', 'Myn hertis lust',
'So ys emprentid in my remembrance', 'Princhesse of youth'[9] and
the enigmatical 'Agwillare habeth'.[10] The first three of these appear

---

[1] Facsimile in *The Musical Quarterly*, xxviii (1942), p. 22; concordance, ibid. xxxviii
(1952), p. 113.

[2] Printed in K. Jeppesen, *Der Kopenhagener Chansonnier* (Copenhagen & Leipzig,
1937), and J. Marix, *Les Musiciens de la Cour de Bourgogne* (Paris, 1937).

[3] Marix, op. cit., p. 93.

[4] See Anglès, *La música en la Corte de los Reyes Católicos*, iii, 1–2 (Barcelona, 1947
and 1951), no. 27, and introduction to iii, 2, p. 23.

[5] Marix, op. cit., p. 240.   [6] Ibid., p. 97.   [7] Ibid., p. 96.

[8] M. Bukofzer, 'An Unknown Chansonnier of the 15th Century', in *The Musical
Quarterly*, xxviii (1942), p. 14.

[9] See M. Bukofzer, 'The First English Chanson on the Continent', in *Music and
Letters*, xix (1938), p. 121.

[10] *Denkmäler der Tonkunst in Österreich*, xi (1), p. 120. See also *The Musical Quarterly*,
xxii (1936), p. 138.

in the Mellon Chansonnier. All of them are written in either the D or the F mode and are cast in *ballade* form—that is to say, they follow the scheme *AAB* with musical rhyme between *A* and *B*. The sources make it plain that the continental scribes were hard put to it to cope with the English words. If they are given at all they are usually corrupt, sometimes beyond hope of sensible emendation, or else they are replaced by French or Italian words. The English songs thus appear in various disguises which make their identification an extremely difficult task. Of the three English songs in the Mellon Chansonnier, 'Alas, alas is my chief song' is related both in words and music to 'Alas departyng' of the Ashmole manuscript, and it is an open question which composition is the earlier.[1] The *chanson* has been tentatively ascribed to Frye, and this ascription is borne out by the cirumstance that the same music occurs in form of a *contrafactum* as the motet 'O sacrum convivium' in Munich, mus. 3232, here with Frye's name.[2] The anonymous 'Myn hertis lust' can be identified with Bedingham's 'Grant temps', the music of which was also adapted to sacred words, 'Beata es'.[3] Both the French and the Latin texts are therefore merely substitutes for the original English *ballade*. The same may be true of 'Gentil madonna' and 'Fortune helas', although no English version has been found thus far.

'So ys emprentid' by Walter Frye has a singularly chequered record. It appears in the Laborde Chansonnier as 'Soyez aprantiz', obviously a strange gallicized paraphrase of the English syllables: the rest of the 'translation' is missing. However, it is carried a little farther in the Monte Cassino manuscript, where it reads 'Soyes aprentis en amours', showing that the text was not intended as a translation of the English version. In several other sources the same *chanson* has been furnished with another French text, 'Pour une suis', which shows no relation to the English lyric. That neither French version is the original is confirmed by the fact that a textless fragment of Ashmole 191, which consists entirely of English songs, is the beginning of the same piece. Finally it reappears in the Trent Codices, here again anonymous, as 'Sancta Maria succurre'.[4] It precedes here a cyclic Mass by Guillaume le Rouge[5] on an undesignated tenor which is identical with that of 'So ys emprentid'. In this case the *contrafactum*

---

[1] Both are transcribed in *The Musical Quarterly*, xxviii (1942), pp. 42 and 45.

[2] See S. W. Kenney, 'Contrafacta in the Works of Walter Frye', *Journal of the American Musicological Society*, viii (1955), p. 182.

[3] Trent Codices, no. 1140.   [4] Ibid., nos. 990 and 1029.

[5] Ibid., nos. 1031–5; see also E. Reeser, 'Een "iso-melische mis" uit den tijd van Dufay', *Tijdschrift der Vereeniging voor Nederlandsche Muziekgeschiedenis*, xvi (1942), pp. 151, 312.

of the *chanson* has been put before the Mass with good reason, though neither discloses the true origin of the music. The tenor appears in the Trent codices[1] another time, again without being designated in any way, in the four-part motet 'Stella coeli exstirpavit'. The extraordinary popularity of Frye's *chanson* appears also from a passage in Ramis de Pareia's *Musica Practica* (1482),[2] which thus fixes the latest possible date for the composition. In this passage the Spanish theorist permits the use of parallel fifths if one of them is diminished, and refers by way of example to 'Soyez aprantiz':

As the example shows, bars 3 and 6 contain parallel fifths which must obviously be modified by *musica ficta*. Frye is also known by the French *chanson* 'Tout a par moy',[3] which was used later on by Tinctoris and Josquin as the basis for other compositions. 'Princhesse of youth', by an anonymous writer, was apparently also well known in its day, as appears from a casual allusion in John Skelton's *The Bouge of Court*. The piece belongs to the last third of the fifteenth century; the *chanson* 'Alone I lyve',[4] which is preserved only in an isolated English fragment, may be of an even later date.

Finally a small but important *chansonnier* in Oporto gives us some Italian *chansons* by Galfridus and Robertus de Anglia, two English composers of the second half of the century who have not yet been

---

[1] No. 204.

[2] Edited by J. Wolf, *Beihefte der internationalen Musikgesellschaft*, ii (1901), p. 65. The passage was also quoted in Aaron's *Lucidario* (1545). Ramis quotes only the text incipit, not the music.

[3] Printed by D. Plamenac in *The Musical Quarterly*, xxxvii (1951), p. 530.

[4] See the *Antiquaries Journal*, xv (1935), p. 1.

definitely identified. Robertus may of course be Morton.[1] 'Che farò io' by Galfridus, and even more 'O fallaze e ria fortuna' by Robertus, stand out for their vivid declamatory rhythm and their happy union of Italian clarity with English melodiousness. They testify to the vigorous interpenetration of styles in the consort of European nations.

[1] Gilbert Reaney suggests that Galfridus may be Frye.—*Ed.*

V

THE TRANSITION ON THE CONTINENT

By RUDOLF VON FICKER

INTRODUCTORY

WE have seen how, in the fourteenth century, there were French and Italian schools, each with its own peculiarities of style, and that England played a conservative part, her music remaining almost unaffected by the daring novelties introduced by the French *ars nova* composers, such as Vitry and Machaut. Even in France this 'new art' was an organic development of thirteenth-century traditions. The music of the Italian trecento, on the other hand, shows a complete breakaway, which might almost be termed a new beginning. Although it is related to the French *ars nova* in matters of technique, its emotional background is entirely different; and it is this which gives it individuality. At the end of the century these three national schools were still independent, and clearly distinguishable from one another. Only during the first thirty years of the fifteenth century was a compromise reached between them; and from their fusion emerged a single musical ideal, valid in both Northern and Southern Europe. The ground was now prepared for the secular musical style of the Renaissance proper: a style whose technique and means of expression were to be cultivated and accepted everywhere.

Thus the fifteenth century must be regarded as a period of transition. At first the medieval forms and technical procedures still persisted; they were indeed intensively cultivated, at times even to the point of exaggeration. But the language of music was undergoing a fundamental change. As in late Gothic art, so in music, this interaction of old and new produced a diversity and a technical refinement which make it very hard to distinguish the origins of the period that followed—the age of Dunstable and Dufay. We must therefore begin by considering the general musical situation in 1400.

The music of the Italian trecento composers had by this time passed its peak, and the later works of Francesco Landini (see p. 77) already show a distinct leaning towards the French *ballade* style; but in spite of these foreign influences his musical language still preserves a sensitive and subjective art of expression. This was indeed the chief artistic contribution of the early Italian Renaissance, and may be ascribed to its breakaway from tradition. The music of Landini's contemporaries and successors already shows the symptoms of decay. It is true that we find certain technical advances in the works of the last of the madrigalists, in particular an enrichment of melodic embellishment. But we find also an affectation and superficiality which were soon to kill the madrigal style altogether. The Italian composers of the early quattrocento were no longer faithful to their national traditions. They surrendered entirely, as we shall see, to the artistic methods of the French and Netherland composers, who from now on dominated Italian music more and more. For the rest of the century Italy's role in music was only subordinate. This fact increases the importance of the part played by England in this final phase of medieval music. The occupation of France, by bringing the most important English composers to the Continent, must have been particularly favourable to an assimilation of musical ideals. England's share in the amalgamation of the different styles, unlike Italy's, must be rated very highly. The expulsion of the English, however, put an end to the period when their influence was at its height on the Continent. The final establishment of the new style was almost entirely the work of the Burgundian and Netherland composers of the second half of the century. Thus at the end of the Gothic period French music still maintained its dominant position. In dealing with the period of transition we shall therefore consider it first.

THE TRANSITION IN FRANCE

With the death of Philippe de Vitry (1361) and of Guillaume de Machaut (1377) the two most important representatives of the French *ars nova* passed away. Their successors contented themselves with taking over and developing the forms created by these two great masters, in particular the new motet and the *ballade*. In spite of developments in technique, especially as regards rhythm, no work of this decadent period reached the artistic level of the classical *ars nova*, much less surpassed it. The growing practice of setting parts of the Mass, however, was of considerable historical significance, since the polyphonic *Missa* (consisting of the five invariable sections of the Mass) was the musical form which occupied in the fifteenth and sixteenth centuries a place of honour comparable to that of the symphony in the eighteenth and nineteenth. Until a few years ago the only early examples known were the Tournai Mass and Machaut's (see pp. 21 and 22); but a far clearer light was thrown on the early history of the form by the discovery of the Toulouse and Barcelona cycles (see p. 21), the fragmentary Besançon Mass,[1] and of certain manuscripts in the chapter libraries of Ivrea and Apt.[2] With the exception of a few fragments, our only other legacy from this period is the Ivrea manuscript, dating from 1360 at the earliest, which throws much light on the motets of Philippe de Vitry, the importance of which has already been noted (see pp. 8–11). Mention has already been made[3] of the French canons to be found in it, which show that this device was cultivated in France as well as in England and Italy. The short canon 'Talent m'est pris'[4] is the nearest French counterpart to the English 'Sumer is icumen in', and seems to have been widely known:

Ex. 60

---

[1] The Besançon fragment is reproduced and partially transcribed by Chailley in *Annales musicologiques*, ii (1954).—*Ed.*

[2] Cf. G. Borghezio, 'Un prezioso codice musicale ignorato', *Bolletino storico bibliografico subalpino*, xxiv (1921), nos. 3–4, and 'Poesie musicali latine e francese in un codice ignorato della Biblioteca capitolare d'Ivrea (Torino)', *Archivum Romanum*, v (1921), p. 173. Contents of the Ivrea manuscript in *Archiv für Musikwissenschaft*, vii (1925), p. 188. Transcription of the Apt manuscript in A. Gastoué, *Le Manuscrit de musique polyphonique du trésor d'Apt* (Paris, 1936).

[3] See p. 16.

[4] Ivrea MS., fo. 52. This canon is found in a different form twice in the Ivrea manuscript, also in Prague, XI. E 9 (see F. Kammerer, *Die Musikstücke des Prager*

- cu li io-li tans est ve - nus Ta - -
- cu cha - le quo cu-cu cu quo cu cu-cu
de chan - ter cu-me le co-qu cu-cu cu-

-lent m'est pris de chan - ter cu-me le co-qu.
cu-cu quo quo-cu li io-li tans est ve - nus.
- cu quo co - cu cha - le quo cu-cu cu quo cu.

(I am in mind to sing like the cuckoo, cuccu cuccu, for the merry season is now come.)

AVIGNON MASS SETTINGS

There are also twenty-four Ivrea Mass settings, in two to four parts, which are of special historical importance. Like all the other compositions in the manuscript, they are anonymous. We can identify the authors of five works, since they appear also in the slightly later Apt manuscript: Chipre, Orles, Depansis, Sert, and Loys. It may be presumed, however, that some of the composers of the remaining pieces are of Italian origin; for the contents of the Ivrea and Apt manuscripts, and particularly of the latter, correspond closely to the musical needs of the papal establishment in its exile at Avignon. (The Popes did not return to Rome until 1377; and even after that there were still French anti-popes at Avignon.) The fact that the polyphonic Mass makes its first appearance in these two manuscripts, and in manuscripts very closely related to them,[1]

Kodex XI E 9 (Augsburg and Brno, 1931)) and in Strasbourg, M. 222 C. 22 (destroyed by fire in 1870), and to the words 'Die Minne fueget niemand' by Oswald von Wolkenstein (*Denkmäler der Tonkunst in Osterreich*, ix (1), p. 183).

[1] Schrade has shown the relationships between the *Ite missa est* of the Toulouse Mass and a troped *Gloria* (fo. 36ᵛ) in Ivrea, between the *Gloria* of the Besançon Mass and a *Credo* (fo. 34ᵛ) in Ivrea, and between the Besançon *Sanctus* and the troped *Sanctus* (fo. 62ᵛ) in Ivrea—relationships so close as to justify his speaking of 'parody' technique: in the second case, parody of the *Gloria* in the *Credo*; in the third, two parodies of a model common to both: cf. 'A Fourteenth Century Parody Mass', *Acta Musicologica*, xxvii (1955), p. 13. The model of the two *Sanctus* was discovered by Roland Jackson in

strengthens the supposition that this type of work represents an independent style, and justifies us in speaking of an 'Avignon school' of music as well as of painting.

In most of these Masses we can indeed detect a deliberate attempt to create a new musical style for this most important part of the liturgy, a style essentially different from that of secular music. An occasional resemblance to the *ars nova* motet is only superficial. It lies chiefly in the frequent use of the hocket, especially in the final Amens of the Glorias and Credos. But the essential features of motet form are purposely avoided. For example, we seldom find a *canto fermo* in the tenor. Again, the characteristic isorhythm of the motet is missing. Instead of the simultaneous use of different sets of words, we find a single liturgical text in all the parts,[1] since the dogmatic significance of the Mass demanded a clear and intelligible musical setting. The division of the words between the parts is not consistent; in the simple conductus-like passages they are sung by all the voices simultaneously. Elsewhere they are written only under the topmost part, which is usually the most richly decorated, or (as is customary in the motet) under the two upper parts. But the chief peculiarity and novelty of this style lies in the melodic shape of the top part, particularly in many of the Glorias and Credos, e.g.:

Ex. 61[2]

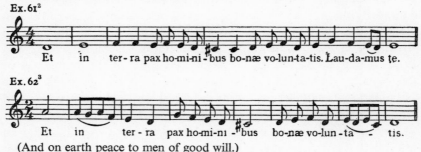

Ex. 62[3]

(And on earth peace to men of good will.)

Here we have a new style of liturgical declamation, which, despite its melodic and rhythmic freedom, retains the vigour characteristic of the plainsong melodies of the *Gloria* and *Credo* by using only one

an *Agnus* at Cambrai (Bibl. Communale 1328, fo. 5): 'Musical interrelations between fourteenth century Mass movements', *Acta Musicologica*, xxix (1957), p. 54. This latter study shows that the separate motets of the Besançon—or, as Schrade and Jackson call it, the Sorbonne—Mass are interrelated, and suggests that an Ivrea *Kyrie* (fo. 16[v]) and *Credo* (fo. 38[v]), and an Apt *Sanctus* (fo. 17), which are similarly interrelated, may also be parts of a very early 'cyclic' Mass.—*Ed.*

[1] The middle voice only of the anonymous *Gloria* on fos. 27[v]–28 has an independent text ('Clemens Deus') grafted on to it in motet style.

[2] Ivrea MS., fo. 16.   [3] Ibid., fo. 27[v].

note to each syllable. Instead of the dance-like triple rhythms of secular music, a simple duple rhythm predominates. No effort is made to make the music conform to the verbal accentuation. Sometimes the syllables are spread out, while at others they are set to quick notes, so that they follow closely on each other. Rhythmically this produces a balancing, compensating effect, making these Masses strangely ascetic and passionless. This new style of church music was clearly an attempt to comply with the Bull of Pope John XXII (1324-5), which strongly condemned the use in church music of secular mannerisms such as the hocket. On the main stream of fourteenth-century music, however, the Bull had no effect. Even in many of these Avignon Masses the greater prolation predominates, after the French manner, e.g.:

Ex. 63[1]

The final Amens are often richly decorated with coloratura passages. The use of the hocket, to which attention has already been drawn, must be regarded only as an outward concession to the prevailing style of the period. This technical mannerism is characteristic of the Avignon school,[2] and occurs less and less as the century draws to its end. The simple declamatory style of the new polyphonic Mass, on the other hand, was adopted by the Italians and Netherlanders, and persisted up to the time of the young Dufay.

FRENCH SECULAR MUSIC

While this specialized type of church music was for the present confined to a few ecclesiastical centres, two traditional forms were becoming extremely widespread—the motet and the French secular song. The reputation of such composers as Machaut was at least as great at the chief foreign courts as in their own country. After his death the demand for music and musicians increased still further;

---

[1] Ibid., fo. 29ᵛ.
[2] The Mass movements of the trecento by Gherardello, Lorenzo, Donato, and Bartholus de Florentia in Paris, Bibl. Nat., ital. 568 and Brit. Mus., Add. 29987, form the Italian counterpart. Cf. also the *Credo* of Machaut's Mass.

poetry and music came more and more to be essential features of court ceremonial. The French kings Charles V (1364–80) and Charles VI (1380–1422), and all the great princes of the period, spared no expense to secure the services of the best musicians. This last age of chivalry culminated in the *Cour amoureuse* instituted in 1401 by Charles VI, in which all the dignitaries of Church and State held offices appropriate to their rank. Their solemn sessions were accompanied by the most splendid ceremonial, of which the most important feature was the performance of new *ballades*, each with a motto-refrain, given to the musicians beforehand by the master of ceremonies. The performer who had shown most skill in singing the praise of the ladies was crowned with a golden circlet.

The exalted spirit of this period is well represented by the exclusively French contents of the Chantilly manuscript, already referred to briefly at the end of Chapter I.[1] This is a copy, made in Italy, of a collection dating from about 1390. It contains chiefly *ballades*, *rondeaux*, and *virelais*, 100 in all; but at the end are some three-part motets—ten Latin and three French. Machaut is represented only by three of his best-known *ballades*, and Landini by two of his French ones. The names of the composers are almost always given; among them are Jean Vaillant, Jehan de Suzay (Suzoy), Solage, Baude Cordier, Grimace, Jo. Galiot, Jacob de Senleches (Selesses), Guido, Jo. Simonis de Haspre (Hasprois), Jo. Cunelier, presumably identical with Jacquemart de Cuvelier, and others. During this period immediately following the death of Machaut Paris and the French court seem still to have been the centres of musical activity.

The words of the *ballades*—a term which we shall use to include also the *virelais* and *rondeaux*—deal for the most part with love, in every possible interpretation of the word. Next, and with increasing prominence, come allegorical and mythological themes, applied to great personages of the time, such as Gaston Phébus, Count of Foix, and John, Duke of Berry. Two *ballades* mourn the deaths of Machaut ('Armes, Amours' by Andrieu) and of Eleanor of Aragon (d. 1382) respectively, while others deal with warlike enterprises. Thus the *ballade* now takes over functions which had hitherto been the monopoly of the motet. Thanks to the simple, clear structure of its verses, each rounded off by the same motto refrain, the *ballade* was able temporarily to compete with the motet, which was complicated and

---

[1] Musée Condé, 1047; for contents see J. Wolf, *Geschichte der Mensural-Notation von 1250–1460* (Leipzig, 1904), i, p. 329. See also G. Reaney's study in *Musica Disciplina*, viii (1954), p. 59.

difficult to understand. In the *double ballade*,[1] however, we find more than one set of words used simultaneously, a practice borrowed from the motet. There are also *ballades* with Latin words, e.g. 'Inclite flos', by Mayhuet de Joan, in honour of the Avignon Pope Clement VII (1378–94), and 'Angelorum psallat' by Uciredor (Rodericus). In the hands of Machaut the *ballade* had still expressed entirely subjective emotions; now, however, adopting the fanciful subject-matter of the motet, it entered the objective field of courtly and aristocratic ceremonial.

In so doing, it also underwent a musical change. It is true that the clear, simple pattern of the Machaut *ballade* was retained in the works of some composers, e.g. Vaillant, Solage, Grimace, and others. In general, however, a special characteristic of the late French *ballade* is an increasing rhythmic complexity. This is evident from the unusually complicated notation used in the principal manuscripts—in addition to Chantilly, one at Modena[2] and another at Turin[3] (see p. 144). Before this time colour was very rarely used; but in these manuscripts red notes are frequently interspersed with the normal black ones, the change of colour signifying an alteration in value. Moreover, the individual parts have different time signatures, which are often interchanged, so that the bar-lines in a modern transcription do not coincide. The rhythmic proportions also differ frequently; while one part is in duple time, another may be in triple. Another feature of this rhythmic complexity is the frequent use of the *punctus syncopationis*. This point of syncopation suspends the normal rhythmic arrangement of a melodic phrase, displacing it by syncopated figures. The correct interpretation of such a complicated piece of notation must sometimes have been very difficult for the performers. Many *ballades*, in consequence, have verbal directions appended, and it is only with their aid that the music can be correctly deciphered.

In fact, these compositions exhibit a rhythmic obscurity which is only comparable with that found in some modern works. The rhythmic balance between the parts is intentionally disturbed, and sometimes completely upset by syncopation, the use of different rhythms, and so on. Each part seems to lead its own rhythmic life. At the same

[1] e.g. Andrieu's lament for Machaut.

[2] Modena, Bibl. Estense, M. 5. 24 (olim lat. 568); for contents see Wolf, op. cit., p. 336, and G. Cesari and F. Fano, *La Cappella musicale del Duomo di Milano*, i (Milan, 1956), p. 109.

[3] Turin, Bibl. Naz., J II 9; for contents see *Archiv für Musikwissenschaft*, vii (1925), p. 212; for detailed discussion see Richard H. Hoppin, 'The Cypriot-French Repertory of the Manuscript Torino, Biblioteca Nazionale, J. II. 9', *Musica Disciplina*, xi (1957), p. 79.—*Ed.*

time it must not be forgotten that the original framework of these works was comparatively simple. Its later transformation was the result of artistic licence on the part of the performers, which gave it, like modern jazz, the maximum rhythmic freedom and diversity. We can only understand and justify this *rythme flamboyant* if we remember the very important social position of the *ballade* in these last days of chivalry. Music and society alike showed a positive aversion to all that was simple, natural, and reasonable. All this encouraged an exaggeration which led to the final exhaustion of the old traditions.[1]

THE TRANSITION IN ITALY

The Modena manuscript also contains for the most part French *ballades*, equally complicated in rhythm; it is noteworthy that most of the composers are Italian. Only single examples of *ballades* by Machaut, Selesses, Simon de Haspre, and Mayhuet de Joan are included. The first and last fascicles of the manuscript are in another hand, and consist almost exclusively of the works of Matteo da Perugia.[2] Of the other Italians Filipoctus de Caserta, who had already figured in the Chantilly manuscript, deserves special mention. He probably worked at the papal court at Avignon. His *Tractatus de diversis figuris*[3] is a short exposition of the new rhythmic problems. He may be regarded as the most important Italian composer of the new school. Anthonellus de Caserta,[4] Conradus de Pistorio (Corrado da Pistoia),[5] Magister Egidius (de Murino), and Johannes de Janua also deserve mention. None of these composers adhered to their national tradition: their ready adoption of the language, form, and technique of the French *ballade* shows the strength of the influence exerted by French culture in Italy at the turn of the century.

This wholesale imitation of the forms current in French society was one of the reasons why even Italy herself gradually lost her understanding and perception of the magnificent tradition of the trecento. The famous Squarcialupi codex[6] (see p. 47) is a later attempt to collect the accessible material of the classical period of the mad-

---

[1] A representative collection of 35 *ballades* will be found in W. Apel, *French Secular Music of the Late Fourteenth Century* (Cambridge, Mass., 1950).

[2] Matteo died in 1418; his works are printed in Cesari and Fano, op. cit.

[3] C. E. H. de Coussemaker, *Scriptorum de musica medii aevi nova series* (Paris, 1864–76), iii, p. 118. The treatise is attributed to Egidius de Murino in some manuscripts: cf. p. 29.

[4] Five *ballades*, one *virelai*, and two *rondeaux* are printed in Apel, op. cit., pp. 31*–44*.

[5] Wolf, op. cit., ii, no. 67: 'Veri Almi.'

[6] Florence, Bibl. Laurenziana, pal. 87.

rigal and to save it from oblivion by preserving it in this splendid volume. It is true that the Modena manuscript contains *ballades* by Bartholomaeus de Bononia (Bartolomeo da Bologna),[1] Dactalus (Bartolinus) de Padua, and Frater Carmelitus, which still show superficial traces of the old trecento technique: indeed they seem to outdo the trecento in their delight in the use of melisma. But the natural flow and clearly defined melodic style of the older madrigals is lacking: the new rhythmic artifices made it impossible. Melisma had lost its expressive power and degenerated into mere technical virtuosity. With the death of Landini in 1397 the basic traditions of the trecento were finally abandoned. Only reminiscences of the old technique are to be found in the works of his successors.

In addition to Bartolomeo and Bartolino, mentioned above, Zacharias (Zaccaria), a singer in the papal chapel, is given a place of honour as a composer in the Squarcialupi manuscript.[2] He appears to have been the oldest of a group of composers of the same name.[3] The motet 'Sumite carissimi' attributed to Magister Zacharias in the Modena manuscript[4] is an example of rhythmical complexity very much in the French manner. Oxford, Bodleian, Canonici misc. 213 (see pp. 47–48 and *infra*) mentions a Nicola Zacharias, who was a singer at the papal chapel from 1420 to 1422, and Antonius Zacharias, who came from Teramo in southern Italy and is also represented by three *ballate* in the Lucca Codex.[5] A number of Glorias[6] and Credos by a composer called Zacar are in Bologna, Bibl. G. B. Martini, Q 15 (see p. 47); it is impossible to say whether he is identical with either of the foregoing.

THE REINA AND TURIN CODICES

The manuscript known as Codex Reina is a collection of secular songs which was probably made in the Venetian territory between *c.* 1390 and *c.* 1440.[7] It consists of a comprehensive selection of works representative of the Italian trecento—many of them otherwise un-

---

[1] Wolf, op. cit., ii, no. 68: ' Que pena.'

[2] Ibid., no. 63: 'Sol mi trafigge'; also in Wolf's transcription of the Squarcialupi Codex (Lippstadt, 1955), p. 332.

[3] Cf. Federico Ghisi in *Archiv für Musikforschung*, vii (1942), pp. 25 ff., and K. von Fischer in *Acta Musicologica*, xxx (1958), p. 188.

[4] Wolf, *Geschichte*, no. 70.   [5] Cf. Chap. II, p. 47.

[6] A fragment of one of these appears anonymously in the Old Hall manuscript, fo. 28ᵛ; see M. F. Bukofzer, *Studies in Medieval and Renaissance Music* (New York, 1950), p. 38, and *infra*, p. 168.

[7] Paris, Bibl. Nat., n.a. fr. 6771; contents in Wolf, op. cit., i, p. 261, and Kurt von Fischer, 'The Manuscript Paris, Bibl. nat. nouv. acq. frç. 6771', *Musica Disciplina*, xi (1957), p. 38. The last part of the Codex was obviously compiled later.—*Ed.*

known—followed by a whole series of French *ballades*. In this collection a significant change of taste is recognizable: the rhythmic artifices
of the court *ballade* are almost entirely avoided. The few examples of
this type of composition which are taken over from the Chantilly and
Modena manuscripts were evidently regarded only as curiosities. The
classical *ballade* of Machaut is now the pattern of excellence. It clearly
served as a model to the composers whose *ballades*, *rondeaux*, and
virelais appear in the Reina manuscript. The accompanying instrumental parts often behave in what may be described as a 'counter'
manner, showing a preference for wide and angular leaps. The voice
parts on the other hand have become once more tranquil and rhythmically simple. The plain concise melodic line of many of these
rondeaux foreshadows the Burgundian *chanson*; indeed a number of
them have been identified by concordances as the work of Dufay and
Binchois. Other French composers represented are Grenon, Legrant,
and Fontaine.

The rhythmic complexity of the *ballade* was undoubtedly brought
to an end by the general disillusionment in France, whose over-
whelming defeat at Agincourt (1415) had brought the nobles to their
senses. Meanwhile, however, the ideals of chivalry were preserved
on a distant island which had remained unaffected by the catastrophe
in the home country; in Cyprus the last kings of Jerusalem, of the
house of Lusignan, were trying to imitate and even to outdo the
French court in extravagant display. Literature and music had for a
long time been cultivated here; and the works of Machaut and
Landini had been received with the highest honours. A representative
selection of the music used at the court of Cyprus is to be found in
the magnificent manuscript compiled in Cyprus between 1413 and
1434, and probably sent to Turin on the occasion of the marriage of
Princess Anne de Lusignan to Louis of Savoy.[1] It contains Mass
movements, cyclic Masses,[2] and motets, the words of the latter sometimes referring to local affairs. These are followed by a collection
of 167 *ballades*, *virelais*, and *rondeaux*, mostly in three parts. Not a
single composer's name is given, and not one work has so far been
found in any other manuscript. This fact alone serves to demonstrate
the isolated musical position of Cyprus. The manuscript attracted
no attention when it reached Italy, since it represented merely an
aftermath of the rhythmically exaggerated *ballade* style which was
already out of date on the Continent. Reference may be made to the

---

[1] See p. 141, n. 3.
[2] Each monophonic Mass cycle unified by identical or similar motifs, according to
Schrade: see *Journal of the American Musicological Society*, viii (1955), p. 67.—*Ed.*

ballades 'Pour haut'[1] and 'Tout homme veut',[2] which show the same leaning towards rhythmic obscurity as their forerunners in the Chantilly and Modena manuscripts. The greatest rhythmic difficulties in the Turin manuscript are found in the *ballades* which include canon, e.g. 'Sur toute fleur'.[3] In the directions given for its performance the old 'proportions' have to be translated into various appropriate rhythmic values. This procedure gives further proof of the way in which rhythmic considerations dominated the music of the late Gothic period.

ISORHYTHMIC MOTETS

Rhythmic principles also play an important though different part in the *ars nova* motet. In the isorhythmic motet (see vol. II, p. 390) the rhythmical pattern of the first section or *talea* serves to determine the formal structure of the whole. It is only however in the transitional period that this technique is fully developed; in the classical motets of Vitry and still more in those of Machaut (see pp. 8–10 and 19–21), the strict isorhythm is mainly confined to the hocket sections.[4] The rhythmic line of the hocket figures, interspersed with rests, positively invited the composer to write isorhythmic variations. Thus the following passage in the *triplum* part of one of Machaut's motets ('Plange / Tu qui'):[5]

Ex.64

appears seven times, always with melodic variations, e.g.:

Ex.65

It is only in the second half of the fourteenth century that we find isorhythm becoming an established principle of form. The melodic development of the individual *taleae* is now entirely subordinate to a

---

[1] Wolf, *Handbuch der Notationskunde* (Leipzig, 1913–19), i, p. 368.
[2] Apel, *The Notation of Polyphonic Music* (Cambridge, Mass., 1942), p. 419.
[3] Wolf, *Handbuch*, i, p. 373.
[4] Cf. the analysis of some of Machaut's motets in *Zeitschrift für Musikwissenschaft*, vii (1924–5), p. 211.
[5] *Werke*, ed. F. Ludwig, ii, p. 79; Schrade, *Polyphonic Music of the Fourteenth Century*, iii (Monaco, 1956), p. 22.

rigid framework dictated by rhythm. The motet 'Apta caro / Flos'[1]
shows the transition to this stage of isorhythmic development. The
hocket, hitherto an important feature of isorhythm, now begins
gradually to fall into disuse. In the Chantilly manuscript we find it has
entirely disappeared from some motets ('Ida capillorum / Portio',
'Degentis / Cum vix') while in others ('Alpha / Coetus', 'Pictagore /
O terra') it has been banished from the vocal parts and serves only
to enliven the instrumental interludes and endings. The rhythmic
caprices of the contemporary *ballade* very seldom appear in these
motets, and then only in a restrained form. Examples are 'Multi-
pliciter / Favore' from the Chantilly manuscript and 'Sub Arturo /
Fons / In omnem' by Johannes Alanus.[2]

This new and persistent use of isorhythm was bound to prejudice
and even to stunt the melodic development of the motet. The method
of setting the texts, which now become increasingly elaborate, approaches more and more closely to the syllabic, declamatory style
already found in many of the Ivrea Masses. The words are fitted into
the ready-made rhythm of the music, thereby losing entirely their
own rhythmic independence. Musical and verbal accentuation are
often sharply opposed, e.g.:

Ex 66[3]

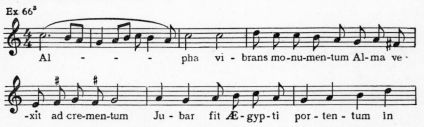

Al - - - pha vi - brans mo-nu-men-tum Al-ma ve ·

-xit ad cre-men-tum Ju - bar fit Æ - gyp-ti por - ten - tum in

([Christ] the Alpha, gleaming sign, did she carry as her nursling while he grew;
[his] radiant glory becomes Egypt's wonder.)

We find in the late Gothic motet the same tendency to concentrate
exclusively on rhythm, and the same taste for what is exaggerated and
unnatural, as in the *ballade*. But the musical results in the two cases
are entirely different: in the *ballade* an obscurity amounting at times
to a loss of balance between metre and rhythm; in the motet, a concentration on rhythmic construction leading to complete atrophy.

While the French subjective type of *ballade*, as has already been
mentioned, found enthusiastic imitators in Italy towards the end of

[1] *Archiv für Musikwissenschaft*, viii (1926), p. 254.
[2] See p. 99.
[3] Chantilly, Musée Condé, 1047, fo. 64ᵛ.

the century, the isorhythmic motet met with little favour there. In the manuscripts of this period (Modena and the Padua fragments[1]) this form is by no means prominent. The Mass, on the other hand, continued to be cultivated by such Italian composers as Matteo da Perugia, Engardus, Zacharias, and Grazioso da Padova,[2] whose works still show traces of the trecento style. It has already been pointed out that this type of Mass represents a reaction against both the spirit and technique of the *ars nova* motet. The exaggerated language, the symbolism, and the harnessing of artistic invention to a given *canto fermo* or to a ready-made pattern, all characteristic of the motet, were unintelligible to the southern temperament. In Italy the composer's own imaginative faculty, and the free exposition of musical subject-matter, remained the chief factors in determining style.

THE NETHERLANDS AND BURGUNDY

At the beginning of the fifteenth century, however, we find the same aesthetic principles gaining ground in northern Europe too. This was due to the employment of a large number of Netherland composers in the papal chapel. One of the most important was Johannes Ciconia,[3] who, like Johannes Brasart, Egidius Velut, and the priest Johannes de Sarto, came from Liège. He was in Italy during the 1360s but returned home in 1372; however, he was appointed a canon at Padua *c.* 1402, and died there in 1411. In addition to his compositions,[4] he wrote an extended treatise, *Nova Musica*, on the general theory of music.[5] Other temporary members of the papal chapel were Nicholas Grenon, Guillaume Legrant, Bartholomaeus Pugnare (Poignare), Pyllois, Pierre Fontaine, Arnold de Lantins, and Guillaume Dufay. Johannes de Lymburgia also seems to have spent some time in Italy. Hugo de Lantins was at various times in Rome and Venice. These composers came from the famous song-schools of Rheims, Tournai, and Cambrai. Their presence in Italy during the first thirty years of the century led to an interchange of musical views with their Italian

[1] Padua, Bibl. Univ., 658, 684, 1115, 1475; Oxford, Bodleian, Canonici Scr. eccl. 229. Cf. *Archiv für Musikwissenschaft*, vii (1925), p. 229; viii (1926), p. 233.

[2] Wolf, *Geschichte der Mensural-Notation*, ii, no. 62; Mass movements by Matteo and Grazioso in Guillaume de Van, *Les Monuments de l'Ars nova* (Paris, 1938).

[3] See pp. 71–74. On his career see Suzanne Clercx in *Revue belge de musicologie*, ix (1955), pp. 48–49.

[4] Thematic index by Wolf, issued as a supplement to *Tijdschrift der Vereeniging voor Noord-Nederlands Muziekgeschiedenis*, vii (1902); to be supplemented by F. Ghisi, in *La Rinascita*, v (1942), pp. 72–103, and *Journal of Renaissance and Baroque Music*, i (1946), pp. 173–91.

[5] Contents listed in Adrien de la Fage, *Essais de dipthérographie musicale* (Paris, 1864). .

contemporaries. Of the latter, Bartholomaeus de Bononia and Zacharias (see p. 143) adopted the new style, as did a number of younger composers: Frater Antonius de Civitate, Antonius Romanus, Nicolaus de Capua, Cristoforus de Monte (Feltre), Matheus de Brixia (Brescia), Bartholomaeus de Bruollis, Do. Vala, and others, such as Beltrame Feragut (Matteo's successor at Milan Cathedral).[1] Of the Netherlanders who presumably remained in their own country the following deserve mention: Richard de Loqueville, who worked in Cambrai from 1412 until his death in 1418, Johannes Franchois de Gembloux, Johannes Rezon, Hubertus de Salinis, Reginald Liebert, Jacobus Vide, and above all Gilles Binchois. The last named was in Paris in 1424 in the service of the Duke of Suffolk, and from 1430 until his death in 1460 was employed at the court of Burgundy.

At the beginning of the century the last representatives of the Avignon school still formed an independent circle, content to maintain the tradition of the polyphonic Mass. The chief composers were Guymont, de Fronciaco, Fleurie, Suzoy (or Suzay), Tailhandier, Perneth (Prunet, Perrinet), and Jacobus Murrin. A manuscript preserved in the cathedral of Apt[2] (Vaucluse) contains late works of this school, and provides a valuable supplement to the Ivrea manuscript. In addition to Masses it contains a few hymns, interesting from the point of view of style. This manuscript is closely related to the Strasbourg manuscript which was destroyed by fire in the war of 1870.[3] The Paris composers Carmen, Cesaris, Tapissier, Baude Cordier,[4] Billart, Briquet (Jean de Villeroy), Bosquet, Guill. Benoit, and Grossim, are the last of the Central French school, which was finally absorbed into the Flemish-Burgundian. The occupation of much of France by the English from 1415 onwards put a check on French enthusiasm for music and the arts. The focal points of musical activity shifted to the ecclesiastical centres already mentioned, and to the rapidly rising duchy of Burgundy, which bid fair to become the sole inheritor of artistic traditions.

The Dukes of Burgundy were already shaping their power politics on modern lines. The ambitious plans of men like Philip the Good envisaged an empire stretching from the North Sea to the Mediterranean. In the artistic sphere the Dukes of Burgundy were already

---

[1] Born at Avignon. Claudio Sartori has identified him with Bertrand di Avignone, cf. *Acta Musicologica*, xxviii (1956), pp. 23–27.—*Ed.*　　　　　　[2] See p. 136. n. 2.

[3] See Charles van den Borren, *Le Manuscript musical M. 222 C. 22 de la Bibliothèque de Strasbourg* (Antwerp, 1924).

[4] Works by these four composers in Reaney, *Early Fifteenth Century Music*, i (*Corpus mensurabilis musicae*, xi).

intent on excelling the French court, by securing the services of the greatest artists. At the same time they encouraged every effort to re-mould tradition in the light of a natural and rational conception of art. In this Burgundian 'waning of the Middle Ages' the new spirit of the coming Renaissance was everywhere apparent. In architecture and the plastic arts the old paths were gradually being abandoned; this is especially noticeable in the style of such artists as Claus Sluter. In the work of Van Eyck, on the other hand, we find a compromise between the sternly spiritual conceptions of medieval art and the natural re-production of the object represented.

In music also we find composers using new technical devices, while the old forms, though to some extent retained, undergo a complete metamorphosis. Thus, while an isorhythmic motet of Dufay or Dun-stable scarcely differs materially in form from one of Machaut's dating from seventy or eighty years earlier, there is nevertheless no comparison between the two as regards melody, harmony, and rhythm. In the final phase of this metamorphosis Continental music was con-siderably influenced by English composers, the external cause being the English occupation of France. As early as 1416 the performances of English choirs had aroused admiration on the Continent. After the death of Henry V in 1422 many English musicians crossed the Channel. The most important of them, John Dunstable, was in the service of the Duke of Bedford, Regent of France. About 1440 Martin le Franc bears witness to strong influence exerted by Dunstable on Dufay and Binchois (see pp. 165 and 184). Later the theorist Tinctoris hails the English composers, headed by Dunstable, as creators of the new art ('novae artis fons et origo').[1] Besides Dunstable we also find on the Continent the names of Leonel Power, Forest, Benet, Beding-ham, Markham, Standley, Stove, Tyling, and others.[2]

SOURCES OF MID-FIFTEENTH-CENTURY MUSIC

An impressive corpus of the work of all these composers, repre-senting different styles, is to be found in five substantial manu-scripts of north Italian origin, dating from about 1440 or 1450: (1) Oxford, Bodleian, Canonici misc. 213;[3] (2) Bologna, Bibl. Univ.,

---

[1] Coussemaker, *Scriptorum*, iv, p. 154; see further, p. 165.
[2] See Chap. VI.
[3] Contents given by G. Reaney in *Musica Disciplina*, ix (1955), p. 74. Selected *chansons* printed in J. F. R. and C. Stainer, *Dufay and his Contemporaries* (London, 1898); Mass movements and motets in Van den Borren, *Polyphonia Sacra* (London, 1932).

2216;[1] (3) Bologna, Liceo Musicale, 37 (now known as Bologna, Bibl. G. B. Martini Q 15);[2] (4) Trent, Castel del Buon Consiglio, 87 and 92;[3] (5) Aosta, Seminario.[4] The Oxford manuscript is chiefly important for the development of the Burgundian *chanson*, on which the other manuscripts throw little light. It also provides a fair number of French, Burgundian, and Italian Masses and motets dating from before 1436. The Bologna University manuscript is a mixed collection, evidently catering only for the local needs of North Italy: it includes Masses of the transition period, non-isorhythmic motets, three of which refer to Venice, and at the end a few Italian and French *chansons*. The composers are for the most part Italians, or Netherlanders resident in Italy.

The manuscript Bologna, Bibl. G. B. Martini Q 15, is the most comprehensive and important of the period. It is arranged in a systematic order: at the beginning is an extensive collection of Mass movements and a few complete Masses, including Dufay's 'Missa S. Jacobi' with the appropriate sections of the Proper. From fo. 190[v] onwards there is an unbroken series of motets. In contrast to the Bologna University manuscript the isorhythmic motet is assigned an important place. The texts refer to various saints, to dignitaries of Church and State, and to political and ecclesiastical events, concerning particularly such North Italian cities as Venice, Padua, Florence, and Vicenza. At the end of the manuscript we find a supplementary section in which the new style of motet to liturgical words (Propers, antiphons, hymns, and Magnificats) is more strongly represented. The French *chanson* is almost entirely absent: it is represented only by a few supplementary pieces. The importance of the Netherland school is evident from the preponderance of works by these composers to be found in this manuscript. A representative number of works by composers active in Italy —particularly Zacharias and Ciconia—are also included, though they make no contribution to the new developments. The older French school, on the other hand, provides only a few works. In both the Bologna manuscripts England is very poorly represented, though her influence had for some time been making itself felt.

In the Trent codices 87 and 92 we find an entirely different state of affairs. The English composers, headed by Dunstable and Leonel Power, are treated at least as generously as the Burgundians. The

---

[1] Contents given by Besseler in *Musica Disciplina*, vi (1952), p. 39.
[2] Contents given by G. de Van in *Musica Disciplina*, ii (1948), p. 231.
[3] Thematic index of Trent 87–92 in *Denkmäler der Tonkunst in Österreich*, vii.
[4] Contents in G. de Van, 'A Recently Discovered Source of Early Fifteenth Century Polyphonic Music', *Musica Disciplina*, ii (1948), p. 22.

Italians, on the other hand, are with a few exceptions entirely absent.[1] As in the Bologna, G. B. Martini, manuscript, Mass movements and a few complete Masses occupy the position of importance which they generally have in manuscripts of the late medieval period; but the large-scale motet of the older type has almost completely disappeared, its place being taken by the simple three-part motet with liturgical words. The *chanson* is more strongly represented than in the G. B. Martini manuscript, but in all the Trent codices it serves for the most part only as a makeweight. Trent 90,[2] which is the work of the German copyist Georg Wiser and was not begun until 1450, resembles 87 and 92 in its choice of composers and of types of work. The later manuscripts—88, 89, and 91—also contain chiefly settings of the Mass, the greater number of which are complete. The *chanson* Mass, based on a secular melody, is prominently represented. We are dealing now with a new generation: the English composers have fallen into the background, leaving the supremacy of the Netherlanders almost unchallenged. Works by Dufay and other older composers occasionally appear, particularly in 88; but in 91 we already meet the new school headed by Ockeghem.

The Aosta manuscript contains 180 pieces, some of which appear twice. It is devoted entirely to sacred music: in addition to Mass movements, which form the bulk of the contents, there are antiphons, motets, Magnificats, &c. Both English and continental composers are represented. Nearly two-thirds of the pieces are found also in other manuscripts of the period; the remaining seventy are *unica*.

Compared with these sources the other manuscripts of the period about 1450 contain a much more limited repertory. Modena, Bibl. Estense, A X. 1, 11 (lat. 471), apart from some hymns and Magnificats, contains only motets, mainly by Dufay and Dunstable. As many of these motets are found nowhere else, this manuscript is of great importance, especially in assessing the importance of Dunstable. Cambrai, 6 and 11 are chiefly concerned with the church compositions of Dufay and Binchois. Florence, Bibl. Naz., Magl. XIX. 112[bis] and Venice, Bibl. Marc., it. IX, 145 confine themselves almost exclusively to the chief composers of the period, the works being mainly of the new type of liturgical motet. Escorial, V. III 24, like the

---

[1] This fact would help to support the view of R. Wolkan, 'Die Heimat der Trienter Musikhandschriften', in *Studien zur Musikwissenschaft*, viii (1921), that the writing of the manuscripts was begun in Lower Austria and finished in Trent. It seems likely that the Munich manuscripts Mus. 3232a and 3154 also originated in Southern Germany.

[2] The contents of Trent, Castel del Buon Consiglio, 93 (thematic index in *Denkmäler der Tonkunst in Österreich*, xxxi) are in the main only a copy of 90.

Oxford Canonici manuscript and Paris, Bibl. Nat., n.a. fr. 4379, is important for the history of the Burgundian *chanson*.[1] Thus, in contrast to the manuscripts just mentioned, those of the Bologna G. B. Martini and Trent represent a type of music already in keeping with the spirit of the new humanism. Here the musical material has been chosen on a comprehensive basis, not dictated by local or personal considerations.

The artistic achievement of the schools already mentioned can naturally best be measured by the works of their great masters. Composers such as Dunstable and Dufay require separate discussion (see Chaps. VI and VII). We shall here examine only the circumstances in which their genius flourished. In the field of secular song the Burgundian *chanson* marks an important development. It has already been noted that the early fifteenth-century *rondeau* or *rondelet*, with its simple and concise style, differs essentially from the complicated *ballade*. In this respect, the Italian *ballata*[2] may have had a stimulating influence, especially on the Netherlanders working in southern Europe. For though in the trecento the *ballata* did not command the same respect as the more pretentious madrigal and *caccia*, it contrived to retain its vitality, e.g. the following example by Zacharias:[3]

Ex 67

---

[1] For the contents and history of these manuscripts see *Archiv für Musikwissenschaft*, vii (1925), pp. 233–44. Escorial, V. iii, 24 has been published in facsimile by Wolfgang Rehm, *Codex Escorial: Chansonnier* (*Documenta Musicologica*, series ii, ii).

[2] See, for example, the *ballate* 'Io son un pellegrin' (A. Einstein, *A Short History of Music*, 5th ed., 1948, p. 211) and 'Con lagrime' (*The Musical Quarterly*, xv (1929), p. 498.)

[3] Modena, Bibl. Estense, M. 5. 24, fo. 23.

(Though I find myself far off in another country, neither time nor place ever part me from you.)

The same simplicity of form and expression is to be found in the early Burgundian *chanson*, though the music is of a different temper. Especially noteworthy is the agreement of verbal and musical rhythm, which, though it seems to us a matter of course, was purposely avoided in the preceding period. The *chansons* of Binchois[1] with instrumental accompaniment may thus be regarded as the oldest genuine examples of the union of poetry and music in accompanied song.

A device appeared quite early in the *chanson*, which was later to assume special importance in the *a cappella* style: that of imitation. Technically it was not new; but it now attained a new aesthetic value. It is commonly found in the form of successive repetitions, in two or in all three parts, of the theme used for the opening words, as in the following example by Do. Vala:[2]

Ex. 68

This imitation makes the beginning of each phrase impressive, both integrating it and giving it prominence, and the parts become of equal importance and mutually dependent. The *ballade*, a solo with accompaniment, was gradually transformed into the *chanson* with all the parts sung, which dominated the second half of the century. Imitation in all the parts, the hallmark of the Renaissance *a cappella* style, was thus fully developed in the *chanson* by about 1450. 'O rosa

[1] *Die Chansons von Gilles de Binchois*, ed. W. Rehm (*Musikalische Denkmäler*, ii) (Mainz, 1957).   [2] Bologna, Bibl. Univ., 2216, fo. 56.

bella' by Johannes Ciconia[1] is one of the earliest examples of this style. The *chanson*, however, in addition to the use of imitation still constantly employed the old homophonic conductus style. Even older devices were occasionally used, especially by Dufay.[2]

The development of the motet and the Mass proceeded in a far more complicated manner. In the early part of the century these two forms approximated more closely in matters of technique. A new type of motet appeared which, though it may have been originated by the Netherlanders of the Liège school and in particular by Ciconia, was used mainly in Italy. This new form abandoned both isorhythm and the *canto fermo*, thereby drawing nearer in formal technique to the polyphonic *Credo* and *Gloria*. On the other hand it used at first a double set of words like the old motets, as well as a canonic introduction (*introitus*), which was sometimes of considerable length. Instead of isorhythm we find—long before its occurrence in the *chanson*—imitation of short phrases complete in themselves, usually in the two upper parts. This innovation is especially common in the great Italian festival motets, both sacred and secular, such as Ciconia's 'O felix templum'[3] and Cristoforus de Monte's 'Plaude decus',[4] composed in honour of the Doge Francesco Foscari in 1423. The important part played by instruments[5]—particularly trumpets—in the performance of these motets is evident from the fanfare-like character of the phrases, which makes them eminently suitable for imitative repetition. See, for instance, the opening of Ciconia's motet in honour of the Paduan lawyer Zabarella, who became bishop of Florence in 1410:

Ex. 69[6]

---

[1] *Denkmäler der Tonkunst in Österreich*, vii, p. 227. Recorded in *The History of Music in Sound* (H.M.V.), iii, together with the setting of the same text attributed to Dunstable (see p. 128).

[2] For an example of canon see Stainer, op. cit., p. 115; for different words in the various parts, ibid., p. 132; for a Latin *canto fermo* in the style of the old French motet, ibid., p. 143.   [3] See pp. 71–72.

[4] *Denkmäler der Tonkunst in Österreich*, xl, p. 6.

[5] See further, pp. 159 and 226.

[6] Bologna, G. B. Martini Q 15, fo. 270ᵛ. Fanfare-like motives are also to be found in other motets by Ciconia, e.g. 'O virum/O lux' (on St. Nicholas), 'O beatum incendium', 'O Padua', 'Venetiae/Michael qui Stenadouros' (Bologna, G. B. Martini, Q 15, fos. 255ᵛ–9).

(*Triplum*: The merits of his virtues raise the noble Doctor to the skies. Therefore let heed be given to the use of the voice . . .

Motetus: Let us sing with sweetest melody, let sweet-toned voices rise to heaven with one accord. Let us make a song [as we play] the lyre.)

In style and construction these works may almost be regarded as forerunners of the Venetian orchestral *canzone* of the early baroque period. Some of the anonymous motets of this kind are evidently related to the Liège school, e.g. 'Lamberte', 'Christi nutu', and 'Gaudeat ecclesia'.[1] In the last of these the vocal line is broken up into short notes of the same pitch, indicating its probable perform-ance by trumpets. The imitative motets by other composers are more vocal in character, e.g. Zacharias's 'Laetetur / Pastor', Brasart's 'Sum-mus secretarius', Bartholomaeus de Brollo's (Bruollis) 'Vivere',[2] and Brasart's 'Fortis cum'.[3] This thematic imitation is also noticeable in the Glorias and Credos of the Ciconia school. In these we find scarcely any difference remaining between the styles of the Mass and the motet. Examples of these festival settings of Mass movements are to be found in Glorias and Credos by Ciconia, Bodoil, Bartholomaeus de

[1] *Denkmäler der Tonkunst in Österreich*, xl, pp. 66, 69, 72.
[2] Van den Borren, op. cit., nos. 48, 36, 51.
[3] *Denkmäler der Tonkunst in Österreich*, vii, p. 97.

Bruollis, Georgius a Brugis,[1] Hugo de Lantins, and Franchois.[2] In the last of these the imitation in the *Credo* at times assumes the character of a fugal exposition.

Even in the isorhythmic motets by the Netherland composers just mentioned we find imitation used, e.g. by Ciconia in the motets paying homage to two bishops of Padua (1405 and 1409)[3] and another in honour of Zabarella, 'Ut te / Ingens',[4] by Hugo de Lantins,[5] and by Franchois. An 'Ave virgo' by Franchois,[6] with its impressive trumpet introduction, is of unusual historical interest. The following quotation will also serve to show the extent to which the late Gothic composers intentionally subordinated the natural verbal rhythm to the rhythmic compulsion of the music:

Ex. 70

(O thou blessed wedded Virgin, mother of thy Maker, thy seat on high . . .)

Although this early occurrence of imitation is of great historical interest, its practice remained local and was not immediately continued. In the first thirty years of the fifteenth century the traditional isorhythmic motet maintained its dominant position. Of the Italians, however, only Antonius de Civitate tried his hand at this form, e.g. in his wedding motet 'Strenua / Gaudeat' (1423).[7] The later representatives of the Paris school, on the other hand, used it in the traditional

---

[1] *Denkmäler der Tonkunst in Österreich*, xxxi, pp. 1, 3, 25, 28, 30.
[2] Van den Borren, op. cit., nos. 13–16.
[3] 'Albane missae / Albane doctor', 'Petrum Marcello / O Petre' (Bologna, G. B. Martini, Q 15, fo. 271ᵛ, 248ᵛ).
[4] Van den Borren, op. cit., no. 27.
[5] Ibid., no. 32.
[6] *Denkmäler der Tonkunst in Österreich*, xl, p. 19. See also below, pp. 235 and 425.
[7] Van den Borren, op. cit., no. 29.

way, e.g. Carmen in his 'Pontifici decori',[1] with a canon in the two
upper parts; Tapissier in his 'Eya dulcis / Vale';[2] Carmen again in
his 'Venite / Salve', Cesaris in his 'A virtutis / Ergo', and Billart in his
'Salve virgo / Vita'[3]—the last presumably identical with the Albertus
Billardi who is found at Notre Dame as early as 1392.[4] Nicholas
Grenon was also active in Paris and in Laon before coming to Cambrai in 1408.[5] The syllabic declamation of his 'Ave virtus / Prophet-
arum'[6] points to an early date. On the other hand his great Trinity
motet 'Ad honorem / Coelorum'[7] cannot very well belong to an earlier
period than the main transition.

The Masses of the Paris school had sunk into an almost abstract
spirituality and rhythmic asperity. The strict conductus is only seldom
met with, e.g. in a *Credo* by Jacobus Murrin.[8] The style of word-
setting approaches more and more to a strongly rhythmic *parlando*,
which is generally limited to the treble part. This is true also of the
Credos by Tapissier and Tailhandier[9] and also of Grossim.[10] A *Gloria*
by Bosquet[11] seems also to belong to the central French school:

Ex. 71

(And on earth peace to men of good will. We praise Thee, we bless Thee, we
worship Thee, we glorify Thee, we give thanks . . .)

This use of clearly pointed rhythms, emphasized by a preference for
duple time, also characterizes the Masses of the early Netherland

[1] Stainer, op. cit., p. 68.   [2] Ibid., p. 187.
[3] Van den Borren, op. cit., nos. 24–26.
[4] A. Pirro, *Histoire de la musique de la fin du XIVe siècle à la fin du XVIe* (Paris,
1940), p. 90.   [5] Ibid., p. 55.
[6] Van den Borren, op. cit., no. 30.   [7] Ibid., no. 31.
[8] Gastoué, *Le Manuscrit de musique polyphonique du trésor d'Apt*, no. 34.
[9] Ibid., nos. 35 and 37.
[10] *Denkmäler der Tonkunst in Österreich*, xxxi, p. 9.
[11] Bologna, G. B. Martini, Q. 15, fo. 75ᵛ.

composers. In the large collection of polyphonic Glorias and Credos contained in the Bologna, G. B. Martini, manuscript this style of writing is still completely predominant. It also gained ground in Italy, as we can see in certain works by Zacharias,[1] Feragut, and Antonius Romanus.[2] In the works of the Italian composers, however, it is significant that the agreement of verbal and musical accent is as far as possible preserved. The syllabic *parlando* style also prevailed in England, as the Old Hall manuscript shows. There is therefore some doubt in assigning works of this kind to a particular school. Almost all the pre-1430 Netherlanders cultivated the style: among them Hugo de Lantins,[3] Velut, Legrant, Hubert de Salinis, Rezon, and Loqueville, Dufay's master. The young Dufay himself also made abundant use of it, e.g. at the beginning of the following *Credo*:[4]

(... the Father Almighty, Maker of heaven and earth; and of all things visible and invisible, and in one Lord. ...)

Several other works by Dufay provide examples of this type of music: a *Gloria*[5] with a hocket-like instrumental interlude in galliard rhythm, two Credos[6] and another *Gloria*.[7] In the last of these the concentration of the melodic line produces an intensity of expression which provides a striking parallel with the vocal line of many of the Ivrea Masses.

[1] *Denkmäler der Tonkunst in Österreich*, xxxi, p. 16.
[2] Bologna, G. B. Martini, Q 15, nos. 17, 18, 27, 29, &c.
[3] *Denkmäler der Tonkunst in Österreich*, xxxi, p. 15.
[4] *Opera Omnia*, ed. G. de Van, fasc. 3, p. 9.
[5] Ibid., p. 4.
[6] *Denkmäler der Tonkunst in Österreich*, xxxi, pp. 73 and 76; the second also in *Opera Omnia*, ed. G. de Van, fasc. 4, p. 16.
[7] *Denkmäler der Tonkunst in Österreich*, xxxi, p. 75.

As far back as the early *ars nova* period instruments had undoubtedly played a large part in the interpretation of these compositions. It seems justifiable to assume that musical conceptions were now governed less by vocal than by instrumental considerations. In solo song the wordless parts were unquestionably performed by instruments; and even in the motets and Masses just referred to the impression of unvocal treatment of the words must have been removed, or at least mitigated, by the fact that the vocal parts were covered by a similar-sounding instrumental accompaniment.[1]

Polyphonic settings of the *Kyrie*, *Sanctus*, and *Agnus Dei*—sections of the Mass which have but few words—are rare at this period. These sections, as we already find in the Ivrea and Apt manuscripts, are often troped, i.e. provided with supplementary words.[2] This device made it possible to set them in the same way as the *Gloria* and *Credo*. But in the Apt manuscript[3] and in the works of the early Netherlanders the old *canto fermo* technique is used, as in the motet, for these parts of the Mass as well as for office hymns. The plainsong melody appears as usual in the tenor, either in long notes or in a simple rhythm, generally trochaic.[4] This procedure leaves the melody almost unchanged, and contrasts strongly with the treatment of plainsong in the fourteenth-century French motet. Examples are provided by the early liturgical motets of Arnold de Lantins, Johannes de Lymburgia, Franchois, Dufay, and Binchois. Dufay took as the *canto fermo* of a three-part *Sanctus*[5] a tenor by Vineux also used in the four-part *Sanctus* by his teacher Loqueville (d. 1418), which follows immediately in the manuscript. He also uses a tenor *canto fermo* in some sections of his 'Missa S. Jacobi'.[6] This Mass, like Reginald Liebert's[7] (see p. 225), contains all the sections of the *Proprium Missae*. The Introit 'Mihi autem', in which the *canto fermo* is in long notes in the tenor, is followed by a *repetitio* (perhaps composed later) which has the *canto fermo* in the top part, using the new technique of melodic coloration (cf. pp. 161–2). In the Masses already referred to there is as yet no sign of the later type of cyclic form. In view of later developments it is

---

[1] For the significant part played by instruments in late medieval music cf. the documentary evidence in Pirro, op. cit., pp. 1–53; also below, p. 226.

[2] There are numerous English troped Kyries of the period 1325–1425.

[3] Gastoué, op. cit., nos. 1 and 11.

[4] The *canto fermo* is often unbroken here, as it is in the sixteenth century in the tenors of secular polyphonic songs.

[5] Bologna, G. B. Martini, Q 15, fo. 19ᵛ.

[6] *Opera Omnia*, ed. G. de Van, fasc. 4.

[7] *Denkmäler der Tonkunst in Österreich*, xxvii (1), p. 1; cf. *Studien zur Musikwissenschaft*, vii (1920), p. 1.

important to emphasize the fact that in the new liturgical motets, and in the Masses of the early Netherlanders already mentioned, the plainsong *canto fermo* is in the tenor.

ENGLISH INFLUENCES

Between 1420 and 1430 we can trace a significant change in the music of the Burgundian-Netherlands school. At the same time English music, which had for long remained in the background, began again to influence continental practice. The works of Dunstable and his contemporaries are discussed in the following chapter. Here we need only mention the essential characteristics of the English influence, in so far as they concern the change of style on the Continent. About 1400 English music was strongly affected, in form and technique, by the achievements of the late French *ars nova*. This is clear from many of the works in the Old Hall manuscript (see pp. 101 and 167). Isorhythm occurs not only in the motet, as in France, but also in Mass movements. Hockets and complicated rhythms, in the style of the late French *ballade* and motet, were also popular. In addition, the syllabic *parlando* style is an essential feature of English motets, and also of many Mass movements, where there is no question of a French model. The development of church music under Henry V must have been largely a matter of adopting the formal principles of the late *ars nova*. These innovations may well have acted as a stimulus, but did not succeed in extinguishing the native English tradition, which was still a living force.

The specifically English features consist in certain peculiarities belonging to an old musical tradition which remained quite unaffected by contemporary technique. In the Old Hall manuscript these features are most apparent in the simple conductus-like pieces, which still show a clear connexion with fourteenth-century practice.[1] In contrast to France plainsong, as a religious symbol, always remained in England the keystone of musical architecture. It did not, as in the French motet, become a mere foundation for the polyphonic structure. The aim was rather to preserve its sensuous qualities, and, indeed, by artistic transformation to heighten them and bring them into conformity with the spirit of the age. At first the plainsong melody was merely presented in a regular rhythmical pattern. Its earliest appearances are in the tenor, but in the Old Hall manuscript it is also found in the middle part, and finally in the upper part, of polyphonic move-

---

[1] Cf. Besseler in *Archiv für Musikwissenschaft*, vii (1925), pp. 219 ff.

ments (see p. 178). When used as the upper part it assumes an increasingly rich melodic form. The single notes of the original melody are still present as the framework, but the result of the so-called 'colouring' of the plainsong is an entirely new melodic line, in which the basic melody is often no longer recognizable.[1] The following extract from a *Sanctus* by Leonel Power[2] will serve to illustrate the final stage of this process of development, which may be followed in detail in the Old Hall manuscript:

Ex. 73

(Hosanna in the highest.)

The original plainsong melody[3] is as follows:

Ex. 74

[1] Cf. A. Orel, 'Einige Grundformen der Motettkomposition im 15. Jahrhundert', in *Studien zur Musikwissenschaft*, vii (1920), pp. 48–101, and R. Ficker, 'Die Kolorierungstechnik der Trienter Messen', ibid., pp. 5–47.

[2] *The Old Hall Manuscript*, ed. A. Ramsbotham, H. B. Collins, and Dom Anselm Hughes (London, 1933–8), iii, p. 66. The middle part (contratenor) is missing in the manuscript in bars 2–5: it is here supplied from Trent Codices, No. 79.

[3] Vatican VIII 'in festis duplicibus' (*Missa de angelis*). The corresponding notes in the upper part of Power's setting are marked with asterisks.

The use of 'colouring' produces here an entirely new form of melody, displaying in its unbroken unity all the essential features of the elaborate melodic style of the English late Gothic period, which found its most pronounced expression in the works of Dunstable. At the same time the way is prepared for a fundamental and universal change: the rhythmical energy which dominates continental Gothic music is here met by a great increase of melodic strength. Rhythmical intensity, never so important in English music as in continental, is now replaced by melodic. This substitution provides the foundation for that decisive change of style discernible in Netherland-Burgundian music about 1430. Practical and theoretical sources alike show that this historically important principle of melodic 'coloration' is of English origin,[1] and that as a form of improvisation it may have existed in England even in the fourteenth century.[2]

This new partiality for melodic shape is closely connected with a particular kind of chordal harmony, also traditionally English.[3] This is the preference for a succession of imperfect consonances of the third and sixth (see pp. 89 and 95), which is so strikingly displayed both in English treatises on descant[4] and in the actual music which has been preserved; it is discussed at length in the next chapter. In the French music of the preceding period the use of a series of imperfect consonances, and especially of sixths, had been so far as possible avoided. This is clearly shown in the hymns in the Apt manuscript,[5] in which—as in fauxbourdon—the plainsong is in the top part. In Apt the guiding principle is still that of 'interchange' (the so-called 'contrary motion' of the theorists),[6] which has no immediate concern for harmonic progression. French musical sources—unlike English— thus provide no clue to the origins of fauxbourdon.[7]

[1] Cf. Ficker, 'Die frühen Messenkompositionen der Trienter Codices', in *Studien zur Musikwissenschaft*, xi (1924), pp. 3 ff.

[2] This seems to be implied by a passage in the treatise *De quatuor principalibus*, frequently attributed to Tunstede, in Coussemaker, *Scriptorum*, iv, pp. 294 ff.

[3] It is mentioned as early as the thirteenth century by Anonymus IV (Coussemaker, *Scriptorum*, i, p. 358) (cf. vol. II, p. 351), and also by Anonymus V (ibid., p. 366).

[4] See M. Bukofzer, *Geschichte des englischen Diskants und des Fauxbourdons nach den theoretischen Quellen* (Strasbourg, 1936), and T. Georgiades, *Englische Diskanttraktate aus der ersten Hälfte des XV. Jahrhunderts* (Munich, 1937).

[5] Gastoué, op. cit., nos. xvii–xxvi.

[6] Cf. *Zeitschrift für Musikwissenschaft*, vii (1924–5), pp. 200 ff.; *Studien zur Musikwissenschaft*, xi (1924), p. 18.

[7] See *infra*, p. 176. For discussion of the disputed origins of fauxbourdon see, in addition to Bukofzer, op. cit., H. Besseler, *Bourdon and Fauxbourdon* (Leipzig, 1950), and R. von Ficker, 'Zur Schöpfungsgeschichte des Fauxbourdon', *Acta Musicologica*, xxiii (1951), p. 93. Cf. also H. Flasdieck, 'Franz. *faux-bourdon* und frühneuengl. *faburden*', *Acta Musicologica*, xxv (1953), p. 111. For a summing-up, see Besseler,

To the Netherlanders fauxbourdon itself remained something exceptional; to be used comparatively seldom. As a general rule they observed the more highly developed style of descant which found its practical realization in, for example, the mature works of Dunstable. In these the conditions were for the first time created for the beginnings of classical linear counterpoint, conforming with harmonic principles.

At the same time, in the Mass movements and liturgical motets of the Netherland school, the plainsong was transferred from the tenor (cf. p. 160 above) to the upper part. In the process it underwent a more or less strong 'colouring', thereby gaining increased melodic significance.[1] As may be inferred from the treatment of plainsong by Leonel Power and other composers in the Old Hall manuscript (see Chap. VI), the English models here, too, played an important part. The self-sufficiency and easy flow of this type of melody must have sounded like an entirely new musical world, especially to continental ears, hitherto accustomed to the pointed rhythms of the syllabic *parlando* technique and to the hockets of the French and Burgundian Masses and motets. The adoption of the new technique brought about a fundamental change in continental composition, namely the comparatively sudden abandonment of forms governed by rhythmic considerations, and their replacement by others predominantly melodic.

The new liturgical motet, with the ornamented plainsong in the upper part, now predominated in the Burgundian school also.[2] The same technique was used in setting sections of the Mass.[3] In this new motet the same words appear in all the parts; and while Gothic music had been intent on contrasting verbal and musical rhythms as sharply as possible, there now appeared that agreement between musical and verbal declamation and accent, in accordance with the sense, which has ever since been the first rule in vocal composition. Instrumental influence, which formed no part of the English tradition, was now greatly diminished and the advent of the *a cappella* style clearly foreshadowed. The old Gothic motet, with its different sets of words,

---

'Das Ergebnis der Diskussion über "Fauxbourdon"', *Acta Musicologica*, xxix (1957), p. 185.—*Ed.*

[1] 'Colouring' of the plainsong as an element in musical construction is quite foreign to southern Europe (Italy, Avignon). If a plainsong melody does appear in the upper part, its outline remains largely unaltered and can always be recognized: see, in addition to the hymns in the Apt manuscript, the *Credo* by Zacharias de Teramo in *Denkmäler der Tonkunst in Österreich*, xxxi, p. 16.

[2] Cf. Orel in *Studien zur Musikwissenschaft*, vii (1920).

[3] Cf. Ficker, *Studien zur Musikwissenschaft*, vii (1920) and xi (1924), p. 35.

fell more and more into disuse.[1] We can see here very clearly the change from rhythmical to melodic treatment: about 1430 the isorhythmic form of the individual sections (or *taleae*) was given up, and replaced by free melodic variation.[2] This principle was especially important in the shaping of the 'cyclic' Mass (see pp. 202 ff.); for the different sections now became 'coloured' arrangements of one and the same *canto fermo*.[3] Each Mass was thus a cycle of large-scale variations.

[1] It continued in use only for special occasions of a political or religious character. One of the last examples seems to be the anonymous motet 'Adoretur / In ultimo / Pacem' (*Denkmäler der Tonkunst in Österreich*, xl, p. 77), written to celebrate the surrender of Bordeaux to Charles VII (30 June, 1451).

[2] This development can be seen already in Dufay's motet in honour of Pope Eugenius IV, 'Ecclesiae militantis / Bella canunt' (*Denkmäler der Tonkunst in Österreich*, xl, p. 26, and *Guglielmi Dufay Opera Omnia*, ed. G. de Van, fasc. ii, p. 82); the date of this work is probably 1436: see *Acta Musicologica*, xxiii (1951), p. 108.

[3] Cf. the analyses of the Masses 'O rosa bella' and 'Le serviteur' in *Studien zur Musikwissenschaft*, vii (1920), pp. 25 and 37.

VI

ENGLISH CHURCH MUSIC OF THE FIFTEENTH CENTURY

By Manfred F. Bukofzer

THE ENGLISH IDIOM

In his historical survey of fifteenth-century music (*Ars Contrapuncti*, 1477) the Flemish theorist Tinctoris declared categorically and not without exaggeration that only the music of the past forty years was worth listening to, and a Spanish theorist even went so far as to assert that music had taken greater strides within that short period than since the birth of Christ. It was, according to Tinctoris, the English school that inaugurated what he called a veritable *ars nova* of the fifteenth century.[1] More precise information about the importance of the English style can be gathered from Martin le Franc's poem *Le Champion des Dames*, in which Binchois and Dufay are said to have followed Dunstable and adopted 'la contenance angloise' and a new practice of making 'sprightly concord' ('frisque concordance'). This report, written while the composers were at the height of their careers (*c.* 1440), clearly implies that the musicians of the time were fully aware of a difference in style between English and continental music, and that it was the assimilation of English elements which brought continental music to the height of its excellence.

What we learn from theorists and poets is borne out by the musical sources themselves. The three most important continental collections —the Trent, Aosta, and Modena manuscripts,[2] containing among them a total of well over 200 English compositions—segregate these from the rest either by presenting them in continuous series of varying length, or by reserving a large section for an exclusively English repertory. Moreover many continental scribes found it necessary to write above their pieces 'Anglicanus' or 'de Anglia', thus making it a special point to state the nationality of the composer, even though his name may not have been known to them. This particular consideration for English music in continental sources bears witness to the high esteem in which it was held.

What was the English idiom which must have struck the ear as a

[1] C. E. H. de Coussemaker, *Scriptorum de musica medii aevi nova series* (Paris, 1864–76), iv, p. 154.   [2] For particulars of these see pp. 150–1.

new style of 'sprightly concord'? This question has given rise to a good deal of controversy, since for us, who look at the music more than 500 years afterwards, the stylistic unity of fifteenth-century music in general weighs more heavily than divergences of national styles. A closer scrutiny of English music reveals three essential traits which characterize the English idiom: (1) the 'block-chord' or note-against-note style with all parts moving in the same rhythm; (2) a strong preference for $^6_3$ chords and full triads; (3) emphatic use of consonant progressions at the expense of unprepared dissonances.

While the last of these is probably not older than Pyamour and Dunstable, the first two belong to a long-established tradition of English music which is in evidence throughout the fourteenth century. The first trait, a survival of the medieval conductus, is seen also in the score notation which, though generally abandoned elsewhere in the fourteenth century, persisted in England well into the fifteenth century. Obviously this form of notation was particularly appropriate if the voices moved in similar rhythm. The delight which English composers took in sonority for its own sake appears in their readiness to increase the number of voices from the normal three to four, five, and even six. From the time of 'Sumer is icumen in', the first six-part composition known, this characteristic is found over and over again in English music. The fondness for thirds and sixths and block chords follows naturally on this. A harmonic idiom that raised the third to a status almost equal to that of the other consonances differs widely from the continental style, in which a succession of full triads was rare at that time. At the beginning of the fifteenth century the English style had passed beyond its primitive stage: far from being a monotonous succession of $^6_3$ chords, it employed full triads in root position in combination with $^6_3$ chords in both parallel and contrary motion, making conspicuous use of the third as a melodic and harmonic interval. The free use of these triads in continental style led on to the development of that four-part writing with a harmonic bass which marks the later works of Dufay. This harmonic type of bass is a most important keypoint for determining the beginning of the Renaissance in music.

English music of this period forms the vital link between the Middle Ages and the Renaissance. Conservative as always, it did not undergo the rapid change from the $^6_3$ style to fuller harmony; but all its current forms, from the Ordinary of the Mass and the isorhythmic motet to polyphonic antiphons and hymns, were pervaded with the conductus style and its sonorous harmonic idiom. This earlier stage is reflected in the Old Hall manuscript[1] and in the Fountains fragment.[2] With these may be included a number of somewhat later manuscripts, notably a fragment at Pembroke College, Cambridge; British Museum, Egerton 3307;[3] Oxford, Bodleian, Selden B 26[4] and Add. C 87; with sundry other collections of carols and secular songs, and smaller fragments. With the single exception of Bodleian, Add. C 87, all the sources quoted present some at least of their contents in the old-fashioned score arrangement. Their extensive repertory of nearly 300 pieces is, as we should expect, mainly liturgical, and even the English carols and Latin cantilenas are mostly religious.

For a long time the English compositions were thought to represent a school of merely local interest and importance, out of touch with the 'international' school of English composers abroad. The works of these writers appear in the Trent, Aosta, and Modena manuscripts, as well as in Munich, Bologna, Florence, and several other European libraries. A comparative study of English and continental sources has revealed that the two schools have much more in common than was hitherto believed. Nearly all the English manuscripts cited above contain compositions that are also known from continental sources, the Old Hall manuscript having no fewer than eleven. Thus the gap between the local and the cosmopolitan groups of English composers does not seem so wide as had been supposed, even if it is true that all English composers, great or small, at home or abroad, show in varying degree their indebtedness to the English idiom.

THE OLD HALL MANUSCRIPT

As we have seen (p. 101) the repertory of the Old Hall manuscript is confined to the early part of the century. In it we meet for the first time in English musical history a long list of named composers: Aleyn, Byttering, Burell, Chirbury, Cooke, Damett, Excetre, Fonteyns, Roy Henry, Gervays (also known as Gervasius de Anglia in Bologna, G. B. Martini, Q 15), Lambe, Leonel Power, Mayshuet, Olyver, Pennard, Pycard, Queldryk, Rowland, Sturgeon, Swynford, Tyes, and Typp. Compositions by Dunstable and Forest, more advanced than the rest, have been inserted by a later hand. Mayshuet can be identi-

---

[1] Edited by A. Ramsbotham, H. B. Collins, and Dom Anselm Hughes, 3 vols. (London, 1933–8).

[2] Brit. Mus., Add. 40011 B. See *The Old Hall Manuscript*, iii, p. xxix; and Manfred F. Bukofzer, *Studies in Medieval and Renaissance Music* (New York, 1950), pp. 86–112.

[3] See pp. 121 and 181.

[4] Published in J. F. R. Stainer, *Early Bodleian Music* (London, 1901), i and ii.

fied with Mayhuet de Joan of the Chantilly manuscript (see p. 105).

Though all the compositions are influenced in various degrees by the first two features of the English idiom they show a surprisingly wide variety in style. The most archaic group has been dealt with in Chapter III: it is written in score, and carries the plainsong usually in the middle voice. Similar compositions occur also in the Fountains fragment, which duplicates six of the Old Hall pieces. The more advanced compositions, inscribed in choirbook arrangement or *cantus collateralis*, show in part a decidely Italian and French influence.[1] That Italian music was actually sung in the Chapel Royal can be proved by an anonymous and fragmentary *Gloria* in the Old Hall manuscript (fo. 28ᵛ) which appears in Bologna, G. B. Martini, Q 15, and other continental manuscripts as a composition by Zacar (see p. 143). Another *Gloria* by him, described in the Bologna manuscript as 'Anglicana', shows like the first no trace of English influence in the music. The meaning of the title is not clear; it may possibly imply that the composer spent some time in England.

ITALIAN INFLUENCE

Italian influence manifests itself clearly in the canonic Glorias by Pycard,[2] in which he applies the technique of the *caccia* to the Mass. The first of these is canonic not only in its tenor but also, as Strunk has shown,[3] in the upper voices, and thus represents one of the rare examples of double canon. The second canon is not specified in the manuscript, but only implied by the double text. The same is true of a canonic *Gloria* by Byttering.[4] Canon for no less than three voices, again unspecified, occurs in an anonymous five-part *Credo*,[5] and the height of structural and rhythmic complexity is reached in another anonymous *Credo*[6] in which the upper three voices are in strict mensuration canon. They enter simultaneously, presenting the same line at different speeds to the accompaniment of two instrumental parts. The piece, which is more remarkable for artificiality than for artistic excellence, may perhaps be ascribed to Pycard, who is very fond of such sophistications.[7] In his treatment of dissonance he adheres, like so many of his fellow composers, to the contrapuntal precepts of *ars nova*. The undisguised clashes between the voices, so

---

[1] See H. Besseler in *Archiv für Musikwissenschaft*, vii (1925), p. 225; Charles Van den Borren, *Études sur le XVᵉ siècle musical* (Antwerp, 1941), p. 98; and Bukofzer, op. cit., pp. 53 ff.   [2] *The Old Hall Manuscript*, i, pp. 84 and 119.

[3] Bukofzer, op. cit., pp. 83–85.   [4] *The Old Hall Manuscript*, i, p. 47.

[5] Ibid. ii, p. 81.   [6] Ibid. ii, p. 101.   [7] Cf. p. 103.

frequent in the Old Hall compositions, are due to the notion that the single parts must be consonant with one voice, normally the tenor, but not necessarily with all the voices. The lively hocket sections found at the end of several elaborate compositions are also a common feature of fourteenth-century music. A *Credo* by Byttering,[1] with two strongly imitative upper voices, belongs also to the *caccia* type, but shows a more complex construction. Here the two instrumental parts form a rhythmic ostinato pattern of seven bars which is stated eighteen times with only slight rhythmic variants, but each time in a different melodic form. This is a continuation of the isorhythmic idea in motet composition, but it is adopted here in the loose fashion in which Italian composers preferred to handle this essentially French device.

The *caccia* was only one of the secular forms that served as models for the Mass settings in the Old Hall manuscript. Another favourite type, characterized by a florid treble melody and two supporting voices, often instrumental, followed the model of the *ballade* and *virelai*. Here the composer concentrated upon the treble, which was composed first, according to the assertion of a contemporary theorist. This type has often been called (rather unfortunately) '*ballade* Mass', though 'free treble style' would be a more satisfactory and accurate term. It is found in the majority of the Mass compositions, for example, in Roy Henry's vigorous *Gloria*,[2] in the setting by Byttering which follows it,[3] and in those of the *Credo* by Damett,[4] Byttering,[5] Cooke[6] and several others. In many Creeds and in some Glorias the words are often divided up between the voices and sung simultaneously in the manner of a polytextual motet. This method of telescoping the movements for the sake of brevity was not considered objectionable from the liturgical point of view current at that time, and it led eventually to truncated settings of the Creed, a text which we should expect to be preserved intact.[7] Telescoped settings occur so often in the English school that they have been taken for an exclusively English characteristic. It is true that they were far less popular in Franco-Flemish music, but they do appear here as early as the pre-Dufay generation. Truncated settings, on the other hand, are possibly exclusively English. They lasted in England up to about 1545.

---

[1] *The Old Hall Manuscript*, ii, p. 203.
[2] Ibid. i, p. 34.
[3] Ibid. i, p. 39.
[4] Ibid. ii, pp. 93 and 261.
[5] Ibid. ii, p. 149.
[6] Ibid. ii, p. 252.
[7] See Dom Anselm Hughes, 'The Text-Omissions in the Creed', in *Missa O quam suavis*, ed. H. B. Collins (London, 1927), p. xxxiii, and Ruth Hannas, 'Concerning Deletions in the Polyphonic Mass Credo', *Journal of the American Musicological Society*, v (1952), p. 155.

ISORHYTHMIC COMPOSITIONS

How thoroughly the composers of the Chapel Royal were familiar with French music in general and with the isorhythmic motet in particular is clear from the inserted motets. These are eleven in number, not counting the polyphonic settings of antiphons in conductus style which stand midway between conductus and motet. No fewer than nine of the eleven motets proper[1] turn out to be isorhythmic. The motet tenors, consisting usually of two or more isorhythmic sections or *taleae*, are written down once only but must be repeated in diminution while the upper voices proceed in sections of identical rhythm but different melody. The extreme artificiality of this form is not at all consistent with the English idiom, less in evidence here than in the conductus settings. 'Arae post libamina',[2] noteworthy for its backward and highly dissonant style, is actually by a French composer, Mayshuet. The isorhythmic 'En Katherinae solemnia' by Byttering[3] can perhaps be associated with the marriage of Henry V and Catherine of Valois. This conjecture is based not so much on the identity of names as on the tenor, which quotes from the St. Catherine respond ('Virgo flagellatur'[4]) only the section 'Sponsus amat sponsam', which alone would be appropriate to such an occasion.

That the insertion of the isorhythmic motets was not altogether haphazard is revealed in a rather surprising way by Damett's 'Salvatoris mater'[5] and Sturgeon's 'Salve Mater',[6] which interrupt the series of *Sanctus* compositions. Both use sections of the same Gregorian *Sanctus* in their tenors, so that they can be regarded as very lavishly troped *Sanctus* settings. But this is not all; the melody of the troped *Benedictus*[7] includes in Damett's tenor only the fragment 'Benedictus Mariae Filius qui ve-', while Sturgeon continues in his motet exactly where his predecessor had left off with '-[n]it in nomine Domini'. This direct connexion between the two tenors can hardly be a mere coincidence.

More noteworthy than the appearance of isorhythmic motets is the fact that even the Mass settings are isorhythmic in twelve cases. The absence of melodic repeats in this technique so greatly obscures the regular recurrence of the same rhythmic patterns in all the voices that

[1] Four of them are fragments not printed in the edition. The Fountains fragment (see p. 105) also contains isorhythmic motets.
[2] *The Old Hall Manuscript*, iii, p. 150.
[3] Ibid. iii, p. 145.　　　　　　[4] *Processionale Monasticum* (Solesmes, 1893), p. 214.
[5] *The Old Hall Manuscript*, iii, p. 40.
[6] Ibid. iii, p. 51.
[7] *Graduale Sarisburiense* (London, 1894), pl. 17*, and Sarum No. 3, ibid., pl. 15*.

even the editors of the music have failed to notice them. Apart from their musical interest they give us valuable clues for the correct restoration of the numerous passages in which the barbarous removal of illuminated initials has spoiled the manuscript.

Although Machaut had already set a precedent for the transfer of motet technique to the Mass, its extensive cultivation is not typical of the continental repertory, where the forms were kept distinct. The merging of forms, such as conductus, *caccia*, isorhythmic motet, and Mass, was characteristic of schools which stood outside the central development and brought about through their conservative outlook novel, if eclectic, forms. The isorhythmic Mass movements of the Old Hall manuscript clearly show this vigorous development of a stimulus originally French. While most of the Masses in motet style are strictly isorhythmic in all voices, others are so only in their tenor, for example, the *Credo* by Swynford.[1] Others try to make the abstract isorhythmic sections really audible through melodic variation, or what has been called 'isomelic' technique. This can be found in Pennard's *Credo* for four voices,[2] which falls into two gigantic divisions of eighty bars each in length, the second of which is a literal repeat in the two lower voices. Only where the duet has words is the music not repeated, and the second statement of the melody is a variant of the first. The last thirty-two bars bring an extended hocket of the corresponding bars of the first statement. Hints of isomelic repeats can also be discerned in Mayshuet's motet, and in the sumptuous *Credo*[3] by an anonymous composer. This begins with a canonic duet typical of the most elaborate motets and is built on an enigmatic tenor, to be sung forwards and then backwards (*cancrizans*).

Some of the isorhythmic Mass movements deviate from the orthodox procedure in the choice of the tenor also. As a rule the tenor is taken from some part of the Gregorian chant, e.g. an antiphon, as in the case of Pennard's *Credo*[4] or a sequence, as in the case of Pycard's *Gloria*.[5] In no case is the tenor derived from the appropriate plainsong of the Ordinary; and there are also tenors of unknown and probably non-Gregorian origin which seem to have been specially composed. Such undesignated melodies occur in the Glorias by Queldryk and Tyes,[6] and the Creeds by Queldryk[7] and others.

---

[1] *The Old Hall Manuscript*, ii, p. 213.
[2] Ibid. ii, p. 241. The *solus tenor* is only a substitute part contracted from the tenor and contratenor.
[3] Ibid. iii, p. [68].
[4] Ibid. ii, p. 241.
[5] Ibid. i, p. 92.
[6] Ibid. i, pp. 109 and 50.
[7] Ibid. ii, p. 252.

LEONEL POWER

With Leonel or Lionel Power (rather more often called by his first name alone in the manuscripts) we reach the leading composer of the Old Hall group, pre-eminent both in the number of his compositions and in their artistic quality. But for the year of his death in 1445[1] little is known about him. Although the large amount of his work in the Old Hall manuscript suggests a close connexion with the Chapel Royal, nothing has come to light in the archives so far. Leonel's entire output consists of Mass compositions and motets, thus confirming the predominantly religious bent of the English school. Some fifty or more of his compositions have come down to us, a number which causes him to rival Dunstable as the best-known English composer of his time. His isorhythmic compositions comprise Masses only, not a single motet proper. This indicates that in his day the greatest and most representative form of Gothic symbolism in music, the poly-textual and isorhythmic motet, was giving way to a new and more strictly liturgical type, an intimate and personal setting of a sacred text (notably antiphons of the Blessed Virgin and verses from the Song of Songs), which either appear with their traditional chants or are quite independent compositions. The trend away from abstract intellectualism towards a more personal and human devotion is characteristic of the age. Thus the fifteen motets all set texts which betoken the intense devotion to the Blessed Virgin of the early fif-teenth century. The new quasi-liturgical motet must be regarded as an extension of the conductus, which it follows in using a single text. The various antiphons and hymns or sequences of the Old Hall manu-script are written in the archaic score arrangement and represent the intermediate stage between conductus and motet. Leonel took an active part in evolving this form in his 'Ave regina coelorum' and 'Beata progenies' in the Old Hall manuscript,[2] and 'Beata viscera' in the Aosta manuscript.[3] The first two carry the plainsong in the middle voice, the last one in the treble.

POWER'S FIRST PERIOD

In his style Leonel is a master of a transitional period. His works can be divided roughly into an earlier and a later group. Compositions

---

[1] He died at Canterbury.

[2] *The Old Hall Manuscript*, i, pp. 151 and 156; also printed respectively in *Sammel-bände der internationalen Musikgesellschaft*, ii (1901), p. 378, and G. Reese, *Music in the Middle Ages* (New York, 1940), p. 413.

[3] The hymn 'Ave maris stella', printed in *Denkmäler der Tonkunst in Österreich*, xxvii (1), p. 78 under the name of Leonel, is anonymous.

in his 'first manner' are definitely more conservative than those of Dunstable. It is not an accident that they belong to the first layer of the Old Hall manuscript, a fact that explains their remarkably dissonant style. Three of Leonel's Mass movements in the Old Hall manuscript are cast in rigid isorhythmic moulds. Only two of them —a Gloria[1] and a Credo[2] —actually appear under his name, but he is also very probably the author of another Gloria.[3] It is inscribed in the middle of a series of Leonel's pieces, and but for its fragmentary beginning we might have had the ascription. Apart from these external points there is an internal one. The beginning has been restored in the printed edition without reference to the analogous isorhythmic section (bar 47): an alternative amendment would make it closely resemble the beginning of Leonel's Credo, which has the same conflicting key signatures and the same clefs. Moreover, these are the only two movements in which the tenor, in spite of its isorhythmic organization, is a continuous melody. In other words, it is treated unusually like the upper voice of an isorhythmic motet. If the ascription is correct, we should have here one of the attempts to combine the single parts of the Ordinary into unified pairs.

Traces only of this tendency are found in the Old Hall manuscript, but it was to become important later on. This may be seen in a paired Gloria and Credo in the Aosta manuscript,[4] of which the former is isorhythmic in all three voices, the latter only so in the tenor, which is stated four times in increasing diminution in the ratio $6:4:3:2$. Since the Gloria is ascribed to Leonel, the Credo, which follows directly in the manuscript, can be confidently ascribed to him also. The beginning of the Credo is also very similar to a setting of the same text by Byttering.[5] The tenor of the Gloria carries no inscription but can be identified as Gregorian: it quotes the first phrase of the Sarum Gloria V from 'Et in terra' to 'glorifica[mus]'. The tenor of the Credo is drawn from the first two phrases of the chant, from 'Patrem' to 'et terrae'. The fact that the two tenors quote plainsongs of the Ordinary is significant because no parallel case is known to exist in the isorhythmic Mass settings of Leonel's time. The style of the pair conforms on the whole to that of Leonel's isorhythmic Masses in the Old Hall manuscript, the Gloria alone suggesting a slightly more advanced treatment of dissonance.

A Gloria for four voices[6] betrays in its melodic flow the hand of a

---

[1] The Old Hall Manuscript, iii, p. [23].
[2] Ibid. ii, p. 194.
[3] Ibid. iii, p. [32].
[4] Nos. 169–70 (fos. 231ᵛ–4). For the incipits see Musica Disciplina, ii (1948), pp. 41 and 44.
[5] The Old Hall Manuscript, ii, p. 203.
[6] Ibid. iii, p. [23].

superior artist, although the erratic harmonic progressions are still essentially those of *ars nova*. The somewhat clumsy handling of the four voices, which often pause merely in order to avoid parallel octaves, should be noted. Clashes between the voices on unaccented beats are especially noticeable in the four-part compositions. A non-isorhythmic *Sanctus* and *Agnus*[1] illustrate this style. They apparently form another pair of related Mass compositions: both are based upon chants from the same Mass (Vatican XVII),[2] both place the *canto fermo* in the tenor with a very similar treatment, and both are sub-divided by means of the same time signatures into four major parts. In one single case, a *Gloria*,[3] Leonel even ventures into five-part harmony: this *Gloria* is closely paralleled by an anonymous *Credo*,[4] of which he may possibly be the author.

In his three-part writing, exemplified by a *Gloria*,[5] a *Credo*,[6] and another *Credo*, incomplete in the Old Hall manuscript but known also from Aosta (No. 173), Leonel shows himself much freer. Moreover, in these presumably early works the *ars nova* style lingers on in the capricious use of proportions, a free use of accidentals, and nervous rhythms which we find also in Roy Henry's *Gloria*. A *Credo*[7] which is preserved also in Bologna, G. B. Martini, Q 15, wavers between consonant and dissonant style: it contains passages of eloquent and impressive turns in melody and harmony, and approaches the composer's later style. Like most English composers, Leonel likes to alternate between full sections for three, four, or even five voices and melodious duets for two soloists, often marked 'duo' in the originals. These duets differ from the full sections in their thoroughly vocal lines, which show hardly any trace of instrumentalism, and are subdivided by characteristic pauses of an entire bar in which the music comes to a complete standstill. The skilful manipulation of contrasting groups of voices which can be seen in Italian music at the turn of the century was put to systematic use by English composers, so that it became an almost stereotyped feature of English music in the fifteenth century.

POWER'S SECOND PERIOD

In his 'second period' Leonel succeeds in writing a smooth and graceful melody, usually in ternary rhythm; and his dissonance treatment displays the reserve of his later contemporaries, approaching a style which is almost consonant. The compositions of this period are

---

[1] *The Old Hall Manuscript*, iii, pp. 76 and 136. The *Sanctus* is also printed in A. T. Davison and W. Apel, *Historical Anthology of Music*, i (Cambridge, Mass.), no. 63.
[2] *Graduale Romanum*, p. 52*; *Liber Usualis* (1950), p. 61.　　[3] *Old Hall*, i, p. 60.
[4] Ibid. ii, p. 125.　　[5] Ibid. i, p. 70.　　[6] Ibid. ii, p. 167.　　[7] Ibid. ii, p. 185.

preserved almost entirely in continental sources, especially the Trent, Aosta, and Modena manuscripts, and include the 'cyclic' Mass on 'Alma redemptoris' (see p. 205), with several motets, mostly unpublished as yet. If this music is compared with Leonel's earlier style a notable advance is seen at once. In no other English master can we see such growth from his first period to his last. The motets of the Modena manuscript, notably 'Anima mea liquefacta est' (two settings), 'Salve sancta parens', 'Quam pulchra', 'Ibo mihi ad montem', 'Salve regina', and 'Mater, ora Filium',[1] represent the latest stage of his music. They all belong to the new type of liturgical motet and are written without reference to a *canto fermo*, except for the 'Salve regina' which introduces the Gregorian melody in the tenor of the last three invocations. Here Leonel abandoned his former ways completely, and absorbed the new consonant style which Dunstable raised to prominence. These motets can in fact hardly be distinguished from those of his more famous colleague except perhaps for one conspicuous trait. Leonel seems even more progressive than Dunstable in the increased use of imitation, as can be seen in this excerpt from 'Anima mea liquefacta est':

Ex.75

---

[1] The last two are printed in *Denkmäler der Tonkunst in Österreich*, vii, pp. 191 and 212.

(When my beloved spoke, I sought him and found him not; I called and he did not answer me.)

This newly attained mastery extends also to four-part writing. Works like 'Ave regina'[1] and particularly 'Gloriosae virginis',[2] in which subtle duets for different voices alternate with full sections, are free from archaism and challenge comparison with anything else written in this period.

DESCANT AND FAUXBOURDON

The various ways of incorporating a plainsong in a polyphonic composition deserve a separate discussion because they enable us to draw valuable conclusions about the actual process of composition. The plainsong could be presented either in extempore or in written form. The first method has been fully described by several English theorists and composers of the early fifteenth century, notably Leonel Power himself, Richard Cotell, several anonymous writers (one known as Pseudo-Chilston), John Hothby, and two Italian theorists, Guilielmus Monachus and Burtius.[3] The improvised treatment of a plainsong in polyphony, traditionally called descant, worked by rules of thumb for two or more singers. While the continental practice was normally restricted to a system of contrary motion with emphasis on perfect consonances, the English composers preferred parallel motion in the $\frac{6}{3}$ style of their national idiom, though at times they also used the continental method. In the system of 'sights' or *discantus visibilis* they developed a simple 'ocular perfection' (Guilielmus

[1] *Denkmäler der Tonkunst in Österreich*, vii, p. 210.

[2] Printed in J. Wolf, *Music of Earlier Times (Sing- und Spielmusik)*, p. 30, but with the fourth voice omitted in error.

[3] Printed in Bukofzer, *Geschichte des englischen Diskants und des Fauxbourdons* (Strasbourg, 1936). See also S. B. Meech in *Speculum*, x (1935), p. 235; T. Georgiades, *Englische Diskanttraktate aus der ersten Hälfte des 15. Jahrhunderts* (Munich, 1937); H. Besseler, *Bourdon und Fauxbourdon* (Leipzig, 1950); and Bukofzer, 'Fauxbourdon revisited', *The Musical Quarterly*, xxxviii (1952), p. 22.

Monachus) which enabled them to imagine the added voices upon the four lines of the staff on which the chant was written. Continental and English descant differed in the type of intervals and motion used, but both placed the *canto fermo* below. Leonel's treatise on descant is outstanding, because it tries to relax the mechanical improvisation of first inversions by the liberal use of contrary motion, his object being to raise popular practice to a higher level of artistry. In his musical illustrations he stresses imperfect intervals, but he does not admit more than three in parallel motion, or six if the intervals change:

Ex.76

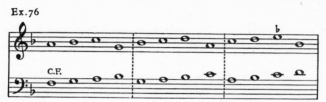

With the spread of English music to the rest of Europe English descant was readily absorbed, but it was transformed into the faux-bourdon. In view of the long-established importance of the treble in continental music it is not surprising that the *canto fermo* was placed in this voice. Transposed to the higher octave the plainsong could now be ornamented by coloration so as to gain the appearance of a melody in free treble style. Whether freely composed or not the melody was accompanied by two lower subsidiary voices moving at the sixth (or octave) and the fourth respectively. This type of harmonization mechanically duplicated the melody at fixed intervals in parallel motion, and for it the term 'false bass' was aptly chosen. In fauxbourdon the improvisation extended in the first place only to the middle voice, which did not need notation but was improvised at the fourth below the melody, as numerous compositions prescribe by the direction 'a fauxbordon'. Fauxbourdon rose to fame with Bin-chois and especially with Dufay, who was perhaps the inventor of the genre; and it enjoyed a great vogue as a primitive and modest type of liturgical music, used especially in the Office. Though the English composers were not unfamiliar with the *canto fermo* in the treble it had not, like English descant, been formalized in a method of im-provisation. It seems that the fauxbourdon fashion reached England only after its appearance on the Continent. Later in the century the term was applied indiscriminately, as it often is still today, to any chain of $^6_3$ chords; but it will be retained here in its original meaning.

METHODS OF CANTO FERMO TREATMENT

In written compositions not bound by the necessarily rigid rules of improvisation any one of the voices could carry the chant. Four methods of *canto fermo* treatment can be distinguished, each calling for a somewhat different approach. The *canto fermo* could be presented (1) as the lowest voice, (2) as a middle voice, (3) as the leading voice in the treble, or (4) in any combination of the foregoing alternatives. If it was placed in the lowest part English descant served as the starting-point for a formal composition such as we find in certain Mass sections of Leonel Power and Dunstable. The method of composition was cumulative, one part being composed at a time, so that the one carrying the chant had to be written first. If the *canto fermo* was placed in the middle, the setting consisted of this principal voice and a supporting one below: in other words it would be a gymel to which a third voice could be added. The underlying gymel structure can be clearly recognized in several compositions of the Old Hall manuscript, especially the Masses and antiphons in conductus style in which the two lower voices reach their cadence in the form $\substack{\text{B–C} \\ \text{D–C}}$ while the highest voice proceeds in fifths parallel with the middle one, as can be seen in Leonel's antiphons cited above (p. 172).

Before the arrival of the fauxbourdon fashion in England the *canto fermo* in the treble was to the English composers just one of the methods of written-out plainsong elaboration, though it was used less often than the other methods. It lent itself to melodic ornamentation more easily in its exposed position as treble than as middle or lowest voice. We find in the Old Hall manuscript not only profuse embellishments, for example in the *Agnus* by Olyver,[1] but also unadorned presentation, as in Excetre's *Gloria*,[2] a curiously archaic composition with many imperfect intervals produced chiefly by contrary motion. As is true of nearly all English compositions it follows the Sarum version of the plainsong (No. 5) more closely than the Roman version (Vatican V). The repeated phrases in the treble of Excetre's *Gloria* have been interpreted as a kind of progressive variation,[3] but they are actually governed by the pre-determined course of the plainsong. In his three-part *Sanctus*,[4] also found in the Trent codices and the Aosta manuscript, Leonel not only turns the chant into a highly flexible figurate melody but also expands it with freely inserted melismas.

---

[1] *The Old Hall Manuscript*, iii, p. 141.
[2] Ibid. i, p. 55.
[3] Van den Borren, *Études sur le XVe siècle musical*, p. 96.
[4] *The Old Hall Manuscript*, iii, p. 66. See Ex. 73 above (p. 161).

A three-part setting of the Communion 'Beata viscera' in the Aosta manuscript (No. 5) shows a much more restrained elaboration of the plainsong, more in the manner of the liturgical compositions in British Museum, Egerton 3307.

The fourth method, which has received little attention as yet, although it can claim to be the most interesting of them all, does not restrict the chant to any one part but presents it in alternation, now in one voice, now in another. This wandering or 'migrant' *canto fermo* presupposes that the single voices function no longer as independent units but as a polyphonic whole. This unified conception of polyphony was the natural outcome of the chordal and emphatically sonorous tradition of English music. It is therefore not surprising that the migrant *canto fermo* was first methodically explored by English composers of the fourteenth and fifteenth centuries, especially the latter. Its occasional use in the music of the Flemish composer Liebert[1] (see pp. 234–5) seems to be due to English contact and coincides with the wave of English influence on continental music.

The Old Hall manuscript supplies us with a considerable number of examples of the migrant *canto fermo*, in which the chant is found moving either between two voices only, or among them all. Cases in point are Typp's *Sanctus*[2] in which the chant appears sometimes transposed a fifth upwards, and the antiphon 'Nesciens mater' by Byttering,[3] who weaves the chant, marked by asterisks in the example below, from the treble to the tenor and from the tenor to the middle voice in an unbroken line. In this example, too, the chant is suddenly transposed, only to resume its original pitch with equal abruptness:

Ex. 77

Ne - sci - ens Ma - ter vir - go vi - - -

---

[1] H. Besseler, *Die Musik des Mittelalters und der Renaissance* (Potsdam, 1931), p. 233.
[2] *The Old Hall Manuscript*, iii, p. 4.
[3] Ibid. i, p. 157. Recorded in *The History of Music in Sound* (H.M.V.), iii.

(Knowing no man, the Virgin Mother brought forth without sorrow.)

Exactly the same technique can be found in several compositions of Bodleian, Selden B 26. In the anonymous 'Speciosa facta es',[1] for example, the melody of the antiphon[2] pervades all the voices, with a slight emphasis on the middle part:

Ex.78

[1] Stainer, *Early Bodleian Music*, i, pls. 92–99; ii, p. 165.
[2] *Antiphonale Sarisburiense* (London, 1901–24), p. 529.

PLATE II

THE EARLIEST ENGLISH PASSION MUSIC
The opening of a three-part Passion according to St. Luke (see p. 181)
(British Museum MS. Egerton 3307, fo. 20)

Migrant *canto fermo* is found also in an anonymous *Agnus* preserved in the English fascicles of the Aosta manuscript (No. 181) and doubtless to be counted among the products of the English school. Similar examples as late as the Pepysian manuscript (see next page) bear witness to the fact that the migrant *canto fermo* was known and used throughout the century.

THE EGERTON AND PEPYS MANUSCRIPTS

The arrival of the fauxbourdon fashion in England towards the middle of the century can first be clearly discerned in the British Museum manuscript, Egerton 3307, dating from the middle of the century. Its place of origin has not yet been definitely determined. While some scholars claim that it was written for St. George's Chapel at Windsor, others believe it to come from Yorkshire, perhaps the abbey of Meaux.[1] Prefixed to an important collection of carols is a series of liturgical compositions for Holy Week, arranged in the order called for by the Sarum Processionale. Among the most interesting items of the manuscript are two polyphonic settings of the Passion choruses, one fragmentary and one complete,[2] which are the earliest extant examples of this form. Composed in stylized fauxbourdon manner, they declaim the words almost exclusively in simple $\frac{6}{3}$ chords. A remarkable Mass, consisting of an incomplete *Kyrie*, with a *Sanctus* and *Agnus*, is written in a slightly more exacting style, and calls at times for a supplementary fourth voice which adds sonority but is otherwise not always essential. The *Sanctus* of this Mass should be compared with a curiously similar *Sanctus* by Binchois[3] which elaborates the same chant. The omission of *Gloria* and *Credo* from this Mass implies that it was composed for weekdays as a *missa brevis*, and this assumption can be proved by the *canto fermo*; for all the movements have in the treble the floriated form of the chants expressly noted in the Sarum Gradual as 'in feriis'. Although the liturgical pieces of the Egerton manuscript contain examples of English descant and of migrant *canto fermo*, treble elaboration in fauxbourdon style predominates, even if the improvisation of the contratenor is never directly called for at any place in the manu-

---

[1] See B. Schofield and M. F. Bukofzer, 'A Newly Discovered Fifteenth-Century Manuscript of the English Chapel Royal', *The Musical Quarterly*, xxxii (1946), pp. 509–36, and xxxiii (1947), pp. 38–51; and Bukofzer, *Studies in Medieval and Renaissance Music*, pp. 113–75. See also R. L. Greene, 'Two Medieval Musical Manuscripts', *Journal of the American Musicological Society*, vii (1954), p. 1.   [2] Cf. pl. II.

[3] Printed in J. Marix, *Les Musiciens de la cour de Bourgogne* (Paris, 1937), p. 182. One Passion and the Mass sections from the Egerton manuscript have been printed in *The Musical Quarterly*, xxxiii (1947), loc. cit.

script. The three voices are written out and move in customary progressions, as is illustrated by the processional hymn for Easter, 'Inventor rutili', which carries the plainsong[1] in the treble.

Ex.79

In - ven - tor ru - ti - li

dux bo - ne lu - mi - nis, qui

cer - tis vi - ci - bus

(Thou leader kind, whose word called forth the radiant light, who by set bounds [dividest night and day].)[2]

Another version of the same composition is preserved also in the Pepysian manuscript,[3] where the section quoted above appears, except for slight variants at the beginning, in identical form. This manuscript may date from as late as 1470, as it contains music by such composers as Banaster (d. 1487) and Hawte. It hardly advances beyond the stage of the Egerton manuscript, as is shown internally by its very old-fashioned style, and externally by the black full notation. It should be noted that apart from the direct overlap in repertory the two manuscripts are also related in respect of their selection of liturgical texts, in particular some from the Sarum Processionale which are not found in post-Tridentine books of the Roman rite. The Pepysian manuscript can be regarded as a later parallel to the Old Hall manuscript, in that it in-

---

[1] *Graduale Sarisburiense*, pl. 104.
[2] Translation in F. E. Warren, *The Sarum Missal* (London, 1913), p. 269.
[3] Cambridge, Magdalene College, Pepys 1236.

cludes, side by side with fine compositions, others in clumsy polyphony which are in all probability the work of provincial composers, perhaps from the North of England.[1] All forms of *canto fermo* treatment occur: some examples use the migrant *canto fermo*, but English descant and fauxbourdon are in the majority. Numerous settings of the Proper of the Mass appear in partial form—that is to say, the solo sections of the chant are set in polyphony, while the choral sections are omitted. This is consistent with medieval practice but was at this time a thing of the past. On the other hand we find Alleluias for three voices in English descant or fauxbourdon style in which, conversely, only the choral sections are composed and the solo sections are omitted. The liturgical function of these would imply that at this time the chorus sang in polyphony, the soloists in plainsong—the exact opposite of the practice just described. A further peculiarity is a number of settings of *Gloria in excelsis*, the verse of the first respond of Christmas matins, *Hodie nobis*: another example of this is in Cambridge, University Library, Add. 5943. Several paraphrases of plainchants (the Lamentations for Tenebrae in Holy Week) composed for one voice as *cantus fractus* in mensural notation, may finally be mentioned as curiosities.

Cantus fractus is found also in MS. VI of Shrewsbury School, a Processional from about the middle of the century, known principally from its non-musical contents, a fragment of an English mystery play.[2] Like the Egerton and Pepysian manuscripts it contains processional hymns and chants, and in addition plainsong insertions in the mystery play[3] and single voices of polyphonic fragments. Several chants are written mensurally and are designated as 'triplex'. These are apparently treble voices of three-part compositions of which the lower voices are lost. As the manuscript allows no space for the other voices, it must have been a part-book with respect to the polyphonic pieces. The appearance of a musical part-book at this early date would be startling, but the manuscript is known to be a part-book of the mystery play and this special purpose may explain the occurrence. The 'triplex' parts sometimes give the impression of being counterpoints to plainsongs. The two most interesting items are unquestionably the Passions according to St. Matthew and St. John, in which only the non-narrative *turbae* and the words of individuals (except

---

[1] Daphne Bird, in an unpublished thesis in Cambridge University Library.
[2] *The Non-Cycle Mystery Plays*, ed. by Osborne Waterhouse in *Early English Text Society*, Extra Ser., civ. See also K. Young, *The Drama of the Medieval Church* (Oxford, 1933), ii, p. 520.   [3] See vol. II, p. 189.

those of Christ) are set to music exactly as in the Passions of the Egerton manuscript. Although the Shrewsbury manuscript has many liturgical texts in common with the Egerton and Pepys manuscripts, there are no concordances with either source.

JOHN DUNSTABLE

It does not detract from the almost mythical splendour of Dunstable's reputation if we say that viewed from the perspective of the English school as a whole his music does not differ from it fundamentally in style. His fame originated on the Continent, and it is not by mere accident that most of his works are preserved in continental rather than in English manuscripts. He wore the laurels that should in justice be shared by men like Leonel Power, Benet, Damett, Pyamour, and others. His fame may also account for the fact that his music was copied more assiduously than that of his colleagues, so that his extant compositions, about sixty, are more numerous than those of any other English master of the period. The little we know of his life throws hardly any light upon his career, though it helps us to understand his European fame. From the date of his death (1453) we can suppose that he was born some time before 1390. According to his epitaph he was a musician, mathematician, and astronomer; and mathematical and astronomical treatises in his handwriting have actually been preserved. An entry in another astronomical writing, formerly in the possession of Dunstable, calls him 'musician to the Duke of Bedford'. As the Duke ruled as Regent in Paris it is probable that Dunstable followed him, and that Binchois and Dufay indeed met him there and learned from him to imitate his 'contenance angloise'.

There is no doubt whatever that Dunstable is of classic stature. In a manner at once authoritative and distinctive he gathered up the features of the English school and gave them the definite stamp which made them famous. He shared perhaps more fully than his colleagues in continental activities in music, and thus served as the proper intermediary between the English and the Franco-Flemish schools. It was because of his classical position that Dunstable shied away from extremes and kept to the middle of the road, clarifying and perfecting the English idiom rather than creating it, as legend has it. His work shows but few signs of growth from early to late style. From the beginning (unlike Leonel) he kept free from the discordances of the harsh *ars nova* harmony, even when he wrote for four voices. With regard to rhythm he adopted the smooth modern style from the outset, and it is only very rarely that his lines display the lacerated design of older melodic practice. It is not the English idiom as such that sets Dunstable apart from his predecessors, but his restricted and novel use of it. His harmonic style is distinguished by an unusually liberal supply of perpetually consonant progressions, verging at times on mono-tony. What could be regarded as a mere poetic licence of Martin le Franc is literally true: 'sprightly concordances' pervade his music and give it the 'angelic sweetness' which passed at the time as the leading characteristic of English music. Unprepared dissonances on the beat, the hall-mark of *ars nova*, are almost eliminated, and even prepared dissonances are relatively scarce. The few remaining dissonances are introduced as melodic ornaments, notably in the various forms of the *cambiata* and *échappée*, e.g.:

Ex.80

or as passing and changing notes. The purging of dissonances from the harmony is a turning-point in the history of dissonance treatment and indeed of contrapuntal writing in general. Dunstable's innovation was therefore not the introduction of the English idiom for which he has been undeservedly praised, but its purification from dissonances. It was unquestionably the new concordant style that accounted for the novelty of Dunstable's music and for the enthusiasm it aroused.

In his melodic progressions Dunstable has been said to favour an underlying pentatonic scale, alleged to be derived from a hypothetical English folksong. Very little evidence can be adduced for this claim. If his melodies were really pentatonic they would avoid semitones; but these appear freely. What strikes the casual observer as vaguely pentatonic is actually caused by the intervals of the English idiom, the triad and the $\frac{6}{3}$ chord. This idiom pervades his music so strongly that the openings of many compositions resemble one another in using the notes of a major or minor triad, and in following with their extension to the sixth. Yet these beginnings, which are so stereotyped as to become conventions, must not be regarded as a personal feature but rather as a general characteristic of the English school, as a few initial motives will show, culled at random from the works of Dunstable and his contemporaries. The illustration also shows how partial the English were to the modes of C, F, and D:

Ex. 81

CLASSIFICATION OF DUNSTABLE'S COMPOSITIONS

The compositions of Dunstable[1] can be classified in seven types, which, though not mutually exclusive, embrace the wide technical range of his music.[2] The first type is a highly stylized extension of English descant, which can be illustrated by two related Mass movements, a *Sanctus* and an *Agnus*,[3] written in a rather old-fashioned style. The second category includes the so-called *ballade* or 'free treble' style, to which Dunstable was predisposed in virtue of his melodic talent. Works in gymel structure form the third class, and isorhythmic motets the fourth. A fifth category comprises the important group of compositions with a borrowed treble in which the chant may be richly embellished or simply harmonized in fauxbourdon fashion. There are only two examples of the latter treatment: the hymn 'Ave maris stella' and a three-part *Magnificat*.[4] The sixth type can be described as the declamation motet: it is characterized by free invention in all the voices and by careful consideration of the declamatory rhythm of the words, often underlined by repeated

[1] Complete edition of Dunstable's works (edited by Bukofzer) in *Musica Britannica*, viii (1953).

[2] See Bukofzer, 'John Dunstable and the Music of his Time', *Proceedings of the Musical Association*, lxv (1938), p. 22, and 'John Dunstable: a Quincentenary Report', *The Musical Quarterly*, xl (1954), p. 29.

[3] *Musica Britannica*, viii, pp. 31 and 33.

[4] Ibid., p. 95.

notes. The last category is formed by compositions with double structure: these depend, as the name implies, on two factors—a borrowed
or freely composed tenor which serves merely as a scaffold for the
entire movement, and a treble as the predominant voice. This twin
or double structure, which should not be confused with double *canto
fermo*, became a distinctive mark of fifteenth-century composition.

Evidently the first, third, and fifth types are identical with the first
three methods of plainsong treatment discussed above (pp. 178 ff.).
It is a sign of Dunstable's reserve that he did not take part in the
experiments with migrant *canto fermo* which his forerunners had
already begun. In compositions of the first type the chant as the lowest
voice did not lend itself readily to embellishment, but in those of the
third type it assumed the character of an embroidered melody. The
only example of the latter is the unusual motet 'Crux fidelis',[1] notable
for its dignified harmonies and the exquisite contour of its lines. The
chant appears in the middle, and when the middle part pauses, in the
treble; and it does not differ in style from the newly written parts. In
his five compositions with the chant in the treble Dunstable draws this
voice into his triadic melodic style and spins it out in florid melismas
of great charm. He goes farthest afield in modifying the chant in the
two motets 'Ave regina' and 'Regina coeli',[2] in which the plainsong
lies hidden at times beneath the luxuriance of his melodic imagination.
This intensely personal and fervent elaboration, which makes the
chant seem like a freely composed line, is an English heritage, upon
which Leonel Power and others have also drawn. This subjective interpretation is in contrast with the objective presentation of the chant
by the Burgundian composers. Yet Dunstable was also familiar with
the restrained type of Burgundian ornamentation: it is probable that
he, the older master, learned in this respect from Dufay, in the same
manner that Haydn learned from Mozart. Such influence is perceptible
in a *Gloria*[3] which presents the plainsong in distinctly balanced phrases
and includes the familiar trope 'Spiritus et alme', set as a duo.[4]

Ex. 82

---

[1] Ibid., p. 103.   [2] Ibid., pp. 99 and 101.   [3] Ibid., p. 16.
[4] The plainsong of both the *Gloria* and its trope can be found in *Graduale Sarisburiense*, pl. 14*.

(Spirit and kindly comforter of orphans. O Lord God, Lamb of God, Son [of the Father] . . .)

It should be noted above how consistently the third is used over and over again as a melodic and harmonic interval. It is introduced on the word 'Deus' in an exposed position after a rest—a device that arrests our attention as surely today as it must have impressed Dufay, who used it in works belonging to his middle period. The beginning of the three-part section on a full triad is noteworthy for its sonority, although only three parts are used, and the suspended seventh on 'Domine' and the unexpected major third on 'Dei' enhance the effect with striking harmonic colour.

By far the largest group of works belongs to the second category, where Dunstable gives free rein to his melodic inspiration. The supporting voices move independently, and they seldom imitate the treble. Many motets of the new liturgical sort with a single text (mostly antiphons of Our Lady) illustrate this type, as for example 'Sancta Maria non est',[1] 'Alma redemptoris', 'Beata Dei genitrix', 'Sub tuam protectionem', 'Salve mater', 'Salve regina' (with the trope 'Virgo mater', again set as a duo) and 'Sancta Maria succurre'. Their great popularity can be inferred from the fact that several of these occur

[1] *Musica Britannica*, viii, p. 121, and Davison and Apel, op. cit., no. 62.

four or five times in the sources.[1] The 'free treble' style appears also in several Masses, e.g.:

Ex. 83[2]

(And on earth peace to men of good will. We praise Thee. . . .)

The exposed position of the third at 'Laudamus te' should again be noted. The suave melody with its charming modulation is accompanied in $^6_3$ style, even to the point of simple consecutives. The opening phrase recalls the *Gloria* Vatican VII, but the resemblances are not literal enough to be considered definite quotations, especially as the rest of the composition turns out to be original writing. The Aosta manuscript contains several other three-part settings of the Mass: a *Gloria* with telescoped text (no. 68), a *Credo* with a strongly syllabic treble in short notes (no. 94), and a *Sanctus* (no. 104). In addition, there is a *Gloria–Credo* pair (nos. 171–2) set in group contrasts for four voices. All these compositions are written in free treble style without reference to the chant.

PLAINSONG AND DECLAMATION

It is difficult at times to decide whether a composition is or is not based upon plainsong. As a great deal of so-called 'Gregorian chant' was still being written in the fifteenth century the process of original composition in plainsong and in mensural music was very much akin, and the composers succeeded so well in assimilating the one to the other that no amount of analysis can definitely extract the borrowed chant unless its model is known. As a rule the cadences give the most valid clue because at these points the plainsong and its mensural elaboration are most often identical. The theory that the works of the English school do not use simple or any embellishment is exploded

---

[1] For references to sources see *Acta Musicologica*, viii (1936), p. 111, and critical commentary to *Musica Britannica*, viii.

[2] *Musica Britannica*, viii, p. 5.

now that the Old Hall manuscript shows the opposite to be true: and the claim that they contain *canti fermi* of 'unknown origin', obscured by embellishment, argues in a circle by assuming the absence of a recognizable plainsong as proving the premise—a dangerous argument from silence. Nor do recurrences of similar melodic phrases which can be found in the course of Dunstable's *Gloria* just quoted, and in many other of his compositions, furnish conclusive evidence of a *canto fermo*: they may be due to unity in style and the formalized methods of composition which worked with stereotyped patterns, cadence formulas, and repetitive ideas. Such repeats can be found in an anonymous *Credo*,[1] which has been said to elaborate an unknown *canto fermo*. The repeats in this composition look, however, quite different from those that would be normally found in a composition based on a plainsong, as for example in Excetre's *Gloria*, mentioned above (p. 178). Triadic patterns in the melody, declamatory sentences, wide leaps and wide range are marks of free invention, though no one of them is necessarily infallible. To deny the existence of freely invented compositions would be to deny a distinct musical trend of the period; for the desire to infuse the chant with individual melody became so strong precisely because free invention had already been widely practised.

The declamatory motet is perhaps Dunstable's most original contribution to the development of form. Here the textual declamation actually generates the musical rhythm, and the numerous repeated notes testify to the predominance of rhythmic considerations over melodic. The declamatory sections stand between extended melismas on the first or last words, which are obviously relics of the *cauda* of the conductus (see vol. II, pp. 326–8). Dunstable broke with the rigidly regular note values and the uniform texture of the conductus, and adopted a looser fabric and a more flexible and varied rhythm. The voices may recite the words either together or successively. Although the treble still predominates, the other voices now gain equality and independence, and for that reason are also supplied with words. The classical and at the same time the most distinctive declamation motet is 'Quam pulchra es',[2] deservedly one of the best known of Dunstable's compositions. We may notice that it also ranks very high in conson-

---

[1] *Denkmäler der Tonkunst in Österreich*, xxxi, p. 90. The English origin of this piece (one of the telescoped settings) can be proved by the fact that it occurs in the Pembroke fragment.

[2] *Musica Britannica*, viii, p. 112; facsimile of the version from Bologna, Bibl. Univ. MS. 2216, ibid., p. xxi; of that from Bologna, G. B. Martini, Q 15, in H. E. Wooldridge, *Early English Harmony*, i (London, 1897), pls. 59–60.

ance. Other compositions of this type, such as 'Sancta Dei genitrix' and 'Salve regina mater mirae'[1] only occasionally have declamatory sections and otherwise incline to the 'free treble' style.

DUNSTABLE'S ISORHYTHMIC MOTETS

Dunstable was so thoroughly steeped in the European musical tradition that he did not venture to ignore the established position of the isorhythmic motet. His compositions of this kind number fourteen, if we include those that are isorhythmic only in their tenor. They are his most complex works, and show as a rule polytextuality and strict isorhythmic construction. The three-part setting of 'Veni Sancte Spiritus',[2] which is built on the first notes of the sequence 'Sancti Spiritus assit', is only partially isorhythmic, because the canon of the enigmatic tenor prescribes *cancrizans* motion, so destroying the exact duplication of the rhythmic scheme. The more famous four-part setting of the text[3] is quoted as late as Gafurius[4] as an example of the rare *modus major perfectus*. It shows the inter-relations of the motet and the trope better than any other example. The tenor voice is given the text and the music of the second and third lines of the hymn 'Veni Creator Spiritus', while the other voices sing simultaneously in the highest voice the words of the sequence 'Veni Sancte Spiritus', in the second voice a trope to it, and in the third voice the hymn-text of 'Veni Creator'. The entire motet falls into three major parts of contrasted tempo, each subdivided into two isorhythmic halves. The two corresponding *taleae* of the tenor are stated three times in progressive diminution in the ratio of 3 : 2 : 1. Although the piece has been frequently and minutely analysed its elaborate use of a borrowed chant in the highest voice has been overlooked. The introductory duets that regularly precede the entries of the tenor are not freely composed but present successively the entire melody of the hymn 'Veni Creator' line by line, with a repeat of the first two. Whenever the *canto fermo* in the tenor pauses for three *longae* the highest voice fills in the gap so that the continuity of the liturgical melody is never broken. Dunstable was obviously bent on hallowing the architecture of the form with liturgical dignity. The consistent use of plainsong in two voices is a unique feature in the entire repertory of the isorhythmic motet.

[1] *Musica Britannica*, viii, pp. 119 and 113.   [2] Ibid., p. 92.
[3] Ibid., p. 88; *The Old Hall Manuscript*, ii, p. 66. Recorded in *The History of Music in Sound* (H.M.V.), iii.   [4] *Practica Musicae* (1496), ii, chap. 7.

All the four-part motets are splendid products of a brilliant and sonorous imagination. In addition to 'Veni Sancte Spiritus' they include 'Gaude Virgo salutata' and 'Praeco praeeminentiae',[1] both noteworthy for hints of isomelic repetition, and 'Salve schema sanctitatis',[2] composed in honour of St. Catherine. The last-named seems to belong to the latest phase of Dunstable's development, by reason of its particularly adroit harmony. The lower voices are remarkably free from the awkward leaps of the usual contra-tenor, and the tenor, taken from the respond 'Virgo flagellatur' (see p. 170) is supported by a lower voice of a real bass character. Dunstable anticipates in this work the advanced type of harmony setting which we do not find fully developed until Dufay's later Masses.

MOTETS WITH DOUBLE STRUCTURE

The seventh and last category comprises works with twin or double structure, such as the motets 'Specialis virgo' and 'Ascendit Christus'[3] and above all two pairs of Mass movements. The first of these consists of a *Gloria* and *Credo*,[4] both based in their tenor on the respond 'Jesu Christe Fili'.[5] The tenor is isorhythmic and remains unchanged in both movements, although the upper parts are freely composed and have no mutual connexion. The pair unmistakably prove Dunstable's desire to unite movements of the Mass in a music-ally unified whole. Within each movement he states the tenor twice, first in augmentation and then, after an intermediary duet, in its original values, 'ut jacet' (as it stands), as can be seen in the following examples, which show the openings of the first and second state-ments of the tenor:

Ex. 84

---

[1] *Musica Britannica*, viii, pp. 74 and 78.   [2] Ibid., p. 81.
[3] Ibid., pp 86 and 148. 'Ascendit Christus' is ascribed to Dunstable in Modena, Bibl. Estense, A X i, 11 (olim lat. 471), to Forest in the Old Hall manuscript (fo. 57ᵛ), where it is incomplete.
[4] Ibid., pp. 35 and 38.   [5] *Antiphonale Sarisburiense*, pl. 249.

(*Triplum*: The Father Almighty, Maker of heaven and earth [and of all things] visible . . .

Tenor: O Jesu Christ, Son of God. . . .)

(*Triplum*: And he shall come again with glory, to judge. . . .

Motetus: Who with the Father and the Son together. . . .

Tenor: O Jesu Christ, Son of God. . . .)

Rhythmic identity and augmentation in the tenor reflect, of course, the technique of the isorhythmic motet. By extending this technique to paired groups of Mass settings, or what may be called the incipient 'cyclic' Mass, Dunstable and Leonel took the decisive step in the creation of the complete tenor Mass.

The second pair of Mass compositions is a *Credo* and *Sanctus* in the Aosta manuscript (nos. 166–7) on 'Da gaudiorum praemia',[1] the verse of the Trinity Sunday respond 'Gloria Patri genitaeque proli'.[2] These two settings are also built upon an immutable isorhythmic tenor, whose rigidity is judiciously counterbalanced by some imaginative and subtle points of imitation between the upper voices. This pairing of movements from the Ordinary led ultimately to the unified cyclic Mass. This significant musical achievement of the English school will be discussed at the end of this chapter.

[1] *Musica Britannica*, viii, pp. 41 and 43.
[2] *Antiphonale Sarisburiense*, pl. 290.

DUNSTABLE'S CONTEMPORARIES AND FOLLOWERS

As a general rule the composers of the English school of Dunstable's time and afterwards follow his concordant style. Though we have the names of many composers the extant compositions of the English school are so often anonymous that it would be rash to propose a chronological order. Only of John Pyamour (d. 1431) is it known that he was active even earlier than Dunstable. He is not represented in the Old Hall manuscript but was an almost exact contemporary of Damett. From 1420, if not before, he was Master of the Children in the Chapel Royal under Henry V (1413–22), and in 1427 was in France in the retinue of the Duke of Bedford, in whose service Dunstable was at this or some later time. The single motet by Pyamour that has survived, 'Quam pulchra es'[1] is in its long melismas reminiscent of the embellished conductus: but in other sections it anticipates the declamation motet. His vocal scoring is unusually thin: duos, and in the three-part sections frequent rests, result in continual thirds and sixths in intricate and delicate alternation and in doublings at the unison. His concordant style, his shunning of harsh appoggiaturas, and his austerely diatonic lines appear surprisingly mature as compared with the music of his contemporaries of the Old Hall manuscript. If it is permissible to judge him by this one example we can claim him as the most gifted composer next to Leonel and Dunstable.

To the names of four better-known members of the English school, John Forest, John Benet, John Bedingham, and John Plummer, can be added those of lesser-known men: Bloym (or Blome), Richard Markham, Neweland, Sandley (or Standley), Souleby, Stove (or Stone?), Tyling, and Wyvell. The oldest of these is probably Forest, whom Hothby mentions together with Leonel, Stove, Dunstable, Fich (or Fith?), Plummer, Morton, and Frye. Forest is known not only from his compositions preserved at Trent and Modena, but also from the Old Hall manuscript, where the motet 'Qualis est dilectus'[2] appears as a later addition. Forest's style is characterized by the judicious contrast of long melismas and short declamatory sections, numerous duos, and a somewhat nervous melodic line with occasional dissonances. The Modena manuscript shows him to be interested in the new type of liturgical motet. In one case he reverts to polytextuality and combines 'Alma redemptoris' and 'Anima mea liquefacta

---

[1] In Modena, Bibl. Estense, A X i, 11 (olim lat. 471), and Trent codices, no. 1526. The opening is published in *The Musical Quarterly*, xxxviii (1952), p. 39.

[2] *The Old Hall Manuscript*, ii, p. 77.

est' in a 'double motet'. Another setting of 'Anima mea liquefacta est' in the Trent codices carries the inscription 'Forest in agone composuit'. The name is erased but still just legible, and the composition is certainly English.[1] 'Tota pulchra es'[2] is a singularly mature declamation motet, in which the words are sometimes set to block $^6_3$ chords; but more frequently the declamatory rhythms are not synchronized in the separate voices, which gives the music a peculiarly restive quality. Only one of Forest's compositions, 'Gaude martyr', is isorhythmic.

John Benet wrote three isorhythmic motets, of which the three-part 'Gaude pia Magdalena'[3] deserves to be known for its vigorous, if somewhat dissonant, handling of the English idiom. One of his settings of the *Sanctus*[4] begins in typical English fashion with a duet alternating between two pairs of voices. The name of the composer is cut off in the manuscript, but the index attributes the piece to Benet. His *Kyrie* trope 'Deus creator'[5] unfolds a duo in strict canon above two instrumental parts, resulting in a four-part setting of great skill and rich sonority. In most of his Mass compositions the treble predominates, and careful attention is given to the declamation: the two supporting parts are sometimes placed in an unusually low register, as for example in a *Gloria* and *Credo* that are known from three sources.[6] Another *Gloria*[7] is conspicuous for its declamatory style: it contrasts strongly with the melismatic form of a *Sanctus* and *Agnus*[8] in Bologna, G. B. Martini, Q 15, which form a pair of related compositions. Benet also made important contributions to the growth of the cyclic Mass form.

The English section of the Modena manuscript, which contains our largest single collection of declamation motets, preserves also two compositions of this type by Stove, about whom we know no more than the reference by Hothby. Both motets set words from the Song of Songs. 'Tota pulchra es' is full of melodic freshness, ingenious use of the scale, and fanciful rhythmic patterns that are often produced by the declamation and then dissolved in long melismas. 'Ibo mihi ad montem', less declamatory than its companion piece, holds a

[1] *Denkmäler der Tonkunst in Österreich*, xl, p. 86. [2] Ibid. xl, p. 80.
[3] Oxford, Bodleian, Add. C 87. [4] Trent codices, no. 1572 [5] Ibid., nos. 107–8.
[6] Trent codices, nos. 904 and 941; Bodleian, Add. C 87; and Munich, mus. 3232a.
[7] *Denkmäler der Tonkunst in Österreich*, xxxi, p. 85.
[8] Facsimile in Wooldridge, *Early English Harmony*, pls. 51–54. The *Sanctus* is printed in J. Wolf, *Geschichte der Mensural-Notation von 1250–1460* (Leipzig, 1904), iii, No. 74, the *Agnus* in *The Oxford History of Music*, ii (1st ed., Oxford, 1905), p. 162. For the facsimile of another *Sanctus* see W. Apel, *The Notation of Polyphonic Music* (Cambridge, Mass., 1942), p. 105.

unique place among these motets because in its lowest voice it states the Gregorian antiphon note for note.[1] So flexible is the rhythm to which the chant is set, and so well is the chant assimilated to the loose texture of the composition that a pre-existing melody—it cannot be called a *canto fermo* because of its rhythmic freedom—would hardly be suspected. Of this combination of the chant with the declamation motet no parallel has so far been discovered.

The large English section of the Aosta manuscript acquaints us with a considerable number of hitherto unknown compositions of the English school, including two new composers, Neweland and Soursby (or Sovesby). They are represented, together with Blome, by three-part settings of the *Sanctus*. All elaborate the plainsong of Sarum No. 5, placed in the old-fashioned way in the lowest voice. There can be little doubt that Soursby is identical with Henry Souleby who is listed as a member of the Chapel Royal in the Wardrobe Books of Henry VI between 1446 and 1452, and also with the 'Anglicanus' of the Trent codices whose name the scribe corrupted to Sorbi. The *Sanctus* by Soursby[2] may be quoted here to exemplify the *Sanctus* settings, which are all very similar, even in the feature (often found in the English school) of writing the tenor in implied augmentation in major prolation:

Ex. 85

---

[1] *Antiphonale Sarisburiense*, pl. 528; *Paléographie Musicale*, xii, p. 361.
[2] Aosta manuscript, No. 180 (fos. 251ᵛ–3).

Other compositions of the English section of the Aosta manuscript are unfortunately anonymous, either because the copyist did not give the name, or because the names were subsequently cut off; but the English origin of several can be verified from parallel sources, such as the Old Hall and Selden manuscripts. However, there are a fair number of compositions left whose English origin is highly probable, not only because they appear side by side with English pieces but also because of their style. These include a four-part isorhythmic motet 'Cujus fructus' on an unidentified tenor; a freely composed motet 'Descendi in hortum' similar to the recently mentioned settings of the Song of Songs in the Modena manuscript; a four-part *Gloria* (no. 150) set as a *caccia* with the treble doubled in canon; a fragmentary *Sanctus* (no. 132) which probably elaborates in the missing treble the chant of Sarum No. 5; two freely composed settings of *Sanctus* (nos. 179 and 183); one or two of *Credo* (nos. 96 and perhaps 174); and two of *Agnus* (nos. 151 and 159). We find here the stereotyped English beginning, duet sections, and effective use of the third or tenth as harmonic intervals.

Other Mass settings of the English school, all fragmentary and anonymous, occur in the Pembroke fragment and in some loose leaves at Magdalen College and University College, Oxford.[1] The Trent codices give among several anonymous English compositions a few single Mass settings in free treble style by Bloym, Markham, and Sorbi.[2] The same source transmits three sacred pieces by one Christofferus Anthony, whose name sounds English. Wyvell, who seems to belong to the generation of Dunstable, is known only by a solitary motet '[Sancta] Maria virgo' in the Pembroke fragment. It is similar to three anonymous compositions of the same antiphon in the Selden manuscript,[3] which retain a conservative and somewhat discordant style, reminiscent of earlier conductus settings. The first 'Sancta Maria' of the Selden manuscript alone has a *canto fermo*

[1] Magdalen College, lat. 266–8, and University College 192. Both sets of leaves come from different periods. The former set contains motets from the late fourteenth (or early fifteenth) century, several incomplete settings of the *Credo* in score notation, the end of a three-part 'Nunc dimittis', and the 'Alleluia, Salve virgo' (also in British Museum, Egerton 3307). The latter set duplicates three Mass sections from the Old Hall manuscript. See Dom Anselm Hughes, *Medieval Polyphony in the Bodleian Library* (Oxford, 1951), p. 52, and the additions by Bukofzer in *Journal of the American Musicological Society*, v (1952), p. 56. Furthermore, both sets contain one leaf each which belonged originally to the same manuscript. Between them they transmit the fragment of a cyclic Mass.

[2] For Markham and Sorbi see *Denkmäler der Tonkunst in Österreich*, xxxi, pp. 94 and 102.

[3] Two are printed in Stainer, *Early Bodleian Music*, ii, pp. 78 and 81; the third is unpublished.

(migrant),[1] the others being freely composed. The first piece of the Selden manuscript lacks the words at the beginning, but they can be identified as the antiphon 'Mater ora filium', also set by Leonel. Neither this piece nor 'Miles Christi', nor several settings of 'Ave regina coelorum mater regis' and 'Nesciens mater', contain any reference to the Gregorian melody. They all look rather old-fashioned and affect a needlessly intricate rhythm, designed apparently to make up for the lack of harmonic interest. The York Mystery Play 'The Wefferes' (Weavers)[2] of the second half of the century contains a few short two-part settings of texts from the Song of Songs in a very primitive style. They are mentioned here not for their very slight musical value but for the interest they have as authentic examples of fifteenth-century stage music.

JOHN PLUMMER

With John Plummer, whose name is spelt variously as Plomer, Polumier, or in other ways, we come to a composer who has hitherto been passed over because very little of his music has so far been known: he must be regarded as one of the most important English composers of the period. He was Master of the Children of the Chapel Royal, in which post he served from 1440 to 1462, presumably the year of his death. As his works are preserved in both English and continental sources he must have gained recognition both at home and abroad. Though only four motets of his have come down to us they reveal a musician of very high rank. They consist of three set-tings of texts from the Song of Songs for three voices—'Descendi in hortum' and two versions of 'Tota pulchra es', and a four-part motet 'Anna mater matris'. The last-named occurs only in Bodleian Add. C 87, the recent discovery of which has substantially added to our knowledge of an obscure phase of fifteenth-century music.

Two conspicuous features mark off Plummer's compositions from those of his contemporaries: the consistently triadic nature of his melody, and the frequent use of points of imitation in all the voices. His melodic ideas are thoroughly English in character and move with a remarkably steady pulse in simple rhythms which indicate the shift from rhythmic to harmonic considerations. The motets from the Song of Songs are typical examples of the declamation motet. Only one of these, the second version of 'Tota pulchra es', is available in print,

---

[1] *Antiphonale Sarisburiense*, pl. 493.

[2] British Museum, Add. 35290. The reader should be warned that the transcriptions in L. T. Smith, *York Plays* (Oxford, 1885), pp. 517 ff., are useless.

and this only in incomplete form.[1] All three are highly melismatic, and at the same time declamatory, in sharp contrast. The declamation moves at times in lively, if plain, $^6_3$ chords, only to be interrupted by imitative melismas in simple harmony. Points of imitation are the most conspicuous feature of 'Anna mater', a piece so original and advanced for its time that it deserves to be quoted at some length. The first treble is marked optional (*ad placitum*) in the manuscript, but it is involved in the imitation, and its omission would make the duets incomplete and impair the structure of the music:

Ex. 86

[1] Stainer, op. cit. ii, p. 168. The complete version has been preserved at Trent and Modena.

(Anna, mother of Christ's mother, look kindly on us, thou that wert worthy to suckle Mary.)

The thoroughly imitative texture of the four parts is an innovation of the highest importance. At the beginning of the century imitation belonged primarily to secular music and only gradually found a place in religious composition: it had not yet become that essential part of the structure which it certainly is in Plummer's motet. For some time it has been maintained that Ockeghem was the first composer of sacred music to introduce structural imitation, in which 'everie part catcheth the point from another',[1] but the claim does not stand scrutiny.[2] It appears now that the English school in general and Plummer in particular must have taken a vital part in establishing this important innovation. The share of English composers in the evolution of imitation seems all the more logical because of their old practice of interchange of parts, which is nothing less than a primitive or incipient form of imitation. It is no mere accident that Plummer is one of the last English composers to make use of interchange of parts: in one section of 'Tota pulchra es' (second version) it even results in invertible counterpoint. It should be noticed that the points of imitation in Plummer's motets do not yet involve any change of harmony: the last fifteen bars in Ex. 86 ring the changes on the common chord of F, and strangely enough all his motets are written in the F mode and nearly all their imitative sections take place in the same settled F major chord. 'Anna mater' hardly ever moves away from that key. It falls into three large divisions with the customary second section in duple rhythm: the music of the two later sections seems to be merely a variant of the first division, and whether this is a deliberate

---

[1] Thomas Morley, *A Plaine and Easie Introduction to Practicall Musicke* (1597), p. 168; ed. R. A. Harman (London, 1952), p. 278.

[2] See Van den Borren, *Études sur le XVe siècle musical*, p. 170.

attempt at variation or only the natural result of the triadic motives is hard to decide. At any rate the predominance of one key or mode and the settled harmonic background indicate that Plummer had reached only a very elementary stage in the development of structural imitation.

The last English composer of sacred music to be mentioned here is Walter Frye, who has sometimes been mistaken for a German. He was better known abroad than at home; most of his works appear in Burgundian sources, and he was probably associated with the Burgundian court in the second half of the century. His compositions include several *chansons*,[1] Masses, and motets. His three- or four-part 'Ave regina coelorum, mater regis' was a favourite motet of the period, and it has been preserved in many continental sources[2] and even in painting.[3] Its popularity is also attested by Obrecht, who borrowed the tenor (and a section of the treble) for a Mass and a motet.[4] In its song-like intimacy, expressive simplicity, and concise harmony Frye's motet closely resembles the *chanson*, and it is not by accident that it occurs in *chansonniers*. The Pepysian manuscript contains another motet of his, a setting of the sequence 'Sospitati dedit' for St. Nicholas. Frye deals with the melody[5] rather wilfully, makes his voices follow irregularly with but few cadences, and (unlike Plummer) does not care for imitation. He revives the conductus style here, but brings it skilfully into conformity with current practice by means of his mellow harmony.

THE MASS AS A UNIFIED WHOLE

In the discussion of Leonel Power and Dunstable we have already seen signs of a disposition to unify the items of the Ordinary of the Mass. The *Missa brevis* of the Egerton manuscript was undoubtedly conceived as a cyclic whole, but apart from the general similarity of style and *canto fermo* treatment the connexion between the movements was liturgical rather than musical, because the plainsongs used were liturgically but not musically related. Such liturgical unification had been known since the days of Machaut's Mass (see p. 22) and was nothing new at the time. But the idea of binding the Ordinary together by one recurring musical element arose only in the first half of the

---

[1] See pp. 131 ff.

[2] See Bukofzer, *Studies in Medieval and Renaissance Music*, p. 310, n. 162; and Plamenac, 'A Reconstruction of the French Chansonnier in the Biblioteca Colombina', *The Musical Quarterly*, xxviii (1952), p. 103; and S. W. Kenney, 'Contrafacta in the Works of Walter Frye', *Journal of the American Musicological Society*, viii (1955), p. 182.

[3] Besseler, *Die Musik des Mittelalters und der Renaissance*, pl. xiii (facing p. 200).

[4] *Werken*, ed. J. Wolf, iv, p. 64 and xvii, p. 141.

[5] *Antiphonale Sarisburiense*, pl. 360; *Variae Preces*, p. 62.

fifteenth century.[1] The means of unification were either more or less consistent motto beginnings for two or more movements, or a pre-existing tenor of liturgical (or later, secular) origin that served as the scaffold for the whole structure. In both methods the pairing of movements was the first step towards a cyclic composition. In a great many examples only the *Gloria* and *Credo*, or the *Sanctus* and *Agnus*, were composed as distinctly related pairs.

The first method can be illustrated by a complete cyclic Mass by Arnold de Lantins,[2] and by many pairs of Mass movements by his Franco-Flemish colleagues. That English composers were also familiar with the idea can be seen from a *Sanctus–Agnus* pair by Benet in Bologna, G. B. Martini, Q 15, and from a *Gloria–Credo* pair by Dunstable (Aosta, nos. 171–2). The Aosta manuscript assigns the composer's name only to the *Gloria*, but it applies without doubt to the *Credo* also. The musical similarity here consists not in a common motto beginning but in the general design and plan of the pieces. Standing both in the F mode they are noteworthy for the adroit use of group contrasts. The beginning is made by two duets for two different pairs of voices, and only after that do all the voices join together in a tutti in very similar manner, marked in both compositions by a change of time signature. The paired arrangement thus achieved is quite evident, clearer in fact than that brought about by motto beginnings which unify only the first few bars and have no bearing on the structure of the composition as whole.

While unification by means of motto or general design appeared first with composers of the Franco-Flemish school, the second method, unification by means of a borrowed or pre-existing tenor, was developed in the English school. Only the latter method really guaranteed structural unity of the whole set of movements, and this fact was quickly recognized by continental composers, who paid their English colleagues the highest form of compliment by adopting the method. For the second time in this century the course of European music was deeply affected by the English composers. The first wave of English influence had brought the chordal and sonorous English idiom to the Continent about 1420; the second, following the first at an interval of no more than fifteen or twenty years, introduced the cyclic tenor Mass which held music under its sway until well beyond the end of the century.

This significant innovation was obviously prompted by isorhythmic

---

[1] On the evidence for a still earlier essay in the linking of Mass movements, see *supra*, p. 137, n. 1; cf. also p. 144, n. 2.—*Ed.*

[2] Van den Borren, *Polyphonia Sacra* (London, 1932), nos. 1–5.

methods of composition; it is no accident that we find so many iso-rhythmic Masses in the Old Hall manuscript. It must be remembered, however, that these were as yet single Mass movements. The idea of tying several movements together by means of a single isorhythmic tenor can be seen first in the works of Dunstable and Leonel. Leonel's isorhythmic *Gloria–Credo* pair is still based on the proper plainsongs of the individual movements and thus forms the link between the earlier practice, seen in Machaut's Mass, and the later, in which the same tenor is made the foundation of several movements, as in Dunstable's pair on 'Jesu Christe Fili'. Because of their borrowed tenor these Masses are by definition compositions with double structure. Strong but unconvincing efforts have been made[1] to show that the Masses of the English school have *canti fermi* of 'unknown origin' in the treble as well. We should be on our guard against identifying as a *canto fermo* what is no more than a natural result of the fact that the trebles of the various movements are counterpoints to the same tenors. The *Credo* 'Jesu Christe' by Dunstable (Ex. 84) has been quoted as an example of such a *canto fermo* in the treble, but the reader will easily be convinced that its existence is quite imaginary.

No complete or cyclic Masses on liturgical tenors occur in the Old Hall manuscript: they appear only in such later sources as the Trent and Aosta manuscripts, and are associated there primarily with Leonel, Dunstable, and their English contemporaries. We find in the English school many isolated Mass compositions which may, of course, be the sole survivors of a pair, or even of a complete Mass. An interesting *Credo* by one Anglicanus,[2] for example, is built upon 'Alma redemptoris', which the tenor states in a fairly floriated form. Strangely enough, the formal subdivisions of the composition do not coincide with those of the liturgical melody: the main break occurs directly after 'Virgo prius', when the tenor is just in the middle of a phrase. This disregard for the melodic structure of the antiphon shows that the presentation of the chant was no longer the point of the com-position, as it had been in English descant, but that it now served as the outer framework for a free composition. It is of no small interest that the motet 'Ascendit Christus' by Dunstable or Forest,[3] which is built upon the same antiphon, breaks off at exactly the same place— a fact which may perhaps give a clue to the composer of this *Credo*. Other compositions of this type include a fragmentary *Gloria* from

---

[1] R. von Ficker, in *Studien zur Musikwissenschaft*, xi (1924), p. 45.
[2] *Denkmäler der Tonkunst in Österreich*, xxxi, p. 92.
[3] Ibid. xl, p. 53, and *Musica Britannica*, viii, p. 148. See p. 192, n. 3 *supra*.

the Pembroke fragment, also anonymous, founded on the respond
'Virgo flagellatur', and a *Sanctus* by Benet[1] which elaborates in its
tenor the respond 'Jacet granum', a specifically English melody in
honour of St. Thomas of Canterbury. The same plainsong underlies
a *Gloria* and *Sanctus*[2] which form a closely related pair in virtue of
the tenor and the identical motto beginnings. Both movements are
probably by Benet also, the *Gloria* being listed in the Aosta manuscript under his name. As the combination of *Gloria* and *Sanctus* is
somewhat irregular it may be surmised that they represent the remains
of a complete cyclic Mass, now otherwise lost. The same may be said
of Dunstable's isorhythmic *Credo–Sanctus* pair on 'Da gaudiorum
praemia'. Another *Sanctus* and *Agnus*[3] on the respond (and verse)
of 'Regnum mundi' constitute a genuine pair. Its author is Driffelde,
about whom nothing is known. He has been considered English,[4]
and his style, as well as his name, seems to confirm the supposition.

THE EARLIEST CYCLIC MASSES

The earliest tenor Mass that has come down to us in complete form
is the 'Missa Alma redemptoris mater' by Leonel Power.[5] In all four
movements—there is no *Kyrie*, as in nearly all cyclic Masses of English
origin—the tenor recurs in strictly isorhythmic fashion. There are two
long sections in triple and duple metre respectively, only the introductory duets standing out of the rigid scheme. In his division of the
antiphon Leonel, like the Anglicanus of the anonymous *Credo*, completely ignores the phrase structure and uses the notes only as structural support. He breaks off arbitrarily in the middle of the word
'po[pulo]' and by so doing wrenches the chant out of its proper
mode. He barely suggests a motto beginning, which indeed is unnecessary in view of the unifying tenor. The Mass as a whole is written
in the typical English idiom, unmistakable especially in the duet sections. There are, however, some noteworthy frictions between the
voices, often caused by the sustaining notes of the tenor. Leonel
differs in this point from Dunstable, who in his Mass 'Da gaudiorum
praemia' (see p. 193) again betrays his classical attitude by setting the
sustained notes in his usual consonant fashion.

---

[1] Trent codices, no. 969.   [2] Ibid., nos. 21 and 982.
[3] Ibid., nos. 973 and 1552.   [4] Wolf, *Geschichte der Mensural-Notation*, i, p. 367.
[5] Printed in *Documenta Polyphoniae Liturgicae*, ser. 1, no. 2 (Rome, 1947), ed. L.
Feininger. There is a startling clash of B♭ against B♮ in the *Benedictus* (bar 105), which
according to the editor is explicitly marked in the manuscript. While the unreliable
Trent codices support this claim, the Aosta manuscript does not: the copyist merely
forgot to insert the key signature of one flat. A B♮ is expressly called for in the tenor,
but only at a later place—which clearly implies that the first B must be flat.

A second complete cyclic Mass is the 'Missa Rex saeculorum',[1] based on an antiphon in honour of St. Benedict.[2] The work is ascribed in the Aosta manuscript (nos. 40 and 65) to Dunstable, in Trent codex 92 to Leonel; whoever its composer, it is a composition of the very highest order. In its omission of the *Kyrie* the Mass resembles the 'Missa Alma redemptoris', but it differs in having a non-isorhythmic tenor, which employs the whole chant. As in the pairs by Benet and Driffelde mentioned above, the rhythm and elaboration of the tenor subject vary from movement to movement, a treatment which allowed greater flexibility and variety, and was in fact the method favoured in the later development of the cyclic Mass. It should be noted that the rigid, as well as the flexible, treatment is evidently as old as the cyclic Mass itself, for either method appears in the two earliest examples on record. A further point of interest is the fact that the primitive stage of the form, the grouping in pairs, is still clearly discernible in the 'Missa Rex saeculorum'. Though the same tenor underlies all the movements, *Gloria* and *Credo* on the one hand, *Sanctus* and *Agnus* on the other, are closely akin in their subdivisions, time signatures, and duet sections. The first pair begins with a long introductory duet anticipating in the *Credo* the melody of the chant and thus effectively preparing the entry of the tenor; while the second pair introduces it at once. The openings of the *Sanctus* and *Agnus*:

Ex. 87

[1] *Musica Britannica*, viii, p. 47.　　　　[2] *Paléographie Musicale*, xii, p. 301.

show that the composer uses great freedom in giving rhythmical shape
to the tenor, but keeps close to the chant melodically. As a rule the
tenor is set out in typical *canto fermo* manner, but sometimes it adopts
the rhythmic animation of the free voices.

A different technique is employed in another Mass printed as the
work of 'Dunstable–Leonel'[1] under the questionable assumption that
the two are one and the same composer. This hypothesis is contra-
dicted by all major sources, which in principle distinguish between
Leonel and Dunstable, some conflicting ascriptions notwithstanding.
The authorship of the work is indeed a troublesome matter: two
movements are anonymous in Trent, where the *Credo* is assigned to
Leonel and the *Sanctus* to Dunstable. Aosta does not give the *Credo*
at all and ascribes the other movements (nos. 145, 154, 155) to Benet.
Only the latter three movements have a motto beginning in common.
It seems that at present Benet has the strongest claim to the authorship. The work is apparently not based on a borrowed tenor: the
melody changes in each movement and the contour does not suggest
a liturgical origin. Composed partly in sustained, and partly in florid
style, it behaves somewhat like the borrowed tenor of a cyclic Mass.
Apart from certain similarities to be found between many freely
composed tenors in the same mode the movements agree only in the
first few notes of the tenor, especially in the *Sanctus* and *Agnus*, where
they even appear in identical rhythm. In other words the first notes

[1] *Denkmäler der Tonkunst in Österreich*, xxxi, p. 119, and *Musica Britannica*, viii, p. 138.

form an isorhythmic motto. While the *Sanctus* and *Agnus* undoubtedly constitute a pair, and are so entered in the Trent codices, the pairing of the *Gloria* and *Credo* is less clear. In favour of joining the two latter movements are the facts that they both begin with a duet section, like the corresponding parts of the Mass 'Rex saeculorum', and that they correspond in other sections also. Whatever the connexion between the pairs may be, the *Sanctus* and *Agnus* offer sufficient evidence that the work stands midway between motto and tenor Mass. The extension of the motto to a freely composed but sustained tenor remains a relatively isolated experiment. Masses on unborrowed tenors do occur in the English school but they did not attain a leading position. The future belonged to the tenor Mass, the typical cyclic Mass of the fifteenth century.

LATER CYCLIC MASSES

English composers of the younger generation continued in the path that Leonel and Dunstable had broken. John Bedingham, who was apparently active during the middle of the century, is known to have written two cyclic Masses. Bodleian, Add. C 87 preserves a fragmentary *Sanctus* which appears in complete form in the Trent codices, but as part of a complete Mass (nos. 225–9). As all its movements are connected by a motto beginning the whole Mass can be ascribed to Bedingham with at least reasonable certainty. The tenor has no designation and does not give the impression of being borrowed. We meet with a different situation in Bedingham's second Mass,[1] which is built not on a liturgical tenor but on the *ballade* 'Dueil angoisseus' by Binchois.[2] It is probable that the Masses on secular motives came somewhat later than those on liturgical tenors. The three Masses on 'O rosa bella'[3] and the unpublished Mass on 'Puisque m'amour' are anonymous, and the mere fact that they make use of English music does not entitle us to regard them as English. Unlike these Masses Bedingham's work is not a very strict *canto fermo* Mass. Although he evidently keeps close to the tenor of Binchois's *ballade* no single voice is consistently borrowed and carried through the entire work. Rather he alludes from time to time to the beginning of the treble and tenor and sometimes even the contratenor of his model, feeling free to quote vaguely and to continue with freely invented passages.

[1] *Denkmäler der Tonkunst in Österreich*, xxxi, p. 127. The edition does not include the 'Benedicamus Domino' (Trent codices, no. 216), which seems to belong to the cycle. It follows directly in the manuscript and begins in all the voices exactly like the section 'Cum Sancto Spiritu'.

[2] Ibid. vii, p. 242; E. Droz and G. Thibault, *Poètes et musiciens du XVe siècle* (Paris, 1924), p. 25; W. Rehm, *Die Chansons von Gilles de Binchois* (Mainz, 1957), p. 45.

[3] *Denkmäler der Tonkunst in Österreich*, xi (1), p. 1.

That the motto which begins all the movements is taken almost literally from the opening of the *ballade* is obvious, but references to the opening of the second part should not be overlooked. Our example shows this beginning with a corresponding section from the *Credo* in juxtaposition:

Ex. 89

(Unhappy heart, which lives obscurely. . .)

(And was incarnate by the Holy Ghost.)

Bedingham here approaches the technique of the so-called 'parody' Mass more nearly than many of his contemporaries, and even if this work cannot be styled an early example of the form it shows the idea in embryo.

The Trent codices also contain a Mass without a title ('sine nomine', or 'innominata' is the customary way of describing such a Mass) by Sandley,[1] who is otherwise known only by the motet 'Virgo praefulgens'.[2] The tenor of this Mass is not a borrowed melody, but a canonic voice which yields the contratenor in a very peculiar fashion. A similarly contrived part can be found in the motet 'Quae est ista' of the Trent codices[3] for which Sandley's authorship has been suggested. Two other English Masses, however, show strict *canto fermo* treatment, one upon 'Requiem aeternam'[4] and the other upon 'Quem malignus spiritus'. The former consists of *Gloria*, *Credo*, and *Sanctus*, of which the *Credo* alone has been preserved completely. The state of the Bodleian fragment indicates that the Mass may have originally included the *Agnus*, now lost. The Mass is for four voices, and in its full triads, occasional imitations, and clear progressions shows considerable ease in four-part writing. The motto beginnings and

[1] Trent codices, nos. 436–40, printed in *Documenta Polyphoniae Liturgicae*, ser. 1, no. 6 (Rome, 1949).
[2] Marix, *Les Musiciens de la cour de Bourgogne*, p. 227 (incorrectly attributed to Binchois).   [3] No. 576.   [4] Oxford, Bodleian, Add. C 87.

the tenor both serve to unify the movements, in all of which the
introit of the Requiem Mass recurs unchanged in sustained notes of
exactly the same rhythm, without any melodic elaboration. The use
of an isorhythmic Mass tenor is extended here to an entire four-part
Mass. The individual movements fall, like the tenor, into three parts
of contrasted time signatures, and all would be of exactly the same
length were it not for the duet sections in which the tenor is silent.

The three-part Mass 'Quem malignus spiritus' is preserved in the
Trent codices[1] and (nearly complete) at Cambridge:[2] it comprises all
the five parts of the Ordinary, including a troped *Kyrie*. Though the
liturgical source of the tenor has so far eluded identification it is
clear that the borrowed chant is stated once in each movement with
a great deal of rhythmic variation but hardly any melodic change.
The first seven notes only of the *canto fermo* recur in identical rhythm
for the first twenty bars of each movement, but the continuation
adopts a strikingly varied rhythm each time. In the following example
the opening bars of the *Kyrie*, *Credo*, and *Agnus* have been superimposed in order to show how the composer managed to give variety
to the same tenor:

Ex. 90

Ky - rie   rex   ge - ni - tor

Pa-   -trem   o - mni-po - ten-tem

Qui   tol -

[*Quem malignus spiritus*]

<hr />

[1] Nos. 897, 935, 962, 963.   [2] University Library, Ii. v. 18.

(*Kyrie*: O Lord, King, Father unbegotten . . .
Credo: The Father Almighty, Maker of heaven and earth . . .
Agnus: Who takest away . . .)

It will be seen that the motto beginning does not apply to the *Credo*, the composer having quoted in the treble the opening of the familiar plainsong. We have here one of the rare instances where the use of a double *canto fermo* in a Mass setting can actually be proved:[1] however, this isolated and short occurrence suggests that the composer was moved to use the plainsong only because at this place it could easily be combined with the principal *canto fermo*. Other quotations occur only when the latter pauses. The rebus 'joy ⌐ langour ■' which occurs in varying forms at each item in the Cambridge manuscript suggests the possibility that the composer may be identical with the Joie of the Trent codices.

Fragments from another cyclic Mass for three voices on an unidentified tenor have been preserved in two leaves from two sets of fly-leaves in Magdalen College and University College, Oxford, mentioned above (p. 197). By a fortunate coincidence these stray

---

[1] For another example, by Regis, see C. Lindenburg, *Het Leven en de Werken van Johannes Regis* (Amsterdam, 1939).

leaves can be matched and give us the *Credo* almost complete and fragments of the *Gloria* and *Sanctus*. The tenor of this Mass is not isorhythmic, and the style of the composition suggests a date of *c*. 1450. From the same period come two fly-leaves in the Coventry Leet Book[1] which contain fragments of Dufay's 'Missa Caput' and of an anonymous cyclic Mass for four voices, presumably of English origin. Its undesignated tenor can be identified as the respond 'Tu es Petrus'.

A Burgundian manuscript at Brussels[2] contains (in addition to some late Masses by Dufay and compositions by Busnois and others) four or more Masses by English composers. One, beginning with the *Kyrie* trope 'Deus creator', is ascribed to a certain Richard Cox (Cockx) about whom we have no biographical information: three others are by Walter Frye. Only one of Frye's Masses, that on the respond 'Nobilis et pulchra',[3] includes a troped *Kyrie* with the same text as that by Cox. The four-part Mass 'Flos regalis' and the three-part Mass on the respond 'Summae Trinitati'[4] omit the *Kyrie* in the customary English fashion. Frye builds his Masses upon *canti fermi* which recur in each movement with some melodic and rhythmic variation without being consistently set off from the other voices. Like Cox he uses motto beginnings, but very little imitation except in some two-part sections. In common with many other English Masses, those by Cox and Frye omit some of the words of the Creed: so do two other Masses in the same manuscript, which make considerable use of $\frac{6}{3}$ style, suggesting their English origin. The plainsong tenor of the Mass 'Summae Trinitati' by Frye stands apart from the others by being almost strictly isorhythmic. Moreover it is found also, though with a different text, in the anonymous motet 'Salve virgo mater pia' of the Trent Codices (no. 240). A closer comparison reveals that the rhythm of the tenor and the motto of the upper voices are identical in both compositions. It is more than probable therefore that they are both by the same author. The motet evidently served as the model of the cyclic Mass since short two- and three-part sections have been bodily taken over. The opening phrase of the motet appears as the motto of all movements, and in the further course of the composition there are obvious references to the model. This application

[1] Facsimile in Bukofzer, 'Caput Redivivum: A New Source for Dufay's Missa Caput', in *Journal of the American Musicological Society*, iv (1951), p. 97.

[2] Bibl. Royale, 5557. See Van den Borren, op. cit., p. 208, and *Acta Musicologica*, v (1933), p. 68. See also S. Kenney, 'Origins and Chronology of the Brussels MS. 5557', in *Revue Belge de Musicologie*, vi (1952), p. 75.

[3] *Antiphonale Sarisburiense*, pl. x. The title and discussion of this and the following Mass in Van den Borren, op. cit., p. 211, need correction.

[4] Ibid., pl. 572.

of parody technique to the cyclic Mass (in combination with a *canto fermo*) is remarkably early. In his parody treatment Frye goes much further than Bedingham does in his Mass 'Dueil angoisseus' (see p. 208), and the only reason why Frye's composition cannot be called a full-fledged parody Mass is that the borrowings seem to be more heavily concentrated in the *Gloria* than in the subsequent movements. However, the example is valuable testimony to the fact that English composers had their share in the development of parody technique.

VII

DUFAY AND HIS SCHOOL

By Charles Van den Borren

THE SIGNIFICANCE OF DUFAY

THE title of this chapter needs a word of explanation. When we use the word 'school' we are tempted to draw a mental picture of the head of this or that school as a master surrounded by his disciples, teaching them his art in a more or less regular course of instruction; and this implies some degree of stability in mutual relationship. Nothing, however, could be less true of Guillaume Dufay (c. 1400–74). The wide extent of his influence arises solely from the fact that in the century in which he lived long-distance communication between composers was more frequent than we might be tempted to suppose. Renowned for the greatness of his genius, Dufay's name was known to all. Sought after by the great ones of the earth, not only in the Church but also in the royal, princely, and baronial courts of the Burgundian Netherlands, of France and of Italy, he moved about from youth to old age with the utmost freedom, riding over hill and dale from one court to another in the retinue of the Pope or the Duke of Savoy on his travels, and taking an active part in the civil or ecclesiastical functions attendant upon these comings and goings.

Thus it came about that he chronicled in song the affairs both great and small of Europe's social and religious life. When barely twenty years old he was called upon to celebrate the wedding of Theodore, son of the Byzantine Emperor Emmanuel Palaeologus, with Cleophe Malatesta of Rimini ('Vasilissa ergo')[1] and in 1423 that of Carlo Malatesta, Lord of Pesaro, with Vittoria di Lorenzo Colonna, niece of Pope Martin V ('Resveillies vous et faites chiere lye').[2] In 1436 he composed the delightful motet 'Nuper rosarum / Terribilis est'[3] for the consecration of the Cathedral at Florence, Santa Maria del Fiore. Another motet, 'Magnam me gentes / Nexus amicitiae / Haec est vera fraternitas',[4] records an agreement made between Berne and

---

[1] *Opera Omnia*, ed. Guillaume de Van and Heinrich Besseler, fasc. 2, p. 1.

[2] André Pirro, *Histoire de la musique de la fin du XIVᵉ siècle à la fin du XVIᵉ* (Paris, 1940), p. 59, and Besseler, 'Neue Dokumente zum Leben und Schaffen Dufays', *Archiv für Musikwissenschaft*, ix (1952), pp. 162–3.

[3] *Opera Omnia*, p. 70.

[4] Ibid., p. 77.

Fribourg to provide help for the Duke of Savoy, who was threatened by the Armagnacs; while the fall of Constantinople in 1453 was commemorated in a series of Lamentations (1454) of which one at least has been preserved, 'Tres piteulx / Omnes amici ejus'.[1] Lastly the motet 'Ave regina coelorum',[2] destined for his own deathbed and containing a personal reference ('miserere tui labentis Dufay'), shows that he was mindful of his responsibilities as a canon both of Cambrai and of Mons.

This continuous association with the living history of his time, due to the abundant recognition of his genius by the most influential persons, explains why his works have been preserved so extensively on the Continent. The most important manuscripts are those which have their origin in Italy, the country which in his youth had been the chief scene of his achievements. It is therefore not at all surprising that modern historians have described the first sixty years of the fifteenth century as 'the age of Dufay'. He was the dominating musical personality of the time, and he blazed the trail for his contemporaries and followers by the richness and variety of his inventions, and the masterly skill with which he turned them to account by synthesis and adaptation—the privilege of all great innovators. It is in this sense, then, that we must understand the expression 'the school of Dufay'.

The greatness of Dufay is before everything else due to this catholicity of outlook. Though a priest and canon and incumbent of many benefices he did not hesitate to entertain his listeners with French *ballades*, *rondeaux*, and *virelais*, where the courtly mind of rhetoricians gave itself free rein, with a spontaneous grace rarely found in the more formal poetry of the second half of the century. Falling under the spell of the Italian tongue, he found accents which sometimes touch the sublime for the purpose of expressing the sweetness and geniality of the language: for example, in his 'Vergine bella'[3] where Petrarch's verses are arrayed in truly ethereal music. In the sphere of sacred music, the motets, Masses, and Mass movements follow one another in his output with continual care for variation of form; and by this means the decorative and expressive quality of the treatment keeps the interest of the subject-matter fresh. Lastly, his refusal to be frozen in immutable formulas shows itself as an essential

---

[1] Pirro, op. cit., p. 84. It occurs in Florence, Bibl. Riccardiana, MS 2794.

[2] Reproduced in F. X. Haberl, 'Wilhelm du Fay', *Vierteljahrsschrift für Musikwissenschaft*, i (1885); transcription by Besseler, *Capella*, i (Kassel, 1950), no. 4. Recorded in *The History of Music in Sound* (H.M.V.), iii.

[3] Ed. Besseler, *Das Chorwerk*, xix, p. 7. See Charles Van den Borren, *Guillaume Dufay* (Brussels, 1925), p. 305. See further, p. 230 *infra*.

characteristic of the man. We may truly say that from beginning to end of his career he was beset by the urge to enrich his art from new points of view, in accord with that advance of technique and aesthetic perception which is seen in the new generation of Ockeghem and Busnois.

THE WORLD OF MUSIC IN DUFAY'S EARLY YEARS

Dufay's entry on the stage about 1420 coincides with the end of a transitional period between the *ars nova* of the fourteenth century and the development of polyphony in the first half of the fifteenth, of which Dufay himself, Dunstable, and Binchois are the most notable representatives. The intervening time produced composers of only second rank, among whom Johannes Ciconia (see p. 147), a native of the principality of Liège, holds a special position in virtue of his reaction against the surrounding vagueness, shown by his search for clarity and logic, the sense of which most of his contemporaries seemed to have lost. In France and Italy the successors of Machaut and Landini were lost in the empty pursuit of subtlety. The notation of the time, especially as it appears in the manuscripts Chantilly 1047 and Modena, Bibl. Estense, lat. 568 (see p. 141), well displays the tendencies of a period when artificiality swamped spontaneous art. The isorhythmic motet, the highest achievement of medieval rationalism, reached its climax during Dufay's prentice years (*c.* 1410–20), with works in which the quasi-mathematical construction arouses more admiration than pleasure. In Italy, the well-spring from which flowed the stream of madrigals, *ballades*, and *cacce* in the fourteenth century steadily dried up: while the last men to employ *ars nova* followed an ephemeral fashion by being content to set French texts of alien interest in a musical style where preciosity contends with pedantry.

It was in a Europe given over to these decadent tendencies that Dufay made his début. He was initiated into the world of music as a choirboy in Cambrai Cathedral, under such masters as Richard de Loqueville and Nicholas Grenon,[1] whose motets and *chansons* seem to be respectable but undistinguished specimens of the Gothic tradition in its declining years. But Cambrai was for him the scene of his apprenticeship to a high and honourable career, since its bishop, Pierre d'Ailly, quickly singled him out from among the alumni of the cathedral. There can be no doubt that he owed the flying start of his brilliant career to the long-sighted patronage of this illustrious

[1] For examples by Grenon, see J. Marix, *Les Musiciens de la cour de Bourgogne* (Paris, 1937), pp. 1 ff. and 233.

churchman—a career which, because of the frequent moves it involved, brought him into touch with widely differing environments, where his receptive nature had splendid opportunities for assimilating the most up-to-date discoveries in musical composition. In other words, Dufay was subjected to a number of influences, the chief being—in addition to the French tradition with which he had been imbued at Cambrai—those of Italy and England. Upon a solid foundation of the French *ars nova*, still redolent of the medieval spirit, foreign techniques were naturalized in his brain: assimilated and applied, they produced a new style, a preparation for the break with the Gothic tradition—a style which the great Netherland school, of which Ockeghem was the chief and best-known exponent in its earlier years, made its own in the latter half of the century.

It is impossible to determine exactly the time that Dufay spent in Italy. There is no doubt that he lived there for many years between 1420 and 1440. Not only would he have met there more than one master of the declining *ars nova*, but he would also surely have established contact with the work of the fourteenth-century composers, such as is contained, e.g. in the famous fifteenth-century manuscript owned by the Florentine organist Antonio Squarcialupi (see p. 47), whom he knew personally. It was from this music, whose charm is lighter and more supple than the French, that Dufay undoubtedly acquired a trend which enabled him to avoid the angularity and complexity of the Gothic style, and to enjoy an easier technique, more free from that rather rugged stiffness which is generally distinctive of French polyphony in the later part of the fourteenth century and the earlier part of the fifteenth.

THE NEW STYLE OF FIFTEENTH-CENTURY MUSIC

On the other hand (as we have already seen) the influence of Dunstable and other English composers was felt by both Dufay and Binchois (see pp. 160 and 165). With Dufay the effect of this influence was chiefly shown in religious music, while the Italians expressed it more usually in the field of secular composition. But on the whole the result is the same: a more imaginative and natural development in melody and, at the same time, an easier and more supple harmonic contact between the contrapuntal voices.

To sum up, what characterizes the polyphony of Dufay's period in contrast to that of the preceding generation is an idea of music more related to human feelings, whose ornamental aspects were completed from now on by a more or less unconsciously emotional element, tending to enlarge the horizon of the creative artist—and that not only in the matter of technique, but also in the power of expression. There can be no doubt that a new era opened with Dunstable and Dufay, in the course of which the delicately wrought miniatures of the older period passed on into a fuller life which more and more resembles the fresco. On the other hand 'art for art's sake', which had made its appearance in the work of the fourteenth century, gave way imperceptibly to a conception in which rules of composition were accompanied by inspiration, the results of which reveal more directly the personality of the composer.

During the first half of the fifteenth century Dufay stands out as the principal witness to this development, without whom the subsequent history of the art of counterpoint would probably have taken a different course. Beside him Dunstable, whose chief activity is closely contemporary with that of Dufay,[1] plays a secondary part in that his representative compositions are confined to a limited sphere. With this limitation we may contrast the catholicism of Dufay, whose compositions range in all directions: we should search in vain for equal versatility in the works (so far discovered or identified) of the English composer. This variety is also lacking in Binchois, the third great name of this generation, a man who thoroughly deserved the esteem in which he was held by his contemporaries, along with Dufay and Dunstable. But while the fame of Dunstable rests chiefly on his church music, that of Binchois comes from his secular *chansons*, which have a distinctive originality.

THE SCHOOLS OF LIÈGE AND CAMBRAI

It is apparent from what has been said that the polyphony of the first half of the fifteenth century grew very largely from international contacts, helped by incorporation of the various techniques used in France, Italy, and England by the leading men—a fact which does not exclude the persistence and active influence of more or less ancient local traditions. For example, the schools of Liège and Cambrai— especially the former—had behind them a distinguished past which, though it unfortunately survives only in isolated examples, proved to be unusually fruitful in the field of instruction. It is impossible to explain the invasion of Italy by the musicians of Liège and Hainault (to which ancient *Comté* Cambrai belonged) during the first quar-

---

[1] There is little ground for the common opinion which considers Dunstable as belonging to an earlier generation, although he died twenty-one years before Dufay.

ter of the fifteenth century without admitting that these men must have undergone a thorough training in their own country, from which they were called to the service of Popes and Italian princes. Ciconia, Arnold and Hugo de Lantins, Brasart, and others came from Liège, while Dufay arrived in Italy fully equipped with the knowledge he had acquired in the choir-school of Cambrai.

The importance of the schools of Liège and Cambrai is shown by the principal manuscripts which contain the polyphonic repertory of the Continent for the first half of the fifteenth century: those compiled about 1430–40 in the black notational system, such as Bologna, G. B. Martini, Q 15,[1] and Bibl. Univ. 2216, or those written slightly later in void or white notation, such as Oxford, Bodleian, Canonici misc. 213, Aosta, or Trent, Castel del Buon Consiglio, 87 and 92. These collections are essentially international in character, though written in Italy, and it is noticeable that they allot the largest space to composers from one or other of these two schools; at the head of them is Dufay—'luna totius musicae', as he was described about the time of his death by Loyset Compère in his motet 'Omnium bonorum plena'.

MOTETS, SACRED AND SECULAR

The types of music written in this period were, in the sphere of sacred music, the Mass and the motet; in secular music, the motet and the *chanson*, the latter term being taken to include differing forms—*rondeau*, *ballade*, *virelai*, &c.—with vernacular texts. In the time of Dufay the motet was still the common property of sacred and secular music, just as it had been in the *ars antiqua* of the thirteenth century and the *ars nova* of the fourteenth. The chief difference in the fifteenth century was that the motet tended more and more to discard French texts in favour of Latin. Most of the Latin texts are drawn from the Proper of the Mass: settings of the *Magnificat*, the Passion choruses, and such liturgical pieces as 'Asperges' and 'Vidi aquam', occur also. Magnificats are usually written in a fauxbourdon style adapted for chanting, e.g. those of Dufay and Binchois. This style is also found in the metrical hymns of the same period, of which Dufay left some specimens. There are other Latin motets beside those for liturgical use, written for special occasions, such as Dufay's 'Nuper rosarum' (1436) (see pp. 214 and 227) for the inauguration of Santa

---

[1] Referred to by its old number, Liceo Musicale 37, in a great deal of musicological literature.

Maria del Fiore, or 'Ecclesiae militantis / Sanctorum arbitrio / Bella canunt'[1] in honour of Pope Eugenius IV.

In secular music the motet, whether political or ceremonial, assumed very different aspects. Sometimes it was written entirely on Latin texts, e.g. the epithalamium 'Vasilissa ergo' or the Berne-Fribourg motet 'Magnam me gentes'; sometimes it combined a French text with a Latin tenor, as in the lament for the Fall of Constantinople: 'Tres piteulx / Omnes amici ejus'. These examples are all from the pen of Dufay, and they betray in both their external nature and their internal structure the intention of getting away from the stereotyped formulas of *ars nova*. These formulas had reached the utmost limits of rigidity under the successors of Machaut in the earliest years of the fifteenth century. With its tenor, contratenor, and two upper voices designed on a purely mathematical plan, the isomelic-isorhythmic motet (see p. 171) actually moved in a closed circle, which had to be broken if the rights of spontaneous inspiration were to be safeguarded. Such men as Dufay and Dunstable recognized this well enough, although they went on making use of the isomelic and isorhythmic formulas, especially when these would improve the structure of their motets. On this firm foundation they reserved to themselves entire liberty to make use of anything that might help them in the matter of development or ornamentation. Dufay in particular employs the technique, which belongs more especially to Dunstable and the English contemporaries, of enriching the Gregorian chant, usually in the upper voice, with embroideries which adorn without destroying its essential melodic qualities.[2] On the other hand, in one and the same piece one finds, in Dufay and his disciples, a melody subjected to repetition but with modifications in detail according to the principle of free variation. It is easy to imagine the importance of this feature when it is realized that the whole of musical development from the fifteenth century has been endlessly nourished by this procedure of varied repetition. While the *canto fermo* is often at the top of the musical edifice, the more usual plan is to entrust it to one of the middle voices, preferably the one immediately above the bass.

In freeing itself from the traditions of *ars nova*, the motet underwent a series of dislocations which materially altered its appearance. The progressive, but far from universal, disappearance of polytextuality, the more and more varied treatment of the tenor, and finally the disappearance of the tenor altogether—these are the essential marks which characterize the process of transformation. We can see here

---

[1] *Opera Omnia*, fasc. 2, p. 82.   [2] See *supra*, pp. 161, 178, and 187.

the phenomena common to all stages of transition, where the simple is followed by the complex. The passage of time imperceptibly works round again to simplicity. This is clear enough if we look forward in imagination to the *a cappella* motet of the sixteenth century, which is a definite witness to the advance in clarity and form attained in the meantime, notwithstanding the occasional survival of the medieval tradition up to the time of Palestrina and Lassus.

METHODS OF MASS SETTING

If in the first half of the fifteenth century the motet appears to be seeking after refinement and thus breaking with tradition, by which it had been too long bound, on the other hand the polyphonic Ordinary of the Mass entered upon a period of unrivalled splendour. The texts of the Ordinary were in prose, unequal in length, and obliged to wear a musical dress in accordance with the practical needs of worship. These facts helped to decide the form of the polyphonic settings of the several sections. The form is quite variable, and it is not in the least surprising that it is related more or less closely to that of the motet—that is to say, it looks for its material and its construction wherever it can profitably find it. Sometimes it makes use of a tenor, treated in different ways according to circumstances; sometimes it does without, thus having recourse to a style of composition hitherto appropriate to secular forms. At other times it employs that homogeneity of rhythm which results from the use of the fauxbourdon in thirds and sixths, or of that succession of concords which is (rightly or wrongly) compared to the old conductus style. In other cases it returns to the technique of the *ars nova* motet, but with less rigour of form. Even the trecento *caccia* could be a source of inspiration, as in the curious *Gloria ad modum tubae* by Dufay, where the text is sung from end to end in canon at the unison, supported in the two lower voices by ostinato figures entrusted to brass instruments, and treated in their turn in canon, or rather in hocket.[1]

Naturally the greater length of the text of the *Gloria* and *Credo* compared with that of the *Kyrie*, *Sanctus*, and *Agnus* had the effect of encouraging that rapid syllabic declamation which eventually became traditional in these two items of the Ordinary. Conversely, the short texts of the *Kyrie*, *Sanctus*, and *Agnus* encouraged a similar conciseness in the music. In other cases this brevity of text led to a longer extension, through the use of a melismatic style or the insertion

[1] *Denkmäler der Tonkunst in Österreich*, vii, p. 145.

of tropes, for example, in Dufay's *Sanctus papale* and its corresponding *Agnus*.[1] The treatment of the Mass in isolated numbers was
particularly favourable to this sort of composition. What was lacking
was that unity of conception which was eventually to weld the polyphonic setting of the Ordinary into one coherent whole, planned on
more or less strict lines. The contrapuntists of the fifteenth century
were, as Chapters V and VI have shown, the first to envisage the possibilities of large-scale compositions designed with the idea of sub-
ordinating the whole to an architectural plan of harmonious proportions free from all inconsistency of style.

DUFAY'S MASSES

Dufay played a prominent part in developing the new form. The
earliest of his Masses on a single tenor appears to be the one which
uses the melody of his own *chanson* 'Se la face ay pale';[2] it is for four
voices. Its early date is suggested by the fact that the tenor is used in
accordance with a method which might be called archaic: it is given
to the lowest voice but one, is preserved there intact without alteration,
and strictly speaking exercises no influence on the thematic material
of the other voices. The work illustrates very well the principle of the
tenor as a foundation: augmented or diminished each time it occurs,
the theme stands out in contrast to the other voices with their greater
abundance of short notes, which add an ornamentation very different
from the plain presentation of the *canto fermo*. The point is not
irrelevant, since as time goes on we find less and less medieval rigour
in the treatment of a *canto fermo*. It became, in fact, increasingly
supple, until by the end of the fifteenth century the thematic thread
of the tenor was woven into the whole web of the counterpoint. This
technique, which is marked by an increasingly frequent use of imitative entry, brought about in its turn the gradual disuse of the Mass
founded on a tenor *canto fermo* and its replacement as the favourite
type in the sixteenth century by the *missa parodia*, or 'parody'
Mass. This change occurred all the more easily since patterns were
found ready-made in the polyphonic motets, *chansons*, and madrigals which provided the necessary material.

In Dufay's 'Caput' Mass[3] the *canto fermo* is taken from the final

---

[1] *Denkmäler der Tonkunst in Österreich*, vii, pp. 148 and 153.

[2] *Opera Omnia*, iii, p. 1. Besseler (ibid., pp. iii and v) maintains that the 'Missa Caput'
is older. The *chanson* 'Se la face ay pale' exists in two versions, one for three voices,
the other for four, both printed in *Denkmäler der Tonkunst in Österreich*, vii,
pp. 251–2.

[3] *Denkmäler der Tonkunst in Österreich*, xix (1), p. 17.

melisma of one of the optional antiphons for Maundy Thursday, 'Venit ad Petrum', which ends with the words: 'Domine, non tantum pedes meos, sed et manus et caput' (Lord, not my feet only, but my hands and my head). This antiphon, which is not part of the Roman rite, is found in several French and English sources. Dufay's tenor is almost identical with the Sarum version—a striking confirmation of the influence of English music on his work.[1] The layout of the parts in the 'Caput' Mass does not differ materially from that in 'Se la face ay pale'. The tenor has no echoes of its theme in the other voices. On the other hand it is intentionally free from the rule of proportion by which (in 'Se la face ay pale') repetitions, whether augmented or diminished, must always keep the exact shape of the first appearance of the theme. In place of the perfect isorhythm resulting from such a system the tenor of the 'Caput' Mass shows a breaking-up of the old symmetry and the use of rhythmic variation, while in the other voices we find arabesques which are broader, more sinuous, in short, less Gothic. In both Masses the unity created by the tenor is confirmed by the use of a brief motto theme in the treble for all the sections.[2]

The same characteristics appear in the Mass 'L'homme armé',[3] which seems to be the earliest written on this famous theme. The melody of the anonymous *chanson* has a stark simplicity and modal unorthodoxy which might appear at first sight unsuitable for a sacred work—a judgement proved false not only by the frequency of its use from the fifteenth century to the seventeenth but also by the striking success attendant on it. Here, as in the 'Caput' Mass, the *canto fermo* appears with variations of rhythm; and an additional subtlety is provided by its introduction backwards in the last section of the *Agnus*. The sections are also linked by a striking motto theme in the treble. Points of imitation occur frequently.

The Mass 'Ecce ancilla'[4] seems to have been written in 1463. The tenor is taken from two antiphons: 'Ecce ancilla' and 'Beata es Maria'.[5] This work, which belongs to the composer's old age, is notable for its modern tendencies. We find a greater number of imitative entries (occasionally drawn out so that we have the illusion of canon), homophonic progressions free from archaic sound,

---

[1] For a full discussion see M. F. Bukofzer, *Studies in Medieval and Renaissance Music* (New York, 1950), pp. 226 foll. See also F. Ll. Harrison, 'An English Caput', *Music and Letters*, xxiii (1952), pp. 203 ff.

[2] On further relationships between the upper parts of the various sections of the Masses 'Se la face ay pale' and 'Caput', see H. C. Wolff, *Die Musik der alten Niederländer* (Leipzig, 1956), pp. 30 ff.—*Ed.*

[3] *Opera Omnia*, iii, p. 33.   [4] *Ibid.*, p. 66.

[5] *Antiphonale Monasticum* (Paris, 1934), pp. 223 and 207.

in some places dominant cadences replacing the old 'fauxbourdon' cadence, and rhythmical experiments which antedate those of Obrecht and Josquin. All this shows clearly how at this period of his life Dufay was gradually freeing himself from the Gothic tradition and exploring the innovations of Ockeghem and his contemporaries.

This new orientation is shown even more decisively in the Mass 'Ave regina coelorum',[1] where Dufay adopts a technique which may be compared with that of the yet unborn *missa parodia*. It draws its thematic material not only from the melody of the antiphon of Our Lady 'Ave regina coelorum'[2] but also from the material derived from it in the troped motet of the same name[3]—unless, indeed, the Mass was composed before the motet, a possibility which should not be ignored. However that may be, in this Mass the tenor is treated with a freedom not found in the preceding examples. In the Mass, as in the motet, the *canto fermo* proliferates through the whole work. This is a great help to unity, no longer hampered by the opposition between the tenor and the other more decorative voices, and still further strengthened by the fact that the melodic contour of the chief theme is directly inspired by the tenor. A work of this kind is comparable to an architectural design of perfect balance, where theoretical construction and imaginative fantasy are both brought into harmonious play.

From the very first, composers of Masses on a *canto fermo* took care not to overwork the tenor. As a general rule the *canto fermo* does not put in an appearance in each section of the Mass until some time has elapsed. The opening of each section consists of a duet by two of the upper voices, which determine in the first few bars the melodic design of the chief theme. There are similar duets at each place where the tenor has rests of greater or less length. It frequently happens also that some subdivisions of the text are without a tenor at all, so that in Masses for three voices there will be duets, in Masses for four voices trios, in which the lighter treatment is contrasted with the more frequent passages in which the *canto fermo* appears. Thus in Dufay's Mass 'Se la face ay pale' the five main divisions are introduced by duets, with the exception of the *Kyrie*; whereas the *Christe eleison, Benedictus*, and second *Agnus* take the form of trios, entirely independent of the tenor theme. It is obvious that composers were anxious to avoid monotony by making use of any methods which might introduce variety without destroying unity.

[1] *Opera Omnia*, iii, p. 91.
[2] *Antiphonale Monasticum*, p. 175.
[3] See p. 215.

A special case must be mentioned where unity is impaired by using as *canti fermi* the proper Gregorian melodies of the *Kyrie*, *Gloria*, *Credo*, *Sanctus*, and *Agnus*. It occurs in the work of a composer who was contemporary with Dufay, Reginald Liebert—a Mass which comprises a complete setting of the Proper as well as the Ordinary.[1] It is a big work for three voices, with the liturgical chant set in the highest voice, in the style of Dunstable. There is no unity in the Gregorian Ordinary beyond a general conformity of style; the different melodies were composed independently of one another at different times, and any resemblances between the separate items are purely accidental. It follows that Liebert's Mass, by its very nature, is devoid of thematic unity. If it gives the impression of unity, that is because the style is consistent from beginning to end; but in spite of the craftmanship with which the composer handles the architecture of his very Gothic style, the result is monotonous.

FRENCH AND ITALIAN SONGS

When we turn from sacred music to secular we find a rich store of French and Italian songs written in the first half of the fifteenth century, though admittedly they are less novel than the Masses or motets. The *chanson* was an art of miniature, bound by the rules of formal rhetoric which, while permitting much variety in detail, would not allow the musician to break its laws and give his inspiration free rein. The music illustrates the verse in a system of musical 'rhymes' which correspond to the metrical form of the poem. Wilful infringement of these conventions was unusual in this period. It was not until the sixteenth century that the art of song-writing was freed and the demands of poetical form became less exorbitant.

The repetition of words and parts of phrases, which was one of the chief instruments of emancipation later on, is found only here and there in the age of Dufay: among the early examples are Ciconia's 'O rosa bella'[2] (see p. 153) and Bartholomaeus de Bononia's 'Morir desio'.[3] Dufay himself seems to have used the method of repetition very sparingly, if we can judge from such of his secular music as is available for study. Indeed he makes a point of avoiding repetition of any kind,

---

[1] *Denkmäler der Tonkunst in Österreich*, xxvii (1), p. 1.

[2] Ibid., vii, p. 227. Recorded in *The History of Music in Sound*, iii.

[3] Oxford, Bodleian, Canonici misc. 213, fo. 137ᵛ. It is chiefly in Italy that we find a text treated in this manner: cf. the examples published by F. Ghisi in *Italian Ars-nova Music*, a supplement to his article under the same title in the *Journal of Renaissance and Baroque Music*, i (1946), p. 3.

not only in his *rondeaux* and *ballades*, where repetition would be against the rules of the form, but also in works such as 'Vergine bella',[1] which seem to require a constant restating of the theme. The illusion of development, especially in the *rondeaux*, is sometimes due on the one hand to refrains which consist of an unusually large number of lines, and on the other hand to the multiplication of instrumental preludes, interludes, and postludes, in which the words are enclosed as in a frame.

THE USE OF INSTRUMENTS

There is no doubt that instruments played an important part in the music of the first half of the fifteenth century. It is a matter that has given rise to much controversy; and the solution is not easy because the manuscripts themselves have little or nothing to say on the point. But we may be quite sure that unaccompanied performance of the vocal music of this period is justified only in the case of motets and portions of Masses in fauxbourdon style. In every case, especially in secular music, voices and instruments seem to have been of equal importance and were used with a freedom and variety entirely in keeping with music of so decorative a character. The composers of this period wanted above all to make the melody and the rhythm of the counterpoint stand out as clearly as possible. It is possible to do this with facility only if we make use of instruments—a practice which is supported by the sculpture and pictures of the time. We must not think of this contrast as an unalterable principle, for many pieces are quite satisfactory when played on a family of instruments of the same timbre. As a general rule each voice was doubled by an instrument: but again, we must not regard this (or any) practice as invariable. We must remember also that performance by instruments alone of music composed primarily for voices, or for voices and instruments, was much more frequent in this period than it would have been in the sixteenth century, when the so-called *a cappella* style was at the height of its development, and when instrumentalists were beginning to have an independent repertory of their own. In short, the manuscripts of the Dufay period suggest that the music was executed with whatever voices or instruments were available at any particular time or place.

In the case of sacred music the problem of instrumentation is

---

[1] See p. 230.

not quite so simple. We do know that instruments were used in churches at this time; but we do not know exactly how, on account of the absence of indications in the manuscripts and the general uncertainty of the text-underlaying. The organ and brass instruments (trombone and trumpet) at all events were mainly used for the accompaniment of Masses and motets, where strings, lutes and woodwind, more suited to the ornaments of secular music, would have been out of place. Yet it is not impossible that they were used on occasion—for example, in the consecration of the new cathedral at Florence, which was an event of sufficient importance to warrant the accompaniment of the motet 'Nuper rosarum' by *tubae*, *fides*, and *tibiae* (brass, strings, and woodwind).[1] And some of Dufay's motets, such as those in honour of the Blessed Virgin ('Salve regina', 'Flos florum', &c.), the tender character of which forbade the use of trumpets, were particularly well fitted for what were then styled *bas instrumens—vielle*, recorder, lute, and so on.[2]

DUFAY'S STYLE AND DEVELOPMENT

It will be of interest to follow Dufay over half a century (1420–70) and to trace in his works the different phases in the development of polyphony. The following extract from the motet 'Nuper rosarum',[3] written in 1436, when he was about thirty-five years old, shows the free and supple way in which he could handle the form. The *canto fermo* (in the two lower parts) is the Introit for a dedication festival, 'Terribilis est locus':[4]

Terribilis est locus iste

---

[1] *Opera Omnia*, fasc. 2, p. xxvii.
[2] For the instruments of this period see Chap. XIII.
[3] *Opera Omnia*, fasc. 2, p. 71.
[4] *Graduale Romanum* (1907), p. [63]; *Liber Usualis* (1950), p. 1250.

(. . . the splendid shrine dedicated [to thee, flowers] have continually adorned. Today the Vicar of Christ and successor of Peter, Eugenius, . . .)

About thirty-five years later Dufay wrote his Mass and motet 'Ave regina coelorum'. Ex. 92, from the second *Agnus*[1] (found also in the motet), has a simplicity, a skill, and an obvious intention to make the music fit the words which present him as a forerunner of Josquin. We may notice particularly the passage at 'miserere', with its plaintive melody and its unusual and expressive accidentals. The more formal style which we find in 'Nuper rosarum' has completely disappeared;

[1] *Opera Omnia*, iii, p. 119.

and the ornamentation has been relegated to the background, so that the newer and more humane elements stand out clearly:

(Thou that takest away the sins of the world, have mercy upon us.)

It is perhaps a little surprising, at first sight, to find composers of the fifteenth century, in spite of their ecclesiastical positions, writing

love-songs. The explanation is, in part, that it was one of the obliga-
tions incurred by a composer when he entered the service of a king
or prince. Added to which, the Middle Ages did not separate church
and lay interests as we (perhaps to our great loss) do now. There was
at this period no taste for that popular poetry which later on brought
the *chanson* of Italy, France, and the Burgundian Netherlands down
to a lower level of morality. Most of the poems set by Dufay, Binchois,
and their contemporaries retain something of the chivalry of the Middle Ages, with its formal clichés and its lack of contact with everyday
life. This conventionalism reached its extreme in Machaut and is still
very charming in the literature of the first half of the fifteenth century.
The language is gracious and picturesque, the thought not yet so involved as it was in its decadence in the days of Ockeghem and Busnois.

Dufay was attracted by the *rondeau*, *ballade*, and *virelai*, and set
them for combinations as varied as they were appropriate, finding in
them a chance to display his exquisite taste. But when we hear his
music performed, we feel that he has not entered fully into the
meaning of the words, except in some instances of his most mature
work. For example, in the *rondeau* 'Adieu m'amour' and the *virelai*
'Malheureulx cueur'[1] he treats the words more expressively than in
his earlier work, where he seems less concerned with expressing the
emotions of the text than with writing beautiful and varied music.
In his later work we find *chansons* in which the themes are airy or
graceful or serious or sad according to the subject-matter. There are
also odes to the New Year, e.g. 'Ce jour de l'an' and 'Bon jour bon
mois',[2] and spring songs, e.g. 'Ce jour le doibt',[3] 'Ce moys de May',[4]
where there is some imitation and music full of life and colour; and
in songs such as 'J'atendray tant qu'il vous playra', 'Pouray je avoir
vostre mercy',[5] and 'Pour l'amour de ma doulce amye',[6] the emotions of love are expressed with a frank and tender elegance.

In 'Vergine bella',[7] the most beautiful of his Italian *canzone*, instead of art conceived for its own sake we see music completely
conformable to the text—the first of the poems to the Virgin written
by Petrarch in *sestina* form. Composed in his youth, it combines
devotion to the Madonna with artistic perfection. There is perfect

[1] Ed. Besseler in *Das Chorwerk*, xix, pp. 22 and 20.
[2] J. F. R. and C. Stainer, *Dufay and his Contemporaries* (London, 1898), pp. 102 and
134.
[3] *Denkmäler der Tonkunst in Österreich*, xi, p. 85, where it appears as 'Le jour s'endort'.
[4] Stainer, op. cit., p. 105.
[5] Ibid., pp. 138 and 152.
[6] Ibid., p. 157. Recorded in *The History of Music in Sound*, iii.
[7] Van den Borren, *Guillaume Dufay*, p. 305; Besseler, *Das Chorwerk*, xix, p. 7.

concord between the faith of the artist in his quest for beauty and
that of the believer kneeling before her whose help he implores. From
this quotation we can form our opinion as to whether it is not superior
to the learned polyphonic settings of the same words by Cipriano de
Rore or Palestrina in the following century:

(I invoke her who always answers favourably; I call her trustingly, Virgin,
be merciful. The extreme unhappiness of human affairs. . . .)

GILLES BINCHOIS

The *chansons* of Binchois form a marked contrast to those of Dufay. We have a great number of them,[1] and they show an uneven quality; furthermore, the great technical variety which we meet in similar works by Dufay is not found in Binchois. But when his inspiration is at its height he is unequalled in making the *chanson* express everything that the limitations of its form allow; here he can surpass Dufay. An example, very striking for the period, is afforded by a series of settings of poems by the best authors of the day, such as Charles d'Orléans ('Mon cuer chante'), Alain Chartier ('Tristre plaisir et douloureuse joye'), and Christine de Pisan ('Dueil angoisseus'),[2] in the selection of which he shows the nicest literary discrimination. We see that his human sensibilities were more developed than Dufay's. Many of his *chansons* leave behind them a haunting melancholy or a tender sweetness—for example, the exquisite *rondeau* 'De plus en plus se renouvelle'[3] and the delightful *ballade* 'Je loe amours',[4] which begins:

Ex. 94

(I praise love, and thank my lady for the fair welcome that I owe them both; For by love I have chosen my lady, by my lady my heart is filled with joy.)

In addition to 'Dueil angoisseus' and 'Tristre plaisir' another fine example of his writing in melancholy vein is 'Ay douloureux disant

[1] Complete edition by W. Rehm, *Die Chansons von Gilles de Binchois* (Mainz, 1957).
[2] Ibid., pp. 25, 40, 45. See also J. Marix, *Les Musiciens de la cour de Bourgogne* (Paris, 1937), p. 65, and Droz and Thibault, *Poètes et Musiciens du XVᵉ siècle* (Paris, 1924), pp. 29 and 25.
[3] Rehm, op. cit., p. 10; Stainer, op. cit., p. 80.
[4] Rehm, op. cit., p. 49; Marix, op. cit., p. 52; and cf. p. 430 below.

helas',[1] with its very low-pitched range for voices. The first section, the refrain, is given here, showing the voices with different signatures —two flats for the lower voices, none at all for the *superius*:

Ex. 95

Ay dou-lou-reux di-sant he-las! De ma pi-teu-se vi-e las, Tres de-si-rant suy de mou-rir

(Unhappy, I cry 'Alas'; weary of my miserable life, I fain would die.)

In striking contrast is the simple gaiety of the well-known 'Filles à marier'.[2]

[1] Rehm, op. cit., p. 8; Marix, op. cit., p. 37.

[2] Rehm, op. cit., p. 52; Marix, op. cit., p. 46; also in A. T. Davison and W. Apel,

DUFAY'S CONTEMPORARIES

Our account of music on the Continent would be incomplete without mention of many composers who, if not so eminent as Dufay and Binchois, yet achieved real celebrity in their own day, as the large number of their works found in contemporary manuscripts bears witness. Italy lies to some extent out of the main stream, if we are to view it as a question of the influence of Dufay upon its composers. The works of Bartolomeo Brolo, Bartholomaeus de Bononia, Zacharias of Teramo, and Zacharias 'cantor Domini nostri Papae' (1420), seem to have been written before his first visit to Italy.

Beyond the confines of Italy were a number of lesser composers who wrote for the Papal Chapel, or for one of the courts of Italy or Burgundy. Many of their *chansons* are worthy to stand beside those of Dufay and Binchois and in many cases may well be earlier in date. A large number are to be found in Oxford, Bodleian, Canonici misc. 213.[1] These lesser-known and mostly rather older composers—Malbecque, Adam, Legrant, Liebert, Cordier, Grossim, and others—show great delicacy in their *rondeaux* and *ballades*. If their work is not always free from clichés the same is true of Dufay and Binchois. Now and again these minor composers strike an original note, e.g. the joyful *rondeau* by Johannes Legrant, 'Entre vous, nouviaux mariés',[2] has an air of the countryside, and Grossim of Paris in his 'Va-t'ent souspir'[3] writes a melody of great delicacy. In more serious subjects, Adam ('Au grief hermitage de plours'),[4] Liebert ('Mourir me voy')[5] and Pierre Fontaine ('J'ayme bien celuy qui s'en va',[6] with an interesting contratenor marked *trompette*) have a striking and noticeable air of melancholy.

In the sphere of sacred music Johannes Brasart, Johannes de Sarto, Johannes Franchois de Gembloux, Johannes de Lymburgia, and H. Battre (of Ciney?) show the degree to which the ideas of the school of Liège had been assimilated. Unfortunately the relatively small number of their works in the manuscripts[7] is not large enough for us

---

Historical Anthology of Music, i (Cambridge, Mass., 1946), no. 70. For emendation and completion of the text, see *The Musical Quarterly*, xxxvii (1951), pp. 518–19. Recorded in *The History of Music in Sound*, iii.

[1] A selection is printed in Stainer, op. cit.

[2] Stainer, op. cit., p. 167.

[3] Ibid., p. 172.

[4] Ibid., p. 57.

[5] Ibid., p. 176.

[6] P. Aubry, *Iter Hispanicum* (Paris, 1908), p. 28.

[7] With the exception of Johannes de Lymburgia, who is plentifully represented in Bologna, G. B. Martini, Q 15, but still not available for study (except for a very few specimens) in modern notation.

to estimate their relative values. Such of their compositions as have been published[1] since the beginning of the century give us, however, some idea of their general character. Guillaume Legrant comes first, with a curious *Gloria* and *Credo*[2] (in both the Oxford and Bologna manuscripts): it is written boldly in a homophonic style without fauxbourdon, with frequent use of augmented fourths in the melodic line, in defiance of theory. The composer was a pontifical singer in 1419, so that these pieces have no dependence upon Dufay. The work of Brasart (who was in the papal employ in 1431) and de Sarto, on the other hand, are reminiscent of Dunstable in the ornamentation of their upper voices. Some of their motets, such as 'O flos flagrans' by Brasart[3] and 'O quam mirabilis' by de Sarto[4], are worthy of a place beside the work of Dunstable and Dufay. Reginald Liebert has been mentioned earlier (see p. 225): his Mass follows the style of Dunstable and Leonel Power. Johannes Franchois deserves mention for his *Gloria* and *Credo* in the Canonici manuscript;[5] also for his motet 'Ave virgo' in Bologna with its instrumental prelude (*Trumpetta introitus*).[6] Both these works show initiative above the ordinary.

ARNOLD AND HUGO DE LANTINS

We have left to the end of this chapter two composers about whom we are fortunate to have fuller information: Arnold and Hugo (Hugho, Hugh) de Lantins. Both came from the province of Liège and both lived in Italy during the first thirty years of the fifteenth century. There, like Dufay, Hugo commemorated the wedding between Cleophe Malatesta and Theodore Palaeologus in 1421. Arnold was a member of the papal choir in 1431, along with Brasart and Dufay. We do not know whether they were brothers or cousins, but we can be fairly sure from the general similarity of their work that they belonged to the same generation.

The differences in their temperaments are reflected in their music. Arnold is contemplative and pours out his soul without paying much heed to technical problems. Hugo is more active and does not shrink from any problem: his composition 'Je suy exent',[7] employs all the

---

[1] Principally in various volumes of *Denkmäler der Tonkunst in Österreich*; and Van den Borren, *Polyphonia Sacra* (London, 1932).

[2] Van den Borren, op. cit., nos. 18–19.

[3] *Denkmäler der Tonkunst in Österreich*, vii, p. 102.

[4] Ibid., p. 215.

[5] Van den Borren, op. cit., nos. 13–14.

[6] *Denkmäler der Tonkunst in Österreich*, xl, p. 19; cf. pp. 156 *supra* and 425 *infra*.

[7] Oxford, Bodleian, Canonici misc. 213, fo. 57; facsimile in W. Apel, *The Notation of Polyphonic Music 900–1600* (Cambridge, Mass., 1942), p. 177.

subtleties of notation current in the first quarter of the century. When imitation was used at this time, it was used sparingly; but Hugo employs the device so often and so continuously that he seems to anticipate Busnois by half a century. Arnold's religious music is an admirable reflection of his contemplative nature, specially noticeable in the *Sanctus* of his three-part Mass 'Verbum incarnatum'[1] and the four-part motet 'Tota pulchra es'.[2] In this extract from the latter the atmosphere of the Song of Songs is captured with a suavity equalled only by the *Sanctus*:

Ex. 96

(And the voice of the turtle is heard in our land.)

If we turn to the secular works of the two composers,[3] the contrast is still evident. Hugo handles the French *rondeau* and the Italian *canzone* with more vivacity than Arnold, and abandons the note of mourning for the joy of life, e.g. 'Prendre convint de tout en gré', 'Joly et gay', and 'Pour resjoyr la compaignye'.[4] But when he deals with the same subjects as Arnold, his ideas are of great

[1] Van den Borren, op. cit., no. 4.
[2] Ibid., no. 41.
[3] Their *chansons* and those of Johannes Franchois de Gemblaco are all printed in Van den Borren, *Pièces polyphoniques de provenance liégeoise* (Brussels, 1950).
[4] Ibid., pp. 39, 52, and 55.

sublimity, as we can see from the opening of the *chanson* 'Plaindre m'estuet':[1]

Ex. 97

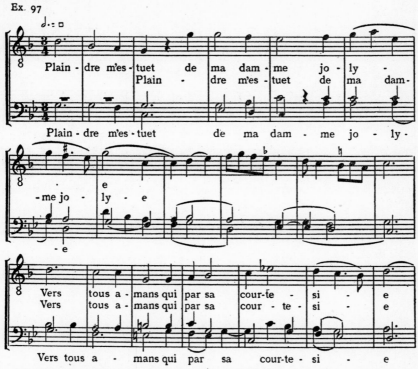

(I had matter of complaint concerning my beautiful lady, against every suitor who, [profiting] by her courtly magnanimity, . . .)

Arnold is most at home in songs of mourning. *Rondeaux* such as 'Puis que je voy, belle', 'Se ne prenes de moy pité' (dated 1428), and 'Las, pouray je mon martire celer'[2] are masterpieces of a very high order, a claim which can be substantiated by the opening of 'Las, pouray je', with its expressive pedal-point and unexpected close in F♯ minor:

Ex. 98

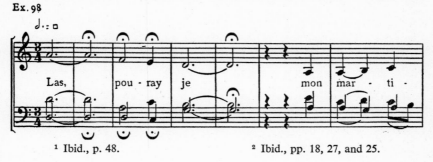

[1] Ibid., p. 48.   [2] Ibid., pp. 18, 27, and 25.

(Alas, shall I be able to conceal my pain, when my heart pricks me with such agony?)

VIII

THE AGE OF OCKEGHEM AND JOSQUIN

By Nanie Bridgman

INTRODUCTION

At the time when Dufay, in his old age, was turning from the subtleties of a Gothic art derived from *ars nova*, to a polyphonic style far removed from the traditional basis of French art, a younger generation of musicians arose, led by Ockeghem (*c.* 1420–95), which adopted these modified values and realized its own aims in strict polyphony and canonic imitation. It is this remodelled style that Tinctoris called 'the *ars nova* of the fifteenth century'. The new style was to enjoy an unbroken development to the farthest possible limits of its growth, attaining to a genuine systematization of counterpoint and giving way, at the end of the sixteenth century, to the accompanied monody successfully advocated by the Italians. The fact that the musicians forming this new school were mostly born in the Low Countries has induced certain musicologists to give it the name of 'the Netherland school'; others, relying on equally valid arguments, prefer to call it 'Franco-Flemish' or 'Franco-Netherland'.[1] Actually, if one accepts the idea of effective influences, one must admit that no school was ever more international; for though these composers came from the North and many of them returned to spend their last years in their native land, they nevertheless lived abroad for the whole of their productive lives and sometimes even their formative periods. Thus one of the most important of them, Ockeghem, was to remain for more than forty years in the French royal chapel. However, there was between them a powerful cultural bond which caused them all to follow the same musical discipline and to distinguish themselves in the same style; and it must be admitted that the most successful workers along these lines were in fact Netherlanders, natives of that 'northern Burgundy' which Charles the Bold had never been able to incorporate with any lasting effect in Burgundy proper and which, at the death of his daughter Mary in 1482, passed into the hands of the House of

---

[1] Gustave Reese, *Music in the Renaissance* (New York, 1954), p. 9. See also Albert Van der Linden, 'Comment désigner la nationalité des artistes des provinces du nord à l'époque de la Renaissance', *La Renaissance dans les provinces du Nord* (Paris, 1956), pp. 11–17.

Austria, while Dijon, the musical centre of the previous generation, reverted to the kingdom of France.

Difficult though it may be to discover the genesis of this Netherland style, it is equally impossible to allow that it arose unheralded about the middle of the century; its characteristic features were already evident before the new generation headed by Ockeghem had made its appearance, as is proved moreover by the latest motets of Dufay. But we know as little as ever about its origins or about the reasons which caused it to arise in the Flemish area, thus making the Low Countries 'the magnetic pole of composition in our continent'.[1] Certainly Charles the Bold, following in this respect in his father's footsteps, had greatly helped the advance of music, all the more as he himself sang, played the harp and 'made up *chansons* and motets'.[2] It is known also that in the great commercial towns such as Antwerp, Bruges, and Cambrai, wealthy citizens maintained an active musical life, and that the cathedral choirs formed excellent schools in which young choristers were brought up on the music of the great masters. But we cannot tell how the mystery of the composer's craft, over and above this instruction in singing, was handed on, nor how the continuity of this polyphonic learning was maintained, for the theoretical treatises of the time expound abstract ideas looking towards the past—towards medieval formalism—rather than towards the splendid possibilities revealed for music in the hands of such men as Dufay or Ockeghem.

We have no documentary information about the syllabus of studies in a medieval choir-school, nor about the educational methods used by its teachers. However, as de Van very truly observes, 'the training of a singer and of a composer merged with each other',[3] and the cathedral music-school was 'not only the conservatoire where the novice was introduced to the basic principles of musical scholarship, but also the workshop in which the master-craftsman produced masterpieces readily understood by his associates'.[4] The principles followed by Josquin in his teaching have moreover been reported to us by his pupil Adrian Petit Coclico, from whom we learn that the Master did not delay his pupils 'in longis et frivolis praeceptionibus' (with long and useless instructions) but that he taught 'per exercitium

[1] H. J. Moser, 'Die Niederlande in der Musikgeographie Europas', *Kongress-Bericht: Internationale Gesellschaft für Musikwissenschaft* (Utrecht, 1952), p. 302.

[2] André Pirro, *Histoire de la musique de la fin du XIVe siècle à la fin du XVe* (Paris, 1940), p. 115.

[3] Guillaume de Van, 'La Pédagogie musicale à la fin du Moyen-âge', *Musica Disciplina*, ii (1948), p. 86.   [4] Ibid., p. 81.

et practicam' (through practical application).[1] It is plain that in such an apprenticeship a good deal was left to those who were capable of teaching themselves, and that more faith was reposed in natural gifts than in instruction. Josquin himself imparted the secrets of his art only to those whom he judged worthy to receive them.[2]

THE NETHERLAND STYLE

What are the characteristics—beyond the composers' nationality, which in any case is sometimes difficult to determine exactly—that enable us to treat the school, headed first by Ockeghem and then by Josquin, as a real unity and thus to distinguish it from the very different world of French music? It should be noted that this completely new style appeared at first only in sacred music; it was in this sphere that the new contrapuntal resources were to make themselves apparent and find their fullest vocal realization. For all these composers—except Busnois, who was first and foremost a Court musician—religious music was endowed with the highest prestige. The two worlds of sacred and profane were still quite clearly separate with Ockeghem; it was Josquin (d. 1521) and his contemporaries who were later to stand for the reconciliation of these two domains into a polyphonic style equally complex for either.

Ockeghem proceeded to rid musical language of all the subtleties of the previous age and attained 'a noble simplicity unknown to Dufay'; furthermore, music was henceforth to be employed 'in the service of the ideas suggested by its text, by means of a harmonious fusion of the decorative and expressive elements'.[3] Perhaps we may detect here the influence of the 'Illustre Lieve Vrouwe Broederschap', which at that time was diffusing throughout the Low Countries a religion with a human touch very different from the dogmatic sterility of the Middle Ages. Moreover from the purely technical point of view, the imitative method of writing (already prefigured by Dufay in his Mass 'Ave Regina') was exemplified, still tentatively but significantly for the future, in certain works by Ockeghem and Busnois. The tenor would sometimes act as a 'spiritual centre' of a composition and provide the substance for the whole of its polyphony; it would no longer provide merely extraneous support to the other voices; the latter would now each in turn take up its thematic material. Josquin in particular developed the possibilities of the imitative style in which the same

---

[1] Adrian Petit Coclico, *Compendium musices* (Nuremberg, 1552), f. Fii v°. Facsimile pub. Manfred Bukofzer, *Documenta musicologica*, ix (Kassel, 1954).   [2] Ibid., loc. cit.
[3] Charles Van den Borren, *La Musique en Belgique* (Brussels, 1950), p. 53.

musical theme is given out by each of the voices in succession; thus
creating 'a free, unified and yet complex contrapuntal organism: free
because it is not tied to a *cantus firmus*, unified because the same
thematic substance penetrates all parts, complex because each part
presents the theme at a different time while the other voices go against
it contrapuntally, avoiding simultaneity in rhythm and metre. This
results in a tonal structure unified harmonically, diversified rhythmically and metrically.'[1] This new style brought about a new technique of composition; instead of thinking of the various parts of a
work successively, composers came to think of them simultaneously.
The method was no longer, as Egidius de Murino had recommended,
to write the tenor first, if composing a motet, or the *superius* if composing a *chanson* ('Qui vult condere modulum fiat primo tenor . . .
Et qui vult condere baladam, rotundellum, viriledum, psalmodium fiat
primo discantus')[2]—nor to consider, like Burzio (Burtius), in which
cases it was best to write the *superius* first and in which the tenor or
the bass ('Qualiter debeant componi cantilene: aut prior incipiendum
sit a suprano vel tenore, aut contrabasso').[3] Pietro Aron attributes to
Josquin and to Isaac the determining influence in this new process of
musical creation, which seems moreover to have coincided with the
appearance of a new procedure in musical notation. For until then it
had been the practice to write in separate parts, each imagined and
worked out in its own right; but about 1500, if Lampadius is to be
believed, men began sometimes to compose directly in score—a
material illustration of the unitary quality henceforth to characterize
musical composition. As a consequence of this new procedure, greater
perfection is to be observed in the relation of the various parts to each
other.[4]

One survival of fourteenth-century *ars nova*, very fashionable
between 1475 and 1525, was the writing of canons in more or less
puzzling terms. The method was to note down one voice-part only and
to conceal the true structure of a composition under a formula whose
meaning had to be guessed. For example, 'Otia dant vitia' meant that
the rests were to be ignored, 'Canit more Hebraeorum' (and also

[1] E. E. Lowinsky, 'Music in the Culture of the Renaissance', *Journal of the History
of Ideas*, xv (1954), p. 531.
[2] *Cantus mensurabilis*, ed. Coussemaker, *Scriptorum de musica*, iii, p. 124. See also
Bukofzer, 'Fauxbourdon Revisited', *The Musical Quarterly*, xxxviii (1952), p. 38.
[3] Lowinsky, 'On the Use of Scores by Sixteenth-century Musicians', *Journal of
the American Musicological Society*, i (1948), p. 20.
[4] See Suzanne Clercx, 'D'une ardoise aux partitions du XVIe siècle', *Mélanges . . .
offerts à Paul-Marie Masson* (Paris, 1955), pp. 157–70, and Lowinsky, 'On the Use of
Scores.'

'Vade retro Satanas') that the music was to be sung backwards, 'Ascende gradatim' that the melody was to be sung one degree of the scale higher each time it recurred. Composers also practised strict canon, as we still understand the term, the most famous example of which is the 'Deo gratias' attributed to Ockeghem, ostensibly for thirty-six voices but really consisting of four canons in nine parts each and never calling for more than eighteen voices to sing together.[1] Strictly mathematical compositions of this kind, leaving very little room for the free flowering of genius, are however much rarer than has often been stated in Netherland polyphony, which, in the hands of such men as Ockeghem or Josquin, was never tied to any system.

MUSICAL FORMS

With Ockeghem the Mass held pride of place, whereas Josquin put most of his audacities into his motets, remaining always more conservative in his Masses. Composers chose for the most part to set the Ordinary of the Mass rather than the Proper, whose text is of course different for each day (the only one to set it was Isaac in his *Choralis Constantinus*), or the Requiem Mass, very few examples of which are found.

During the first half of the fifteenth century the cyclic Mass was still infrequent; but about the middle of the century, as we have seen in earlier chapters, musicians sought to provide a thematic link between the various numbers, either by means of an initial motive recurring at the beginning of each, or by the use of a *canto fermo* repeated throughout the work, usually in the tenor. This *canto fermo* might be taken from plainsong or from a *chanson*; or it might be the composer's own invention, as in Josquin's Masses 'La sol fa re mi' and 'Hercules dux Ferrarie',[2] the theme of the latter of which is based on the vowels in its title: e u e u e a i e, *re ut re ut re fa mi re*:

Ex. 99

[1] Printed in Riemann, *Handbuch der Musikgeschichte*, ii, 1 (Leipzig, second edition 1920, p. 237).   [2] *Werken*, ed. Smijers, *Missen*, i, no. 2, and ii, no. 7.

Gradually, in the course of the sixteenth century, the *canto fermo* technique was to give place to that of the *missa parodia*, but this way of writing was still rare even with Josquin, and it was not until the next generation that it was adopted almost exclusively.

The motet, though not such a favourite with composers, was frequently their chosen vehicle for all kinds of learned contrapuntal technicalities. Busnois scattered canonic imitations and subtle modulations in his motet 'In hydraulis,' which was a homage to Ockeghem; similarly Compère's motet 'Virgo caelesti' (in Petrucci's *Canti B*, Venice 1502) is skilfully constructed on a tenor which thrice repeats the notes of the hexachord *ut re mi fa sol la*, each time in shorter note-values:[1]

[1] Transcribed by Albert Smijers.

(Virgin made glorious by bearing a heavenly offspring, thou who dost alway have compassion on the human race, look upon thy servants who continually dedicate themselves to thee, Virgin Mary.)

With Josquin and his generation the motet began to take first place. The texts available for it, more varied than those of the Mass, enabled musicians to satisfy the ideal they were henceforth to follow, one whose tendency was to regard the text as the source of musical inspiration. The motet may thus be considered as the earliest form to express the ideas of the Renaissance—a free form in which each section of the text had music of its own, penetrating as deeply as possible into the meaning of the words.

At the same time the *chanson* carried on the tradition of the Burgundian court in a kind of 'autumn of the Middle Ages', as Huizinga has very aptly termed it.[1] Set invariably to French words—very few *chansons* have Flemish texts, for these 'Netherlanders' were mostly

---

[1] *Herfsttijd der Middeleeuwen* (Haarlem, 1919); English edition, *The Waning of the Middle Ages* (London, 1924). See also Heinrich Besseler, *Bourdon und Fauxbourdon* (Leipzig, 1950), p. 207.

French-speaking—it certainly owed many of its refinements, and also of its limitations, to the French culture of the Dukes of Burgundy. In the time of Ockeghem and Busnois the *ballade* (still favoured by Dufay) gave way to the *rondeau* and the *bergerette*, and these were the forms in which composers henceforth preferred to write. The complex framework of the *rondeau* was reduced to two simple types, the *rondeau-quatrain* with a four-line refrain and the *rondeau-cinquain* with one of five lines. Only the words of the refrain were written under the music, and no treatise helps us to solve the delicate problem of how to distribute the rest of the poem. We may, however, suppose that the scheme used in the thirteenth century, *ABaAabAB*, was still valid, as is suggested by Hayne's famous *chanson*, 'De tous biens plaine'.[1]

Ex. 101

De tous biens plaine est ma mais-tres - se, Chas-cun lui doit tri - but d'on-neur; Car

---

[1] Knud Jeppesen, *Der Kopenhagener Chansonnier* (Copenhagen & Leipzig, 1927), p. 7; this version occurs with trifling variants in other manuscripts, notably Dijon MS. 517 (formerly 295), reproduced in Ambros, *Geschichte der Musik*, ii (Leipzig, 3rd ed., 1891), p. 576, and Droz, Rokseth, and Thibault, *Trois chansonniers* (Paris, 1927), i, p. 20. Petrucci (*Odhecaton*, No. 20) prints a version with an additional part: see the modern reprint and Smijers, *Van Ockeghem tot Sweelinck*, v (Amsterdam, 1939), p. 144.

Text		Music
a	*De tous biens plaine est ma maistresse,*	
b	*Chascun lui doit tribut d'onneur;*	A
b	*Car assouvye est en valeur*	
a	*Autant que jamais fut déesse.*	B
a	En la veant j'ay tel léesse	
b	Que c'est paradis en mon cueur.	A
a	*De tous biens plaine est ma maistresse,*	
b	*Chascun lui doit tribut d'onneur.*	A
a	Je n'ay cure d'aultre richesse	
b	Si non d'estre son serviteur,	A
b	Et pource qu'il n'est chois milleur	
a	En mon mot porteray sans cesse:	B
a	*De tous biens plaine est ma maistresse,*	
b	*Chascun lui doit tribut d'onneur*	A
b	*Car assouvye est en valeur*	
a	*Autant que jamais fut dèesse*	B

(All good things are found in my mistress, every man must pay her honour; for she is perfect in beauty as any goddess ever was. When I see her I feel such joy that there is paradise in my heart. All good things are found in my mistress, every man must pay her honour. I care for no other riches but only to serve her, and since there is no better choice, I shall continually bear her as my device. All good things are found in my mistress, every man must pay her honour; for she is perfect in beauty as any goddess ever was.)

The *bergerette*, which was simply a kind of *virelai*, tended to secure a place for itself alongside the *rondeau*, whose structure it more or less reproduced. Its middle stanza, however, had no refrain (though some critics think there was one, at least in most cases);[1] moreover this stanza was freer in rhymes and in length of lines. Its formal plan (*AbbaA*) was less monotonous than that of the *rondeau*, and this may have been the reason for its success, as it had not even the attraction of novelty. Not indeed that it enjoyed any greater vogue than the *rondeau*; among the secular works of Busnois, as against 41 *rondeaux*, there are only 13 *bergerettes*,[2] and only 15 out of the 106 items of the Laborde *Chansonnier*, from which the following example is taken:

Ex 102

[1] R. W. Linker and G. S. McPeek, 'The Bergerette Form in the Laborde Chansonnier', *Journal of the American Musicological Society*, vii (1954), pp. 113 ff.

[2] Catherine Brooks, 'Antoine Busnois, Chanson Composer', *Journal of the American Musicological Society*, vi (1953), pp. 124–7.

(O fair Diana, shining and very beautiful, whose rays reach resplendently as far as Phoebus who illuminates the world.)

Obviously these *formes fixes*, inherited from the past, provided the composer with a rigid framework which left him no scope for such musical development as was possible within the ample outlines of the Mass and the motet; a musician such as Ockeghem was always constricted when writing *chansons*, whereas the graceful but slighter talent of Busnois was quite at home in them. The *chanson* was in that age a 'minor form' which confined itself, as Martin Le Franc had already remarked, to 'bergerettes doulces et assez legierettes'.[1] Still, composers did their best to move with the times; they gave the *chanson* a solid harmonic structure, in which unprepared dissonances became the exception and the asperities of the previous age disappeared. In the matter of polyphony, imitation became more frequent, as we have already seen in connexion with church music; the beginning of this piece from the Copenhagen *Chansonnier*[2] is typical:

Ex. 103

---

[1] Pirro, op. cit., p. 115.   [2] Jeppesen, op. cit., p. 56.

(Upon my soul, my love)

Here again things were a little different for Josquin's generation. Whereas the first two collections published by Petrucci, the *Odhecaton* in 1501 and *Canti B* in 1502,[1] still contain a high proportion of *chansons* in fixed forms, his *Canti C* (1504) exhibit a larger number written to poems of a freer type, having no set construction and differing one from another. Josquin's, for instance, almost all belong to this category. All things considered, therefore, the end of the fifteenth century may be taken as the culminating moment of that desire for emancipation which characterized the Renaissance; henceforth musicians would get rid of both the *canto fermo* and the *formes fixes*, and their musical creations would be free from hampering restrictions.

THE PERFORMANCE OF MUSIC

Sacred and secular music each had a different method of interpretation; it was in church that performance first developed more and more firmly along choral lines, leading ultimately to the 'chorus-conscious'[2] music of Ockeghem and Josquin, and to *a cappella* performance. Polyphonic choral music was quite foreign to the medieval tradition, which knew only of choral singing in unison; and the beginnings of choral polyphony coincided with the beginnings of the musical Renaissance, with its ideal of homogeneous sonority.[3] This does not mean that instruments were not heard in church; numerous documents provide evidence to the contrary. In 1503, at the Easter Mass heard by Philip the Handsome at Bourg, 'there came with the choristers Maistre Augustin, playing upon his cornett, the which did one good to hear'; and a few months later, at a Mass attended by the same prince at Innsbruck, 'the Gradual was intoned by the King's sackbuts, who also played the "Deo gratias" and the "Ite missa est",

[1] There is a modern edition of the *Odhecaton* by Helen Hewitt and Isabel Pope (Cambridge, Mass., 1946).

[2] Bukofzer, 'The Beginnings of Choral Polyphony', *Studies in Medieval and Renaissance Music*, p. 189.   [3] Besseler, op. cit., p. 190.

and my Lord's choristers sang the Offertory'.[1] While Schering's theory, according to which some Masses were performed on the organ alone,[2] is now abandoned, this instrument certainly played its part; but the accounts given by chroniclers frequently leave it uncertain what exactly that part was—for example when one of them states that the organ supported the voices of the choir at the reception of Bishop Guillaume Chartier at Notre Dame, Paris, in 1447.[3] Moreover the chroniclers concerned with church ceremonies usually mention only the prowess of the choristers. Among these, the Flemings had certainly earned a noteworthy reputation, if we may judge by the large number of them filling posts in the Pontifical chapel; and Charles the Bold, as Molinet says, collected 'the best-famed choristers in the world, and kept a chapel furnished with voices so harmonious and delectable that, bating the Heavenly glory, there was no other delight to be compared therewith'.[4] The Mantuan poet Teofilo Folengo in his *Macaroneae* (published in 1516 under the pseudonym of 'Merlinus Cocaius') describes the Flemish choristers as 'excellent in their art' and adds that they, 'having drunk good wine, begin to sing with vibrant voices, the which their throats may very easily send forth as they are all strong and robust in the breast'. In another place he remarks of a singer: 'You would say on hearing him that he must be a Fleming, for his gullet is disposed as it were a great organ-pipe. It is nothing for him to reach gamma-ut; he will sing lower, down to the very bottom of the cellar.'[5] Ockeghem himself was mentioned by Tinctoris as one of the finest *bassi contratenoristae* of his time.[6] References such as these enable us both to imagine what splendid performances these men must have given and also to understand why, with such 'instruments' at their disposal, composers such as Ockeghem or Josquin could invent such powerful constructions in vocal polyphony, and why this art arose first in these northern lands. But whereas the ideal of choral music was carried out to the full in the Church, secular music was slow to adopt the new style; writers of *chansons* confined themselves for the most part to a single voice

---

[1] G. Van Doorslaer, 'La chapelle musicale de Philippe le Beau', *Revue belge d'archéologie et d'histoire de l'art*, iv (1934), pp. 51 and 52.

[2] Arnold Schering, *Die niederländische Orgelmesse im Zeitalter des Josquin* (Leipzig, 1912).

[3] Pirro, 'Remarques sur l'exécution musicale de la fin du 14e au milieu du 15e siècle', *I.S.M.R. Congress Report, Liège 1930*, p. 57.

[4] Pirro, *Histoire de la musique*, p. 117.

[5] French translation (Paris, 1606), livre 1er, p. 32, and livre 21e, p. 648. Quoted by Pirro in *Tribune de Saint Gervais*, i (1895), p. 14.

[6] *De inventione et usu musicae*, ed. K. Weinmann (Regensburg, 1917), p. 33.

accompanied by instruments—a type of performance which moreover was not forbidden in sacred music, since Crétin, in his *Déploration* on the death of Ockeghem, relates that Hayne sang the motet for the dead, 'Ut heremita solus', accompanying himself on the lute.[1] Conversely, it is certain that *a cappella* performance was not entirely unknown in secular music, as is sufficiently proved by the new structure of *chansons* at the end of the fifteenth century, in which the unsingable contratenor parts found earlier in the century almost cease to occur.[2] Directions such as those in an Italian manuscript copied in 1502, in which each of the four parts of a *frottola* bears precise indication of its singer—'pro puero, pro alto, pro tenorista, pro basso'—also constitute clear evidence for the *a cappella* performance of secular music.[3]

With these two ways of performance there went also two ways of writing manuscripts: for music to be performed by church choirs there were large choir-books intended to be read by all the singers together at the lectern, the various parts being noted on opposite pages, whereas the *chansonniers*, those invaluable source-books for our knowledge of private music-making, frequently have each part noted in a separate book for each performer to rest on his knees. There is an abundance of manuscript sources in which the *monumenta* of Netherland music are preserved, not only in the Low Countries but in foreign libraries.[4] An important contribution to the stock is the remains of the Burgundian ducal library, notable items in which are the *chansonniers* made for Margaret of Austria and the fine books written by the most famous copyist of the age, Pierre van den Hove, called Alamire (d. about 1534), whose musical calligraphy is one of the most beautiful of its kind.

Although the progress of music-printing in the Netherlands was notably slow in comparison with that in Italy, France, and Germany (its earliest example was Tielman Susato's *Premier livre des chansons à quatre parties*, Antwerp, 1543), the Venetian printer Petrucci chose for his first collection of printed music, entitled *Harmonice musices odhecaton A*, a repertory largely made up of Netherland works—i.e.

---

[1] *Déploration sur le trépas de Jean Ockeghem*, ed. Thoinan (Paris, 1864), p. 34. The motet, originally published by Petrucci in his *Motetti C* (Venice, 1504), was reprinted by Schering in *Geschichte der Musik in Beispielen* (Leipzig, 1931), no. 52.

[2] Jeppesen, op. cit., p. xlix.

[3] Nanie Bridgman, 'Un manuscrit italien du début du XVIᵉ siècle à la Bibliothèque nationale', *Annales musicologiques*, i (1953), p. 244, no. 93; and 'La Frottola et la transition de la frottola au madrigal', *Musique et poésie au XVIᵉ s.* (Colloques internationaux du CNRS, sciences humaines, v) (1954), p. 69.

[4] See Van den Borren, op. cit., pp. 470 ff., and Reese, op. cit., pp. 97 ff.

chansons to French words in the Burgundian style—and throughout his activities, which closed in 1520, out of the 49 books that he published, some 30 were devoted to the musicians of this school.[1] We have to wait for Attaingnant's first collection (Paris, 1527) in order to find a repertory of *chansons* specifically French in style as well as by language.

OCKEGHEM AND HIS CHURCH MUSIC

The musicians of this generation may appropriately be grouped round Ockeghem and Busnois, for each perfectly illustrates one of the two poles of musical creation, religious and profane. Ockeghem—continuing the tradition of his great predecessors—as a churchman, composed for the Church, whereas Busnois, a Court musician, wrote for Court diversions. Tinctoris expressed a joint admiration for both of them as 'praestantissimi ac celeberrimi artis musicae professores' when he dedicated to them his *Liber de natura et proprietate tonorum*.[2]

Johannes Ockeghem, born about 1420, was a *vicarius* at Antwerp cathedral in 1443–4, a chorister to Charles of Bourbon at the ducal chapel of Moulins from 1446 to 1448, and then, from 1452 until his death in 1495, attached to the royal chapel of France, first as chorister and then as choirmaster; he there served three kings, Charles VII, Louis XI, and Charles VIII. There had also been conferred upon him one of the highest posts in the kingdom, that of treasurer of the abbey of St. Martin at Tours. His death inspired tributes from both poets and musicians, the most celebrated evidences of their respect being Guillaume Crétin's already mentioned *Déploration* and the musical epitaphs by Josquin (to verses by Molinet) and Lupi (to a text by Erasmus).

Their praise is amply justified by the composer's surviving works. He has too often been considered as 'a pure cerebralist almost exclusively preoccupied with intellectual problems', for whom 'expression was. . . . a secondary consideration'.[3] In fact, in the fourteen Masses and one separate *Credo* by him which have come down to us,[4] beauty

---

[1] Claudio Sartori, *Bibliografia delle opere musicali stampate da Ottaviano Petrucci* (Florence, 1948). [2] Ed. Coussemaker, *Scriptorum*, ix, p. 16.

[3] Cecil Gray, *The History of Music* (London, 1928), p. 62.

[4] Ockeghem's Masses have been reprinted complete by Plamenac in the first two volumes of his edition of the composer's *Collected Works* (i, Leipzig, 1927; ii, New York, 1947). Plamenac also prints (ii, p. 98) the Mass 'Pour quelque paine', attributed to Ockeghem in Brussels, Bibl. royale, MS. 5557, though a Vatican manuscript, Capp. Sist. Cod. 51, gives it to 'Cornelius heyns'. He omits the Mass 'Le Serviteur', printed as Ockeghem's in *Denkmäler der Tonkunst in Österreich*, xix (1) (1912), believing it to be by Guillaume Faugues. There are also a number of reprints of separate Mass-movements (e.g. the Kyrie and Agnus Dei III of 'L'homme armé' in Davison and Apel, *Historical*

is never sacrificed to technical display, and, whether or no it were the composer's aim, his Masses produce an impression of powerful grandeur which is emotionally very telling. As Křenek very well puts it, 'it is this ability of evoking not only intellectual interest, but also immediate emotional reactions under completely changed social and psychological circumstances, which proves that Ockeghem's music is still alive'.[1] It is very difficult to define the essential character of his work, for no artist has given greater evidence of freedom in his writing than this composer who, as Van den Borren very truly noted, 'was bound by no system' but looked sometimes back, sometimes forward. His treatment of dissonances may appear to be a trace of the old style which Tinctoris condemned when calling for the reduction of dissonant elements, but for all that, he used them so unexpectedly that his work did much more to renew the language of music than the more conventional harmony of Obrecht a little later.[2] Moreover, while he retained from the Gothic period the practice of linear writing for each voice separately, his polyphonic texture is an inseparable union of parts into a whole and proves in itself that he thought of the various parts simultaneously in the manner characteristic of the new age. Although all the parts have functions of equal importance and are subtly connected, the device of imitation is infrequently employed in his Masses and never becomes a mechanical routine; rather is his polyphonic texture shot through with passing contrapuntal ingenuities, each of them occurring at the bidding of his invention as the occasion demanded. It is therefore wrong to consider Ockeghem, as Riemann did, as the 'father' of the continuously imitative style.[3] In this repugnance on Ockeghem's part towards a procedure which was to be particularly dear to his Netherland countrymen, we may perhaps discern the influence of the French environment in which he spent more than forty years, and which was musically marked by constant unwillingness to adopt the imitative style, as may be verified by a study of the purely French music of the sixteenth century.

In the only Mass which he composed on an exclusive basis of canonic imitation (the 'Missa prolationum') the strict constraint which he imposed on himself did not in any way hinder the spontaneous expansion of artistic feeling; and this although anyone might

Anthology of Music, i, No. 73), and the 'Missa Mi-mi' has been published complete by Besseler in *Das Chorwerk*, iv.

   [1] Ernst Křenek, *Johannes Ockeghem* (New York, 1953), p. 67.

   [2] Křenek, 'A Discussion of the treatment of dissonances in Ockeghem's Masses as compared with the contrapuntal theory of Johannes Tinctoris', *Hamline Studies in Musicology*, ii (St. Paul, Minn., 1947).   [3] *Handbuch der Musikgeschichte*, ii, 1, p. 233.

have felt paralysed in the narrow framework of this contrapuntal exploit, in which two pairs of voices sing two different canons simultaneously. The 'Missa cujusvis toni' is another example of Ockeghem's virtuosity, as it can be sung in the first, third, fifth, or seventh mode according to the clefs prefixed; but it is none the less a work of art. To these two Masses, composed freely, without *canti fermi*, should be added the 'Missa Mi-mi' or 'Quarti toni', whose unifying factor is the descending fifth from E to A (*mi* in the natural and soft hexachords),[1] stated by the bass at the beginning of each section; this remains one of his finest works, with no recourse to musical sophistications. The Masses 'Sine nomine' and 'Quinti toni,' for three voices, are also freely composed but derive a certain unity from the initial motive beginning each section. Elsewhere Ockeghem did not disdain the method of composition on a *canto fermo*. Only two of his *canti fermi* are liturgical in origin: 'Caput'[2] and 'Ecce ancilla Domini', whereas five are taken from secular *chansons*: 'Au travail suis' (either by Barbigant or Ockeghem's own),[3] 'De plus en plus' (by Binchois), the popular 'L'homme armé', and two *chansons* by the composer himself, 'Ma maîtresse' and 'Fors seulement'. In 'L'homme armé' the tune is reproduced literally without variation, and the tenor, not being subjected to imitative treatment, does not infuse its substance into the other parts; on the other hand 'De plus en plus' and 'Au travail suis' are treated very freely indeed, and in the latter there are examples of imitation based on the tenor. In the former, the long duet-passage at the end of 'Pleni sunt,' with its free rhythms, is characteristic of Ockeghem, who was very fond of melodies floating for a long time 'in suspense' before coming to rest on the final cadence. The two five-part Masses, 'Sine nomine' and 'Fors seulement,' consist only of *Kyrie*, *Gloria*, and *Credo*. In the latter, which is certainly a work of the composer's maturity, he uses the *superius* part of his own three-part *chanson*[4] not only as a tenor *canto fermo*, but also treats the theme imitatively in the upper parts, e.g. at the beginning of the

---

[1] There are 'Mi-mi' Masses by de Orto, Pipelare, and other composers of the period. The first *Agnus* of de Orto's is printed in Ambros–Kade, *Geschichte der Musik*, v (Leipzig, 1889), p. 198.   [2] See the analysis of this Mass in Bukofzer, op. cit., pp. 278 ff.

[3] On the authorship of this *chanson*, see Dragan Plamenac, 'A Postscript to Volume II of the Collected Works of Johannes Ockeghem', *Journal of the American Musicological Society*, iii (1950), p. 33.

[4] Printed without words in O. J. Gombosi, *Jacob Obrecht* (Leipzig, 1925), p. 12 of the musical appendix, and F. J. Giesbert, *Ein altes Spielbuch* (*Liber Fridolini Sichery*) (Mainz, 1936), p. 2, and with words and variant musical text in Droz and Thibault, *Trois chansonniers français du XVᵉ siècle* (Paris, 1927), p. 48. The melody was a favourite of the time; Gombosi, op. cit., p. 16, mentions 32 *chanson* settings and there are 'Fors seulement' Masses by Obrecht, Pierre de la Rue, and Pipelare.

Kyrie.[1] Portions of the other parts of the *chanson* are also used, in accordance with what was later to be the principle of the *missa parodia,* as in this passage at the beginning of the second *Kyrie.*

Ex. 104

His Requiem Mass, mentioned in Crétin's *Déploration,*

> La messe aussi exquise et tres parfaicte
> De Requiem par ledict deffunct faicte,[2]

(Also the exquisite and most perfect Requiem mass written by this man who is dead.)

[1] Recorded in *The History of Music in Sound* (H.M.V.) iii.   [2] Ed. Thoinan, p. 34.

is one of his most important works from an historical point of view,
since it is the oldest Mass for the Dead that has so far come down to
us (Dufay's being lost). It is also one of Ockeghem's most expressive
compositions, each of its numbers being given a different hue. The
Tract ('Sicut cervus', instead of 'Absolve, Domine' as in post-Tridentine
Requiems) is notable for its particularly remarkable lyric quality; the
words 'fuerunt mihi lacrimae meae' are (as Plamenac says)[1] set 'in a
clearly descriptive manner', with short phrases in the tenor suggestive
of sobbing:

Ex. 105

(My tears have been my meat day [and night].)

The rest of Ockeghem's work for the Church consists of only nine
motets. The opening of 'Alma redemptoris mater' may be quoted as
a typical example of his use of a Gregorian *canto fermo*:[2]

Ex. 106

---

[1] *Ockeghem: Collected Works*, ii, p. xxxiii.
[2] Besseler, 'Von Dufay bis Josquin', *Zeitschrift für Musikwissenschaft*, xi (1928),
p. 21, and *Altniederländische Motetten* (Kassel, 1929), p. 5.

(Bountiful Mother of the Redeemer.)

This work, the culminating point of the old master's maturity, displays an artistic character quite different from that of Dufay's motet on the same theme.[1] The alto sings an ornamented version of the antiphon.

Ex. 10.

OCKEGHEM'S CHANSONS

Ockeghem's twenty *chansons*, though they do not include such outstanding masterpieces as this, nevertheless reflect the great diversity of his genius. On the one hand there is the beautifully plastic theme of 'D'un autre amer';[2] on the other, the syllabic declamation of 'Ma bouche rit'[3] and 'Malheur me bat'[4]. Imitative writing is more frequent in them than in the Masses; it is here that we must look for proof that Ockeghem played a part in the development of this style. Sufficient

---

[1] Dufay's composition has been reprinted several times—most accessibly in Davison and Apel, *Historical Anthology of Music*, i (Cambridge, Mass., 1946), no. 65.

[2] Published by Droz, Rokseth, and Thibault, *Trois Chansonniers* (Paris, 1927), p. 72, and by Smijers, *Werken van Josquin des Prés, Missen*, ii, p. 140.

[3] *Odhecaton*, no. 54; also reprinted by Gombosi, *Jacob Obrecht* (Leipzig, 1925), app. p. 6, and in *Trois Chansonniers*, p. 9.

[4] *Odhecaton*, no. 63.

evidence of the fact would be 'Petite camusette', the beginning of which is constructed in accordance with the strictest imitative principles,[1] or 'Prenez sur moi votre exemple amoureux',[2] which constitutes a *tour de force* in the building-up of a complicated canon, and was thought by Isabella d'Este worthy to be inlaid on the walls of her private chamber.

BUSNOIS

Antoine de Busne, known as Busnois, who was a priest, a poet, and a musician, entered the service of Charles the Bold in 1467 and was a member of the Burgundian ducal chapel until 1482. He died in 1492 at Bruges, where he filled the post of *rector cantoriae* at the church of Saint-Sauveur.[3] It is customary to regard him primarily as a writer of *chansons*, and certainly his most signal successes are in this field—seventy-seven compositions whose beauty of melodic line, subtlety of rhythm, sense of harmonic colour and judicious use of imitative writing are evidence of remarkable variety and originality.[4] The theme of elegiac love inspired him to a series of delicate little masterpieces, bearing witness to the refined culture of the Burgundian court of which he is the most characteristic representative. Though in the field of church music he had not Ockeghem's range, still there are numerous examples of his personal style among his motets.[5] He was fond of surprising effects which hold the listener's attention; and his humanism, inclining both to pedantry and to childishness, induced him to seek deliberately after strangeness. Two of his nine motets are freely composed, five make use of plainsong tenors, and the two most original, 'In hydraulis'[6] and 'Anthoni usque limina',[7] employ as *canti fermi* themes freely invented in accordance with what was soon to be a frequent practice. The former, whose *seconda pars* is a homage to Ockeghem, is one of his most ingenious; it is built upon a tenor of three notes repeated like an ostinato. The motet in honour of St.

---

[1] Gombosi, op. cit., p. 8.

[2] *Trois Chansonniers*, p. 1, and Jeppesen, op. cit., p. 62.

[3] G. Van Doorslaer, op. cit., p. 30.

[4] George Perle, 'The Chansons of Antoine Busnois', *The Music Review*, xi (1950), p. 89, and C. Brooks, op. cit., p. 111.

[5] E. H. Sparks, 'The Motets of Antoine Busnois', *Journal of the American Musicological Society*, vi (1953), p. 216. 'Regina coeli' and 'Anima mea liquefacta est' are printed in Smijers, *Van Ockeghem tot Sweelinck*, i (Amsterdam, 2nd ed., 1952). The Mass 'L'homme armé' is printed by Feininger, *Monumenta polyphoniae liturgicae*, series i, i, fasc. 2.

[6] *Denkmäler der Tonkunst in Österreich*, vii, p. 105.

[7] Facsimile and transcription in C. L. W. Boer, *Het Anthonius-motet van Anthonius Busnois* (Amsterdam, 1940).

Anthony is one of the most curious written in that age; its tenor consists of a single note D, recurring at intervals in accordance with the demands of a canon, the somewhat obscure formula for which is written on a scroll also bearing the drawing of a bell, so that it is possible, as Fétis thought, that this tenor was actually intended to be played on a bell.[1] But all this technical ingenuity is too often attained at the expense of that inner life which suffuses the religious works of Ockeghem. Nevertheless we must admit that Busnois was one of the most typical representatives of this transition period between Gothic and Renaissance art.

MINOR CONTEMPORARIES

To give a completely accurate picture of the musical life of this time we should mention a number of minor but by no means negligible composers, though a study of their works would add nothing essential to the knowledge already acquired from those of their two great contemporaries. For instance, there was Caron—frequently quoted by Tinctoris[2]—who is known to have lived at Cambrai and doubtless spent some time in Italy also; he wrote Masses and, more notably, *chansons* the most famous of which, 'Hélas que pourra devenir', is found in no fewer than sixteen sources.[3] Tinctoris also speaks of Guillaume Faugues, whose extant work consists exclusively of Masses —one of them, on 'L'homme armé', written entirely in canon[4]—and Johannes Regis (*c.* 1430–85) who left eight motets, two Masses, and two *chansons*.[5] Hayne van Ghizeghem, who was personal valet to Philip the Good and afterwards to Charles the Bold, as well as being a member of their chapel, was exclusively a composer of *chansons*;[6] in these he sometimes equals the grace of Busnois, and one of them, 'De tous biens plaine', quoted above as Ex. 101, was among the most famous of its age. Jacob Barbireau, who from 1448 to 1491 was choirmaster of Notre-Dame at Antwerp, left only three Masses, one motet, and three *chansons*.[7]

[1] C. Van den Borren, *Études sur le XVe siècle musical* (Antwerp, 1941), p. 239.

[2] Coussemaker, *Scriptorum*, iv, pp. 77, 146, 152, 154, 172, 200.

[3] Plamenac, 'A Reconstruction of the French Chansonnier in the Biblioteca Colombina, Seville', *The Musical Quarterly*, xxviii (1952), p. 108. The 'L'homme armé' Mass is in Feininger, op. cit., series i, i, fasc. 3.   [4] Feininger, op. cit., series i, i, fasc. 4.

[5] *Opera Omnia*, ed. C. W. H. Lindenburg (American Institute of Musicology, 1956); see also C. W. H. Lindenburg, *Het leven en de werken van Johannes Regis* (Amsterdam, 1939).

[6] Sixteen of his *chansons* are printed in Marix, *Les Musiciens de la cour de Bourgogne* (Paris, 1937).

[7] *Opera Omnia*, ed. Bernhard Meier (American Institute of Musicology, 1954 and 1957); see also J. Du Saar, *Het leven en de composities van Jacobus Barbireau* (Utrecht, 1946).

THE PERIOD OF JOSQUIN DES PREZ

Another generation of musicians, living at the turn of the century, is centred for us—as the previous generation is upon Ockeghem—on Josquin des Prez, one of the greatest composers of all time, whose life (spent almost entirely outside his own country) and whose works are both the type and the highest point of the style of his age.[1] He is usually said to have been born in Hainault about 1450, but it seems that we must adopt an earlier date, since from 1459 until 1472, under the name of 'Juschino de Frantia', 'Judocho Frantia', or 'Iustino', he was in the choir of Milan Cathedral, whence in 1472 he was called to the chapel of Duke Galeazzo Maria Sforza.[2] In 1479 he was still at Milan, in the service of Cardinal Ascanio Sforza, then from 1486 to 1494 at the Papal chapel, and in 1499 at the court of Ercole d'Este of Ferrara. In 1501 he was in France, then back at Ferrara in 1503, then again until 1515 in France, probably attached to Louis XII's chapel. His last years were spent as provost of the chapter at Condé, where he died in 1521.

Few musicians have enjoyed as great a reputation as Josquin; it would be a hopeless task to attempt to quote all the encomiums that were bestowed upon him. But it is instructive to find evidence of his celebrity dating from long after his death, showing that his genius was honoured in all periods. In an important though still not well known manuscript, copied in Italy at the very end of the sixteenth century, there occur, along with *ricercari* and works by the madrigalists, three Masses by Josquin—chosen, curiously enough, from among the more archaic in style of his productions.[3] It is quite natural to find his pupil Petit Coclico, or his contemporaries Compère, Glareanus, Spataro, Lampadius, Gafurius, Castiglione, or Luther referring to him in terms of the highest praise; but it is more surprising that in 1711 Andrea Adami[4] should still have regarded him as 'il lume maggiore di questa gran scienza, dal quale imparono tutti i contrapuntisti che vennero dopo di esso' (the greatest luminary of this great science, from whom have learned all the contrapuntists who have come after him), adding: 'non v'ha dubbio che fu Josquin uomo di gran talento di cui parla e

[1] Complete edition, ed. Albert Smijers (Amsterdam and Leipzig, 1921–56).

[2] Sartori, 'Josquin des Prés, cantore del Duomo di Milano', *Annales musicologiques*, iv (1956).

[3] 'L'homme armé super voces musicales', 'La sol fa re mi', and 'L'homme armé sexti toni' (*Kyrie* and *Gloria* only) on pp. 367, 377, and 384 of the 'Bourdeney-Pasche' manuscript, so called from the names of its last two owners, acquired by the Bibliothèque nationale de Paris in 1955 (Rés. Vma. MS. 851).

[4] *Osservazioni per ben regolare il coro dei cantori della Cappella Pontifica* (Rome, 1711), p. 160.

parlerà sempre la fama' (there is no doubt that Josquin was a man
of great talent of whom fame always speaks—and always will).

It is indeed true that whatever type of composition Josquin attempted, he gave evidence of genius in all of them, the wealth of his imagination and the diversity of his style being a source of constant surprise. He was the first to satisfy in any degree the Renaissance ideal,
whose aim was the expression in music of all the moods of a text
('omnium affectus exprimere', as Coclico said); in this he was a worthy
forerunner of Lassus. We never find in him that 'inner emptiness' of
which the music of this period has sometimes been accused.[1] He was
a master both of expression and of contrapuntal art; it is impossible
to characterize his genius merely by analysing the methods of his
musical rhetoric, for his 'Netherland mysticism' is as likely to find its
outlet through a conservative technique as through works looking
towards the future. The inmost secret of his art is to be sought in the
depth of his religious feeling, for his *chansons*, despite the skill he
shows in them, figure in his work only as 'cantus parvus'.[2] His motet
'Ave verum', the first part of which is given below, is a good example
of what a composer's inner resources may achieve with the simplest
of means, and would amply justify our speaking of 'the Josquinian
miracle'.

Ex. 108.

[1] M. Françon, *Poèmes de transition, XVe–XVIe siècles* (Cambridge and Paris, 1928
p. 29.
[2] Walter Wiora, 'Der religiöse Grundzug im neuen Stil und Weg Josquins des Prez'
Die Musikforschung, vi (1953), p. 23.

(Hail, true body of Christ, born of the Virgin Mary. Truly you suffered and were sacrificed on the cross for man.)

Long before Palestrina, Josquin showed himself keenly concerned to meet the requirements of verbal intelligibility, and in his compositions the demands of clarity are always satisfied, thanks to careful articulation and absence of entangled melismata.[1] This, however, did

---

[1] Lowinsky, 'Zur Frage der Deklamationsrhythmik in der a cappella Musik des 16. Jahrhunderts', *Acta musicologica*, vii (1935), p. 62.

not prevent him from achieving a supple melodic line; he would sometimes allow a voice to expand upon a long expressive scale-passage, as in his 'Salve regina' the altus does upon the word 'regina'.[1] It was the same desire for clarity that frequently induced him to lighten the complex substance of his contrapuntal structure by dividing a quartet of voices into alternating duets, a procedure usually considered specially characteristic of his writing. One can study in his work every feature of the period: form of cadences,[2] distribution of voices,[3] use of imitation, homorhythm and dissonant intervals, gradual abandonment of the church modes. But the variety of the means he employed in all these fields, and the ease with which he combined the old with the new, make it very difficult to establish a chronology of his works or to follow the evolution of his style.[4] He stands before us as a complete musician, never bound by a system or a formula, capable of any audacity and any (doubtless unconscious) revolt against the principles laid down by theorists.

JOSQUIN'S MASSES

In the score or so of Masses by Josquin which have come down to us, despite a deliberately conservative style, we find all the procedures then in use for composing a Mass, but so renewed and enriched that these works occupy a very important place in the history of the form. A consideration of the various aspects of Josquin's use of the *canto fermo* would comprise in itself a study of no little complexity. Some of these Masses are based on themes of his own invention, some make use of secular *chansons*, and others again use liturgical melodies. On the one hand there are the Masses 'La sol fa re mi',[5] 'L'homme armé sexti toni'[6] and 'L'homme armé super voces musicales',[7] in which Josquin keeps to the traditional treatment of the *canto fermo*, but makes it more flexible and diversifies it by transformed statements of the theme; on the other, the Masses 'Malheur me bat'[8] and 'Fortu-

[1] *Werken*, ed. Smijers, *Motetten*, iii, p. 26.
[2] M. E. Brockhoff, 'Die Kadenz bei Josquin', *Kongress-Bericht . . . Utrecht 1952*, pp. 86–95.
[3] Helmuth Osthoff, 'Besetzung und Klangstruktur in den Werken von Josquin des Prez', *Archiv für Musikwissenschaft*, ix (1952), pp. 177–94.
[4] Van den Borren, 'À propos de quelques messes de Josquin', and H. Osthoff, 'Zur Echtheitsfrage und Chronologie bei Josquins Werken', *Kongress-Bericht . . . Utrecht 1952*, pp. 79 ff. and 303 ff.
[5] *Werken*, ed. Smijers, *Missen*, i, no. 2.
[6] Ibid., no. 5.
[7] Ibid., no. 1. The beginning of the *Sanctus* is recorded in *The History of Music in Sound*, iii.
[8] Ibid. ii, no. 8.

nata desperata',[1] which look forward to the technique of the *missa parodia*—a technique he was to use in its developed form for the Mass 'Mater patris',[2] a free *parodia* on a motet by Brumel. The same diversity in treatment of *canti fermi* is to be observed in the Masses on Gregorian themes. Whereas the Mass 'De beata virgine'[3] has no tenor properly to be so called, but passes the liturgical melodies (taken from the Gregorian Masses IX and IV)[4] from one voice to another, the Mass 'Da pacem',[5] on the contrary, keeps to the old tradition of a tenor often in long note-values, and also contains academic and well-constructed canons which are in no way a hindrance to expressiveness, as is evident from the *Incarnatus*, described by Pirro as 'an act of fervent meditation'. The Mass 'Pange lingua',[6] in which the hymn-melody is broken into thematic fragments, with subtle variants, treated imitatively by four parts always of equal importance, represents the highest peak of Josquin's art, and justifies all the epithets applied to it by Ambros.[7] The second *Agnus Dei* is the supreme manifestation of Flemish mysticism in music of Italian limpidity and sweetness:

Ex. 109

[1] *Werken*, ed. Smijers, *Missen*, i, no. 4.
[2] Ibid. iii, no. 12.
[3] Ibid., no. 16, and *Das Chorwerk*, xlii.
[4] *Liber Usualis* (1950), pp. 40 and 25.
[5] *Werken*, *Missen*, iv, no. 19 and *Das Chorwerk*, xx.
[6] Ibid., no. 18, and *Das Chorwerk*, i.
[7] Ambros-Kade, *Geschichte der Musik*, iii (Leipzig, 1889), p. 223.

(Grant us thy peace.)

These Masses enjoyed the greatest popularity, as witness the publications of Petrucci. It was in fact with a volume by Josquin that the Venetian publisher inaugurated the series of his collections of Masses in 1502, and he not only published two more books in 1505 and 1514, but also reissued the first two books in 1515 and 1516.

JOSQUIN'S MOTETS

Josquin's motets contain the best of his work. In these, stimulated by a continual diversity of texts, offering him a very wide scope, he gave more evidence of independence of the current musical system than in his Masses. The latter are usually for four voices, but Josquin in his motets, though still fond of this layout, shows greater variety and writes for three to six voices, never feeling encumbered by the complexity of six-part writing which in no way impeded his natural genius. Although he does not completely abandon the old *canto fermo* technique, he often substitutes for it that of continuous imitation, the principle which was to be fundamental to the creative work of his successors, in which each section of the text has its own melody, imitated by each voice in turn, as in the two extracts here given from 'Ave Maria . . . virgo serena'.[1]

Ex. 110

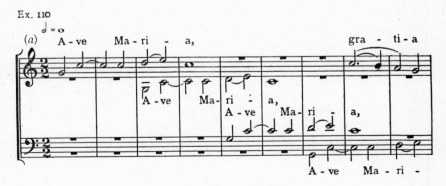

[1] *Werken, Motetten*, i, p. 1.

(Hail Mary, full of grace, the Lord be with thee, O serene Virgin.)

(Hail thou, whose nativity was our feast, a light rising like the morning star, coming before the true sun.)

The highly evocative text of the psalms—Josquin's polyphonic settings of which are perhaps the earliest examples of their kind—suited his expressive style.[1] Among them, the five-part 'Miserere', written for Ercole d'Este and printed by Petrucci in 1519, is built on a very simple *canto fermo* repeated one degree lower each time in the first and third sections, one degree higher each time in the second section.[2] The publisher Johannes Ott questioned whether anyone could hear it unmoved and without having his attention forcibly drawn to the

[1] A short but typical psalm motet, 'Tribulatio et angustia', is recorded in *The History of Music in Sound*, iii.
[2] *Werken*, ed. Smijers, *Motetten*, ii, p. 58.

words of the Prophet, seeing that its sounds correspond so exactly to the feelings of a man overcome with remorse, and that its persistently imploring tone so well indicates regrets and hope.[1] Josquin kept to the tradition of the motet with double text, sacred and profane, when he associates both words and melody of the *chanson*, 'D'un autre amer', with the Latin words 'Nobis esset fallacia'. His five-part 'Stabat mater', in which the tenor is that of Agricola's *chanson* 'Comme femme desconfortée', is one of his most remarkable works;[2] but here the function of the borrowed theme is rather to evoke emotion by verbal symbolism than to provide a musical basis.

JOSQUIN'S SECULAR MUSIC

Traces of Josquin's travels in Italy are to be found in his essays in the form then in vogue there, the *frottola*;[3] but this was an essentially indigenous type of composition and drew from him only three not very significant examples. The only one striking the genuine note is 'El grillo è buon cantore', with its witty imitation of the cricket.[4] On the other hand his fifty-two settings of French words establish him as one of the most important composers of *chansons*. He more or less gave up the fixed forms of the *rondeau* and *bergerette*; though some of his *chansons* are still constructed with repeated elements, in accordance with an indefinite variety of patterns: *AbA*, *AbA'*, *aab*, *aabbc. . .*, &c. But there are numerous *chansons* composed freely, in the same way as a motet. These offer solutions of a whole series of contrapuntal problems with numerous canons, and Josquin seems in them to be concerned less with expressiveness than with technical mastery. None the less in 'Cueurs desolez', for five voices, the *quinta vox*, singing the theme 'Plorans ploravit in nocte' from the Lamentations, adds to the dramatic feeling;[5] and the same kind of symbolism is found in his elegy on the death of Ockeghem, 'Nymphes des bois', where the tenor sings the melody of the Introit 'Requiem aeternam', a further visual symbolism being added by writing the piece in black notes.[6] The *chansons* are the only part of Josquin's work in which those features make themselves apparent which were later to characterize French music in the sixteenth century; 'Petite camusette'[7]

---

[1] Preface to the *Secundus tomus novi operis musici* (Nuremberg, 1538).
[2] *Werken*, ed. Smijers, *Motetten*, ii, p. 51.
[3] See Chapter XI.
[4] Recorded in *The History of Music in Sound*, iii.
[5] *Wereldlijke Werken*, p. 72.
[6] Ibid., p. 56.
[7] Ibid., p. 43.

shows the gulf between this style and that of the older Burgundian type of *chanson*:[1]

Ex. III

[1] Another characteristic example, 'Je ne me puis tenir d'aimer', is recorded in *The History of Music in Sound*, iii.

(Little snub-nose, you're my death. . . . Robin and Mary are off to the beautiful woods.)

OBRECHT

Beside Josquin, Jacob Obrecht occupies a somewhat special place, because, to begin with, he was the only true Netherlander of the group.[1] Born about 1450 and probably descended from a Bergen-op-Zoom family, it was in this town that he held his first post, about 1476—that of choirmaster to the Guild of Our Lady, where he is supposed to have had Erasmus for a pupil.[2] He was afterwards in turn at Cambrai (1484–5), Bruges, Ferrara, and Antwerp (1492–6), and he died of plague at Ferrara in 1505. Of all the musicians of this generation, he is the one in whom many have claimed to see the greatest resemblance to Josquin; but actually his music, though always pleasant, tends to sound facile, so that one is not surprised to learn that he could compose a Mass in a single night, as Glareanus states.[3] He often extends his ideas by interminable sequences, instead of seeking more skilful solutions; witness the *Gloria* of his Mass 'Ave regina caelorum':[4]

Ex. 112

---

[1] A collected edition of Obrecht's works, edited by Johannes Wolf, has been published in thirty volumes (Amsterdam and Leipzig, 1908–21). A number of compositions which have come to light since in the library of Segovia Cathedral (see *Acta Musicologica*, viii (1936), pp. 6–17), notably songs to Dutch texts, have been published by Smijers in *Van Ockeghem tot Sweelinck*, iii (Amsterdam, 1941). A new collected edition *Opera omnia*, begun by Smijers, is in progress.

[2] Glareanus, *Dodecachordon* (Basle, 1547), pp. 256 and 456.

[3] Ibid., p. 456.

[4] *Werken*, ed. Wolf, *Missen*, iii, p. 146.

(We praise Thee, we bless Thee, we worship Thee, we glorify Thee.)

Obrecht was not very progressive and kept to a rather outdated style, making little use of imitation but frequently employing *canti fermi* in long note-values and showing a certain fondness for polytextual motets. All the same, he belongs indubitably to the generation of the transition period; he is to be distinguished from the Ockeghem group by a strong feeling for tonality, abandonment of the fixed forms, a taste for clear harmony, and the effort to preserve unity by repeating the same motive—with variations—in the different voices. But it is not so much on account of learning as through his graceful and flexible melody and by his sincere and serene piety that Obrecht is to be ranked with the first musicians of his day.

His Masses constitute more than two-thirds of his output, and the best part of it. Petrucci published a volume of five of them[1] as early as 1503, only a year later than the first book of Josquin's. In the Masses—mostly for four voices—while the *canto fermo* principle is predominant, construction on this basis is varied in all sorts of ingenious ways.[2] The theme may appear complete, even repeated, in the tenor or superius, but most frequently the melody is divided into several sections, introduced one at a time in successive movements, and not stated complete until the end of the work, as in 'Malheur me bat'[3] and 'Maria zart'. These *canti fermi* are chosen in almost equal number from liturgical melodies or secular songs, the latter including not only French *chansons* but German and Flemish pieces also (e.g. 'Maria zart', 'Schoen lief', and 'Der pfoben swancz'[4]). The title of the

---

[1] Reprinted as the first volume of *Opera omnia*, ed. Smijers (Amsterdam, 1953–7).
[2] M. Kyriazis, *Die Cantus-Firmus Technik in den Messen Obrechts* (Bern, 1952). See also on Obrecht's Masses, B. Meier, 'Zyklische Gesamtstruktur und Tonalität in den Messen Jacob Obrechts', *Archiv für Musikwissenschaft*, x (1953), pp. 289–310.
[3] *Werken, Missen*, i, p. 141; *Opera omnia*, i, p. 173.
[4] The last is printed by Wolf (*Werken, Missen*, v, p. 1) as a 'Missa sine nomine', but identified by Gombosi, *Jacob Obrecht: eine stilkritische Studie* (Leipzig, 1925), p. 116.

'Missa Graecorum' is still an unsolved riddle,[1] and the Mass known as 'Carminum' is curious in that it makes use not of one but of several *chansons*. It belongs, moreover, to the work erroneously published by Wolf as a Mass 'Adieu mes amours', and it would be preferable to combine these two, as Smijers proposed to do in his new edition of Obrecht's works, under the common title 'Missa diversorum tenorum'.[2] The 'parody' principle may be observed in the Masses 'Fortuna desperata', 'Fors seulement',[3] and 'Rose playsant', in which the composer borrows from all the parts of his model. The Mass 'Si dedero'[4], also written on this principle, has the further interest of being one of the earliest to be based on a motet instead of one of the secular *chansons* which had hitherto been the only polyphonic models. The remarkable Mass 'Sub tuum praesidium'[5] employs the Gregorian antiphon throughout but introduces other texts and melodies in honour of the Virgin in the *Credo* and following numbers. Its *Kyrie* is for three voices; by the successive addition of one more voice in each number, so that the final *Agnus* is for seven, the Mass is gradually built up to a massive edifice.[6] The following example is taken from the *Agnus* III:[7]

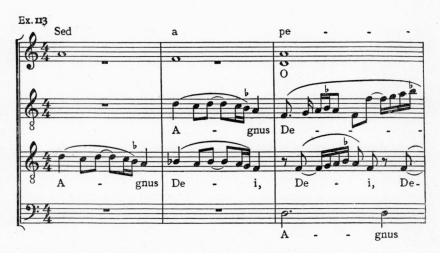

Ex. 113

---

[1] *Opera omnia*, i, p. 69.

[2] Smijers, 'De Missa Carminum van Jacob Hobrecht', *Tijdschrift voor Muziekwetenschap*, xvii (1951), pp. 192–4.

[3] *Werken, Missen*, i, p. 85; v, p. 133; 'Fortuna desperata' also in *Opera omnia*, i, p. 113.

[4] *Werken, Missen* iii, p. 1.

[5] Ibid., ii, p. 1.

[6] See the detailed study of Obrecht's masses in Peter Wagner, *Geschichte der Messe* (Leipzig, 1913), pp. 114–39.

[7] *Werken, Missen*, ii, p. 36.

In his nineteen motets Obrecht frequently uses a *canto fermo*, as in the three settings of 'Salve regina', one of which—that for six voices[1]—felicitously exploits the contrast of the three high voices with the three lower. He revived and even exaggerated the nearly obsolete practice of setting more than one text at a time in the five-part Christmas motet 'Factor orbis',[2] in the second section of which each voice sings a different liturgical text—sometimes to the associated melody. Very characteristic of Obrecht's limpid later style is the four-part 'Si oblitus'.[3]

The Passion for four voices attributed to Obrecht in some sources,[4] would seem more probably to be the work of Antoine Longueval or Longaval, who was a chorister in the French royal chapel from 1504 to 1522 and appointed its choirmaster in 1517.[5] This Passion, its text compiled from all four Gospels, is in reality an extended motet and the earliest of a whole series of 'motet-Passions'.

Seventeen of Obrecht's thirty-one secular pieces are set to Dutch words,[6] which seems an unexpectedly high proportion until we remember the composer's nationality; the fact that only eight of his *chansons* have French words is sufficient proof of his special position. In this connexion it is worth observing that the arguments adduced by Lenaerts, to explain why these so-called Netherlanders so seldom set

[1] *Werken, Motetten*, p. 1; *Opera omnia*, ii, p. 1.

[2] *Motetten*, p. 15.

[3] Ibid., p. 9; recorded in *The History of Music in Sound*, iii.

[4] Ed. D. de Lange (Amsterdam and Leipzig, 1894); also in *Werken, Passio*.

[5] M. Brenet, *Les Musiciens de la Sainte-Chapelle du Palais* (Paris, 1910), pp. 65, 68 ff.; Smijers, 'De Matthaeus-Passie van Jacob Obrecht', *Tijdschrift der Vereeniging voor Nederlandsche muziekgeschiedenis*, xiv (1935), p. 182.

[6] Ten of them in Smijers, *Van Ockeghem tot Sweelinck*, iii.

texts in their own language, are not valid for Obrecht who, though he
had spent a great part of his life abroad, nevertheless chose Dutch for
his secular compositions in spite of the fact that the language was not
at all widely diffused.[1] It is better to admit quite simply that composers
usually prefer their native tongue, and that this may be taken as a
fairly sound criterion by which to decide their national origins.
Obrecht's stay in Italy is recalled only by two *chansons* to Italian
words, one of them being the delightful 'Tortorella'. There are also
four pieces without titles or words, impossible to classify in any
special genre and not displaying the features of an essentially instrumental style either.

ALEXANDER AGRICOLA

Among Josquin's contemporaries, Alexander Agricola is one of
those whose musical personalities remain clearly defined beside that
of the master. The fact that he was frequently referred to by his Christian name alone sometimes makes it difficult to identify him, and we
are uncertain also of his origin since he was described as 'de Alemania'
whereas his epitaph says: 'quis Belgam hunc traxit ?' It is probable,
however, that he came from Flanders.[2] From 1472 to 1474 he was at
Milan in the service of Duke Galeazzo Maria Sforza, moving thence
to Florence and afterwards to Cambrai (1475–6), then returning again
to Italy. In 1500 he appears for the first time on the list of musicians
serving Duke Philip the Handsome, who 'retained Alexander Agricola
as chaplain and chorister in his chapel, over and above the regular
number'.[3] He is also mentioned among the members of this choir in
the last list drawn up (1506) at Valladolid, where it is thought he died
the same year.

His output includes nine Masses, two settings of the Creed, some
twenty-five motets, and ninety-three secular settings of French, Italian,
and Flemish words.[4] Five of his Masses were published by Petrucci
in 1504, among which the Masses 'Malheur me bat' (on Ockeghem's
chanson) and 'Je ne demande' (on one by Busnois) are especially
remarkable for the freedom with which the *canto fermo* is treated:
Agricola changes its rhythm, decorates it, simplifies it, and sometimes
even leaves it out altogether.[5] His motet 'Si dedero', though written

---

[1] R. Lenaerts, *Het Nederlands polifonies lied in de 16e eeuw* (Antwerp, 1933), p. 114.
[2] Gustave Reese, *Music in the Renaissance*, p. 207.
[3] G. Van Doorslaer, *La Chapelle musicale de Philippe le Beau*, p. 47.
[4] Complete list in Paul Müller's article in *Die Musik in Geschichte und Gegenwart*, i
(1949), cols. 159–60.
[5] *Kyrie* and *Agnus* II of 'Je ne demande' have been reprinted in Gombosi, op. cit.,
musical appendix, pp. 68–73, and an excerpt from the *Gloria* in Besseler, *Musik des*

in a rather elementary manner—a tenor accompanied mostly in parallel movement—seems to have enjoyed considerable celebrity, since it
is found in twenty-two different sources.[1] The fact that he sometimes
set the same music indifferently to a motet-text and to secular *chanson*-
words (e.g. his motet 'Ave que sublimar ad sidera' is identical with
one of his two *chansons* 'Comme femme') may point to his having
cared little for the expressive content of words; and certainly in many
of his *chansons* he is ingenious rather than moving. He occupies a
place of the first importance in the field of new rhythmic ventures,
and he often ornaments in an instrumental style. As an example of
this we may quote his four-part setting[2] (in Petrucci's *Canti C*, 1504)
of the tenor of Hayne's 'De tous biens plaine' (see Ex. 101) in which
the accompanying counterpoints are broken into short detached
motives:

Ex. 114

Mittelalters und der Renaissance (Potsdam, 1931), p. 240. The *Kyrie* from 'Malheur me
bat' is also reprinted in Gombosi, p. 57, and (*Kyrie* I only) in Peter Wagner, op. cit.,
p. 271; Pirro, op. cit., p. 204, gives a substantial excerpt from the *Sanctus*.

[1] See Helen Hewitt's edition of the *Harmonice musices odhecaton*, no. 56. See also
Nanie Bridgman, 'Un manuscrit italien du début du XVIᵉ siècle', in *Annales musicologiques*, i (Paris, 1953), no. 23.

[2] This exists in Cod. Cap. Giulia (Rome) in a three-part version. Gombosi, op. cit.,
pp. 42–43, advances reasons for believing the additional part to be by a later hand.

In his other setting in three parts, the same melody is accompanied in a quite different style, in equal notes suggesting keyboard technique.[1] Similarly there have come down to us three different versions of 'D'un autre amer' and two of 'Tout a par moy',[2] bearing witness to the versatility of his talent and to the lively imagination which prompted his ingenious variations. He seems to have been particularly fond of giving the tenor of a French *chanson* Latin words which provide a symbolic commentary on the French text: e.g. 'Belle sur toutes'/'Tota pulchra es' in the *Canti* C,[3] 'Revenez tous regrets'/'Quis det ut veniat'[4] 'L'heure est venue de me plaindre'/'Circumdederunt me gemitus mortis'.[5] Finally, like most of his fellows, Agricola did not remain indifferent to Italian music; he composed not only a *frottola*, 'Amor che sospirar,' adopting therein the homophonic style of the Italians, but also some *canti carnascialeschi* such as the 'Canto de' facitori d'olio'.[6]

Although the search for novelty and originality of which we are conscious in Agricola was not always crowned with success, it explains the favoured place that Petrucci, reflecting the opinion of his customers, gave this composer in his collections.

HEINRICH ISAAC

Another musician, Heinrich Isaac, stands in the forefront of the picture, first because of the diversity of his talent and the influence he exercised, especially on the development of German music, and also because of the international character not only of his life but of his work. His own nationality has often been disputed. Nachtgall (Luscinius) called him 'ex Germanis nostris',[7] in Italy he was sometimes known as 'Arrigo Tedesco', whereas Paolo Cortese described him as 'Gallus'. But as he referred to himself in his will as 'de Flandria', there seems to be no reason to contradict him. He was summoned to the court of Lorenzo de' Medici, probably not later than 1479, to replace the organist Squarcialupi,[8] but left Florence after the death of his patron in 1492 and a year or two later entered the service

[1] Quoted by Pirro, op. cit., pp. 208–9.
[2] The former are printed in Smijers, *Van Ockeghem tot Sweelinck*, iv, pp. 101, 103, and 105, one of the latter, ibid., p. 107, and *Werken van Josquin des Prez, Missen*, iii, p. 56.
[3] Printed by Schering, *Geschichte der Musik in Beispielen* (Leipzig, 1931), no. 53.
[4] Printed by Maldeghem, *Trésor musical: Musique profane*, xi, p. 43.
[5] *Odhecaton*, no. 81.
[6] Federico Ghisi, *I Canti carnascialeschi nelle fonti musicali del XV e XVI secolo* (Florence, 1937), p. 48.
[7] *Musurgia* (Strasbourg, 1536), p. 94.
[8] L. Parigi, *Laurentiana, Lorenzo dei Medici cultore della musica* (Florence, 1954), p. 25.

of the Emperor Maximilian, who appointed him court composer in 1497. He continued none the less to spend time abroad at Constance, Ferrara, and especially Florence where, from 1512 onwards, he was Maximilian's diplomatic agent; he died there in 1517.[1]

In his secular works Isaac provided arguments for all the nationalities in turn attributed to him, by the ease with which he interpreted German, French, or Italian words. He was the only one of these Northern musicians able to endow the *canti carnascialeschi* so dear to Lorenzo[2] with the true Florentine touch, and some of his *frottole* are among the best of their kind—for instance 'Morte che fai', which he wrote to a *strambotto* by the poet Aquilano.[3] For these he mostly chose the homophonic style suitable to the solo voice with lute accompaniment which at that time was prevalent in Italy. It was he who set to music the lament by Angelo Poliziano on the death of Lorenzo, 'Quis dabit capiti meo aquam'.[4] His French *chansons* show, by the use of popular songs such as 'A l'ombre d'un buissonnet', 'Mon père m'a donné mari' or 'Et qui la dira',[5] that in this domain also he had completely assimilated not only the spirit of the language, but also the usual musical style of his Romance-speaking colleagues, with a predominance of contrapuntal, imitative writing. But his German secular songs are the most numerous, and also the most successful. In these works, mostly for four voices and built on a tenor, Isaac brought into being for the first time a genuine German type of art-song, ranging from the tender beauty of 'Freundtlich und mild' to the comedy of 'Es het ein Baur ein Töchterlein',[6] in which he successfully alternated homophony with polyphonic passages in which the different voices borrow the principal melody. In the famous 'Isbruck, ich muß dich lassen', in which the superius has a melody

Ex. 115

Is - bruck, ich muss   dich   las - sen,   Ich fahr do-hin

---

[1] Pirro, op. cit., p. 195, and H. J. Moser, *Geschichte der deutschen Musik*, i (third edition, Stuttgart, 1923), pp. 375 ff.   [2] See Chapter XI.

[3] Published by Nanie Bridgman, 'Un manuscrit italien', *Annales musicologiques*, i, p. 263.

[4] *Denkmäler der Tonkunst in Österreich*, xiv, p. 45.

[5] The first two are printed ibid., pp. 96 and 74, the last in the modern edition of the *Odhecaton*, no. 11.

[6] *Denkmäler der Tonkunst in Österreich*, xiv, pp. 10 and 7.

(Innsbruck, I must leave thee. I take my way into a strange land. My joy is taken from me and I know not how to recover it where I am banished.)

probably of popular origin, he prefigures the German chorale with its homophonic style and its short phrases separated by silences. The final melisma of this song, in parallel fourths, expresses sadness with the subdued sentiment characteristic of German popular art. In another, probably earlier version of the song,[1] the melody is heard in the tenor and imitated canonically; this version appears note for note as the *Christe secundum* of his 'Missa Carminum', based on several German songs.[2]

Petrucci printed five 'Misse henrici Izac' in 1506; four of them are *chanson*-Masses,[3] and German publishers—Petrejus, Grapheus, Ott,

[1] Recorded in *The History of Music in Sound*, iii.

[2] Published posthumously by Rhaw in *Opus decem missarum* (Wittenberg, 1541), and reprinted by Reinhold Heyden, *Das Chorwerk*, vii.

[3] Wooldridge printed the *Agnus* of one of them, 'Charge de deuil', typical of Isaac's mastery in the completely imitative style, in *The Oxford History of Music*, ii (Oxford, 1905), p. 257. The *Kyrie* of 'Quant j'ay au cor' is printed in *Van Ockeghem tot Sweelinck*, vi, which also contains examples of Isaac's French, German, and Italian songs.

and Rhaw—who brought out others during the first half of the sixteenth century, also favoured his *chanson*-Masses. But actually, as
Glareanus noted, Isaac himself preferred liturgical themes, on which
he based his most characteristic Masses.[1] His most important work
in this field is certainly his series of settings of the Proper of the Mass
for the whole year, according to the Constance Gradual. He died
before he could finish this *Choralis Constantinus*, which was completed
by his pupil Ludwig Senfl. The publisher Formschneider issued it at
Nuremberg in three books, in 1550 and 1555.[2] The historical importance of this work is very great; apart from William Byrd, no other
composer has tried his hand at so gigantic an undertaking. It is
written in an indubitably 'Netherland' style, with nearly all the
entries in imitation, skilful and varied throughout, and alternating
with homophonic passages; the composer has managed to invest the
plainsong melodies with new life, by varying and amplifying them,
never doing violence to the expressive content of the text. Sometimes
he strains after rhythmic complexities,[3] but in general he keeps to a
beautifully simple style of counterpoint, as in the Alleluia for the
Common of Apostles:[4]

Ex. 116

---

[1] *Dodecachordon*, p. 460. On Isaac's Masses, see Peter Wagner, *Geschichte der Messe*,
pp. 280–312; five of them have been edited by Louise Cuyler (Ann Arbor, 1957).

[2] The first two parts have been edited by Bezecny and Rabl, and by Webern, in
Denkmäler der Tonkunst in Österreich, v (1) and xvi (1), the third by Louise Cuyler
(Ann Arbor, 1950). See also P. Blaschke, 'Heinrich Isaaks Choralis Constantinus',
Kirchenmusikalisches Jahrbuch, xxvi (1931), p. 32; O. zur Nedden, 'Zur Musikgeschichte
von Konstanz um 1500', *Zeitschrift für Musikwissenschaft*, xii (1930), p. 449;
A. Thürlings, 'Heinrich Isaac in Augsburg und Konstanz', *Denkmäler der Tonkunst
in Bayern*, iii (2), p. xcix, and W. Gerstenberg's review of Cuyler, op. cit., *Die Musikforschung*, vii (1954), p. 116.

[3] Above all in 'De radice Jesse' with its different mensuration in all four parts
simultaneously and frequent changes of mensuration within each part: see *Denkmäler
der Tonkunst in Österreich*, xvi (1), p. 194; facsimile of original notation in Apel, *The
Notation of Polyphonic Music* (Cambridge, Mass., 1942), p. 173. Glareanus cites the
same piece as an example of extreme mensural complexity in the *Dodecachordon*, but
with a different text: 'Conceptio Mariae virginis'.

[4] Part iii, p. 78 of Louise Cuyler's edition. The *Choralis Constantinus* is discussed
further in vol. IV, Chapter III.

Isaac also left a fair number of pieces in a definitely instrumental style; yet, organist of Florence Cathedral though he was, he seems to have completed only one work for organ, written at the request of Martin Vogelmayer, himself organist at Constance.[1] The rest of these instrumental works, such as the charming 'Der Hundt',[2] were probably intended for small wind or string consorts.

Isaac was one of the most significant figures of his generation. His contemporaries recognized from the first that he had an inventive facility all his own. An undated letter (probably of about 1500), addressed to Ercole d'Este by someone signing himself 'Gian', sets Isaac and Josquin against each other, and while admitting that Josquin 'compone meglio' (composes better), nevertheless gives the preference to Isaac who 'farà più spesso cose nove' (will compose new things more often).[3] His pupil Ludwig Senfl was doubtless right when he wrote, 'Er ist in aller Welt bekanndt'; for the diffusion of his music was so wide that Moser, writing of the geographical distribution of his works in manuscript, expresses it in the formula 'from Portugal to Pomerania and Poland'.[4] Furthermore, he exerted such an influence on German music that some historians in that country have thought

[1] *Denkmäler der Tonkunst in Österreich*, xvi (1), p. 241, printed p. 229.

[2] Ibid. xvi (1), p. 225, xxxvii (2), p. 75, and *Carmina* (Hanover, 1929), ed. H. J. Moser, p. 7.

[3] E. Van der Straeten, *La Musique aux Pays-Bas*, vi (Brussels, 1882), p. 87.

[4] 'Die Niederlande in der Musikgeographie Europas', *Kongress-Bericht . . . Utrecht 1952*, p. 299.

fit to claim him as one of their own: 'dafür gewannen wir den Nieder-
lander Heinrich Isaac . . . ganz als den unsern'.[1]

It was at this period that there arose in Germany, in the musical
environment fostered by the Emperor Maximilian,[2] the earliest generation of German musicians to abandon their conservative principles
and adapt the resources of the polyphonic style to their own genius.
It would be going too far to give the whole credit for this transformation to a single man, but it cannot be regarded as a pure coincidence
that German musical conservatism came to an end at the time of
Isaac's attachment to the court of Innsbruck; the transformation was
already adumbrated, but he certainly accelerated it.

GERMAN COMPOSERS

It is surprising to note how far Germany stood from the great
polyphonic art, throughout the fifteenth century, confining herself to
the creation of an essentially national vocal music, the three most
important collections of which are the *Lochamer Liederbuch*,[3] the
Schedelsches Liederbuch[4] and the *Glogauer Liederbuch*.[5] Even in these,
however, there may already be observed—besides their very marked
Teutonic character whose homophonic style suggests a folk-origin—
some influence of Netherland technique, especially in the two last-
named collections, where the imitative style is frequently employed.[6]
In the sixteenth century these songs were to be the stock on which
German composers (and also, as we have seen, Isaac himself) drew for
their polyphonic works. Early in that century the printers Oeglin
(Augsburg, 1512), Schoeffer (Mainz, 1513), and Arnt von Aich
(Cologne, *c*. 1519) published similar collections of German songs
in accordance with the same tradition, which was to continue as late
as 1545. And although works by Josquin, Agricola, and Isaac appear
in the four manuscripts which form the most important sources of
German polyphonic church music (Berlin, Deutsche Bibl. 40021
(formerly Z 21); Munich, Staatsbibl. Mus. 3154; Leipzig, Univ. Bibl.
1494,[7] and Breslau, Mus. Inst. der Univ. 2016), the German composers included in these sources—Adam of Fulda, Johannes Aulen,[8]
Balthasar Harzer (Resinarius) (a pupil of Isaac), Paul Hofhaimer,

---

[1] J. Müller-Blattau, *Geschichte der deutschen Musik* (third edition, Berlin, 1942), p. 72.
[2] On music at Maximilians's court, see W. Senn, *Musik und Theater am Hof zu
Innsbruck* (Innsbruck, 1954).   [3] See p. 372.   [4] See p. 374.   [5] See p. 368.
[6] H. Osthoff, *Die Niederländer und das deutsche Lied* (Berlin, 1938).
[7] Published by Rudolf Gerber as *Der Mensuralkodex des Nikolaus Apel* (*Das Erbe
deutscher Musik*, xxxii–xxxiv) (Kassel and Basle, 1956).
[8] Aulen's three-part Mass, which appears in two manuscripts, has been reprinted
in *Das Chorwerk*, xxxi.

Conrad Rupsch, Paulus de Rhoda, Finck, and others—do not seem
to have derived much profit from the association. Conservative
though they were by the side of the great Netherlanders, they did
indeed show evidence of beginning to strike out a line for themselves
in the polyphonic field, but it was chiefly in emulation of the earlier
generation, that of Dufay.

All the same, three of them deserve notice. Adam of Fulda (*c.*
1445–1505) was both composer and theorist, first at the court of
Torgau and then as a teacher in the University of Wittenberg. He is
known chiefly for his treatise *De musica* (1490) in which he names
Busnois as 'worthiest example' for imitation; but he also left a
number of vocal pieces, one of which, 'Ach hülff mich layd', was said
by Glareanus (who published it with Latin words: 'O vera lux et
gloria') to be 'elegantissime composita ac per totam Germaniam
cantatissima'.[1] Two others, 'Ach Jupiter' and 'Apollo aller Kunst',
indicate by their choice of words the composer's classical leanings.
In his church music he clings to the old *canto fermo* technique, sometimes placing the *canto fermo* in the tenor as in his four-part Mass in
the Berlin manuscript[2] and the anonymous setting of 'Pange lingua'
in Leipzig 1494 attributed to him by Riemann,[3] far more often in the
superius, in long notes of equal value, accompanying it with independent non-imitative parts, as in his setting of 'Veni creator
spiritus':[4]

Ex. 117

[1] *Dodecachordon*, p. 262.
[2] *Kyrie* printed in W. Niemann, 'Studien zur deutschen Musikgeschichte des XV.
Jahrhunderts', *Kirchenmusikalisches Jahrbuch* (1902), pp. 35–38, with sixteen other compositions by Adam of Fulda.
[3] *Das Erbe deutscher Musik*, xxxii, p. 54.
[4] Ibid., p. 28, and Niemann, op. cit., pp. 13–15.

Heinrich Finck (*c.* 1445–1527) spent much of his career in Poland, and his great-nephew the theorist Hermann Finck, in his *Practica musica* (1556), attached great importance to this foreign residence in the musical formation of one 'cujus ingenium in adolescentia in Polonia excultum est'. He afterwards moved to the court of Wurtemberg until 1513, and then to Vienna, where he remained until his death; his works were not published until later.[1] In his secular vocal pieces (which owe much to Isaac) he displays great skill, making judicious use of imitation, and sometimes much expressive power—his love-songs are among the best in German secular art. His three surviving Masses, based on Gregorian melodies, range from a simple three-part Mass 'De beata Virgine' in the Regensburg manuscript[2] to the imposing Mass for six voices called 'Missa in summis', a work of his maturity,[3] in which he uses the imitative style more amply and shows himself an adept in more modern procedures. The energetic but somewhat crabbed counterpoint of his religious music, and his working of short detached motives, suggest an affinity with Alexandra Agricola. But when we can put our fingers on undoubtedly early work of Finck, such as the pieces preserved in the Berlin and Leipzig manuscripts, which date from the turn of the century, we find him—like the other German composers represented in the same manuscripts—basing his work on *canti fermi* in long notes of equal value and writing basses which tend to run in sixths or tenths with a higher part. When he introduced such a long-note *canto fermo* with imitations in diminished values, as in this 'Iste confessor'[4] from the collection of his hymns published posthumously by George Rhaw in

---

[1] *Schöne ausserlesene lieder des hochberümpten Heinrici Finckens . . . lustig zu singen vnd auff die Instrument dienstlich* (Nuremberg, 1536). These thirty songs, with German texts, with some hymns and motets—and some compositions by Hermann Finck—were reprinted by Eitner in *Publikationen der Gesellschaft für Musikforschung*, Jg. 7 (viii) (1879). Some of his hymns are reprinted in *Das Chorwerk*, ix and xxxii.

[2] MS. B. 117. Reprinted in Ambros-Kade, op. cit., v, pp. 247–79.

[3] Stuttgart, Landesbibl. MS. 28. Printed in *Das Chorwerk*, xxi, with the title 'Missa in summis' added by the editor.

[4] Reprinted in *Das Chorwerk*, ix, p. 22.

1542, he was laying the foundations of what we now recognize as a favourite German device in the treatment of hymn-melodies:

Ex. 118

(He, the hallowed Witness of the Lord. . . .)

Paul Hofhaimer (1459–1537), regarded in his time as the greatest organist in Germany, seems to have been one of the few musicians of his country to enjoy an international reputation. He was for a long time in the service of Maximilian, who knighted and ennobled him; on the Emperor's death in 1519 he moved to Salzburg, where he remained as cathedral organist until his death.[1] Church musician though he was, he left only three pieces for his own instrument[2] and very little church music. Among his motets, the 'Tristitia vestra' published by Rhaw in his *Tricinia* (1542)[3] shows him developing the method of Ex. 118 in a way even more markedly anticipating later German hymn-treatment; the *canto fermo* in long notes (in the highest part) is cut into short sections, each introduced by imitation (in diminished values) in the other parts. He excelled in the secular song,[4] sometimes employing imitative polyphony as in the often reprinted 'Mein's traurens ist',[5] sometimes in almost purely harmonic, decorated note-against-note style. Most of them, however, belong rather to the preceding century than to the new style, and are notable not for the long melodic lines of the Netherlanders, but for the short phrases with frequent cadences characteristic of the fifteenth-century German song-writers. At the end of his life Hofhaimer, a friend of Vadian and other humanists, took part in the experiments in setting Horatian metres quantitatively in four-part harmony (see Chapter X, pp. 370–1). His *Harmoniae poeticae* (Nuremberg 1539) were completed after his death by Senfl; these settings, with their renunciation of all specifically musical interest, are a flat denial of Netherland aesthetic.[6]

Meritorious though these three composers were, they cannot in any way compete with Isaac, who, by reason of the diversity and modernity of his talent, must be considered the earliest great musician in Germany.

PIERRE DE LA RUE

It would be unjust to deny Pierre de la Rue a special place among his contemporaries, for, though he did not share the adventurous life

---

[1] H. J. Moser, *Paul Hofhaimer* (Stuttgart and Berlin, 1929).

[2] Printed in Moser, op. cit., pp. 8, 17, 34, and in his *Frühmeister der deutschen Orgelkunst* (Leipzig, 1930), pp. 9, 16, 48. See also pp. 436–7.

[3] Reprinted by Riemann, *Handbuch*, ii/1, p. 194, and Moser, *Paul Hofhaimer*, Nachtrag, p. 22.

[4] See the musical appendix to Moser, *Paul Hofhaimer*, also issued separately as *91 Tonsätze des Kreises von Paul Hofhaimer*. Moser published important addenda and corrigenda to his book, and two more compositions, in *Zeitschrift für Musikwissenschaft*, xv (1932), pp. 127–38.

[5] Moser, *Paul Hofhaimer*, p. 72, Ambros-Kade, op. cit., v, p. 303, Davison and Apel, op. cit., No. 93.

[6] The *Harmoniae poeticae* have been edited by Achleitner (Salzburg, 1868). A number of examples are given by Liliencron, 'Die horazischen Metren in deutschen Kompositionen des 16. Jahrhunderts', *Vierteljahrsschrift für Musikwissenschaft*, iii (1887), musical appendix, pp. 49–91. See also *Proceedings of the Musical Association*, xlvi (1919), p. 83.

and international fame of the greatest among them, he often equalled their achievements. He was one of the musicians whom Petrucci honoured by publishing a collection of their works (*Misse Petri de la Rue*, 1503)—sufficient proof of the reputation he enjoyed.

The name of 'Pierchon de la Rue' appears in 1492 in the list of choristers in the future Emperor Maximilian's chapel, where he was to remain over a period covering the reign of Philip the Handsome and the regency of Margaret of Austria and extending into the Archduke Charles's time. In 1516 he retired to Courtrai, dying there in 1518. As a result of this quiet life—which, except for two journeys to Spain, was spent mainly in Brussels and Mechlin—his work is marked by a gravity and austerity well suited to please the Regent Margaret, who had two manuscripts of his Masses copied and illuminated for her own use. The *chanson* was not his strong point; at any rate he does not display the vivacity and lightness of touch one is accustomed to expect in works of this type. On the other hand, he was able to convey the melancholy of 'Pourquoy non veuil-je morir' by means of unexpected chromaticisms, by using the bass in its most sombre register (down to B flat below the bass stave), and by a beautiful, simple melodic line unspoiled by contrapuntal artifice.[1] Similarly in a *chanson* attributed to him in the Florentine manuscript, Ist. mus. 2439, 'Plorer, gémir, crier et braire', the note of lamentation is struck by using as thematic basis the Introit 'Requiem aeternam' in free canon between the two lower voices.[2]

La Rue's austere art was better suited to the seriousness of the motet; but he excelled above all in the writing of Masses. More than thirty-five by him are known, in which he displays no less learning than elevation of style.[3] The 'Missa pro defunctis'[4] is certainly the most remarkable of them; its earlier movements are written for four male voices in their lower register, but it lightens in the Tract and Communion through the introduction of a soprano part. Perhaps because

---

[1] *Odhecaton*, no. 15, and *Das Chorwerk*, iii, p. 29.

[2] Extract published by Pirro, *Histoire de la musique*, pp. 229–30.

[3] Seven of them have been printed in A. Tirabassi, *P. de La Rue, Liber Missarum* (Malines, 1941). Expert published the Mass 'Ave Maria' in *Les Maîtres musiciens de la Renaissance française*, Feininger, 'Ave Sanctissima' in *Documenta polyphoniae liturgicae*, series I, B. The *Kyrie* of 'Incessament' is printed in *Van Ockeghem tot Sweelinck*, iv, the *Sanctus* of 'Tous les regres' in Ambros-Kade, op. cit., v, p. 137, the *Kyrie* of one of Pierre's 'L'homme armé' Masses in Davison and Apel, op. cit., no. 92, the first *Kyrie* of 'Nunquam fuit' (='Nunca fué') in H. C. Wolff, *Die Musik der alten Niederländer* (Leipzig, 1956), p. 259, and the *Kyrie* of 'De sancto Antonio' in Schering, *Geschichte der Musik in Beispielen* (Leipzig, 1931), no. 65.

[4] Printed in *Das Chorwerk*, xi. The Introit is recorded in *The History of Music in Sound*, iii.

he was untouched by Italian influences, no fresh air blows through his melodies, which tend to be in conjunct motion and never attain the winged flight of Josquin's—in comparison with whom his gifts are less varied and his music lacking in life. He doubtless reflects the atmosphere of pious austerity surrounding Margaret of Austria; the serious tone in which he excelled must have suited the mood of that Princess, whose life had suffered early bereavement.[1]

LOYSET COMPÈRE

There could be no greater contrast to Pierre de la Rue's serious talent than the merry fancies of Loyset Compère, who excelled in the writing of *chansons* and died in 1518 as a Canon of St. Quentin. Only two complete Masses by him have survived: 'L'homme armé', a *canto fermo* Mass, with a wealth of canon and imitation, and an embryonic 'parody'-Mass on Hayne's *chanson* 'Alles regrets'.[2] The rest of his church music consists of a *Kyrie*, *Gloria*, and *Credo* preserved in the archives of Modena cathedral (MS. mus. 4, fos. 26ᵛ–30), a *Credo* 'Mon père' (published by Petrucci in his *Fragmenta missarum*, 1505), four Magnificats, and twenty-six motets. Among these last, pride of place must be given to the famous 'Omnium bonorum plena', based symbolically on the tenor of Hayne's *chanson*, 'De tous biens plaine' (Ex. 101), whose words are of course the translation of its Latin text. This motet, often called 'the Prayer for the Choirmen', has indeed a second part consisting of a prayer to the Virgin to intercede for the salvation of singers, a list of whose names from Dufay down to himself is given by the composer, thus providing a kind of register of the musicians famous at the time. The subtlety with which Hayne's *rondeau* is here used—adapted to a ternary rhythm in the first part and restored to its own binary in the second—the rhythmic and melodic variety, and Compère's own delicate charm, would in any case suffice to give interest to the work.[3] Compère also carried out a scheme of three series of eight motets each, as substitutes for the Mass, each motet being intended to replace a liturgical section of the Mass text—probably in Low Masses. Thematic analogies may

---

[1] Jozef Robyns, *Pierre de la Rue, circa 1460–1518, een bio-bibliographische studie* (Brussels, 1954).

[2] Masses and Mass-fragments published by L. Finscher, *Loyset Compere: Opera Omnia*, i (American Institute of Musicology, 1958).

[3] See Van den Borren, *Études*, pp. 231 ff. Published in *Denkmäler der Tonkunst in Österreich*, vii, p. 111

even be detected between some of these motets, thus establishing a
unity which recalls that of the Mass itself.[1]

In his French *chansons* Compère appears somewhat old-fashioned,
because of his continued fidelity to the old fixed forms. For all that,
he was the composer most drawn upon by Petrucci in the *Odhecaton*,
which contains no fewer than sixteen of his pieces.[2] He was moreover
the favourite musician even in a German book of songs collected and
published about 1530.[3] Indeed he was more at ease in the *chanson*
than any other musician of his time and he is one of those who may
without injustice be included in a purely French school, for he derived
from his residence in France—where in 1486 he was a member of the
Royal chapel—a sense of comedy, even downright buffoonery, and
that narrative manner, so dear to the French because it gives the
words the principal role. This somewhat dry *parlando* style is well
represented by 'Et dont revenez vous' with its ten syllables on the
same note; but Compère was also capable of conveying melancholy,
as in 'Sourdez regrets'[4] or 'Chanter ne puis'. Like Agricola he was
fond of using a Latin text in the tenor to underline the meaning of the
French words of the superius: e.g. 'Le corps'/'Corpus meum', 'Male
bouche'/'Circumdederunt me viri mendaces'[5]. Italy, where in 1475
he was in the service of the Duke of Milan, prompted him to write
a few witty *frottole*: 'Che fa la ramacina' is a very successful little
rhythmic *divertissement*.[6]

MINOR COMPOSERS

A number of composers with less sharply defined personalities
have none the less their place in the history of music, if only because
they represent the average art of their time. Some of them, moreover,
enjoyed contemporary reputations surprising to us but not after all
unfounded.

If we were to attach any credit to Petrucci's judgement, we should
have to allow an important place to Marbriano de Orto. The Venetian
publisher, besides including motets, a setting of the Lamentations,

[1] Jeppesen, 'Die drei Gafurius-Kodizes der Fabbrica del Duomo Milano', *Acta
musicologica*, iii (1931), p. 16.

[2] One of them, 'Nous sommes de lordre desaynt babuyn', is recorded in *The History
of Music in Sound*, iii.

[3] Bridgman, 'Christian Egenolff, imprimeur de musique', *Annales musicologiques*, iii
(1955), p. 77.

[4] Published by Maldeghem, *Trésor musical: musique profane*, xxiii, p. 17.

[5] *Odhecaton*, nos. 67 and 46.

[6] Published in *Das Chorwerk*, xliii, p. 9, and R. Schwartz, *Ottaviano Petrucci. Frottole,
Buch I und IV* (Leipzig, 1935), p. 92.

and *chansons* by this composer among his collections, brought out a volume of his Masses in 1505, and used his 'Ave Maria' as the opening item of the *Odhecaton*. De Orto was in the Papal service from 1484 to 1494, then returned to the Netherlands, becoming chorister to Philip the Handsome in 1505 and first chaplain to Charles V in 1515; he died at Nivelles in 1529.[1] But, though his writing is always correct and his style often expressive and broad, though he often used procedures rendered notable by Josquin, and though (in Pirro's words) 'he served God, art and the world with equal good fortune', he never rose above the level of honourable mediocrity.

Johannes Ghiselin enjoys the distinction of having been chosen by Petrucci next after Josquin and Obrecht for the publication of a volume of Masses, but is otherwise quite unknown under that name. However, as there is, in a manuscript at Florence, a *chanson* assigned to 'Jo. Gysling alias Verbonnet', we may suppose that he was the same person as the Verbonnet who is found in 1491, 1503, and 1535 at the court of Ferrara.[2] His five Masses, based on *chansons*, are somewhat lacking in inspiration—too repetitive, too regular in melody, and monotonous in development. His motets and *chansons* are to be found in Petrucci's collections (especially the *Canti C*); and the one piece of his in the *Odhecaton*, 'La Alfonsina'—apparently intended for instrumental performance—was perhaps composed in honour of Alfonso I, Duke of Ferrara.[3] The manuscript Panciatichi 27 in the Biblioteca Nazionale at Florence contains a piece by Ghiselin in which the famous theme of 'La Spagna' occurs.[4]

Gaspar van Weerbecke, born at Oudenarde, was in orders at Tournai and in 1469 *rector* at S. Gottardo in Milan; he then served in the Papal choir; in 1490 he was director of the chapel choir at Milan and later entered the service of Philip the Handsome (1495–7), returning finally to the pontifical chapel from 1499 to 1509. His contemporaries seem to have regarded him with the highest esteem. Petrucci published five of his Masses (*Misse Gaspar*) in 1507, a sixth in *Missarum diversorum auctorum liber primus* (1508), a setting of Lamentations[5] (in his *Lamentationum liber Secundus*, 1506), nine of his motets in the collection of thirty-three *Motetti A* (1502), and a few more in the subsequent collections of 1503 and 1505. Franchinus

---

[1] Pirro, *Histoire de la musique*, pp. 214–15.

[2] Ibid., pp. 223–4.

[3] Hewitt, *Harmonice musices Odhecaton*, p. 76.

[4] On 'La Spagna', see Gombosi, *Compositione di Meser Vincenzo Capirola* (Neuilly-sur-Seine, 1955), p. xliii. The opening of Ghiselin's piece is printed on p. 1.

[5] Reprint in Schering, *Geschichte der Musik in Beispielen*, no. 58.

Gafurius secured a Mass and nineteen motets by him as part of the collection of manuscripts made for Milan Cathedral in 1490, and another is quoted as an example by Sebald Heyden in his treatise *De arte canendi* (1540). Other compositions have remained in manuscript, among them the 'Missa Princesse d'amorettes' which Pirro regarded as his most remarkable work.[1] His predominant qualities were clarity, simplicity, and euphony, but he could also manage canon skilfully, and was a master of the rhythmic complexities of Netherland practice. He left very few secular works, apart from 'La Stangetta' (*Odhecaton*, No. 49) which in any case is not certainly his. For this reason among others it is not very likely that he was the same person as the 'Japart' by whom, on the other hand, only secular compositions are known.[2]

Mathieu Pipelare of Louvain, choirmaster at 's-Hertogenbosch (*c.* 1497–*c.* 1500),[3] was honoured by having his Mass 'L'homme armé' chosen for inclusion in the only collection of Masses published by Antico (Rome, 1516). In a motet by him on the Seven Sorrows of Our Lady, 'Memorare mater Christi',[4] not only does each of the seven voices represent one of the Sorrows, but the symbolism is strengthened by giving the third voice the tenor of the Spanish *villancico*, 'Nunca fué pena mayor'. Some Masses and a 'Salve Regina' by him in manuscript at Munich and Jena show the ingenuity of the craftsmanship, for example, in his statement of the 'Salve' theme by the contra only and in his alternation of dialogue with long solo phrases; or again by the way in which he ensures the unity of his Mass 'Dixit Dominus' by means of a motto-motive at the beginning of each movement. But one notices also that he sometimes spoils good themes by excessive scholasticism, even verging on mannerism.

Although Mathieu Gascongne, described as a priest of Cambrai in a document of 1518,[5] is claimed by some writers as a Frenchman, his work shows greater affinities with the Flemish style, on whose rhetorical resources he drew fully for the treatment of even the least promising of themes. He did not overdo repeated notes and could invent themes of a certain breadth and sustained inspiration. A few motets by him have survived—one of them dedicated to the King of

---

[1] *Histoire de la musique*, p. 212. Facsimile of the *Kyrie* in *Die Musik in Geschichte und Gegenwart*, iv (1955), col. 1409; transcribed by Smijers, *Van Ockeghem tot Sweelinck*, vi, which also contains two of the motets printed by Petrucci in his collection of 1503.

[2] Pirro, ibid., p. 214. See also G. Croll, 'Gaspar van Weerbecke', *Musica Disciplina*, vi (1952), p. 67.

[3] Smijers, 'De Illustre Liewe Vrouwe Broederschap te 's-Hertogenbosch, *Tijdschrift der Vereeniging voor Nederlandsche muziekgeschiedenis*, xiii (1929), p. 215.

[4] Published by Maldeghem, *Trésor musical: musique religieuse*, xi (1875), p. 31.

[5] Michel Brenet, *Les Musiciens de la Sainte-Chapelle du Palais*, p. 69.

France,[1]—some Masses and three *chansons*.[2] His Mass 'Pourquoi non', based on a *chanson* by Pierre de la Rue, is not unworthy of its model, and an impression of strength is left by his Mass 'Vos qui in turribus'. His work forms a kind of link between the Netherland style and the French style properly so called.

For all the great reputation of Tinctoris (*c.* 1435–1511) as a theorist, he can be given only minor rank as a composer. His eleven treatises, though accepting old-established rules, still leave room for the new spirit; but the musical examples with which he illustrates them (undoubtedly written by himself) bear witness to more craftsmanship than talent.[3] Nor is there any greater sign of inspiration in his four Masses, his cycle of Lamentations, his two motets and his five *chansons*.[4] This, however, in no way affects the importance of his theoretical work, which remains among the most significant produced in that period.

Worthy of remembrance—though we must be content merely to mention their names—are Johannes Stokhem, Crispin van Stappen, Benedictus de Opitiis, Antoine Divitis, Nicolaus Craen, and Noel Baldwin. And still more would have to be added if we wished to include all the musicians of this incredibly prolific generation.

NETHERLAND ART IN FRANCE

The question of France's share in this so-called Netherland phase of musical history is difficult to decide since nearly all the musicians with whom we have hitherto dealt were French-speaking, many of them spent an important part of their career in France, and their cultural ties with France were in fact much more real than the artificially forged links which bound them to the Holy Roman Empire. There would not even be any question of a distinction between Netherlanders and Frenchmen were it not that the latter, from the end of the fifteenth century onwards, showed a certain distaste for the polyphonic complications of the North, and developed instead a style already adumbrating what was to be typical of French

---

[1] Published by Rokseth, *Treize motets et un prélude pour orgue* (*Publications de la Société française de musicologie, I[e] série*, v), p. 12. See also p. xiii.

[2] One *chanson* published by Charles Bordes, *Chansonnier du XVIe siècle* (Paris, n.d.), no. viii; two others by Expert, *Les Maîtres musiciens de la Renaissance française*, v (Paris, 1897), pp. 1 and 49.

[3] Published by Coussemaker, *Scriptorum de musica medii aevi,* iv (Paris, 1876), pp. 1–200.

[4] The 'L'homme armé' Mass has been published by Feininger, op. cit., series i, i, fasc. 9, the *Agnus* from it by Smijers, *Van Ockeghem tot Sweelinck*, iv.

music in the sixteenth century. We are thus concerned here not merely with musicians born in France, but with men who made their mark exclusively in France and whose style answered to the aesthetic demands of France.

The fact that half the career of Antoine Brumel was passed in France (at Chartres, Laon, Paris, and Lyons) would in itself be enough to justify our dealing with him here; but in addition, his style shows greater kinship with the French composers than with those of the Low Countries. His work for the Church looms larger than his secular music, which consists only of a few *chansons* as against some thirty motets and sixteen complete Masses, five of which were published by Petrucci in 1503.[1] Their qualities justify the choice; but what interests us in Brumel is not so much that we find in him, though with less genius, the methods used by Josquin (the imitative style and the division of voices into two pairs), nor that his Mass 'De Beata Virgine' is nearly as fine as Josquin's, nor that he could acquit himself skilfully of the task of writing polyphony in twelve parts in the Mass 'Et ecce terraemotus', nor that he could construct a double canon in the Mass 'A l'ombre d'ung buyssonet'. It is on the contrary, more important to identify the qualities that differentiate him from his great contemporaries, and to note that he was the first to apply to the Mass a style hitherto reserved for the *chanson*. The modern editor of his Mass 'L'homme armé' observes very truly that the *Confiteor* 'could pass for a secular, almost frottolesque piece'.[2] Brumel certainly seems less concerned than his contemporaries to display his learning; in the same Mass he often contents himself with letting the outer parts move in consecutive tenths, in accordance with a practice approved by Gafurius in his *Practica Musicae* but usually kept for more modest compositions. The opening of the *Credo* is typical:

Ex. 119

[1] *Antonii Brumel Opera Omnia*, ed. Armen Carapetyan (*Corpus mensurabilis musicae*, v); 'Missa de Beata Virgine', published by Antico in *Liber XV missarum electarum* (Rome, 1516), reprinted by Expert, *Les Maîtres musiciens*, viii (1898).
[2] *Opera Omnia*, i, p. iv.

(Father Almighty, Maker of heaven and earth, and of all things visible . . .)

His love of clarity and simplicity often leads him to write the simplest
note-against-note counterpoint, as in the 'Missa super Dringhs',[1] in
which the text is declaimed to reiterated chords in the French manner.
He seems to have been already aiming at the ideal in which the
musical composition is subordinated to the intelligibility of the words.

Antoine de Févin (c. 1470–c. 1512), born at Arras, was a chorister
of Louis XII, who in a letter of 1507 gave high praise to his *chansons*
—which may well surprise us when one considers their somewhat
superficial facility. Févin's output comprises fifteen *chansons*, three
Magnificats, Lamentations, some thirty motets, and a dozen Masses.
Three of these last were published by Petrucci (Fossombrone, 1515),
three by Antico in his *Liber quindecim Missarum* (Rome, 1516), and
a lute version of the Mass 'Ave Maria' was printed by Girolamo
Scotto as late as 1546. It is curious that there should have been such
a rage for him; for, though his Mass 'Sancta Trinitas' (based on one
of his own motets)[2] shows a certain depth, his counterpoint in the
Masses 'Ave Maria' and 'Mente tota' (on motets by Josquin) is

---

[1] Published by Petrucci in *Missarum diversorum auctorum liber primus* (1508); excerpts
reprinted in Wooldridge, *Oxford History of Music*, ii (1905), p. 246, Peter Wagner,
Geschichte der Messe (Leipzig, 1913), p. 176, and Schering, *Geschichte*, no. 64.

[2] Reprinted by Rokseth in her edition of Attaingnant's *Treze Motetz* of 1531 (Paris,
1930), p. 28; see *infra*, pp. 456–7. The opening of the *Kyrie* of the Mass 'Sancta Trinitas'
was given by Wooldridge, op. cit., p. 261. 'Ave Maria' has been edited by J. Delporte,
Collection de polyphonie classique, xlvii, 'Mente tota' by Expert, *Les Maîtres musiciens*,
ix.

slight to the point of vacuity, especially in the latter, a passage from
which shows his excessive reliance on two-part syllabic declamation:

Ex. 120

(And was incarnate by the Holy Ghost of the Virgin Mary.)

In this Févin points the way to the rather frivolous type of *chanson-
Mass* favoured by Certon, Sermisy and other French composers
during the second quarter of the century. Evidently there were people
who found the style attractive, notwithstanding, since Févin's compositions fill the greatest space in MS 1760 of the Pepysian Library
at Magdalene College, Cambridge; and the somewhat insipid grace of
his motet 'Descende in hortum meum' has not prevented it from
enjoying a certain celebrity even down to our own time.[1]

Jean Mouton (*c*. 1470–1522), born at Samer, and in the service of
both Louis XII and Francis I, was the most worthy of Josquin's successors; for, though he had like Févin a vocal style 'facili fluentem
filo' as Glareanus put it,[2] he combined with it a contrapuntal skill
which, never being exploited for its own sake, in no way spoiled the
beauty of his melodies. He wrote little secular music. 'La la la l'oysillon
du bois' possesses a simple delicacy altogether personal to him and
exactly suited to the popular type of words,[3] whereas his 'Déploration' on the death of Févin, 'Qui ne regrettroit le gentil Fevin',
written in double canon, shows quite a different aspect of his talent.[4]

[1] First published by Kriesstein of Augsburg (1540); reprinted by Ambros–Kade,
op. cit., v, p. 208, and in a practical edition by Expert (Collection Henry Expert No.
2990). For a full bibliography, see B. Kahmann, 'Antoine de Fevin, a bio-bibliographical
contribution', *Musica Disciplina*, iv (1950), pp. 153–62, and v (1951), pp. 143–55.

[2] *Dodecachordon*, p. 464.

[3] Published by Expert, *Extraits des Maîtres musiciens de la Renaissance française*,
no. 3074.

[4] Published by Plamenac, 'Deux pièces de la Renaissance tirées de fonds florentins
Revue belge de musicologie, vi (1952), p. 12.

Petrucci published a volume of five of his Masses, *Missarum Joannis Mouton Liber I*, in 1508 and reissued it in 1515; Antico published two in his *Liber quindecim Missarum* of 1516; Attaingnant two in his *Primus liber viginti missarum musicarum* (Paris, 1532) and Moderne one (*Liber decem missarum*, Lyons, 1540); a few more have come down to us in manuscript. Nearly all of them draw upon liturgical themes; only four are based on *chansons*. Their methods range from that of the *canto fermo* Mass to the full *missa parodia* procedure of 'Quem dicunt homines', based on a motet by Richafort. His 'Missa L'homme armé' contains canons for two, three, four, and even seven voices. Mouton shows his fondness for canon also in some of his motets: 'Nesciens mater' and 'Ave Maria gemma virginum', both for eight voices, consist of quadruple canons in which there is never an unskilful harmonic clash;[1] Glareanus printed a four-part mirror-canon, 'Salve mater salvatoris'[2] in the *Dodecachordon*; in 'Ave Maria'[3] the canon is worked in two of the voice-parts only. Mouton was always attentive to the mood of his text, and equally capable of conveying the naïve gaiety of 'Gaude virgo Catherina' with its dance-rhythm, the rustic charm of 'Noë noë psallite'[4] and the solemnity of 'Quis dabit oculis nostris',[5] written on the death of Anne of Brittany; but the mood best suited to him was the serenity found in his Antiphons of the Virgin.[6]

Elzéar Genet (*c.* 1470–1548), known as Carpentras from the name of his native town,[7] after serving Louis XII, was sent by that King to Leo X to be director of the papal chapel. On entering the Pope's service he gave up the *frottole* he had been composing,[8] and took to sacred music, bringing out between 1532 and 1537 a book of Masses, one of Lamentations, one of hymns, and one of Magnificats, all published at Avignon at his own expense. His reputation was due mainly to his Lamentations, which long continued to be sung in the papal chapel; they contain passages in fauxbourdon, others in imita-

---

[1] Published by Smijers, *Treize livres de motets parus chez Pierre Attaingnant en 1534 et 1535*, iii (Paris, 1936), pp. 43 and 173.

[2] Published by Schering, *Geschichte der Musik in Beispielen*, no. 66.

[3] Published by Boepple, *Dessoff Choir Series*, no. 40 (New York), and Expert, *Extraits des maîtres musiciens*.

[4] Published by Smijers, *Treize livres de motet* ii (Paris, 1936), p. 86.

[5] Published by Casimiri and Dagnino, *Monumenta polyphoniae italicae*, ii, p. 113.

[6] Paul Kast, *Studien zu den Messen des Jean Mouton* (Frankfurt, 1955); R. Dammann, *Studien zu den Motetten von Jean Mouton* (Diss. Freiburg, 1952: unpublished).

[7] For biographical detail, see Lee Rigsby, 'Elzéar Genet, a Renaissance Composer', in *Studies in Music History and Theory* (Florida State University Studies, No. 18, 1955).

[8] Three *frottole* were published in Antico's *Canzoni . . . et frottole. Libro tertio.* (Rome, 1517); reprinted by Alfred Einstein (*Smith College Music Archives*, iv), pp. 10 16, and 22.

tion, and the traditional vocalizations on the Hebrew letters; their very French clarity was well suited to the tendency soon to be recommended by the Roman Church and exemplified by Palestrina:[1]

Ex. 121

(Her adversaries are the chief, her enemies prosper.)

NETHERLAND ART IN EASTERN EUROPE

The Netherland polyphonic style became predominant in all European countries, each of which adapted it to its own genius with more or less felicity, preserving more or less of its own character. It is interesting to note that in Hungary and the Slavonic countries, where native folk-music was most fully alive and eastern Catholicism already possessed of a musical language of its own, the study of counterpoint found no very fruitful soil in which to develop. But it should also be remembered that the disturbed history of these countries left them little scope to realize the full possibilities of their talents.

[1] For excerpts from the Lamentations, see Ambros–Kade, op. cit., v, pp. 212–24.

In Dalmatia the chief influence to be observed is that of Italian music, whereas in Bohemia—Prague being an active centre of international culture—there are evidences of an early contribution from native Czech musical sources to polyphonic composition;[1] there still exist fragments of Masses and motets based on Bohemian folksongs and unaffected by any foreign influence.[2] The *Speciálnik* manuscript in the Hradec Králové museum library, though copied in 1611, consists entirely of works dating from at least a century earlier; in it are found, besides the Netherlanders Agricola, Tinctoris, Lannoy and Pullois, two Czech composers, Gontrášek and Tomek. Many of the pieces have Czech words, and the *canto fermo* is often a Hussite hymn or a native song. But the fall of the kingdom in 1620 put an end to this artistic movement in Bohemia.

Netherland polyphony found its way very early into Poland; contrapuntal writing was practised early in the fifteenth century by Mikołaj z Radomia (Nicholas of Radom), said by Ludwig[3] to have been 'familiar with the most progressive technique'. In 1451 Stanislas of Cracow wrote his *Musices Compendium*, and King John Albert about 1492 summoned to his court the German musician Heinrich Finck (see *supra*, p. 286), who was to remain in Poland until 1506. The line of great Polish musicians begins with Mikołaj z Krakowa (Nicholas of Cracow), first mentioned in the rectoral records of Cracow University in 1488. Compositions by him, marked 'N. C.', occur in the organ tablature of Jan z Lublina (John of Lublin)[4] and in another belonging to the monastery of the Holy Ghost at Cracow;[5] these two manuscripts, dating from *c.* 1537–48, contain numerous works by Polish musicians as well as by foreigners, and dances of Polish origin as well as German and Italian ones. The opening of Mikołaj's most famous secular song, 'Aleć nade mną Wenus', some-

---

[1] The real beginnings of Czech polyphony are the two-part pieces preserved in the Vyšebrod (Hohenfurt) Codex H 42 (1410) and the *Jistebnický Kancionál* (*c.* 1420).

[2] See Dobroslav Orel, 'Počátky umělého vícehlasu v Čechách', *Universita Komenského v Bratislave* (*Filozofická fakulta*), i (1922), p. 145, and his 'Stilarten der Mehrstimmigkeit des 15. und 16. Jahrhunderts in Böhmen', *Festschrift für Guido Adler* (Vienna, 1930), p. 149.

[3] 'Die mehrstimmige Messe des XIV. Jahrhunderts', *Archiv für Musikwissenschaft*, vii (1925), p. 430. The Polish literature on Mikołaj is naturally considerable: see in particular 'O utworach Mikołaja Radomskiego', *Polski Rocznik Muzykologiczny*, ii (1936), pp. 87–94, which gives the most important references.

[4] Three examples printed in Zofia Lissa und Jozef Chomiński, *Muzyka polskiego odrodzenia* (Warsaw, 1953), pp. 42, 45, and 146; see also Adolf Chybiński, *36 tanców z tabulatury organowej Jana z Lublina* (Cracow, 1948).

[5] Zdzisław Jachimecki, 'Eine polnische Orgeltabulatur aus dem Jahre 1548', *Zeitschrift für Musikwissenschaft*, ii (1920), p. 206.

times described by Polish historians as a 'madrigal', deserves quotation:

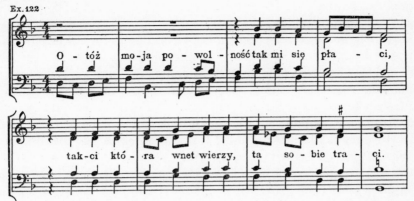

Ex. 122

O - tóż mo-ja po - wol - ność tak mi się pła - ci, tak-ci któ - ra wnet wierzy, ta so - bie tra - ci.

(Lo, my slowness is its own reward, for she who believes at once is lost.)

Cracow had become the centre of Polish musical activity by the end of the fifteenth century, and several theoretical works were published there about 1519; the most famous of these, the *Opusculum musice* of Sebastjan z Felsztyna (Sebastian de Felstin), was several times re-issued. None of these treatises, it is true, has anything to say on the problems of counterpoint so dear to Western theorists; they would seem to have been compiled for the use of singers. Sebastjan (*c.* 1480–*c.* 1544) also left some church compositions based on Gregorian tenors, in homophonic style and with hardly any use of imitation. The opening of his 'Alleluia ad Rorate cum Prosa'[1] is typical:

Ex. 123

Al - le - - - - - - - lu - ia

This musical movement was to culminate at the middle of the six-teenth century in what is generally regarded as the golden age of Polish music, greatly encouraged by the establishment at Cracow in 1543 of a Collegium Rorantistarum for King Sigismund I's chapel.[2]

Hungary, in the reign of Matthias Corvinus (1440–90), enjoyed a musical life unsurpassed by that of any Western court and marked by the same international character. Beatrice of Aragon had intro-

[1] Quoted by Jachimecki, *Historja muzyki polskiej* (Warsaw, 1920), p. 45.

[2] Jachimecki, *Muzyka polska*, i (Cracow, 1948). Lissa and Chomiński, op. cit.

duced Italian culture there, and many celebrated composers lived for longer or shorter periods in Hungary: Johannes Stokhem (of whose presence at Buda we know through Tinctoris), Erasmus Lapicida,[1] Jacobus Barbireau, and the famous Piero Bono, 'chitarista rarissimus', whom Tinctoris esteemed above all others for his improvisations.[2] In 1483 the Papal envoy judged the choir of the Hungarian royal chapel, at that time directed by Johannes Stokhem, to be better than the Papal choir itself. One of its members may have been the Flemish singer Jean Cornuel, known as Verjus, who was afterwards a *vicarius* at Cambrai; but we cannot be certain that he ever travelled to Hungary as Molinet suggests.[3] It is also probable that the countertenor Roger de Lignaquercu, a former member of the Papal choir, was at that time in Matthias Corvinus's service.[4] Under the last two Jagellon kings (1490–1526), although the country was less prosperous, music continued to play an important part in Court life, and from 1490 the chapel choir had as one of its members Thomas Stoltzer (*c.* 1470–1526), one of the most important and prolific of German composers, by whom we have 150 church compositions, nine psalms, and eleven German songs in which one recognizes the characteristic style of his countrymen Finck, Hofhaimer, and Isaac.[5] On the other hand very little by Hungarian composers has survived, so that we cannot speak of a properly Hungarian school.

CONCLUSION

The moment was at hand, after the death of Josquin and the disappearance of this generation of transitional composers, when France was to make a clean break with Netherland hegemony; such musicians as Janequin and Sermisy, with their short phrases, their succinct melodies, their extreme care to avoid interlacing of parts, and their syllabic declamation designed to ensure above all the intelligibility of the words, are far removed indeed from the aesthetic principles of the great Flemish master. In the Low Countries on the other hand the tradition was to continue and Josquin to be worthily represented by his pupil Gombert, by Clemens non Papa, and by Thomas Créquillon, that great precursor of Lassus.

[1] O. Wessely, 'Neues zur Lebensgeschichte von Erasmus Lapicida', *Anzeiger der phil.-hist. Klasse der Österreichischen Akademie der Wissenschaften.* Jg. 1955, No. 7, p. 85.
[2] E. Haraszti, 'Pierre Bono, luthiste de Mathias Corvin', *Revue de musicologie*, xxxi (1949), pp. 73–85.
[3] Droz, 'Notes sur Me Jean Cornuel dit Verjus, petit vicaire de Cambrai', *Revue de musicologie*, vii (1926), p. 178.
[4] Pirro, 'Jean Cornuel, vicaire à Cambrai', *Revue de musicologie*, vii (1926), p. 200.
[5] Stoltzer's work is discussed in vol. IV, Chapter III.

IX

ENGLISH POLYPHONY (c. 1470-1540)

By FRANK LL. HARRISON

ENGLISH AND CONTINENTAL STYLES

IN a famous passage in the dedication of his *Proportionale Musices* (before 1476)[1] the Flemish theorist Tinctoris credited the English school of the first half of the fifteenth century, headed by Dunstable, with being the originators of what seemed a 'new art' of music. He went on to observe that contemporary English music, on the other hand, was conservative and lacking in imagination when compared with that of the French 'moderns' Ockeghem, Busnois, Regis, and Caron, and supported this criticism by retailing a current saying: 'The English jubilate, the French sing.'[2] The truth of Tinctoris's observations is borne out by the music, for conservative design and florid style were the most characteristic features of English composition from the death of Dunstable to the Reformation. During this time choral music in the larger forms was designed on the 'classical' *canto fermo* principle of the mid-fifteenth century, and used a highly decorative and ornate counterpoint, normally in five or six parts and sometimes in seven or eight. By the early sixteenth century this late Gothic style was so firmly established that during the next fifty years it was able to absorb such typically Renaissance elements as imitative and antiphonal texture without suffering any fundamental change. The transition from late Gothic to Renaissance in English choral music, as in the other church arts, was not fully accomplished until the establishment of the English liturgy in 1549 abolished the ritual and ceremonial of which the florid style was one of the chief ornaments.

RENAISSANCE ELEMENTS IN ENGLISH MUSIC

This style of polyphony has obvious analogies with that of the last period of English Perpendicular architecture. Each was the final phase of the Gothic in its medium, and both expressed the late medieval trend towards the adornment of devotion by the most elaborate and

---

[1] C. E. H. de Coussemaker, *Scriptorum de musica medii aevi nova series* (Paris, 1864–76), iv, p. 154; English translation in O. Strunk, *Source Readings in Music History* (New York, 1950), p. 195.

[2] I take *jubilare* to mean 'to sing in a florid manner' rather than 'to shout', as Strunk translates it.

decorative forms of art and craft. The spirit which transformed the musical style of the early fifteenth century into the large-scale forms of the early Tudor period, combining the calculated framework of the *canto fermo* with the finest detail of melodic line and rhythmic movement, was the same as that which translated 'the fan-vault from the small scale of a cloister into the terms of the height and width of a nave', a feat which was not achieved until the late fifteenth century. Both of these developments represent the union of a 'practical, matter-of-fact spirit with a sense of mystery and an almost oriental effusion of ornament'.[1]

Just as Renaissance elements made their appearance within the visual arts during the first half of the sixteenth century (notable examples are Henry VII's tomb in Westminster Abbey, designed in 1512 by Pietro Torrigiani, and the screen and choir-stalls of King's College, Cambridge, made between 1531 and 1536), so the change in musical style which accompanied the Reformation was anticipated in secular music and in some of the smaller forms of church music. Under Henry VII the medieval carol was transformed in musical style and turned to court use as domestic music. Both Henry VII and Henry VIII emulated in their 'revels' the entertainments of the Renaissance courts on the continent. Pageants and interludes, for which some of the surviving secular music was probably composed, were played by the chapel men and children, and were later taken up, in the form of Latin and English plays with music, by colleges and schools such as Magdalen, Eton, and St. Paul's. Sacred music in Renaissance style was introduced into Henry VIII's chapel in 1516,[2] and between 1519 and c. 1528 the king acquired a collection of church music by Franco-Netherlandish composers.[3] Though the Renaissance techniques of imitative, antiphonal, and homophonic writing played an increasing part in English settings of shorter liturgical forms, the persistence of the florid style and *canto fermo* method delayed until the mid-sixteenth century the arrival of the fully imitative style which continental composers had developed by the 1530's.

[1] Nikolaus Pevsner, *An Outline of European Architecture* (London, 4th edition, 1953), p. 105.

[2] The date of Brit. Mus., Royal 11. E. xi, which contains music by Benedictus de Opitiis, formerly organist of the Church of Our Lady in Antwerp, who became Henry VIII's court organist in March 1516, and Richard Sampson, who was in Antwerp in 1511, became Dean of St. Stephen's, Westminster in 1520, Dean of the Chapel Royal in 1523, and was afterwards Bishop of Chichester.

[3] Brit. Mus., Royal 8. G. vii; the collection includes a secular motet 'Fama malum' and five settings of Dido's lament 'Dulces exuviae', one of which is by Josquin (printed in *Das Chorwerk*, liv, p. 5).

CHORAL FOUNDATIONS

The two centuries before the Reformation saw the founding of many of the choral institutions which have ever since played an important part in English musical life. It was chiefly in these new collegiate churches, colleges, and household chapels that the foundations of the English choral tradition were laid, and their lead was followed in turn by most of the secular cathedrals and greater monasteries. The chapel of the royal household, later known as the Chapel Royal, originally a small group of chaplains and clerks, was enlarged by Richard II and Henry IV, and under Henry V consisted of a dean, twenty-seven chaplains and clerks, and sixteen choristers. By the mid-fifteenth century a Master of the choristers had been appointed, and in 1483 the household chapel was incorporated by Edward IV, whose ordinances provided for twenty-four chaplains and 'gentlemen clerks', that is, singers with the household rank of 'gentleman', eight children and a Master. Henry VIII increased the number of choristers to twelve and maintained some twenty gentlemen. Some other household chapels, such as those of John of Gaunt (d. 1399), John, Duke of Bedford (d. 1435), Humphrey, Duke of Gloucester (d. 1447), Henry Percy, fifth Earl of Northumberland (d. 1527), and Cardinal Wolsey (d. 1530), were comparable with the royal chapel in size, but were personal institutions which did not outlive their owners. On the other hand, some royal and noble patrons gave permanent form to family chapels which they incorporated as collegiate churches with a head (variously called dean, warden, or master), canons or chaplains, clerks, and choristers. Among the more important of these foundations were the chapel of St. George at Windsor, established by Edward III in 1348 and refounded on a larger scale by Edward IV in 1483 with a new chapel and a choir of thirteen clerks and thirteen choristers; the chapel of St. Stephen at Westminster, also founded by Edward III in 1348, which had thirteen vicars, four clerks, and six choristers; the Lancastrian chantry College and Hospital of St. Mary Newarke in Leicester, founded by Henry, Duke of Lancaster, in 1355 with thirteen vicars, three clerks, and six choristers; the Yorkist chapel at Fotheringhay, endowed in 1410–11 by Henry IV and Edward, Duke of York, with a choir of four 'gentlemen-clerks', four 'yeomen-clerks', and thirteen choristers; and the collegiate church of Tattershall established by Ralph, Baron Cromwell, in 1439, where there were six clerks and six choristers.

A chapel choir was also a permanent part of the larger educational foundations of this period. William of Wykeham, Bishop of Winchester, provided for daily services to be sung by three clerks and sixteen boys at New College, Oxford (opened in 1386), and at Winchester College (opened in 1393), while Henry VI's colleges of Eton and King's, Cambridge, founded in 1440–1, each had ten clerks and sixteen choristers. These examples were followed by William Wayneflete, Bishop of Winchester, in his foundation of Magdalen College (opened c. 1480), which had eight clerks and sixteen choristers, and by Cardinal Wolsey in the most lavish establishment of the period, Cardinal College (later Christ Church), Oxford, which originally had twelve clerks and thirteen choristers. In all these institutions an *informator* was provided to train the choristers in polyphony.

The development of polyphonic choral music in the secular cathedrals is indicated by the appointment of one of the vicars as *informator choristarum*. Salisbury appointed John Kegewyn to this post in 1463, and in 1477 Lincoln engaged William Horwood to teach plainsong and the fundamentals of polyphony, detailed as 'pryksong, faburdon, diskant and cownter', as well as the organ and 'clavychordes'. Two years later Richard Hygons undertook to train the choristers of Wells in plainsong, measured music, descant and, if they showed aptitude, in playing the organ, and to supervise the house in which they lived. A parallel development of equal importance was the founding by monastic cathedrals and larger abbeys of a choir of men and boys, distinct from their regular choir of the monks of the community, to sing polyphonic music in the Lady-chapel and nave for the benefit of lay worshippers. By the end of the fourteenth century Worcester had a Lady-chapel choir, which was enlarged and endowed in 1478 under John Hampton as *informator*. Between 1400 and the dissolution of the monasteries in 1537–40 the existence of similar establishments is recorded at Durham, Canterbury, and Winchester cathedrals, and at the abbeys of Westminster, St. Albans, Gloucester, Muchelney, Glastonbury, and Waltham.[1]

LITURGICAL FORMS

The forms of choral polyphony for which the florid style was invariably used were the festal Mass, the large votive antiphon, and the *Magnificat*. In a festal Mass a plainsong melody from the ritual of a feast was used as the *canto fermo*; this tradition of liturgical relevance was certainly one of the factors in the late survival of the *canto fermo*

[1] For sources and a more detailed treatment of the institutions mentioned in this section see F. Ll. Harrison, *Music in Medieval Britain* (London, 1958), chaps. I, IV.

Mass in England. The votive antiphon was identical in liturgical form with the Mary-antiphons which are sung in their seasons at the end of Compline in the Roman rite, though it differed in its ritual position and treatment, and was not limited to the four seasonal texts of the Roman use. The English antiphon, forerunner of the anthem and called by the same name, used both metrical and prose texts from a variety of sources, and was the main part of an act of evening devotion, separate from the regular services in choir, which took place in the Lady-chapel or other votive chapel, or in the nave, according to its devotional object. A large votive antiphon resembled a single movement of a festal Mass in scale and design, though its use (not invariable) of a plainsong *canto fermo* had a structural function only, and was not intended to secure liturgical appropriateness, for the title of the chant was not normally given in the manuscripts. In settings of the *Magnificat*, sung at Vespers on greater festivals, only the even-numbered verses were composed, beginning with 'Et exsultavit', the others being sung in plainsong.[1] The polyphonic verses were composed on ornamented and extended forms of the plainsong tone with which they alternated.

The Mass and antiphon were also written in simpler styles with more modest dimensions. Many shorter Mass settings were composed for the Lady-Mass ('Missa de Beata Virgine'), which was sung every Saturday in choir, and also in larger churches daily throughout the year in the Lady-chapel.[2] The *Kyrie*, *Gloria*, and *Credo* of a shorter Mass were sometimes written *alternatim*, that is, for alternating plainsong and polyphony.

All other forms of polyphony were designed to replace part of the plainsong of the ritual. Unlike the continental repertory, English polyphony of this period did not include 'motets', that is, pieces which were not an integral part of the liturgy but could be inserted into a service at certain points.[3] Consequently the term 'motet' has no useful application in English music of the time, and did not in fact become customary in English usage until after the Reformation. The chief liturgical forms of pre-Reformation choral polyphony were the ritual (as distinct from votive) antiphon; the respond, hymn and prose of the Office; the Alleluia and sequence of the Lady-Mass; the Passion; and certain items of processional music, mostly for Palm

[1] Cf. p. 324.
[2] For the ritual of the weekly and daily Lady-Mass see *Missale ad Usum Insignis et Praeclarae Ecclesiae Sarum*, ed. F. H. Dickinson (Burntisland, 1861–83), cols. 769*–782*.
[3] For some exceptions see Harrison, op. cit., 339, 345.

Sunday, Holy Week, and Easter. Normally only the solo parts of a responsorial chant were set in polyphony, while hymns and sequences were set *alternatim*. In the Passion, liturgically a ceremonial reading of the Gospel, polyphony was applied to the words of the *turba* and of characters other than Christ and the Evangelist, that is, to those parts which were sung *alta voce* in a plainsong performance and were indicated by the letter *a* in the service-books.[1] The sections which were left in plainsong are essential to the liturgical and musical completeness of all these forms, as of the *Magnificat* and *alternatim* Mass.

THE ETON CHOIRBOOK

The most important manuscripts of the earlier part of this period are the large choirbooks at Eton College, Lambeth Palace, and Gonville and Caius College, Cambridge.[2] The Eton book, in writing and illumination the finest surviving English musical manuscript, was written for the College choir between *c.* 1490 and 1502;[3] the Lambeth manuscript, of unknown provenance, may be dated *c.* 1510,[4] while the Caius College book was written, most likely for St. Stephen's, Westminster, by Edward Higgons,[5] who became a canon there in 1518. The Eton collection originally contained sixty-seven votive antiphons to the Virgin for the daily observance enjoined by the college statutes, together with twenty-four Magnificats, a Passion by Richard Davy, and a thirteen-part setting of the Apostles' Creed in the form of a round on a *canto fermo* by Robert Wylkynson. The disappearance of nearly half the original two hundred and twenty-four folios has meant the complete or partial loss of twenty-nine antiphons, one of which can be supplied from the Lambeth book, of twenty Magnificats, two of which are complete in other sources, and of the earlier choruses of the Passion. Among the pieces listed in the index, which has made it possible to reconstruct the original state of the manuscript, is a setting of 'Gaude flore virginali' by Dunstable, his only recorded five-part work, and unfortunately one of the total losses. The working lives of the other twenty-four composers cover the period from *c.* 1460, seven years after Dunstable's death, to *c.* 1520, and the

[1] *Missale Sarum*, cols. 264–72.

[2] Eton College, 178; Lambeth Palace, 1; Cambridge, Gonville and Caius, 667.

[3] For discussion of the manuscript and catalogue of the original and present contents see F. Ll. Harrison, 'The Eton Choirbook', *Annales musicologiques*, i (1953), p. 151. The music is printed complete in *Musica Britannica*, x–xii.

[4] For list of contents see *Musica Britannica*, x, p. 142.

[5] At the end of the manuscript is written 'Ex dono et opere Edwardi Higgons huius ecclesie canonici'.

institutions they represent include at least ten of the more important choral foundations in the country. Since the work of most of these composers has only recently been made available for study and performance, it may be useful to give a complete list, with the dates and places of their activity, as far as they have been established, and the extent of their original contribution to the manuscript:

Name	Institution	Dates*	Original no. of works in Eton MS.
John Browne. . .	..	..	15
Walter Lambe . .	St. George's, Windsor	1479–99	12
Richard Davy . .	Magdalen and Exeter	1491–1506	10
Robert Wylkynson. .	Eton	1496–1515	9†
William Cornysh (junior)‡	Chapel Royal	1496–d. 1523	8
Robert Fayrfax . .	St. Albans and Chapel Royal	1496–d. 1521	6
Edmund Turges . .	..	..	5
William Horwood . .	Lincoln	1476–d. 1484	4
Fawkyner . . .	..	..	3
Baldwyn . . .	..	..	2
William Brygeman .	Eton	1503	2
Nicholas Huchyn . .	..	..	2
Hugo Kellyk. . .	..	..	2
(John) Sygar . .	King's College, Cambridge	1419–1515	2
Gilbert Banester . .	Chapel Royal	1478–d. 1487	1
Robert Hacomplaynt or Hacomblene . .	King's College, Cambridge	1472–d. 1528	1
John Hampton . .	Worcester	1484–1522	1
Holyngborne . .	..	..	1
Richard Hygons . .	Wells	1459–c. 1509	1
(Robert) Mychelson .	St. George's, Windsor	1495–9	1
Nesbett§ . . .	..	..	1
William, Monk of Stratford ‖ . . .	..	..	1
Edmund Sturton . .	..	..	1
John Sutton . . .	Magdalen and Eton	1476–9	1

* The dates of composers in this chapter are in many cases based on new research in archives and printed sources; for details see Harrison, *Music in Medieval Britain*, chaps. I, IV.

† Two of these were added to the manuscript between 1502 and 1515.

‡ See p. 345.

§ Probably the J. Nesbet who composed a *Benedicamus* in the Pepys MS. (see above, p. 182).

‖ There is a single part of a song 'O my lady dure' by 'Parker monke of Stratforde', who may be the same man, in the British Museum MS. Royal App. 58, of the early sixteenth century (after 1504). Stratford in both cases is presumably Stratford-atte-Bowe.

THE DEVELOPMENT OF THE FLORID STYLE

Leaving Dunstable's lost work and Wylkynson's additions out of account, the Eton music covers a period of some forty years after *c.* 1460, during which three stages in the treatment of the florid style may be distinguished. The first is represented by the work of Horwood, Banester, Hygons, and perhaps Kellyk; in the second stage and high point of the style the chief figures are Browne, Lambe, Davy, Fawkyner, and Wylkynson; Fayrfax and Cornysh, who show a trend towards less florid writing, represent the third stage. These phases of style form the links in a chain of development from Dunstable to Taverner, long supposed to have vanished or not to have existed. The rhythmic and melodic style of the first group took on a new exuberance and breadth of line as compared with the style of Dunstable and his contemporaries, and five-part writing became normal. The texture was still virtually non-imitative; the form, while keeping the traditional division into two sections, in triple and duple measure, assumed larger proportions. The tenor remained the basis of the structure, though a plainsong *canto fermo* was used in only one of the antiphons by this group, Hygons's 'Salve regina':

Ex. 124

(We banished sons of Eve cry to thee. We sigh, lamenting and pleading . . . .)

The tenor is the neuma 'Caput' from the Maundy Thursday antiphon 'Venit ad Petrum' on which Dufay, Ockeghem, and Obrecht wrote their 'Caput' Masses.[1] The piece is written in the 'high clefs', with the plainsong at the original pitch, so that transposition down, probably by a fourth, is implied. In works in the florid style, as in longer works of the Dunstable period, 'full' sections written for all the parts alternate with 'solo' sections for a smaller number of (probably single) voices. The first group of Eton composers occasionally used imitation in solo sections, as in this passage from the same work as Ex. 124:

Ex. 125

[1] See F. Ll. Harrison, 'An English "Caput"', *Music and Letters*, xxxiii (1952), p. 203.

(Eternal gate of glory, be thou a refuge to us in the presence of the Father and the Son.)

which typifies the more elaborate style of a solo as compared with a full section. The contrast is heightened by the absence of the slower moving *canto fermo*, which normally appears only in full sections, in keeping with earlier practice.

John Browne is the outstanding member of the second group and ranks among the greatest composers of his age. He takes pride of place at the beginning of the manuscript with the eight-part 'O Maria salvatoris mater', and also wrote for the collection a seven-part *Magnificat*, four six-part antiphons, five antiphons and two Magnificats in five parts, and an antiphon and *Magnificat* in four parts. What remains of this imposing contribution shows imagination and technique of the highest order. A passage from the 'Stabat Mater', one of the finest and most expressive of his works, illustrates

PLATE III

THE ETON CHOIRBOOK

Eton College MS. 178, opening h 2, left-hand page, showing the treble, tenor, and contratenor of Lambe's 'Salve regina' (see Ex. 127 (*a*))

the energy of his counterpoint and the dramatic force he could bring
to the treatment of his text:

(Then the clamorous throng shouts: Crucify him.)

Characteristic of his varied resource are the internal imitation, the combination of duplet and triplet quavers, the sonority of the held chords, the 'thematic' use of four descending notes in varied rhythm, the use of E flat in a cadence on F, and the simultaneous sounding of B flat and B natural.

Thirteen of the seventeen complete antiphons by Browne, Davy, Fawkyner, and Wylkynson are based on a plainsong *canto fermo*. Lambe's treatment of plainsong, however, is quite individual. In the fragmentary 'O regina caelestis gloriae' two Epiphany chants, both identified in the manuscript, are sung simultaneously, while in three other antiphons he continued the earlier technique of 'migrant' plainsong, with and without ornamentation. His most extended example of this method of weaving a polyphonic texture with plainsong material is the 'Salve regina':[1]

Ex. 127 (a)

[1] See pl. III.

(Our life, our sweetness, and our hope, hail!)

(Gentle virgin, pious virgin, sweet virgin, O Mary.)

The second quotation shows the division of a part into two of equal range, frequent in the florid style. In Eton the parts are marked 'semel' or 'gemel' without any apparent distinction between these terms, while in later manuscripts 'gymel' was the usual indication.

The antiphons by Davy and Fawkyner typify the style at its most ornate and decorative, particularly in solo sections. The following is from Davy's 'O Domine caeli terraeque', a work which can be almost exactly dated, as the scribe has noted that it was composed in one day at Magdalen College, Oxford, where Davy was *informator* in 1491–2:

Ex. 128

(He asserted one true God in persons [three].)

DAVY'S 'PASSION'

The contrast between Davy's antiphons and his setting of the *St. Matthew Passion* shows how difference of liturgical function affected musical style. Each chorus of the Passion, which is in duple measure throughout, is composed on a free tenor with continuously varied melodic line and restrained rhythm, while the comparative sobriety of the contrapuntal style, which is related to that of the 'carols of the Passion',[1] makes it perfectly suited to the content of the words:[2]

Ex. 129

[1] See below, p. 345.
[2] The final chorus 'Vere filius Dei' is recorded in *The History of Music in Sound* (H.M.V.), iii.

(But they cried out the more, saying, Let him be crucified. When Pilate saw that he could prevail nothing, but that rather a tumult was made, he took water, and washed his hands before the multitude, saying, I am innocent of the blood of this just person.)

ANTIPHONS BY FAYRFAX AND CORNYSH

Three of the five antiphons which Fayrfax contributed to the Eton book have unfortunately been lost. His five-part 'Salve regina' and four-part 'Ave lumen gratiae' (which survives in part) illustrate the less ornate treatment of the florid style and the more frequent pursuit of short points of imitation which are characteristic of his antiphons in later sources.[1] Cornysh's 'Salve regina' was apparently the most widely known of his antiphons, all of which were in the Eton collection,[2] for it appears in the Scottish choirbook known as the 'Carver' manuscript[3] and in two other manuscripts, also of later date than

[1] For list of his works and their sources see Dom Anselm Hughes, 'An Introduction to Fayrfax', *Musica Disciplina*, vi (1952), p. 89, and Edwin B. Warren, 'The Life and Works of Robert Fayrfax', *Musica Disciplina*, xi (1957), p. 134.

[2] A lost antiphon 'Altissimi potentia' by Cornysh, not in the Eton index, is listed in the remains of an index to a triplex part-book preserved in the binding of the printed book 62. f. 8 (De Riminaldis, *Consiliorum Volumen Secundum*, Lyons, 1558) in the library of Merton College, Oxford.   [3] See below, p. 337.

Eton.[1] It is representative of his larger works in its oscillation between florid and relatively simple vocal lines, the expressiveness of its less florid melodies (the opening trio is a good example), the absence of *canto fermo* design, and the use of imitation in both full and solo sections, as in the last chorus:

Ex. 130

(Sweet Mary, hail!)

[1] Brit. Mus., Harley 1709 (mean) and Add. 34191 (bass, incomplete).

Cornysh's use of B flat against F sharp, which also occurs earlier in this work, is notable.

SHORTER ANTIPHONS

Cornysh's four-part 'Ave Maria mater Dei', written in duple measure and with unadorned melodic style, is the only Eton antiphon which approaches the manner of the contemporary carol. Other examples of the shorter votive antiphon occur in the British Museum manuscript Add. 5665, both in its original layer (probably before 1477), which consists chiefly of carols,[1] and in the later additions (*c.* 1500), which comprise a variety of liturgical forms. Some of the antiphons in this manuscript were composed in a developed descant technique with the plainsong in the middle voice, others are independent of the plainsong. The difference of method may be illustrated by two settings of 'Nesciens mater' composed or copied by John Trouluffe (Canon of St. Probus' Church, Exeter, for some time between 1465 and 1478), who was associated with Richard Smert (Vicar-choral of Exeter Cathedral, 1428–*c.* 1474; rector of Plymtree, near Exeter, 1435–77) in compiling the original part of the manuscript:[2]

Ex. 131

(a)

---

[1] Printed in *Musica Britannica*, iv, pp. 62–109, 115.

[2] Add. 5665, fos. 54ᵛ, 56ᵛ; the second section (from 'ipsum regem') of the latter setting is in triple measure.

(b)

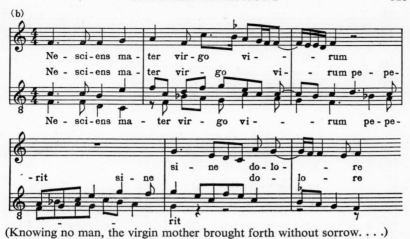

(Knowing no man, the virgin mother brought forth without sorrow. . . .)

The middle part of the former setting is written in plainsong notation, which must be sung in even notes—semibreves in the original notation. This method of writing on the 'monorhythmic' form of the plainsong was used by English composers until the Reformation for such liturgical forms as the respond, hymn, sequence, and ritual antiphon.

A RITUAL ANTIPHON

The Lambeth choirbook contains an interesting item in the form of a comparatively elaborate setting of the ritual antiphon 'Vidi aquam egredientem', sung at the aspersion before Mass on Sundays from Easter to Pentecost.[1] The first two words were given in plainsong by the precentor; after the antiphon came the psalm-verse 'Confitemini Domino', followed by a repeat of the antiphon, the *Gloria patri*, and finally a partial repeat of the antiphon, from the words 'Et omnes ad quos pervenit aqua ista'. The setting in the Lambeth manuscript is a virtually free one, quoting from the plainsong only at the beginning and at the first word of the psalm-verse:[2]

Ex. 132

[1] See *Missale Sarum*, ed. Dickinson, col. 33**.
[2] Lambeth Palace, 1, fos. 44v–45; plainsong from *Graduale Sarisburiense* (ed. Frere), pl. 116.

per-ve-nit........*Ps.* Con-fi-te-mi-ni Do-mi-no quo-ni-am bo-nus: quo-ni-am

in sae-cu-lum mi-se-ri-cor-di-a e-jus.

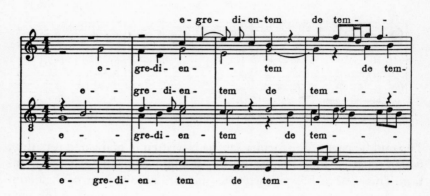

e-gre-di-en-tem de tem-

e-gre-di-en-tem de tem-

e-gre-di-en-tem de tem-

e-gre-di-en-tem de tem-

-plo a la-te-re dex-

-plo a la-te-re dex-te-

-plo a la-te-re dex-te-

-plo a la-te-re dex-te-

-te-ro, al-le-

-ro, al-le-lu-

-ro, al-le-ro, al-

-ro,

End of *Gloria patri*

(I saw water flowing from the temple, out of the right side, and all to whom [this water] came. .... *Ps*. O give thanks unto the Lord; for he is good: because his mercy endureth for ever.)

THE *MAGNIFICAT*

Of the twenty-four Magnificats originally in the Eton manuscript only those by Horwood, Kellyk, Lambe, and William of Stratford are now complete, though two others, by Nesbett and Fayrfax (the setting known as 'Regale'),[1] can be supplied from other sources. For the period up to *c.* 1520 there are eight further settings in the Lambeth and Caius College books, the Fayrfax 'Regale' being in both. The *Magnificat* shared with the Mass and antiphon the contrast between full and solo sections. The normal plan, seldom varied, was to write full sections for the second, sixth, and tenth verses and the second verse of the *Gloria patri*, and solo sections for the words 'dispersit superbos' in the sixth verse and sometimes for 'et in saecula' in the *Gloria* as well as for the fourth and eighth verses. The change from triple to duple measure was invariably made at the sixth verse ('Fecit potentiam'). Since the tenor of each full section was an elaboration of the plainsong, certain melodic idioms reappeared in all Magnificats in the same tone, and this re-working of similar material remained a characteristic of the *Magnificat* throughout its history. This feature,

[1] The 'Regale' *Magnificat* has been edited by Dom Anselm Hughes (London, 1949); the second verse and *Gloria* are recorded in *The History of Music in Sound*, iii.

and also the increasing elaboration of treatment, may be seen in the beginnings of Magnificats by Nesbett, Horwood, Cornysh, and Prentes (probably Henry Prentyce, gentleman of the Chapel Royal in 1509 and 1511), all on the eighth tone:[1]

Ex. 133

[1] (*a*) Edinburgh, National Library, Adv. 5. 1. 15, no. 13; (*b*) Eton, 178, opening z. 2; (*c*) Cambridge, Gonville and Caius, 667, p. 114; (*d*) ibid., p. 130.

(c) CORNYSH

(d) PRENTES

(And my spirit has rejoiced. . . .)

THE YORK MASSES

No complete festal Masses earlier than the Fayrfax–Cornysh period
have survived, though a number of leaves from a choirbook preserved
in the York Diocesan Registry contain incomplete Masses of the late
fifteenth century, including parts of a four-part Mass by John Cuk[1]
on 'Venit dilectus meus' (an antiphon on the feast of the Assumption of
the Virgin), of a *Kyrie* by Horwood, and of some anonymous shorter
Masses.[2] There are also shorter Masses and Mass-movements by 'Sir'
Thomas Packe (perhaps the Thomas Pykke who was a clerk at Eton
from 1454 to 1461), Edmund Sturges (presumably the Turges of the
Eton manuscript), and Henry Petyr,[3] in the later part of Brit. Mus.
Add. 5665. In Cuk's Mass the *canto fermo* appears in the tenor in
paraphrased and abbreviated forms, and not in every full section. In an
anonymous four-part *Gloria* and *Credo*, set *alternatim* and in duple
measure with some use of imitation, a phrase based on the short
versicle 'Custodi nos, Domine', which was sung after the Compline
hymn daily except on double feasts, functions as a recurring theme in
various voices.[4] Another anonymous *Gloria–Credo* pair in the York
leaves, also an *alternatim* setting, is composed on one of the melodies
called 'squares',[5] which were used as material for Lady-Masses until
the Reformation. The tenor of the following passage is based on the

[1] A John Cooke was *succentor vicariorum* at York in 1452–5; see F. Harrison, *Life in
a Medieval College* (London, 1952), p. 300.
[2] See Hugh Baillie and Philippe Oboussier, 'The York Masses', *Music and Letters*,
xxxv (1954), p. 19.
[3] B.Mus., Oxford, 1516, having 'spent 30 years in the study and practice of music'.
[4] The *Gloria* is recorded in *The History of Music in Sound*, iii.
[5] See p. 336.

same melody as the 'Christe eleison' from Ludford's Lady-Mass for
Tuesday quoted on p. 336 below:

Ex. 134

(And He shall come again with glory to judge. . . .)

FESTAL MASSES

The five Masses by Fayrfax, all for five voices, which have come
down to us complete were copied into both the Lambeth and Caius
College choirbooks, which also contain Masses by Nicholas Ludford
(at St. Stephen's, Westminster, at its dissolution in 1547–8, and probably from *c.* 1520)[1] and (William?) Pashe.[2] No Masses by Cornysh
have survived, though we know from a King's College inventory of
1529[3] that the college possessed Masses by him. Fayrfax's 'Regali ex
progenie', on an antiphon for the Nativity of the Virgin, and 'O quam
glorifica', on a hymn for the Assumption, can be approximately dated,
for the former was copied into a lost King's College manuscript in
1503–4[4] and the latter was composed for the degree of Doctor of
Music at Cambridge in 1504.[5] His 'Tecum principium' is based on a
Christmas antiphon, the 'Albanus' Mass on nine notes to which the
word 'Albanus' is set in an antiphon for the feast of St. Alban,[6] while

---

[1] See Hugh Baillie, 'Nicholas Ludford', *Musical Quarterly*, xliv (1958), p. 196.
[2] According to W. H. Grattan Flood in *Early Tudor Composers* (London, 1925),
pp. 80–81, William Pasche was a member of the chapel of Anne, Duchess of Exeter
(d. 1480) in 1476, and died in 1525.
[3] Printed in F. Ll. Harrison, *Music in Medieval Britain*, Appendix IV.
[4] King's College Accounts.
[5] In the Lambeth manuscript it is headed 'O quam glorifica Doctor Feyrfax for his
forme in proceadinge to bee Doctor'.
[6] The 'Albanus' theme is the same as the first phrase of the tenor of Dunstable's

'O bone Jesu', which is a votive Mass of Jesus rather than a festal Mass, makes some use of 'parody' technique by taking material from the beginning and end of his votive antiphon with that text.[1] The four *canto fermo* Masses differ considerably in their treatment of the plainsong, the number of statements ranging from one in each of the four movements in 'O quam glorifica', and the orthodox two in each movement in 'Regali', to twelve in all, some used in solo sections, in 'Tecum principium', and in 'Albanus' an ostinato scheme of forty statements, including inverted and retrograde forms, of its short theme. As a rule each movement of a festal Mass began with a solo section based on the first few notes of the *canto fermo*, anticipating its entry in the first full section:[2]

Ex. 135

motet 'Albanus roseo/Quoque ferendus/Albanus', printed in *Musica Britannica*, viii, p. 58. See Dom Anselm Hughes, 'An Introduction to Fayrfax', p. 99.

[1] For a discussion of the Masses of Fayrfax see ibid., pp. 96–104.
[2] Lambeth Palace, 1, fos. 4v–5.

and the same passage was usually adapted to make a common opening
for the four movements. In 'Tecum principium' Fayrfax varied this
device by beginning each movement with a new point written on the
opening of the plainsong.

Four festal Masses by Ludford have survived complete.[1] The
orthodox *canto fermo* design is used in the six-part 'Benedicta', which
is unusual in being based on the verse of a respond ('Beata es' for the
Assumption), in the five-part 'Christi virgo', on a respond for the
Annunciation, and in the five-part 'Lapidaverunt', on an antiphon for
the feast of St. Stephen. 'Videte miraculum', for six voices with two
interweaving treble parts, has some special features in the treatment
of the *canto fermo*. The respond for the feast of the Purification on
which it is based has one statement in each movement, which is
divided according to the three sentences of its text. The chant of the
second sentence ('Stans onerata') appears in the *Gloria* in monorhythmic form as the treble part of a quartet, in the *Credo* in close imitation
at the unison:[2]

Ex. 136

---

[1] The Merton College index referred to above (p. 318, n. 2) lists three Masses by Ludford
which have not survived: 'Tecum principium', 'Requiem eternam', and 'Sermone blando'.

[2] Cambridge. Gonville and Caius, 667, pp. 35–36; plainsong from *Antiphonale
Sarisburiense* (ed. Frere), pl. 395.

(*Plainsong*: Behold a miracle: (she) standing laden. . . .
    (*a*) : Who takest away the sins of the world. . . .
    (*b*) : And was incarnate by the Holy Ghost of the Virgin Mary.)

and in the *Benedictus* in monorhythmic form as the tenor of a quartet.
The *canto fermo* of the *Agnus Dei* from the first 'miserere' to the end
is not the respond but its verse 'Haec speciosum forma', which has
not been used earlier in the Mass.

    The Mass 'O quam suavis' by John Lloyd or Fluyd[1] (Chapel Royal
1511; d. 1523) is also based on a particularly long plainsong, the

---

[1] The problem of the authorship was solved by Thurston Dart. At the beginning of
the puzzle-antiphon which precedes the Mass is 'Hoc fecit iohannes maris' (i.e. 'of the
flood'). The Mass has been edited by H. B. Collins (London, 1927).

antiphon to the *Magnificat* at first Vespers on the feast of Corpus Christi. In this case the four movements are constructed on only two statements of the chant. The work is most remarkable, however, for the Latin 'canons', or riddles, which must be solved before the lengths, and in some cases the order, of the notes of the tenor can be determined, and which demonstrate the composer's ingenuity in applying numerical progressions and arrangements to musical rhythm.[1] Unlike the mensural subtleties, involving elaborate cross-rhythms, in some pieces in the Old Hall manuscript, these puzzles are external to the actual sound of the music, which conforms to the less ornate treatment of the florid style practised by Fayrfax and Ludford.

OTHER FESTAL MASSES

Of the two important sources of festal Masses of the first half of the sixteenth century, the 'Forrest–Heather'[2] and Peterhouse part-books,[3] the latter is unfortunately without its tenor book. The Forrest–Heather set contains eighteen Masses, including four by Fayrfax, three by John Taverner (Tattershall College, 1525; Cardinal College, Oxford, 1526–30), two by Hugh Aston (B.Mus., Oxford, 1510; St. Mary Newarke College, Leicester, 1525–48), two by Thomas Ashewell (Lincoln, 1508; Durham, 1513), and one each by Avery Burton (Chapel Royal, 1494–1526), William Rasar (King's College, 1509–15), and John Norman (St. David's Cathedral at some time between 1509 and 1522; Eton, 1534–45). The discovery of Aston's connexion with St. Mary Newarke disposes of his suggested identification with Hugh Ashton (d. 1522), Archdeacon of York and Canon of St. Stephen's, Westminster. Aston's four surviving complete works,[4] the 'Te Deum' Mass for five voices, the six-part Mass 'Videte manus meas', on the *Magnificat* antiphon for Tuesday in Easter Week, and the five-part antiphons 'Te matrem Dei laudamus'[5] and 'Gaude virgo mater Christi', show an imaginative and technically accomplished handling

---

[1] See H. B. Collins's Introduction to his edition, pp. xxi–xxx.

[2] Oxford, Bodleian Libr., MSS. Mus. Sch. e. 376–81. The last seven Masses were added by William Forrest, petty canon of Christ Church, Oxford, and chaplain to Queen Mary; the books were given to the Music School by William Heather (d. 1627), founder of the Professorship of Music. For list of contents see Dom Anselm Hughes, *Medieval Polyphony in the Bodleian Library* (Oxford, 1951), pp. 43–44.

[3] Cambridge, Peterhouse, MSS. 31–32, 40–41, compiled between c. 1540 and 1547. For list of contents see Dom Anselm Hughes, *Catalogue of the Musical Manuscripts at Peterhouse, Cambridge* (Cambridge, 1953), pp. 2–3.

[4] His choral works are printed in *Tudor Church Music*, vol. x.

[5] This is the original text of 'Te Deum laudamus', printed ibid., p. 99. The latter text (which is not that of the *Te Deum*) turned the Mary-antiphon (itself an imitation of the *Te Deum*) into an antiphon to the Trinity.

of the florid style. The 'Te Deum' Mass approaches variations in form, for it makes almost continuous use of a short *canto fermo*, the chant of the second verse of the *Te Deum*, which appears twenty-six times in various voices. Appropriately, the 'Sanctus' verse of the *Te Deum* is the *canto fermo* of the *Sanctus* of the Mass (the texts are identical), while the first verse of the *Te Deum* is used only to form the basis of the common opening of the other three movements.

An equally enterprising treatment of *canto fermo* material is found in Thomas Ashewell's fine Mass on the well-known Advent antiphon 'Ave Maria', which is preserved in the Forrest–Heather books. Ashewell followed the method of Fayrfax in the 'Tecum principium' Mass (the plainsong has the same opening notes) by setting the initial notes of the *canto fermo* in a different way at the beginning of each movement. He also used the complete *canto fermo* as the basis of some of the solo sections. At 'Et incarnatus' it is in the bass, in the *Benedictus* it is in the mean, and at 'in nomine Domini' it is in the treble, transposed up a fifth. The variety of his treatment may be judged from these quotations, which include an elaborate and sonorous full section from the *Gloria*:[1]

Ex. 137

[1] Plainsong from *Antiphonale Sarisburiense* (ed. Frere), pl. 5.

(b)

(c)

(d)

(*Plainsong*: Hail Mary, full of grace, the Lord be with thee, blessed art thou among women, Alleluia.)

LUDFORD'S LADY-MASSES

The seven short Masses by Ludford in the part-books Royal Appendix 45–48 in the British Museum are of special musical and liturgical interest, for they are the only surviving complete set of Lady-Masses for the days of the week. One of the part-books contains the plainsong of the Offertories and Communions (the Introits and Graduals are not given), of the solo parts of the Alleluias, and of alternate verses of the Sequences. In addition, it has melodies in measured notation for the *alternatim* performance of the Kyries, and also for *alternatim* parts of the Glorias and Credos except for the Masses on Wednesday and Friday, when the *Gloria* and *Credo* were sung throughout in vocal polyphony, as were the *Sanctus* and *Agnus Dei* every day. This book was almost certainly used at the organ, perhaps with extempore elaboration of the plainsongs (in monorhythm) and *Kyrie* melodies, for the other books supply three-part polyphony for the parts of the ritual which it omits. The movements of the Ordinary are composed on ornamental forms of the melodies called 'squares'. Ludford's Tuesday Mass is based on the same 'square' as the York Mass quoted earlier, and three settings by Taverner of its 'Christe' section[1] have been preserved in a manuscript of the early seventeenth century. The *alternatim* treatment of Ludford's Kyries, in which the 'square' is followed by the polyphonic setting of its ornamented form, may be compared with that of the Sequences, in which the first verse of each pair has a plainsong statement, probably set extempore on the organ, while the second has vocal polyphony on the ornamented plainsong:

Ex. 138

(a)

---

[1] Printed in *Tudor Church Music*, iii, pp. 56–57. For discussion of two manuscript sources of these 'common-property' *Kyrie* melodies see M. F. Bukofzer, *Studies in Medieval and Renaissance Music* (New York, 1950), pp. 191–2. Other instances of their use are the Lady-Masses 'Apon the square' by William Whytbrook and William Mundy in Brit. Mus. Add. 17802–5. See Harrison, *Music in Medieval Britain*, pp. 290–2.

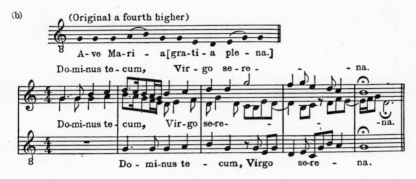

MUSIC IN SCOTLAND

Scottish institutions in which polyphony is known to have been sung during this period include the cathedrals of Aberdeen and Dunkeld, the College of St. Salvator (founded 1450) at St. Andrew's University, King's College at Aberdeen (founded 1495), St. Mary's Church at Crail (raised to collegiate status in 1517), and the Augustinian Abbey of Scone. The only surviving manuscripts are the 'Carver' choirbook (Edinburgh, Nat. Libr., Adv. 5.1.15), which contains Masses, antiphons, and Magnificats,[1] and a set of part-books,[2] traditionally associated with Dunkeld, containing antiphons, with two Masses added at the end. Notes in the choirbook tell us that Robert Carver was a Canon of Scone who was in his fifty-ninth year in 1546, and that he composed the following pieces in the manuscript: a Mass of St. Michael 'Dum sacrum mysterium' for ten voices, a Mass on 'L'homme armé', the only British example known, for four voices,[3] three unnamed Masses for four, five, and six voices, and two antiphons, 'Gaude flore virginali' for five voices and 'O bone Jesu' for the remarkable number of nineteen.[4] Contact with French and

---

[1] For list of contents see *Musica Britannica*, x, p. 142.
[2] Edinburgh, Univ. Libr. MS. Db. I. 7.
[3] Printed by Kenneth Elliott in *Musica Britannica*, xv, p. 30.
[4] See *Musica Britannica*, xv, p. 87.

English music is shown by the presence in the book of Dufay's Mass
'L'homme armé' and of compositions, here anonymous, by Cornysh,
Fayrfax, Lambe, and Nesbett. Carver's own work, though not that of
a composer of the first rank, is earnest and competent, as the opening
of his 'L'homme armé' Mass may suggest:

Ex. 139

(And on earth peace to men of good will. We praise thee . . .)

The antiphons in the Dunkeld part-books give further evidence of the
cultural connexions between Scotland and France. Though all are
anonymous, their style suggests that they are by continental composers, and this is supported by three identifications, for among them

are Josquin's 'Benedicta es', Jaquet of Mantua's 'Ave virgo gloriosa', and a setting of 'Virgo clemens et benigna' by an anonymous composer which is also found in a Florentine manuscript.[1]

JOHN TAVERNER

The characteristics and achievements of this great period in English choral music are summed up with remarkable comprehensiveness in the work of John Taverner.[2] The liturgical range of his compositions may be seen in the following list of his complete works, arranged according to their liturgical categories:

Festal Mass. 'Corona Spinea' (*canto fermo* not identified), 'Gloria tibi Trinitas' (on a Trinity antiphon) and 'O Michael' (on the respond 'Archangeli Michaelis interventione') à 6; sections à 3 from a *Sanctus*, a *Benedictus*, and an *Agnus Dei*.

Shorter Mass. 'Mater Christi' (derived from his antiphon), 'Meane Mass' (printed as 'Sine nomine') and 'Small Devotion' (using material from his antiphon 'Christe Jesu') à 5; 'Playn Song' and 'Western Wynde' à 4; *Kyrie* 'Leroy'[3] à 4; three Christes à 3 for the Lady-Mass.

Votive Antiphon. 'Ave Dei patris filia' (on the *Te Deum*), 'Gaude plurimum', and 'O splendor gloriae' à 5.

Short Votive Antiphon. 'Ave Maria' (two parts missing), 'Fac nobis' (antiphon of the Name of Jesus; two parts missing), 'Mater Christi', 'Sancte Deus' (two parts missing), and 'Sub tuum praesidium' (two parts missing) à 5; 'Christe Jesu pastor bone' (probably originally an antiphon of St. William of York beginning 'O Wilhelme pastor bone')[4] à 4; 'Prudens virgo' and 'Virgo pura' à 3 are probably extracts from Mary-antiphons.

Magnificat. Three settings: on the first Tone à 6, on the second Tone à 5, on the sixth Tone à 4.

Te Deum. *Alternatim*, beginning 'Te eternum patrem', à 4.

Respond. Two settings of 'Dum transisset' à 5 and a version of one of these à 4; 'Audivi', 'Gloria in excelsis' (the verse of 'Hodie nobis caelorum rex') and 'In pace' à 4; two Alleluias à 4 for the Lady-Mass.

Sequence and Tract. 'Jesu spes poenitentibus' (third verse of the sequence 'Dulcis Jesu memoria' for the Mass of the Name of Jesus), 'Traditur militibus' (sixth verse of the sequence 'Coenam cum discipulis' for the Mass of the Five Wounds of Jesus) and 'Tam peccatum' (fourth verse of the Tract 'Dulce nomen Jesu Christe' for the Jesus-Mass in Lent) à 3; 'Ecce mater Jerusalem' à 2 (à 3, one part missing?) is probably from a sequence.

Prose. 'Sospitate dedit aegros' à 5.

(Not determined.) 'Quemadmodum' (no further text) à 6.

---

[1] See E. Lowinsky, 'A Newly Discovered Sixteenth-Century Motet Manuscript at the Biblioteca Vallicelliana in Rome', *Journal of the American Musicological Society*, iii (1950), p. 229.

[2] Printed in *Tudor Church Music*, i and iii.

[3] A name given to one of the 'squares'.

[4] Text in *The York Processional*, ed. W. G. Henderson (Surtees Society, vol. 63), p. 196.

(Wrongly attributed.) 'Rex amabilis' is by Fayrfax, from the antiphon 'Maria plena virtute'; 'Tu ad liberandum' and 'Tu angelorum domina' are by Aston, from 'Te matrem Dei laudamus';[1] 'Esto nobis' is by Tallis, from 'Ave Dei patris filia'.[2]

In Taverner's larger works the new techniques of imitation, canon, ostinato, and sequence are fully assimilated into the ornate line and texture of a style which is considerably more florid than that of Fayrfax and Ludford. His treatment of *canto fermo* design is orthodox, though the *canto fermo* is occasionally used in solo sections, and in 'Gloria tibi Trinitas' it is in the mean throughout. The ingenious imitations and convenient disposition of the four voices in the setting of this theme in the *Benedictus*,[3] to the words 'in nomine Domine', led Thomas Mulliner to transcribe it into his anthology of organ pieces;[4] thus Taverner's 'In nomine' became the ancestor of a long race of instrumental and keyboard 'In nomines', all on the 'Gloria tibi Trinitas' plainsong, which continued until Purcell. In his shorter Masses and antiphons Taverner relied chiefly on imitative, chordal, and antiphonal methods of writing. In the 'Western Wynde' Mass he achieved both strictness of form and variety of style by applying to the Mass the technique of variations. This work is a series of thirty-six treatments of the secular tune, nine in each movement, in which he exploited all the resources of imitative and differentiated texture, of melodic sequence and of ostinato accompaniment, to produce an impressive demonstration of the art of contrapuntal variation. The title of the 'Playn Song' Mass refers to its rhythmic style, for the note-values are confined to the breve and semibreve, with an occasional minim. As in all Masses of this period, the *Sanctus* and *Agnus Dei* are set to extended melodic lines, making the four movements about equal in length.

When he adopted the *Te Deum* as the *canto fermo* of his 'Ave Dei patris filia', Taverner, unlike Aston in the 'Te Deum' Mass, used all five melodies of the plainsong. The settings of 'Dum transisset' are examples of a new method of setting responds on the monorhythmic form of the chant (usually written in plainsong notation), treating the choral rather than the solo sections, and thus reversing the previous practice of singing the soloists' opening and verse in polyphony and the choral sections in plainsong. This exchange of roles also took

---

[1] Printed in *Tudor Church Music*, x, pp. 107–9.
[2] Printed ibid., vi, p. 166.
[3] Recorded in *The History of Music in Sound*, iii.
[4] *Musica Britannica*, i, p. 30.

place in settings of the Alleluia for the Lady-Mass, as in Ludford's cycle and in Taverner's Alleluia 'Veni electa' for the Thursday Mass:

Ex. 140

(Repeat Soloist's beginning of 'Alleluia' as above)

The older method was retained in certain responds which had a special ceremonial context, such as 'Audivi vocem' at Matins on All Saints' Day, 'In pace in idipsum' at Compline during the first three weeks in Lent, and the verse 'Gloria in excelsis' of the respond 'Hodie nobis caelorum rex' at Matins of Christmas Day, which took place before Midnight Mass. Taverner's setting of 'Audivi', like his 'Veni electa', is an example of florid counterpoint on the plainsong:

Ex. 141

(I heard a voice [coming] from heaven: [come all ye] most wise [virgins], store
up the oil [in your vessels, for] the bridegroom will come.
At midnight [a shout arises] . . . Behold the bridegroom comes.)

A prose was an insertion into a respond sung at first Vespers on the
feasts of certain saints. It had the same form as a sequence and was
normally performed by a small group, the choir repeating the music
of each line to its final vowel. The prose of St. Nicholas 'Sospitati dedit
aegros' was a unique case in two respects: it was sung at Matins (a
different prose was sung at first Vespers), and was performed throughout by the whole choir. Since Taverner treats every verse, his setting
assumes the form which has been called a 'variation-chain' when

applied to a sequence. It concludes with a *canto fermo* treatment of
the final words 'Sospes regreditur' of the respond 'Ex ejus tumba'
into which the prose was inserted as a troping elaboration of the
word 'sospes'.

A PROCESSIONAL ANTIPHON

Another instance of the influence of an unusual ritual situation on
the polyphonic treatment of a text is the antiphon 'Christus re-
surgens', which was sung with the verse 'Dicant nunc Judaei' when the
crucifix was carried in procession after it was taken from the *sepul-*
chrum on Easter Sunday morning. The two senior persons present
began the antiphon, and both the antiphon and the verse were sung by
the whole choir. The setting by Thomas Knyght (Salisbury, 1529–49)
adopts the 'respond' method of counterpoint on the monorhythmic
plainsong, in this case written in measured notation since there are
occasional minims and semiminims (quavers and semiquavers in
the values of the transcription):[1]

Ex. 142

Beginners

¹ From Brit. Mus., MSS. Add. 17802–5, a collection of polyphony for the Sarum rite,
probably compiled in the reign of Queen Mary (1553–8).

(Christ being raised from the dead dies no more . . .
Let the Jews now say how. . . .)

CAROLS AND SECULAR MUSIC

Though the carol kept its characteristic form of verse and burden[1] throughout this period, the influence of Renaissance ideas affected both its musical style and its social function. In the fifteenth century sacred polyphonic carols seem to have provided the special music which the customs of secular churches permitted on the festivals between Christmas and the Epiphany, while political and convivial carols were probably sung at evening recreations of secular communities. Later in the century sacred, courtly, and amorous carols became part of the domestic music of the royal court; an account of a royal banquet in 1487 tells us that there were present 'the Deane and those of the King's Chapell, which incontynently after the King's first course sange a Carall'.[2] The collection known as the 'Fayrfax Book' (Brit. Mus., Add. 5465) includes carols of the Passion, carols in praise of Henry VII and of Prince Arthur (d. 1502), and carols of love; among the composers are Banester, Browne, 'William Cornyssh, Junior',[3] Davy, Fayrfax, Turges, Richard Hampshire (Chorister at Windsor, 1474; Scholar of King's College, 1484; clerk there, 1486; clerk at Windsor, 1489–99), and William Newark (Chapel Royal, 1477–1509).[4] Their carols are written in duple measure, and the burden was

---

[1] See *supra*, pp. 121–3.

[2] J. Leland (ed. T. Hearne), *Collectanea*, iv (1774), p. 237.

[3] The elder William Cornysh was Master of the Choristers at Westminster Abbey from 1479 to 1491 and died in 1502. See E. Pine, *The Westminster Abbey Singers* (London, 1953), pp. 19–20.

[4] The other composers mentioned are Sir Thomas Phelyppis, Sheryngam, and Tutor, presumably the John Tuder of the Pepys manuscript.

now usually shortened on its returns, as in Banester's 'My fearfull dreme':[1]

Ex. 143

where the small note indicates the beginning of the burden after the first and subsequent verses.

The early Tudor period saw the beginnings of secular court polyphony in forms other than the carol. The manuscript Add. 31922 in the British Museum contains vocal and instrumental pieces by King Henry VIII,[2] Cornysh, Dunstable, Fayrfax, Lloyd, Thomas Farthyng (chorister at King's College, 1477–83; clerk there 1493–9; then probably in the household chapel of the Countess of Richmond and Derby,

[1] Add. 5465, f. 77ᵛ.
[2] Printed in Lady Mary Trefusis, *Songs, Ballads and Instrumental Pieces composed by King Henry VIII* (Oxford, 1912).

Henry VII's mother; Chapel Royal, 1511–20), Kempe (probably John
Kemp, at Westminster Abbey as lay singer in 1500 and as teacher of
the choristers, 1501–1508 or 9),[1] and Rysby (probably Henry Rysby,
clerk at Eton from 1506 to 1508).[2] In addition there are a few Franco-
Flemish *chansons* of which only the opening words are given.
Cornysh's 'Adieu mes amours' and Farthyng's 'The thowghts within
my brest' illustrate the influences at work at the birth of the secular
song of the English Renaissance. The former is clearly an imitation
of the contemporary French *chanson*, while the latter represents a
simpler and perhaps native style, which may be a development of the
lost songs of the court minstrels:[3]

Ex. 144
(a)

[1] E. Pine, *Westminster Abbey Singers*, p. 28.
[2] The other composers mentioned are Doctor Cooper and Wylliam Daggere. For a
discussion of the puzzle-canons and rounds in this manuscript see J. Stevens, 'Rounds
and Canons from an Early Tudor Songbook', *Music and Letters*, xxxii (1951), pp. 29–
37. The contents of the early Tudor song and carol manuscripts will be edited by Stevens
in *Musica Britannica*.
[3] (*a*) Add. 31922, fo. 15ᵛ; (*b*) ibid., fo. 29ᵛ.

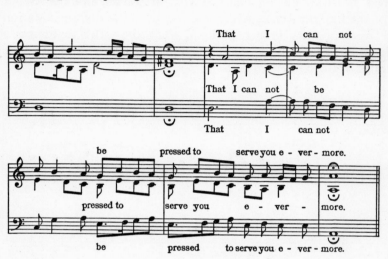

By 1530 both the carol and the secular song were more widely cultivated as household music, for the only collection of polyphony printed in England before the Reformation, the *XX Songes ix of iiii partes and xi of thre partes*, which was issued in that year, comprised a setting of 'Pater noster' followed by sacred and secular carols, songs and instrumental pieces.[1] This famous print, though it had to wait many years for a successor, marks the opening of the great era of Tudor and Stuart domestic music, as well as the close of the history of the medieval carol.

[1] Only the bass part-book (cf. pl. IV(*b*)) and first page of the triplex (British Museum, K. 1. e. 1) and first and last pages of the medius (Westminster Abbey Library) are extant; facsimiles of the contents and four other pages in E. B. Reed, *Christmas Carols printed in the Sixteenth Century* (Cambridge, Mass., 1932): the composers given are Ashewell, Cornysh, (Robert) Cowper, Fayrfax, (John) Gwynneth, (Robert) Jones, (Richard) Pygot, and Taverner. For biographies of Cowper, Gwynneth, Jones, and Pygot see Grove's *Dictionary of Music and Musicians* (London, 5th edition, 1954).

X

EUROPEAN SONG (1300-1530)

By WALTER SALMEN

INTRODUCTION

WHILE for some forms of medieval music the period from 1300 to 1530 can represent no more than a merely external demarcation, in the field of song it is possible to regard this period as an organic unity. This epoch, which we may call the later Middle Ages, saw the gradual passing of the art-song of the early and high Middle Ages as well as the growth of modern forms and styles originating in the towns. The polyphonic art-song was enjoying its first flowering in this period. It blended into one the whole rich treasury of medieval song from the simplest popular song to the most subtle love-song. From the point of view of our immediate inquiry, however, this period is even more significant, as from the beginning of the fourteenth century it is possible for the first time to speak of European song in an historical setting which embraces all levels and classes. The German colonization of Eastern Europe which developed in the later Middle Ages opened up the whole of Europe to the Russian border for the first time, bringing the Slavs, the Balts, and the Magyars at any rate partially into the consort of Western culture.[1] A great unity embracing all the common forms and styles of popular song, as well as the songs of the upper classes, now extended from Portugal to the Ukraine.

Nothing throws more light on the lively European intercourse between the nations at this time than the active mediation effected by the *histriones* and wandering *cantores*. Towards the end of the fourteenth century, for example, we find *ystriones* from Bohemia and Germany at the court of Juan I of Aragon,[2] while between 1400 and 1410 singers and instrumentalists from Poland, Lithuania, Sweden, Bohemia, Portugal, France, Rumania, and Flanders sojourned in the Marienburg in East Prussia, the citadel of the Teutonic Order.[3] In

[1] For details see W. Salmen, *Die Schichtung der mittelalterlichen Musikkultur in der ostdeutschen Grenzlage* (Kassel, 1954).

[2] H. Finke, 'Zur Korrespondenz der deutschen Könige und Fürsten mit den Herrschern Aragons im 14. und 15. Jahrhundert', *Spanische Forschungen der Görresgesellschaft*, v (1935), pp. 473 f., and H. Anglès, 'Es Cantors i Organistes Franco-Flamencs i Alemanys a Catalunya els Segles XIV–XVI', *Gedenkboek D.F. Scheurleer* (The Hague, 1925), pp. 49 ff.

[3] J. Müller-Blattau, *Geschichte der Musik in Ost- und Westpreußen* (Königsberg, 1932), p. 13.

the fifteenth century the importance and influence of the works of Guillaume de Machaut extended from Portugal to Poland.[1] Oswald von Wolkenstein also roved about as a minstrel between East and West,[2] while eruptive mass movements like that of the flagellants in 1349, who, starting from Italy, forced their way as *gesta rusticorum* as far as Poland and England, strengthened the ties between the nations, over and above the common European stratum of song. Great bands of pilgrims journeyed annually, especially from Central Europe, to Santiago de Compostella and other places of pilgrimage. Tunes and songs of all kinds travelled with them and the local people made them their own by translating them, by modifying them in transmission, and by *contrafacta*. Thus no category of music so well documents the supranational coherence of Europe at this period as the European song, the influence of which extended beyond the sphere of the Latin rite.

European song between 1300 and 1530 may be classified according to the cultural areas, prevailing styles, and strata of the population. It must be considered historically, ethnologically, and sociologically. To understand song in this period in its true context and fundamental qualities its history must be studied systematically and as a whole. Many of its forms and melodic patterns belonged to Europe as a whole; some of its features were confined to smaller areas and acquired typical local inflections; many of the songs were universal property; others were the specific possession of particular classes, professional groups, individual strata of the population.[3] At this period Western culture already embraced a complex, highly stratified world. All classes, the governing and the educated as well as 'the people' in the narrower sense of the word, helped to sustain the tradition of song: the historian of the genre must therefore begin at the lowest levels and work his way upwards. The songs of the later Middle Ages are connected with custom and tradition and nature, with religious observances and entertainment at the courts and monasteries and in the middle classes. The songs of the knightly class are unintelligible apart from those of the people, and vice versa, since the social groups of the Middle Ages were not isolated from one another horizontally or vertically but interacted on one another. In addition

[1] F. Gennrich, 'Zur Machaut-Forschung', in *Zeitschrift für romanische Philologie*, l (1930), pp. 351 ff.

[2] W. Salmen, 'Werdegang und Lebensfülle des Oswald von Wolkenstein', *Musica Disciplina*, vii (1953), p. 147.

[3] W. Wiora, *Europäischer Volksgesang* (Cologne, 1952), offers a survey of the types of song common to all Europe.

to the European contacts between the nations there were the relationships between the various strata of society, of which Ex. 145 affords some examples:

Ex. 145

(a) Netherlands, 14th Century, Hulthem MS, Tagelied

Ons comt noch huden een salych dach...

Upper Germany, 1430, H. Laufenberg, Christmas Song

In einem kripfly lag ein kind...

Lower Germany, c. 1470, Rostock Ldb., Student Song

Filia vis militem...

Nuremberg, 1540, G. Forster II No. 43, Drinking Song

So truncken sie die liebe lange nacht...

Bohemia, 1512, Cantio de s. Wenceslao

Gaude, felix Boemia...

Pseudo-Neidhart, 15th Century, 'Der dorn stein'

Darczu stet der walt mit laub bekronet...

O. von Wolkenstein, 1426, Narrative Song

durch Harmanei in Persia...

Nuremberg, 1455, Lochamer Ldb., Love Song

Nw tut er doch als ein rechter schalck...

(b) France, c. 1300, Jehannot de L'Escurel, Ballade

De belle et bonne au cuer vrai...

Spain, 14th Century, Codex de Las Huelgas, Hosanna trope

Personet nunc tinnula...

Thus in the Spanish *Cancionero musical de Palacio* (*c.* 1500)[1] a great number of common European elements appear as well as Spanish peculiarities of style and character; songs of the common people appear alongside those of the aristocratic classes.

The following discussion is confined in the main to Germany as the geographically central land where contact with the songs of other European nations had the most fruitful results, and where even until 1500 songs of all kinds were undoubtedly the central feature of secular musical life. We shall also discuss the music of the nations of eastern Europe and the Iberian peninsula; but the history of song during this period in England, France, and Italy is dealt with separately in other chapters of this volume.

POPULAR SONG

The music of the socially and spiritually basic strata of society forms the foundation of every specialized musical culture. In the later Middle Ages it was considerably more important than later on. Relics of primitive times survived in snatches of verse-melody, religious invocations and recitative-like, melismatic melodies *ane wort* (without words); more highly developed strophic forms had also developed in great profusion. Since the common people sang without reference to writing, and records of popular song are therefore scanty and usually inadequate owing to the imperfect notation, recent oral tradition seems a more fruitful source for the musical historian. Remote country districts in eastern Europe, in the Alps or the Spanish highlands supply adequate material of medieval origin. By reasoning *a posteriori* it is possible to gain from this material a vivid picture of the variety and abundance of medieval folksong. Its ingredients and practices, its peculiar keys and rhythms, cannot be fitted into the theoretical systems of the time.[2]

---

[1] Ed. H. Anglès (Barcelona, 1947 and 1951).
[2] Cf. W. Salmen, 'Vermeintliches und wirkliches Volkslied im späten Mittelalter', *Kongreßbericht Lüneburg 1950*, pp. 174 ff., W. Wiora, 'Alpenländische Liedweisen der

The main recorded sources of popular songs with melodies from the Middle Ages are: the flagellant songs of 1349 recorded by Hugo von Reutlingen (ed. Runge, Leipzig, 1900); the St. Blasius MS. 77 of 1439 (ed. Moser-Quellmalz, 1934); the *contrafacta* of Heinrich Laufenberg, *c.* 1430 (reprinted in Böhme's *Altdeutsches Liederbuch*, Leipzig, 1877); the *Hohenfurter Liederbuch* from the second half of the fifteenth century (ed. Bäumker, Leipzig, 1895).[1] There are also single items in various collections of urban origin from the *Lochamer Liederbuch*[2] to Georg Forster's *Frische Teutsche Liedlein* (Part II, 1540).[3] The latter examples appear, however, in stylized versions, which considerably lessens their value as sources. As an example may be quoted the 'Tannhäuser Ballad' in a simple three-part arrangement from the Mensural Codex of 'M.L. of Innsbruck', which originated between 1480 and 1520.

Ex. 146

Tan - hau - ser Ir seit mir lieb

(Tannhäuser, you are dear to me.)

There are practically no direct records of the medieval popular song of the western Slavs and Hungarians. On the other hand, in Spain

Frühzeit und des Mittelalters im Lichte vergleichender Forschung', *Angebinde für J. Meier* (Lahr, 1949), pp. 169 ff., and H. Anglès, 'Das spanische Volkslied', *Archiv für Musikforschung*, iii (1938), pp. 331 ff. The theorist Jerome of Moravia speaks characteristically of the *layci cantus maxime irregulares*.

[1] See also the article 'Hohenfurter Handschriften', *Die Musik in Geschichte und Gegenwart*, vi (1957), col. 578.

[2] Published in facsimile by K. Ameln (Berlin, 1925).

[3] Reprinted in *Das Erbe deutscher Musik* (*Reichsdenkmale* xx), i (Wolfenbüttel, 1942).

quite early collections of music include popular songs, for example in
the fourteenth century the *Llibre Vermell*, of Montserrat, where they
appear in the form of popular vocal canons (*caça*).[1] The *De Musica
libri Septem* of Salinas (Salamanca, 1577) is, however, the first reliable
source of any size. It contains several *canti antiquissimi*, such as the
following archaic couplet:[2]

Ex. 147

Las ma-ña-nas de.a - bril   dul-ces er- an   de dor - mir.
(April mornings were sweet for sleep.)

As in the history of the *Minnesang*, so also in that of popular song, the
increasing urbanization and Christianizing of central Europe in particular brought about far-reaching changes, since the structure and way
of life of the people were very largely transformed by these processes.
Natural ties were loosened over a wide area and this led to the atrophy
or modification of traditional customs and some of the spheres in
which popular song had been an active force. Popular song for-
feited its old place in the main spheres of life and was reduced to the
level of mere entertainment. Hitherto songs associated with traditional customs had predominated; now the love-song and the narrative song came to the fore: a process which, especially in the lower
classes in and near the towns, ran parallel with the almost complete
abandonment of recitative-like and melismatic elements in favour of
strophic songs and compact patterns. The universal rationalistic
trends of the age encouraged, in particular, the development and dis-
semination of symmetrical, archlike melodic patterns which were also
assimilated by the Slavs, Balts, and Magyars as a result of the German
colonization of eastern Europe. To begin with, however, only certain
isolated areas of eastern Europe were affected.

To get a real idea of the abundance and vitality of medieval popular
song one should consider the high artistic skill of the finest singers in
the countryside, the freedom with which they approached problems
of form, and the wealth of improvisation which the singing contests
and competitions revealed.[3] In addition to this one should take into

---

[1] Ed. G. Suñol in *Analecta Montserratensia*, i (1917), pp. 100 ff. and also Ursprung,
Zeitschrift für Musikwissenschaft, iv (1921–2), pp. 136 ff.

[2] For further examples see F. Pedrell, *Sammelbände der internationalen Musikgesellschaft*, i (1899–1900), pp. 381 ff.; H. Anglès, *Archiv für Musikforschung*, iii (1938), pp.
331 ff. and J. B. Trend, *The Music of Spanish History to 1600* (London, 1926), Exs. 36–42.

[3] Cf. R. Hildebrand, *Materialien zur Geschichte des deutschen Volkslieds* (Leipzig,
1900), pp. 76 ff.; L. Uhland, *Alte hoch- und niederdeutsche Volkslieder*, ii (Stuttgart,
1866), pp. 206 ff.

account the profusion of the various forms of polyphony and *vber-singen*.[1] Today such features as these survive to any extent only in Spain and the remoter areas of eastern Europe where the people still constitute an organic society and have not yet been levelled down into a uniform mass.

POPULAR RELIGIOUS SONGS

In the course of this development the religious invocation, which was associated chiefly with processions and pilgrimages, remained relatively unaltered. As an established type and basic stratum of popular song it can be traced back to fourteenth-century sources. Rhyming refrains which were originally introduced with a magic intention, as well as certain melodic shapes, suggest a primitive origin. The most widespread form is that of the short-rhymed couplet with refrain, the content usually being a prayer:

Ex. 148

Nu   ist dîv betfart   so here: Crist raît sel-ber gen Je - ru - sa-leme.

Er fûrt an crutz an   si - ner hant. Nu helf uns der   hai - lant!

(Now the pilgrimage is exalted: Christ Himself rides toward Jerusalem. He carries a cross in his hand. Now may the Saviour help us!)

As is proved by the *Hohenfurter Liederbuch* and the liturgy of the flagellants of 1349, the singing of these short strophic songs 'in church processions and processions with the Cross', was divided between the precentor and the responding retinue of the faithful.[2] The pilgrims' invocation of Santiago de Compostella, 'Herru Sanctiagu', of which there is documentary evidence as far back as the twelfth century, and the crusaders' invocation 'Sant Marî, muoter unde meit', show that this form was current throughout the Christian world. From the fourteenth century onwards there was a clear tendency to expand the short form of invocation into longer invocations to the saints or into Christobiographical invocations.[3] Earlier religious songs such as 'Er-

---

[1] R. Batka, 'Cantus fractus vocibus', in *Mitteilungen des Vereins für Geschichte der Deutschen in Böhmen*, xlv (1906), pp. 5–10, and cf. *Basler Zeitschrift für Geschichte und Altertumskunde*, xxv, p. 54, for the report of the Castilian nobleman Pero Tafur of 1438 on the *kunstgemäß dreistimmig* singing of the common people in the Aargau.

[2] In the Bavarian Chronicle of Joh. Aventinus we read:
                    so sang etwa einer ein ruef vor,
                    die andern sangen alle nach.

[3] E. Fredrich, *Der Ruf* (Diss. Berlin, 1936), p. 35.

standen ist der heilige Christ' also document this tendency to expansion of the invocation; clerics concerned with the cure of souls took a considerable interest in this development and even themselves composed more artistic invocations on the basis of traditional resources and formulae.[1] In particular, the *Hohenfurter Liederbuch* contains examples in which popular melodies are used (fos. 1–64). The rise of the vernacular hymn, which was related to this development, was promoted above all by the eruptive mass movements of the fourteenth century which throughout Central Europe helped to fulfil the popular demand to be allowed to sing in Church *in linguaggio suo*. This aspiration was particularly evident in Bohemia and Poland, where Western forms and patterns usually stood sponsor to local developments.[2] Archaic strata were washed to the surface by pressure from below and, in particular, worship of the saints in warm spiritual tones, saturated with mystic emotion, enjoyed a period of flowering before the Reformation.[3] How great the number of invocations, pilgrim songs, and Christmas and Easter hymns must have been is indicated by a passage in Georg Witzel's *Psaltes ecclesiasticus* of 1550:

> On this crusade the beautiful Easter songs were sung in Latin and German. Our forefathers knew a number of special devotional hymns designed for this purpose: over fifty in all.

The Catholic songbooks of Beuttner, Coler, and Korner from the beginning of the seventeenth century offer gleanings from this harvest of popular religious music.

Devotio moderna and other lay movements of pre-Reformation times set out to achieve a matured simplicity in daily life and singing, and thus helped to infuse a middle-class spirit of personal devotion and edification into religious song. Songs in honour of Mary and Christ flourished above all in convents in the Netherlands and Low Germany, everything worldly being understood in an otherworldly sense.[4] Since new tunes were composed only in the rarest cases, the best-known popular tunes of all kinds were used for the *dick hübschen Liedli*. The Minorite orders of both sexes and the lower

[1] Some items in the Spanish *Llibre Vermell* also owe their origin to this endeavour to create or provide *honestas ac devotas cantilenas* for pilgrims (cf. Suñol, op. cit., p. 106).

[2] Cf. for example the Polish *patrium carmen* from the fourteenth-century 'Bogurodzica' (*Archiv für slavische Philologie*, i, 1876, p. 75), a song to the Virgin Mary in tripartite strophic form, or the Czech St. Adalbert's song 'Hospodine pomiluj ny'.

[3] For a general introduction see Hoffmann von Fallersleben, *Geschichte des deutschen Kirchenliedes* (Hanover, 1861), pp. 73 ff.

[4] More precise details in W. Salmen, *Kongreßberichte Utrecht* (1952), pp. 340 ff. and *Bamberg* (1953), pp. 187 ff.; and in the edition of the *Liederbuch der Anna von Köln* (Düsseldorf, 1954).

ranks of the town clergy took a particularly active part in this development. Whether it was the Franciscan Nikolaus von Kosel working for the people in Silesia, or Dirk von Zwolle in the Netherlands, or the White Cross knight Heinrich Laufenberg at Strasbourg, or Father Ladislaus in Poland (Ex. 149)—all of them were intent on pouring a Christian content into the abundance of late medieval popular

Ex. 149

(Judas sold Jesus for miserable money.)

song. Dance songs (Ex. 151*a*), love songs, morning songs, ballads, and so on, were all adopted so long as the melody satisfied the requirements of the *contrafactum*.

NARRATIVE SONGS

In the later Middle Ages the narrative song was another outstanding type of song with a style and stamp of its own, to which both the professional singers among the people and also particular cultured groups contributed. This group of songs includes ballads or romances, legends, topical political songs, satirical songs and, in the sixteenth century, the printed news-song. Everywhere, whether in Hungary or in Lithuania, in Germany or in Portugal, the old heroic epics, the *cantares de gesta* sung by *juglares épicos* to short verse-melodies,[1] were all declining at this time, and the folk ballad and romance were being partially transformed or substantially remoulded into the style in which the political song was sung. This development also ran on parallel lines in most European countries, though occasionally at slightly different times; changes in the structure of society exerted a decisive influence on this process.[2] Strong dance-like traits, particularly in the Spanish romance of the fifteenth and sixteenth centuries, in the measure of the *redondilla mayor*, and in certain German ballads, point to a physico-spiritual unity in the performer's approach to the narration, which survives to this day in the typical stepping

[1] See vol. II, p. 222.
[2] Cf. Z. Kodály and D. Bartha, *Die ungarische Musik* (Budapest, 1943), pp. 39 ff. and D. Díaz-Plaja, *Historia General de las Literaturas Hispánicas*, i (Barcelona, 1949), p. 318.

motions of singers in the Faroes.[1] Subject and music both suggest
supra-national connexions which, though established to some extent
by wandering *histriones*, had deeper roots,[2] especially when the songs
dealt with topics of universal human interest or where the melodies
were founded on the basic formulae of the old European epic.[3]

The fourteenth to sixteenth centuries were also the Golden Age of
political and topical songs. Partly as a result of the material and cultural tastes of the middle class, all the outstanding events of political and private life were celebrated in song; historical events were
usually not recorded in chronicle fashion, but 'composed in songs'.[4]
The 'lively journeyman' (*frische Geselle*), the 'free knight' (*freie
reuter*), the students and mercenaries who usually announced their
authorship in the last verse of these *newen Lieder*, were types per-
sonifying a particular outlook on life. Being intended for a wide public,
these songs were written entirely for effect, not least because they were
often used as weapons in the struggle to influence public opinion in
the religious and political disturbances of the later Middle Ages.[5]

Ex. 150

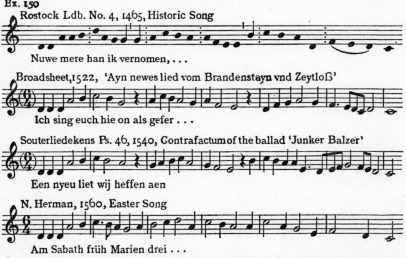

Rostock Ldb. No. 4, 1465, Historic Song

Nuwe mere han ik vernomen, . . .

Broadsheet, 1522, 'Ayn newes lied vom Brandensteyn vnd Zeytloß'

Ich sing euch hie on als gefer . . .

Souterliedekens Ps. 46, 1540, Contrafactum of the ballad 'Junker Balzer'

Een nyeu liet wij heffen aen

N. Herman, 1560, Easter Song

Am Sabath früh Marien drei . . .

---

[1] On the dance song in general see W. Wiora and W. Salmen, 'Deutsche Tanzmusik
des Mittelalters', *Zeitschrift für Volkskunde*, 1 (1953); on sung dances in the Christmas
ceremony of rocking the cradle see W. Salmen, in *Kirchenmusikalisches Jahrbuch*, xxxvi
(1952), pp. 26 ff.

[2] Cf. the geographical distribution of the older ballads in *Deutsche Volkslieder mit
ihren Melodien*, i (Berlin, 1935); or, for a single example, R. Menéndez Pidal, 'Das Fort-
leben des Kudrungedichtes', *Jahrbuch für Volksliedforschung*, v (1936), pp. 85–122.

[3] Cf. W. Wiora, *Europäischer Volksgesang*, p. 16.

[4] A. Haas, 'Das pommersche Herzogshaus im Volksliede', *Baltische Studien*, N.F.,
xxxix (1937), p. 37.

[5] A great number of examples in R. v. Liliencron, *Die historischen Volkslieder der
Deutschen vom 13. bis 16. Jahrhundert*, i–iv (Leipzig, 1865–9).

They were performed in an expressive, sustained style, and consisted of 4–8 line stanzas; the vocal compass was large; the melodies had a touch of recitative; the rhythm was usually free. All these characteristics are illustrated in a song (Ex. 150) describing an event which took place in 1465, which happens to be extant exactly as it was sung and also in stylized versions in mensural notation. The legends, which were sung mostly by blind singers *per solum usum* and contained the lives of saints, stories of miracles, and so on, form a subsidiary branch of the narrative song.

THE MINNESANG OF THE LATER MIDDLE AGES

While popular song formed the basis of medieval song, courtly and clerical circles developed the apexes of the pyramid, to use a metaphor that well describes the nature of this complex genre. In the fruitful periods, however, the song-writers at the top of the pyramid did not lead a separate, esoteric life of their own, but always kept in touch with the simple songs of the people. In the fourteenth century courtly aristocratic life and the *Minnelied* that was woven into it did not die out but were joined on an equal footing by the burgher and the middle-class song which impelled the *Minnesang* into the last phase of its development. The *Minnesang* was an aristocratic, formally strict lyric of high quality, peculiar to one class, designed for the *wolgemuot* entertainment of a knightly aristocratic society unified in style and outlook. As a means of education in *wort unde wîse*, as a secular form of art for the refinement of courtly manners, it enjoyed its prime under the Hohenstaufen. The *Frauendienstlied* (song expressing the knight's homage to his lady), the morning song,[1] and the crusader's song were its main forms, in which class characteristics, personal qualities and popular elements were all combined, fused into one by a high ethical outlook. Since the Western chivalry of the Middle Ages represented a great community bound by ties of kindred and such common experiences as the Crusades, its lyric poetry also contained many supra-national elements of theme, form, and melody (cf. Ex. 145). Even after the Germans had colonized eastern Europe, however, the nobility in Europe beyond the Elbe was still very largely excluded from this 'courtly song' (*hovelîchen singen*). Admittedly there were a few offshoots in eastern Europe when the form was already dying but they failed to take root and bore no fruit.[2] The semi-Slav

---

[1] See vol. II, pp. 242–3.

[2] Details in R. Heckel, *Geschichte der deutschen Literatur in Schlesien* (Breslau, 1929), p. 45; F. Karg, *Das literarische Erwachen des deutschen Ostens im Mittelalter* (Halle,

Prince Wizlaw III of Rügen (d. 1325), seventeen of whose songs and maxims have been handed down in the *Jenaer Liederhandschrift*[1] in fairly exact notation, is the sole exception. His melodies are thoroughly indigenous, though in their construction they show clear signs of the later courtly style. Some examples of his work reveal with particular clarity how, about the year 1300, popular melodies were being stylized and sublimated to accord with specifically class conceptions.

The *Minnesang* is essentially unwritten monody. Everything in it is designed for singing. *Singen unde sagen* were taught by a master from whom the pupil learnt, by listening, the forms, formulas, and simple patterns which it was then his task to elaborate in a deeply felt, expressive performance. The extant sources from the fourteenth and fifteenth centuries, song manuscripts which, like the Jena and Colmar[2] *Liederhandschriften* contain predominantly gnomic poetry, offer almost nothing of this deeply subjective, expressive side of the *Minnesang*. These later compilations usually contain simplified, faded tunes flattened down to the level of the *Meistersang* and, as Josef Görres put it so well as long ago as 1817, they are related 'by miserable tokens . . . in a merely conventional way to what is to be expressed'. What part the accompanying instrument played in the performance and whether the song was rendered strictly by one voice only, remains an open question. In its later evolution the *Minnesang* assumes many forms; it usually consists of tripartite stanzas[3] and in the *Leich*[4] and *Spruch* (maxim) it is rich in melismata. The *Leich* died out in the fourteenth century. Master Alexander[5] provided the mature examples of it at the end of the thirteenth century.

Already in the thirteenth century the decline of the *Minnesang* began with the intrusion of uncourtly characteristics and the assimilation of elements from the rustic, minstrel, and middle classes. Neidhart von Reuental[6] (d. 1250) led the way in the development of the pastoral, rustic offshoots of the *Minnesang*,[7] and he was followed in

1932), p. 8; J. Trostler, 'Die Anfänge der ungarischen Persönlichkeitsdichtung', *G. Petz-Festschrift* (Budapest, 1933), p. 288.

[1] Ed. Holz, Saran, and Bernoulli, 2 vols. (Leipzig, 1901). See vol. II, p. 253, n. 2.

[2] See P. Runge, *Die Sangweisen der Colmarer Handschrift* (Leipzig, 1896).

[3] This construction was also the basis of the poetry composed by the wandering scholars and the middle-class poetry of the Western Slavs, cf. J. Feifalik, 'Altčechische Leiche, Lieder und Sprüche des 14. und 15. Jahrhunderts', *Sitz.-Berichte der k. k. Akademie, Wien*, xxxix (1862), pp. 627 ff.   [4] See vol. II, pp. 257 ff.

[5] Cf. *Die Musik in Geschichte und Gegenwart*, i, cols. 311–13; *Denkmäler der Tonkunst in Österreich*, Jg. xx. (2), vol. xli.   [6] See vol. II, p. 256.

[7] Ed. Schmieder and Wiessner in *Denkmäler der Tonkunst in Österreich*, Jg. xxxvii, vol. lxxi; also Runge, *Die deutsche Liedweise* (Vienna, 1904).

the fourteenth and fifteenth centuries by a great number of pseudo-Neidharts who imitated him in this popular style. Owing to his imitators 'Neidhart' became a general label applicable to any song connected with nature and with the elemental in word and sound.[1] Whereas, however, Neidhart von Reuental was still a *hêr* and a knightly observer of peasant life, in his imitators emphasis on the seamy side of life and the purely physical increases perceptibly. Smoothly flowing lines and dance-like rhythms, particularly in the summer songs, are the characteristics of these late flowering imitations of the *Minnesang*.[2]

The four *Minnelieder* of Eberhard Cersne of Minden, dating from 1404,[3] and the MS. Berlin 922 (*c.* 1410)[4] represent another strand in the pattern of the later courtly *Minnesang*, with their long, ingenious stanzas. As the results of an effort to restore an already dying form, these songs show some poetic and melodic characteristics of the thirteenth century, but they were in fact a passing phenomenon, the over-elaborate products of a decadent style, marking a transition to the love-songs of the urban middle-class.

THE MEISTERGESANG OF THE MIDDLE AND UPPER CLASSES

The *Meistergesang* of the fourteenth to sixteenth centuries was not merely a late product of the *Minnesang* but a genre of its own.[5] Admittedly it took over a good deal from the *Minnesang*, especially in matters of form and melody, but there was so much that was new in its predominantly ethical valuation of singing, as opposed to the more aesthetic approach of courtly art, in the workmanlike approach of this purely urban art, in the 'tones' it uses, in the subordination of secular themes to religious ones, and in its emphasis on the reason, that a clear-cut distinction must be made between the two types.

This learned art of the middle class and the aristocracy originated mainly in the Middle Rhine where, according to Meister Regenbogen, *die besten senger sîn*. It was evidently Heinrich von Meissen (d. 1318), usually known as Frauenlob,[6] who became the ancestor of the first German fraternity of *gesanges meistern*. Mainz began with the foundation of a religious brotherhood of singers in close association with

---

[1] For an example of the close intertwining of Neidhart's style with popular song and that of the wandering singers, see J. Meier, 'Minnesang und Volkslied', in *Jahrbuch für Volksliedforschung*, vii (1941), pp. 1–4; in folk ballads too, the minnesingers still played a part at least as legendary figures: cf. for example, *Deutsche Volkslieder* (Berlin, 1935), nos. 12, 15, 16.

[2] H. Naumann and G. Weydt offer an excellent selection of the texts of the *Herbst des Minnesangs* (Berlin, 1936), including rural, social, didactic and parodistic examples.

[3] Ed. Wöber (Vienna, 1861).   [4] Ed. Lang and Müller-Blattau (Berlin, 1941).

[5] B. Nagel, *Der deutsche Meistersang* (Heidelberg, 1952), p. 20.

[6] See vol. II, p. 258.

the Church, like the Italian *laudesi*, the French *confréries* and *puys*, and the *Contistori del gay saber* founded in 1323 and revived in Barcelona in 1414, and finally the Portuguese *dezidores*. In this way an art of cultivated singing that had hitherto been free was led on to scholastic paths; mastery of rules and techniques was now required in place of the old spontaneity, and a certain measure of religious learning and familiarity with the *septem artes liberales* was also presupposed. The relationship between knight and page now became that of master and apprentice.

The association of *Minne* with God and the Virgin Mary and the adaptation of the traditional art of the knightly class to the ecclesiastical system is already apparent in Frauenlob, who still considered himself a court singer and deliberately composed in the old style.[1] His art and that of the generations that followed him is based on the words of the song. Emphasis is laid on the sense (*sin*) and there is a striving for philosophical and theological profundity which inevitably brings the text into the foreground and takes the natural vitality out of the singing by burdening it with thought. Everything in this art can be acquired by learning and can therefore be summed up in rules and examples, for 'sang ist eine wyse meisterschaft' (Colmar No. 111). Unlike the *Minnesang*, the *Meistersang* was therefore dependent on documents such as the *gross buch von Mencz*, which has not survived.

'The world has come to autumn' (*Diu werlt ist ûf daz herbest komen*) (Frauenlob): this sentence reflects the feeling that was general among these middle-class singers, the feeling that they were witnessing the decline of the old ethical and social ideals which they would like to have seen preserved.[2] 'Highly intelligent and scholarly people, such as doctors, knights and barons, nobles and other intelligent men'[3] therefore shut themselves off from the outside world and sang in small circles 'in number and measure' (*in zal und mas*). Thus poetry became 'the affair of the middle-class guilds'.[4] Didactic poetry of a scholastic cast and eulogies were the content of their solemn sessions, which were based on a prescribed ceremonial.[5] The singing was strictly monophonic, without instrumental accompaniment; in fact,

---

[1] I. Kern, *Das höfische Gut in den Dichtungen Heinrich Frauenlobs* (Berlin, 1934), pp. 7 ff.

[2] W. Rehm, 'Kulturverfall und spätmittelhochdeutsche Didaktik', *Zeitschrift für deutsche Philologie*, lii (1927), pp. 300 ff.

[3] P. Notz, *Die Meistersinger in Iglau* (St. Pölten, 1942), p. 3.

[4] J. Görres, *Altteutsche Volks- und Meisterlieder* (Frankfurt, 1817), p. iii.

[5] Muskatblüt says (54, 40 ff.): 'gesang ist ein man, der zucht und scham zu aller zit dût leren. gesang ist ein vrsprung gûder sache' (song should always teach propriety and modesty: song is a source of good).

instrumental music of any kind was considered in bad taste, since 'Die tommen hörent pfiffen gern' (Colmar, No. 43), or:

> Was thöne gont nü vs eim ror,
> gar offenbor,
> das achtent wise meister nit ein hor
> wann gütten sang, den hörn si gern (*ibid.*).

(Wise masters pay no heed to sounds from a pipe, but they gladly listen to good singing.)

The most important musical source for the fourteenth and early fifteenth centuries is the Colmar Manuscript (Munich Cgm 4997). It contains 107 melodies by 36 writers and was in the possession of the Colmar guild of mastersingers from the sixteenth century onwards.[1] It is the basic song-book, the first great tablature that has been preserved and it contains above all the 'tones' of the twelve legendary founders of the *Meistersang* who are first mentioned by Rumelant of Swabia about 1275. The Donaueschingen Manuscript (Fürstenberg-ische Hofbibliothek No. 120) which contains twenty-one 'tones'[2] is closely related to this source. A singer had to master the standard 'tones' of these twelve 'ancestors' before he could qualify as a *Meister*. In the guilds all new songs had to follow these melodic models and their metrical schemes: no independent invention of any kind was permitted. That this still held good in the fifteenth century is apparent from some lines about a contest 'for the wreath' (*umb das Kränzlein*), the climax of the Sunday session:

> ein junger man, der niht vil gît,
> mit im sô wil ich singen
> umb einen hübschen rôsenkranz;
> und trit er an der meister tanz,
> singt er uns ûz zwelf meister guot,
> sô mag im wol gelingen.[3]

(I'd like to compete in singing for a pretty rose-garland with a young man who does not say much; and if he enters for the master-dance and sings songs from the twelve masters, he may very well succeed.)

This *gedoene singen* naturally had a devastatingly constricting effect on poetic thought. The organic unity of 'word and tune' (*wort unde wise*) in the *Minnesang* vanished; its place was taken by a mechanical

---

[1] F. Eberth, *Die Minne- und Meistergesangweisen der Kolmarer Liederhandschrift* (Diss. Göttingen, 1932), p. 15.

[2] Cf. *Die Musik in Geschichte und Gegenwart*, iii, cols. 667–9.

[3] Uhland, *Alte hoch- und niederdeutsche Volkslieder*, ii, p. 313. As late as 1549 Jörg Wickram refuses to recognize all those 'die so do singenn anderi tön dann so vonn den zwölf Meisterenn gedicht' (who sing other tones than those of the twelve masters).

syllable-counting technique, by expressionless, formula-ridden melodies which provided sounds for the words but were not organically related to them.[1] These 'tones', of which the nucleus usually consisted of merely one or two lines or more extended patterns, as in Ex. 145, possessed definite techniques for expanding these small groups of lines and combining them with extensive maxims or lays. Sequence, matching, and the mosaic-like joining of melodic fragments constituted the secret of this exclusive, type-ridden *holdselige Kunst*. The tripartite stanza, its periods forming a strictly regular structure, was the most usual form.[2]

Singers mostly used the middle register of the voice, and sang at a comfortable tempo in a regular, speech-like rhythm with no emotional outbursts. There was little original power in this singing. The guild-masters only rarely drew on popular song, though (exceptionally) the following *wyse* of Frauenlob (Ex. 151*b*) is obviously based on a popular dance-song of the Middle Ages (Ex. 151*a*):

Ex. 151

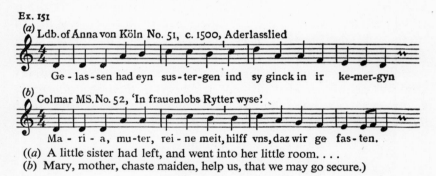

(a) Ldb. of Anna von Köln No. 51, c. 1500, Aderlasslied

Ge - las - sen had eyn sus - ter-gen ind sy ginck in ir ke-mer-gyn

(b) Colmar MS. No. 52, 'In frauenlobs Rytter wyse'.

Ma - ri - a, mu-ter, rei - ne meit, hilff vns, daz wir ge fas-ten.

((*a*) A little sister had left, and went into her little room. . . .
(*b*) Mary, mother, chaste maiden, help us, that we may go secure.)

The *raizer vnd schamparen lieder* were attacked by the guild singers most emphatically. The art of the Netherland *Rederijkers*, the fruits of which are partly preserved in the fourteenth-century Gruythuys Manuscript, was musically related to the German *Meistersang* in spite of even deeper French influences.[3]

Ex. 152

So vruechdenrijch Was nie mijn zin Vrauwe ze-ker-lijch Dan al sich bin

[1] Cf. Nagel, op. cit., pp. 19 and 69 ff.
[2] Ibid., p. 79.
[3] Cf. C. Lindenburg, 'Notatieproblemen van het Gruythuyzer handschrift', *Tijdschrift voor Muziekwetenschap*, xvii (1948), pp. 44–86.

Bi dir, In dir, Dan tzwi-fel ghein: Want ich ben dijn. Ende niemens meer:

Dijns li-dens pijn Doet mir so seer Den tzijt Her lijt Ich dir ghemein.

(Dear lady, my mind has certainly never been so full of joy as when with you and in you; then doubts vanish; for I am yours and belong to none else: your painful suffering gives me much anguish ever since I lay with you.)

From the Rhine the *Meistersang* gradually moved eastwards during the fifteenth and sixteenth centuries and about 1600 it even established itself in several German towns in Bohemia and Moravia.[1] The Slavs did not adopt it, however, and even in central Germany it was confined to a few of the larger cities, among which Strasbourg, Augsburg, Nuremberg, and Ulm became important centres. With the economic rise of the artisan class these cities obtained almost complete control of the art. Hans Folz (died *c*. 1515) and Hans Sachs (d. 1576) were the most outstanding figures. In spite of isolated impulses emanating from such masters as Michel Behaim (1416–74) who remained outside the strictly enclosed guilds, the *Meistersang* remained historically insignificant. Even Adam Puschmann's collection of the standard 'tones' in a *Singebuch*[2] intended for the instruction of the young (1584–8) was unable to arrest its gradual decline. Although such masters as Hans Folz burst the narrow confines of the authoritarian 'tones' of the twelve original masters and the Reformation also gave the art a certain fillip, the mannerism and spiritual barrenness of the form spread so widely that it may be considered to have died out by the middle of the sixteenth century.

INDEPENDENT SONG WRITERS

A number of masters of the fourteenth and early fifteenth centuries, some known, some anonymous, unconnected with schools and guilds and not classifiable as *Minnesinger* or *Meistersinger*, must be considered as the more important promoters of the development of the art song. All had vital qualities of their own which enabled them to mediate to some extent between the common people and the upper classes and to prepare the way for later developments. They infused

---

[1] Cf. Salmen, *Die Schichtung der mittelalterlichen Musikkultur in der ostdeutschen Grenzlage* (Kassel, 1954), chap. 'Der Meistergesang', pp. 89 ff.

[2] Ed. G. Münzer (Leipzig, 1906).

new life from below into the later courtly *Minnesang* by blending it
with middle-class ingredients. Mülich of Prague, who was active
during the reign of John of Luxembourg (1310–46), is the earliest
of these individualists. His *rey* breathes a natural freshness and
courage:

Ex. 153

Un sicht man a-ber bey-de, den an-ger vnd die hey-de in
man-ger han-de ley-de; was ri-cher au-gen-wei-de, daz ist ver-dor-ben
in dez mey-en cley-de! daz ko-met von des ar-gen win-ters nyt.

(And one again sees both meadow and heath suffer in many ways; what had
been a lovely sight for our eyes in the garb of May is now destroyed. This has
been done by the envy of evil winter.)

Count Peter von Arberg (*c.* 1350) is particularly notable on account of
the animated and expressive 'Grosse Tageweise', which he modelled
on a *Tagelied* current in the later Middle Ages.[1]

The work of the Monk of Salzburg (end of the fourteenth century),
whom the Colmar Manuscript actually reckons among the 'masters',
evidently because of his high artistic power and great popularity
which lasted into the sixteenth century, also has a strongly individual
flavour. Although he made a name for himself in the field of religious
poetry, as a translator of Latin hymns and sequences, and also had
an exemplary influence as the creator of 'tones', he is especially outstanding as a notator of the common tunes of the Alpine regions and
as a singer of homespun melodies (see Ex. 154). He takes specimens of
ordinary Alpine music and refashions them in the style of the courts
and cities. As a cleric he makes a special point of simplicity in song,
returning to some extent to pre-*Minnesang* forms of aristocratic song
and dance. In his work traces of archaic triadic melody, primitive
wind music decidedly folkish in cast, the primitive practices of simple
descant or *vbersingen*, even basic elements from the religious invocation,[2] are found alongside the 'tones' of the Mastersingers, such

[1] Cf. Salmen, *Kongreßbericht, Bamberg 1953*, Melodietafel, No. 1.
[2] E. Fredrich, op. cit., pp. 139 ff.

as the *güldin ABC* of a conservative twelve-part *Leich* in double strophes:

Ex. 154

Zart lib-ste frau in li-ber acht, wünsch mir ain lib-lich, frö-lich nacht,

wann so mein hercz dein treu be-tracht, das freuet all mein kraft vnd macht

(Dearest lady [whom] I hold in tender regard, wish me a happy and joyful night. When my heart thus beholds your constancy, all my strength and power rejoice.)

While Hugo von Montfort (1357–1423) and his page Burg Mangolt who 'made the tunes' (*die weysen hat gemachen*) held fast to the old ideals of chivalry and loyally preserved some elements of the *Minne-sang*,[1] his contemporary Oswald von Wolkenstein (1377–1445) became one of the greatest of German song-writers. He no longer composed *Minnelieder* but love-songs charged with intense personal experience; on his long journeys through Europe he picked up the art song of other nations and remoulded it in his own style,[2] thereby enriching his native inheritance. Since he no longer recognized the binding force of the old maxims and ways of life, he was free to be himself and to put the antiquated models of the past behind him. He combined a mastery of sophisticated forms with a folk-like originality and Italian and French techniques with the German tradition of minstrelsy. Belonging as an *edler und vester Ritter* to the aristocratic upper class, he established supranational and supra-class connexions after 1400 from which sprang the beginnings of the middle-class social song (*Gesellschaftslied*). He also provided some of the earliest examples of the polyphonic *Lied* and thus he had an exemplary influence parti-cularly on musical circles of the middle class. Free from the tyranny of rules, his language is heartfelt and full of warm humanity, though, in accordance with his character, it is also marked by harsher traits. He stands at the outset of the newer German song.

[1] Ed. P. Runge (Leipzig, 1906).
[2] W. Salmen, 'Werdegang und Lebensfülle des Oswald von Wolkenstein', *Musica Disciplina*, vii (1953), p. 147.

THE LATIN LYRIC

Concurrently with the vernacular lyric of the Middle Ages, the Middle Latin lyric was cultivated by the *literati*. It covered a wide field, ranging from the sequence, the conductus, the *cantio*, and the trope to the student song and the humanistic ode. Although produced in great quantity after the fourteenth century, it had by then already lost much of its individual force and was attempting to imitate the vernacular lyric that was now springing up. This is shown by the off-shoots of the conductus in the fourteenth century (a form which is still significantly prominent in the manuscript from the convent of Las Huelgas),[1] by its successors which may be collectively described by the general term *cantio*, by the transformations of the sequence, and so on.[2] In Germany, Bohemia, or Spain one form often passed into the other, as is shown by examples in the MSS. Erfurt Bibl. Amploniana Q 332, Engelberg No. 314 or, in the sixteenth century, by the *Cantional Franus*.[3] Another example is the *Glogauer Lieder- und Musikbuch*[4] in which hymns, responses, sequences, and antiphons are arranged and remoulded like German song-tunes.

Wherever the Roman Church penetrated eastern Europe more deeply, the clergy used an increasing number of metrical Latin texts for an increasing number of festivals. How much scope there was for this becomes clear if one remembers that at the time of Charles IV (1347–78) there were 150 feast-days and holidays in Bohemia and nearly 1,200 persons engaged in liturgical singing in the churches of Prague.[5]

Many new works were written for the Proper of the Mass. *Benedicamus* tropes, Alleluias and other tropes all gave expression to the late medieval delight in feast-days, and were typical of the sumptuous elaboration of public worship. Names like Bishop Conrad I of Breslau

Ex. 155

De-cet hu-jús cun-ctis ho - ris　fe - sti vo-ce　dul - ci - o - ris　fa - ce - re

me - mo - ri - am

(Meet is it, through the day, to celebrate in song this delightful feast.)

---

[1] See vol. II, p. 314.

[2] Cf. J. Handschin, 'Peripheres', *Mitteilungen der Schweizerischen Musikforschenden Gesellschaft*, ii (1935), pp. 24–32.　　　[3] Ed. D. Orel (Prague, 1922).

[4] Ed. H. Ringmann and J. Klapper, *Das Erbe deutscher Musik*, iv and viii (Kassel, 1936–7).

[5] R. Batka, *Die Musik in Böhmen* (Berlin, 1906), p. 7.

(1417–47), the Sagan abbot Martin Rinkenberg (d. 1489), Magister
Zaviše and J. von Jenstein in Bohemia (Ex. 155), Abbot Franz Gais-
berg of St. Gall (1504–26),[1] stand out among many others, especially
in the history of the sequence and antiphon. Rhymed prayers were
used more for private devotions,[2] like many of the contemplative
Marian songs such as 'O Maria pia' in the 'Brabant ton her peter von
Sassen' of the Monk of Salzburg (Colmar MS. Nos. 7–8). Religious
plays, designed partly for liturgical use, partly for the entertainment
of the common people, spread from Spain to Prague[3] with many
lyrical interpolations based on medieval texts common to all Europe.

The non-liturgical *cantio* was the most productive branch of all this
copious activity. It shows a genuine revaluation of Christian singing
in the later Middle Ages, in which popular song of all kinds played a
creative part. The *cantio* represents the final blossoming of a class-
conditioned religious art which was cultivated by students, clerics,
scholars, and middle-class fraternities. *Cantiones* were not tropes but
free monophonic Latin songs, with a religious content. On special
feast-days only it was the custom to sing in two simple parts (see
Ex. 157). The cult of the Virgin Mary and the Christmas festival
were organized on a lavish scale. In particular, Christmas stimulated
the composition of primitive, dance-like melodies expressing joy and
jubilation (Ex. 156). Secular forms of the dance song and melodic types

Ex. 156

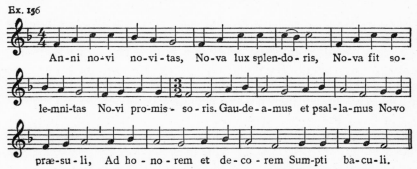

An-ni no-vi   no-vi-tas,   No-va lux splen-do- ris,   No-va fit so-

le-mni-tas No-vi pro-mis - so - ris. Gau-de - a-mus et psal-la-mus No-vo

præ-su - li, Ad ho - no - rem et de - co - rem Sum-pti ba-cu-li.

(Now is the new year's new beginning, now a new and glorious light, a new
festivity is kept, for a new patron. Let us rejoice and strike the strings for a new
lord, to honour as is fitting his assumption of office.)

such as the *rondeau* without inner refrain were mostly used for

[1] F. Labhardt, 'Zur St. Gallischen Sequenztradition im Spätmittelalter', *Kongreßbericht Basel, 1949*, pp. 176 ff.
[2] J. Gmelch, 'Unbekannte Reimgebetkompositionen aus Rebdorfer Handschriften',
P. Wagner-Festschrift (Leipzig, 1926), pp. 69–80.
[3] See vol. II, Chap. VI, and E. Schuler, *Die Musik der Osterfeiern, Osterspiele und
Passionen des Mittelalters* (Kassel, 1951).

this purpose.[1] Since they contain the repertories of school choirs and *Bruderschaften*, the most important sources of this period are the Mosburg Gradual of 1360 (Munich MS. Univ. Bibl. 156), the Engelberg MS. 314 (late fourteenth century), the *Jistebnický Kancionál* of 1420 (see Ex. 157),[2] and the *Neumarkt Cantional* of the mid-fifteenth century.[3]

Ex. 157

In hoc an-ni cir-cu-lo vi-ta da-tur sæ-cu-lo,

na-to no-bis par-vu-lo per vir-gi-nem,

na-to no-bis par-vu-lo per vir-gi-nem Ma-ri-am.

(Now as the year comes round, life is given to the world, for a child is born to us of a virgin, for a child is born to us of the Virgin Mary.)

The Latin lyric of the unattached student intelligentsia of the medieval city is also unintelligible without reference to rural and urban popular song. *Cantilenae* for the convivial meal, comic songs, and satirical songs attend the history of student life from the High Middle Ages to modern times.[4] These *cantilenae* were light-hearted compilations of songs of every type, varying in quality according to the ability of the compiler.

Finally, mention must be made of a branch of Latin lyric poetry brought into being in the sixteenth century for didactic reasons. This was the didactic metrical ode: the incentive came from the cultured aristocracy, though there was no genuine reality behind it. Originating in German humanistic circles, its sphere of influence was almost entirely restricted to the universities. Free from the compulsion of

---

[1] For an example see the melody-table in W. Salmen, 'Über das Nachleben eines mittelalterlichen Kanonmodells', *Die Musikforschung*, vii (1954), p. 55.

[2] See also vol. II, p. 335.

[3] Cf. H. Spanke, 'Das Mosburger Graduale', *Zeitschrift für romanische Philologie*, li (1930), pp. 582–95; *Analecta Hymnica*, xx, No. xii–xxii; A. Schmitz, 'Ein schlesisches Cantional aus dem 15. Jahrhundert', *Archiv für Musikforschung*, i (1936), pp. 385–426; J. Handschin, 'Die Schweiz welche sang', *Festschrift für K. Nef* (1933), pp. 102–33; Z. Nejedlý, *Dějiny předhusitského zpěvu v Čechách* (Prague, 1904); for further sources see *Die Musik in Geschichte und Gegenwart*, ii, cols. 780 ff.

[4] For examples from this period cf. *Glogauer Liederbuch*, Nos. 101 and 215 (*Das Erbe deutscher Musik*, iv, p. 15, and viii, p. 60); H. Walther, 'Kleine mittellateinische Dichtungen aus zwei Erfurter Handschriften', *H. Degering-Festschrift* (Leipzig, 1926), pp. 296–315; Feifalik, op. cit., p. 720; in the *Cantional Franus*, 'Dorothea coronata' (ed. Orel, p. 132); H. J. Moser, *Geschichte der deutschen Musik*, i (Stuttgart, 1920), p. 170.

measured rhythm, these compositions were sung *secundum naturas et tempora syllabarum et pedum* (P. Tritonius, 1507) of the text:

Ex. 158

Mae - ce - nas a - ta - vis e - di - te re - gi - bus, o et præ - si - di-

um et dul - ce de - cus me - um,

(Maecenas, descended from kingly ancestors, O my guardian, my pride and joy!)

Written in note-against-note chordal style with the melody usually in the treble, with deliberate simplicity, emphasis was laid on good declamation and pregnant themes. Well-known composers such as Ludwig Senfl, Paul Hofhaimer, Wolfgang Greffinger, and Joachim a Burck devoted themselves to this branch of Latin song in the first half of the sixteenth century. Their influence extended as far as Cracow and Transylvania.[1]

THE ART SONG OF THE FIFTEENTH AND SIXTEENTH CENTURIES

In central Europe the culture of the later Middle Ages received its deepest impress from the towns. Increasing social differentiation, economic ambitions, changes in political organization all encouraged the rise of the middle class in the fourteenth century. This new middle-class world, which was such an important factor in establishing the foundations of musical culture in Germany and eastern Europe, was created by elements from the country and from the upper classes,

[1] Cf. H. J. Moser, *Paul Hofhaimer* (Stuttgart, 1929), pp. 162 ff.; R. von Liliencron, 'Die Horazischen Metren in deutschen Kompositionen des 16. Jahrhunderts', *Viertel-jahrsschrift für Musikwissenschaft*, iii (1887), pp. 26–91; A. Chybiński, 'Über die polnische mehrstimmige Musik des XVI. Jahrhunderts', *H. Riemann-Festschrift* (Leipzig, 1909), p. 345; B. Szabolcsi, 'Die metrische Odensammlung des Johannes Honterus', *Zeitschrift für Musikwissenschaft*, xiii (1931), pp. 338–40.

which were, temporarily at any rate, in decline. The medieval town was a community behind walls, in which talents and riches were gathered in hitherto undreamt-of profusion. Music emerged spontaneously, with its own style and forms, as an adornment of this new life and as the handmaid of divine worship. The home, the inn, the market, and the street became the main centres of singing; games, festivals, customs, and entertainments provided the occasions.[1]

From the period around 1360 the *Limburg Chronicle* reports in detail how, after the disasters and catastrophes of the middle years of the century, new creative energies were stirring throughout Germany and life began to pulsate again. Song was no exception; in fact, the new type of short, normally tripartite middle-class household song (called the *widersenge, mit drên gesetzen*), after the style of 'Ach, reinez wip von guder art', consisting of two main sections (*Stollen*) and an 'aftersong' (*Abgesang*),[2] now began to flourish and for more than two hundred years it formed a basic constituent of the music-making of middle-class amateur circles and of court choirs alike. From the second half of the fourteenth century song acquired a new standing and significance in the free, less class-ridden social life of the time. It liberated itself entirely from natural ties and class criteria and became an intrinsic part of the social life of the age, keeping pace with every change of fashion. With the adoption of a regulated polyphony its artistic level rose ever higher. Song was the most vital element in German musical life up to 1500. Through the polyphonic song Germany first emerged as an independent force in European music.

The first considerable collection of middle-class song for the home, from the opening stage of its development, is the *Lochamer Liederbuch* (1452–60) from Nuremberg.[3] A study of its contents, which were contributed by amateurs, clerics, mastersingers, and instrumentalists, shows most clearly which paths of development were taken during the first hundred years and the nature of the foundations of this rich tradition of urban song in Germany. In the notation and style of the tunes the mensural conception is here for the first time fully

---

[1] On the general joy in singing at that time a *Christliche Ermahnung zum frummen Leben* of 1509 says: 'wan zwo oder drie zusammen kommen, so müssen sie singen, und sie singen alle bey der Arbeit in Haus und Feld, bei Gebet vnd Frummigkeit, in Freud und clag bey trauer und gelag' (when two or three come together they have to sing, and they all sing at work in house and field, at prayer and devotion, in joy and sorrow, mourning and feasting).   [2] Cf. vol. II, p. 252.

[3] On the general development up to 1450 and the *Lochamer Liederbuch* see W. Salmen, *Das Lochamer Liederbuch* (Leipzig, 1951). The *Liederbuch* has been published in facsimile by Konrad Ameln (Berlin, 1925).

developed in this field, and the peculiarly German type of song firmly established. One can see how from a conglomeration of the most varied influences of *Minnesang* and *Meistersang*, popular song and non-German forms, there gradually arose in Upper Germany a mature type of song, homogeneous in mood, outlook, forms of expression and language, and middle-class in character. Nuremberg was its chief centre. In addition to developing the usual prototypes, Western models were also drawn on in the polyphonic treatment:

Ex. 159

(Winter is about to go; this year it has been very long for me; summer is coming with promise of joys, and my mind rejoices.)

In the towns the type of song known as the 'tenor song' (which Hoffmann von Fallersleben also called the *Gesellschaftslied*) had developed. The tenor song is a peculiarly German form which remained current until after 1550. The *canto fermo*, whether popular song or art song, lies in the middle in the tenor or sometimes the baritone register. Two or more instruments play around it, but, after 1530, these were sometimes replaced by voices. As a solo song it is usually characterized by expressive, vigorously individual and fluid rhythm (cf. Ex. 159). It is concerned with the subtleties of love, in the treatment of which it makes a creative, not a purely mechanical, use of the heritage of chivalry. Simpler popular songs could also be stylized and arranged in this manner, though this development, influenced by the humanist movement, occurred to any considerable extent only in the sixteenth century. This mode of composition, which reached its highest flowering around 1500, was taken as a model even in the widely scattered townships of eastern Europe.[1] As middle-class collections for daily use the *Rostocker Liederbuch* of 1465, the song book of the doctor Hartmann Schedel, and the *Glogauer Lieder- und Musikbuch* of the second half of the fifteenth century contain all sorts of variants of the tenor song in *Bar* form (that is, the form consisting of two *Stollen* with *Abgesang*). The later development of the tenor song was greatly influenced, especially as regards polyphonic texture, by the first and second generations of Netherlanders, who, through Heinrich Isaac, made a direct impact on German song.[2]

While the middle-class art song was usually composed anonymously up to 1500, after the turn of the century well-known composers came forward in increasing numbers to show their skill in writing court tunes (*Hofweisen*) and popular songs of an urban character. Above all in the court choirs of Heidelberg, Stuttgart, Augsburg, and the choir of Maximilian I, which wandered from one imperial city of southern Germany to another, the metrically smooth, didactic court song (*Hofweise*) of humanistic origin was developed in four- and five-part polyphony with all the tokens of a fastidious product of the cultured class. The spiritual homogeneity of this type of song was increased by the abundance of textual and melodic formulas that were available. Plays on rhymes, short lines interspersed with pseudo-classical allegories, plays on monograms and the like, are frequent, as for example in the following stanza:

> Ir ist mein hertz/mit schertz vnnd freid/
> durch sie ich leid/ ob ich erlost möcht werden/
> Früntlich/ thût sich/ in eren/ meren/ mein gunst gen ir/
> als schir/ ich denck der weis vnd perden[3]

(Hers is my heart with jest and joy; on account of her I suffer [lest] I obtain release. My favour towards her increases in friendly and honourable fashion when I think of her speech and gestures.)

The tenors were assembled mosaic-fashion by the *phonasci* (as Glareanus calls them)[4] from universally current patterns in accordance with a uniform style.[5] Certain felicitous inventions such as 'Ich

---

[1] Cf., for example, *Cantional Franus*, fo. 355b (ed. Orel, pp. 179–81), or *Zeitschrift für Musikwissenschaft*, v (1923), pp. 481–4.

[2] H. Osthoff, *Die Niederländer und das deutsche Lied* (Berlin, 1938).

[3] From Peter Schöffer's *Liederbuch* (Mainz, 1513), tenor part-book, fo. 10.

[4] *Dodecachordon*, ii, chap. 38, pp. 174 ff.

[5] C. Reinhardt, *Die Heidelberger Liedmeister des 16. Jahrhunderts* (Kassel, 1939).

stund an einem Morgen' appear in almost all the collections of
the period. One of these universally popular tunes is the heart-felt
'Entlaubet ist der Walde', which exactly catches the mood of the poem:

Ex. 160 THOMAS STOLZER

(The wood is stripped of leafage against this winter cold.)

The urban or aristocratic art song reached its zenith in the work of
Paul Hofhaimer (who, without abandoning polyphony, developed a
more chordal style), Heinrich Finck, with his intensely passionate
love-songs, Ludwig Senfl and Caspar Othmayr. Senfl, in particular,
had at his command a wide range of styles from the simple note-
against-note setting to fully developed imitations in from three to six
parts, and even quodlibet-like combinations of several basic tunes
in masterly alliance:

Ex. 161

Syllabic setting based on verbal stress is most marked in his work, under humanistic influence, while as a *synphonet*[1] he is distinguished by fullness of sound and delight in colour, together with masterly treatment of ornamentation. His collection of some 270 songs is representative of chamber music at its best at the south German courts of the Emperor Maximilian I and Duke Wilhelm IV of Bavaria. But quasi-popular dance-songs in allemande-rhythm, ingratiatingly fresh, also appear in his work.

Popular song occupied an even greater place in the work of Othmayr (d. 1553). He succeeded in constructing a concertante type of song which divided the basic melody between treble and tenor. The *bicinium*-like treble-tenor song which evolved in this way, as in Ex. 162

Ex. 162

(If it isn't dark in the vault, don't knock at the door.)

[1] Glareanus's word for a composer who can add parts 'according to the laws of art', in distinction from the *phonascus* who can invent a new tenor.

—the technique is derived from Josquin des Prez—led the German polyphonic song to the stage where, after 1550, it came under Italian influence. Smoother, more marked rhythms give his settings of popular songs in particular a fresh, full-blooded character. Since the old 'court tunes' (*Hofweisen*) had very largely lost their vitality, Othmayr raised the popular song into the sphere of serious composition. Songs with didactic, emotional, religious, topical or burlesque content were strung together in motley sequence and for the last time new life was infused into the late medieval art song of town and court. After the middle of the sixteenth century the traditional *Tenorlied* held its ground most tenaciously in the settings of Protestant chorales, while the *geselliges Lied* (social song) succumbed to the fashions of Italy and the Netherlands. In his five books of *Frische Teutsche Liedlein* (1539–56) Georg Forster gathered in the harvest of this rich period, apprehending that its end was near.[1]

POLYPHONIC SONG IN SPAIN

The art of song in the Iberian peninsula was in no way inferior in quality to the German polyphonic song in its heyday, though it differed from it in many respects. In Spain and Portugal during the fourteenth to sixteenth centuries the courts were the centres of musical life. As many foreign musicians were guests at these courts, French influence was predominant.[2] French and, later, Italian song almost completely dominated the art of the Spanish aristocracy until the middle of the fifteenth century. Then, from sporadic beginnings under the 'Catholic monarchs' (Ferdinand and Isabella), more traditionally Spanish paths began to be taken and this made it possible very largely to break away from foreign models. According to one chronicle, at the *grandes fiestas* at the courts of Seville, Valladolid, Toledo, Segovia, Barcelona, Saragossa, Valencia, and Medina del Campo around 1448 'lays, e delays, e virolays, e chazas, e rondelas, e conplayntas, e baladas, chanzones de toda el arte que trovan los franzeses'[3] were sung and played in court society. From 1400 these court songs were collected in Castilian in *cancioneros*, of which the *Cancionero musical de Palacio* is the most important from this period.[4] The *Cancionero de Palacio* gives us the late fifteenth-century repertory of polyphonic

[1] Further sixteenth-century sources are enumerated in the bibliography.

[2] Cf., for example, the repertory of the Chantilly MS., Musée Condé No. 1047, *Musica Disciplina*, viii (1954), pp. 88–95, and also Anglès, *La música en la Corte de los Reyes Católicos*, i (Madrid, 1941), pp. 14 ff.

[3] Anglès, ibid., p. 26.

[4] Ed. Anglès (Barcelona, 1947–51); further sources are listed by Anglès in *Theodor Kroyer-Festschrift* (Regensburg, 1933), pp. 62–68.

song at the court of the *Reyes Católicos*, under whose rule a truly Spanish art-music first evolved. The *villancico amoroso* and *religioso*, the *romanze* and the *estrambote* are the predominant forms, but even archaic couplets are found:[1]

Ex. 163

(I would not be a nun, not I, for I am a girl who falls in love.)

The *villancico*[2] is the Spanish counterpart of the Italian *frottola*.[3] The melody lies in the highest part, with mainly note-against-note accompaniment by two or three other voices in a well-balanced texture. Juan del Encina was one of its leading masters:

Ex. 164

(Let us be merry, and that truly; for grief comes without our going to seek it.)

[1] Cf., as a German parallel, J. Zahn, *Die Melodien der deutschen evangelischen Kirchenlieder*, i (Gütersloh, 1888), no. 126.

[2] See Isabel Pope, 'Musical and Metrical Form of the Villancico', *Annales musicologiques*, ii (Paris, 1954).   [3] See Chap. XI.

One also comes across simple settings with imitative part-writing in the Flemish style:

Ex. 165

Malos adalides
(Evil leaders have they been.)

These settings differ from the French and the Flemish mainly 'por la amabilidad de su texto, por el resabio popular español de sus temas musicales y por su técnica simplicísima que a primera vista uno tomaría por muy arcaica y primitiva, más aun de lo que ella lo es en realidad' (by the charm of their texts, the Spanish flavour of their musical themes and the very simple technique which one would at first glance take to be very archaic and primitive—though they are by no means so in reality).[1] Elements of Castilian popular song can be traced in all these severe and simple settings; for the Spanish art-song, organically based on native popular song, developed away from the imported art of France and Italy, and it is this that gives it its peculiar charm and raciness. After 1516 conditions changed with the advent of the Habsburgs.

THE BEGINNINGS OF THE PROTESTANT HYMN

Although the Reformation had scarcely any influence on the polyphonic art-song of the towns and courts before 1540, in the field of the monodic German song it had all the greater effect on a development which had already begun in the fifteenth century: the endeavour to adapt the vernacular song to the purposes of divine worship. Christian and sectarian lay movements, above all that of the Bohemian Brethren and that of the followers of Jan Huss (1369–1415), notably led the way in this field. Using Latin hymns and sequences, Czech and German popular songs from every stratum of society, in a sober and strictly Biblical spirit they created syllabic melodies which found their way, with the necessary changes of text, into their song-books. By removing the old familiar characteristics and freedoms of the traditional song they constructed simple and severely impersonal tunes for

[1] H. Anglès in *Spanische Forschungen der Görresgesellschaft*, viii (1940), p. 340.

divine service and family prayers. The congregational hymn (*Gemeindelied*) became a style on its own.

Luther pursued this line with greater power and intensity. While at the same period the Catholic Church generally continued to oppose vernacular singing in Church, Luther gave it a central place in the service, unlike Zwingli who opposed it to begin with.[1] Luther and his collaborators drew freely on the abundant variety of German song of the later Middle Ages, recoining it *christlich corrigiert*, since, as Luther himself said, 'the devil should not be allowed to keep all the best tunes for himself'. After 1524 *Enchiridien* and *Gesangbücher* appeared one after another, disseminating the Lutheran hymn in all directions.[2] Even the broadsheet was eagerly used as a means of propagation:

Ex. 166

Sanct Pau-lus die Co-rin-thi-er, Hat vn-ter-weist in rech-ter lehr.

So bald er a-ber von jm kam, Da fien-gen sich vil sec-ten an.

(Saint Paul instructed the Corinthians in true doctrine. But directly he left them numerous sects sprang up.)

In this way universally current melodies were removed from the process of natural evolution, given fixed rhythm, and stylized as printed hymns. When the hymn was set polyphonically, the principles of the secular tenor song still held good. In so far as they joined the Reformation movement, the peoples of eastern Europe eagerly made the most of this tendency which did so much to emancipate them and strengthen their national self-consciousness. As early as 1530, for example, Lutheran chorales were being sung in Polish in the Marienkirche at Thorn. Hymn-books from central Germany were used as the basis for Lithuanian, Slovak, and other translations in the sixteenth century. In this way a number of fifteenth-century German songs were passed on to the peoples of eastern Europe.[3] They were taken as models and imitated in many ways. Thus the old German song of the fourteenth, fifteenth, and sixteenth centuries was transformed and entered a new phase of development.

[1] A. Geering, *Die Vokalmusik in der Schweiz zur Zeit der Reformation* (Aarau, 1933), pp. 31 ff.

[2] See vol. IV.

[3] Cf. Ex. 11 in Salmen, *Die Schichtung der mittelalterlichen Musikkultur in der ostdeutschen Grenzlage* (Kassel, 1954).

XI

SECULAR VOCAL MUSIC IN ITALY
(c. 1400–1530)

By Everett Helm

INTRODUCTORY

BETWEEN the brilliant period of the trecento *ars nova* and the even
more brilliant period of the sixteenth-century madrigal Italy produced
little or nothing of first-rate musical importance. No Italian composer
of that time could be mentioned in the same breath with Dunstable,
Dufay, Binchois, Ockeghem, Obrecht, Isaac, or Josquin des Prez; no
Italian form made a direct impression on the main artistic production
of Europe. By the end of the fourteenth century *ars nova* was all
but exhausted. It had been, in any case, more an end than a beginning, predominantly medieval in character although charged with a
certain freshness and elasticity, foreshadowing things to come. The
frottola forms of the late fifteenth and early sixteenth centuries, while
important as forerunners of the madrigal, were yet on too low an
artistic level to compete with contemporary Franco-Flemish music
in terms of quality and international importance. And between the
music of Landini and the *frottola* composers lies a comparatively arid
stretch of some eighty years, during which Italy could claim no direct
part in the development of the art.

It appears odd, at first glance, that fifteenth-century Italy, which
saw the painting of Masaccio, Fra Angelico, Gozzoli, Fra Filippo
Lippi, Ghirlandaio, and Mantegna, the sculpture of Donatello, Della
Robbia, and Verrocchio, the architecture of Brunelleschi, Alberti, and
Bramante, should be ineffective in the field of music; yet there is an
almost exact parallel in the more closely connected field of literature.
The bright promise which Italian literature held during the time
of Petrarch was not fulfilled in the immediately succeeding generations; the freshness of the trecento gave way to a quattrocento anti-
quarianism which drained the red blood from Italian poetry for nearly
a hundred years. The first effect of the classical revival in literature
was the almost complete abandonment of the vulgar tongue in favour
of Latin. The beautiful, flowing Italian of Petrarch was succeeded by
stilted, devitalized imitations of Lucretius, Quintilian, and Ovid.

In the latter part of the fifteenth century Italian re-emerged as a literary language and challenged the supremacy of Latin. Much credit for this change is due to Lorenzo de' Medici, who, although completely trained and grounded in Latin and the ancient classics, escaped the cult of pedantic imitation. Not only did he defend Italian, declaring in an essay that the vernacular was the artistic equal of Latin, just as Petrarch was of Ovid; he himself also wrote Italian poetry of no small merit. Many of his poems are neo-Petrarchian, but he found his happiest expression in the more popular forms of *ballate* and carnival songs. Here the energizing influence of the common people, excluded for a time from Italian literature, became again apparent. It is no coincidence that at this moment Italian secular music once more began to flourish and the development leading directly to the Italian madrigal began.

POPULAR MUSIC AND COURTLY IMPROVISATION

Before considering the pre-madrigal forms, a word should be said concerning popular poetry and music during the fifteenth century. Contact between popular and artistic forms was virtually non-existent, since the people were in no way equipped to follow the humanists in their Greek and Latin preoccupations, nor did the humanists give any consideration to the vernacular forms of the plebs. There were, however, vast quantities of popular poems and rhymes produced during the fifteenth century, nearly all of them designed as lyrics for musical performance. One type of poem was the *ballata* or *canzone a ballo*, a song meant to accompany dancing. Many of these appear to be vulgarizations of *ballate* written by Dante, Boccaccio, and Sacchetti in the preceding century. Special dance-songs were available for practically every festivity, from public dances in the square to weddings, carnival processions, and May Day tournaments. There existed as well an enormous quantity of love poetry, written in forms called *rispetto, strambotto, stornello, fiore, ciure, villotta, canzuna,* &c. Names and dialects of these forms vary considerably from one region to another, but similarities of imagery, phraseology, and style indicate common sources of origin, lost in the more remote past. Unfortunately the music to which such poems were sung has not been preserved in its original form, though when we arrive at the music published early in the sixteenth century we shall see that certain pieces show traces of considerable antiquity.

Besides popular poetry and music the fifteenth century produced a large quantity of courtly poetry, written by amateurs and dilettantes, stereotyped in its expression (generally pseudo-Petrarchian) and largely anonymous. Music was improvised to these verses either by professional singers or by those members of the court who had musical ability; the usual accompaniment was on the lute. One poet of some literary attainment took up these forms of doggerel and transmuted them into something approaching artistic creation. This was Leonardo Giustiniani (d. 1446), reputed author of the poem 'O rosa bella' (see pp. 128 and 153). Giustiniani himself was famous for his improvisation; unfortunately no composition of his has come down to us. He is generally considered to have been instrumental in developing and fixing the form of the *strambotto*, a form we shall meet with presently.

The music performed before the refined society of the Italian courts during the fifteenth century was the music of Franco-Flemish composers—the internationalists who dominated European music throughout the century. Not only did the music of foreigners supply all demands; even more astonishing is the fact that nearly all the practising musicians of the century were French, German, English, Spanish, or Flemish. The registers of the Papal chapel disclose scarcely one Italian name; instrumentalists of all kinds were chiefly imported, as were music tutors in the houses of the nobility. As if to emphasize the dominant position of foreign composers, the first part-music printed in Italy (and in the world) consisted almost exclusively of Franco-Flemish compositions.[1]

The re-emergence of Italian music dates from about 1480 and takes two principal forms. The first is the Florentine carnival song (*canto carnascialesco*) created largely by Lorenzo de' Medici; the second is the Mantuan *frottola*, stimulated principally by Isabella d'Este.

CARNIVAL SONGS

During the time of Lorenzo the Magnificent (1448–92) the Florentine carnival attained a brilliance unknown before or since. He found the old celebrations too sober for his tastes and invented new forms, more sumptuous and more artistic than before, replacing the less spectacular processions with magnificent parades, including elaborate floats. He himself wrote carnival poetry, and commissioned Poliziano, who was attached to his court, to do the same; the old *canzone a ballo* he supplanted with carnival songs, *trionfi* and *carri*—forms which he may be said to have invented in their classic form. These pieces, as regards their texts, are a curious combination of pseudo-popular traits and typical Florentine cynicism. Nearly all are amorous in

[1] See p. 253.

intent, and many are obscene. Women are urged to set not too much store by their virtue; wives are admonished to enjoy themselves even if their husbands are cuckolded in the process; and the populace in general, young and old, is reminded of the transitory nature of earthly pleasure and of the irresistible passing of time. Over the gaiety of burlesque and uninhibited enjoyment one hears the melancholy note of Lorenzo's own line 'di doman non c'è certezza' (dance and be happy today, for the morrow is uncertain).

The *canti carnascialeschi* proper most frequently take the form of narrative portrayals of popular types: hermits, beggars, pilgrims, and artisan classes such as masons, tailors, woodcarvers, oil vendors, &c. Many *canti* open with a statement of what class or type of character is being represented: 'Donne noi siam giovanni', 'Siam galanti di Valenza', 'Noi siam tre pellegrini', &c. These pieces abound in *double entendre*, not to mention outright obscenities, designed to amuse the public. The anonymous 'Canto di donne che cacciano si conigli' (song of women hunting rabbits) begins as follows:

Ex. 167[1]

(We are all young women who hunt, and we never ask for any other kind of exercise.)

Six stanzas follow, describing the manner of hunting and giving advice to other women on how to catch rabbits, pointing out that many famous women have followed this trade and recommending it as being most rewarding. The thinly veiled meaning is clear.

A special type of song is the *canto dei lanzi*. The *lanzi* were German mercenary soldiers imported into Italy, renowned for their

[1] P.-M. Masson, *Chants de carnaval florentins* (Paris, 1913), pp. 79–80.

drinking, their poor Italian, and their ability to play wind instruments. In many carnival songs they are caricatured both in their customs and in their speech. The texts are a garbled mixture of German and Italian dialects, with their barbaric pronunciation of Italian imitated as well, so that many of these texts are today quite incomprehensible.

The most elaborate aspects of the Florentine carnival were the *trionfi* and *carri*. These were large, impressive displays representing mythological deities, imaginary victories, and allegorical virtues. The names alone gave a clear idea of the subject-matter: allegorical *carri* representing the four humours, the *quadrivium*, the four seasons of the year, 'il trionfo della Dea Minerva', 'il trionfo di Arianna e Bacco', 'il trionfo de' diavoli'. The last named, by Alexander Coppinus, may serve as an example of the prevailing style in Florentine carnival music:

Ex. 168[1]

[1] Masson, op. cit., pp. 74–77.

(From the joyless grottoes where neither day nor pure light shines, but only eternal night and dark mists, we women have fled and have come to show you for your good our cruel fate.)

One is struck immediately by the breadth of the style, coupled with the comparative simplicity of the means. The harmonies are elementary; counterpoint is restricted to the two short duets. As a matter of fact, this *trionfo* is more complicated, by reason of these duets employing imitation, than the majority of *canti*, which are frequently composed exclusively of block harmonies, with occasional passing notes. It is noteworthy that in this music three-part writing is replaced by four-part; only the very earliest pieces of Lorenzo's time are for three voices.

This is music *par excellence* for outdoor performance, and to appreciate its true quality it must be imagined in that setting. Greater brilliance was added by the use of instruments; contemporary documents mention the participation of lutes, *chitarre*, and rebecs among the strings, bombards, *pifferi*, *corni*, *trombe*, and *tromboni* among the wind instruments.

The standard procedures and over-all traits of this music may be summarized as follows:

1. Simultaneous attack in all voices at the opening, followed by a series of broad chords.

2. Predominance of homophonic writing, lightly ornamented from time to time by passing and other ornamental notes.

3. Clear delineation of phrases. Simultaneous attack in all voices is the rule for each new phrase of text. Clear-cut cadences at the end of each phrase of text; frequent use of pauses on final notes; frequent use of rests between phrases.

4. Occasional insertion of duet or (less frequently) trio passages, employing the most rudimentary forms of imitation.

5. Predominance of duple time in the opening and principal portion of most pieces. Introduction of triple time towards the close of the piece; in some instances this is retained to the end, while in others the closing bars revert to duple time.

6. Monotony and limited range of the harmony. Tonic, dominant, and subdominant constitute the harmonic material for most of this music, with an occasional use of the supertonic, with minor or major third. (We are justified in using these terms in connexion with music written long before the harmonic system was codified, since the effect of the music is eminently harmonic.)

7. Absence of modulation. The only approach to modulation is the not infrequent semi-cadence (cadence on the dominant, preceded by its own dominant).

8. Melodic monotony. It is no exaggeration to say that much of this music is non-melodic. Although vertically conceived, it does not, like the *frottola*, consist of a tune in the top voice supported by the other voices. The *cantus*, indeed, is scarcely more important than any other voice; it moves generally in a limited range and lacks the quality of tunefulness. The monotony of range is further increased by frequent crossing of the upper two voices. The bass is in a sense the most important voice, for it supports the harmony which seems to be erected on it. It is the most active part in terms of motion, moving often by fourths and fifths. The intent of carnival music was clearly declamatory, not melodic, and this declamatory style had important repercussions in later madrigal compositions, many of which were also intended for outdoor performance.

The *canto carnascialesco* is the first strong statement of Italian national style, which from this time forward entered into direct competition with the international style of the Netherlanders and eventually, toward 1560, vanquished it. In practically every respect it is the antithesis of the Franco-Flemish style represented by the *Odhecaton*. Its qualities are precisely those which are innately and firmly Italian. Here is the technique of fresco, with its broad, flat strokes as opposed to the miniature work of the northern composers. Here are simplicity and directness instead of complication and artifice. Expressed in musical terms, here is homophony instead of polyphony; vertical in place of horizontal construction; sharply delineated phrases instead of textual continuousness; square-cut rhythm instead of a complex, undulating rhythmic flow.

It is notable that from the very beginning this new Italian style left its imprint upon northern composers. Indeed, there is a curious anomaly in the fact that some of the first and best carnival songs were composed by Heinrich Isaac, whom Lorenzo the Magnificent employed as his principal musician.[1] Isaac, the composer of complicated Masses and delicate *chansons*, wrote for Lorenzo in a purely Italian style, indistinguishable from the work of native Italians save by its workmanlike quality. He was among the first of a long line of foreign composers, mostly Netherlanders, who brought to Italy their superior technical equipment and their northern styles, and who ended by adopting, to a greater or lesser degree, the characteristic stylistic elements of Italian national music—a line which includes such figures as Josquin, Arcadelt, Verdelot, Cipriano de Rore, and Lassus.

Lorenzo the Magnificent died in 1492, and with him disappeared the brilliance of carnival. Until 1498, when the Medici house was restored, the once gay city moaned and lamented under the influence of Savonarola. Instead of splendid *carri* and *trionfi* the carnival time was given over to religious processions and sermons. During the carnivals of 1497 and 1498 the public was entertained by two enormous 'bonfires of vanities', organized by the reforming priest. To these bonfires long lines of children brought every sort of musical instrument and quantities of 'lascivious music', which were consigned to the flames during the singing of devout *laudi* and psalms. It is certain that most of the manuscripts of Medicean carnival music were destroyed in these fires.

With the Medici restoration the older type of carnival was brought back, but never with the same brilliance or whole-hearted participation. The influence of Savonarola was not easily shaken off; the people as a whole took less and less part in carnival celebrations, which were continued largely by the aristocracy. The music changed corre-

[1] See *supra*, p. 279.

spondingly; appealing to a more select group it became more literary and more ingenious. Expressed in other terms, the late carnival song moved in the direction of the madrigal.[1]

LAUDI

During the time Savonarola was in power many former carnival songs, originally with worldly and even obscene texts, were converted into *laudi*[2] by the substitution of new and sacred words.[3] This kind of expropriation by the church is, of course, by no means limited to the *lauda*; we see the sixteenth-century French *chanson*, for example, converted in the same way, often with the alteration of only a few key words. Not all *laudi* were converted carnival songs; on the contrary, even such men as Lorenzo de' Medici wrote *laudi* which were given their own settings by court composers, and a religious play on the subject of St. John and St. Paul. (Unfortunately Isaac's music to the play has not been preserved.) When original music was composed, it was either in the style of secular music or it was of extreme simplicity in harmony and texture.

A large collection of polyphonic *laudi* from *c.* 1500 has been published by Knud Jeppesen.[4] Its contents show that certain *frottola* composers turned their attention also to *laudi*, composing them in much the same style as their secular works. There are, however, a number of pieces which have a distinct style of their own, characterized by a certain seriousness and tenderness (resulting in part from an expressive use of suspensions in the cadences), an openness of texture, and a simplicity of means. Short pieces such as the following —few of them are very much longer—demonstrate that a typically Italian style was emerging also in the field of religious music. The composer is D. Philippo:

Ex. 169[5]

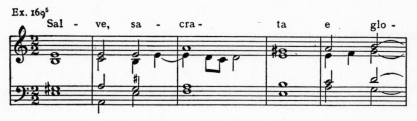

---

[1] See the 'Canto de' diavoli' (text by Macchiavelli) in Masson, op. cit., p. 12, and the 'Trionfo del Broncone' in F. Ghisi, *I canti carnascialeschi* (Florence, 1937), p. 76.

[2] Cf. vol. II, pp. 266–9.

[3] Cf. Ghisi, 'Strambotti e laude nel travestimento spirituale della poesia musicale del quattrocento', *Collectanea Historiae Musicae*, i (Florence, 1953), p. 45.

[4] *Die mehrstimmige italienische Laude um 1500* (Leipzig, 1935).   [5] Ibid., p. 1.

(Hail, holy and glorious emblem, on which the Lord of all was crucified.)

There is no reason to ignore the probability that certain elements of the *lauda*, both technical and emotional, went into the shaping of the early madrigal. The madrigal, admittedly a composite of other forms and commonly described as a simple amalgamation of motet and *frottola*, appears in fact to be a mixture of certain traits from the carnival song, the *lauda*, the *frottola*, the French *chanson*, and the motet. The direct path to the madrigal, however, is by way of the *frottola*, which we shall now consider.

THE *FROTTOLA* FORMS

The companion piece to the Florentine carnival song is the Mantuan *frottola*, which made its appearance more or less simultaneously with the new carnival music of Lorenzo's time. It is difficult, if not impossible, to say which of these two forms preceded the other, or in what ways they may have influenced each other. In manuscripts of the late fifteenth and early sixteenth centuries they are frequently found in the same volume; the MS. Panciatichi 27 of the Biblioteca Nazionale of Florence (early sixteenth century), for example, contains *frottole*, carnival songs, *laudi*, and sacred music.

The year 1480 is as far back as one could logically date the beginnings of *frottola* composition, and it was about the same time that composition of the classic type of carnival song began. The great volume of *frottole*, however, comes only towards the end of the fifteenth century and in the first two decades of the sixteenth.

The *frottola* forms grew naturally out of the tradition of improvised song. The principal patron of the *frottola* in its first bloom was the celebrated Isabella d'Este, who in 1490 went to Mantua as the wife of the Marchese Francesco Gonzaga and soon established an international reputation for her intelligence, her culture, and her sincerity. Following the lead of Lorenzo de' Medici, she did much to establish the Italian language as a vehicle for music, and even more than Lorenzo was responsible for the emergence of typically Italian music in the sixteenth century. In her small but brilliant court, where she herself performed on the clavichord, she not only cradled the new Italian musical art but also strove constantly to improve its quality. She saw the *frottola* as the national answer to the Franco-Flemish *chanson*,[1] and urged both poets and musicians to cultivate the new forms. She saw artistic possibilities in the pseudo-popular *strambotto* and *barzelletta* (*frottola*), in the *oda* and the *sonetto*, and she employed as court composers not *oltremontani* but two native Italians (a rare choice at that time), Marchetto Cara and Bartolomeo Tromboncino, whose fame soon spread throughout Italy and beyond. These composers were no Josquins or Isaacs; but they had precisely the equipment required to start the movement of Italian music. Their very lack of the technique necessary for creating complicated music was a safeguard for the new art; it removed the temptation to become obscure, over-learned, and turgid.

The *frottola* is at best a second-rate form of art, as regards both the texts and the music. It is the work of hack poets and inferior musicians. It is artificial and banal, devoid of technical prowess or serious emotion. It is repetitious, stereotyped, and cliché-ridden. But the musical and poetic styles are in perfect harmony and the *frottole* embody one very important feature, which in them is almost an innovation—straightforwardness of rhythm; this will be discussed below.

Up to this point the terms '*frottola*' and '*frottola* forms' have been used in a generic sense, to designate a whole group of forms related in style. In addition to this general use, the word *frottola* has a specific

[1] On the musical relationship between *chanson* and *frottola*, cf. Disertori's prefatory study to the 1954 reprint of Petrucci (see n. 1 on next page), pp. xxxvii ff.

meaning as the name of a definite form, distinct from the others, within the family. In the succeeding pages the context will indicate which meaning is to be attached to the word. The family of *frottola* forms includes the *frottola* proper, the *oda*, the *strambotto*, the *capitulo*, and the *sonetto*. The eleven books of *frottole* published by Petrucci during the first two decades of the sixteenth century[1] form the main repository of *frottola* music, and also show clearly the development towards the madrigal.[2]

(i) *The Frottola.* The *frottola* as a poetic form is distinguished by a refrain which is sung at the beginning of the piece and after each stanza. The stanzas themselves are usually of six or eight lines, each line of eight syllables; the metre is trochaic. A typical rhyme scheme is:

> *Refrain*:   a b b a a b
> *Stanza 1.*   c b c b b a
> *Stanza 2.*   d e d e e a

which shows the device in which this poetry abounds—the carrying over of a rhyme from one stanza to another. Four-line and eight-line *frottole* are also found, always with the characteristic metre and always with refrain.

(ii) *The Oda.* This is not the Latin ode of Horace, but rather a form designed specially for *frottola* music, making its appearance first in the *frottola* books. It is a poem of several four-line stanzas, without refrain. The last line of each stanza usually varies in length from the first three, which contain seven syllables each. The metre is iambic.

(iii) *The Strambotto.* The origin of the *strambotto* is to be found in the folk-poetry of more remote times; its birthplace is believed to be Sicily. In the early fifteenth century it was the form of the famous *giustiniana*, whose memory seems to have almost vanished by 1500. The *strambotto* consists of eight lines, each of eleven syllables, divided into four pairs of two lines each; there is no refrain. The rhyme scheme is either *a b a b a b c c* (the *ottava* form of later times) or *a b a b a b a b*. *Frottola, oda,* and *strambotto* are the three most common forms in

---

[1] Books I and IV, ed. Rudolf Schwartz, have been reprinted as Jg. viii of *Publikationen älterer Musik* (Leipzig, 1935), Books I, II, and III, transcribed by Gaetano Cesari and ed. Raffaello Monterosso, as *Instituta et Monumenta*, series I, i (Cremona, 1954). (The latter perpetuates Petrucci's erroneous numbering.)

[2] I should like here to express my thanks and gratitude to the late Alfred Einstein for allowing me to consult his complete collection of *frottola* transcriptions and to reproduce examples from them.

the early publications of Petrucci. The *sonetto*, however, occupies an increasingly important place as successive books appear.

(iv) *The Sonetto*. The *sonetto* has the regular sonnet form: fourteen lines to a stanza, five feet to the line, in iambic metre. It consists of one stanza without refrain.

(v) *The Capitulo*. The *capitulo* or *terza rima* appears in the index of Petrucci's fourth book under the heading *Sonetti*. Actually, the two forms are quite distinct, although they are cast in the same metre. The *capitulo* is a series of terzines connected by a chain rhyme scheme *a b a*: *b c b*: *c d c*: *d e d*, &c.

(vi) *The Canzona*. The *canzona*, a favourite form of Petrarch's and always an aristocrat among verse forms, is rare in Petrucci's early books but in the course of their publication assumes an increasingly important place. Free in construction, it consists of an undetermined number of stanzas, composed of lines which may vary among themselves in length; rhyme scheme is also free. A single *canzona* stanza is in effect a madrigal.

(vii) *Lesser Forms*. Several less important forms are found in pre-madrigal poetry. There are Horatian odes and occasionally other pieces of Latin verse, such as Dido's farewell from the fourth book of the *Aeneid*, an excerpt from the *Heroides* of Ovid, and some medieval Latin pieces. Petrucci's fourth book includes an air for the singing of Latin verses ('Aer de versi latini'). These few pieces indicate that although the Latin tongue was not entirely forgotten, it occupied a very unimportant place in *frottola* literature.

Other Italian forms found in Petrucci's books are the *canzonetta* and *villota*. The former is a general term for little songs with refrain, without fixed rhyme scheme, usually with lines of seven or eleven syllables. The *villota* has its origin in the trecento *caccia* and is characterized by a distinctly popular flavour. Musically as well it continues the *caccia* style in its frequent use of imitation. It consists of one stanza, having an undetermined number of lines, comprising varying numbers of syllables. The form has not yet been adequately studied. In a spirit of misguided nationalism Torrefranca assigned to the fifteenth-century *villota* an importance and a role incommensurate with known facts.[1]

A considerable number of *canti carnascialeschi* appear also in the Petrucci prints. These have been identified and catalogued by Ghisi in his useful book on the carnival song.[2] The presence of a small

[1] Fausto Torrefranca, 'I primordi della polifonia del Cinquecento', *Nuova Antologia*, ccclxxvi (Rome, 1934), p. 107. [2] F. Ghisi, op. cit., pp. 126–44.

number of pieces with Spanish texts draws attention to the existence
of a Spanish court in the kingdom of Naples.

DEVELOPMENT OF THE *FROTTOLA*

Riemann considered the *frottola* poetry as the outgrowth of preceding popular forms and maintained that the *frottola* is in reality
nothing but a popular dance-song. The similarity of many *frottole*
to the earlier *ballata* form[1] must not be overlooked. But whatever
part the *ballata* may have played in the background of the *frottola*,
its influence had largely disappeared by the time of Petrucci's publications.

Frottole were cultivated mainly for or by the nobility. They
flourished chiefly in the courts of northern Italy, especially in Mantua,
Ferrara, Venice, Urbino, and Florence. Einstein[2] has pointed out the
significant fact that those cities in which the *frottola* flourished were
the very ones in which Pietro Bembo, the cardinal and poet, was influential. The part which he played in the development of the *frottola*
and the eventual creation of the madrigal was undoubtedly an important one. There can be little doubt that he influenced poets and
musicians alike, by word and example, to create works of a higher
order, leading in the direction of the madrigal. The fact that *frottola*
production was carried on frequently under his aegis is another indication that the poetry was anything but popular, despite occasional
folk-like reminiscences in certain pieces.

Between 1504 and 1514, the ten years during which Petrucci published his eleven *frottola* collections, a considerable development may
be observed in the quality of the texts. The first book, entitled simply
Frottole libro primo, contains a majority of true *frottole*, of which
there are 40, as against 11 *ode*, 6 *canzonette*, 2 Latin odes, and 3
miscellaneous forms. The second book (1504) contains 37 *frottole*,
14 *ode*, and 2 *sonetti*; in it appears the first poem of literary quality—
Poliziano's 'Piangete mecho amanti'.

Book III ('1504'=1505) shows an increase in the number of literary
poems, containing the first work of Petrarch to appear in Petrucci's
collections, 'Ite caldi sospiri', as well as Poliziano's 'Piangete occhi
mei lassi', and a *frottola* by Calmeta, 'Nacque al mondo per amare'.
Its contents are 48 *frottole*, 8 *ode*, 1 *sonetto*, and 5 miscellaneous.[3]

---

[1] See *supra*, p. 65.
[2] Alfred Einstein, 'Das elfte Buch der Frottole', *Zeitschrift für Musikwissenschaft*,
x (1927–8), pp. 613–24.
[3] Josquin's 'El grillo', from Book III, is recorded in *The History of Music in Sound*
(H.M.V.), iii.

The fourth book (1505) is the only one which bears a more exact title: *Strambotti, Ode, Frottole, Sonetti, Et modo de cantar versi latini e capituli Libro quarto*. A considerable change has occurred since the third book. A newcomer, the *strambotto*, has entered the picture and occupies the greater portion of the book. The sonnet forms (including the *capitulo*) are present in greater number than heretofore and in that respect represent an advance in taste. However, none of the poems has a known literary origin and, indeed, the general quality of the verse is low. The collection contains 47 *strambotti*, 19 *frottole*, 14 *ode*, and 9 *sonetti*. The appearance of *strambotti* in such great number is noteworthy, for although their artistic value is low indeed, from this form developed the later *ottava rima*, which was utilized in important works of literature and was set frequently by madrigal composers.

The fifth book (1505) again bears a simple title, *Frottole, Libro Quinto*, and contains two poems of literary character—Galeotto de Caretto's two *frottole* 'Pace hormai che a discoprire' and 'Se gran festa me mostrasti'. This poet had considerable personal contact with the Mantuan court, and the presence of his works in the *frottole* collections forms another link in the chain of evidence pointing towards the leading role played by Mantua and by Cardinal Bembo in the development of the *frottola* toward the madrigal. *Frottole* again predominate in this book, there being 45, as against 6 *strambotti*, 7 *ode*, and 3 *sonetti*. *Frottole Libro Sexto* (1505) contains 47 *frottole*, including 'Lassa donna i dolce sguardi' of Carreto, 9 *strambotti*, 5 *ode*, 2 *sonetti*, and 3 miscellaneous.

In the seventh book (1507) the literary atmosphere becomes more pronounced. Petrarch is represented by three *stanze di canzona*: 'Si e debile il filo', 'Che debbio far che mi consigli', and 'S'il dissi mai che venga'. There is also a *canzona* of Bembo himself, 'Non si vedra gia mai', and a *frottola* of Poliziano, 'Io non tho perche non lho'. The contents of this book are unusually varied: 32 *frottole*, 9 *strambotti*, 10 *ode*, 4 *stanze di canzona*, 3 *canzonette*, 2 *capituli*, 4 *sonetti*, 1 *sestina*, and 2 miscellaneous.[1] The appearance of the *stanze di canzona* is important, for in the moment that a composer selects one stanza only as the basis of his composition, he is in effect composing a madrigal.

In the eighth book (1507) only one text appears to be identifiable with a literary source—namely, the lines from the third book of Vergil's *Aeneid*, 'Dissimulare etiam sperasti'. From a literary point

---

[1] Demophon's *frottola*, 'A che son hormai conducto', from Book VII, is recorded in *The History of Music in Sound*, iv.

of view this book seems to represent a retrogression. It has 34 *frottole*, 9 *strambotti*, 6 *ode*, 3 *sonetti*, 2 *canzone*, and 4 miscellaneous.

Petrarch is represented again in the ninth book (1508) by two poems: 'O tempo o ciel volubil' and a *sestina*—the first of his to be set to music—'Mia benigna fortuna'. In this book we find 39 *frottole*, 5 *strambotti*, 9 *ode*, 3 *capituli*, 2 *sonetti*, 2 *ottava rime*, and 5 miscellaneous.

Unfortunately no complete copy of the tenth book has been found, although it is possible that one may yet be discovered when the libraries of Europe have been thoroughly catalogued.[1] The loss is the more lamentable because of the great disparity between the ninth and eleventh books. We find here what might almost be termed a revolution in taste, and the discovery of the tenth book might throw some light on the process by which the change was accomplished. In the ninth book, and indeed in all books preceding the eleventh, poetry of a literary nature is found only in isolated instances. However, in the eleventh book, published in 1514, six years after the ninth, we find ourselves at once in a literary milieu; six well-known poets are represented, and twenty-five of the seventy pieces have known literary origins. Petrarch is represented by no fewer than twenty poems; Bembo, Sannazaro, Tebaldeo, Mutio Justino Politano, and Pietro Barignano each by one. It is the first appearance in music of Sannazaro, who later became a favourite of the madrigalists.

The number of poems by Petrarch in this book may well reflect a conscious resolve by the composers to set texts of higher quality and may indicate a reaction against the insipid *frottola* texts hitherto in vogue. Even though the music was scarcely suited to the finished and lyrical texts of Petrarch, the satisfactory setting of his texts became a goal, if not an achievement, of the frottolists, and the noble tone of his poetry induced a striving after a corresponding nobility of tone in the music. Yet the time was still distant when the madrigal would have progressed to such a point that it could be a companion, rather than a beast of burden, for Petrarch's works.

Before 1514 only one known collection was published by a competitor of Petrucci, and it contained chiefly reprints from Petrucci's collections. This was the *Canzoni nove*, printed in Rome by Andrea Antico (1510). Between the date of Petrucci's eleventh book and the first known edition of madrigals (1530) various publishers brought out

---

[1] The only trace of this publication consists of fragments of the alto and bass parts, preserved in the Biblioteca Colombina, Seville. Jeppesen, 'Die neuentdeckten Bücher der Lauden des Ottaviano dei Petrucci', *Zeitschrift für Musikwissenschaft*, xii (1929–30), pp. 73 ff., suggests that both the ninth and eleventh books may be reprints of earlier editions.

books of *frottole* and related forms. Many of the pieces were reprints from Petrucci: poems of literary quality, especially Petrarch's, continued to be included. Yet with one exception no collection rivalled Petrucci's eleventh book in literary splendour. The exception was Petrucci's own book *Musica de messer Bernardo Pisano sopra le canzone de Petrarca* of 1520. Besides including *canzone* by Petrarch, this noteworthy publication, unfortunately lost, contained one of the first settings of stanzas from Ariosto's *Orlando Furioso*, later a rich fund for madrigal composers. Other important publications for the development of the *frottola* include Antico's *Frottole libro tertio* of 1517,[1] the first to contain poetry by Castiglione; and a 1519 publication of Laneto[2] which contains, besides three poems of Petrarch and an excerpt from Vergil, a poem of Michelangelo, 'Come haro donque', set by Tromboncino.

RELATION OF TEXT AND MUSIC

For the general run of *frottola* poetry the music is an ideal companion; indeed, it can scarcely support the weight of Petrarch's and other literary texts. This music is in a sense non-expressive—often pleasant, sometimes *gauche*, but never passionate. It renders the anguished complaint of the lover dying of grief with the same cheerful banality that praises the beloved's eyes. This is as it should be, for the suffering and the rapture indicated by the words are in reality mock suffering and mock rapture, expressed in standardized clichés. Sentimentality has no place in the *frottola* as it has in the early madrigal; the *frottola* is pointed, often epigrammatic, frivolous, banal.

The fact that the same music must serve for several or many stanzas precludes a close relationship between music and text. In nearly all forms the music is short and is repeated as often as necessary to get through the entire text. In the *oda*, for example, the first stanza is set and the same music repeated for successive stanzas. In most *strambotti* only the first two lines are set and this music is repeated three times; through-composed *strambotti*, however, do exist. In the *frottola*, the same music serves for the refrain and for the stanza, and since the stanzas are longer than the refrain repetition occurs within even this amount of music.

The musical rendering of text accent and prosody ranges from the exact to the practically non-existent. In some pieces, notably *ode*, the

---

[1] Reprinted by Einstein (Northampton, Mass., 1941).
[2] *Fioretti di Frottole Barzelette Capitolo Strambotti e Sonetti Libro Secondo, Stampato in Napoli*, &c.

music is a faithful servant to the rhythm and accent of the text. In many *strambotti* the two appear to be conceived with no relation to each other. Most *frottole* proper fall somewhere between these two extremes. The problem of text-underlaying is in some instances practically insoluble. Most Petrucci *frottole* have the complete text only in the top voice, the cantus; the other voices have only the first words. Even in the top voice the underlaying is inexact, and the text syllables do not accompany their corresponding notes. It has been suggested that the words were so printed as to enhance the appearance of the page. It is more likely that the technique of music-printing had not yet reached the point at which exact underlaying was possible. Nor was it considered a necessity; singers of that period were instructed and trained in *prima vista* syllabification, which enabled them to correlate music and text.

Much speculation has revolved around the question of instrumental participation in *frottola* music. The fact that often only the top voice carries the full text has led some scholars to conclude that *frottole* were performed by a solo voice accompanied by instruments. The musical structure itself very often seems to support this contention; in many *frottole* the top voice is the only one which has rests between phrases, while the three lower voices carry on, perhaps throughout an entire piece, without interruption. In addition, the top voice is usually the most melodious, being sometimes a real tune. There is little doubt that *frottole* were often performed by a solo voice accompanied by instruments. The fact, however, that certain pieces published by Petrucci are found in contemporary manuscripts with full text in each voice indicates that they were also sung without accompaniment. Further evidence is supplied by the title-page of Antico's *Canzoni nove*, which shows four persons singing without instruments. Moreover, closer examination of the lower voices in many pieces reveals that, even though they may be devoid of rests, they are entirely singable and form clear cadences. The truth of the matter would seem to be that in publishing *frottole* Petrucci and his successors were supplying raw material for adaptation in various ways, depending upon the resources available. A common method of performance was with solo voice and lute, in which case the alto part might be simply omitted and the tenor and bass intabulated (i.e. notated) for the lute. The fact that both Tromboncino and Cara were famous for singing to the lute points to the popularity of this kind of performance. Certain pieces appear to have instrumental interludes or postludes or both, suggesting another kind of instrumental participation

—either constant doubling of the voice parts by instruments or alternation of vocal and instrumental sections.

Pictorialism, employed constantly in the madrigal, is rare in the
frottola. Occasionally a word like 'fugge' (flees) will be accompanied
by quicker notes in the music; in general, however, such words as
'vivo', 'morto', 'catena' (chain), 'alto' (high) and the like are not
given special treatment. (It goes without saying that whatever
pictorialism there is is valid only for the first stanza of text.) A few
pieces display a device frequently used in the madrigal—the translation of solmization syllables, when they occur in the text, by their
corresponding notes (e.g. the word 'sola' is set by G (*sol*) and A (*la*)).
A few *frottola* pieces contain imitations of animal sounds or other
sounds of nature, foreshadowing the French *chanson*, which was probably influenced by the *frottola*. Among them are *historiettes*, similar
in style and spirit to the early *chansons* of Certon and Janequin.
A particularly charming one is found in Petrucci's seventh book (no.
44) imitating the crowing of the cock:

Ex. 170

(Almost always before dawn the cock sings 'cu cu ru cu'.)

MUSICAL STYLE

The most immediately striking feature of the *frottola* (the word is used here in its generic sense) is its four-part harmonic structure. Here, for the first time in musical history, composers hit upon the principle which later became standard and which today still forms the basis of instruction in harmony. At the end of the brief *frottola* period the principle of four-part harmony was again largely abandoned. In the madrigal the predominance of imitation implies the melodic equality of the several voices; only in the lesser forms (*villanella, canzonetta,* &c.) does one see a partial continuation of *frottola* style. And the advent of the *basso continuo* style about 1600 reduced music to its basic elements—a single melodic line and a supporting bass.

Despite outward dissimilarities there is a curiously close parallel between the *frottola* and *basso continuo* styles. The *frottola* consists basically of two melodic lines, soprano and bass; the soprano carries the tune while the bass, moving often by leaps, supplies the harmonic foundation. Between these two the alto and tenor move about to fill in the harmony. In the typical *frottola* (the word is used here to designate the specific form) the two middle voices are quite active, giving at first glance the impression of considerable counterpoint. Closer examination, however, shows that the activity is of a specious kind; the voices are not making real polyphony but rushing about from one harmony note to another, often filling in larger intervals with passing notes, and constantly crossing each other, either to produce movement or to avoid parallel fifths or octaves.[1] (One characteristic of the style is the upward leap of an octave by the bass voice to take the fifth of the final chord, crossing above an upper voice which takes the fundamental note.) Such random crossings, it is clear, have an entirely different motivation and effect from the controlled crossings of the Palestrina period, which are a natural, almost inevitable, consequence of the independent flow of the several voices. In some instances the middle voices continue from beginning to end without any rest whatsoever,[2] suggesting also by their contour instrumental performance.

The structure of the *frottola* forms is therefore essentially homophonic, even when their homophony is disguised by superimposed movement. Pure homophony, in the form of note-against-note passages, is by no means rare, appearing as a contrasting passage in an

---

[1] Petrucci, Book I, no. 44 (corrected numbering).   [2] Ibid., Book I, no. 6.

otherwise ornamented *frottola*, or constituting the principal technique, especially in the *oda*, of which the following (from Petrucci's second book) is an example:

(Weep with me, ye lovers, for my grief is extreme; and I suffer every hour for loving too much.)

Vocalizes in the top voice, such as the one which closes the last phrase of the above *oda*, are not uncommon and serve to underline the melodic importance of the cantus. In a few *frottole* the cantus may hold the last note while the other voices make a series of plagal cadences—a common practice in the madrigal.

Imitation plays a small part in *frottola* technique, and when it occurs, it is generally of a primitive nature. A kind of buried imitation is sometimes employed, in which a short motive is passed from one voice to another within, rather than at the beginning of, the melodic phrases; since these motives are of a neutral character, such imitation goes almost unnoticed.[1] Imitation employing the head of the motive is comparatively rare, especially in the earlier *frottola*. Such a piece as 'O, Dio, che la brunetta mia'[2] is exceptional among the early Petrucci pieces, being constructed of a series of points of imitation, which are, however, not carried out with exactitude. As the *frottola* developed, imitation played an increasingly important role; moreover, the homophonic and contrapuntal sections within a given piece tended to become more distinct and more sharply differentiated.

The following example, published in 1518,[3] is instructive for the development of the *frottola*; it is by Cara, one of the original frottolists and a native-born Italian. It presents a curious combination of old and new traits: the opening in strict imitation but with the entrance of the tenor over-long delayed; the buried imitation in bars 12–13 (tenor-cantus-bassus); the rather awkward use of imitation in bars 20–27; the sharply contrasting passages (bars 14–18 and 30–40) in declamatory, note-against-note style, foreshadowing madrigal practice; the attempt at varying the texture by momentarily reducing the number of voices (bars 20–28); the almost complete abandonment of the 'decorative' technique of filling in intervals with passing notes; and the sober, serious tone, so foreign to the early (and more typical) *frottola*:

Ex. 172

Quan - do lo po - mo vien da lo po-ma - ro S'el

Quando lo po

Quando lo po

Quando lo po

non e ma-tu - ro si pos-sei mai ma-tu - ra-re la

[1] Petrucci, Book I, no. 44.

[2] Ibid., Book I, no. 40.

[3] *Frottole*, Book II, published by Jacomo Mazochio (Rome, 1518).

(When the apple comes from the apple-tree, if it is not ripe it still may ripen one day. In the moonlight the heart struggles with itself, one foot in the water.

the other in the boat, one arm round the neck and the hand in the bosom.
O traitress, why dost thou not wish me well?)

The typical pattern of decorated homophony has here been replaced
by a texture in which all voices are of equal melodic and rhythmical
importance, and in which the predominance of evenly marching minims
imparts a severe character to the music. From the purely aesthetic
standpoint, such a piece, already half a madrigal, is less satisfactory
and less perfect than the early *frottola*. As a step towards the madrigal,
however, it represents a significant development and shows that the
madrigal was by no means the exclusive creation of the Netherlanders.

In relation to Netherland practice the *frottola* appears as a closer
approach towards the major-minor system; it is nearer to the modern
tonal system, indeed, than is the early madrigal which follows it,
partly because of the predominance of tonic, dominant, and subdominant, and partly because of the harmonic bass which moves on
the whole more slowly than the other parts and employs passing notes
less frequently to fill in larger intervals. Triads in fundamental position
form the basis of the harmony and are found on nearly every strong
beat (the first and third minims in a four-minim bar). Empty fifths are
avoided, except in final cadences, and smoothness of part-writing is
often sacrificed to the well-being of the vertical structure. One of the
main charms of the *frottola* lies in its combination of tonal and modal
harmonies, the frequent use of dominant-tonic establishing a more
or less firm tonal background for modal procedures. The Dorian and
Mixolydian modes are in the majority.

The rhythmic as well as the harmonic-structural aspect of the
frottola represents, for its period, a new departure. In striking contrast to the often complicated rhythms of Netherland polyphony, the
Italian *frottola* displays a straightforwardness and definiteness of
rhythm and phrasing which may well be its closest tie with popular
music. The strong beats are well-marked not only rhythmically but
also by the harmonic progressions, which as a rule move regularly
from weak to strong beats. The phrases are on the whole clearly defined
and are often composed of four bars (i.e. four groups of four minims)[1]
although three-bar phrases are common.[2] Rhythmic clarity is fur-
thered, too, by the fact that in nearly all *frottole* the voices begin
together in the same rhythmic pattern, as they do also in many intermediate phrases.

Syncopation is rare in the *frottola*—whether in the individual

---

[1] Petrucci, Book I, nos. 3 and 13.
[2] Ibid., Book I, no. 67, Book IV, no. 61.

voices or in the structure as a whole. The nervous subdivision of the beat which characterizes the Burgundian *chanson*, as well as the rhythmic complexity not only of the individual voices but also of the entire fabric which marks the works of Ockeghem, are both entirely foreign to *frottola* style. All four voices have the same time-signatures, and generally all four move in the same over-all rhythm, although occasionally one voice may momentarily be in another rhythm.[1] A number of pieces are built on the alternation of $\frac{6}{2}$ and $\frac{3}{1}$ bars.[2]

Mention has been made of the fact that in certain pieces, notably the *oda* and the note-against-note *frottola* passages, the text determines the musical rhythm fairly exactly. As a result the rhythm is often dull, reflecting the monotony of the text. The late *frottola* and early madrigal show a reaction against this plainness in rhythm and phrasing, which was in its turn a reaction against the too great complication (according to Italian standards) of fifteenth-century Netherland style. Those *frottola* passages in which text rhythm governs the musical are indicative of the primary importance which madrigalists later attached to the text. In some (apparently older) *strambotti*, on the other hand, there seems to be little or no relationship between verbal and musical rhythm, and the exact adjustment of text and music appears to be a matter of relative indifference, occasionally presenting almost insuperable problems.[3]

CONCLUSIONS

The *frottola* composers are small in stature compared with their Netherland contemporaries. Cara, Tromboncino, Alessandro Mantovano, Don Michele Vicentino, Carpentras, Michele Pesenti are names which individually cannot stand beside those of Isaac, Obrecht, and Josquin des Prez. Yet they were instrumental, collectively, in shaping a new style, and they did more than has been generally recognized in the formation of the madrigal itself.[4] Among the first known madrigal collections both Cara and Tromboncino are represented. The influence of the open Italian style on the Netherlanders themselves, especially those (the large majority) who visited or lived in Italy, is patent in their works; and the importance of *frottola* forms for the early French *chanson* is a subject which demands further investigation.[5]

---

[1] Ibid., Book IV, no 61 (cantus).   [2] See Ex. 170 above (p. 399).

[3] e.g. Book IV, no. 53.

[4] Cf. Everett Helm, 'Heralds of the Italian Madrigal', *The Musical Quarterly*, xxvii (1941), p. 306.

[5] Cf. Helm, 'The Sixteenth-Century French Chanson', *Proceedings of the Music Teachers' National Association* (New York, 1942).

XII

THE INSTRUMENTAL MUSIC OF THE MIDDLE AGES AND EARLY SIXTEENTH CENTURY

By YVONNE ROKSETH

THE TWELFTH AND THIRTEENTH CENTURIES

LITTLE instrumental music earlier than the fifteenth century survives, though the literature of every country shows how great a part it played. Whether in the castle or in the market-place, the minstrels had only to start tuning their instruments for people to gather round. Why, then, has so little written music survived to enlighten us about the works they performed?

There are two reasons. In the first place these instrumentalists undoubtedly had a large repertory of dance music, quite distinct from vocal music. Now this music, so far as it was written down, has disappeared as a result of the wandering life of the minstrels, and also because of the purely empirical character of their skill. Even in our own day many players in the remoter parts of Europe cannot read music, still less copy it; they pass on by ear traditional pieces which they play from memory.

But there is another, more general, explanation for the scarcity of instrumental music in the manuscripts. A very large proportion of the music that we take to be vocal, because it is provided with words, was in fact the common property of singers and of instrumentalists. The distinction between vocal and instrumental music, which was to become more and more precise during the fifteenth and sixteenth centuries, owing above all to the special development of music for organ and lute, was not yet clearly drawn in the twelfth and thirteenth. Even when it had sacred or secular words the melody was not connected in the minds of its composers or interpreters with the voice any more than with this or that instrument. It existed, so to speak, in itself, in an absolute sense unconcerned with the contingencies of performance. It may be that one method of execution was preferred to another— for example, noisy instruments were thought undesirable in church —but in this matter public taste and demand were still in process of formation. One thing is certain: the discrimination of timbres, with all the evocative associations with which we surround them today, was still only very rudimentary before the fifteenth century. This faculty was to be slow in awakening. As late as the eighteenth century Handel was to write trio sonatas that could be played by two oboes, two flutes, or two violins indifferently, and Couperin was to offer similar alternatives. Even today do we not tolerate all sorts of arrangements of masterpieces which distress only the purists?

INSTRUMENTS IN THE *LAIS* AND ROMANCES

Many literary texts, especially French—since France led the way in music during the period we are studying—are available to prove to us that most kinds of music were susceptible of instrumental interpretation. Some of these kinds were particularly cultivated by the minstrels. Thus the *lais*, of many of which both music and words have survived,[1] were played on the most varied instruments. Wace, the Anglo-Norman trouvère who wrote his *Brut* for Queen Eleanor of England in 1155, describes a concert in which could be heard '*lais* played on viols, harps, rotes, bagpipes, panpipes,[2] bells and shawms'.[3]

> Lais de vieles, bones notes,
> Lais de harpes, lais de rotes,
> Lais de corons, lais de fretels,
> Lais de timbres, de calamels . . . .

In another Arthurian romance, written in Catalonia in the Provençal language, the palace jongleurs play on their viols not only *lais* but also *descorts*, *dansas*, and *chansons de geste*.[4] Innumerable verse chronicles might be drawn on to lengthen the list of similar references. They show a constant interchange of the terms 'to sing' and 'to play the viol'.[5] Similarly *vieler* or *harper* and *faire lais* may be synonymous.[6]

People were certainly delighted to hear the viol or harp play a favourite tune but they also enjoyed hearing them add their sounds to a human voice. A girl or a student sings, while a jongleur accompanies on a bowed vielle.[7] Alone in her chamber, Queen Yseut softly sings a love-song, attuning her voice to the harp whose strings she

[1] Cf. vol. II, pp. 247–50.   [2] On *fretels*, see p. 479.

[3] Ed. by Leroux de Lincy (Rouen, 1838), ii, p. 112.

[4] *Jaufré* (c. 1226), ed. by Cl. Brunel (Paris, 1943), lines 9812 ff.

[5] For instance in *Durmart le Gallois* (ed. Stengel, Stuttgart, 1873, line 370) and in *Roman de la Poire* by Messire Thibaut (ed. Stehlich, Halle, 1881, lines 1130 ff.).

[6] Continuation of *Perceval* by Gerbert de Montreuil, ed. Potvin., iii (Mons, 1866), line 10,669; *Durmart le Gallois*, lines 3225 ff.

[7] *Guillaume de Dole* by Jean Renart (c. 1200), ed. Servois (Paris, 1893), lines 1834 ff.; cf. lines 2216 ff.

plucks.[1] In *Galeran* (*c*. 1200) Fresne accompanies herself on a harp
with silver strings and ivory pegs.[2] To handle a viol while singing is a
laudable feat in which certain heroes excelled.[3] Or sometimes they are
content to play on the viol the refrains of their songs, as a jongleur-
magician does in one of the tales of the Round Table, thus making
prisoners of many of his listeners.[4] Minstrels who can match their
voices with the sounds of the flute they play themselves are admired.[5]
We hear of trios in which a voice joins, for instance, with harp and
buisine (primitive trombone).[6]

DANCE FORMS

Fairly closely related to the *lai* in musical structure is a form which
probably originated in Provence towards the end of the twelfth century under the name of *stampida* or *estampida*, and spread through
France very quickly as the *estampie*. The *estampie* was at first vocal,
probably a dancing-song; but in the course of the thirteenth century it
was more and more often performed instrumentally. Johannes de
Grocheo, who lived in Paris at the end of the century, looked upon
it as a dance and described it among the three forms 'commonly
played before rich people at feasts and games'.[7] The name of *stantipes*
given it by Grocheo is the result of his efforts to find a Latin equivalent for *estampie*. (The etymologies proposed by Moser[8] and Sachs[9]
seem to be needlessly complex and to ignore the question of dates.)
Others who followed Grocheo devised other translations: *estampeta*
(Robert de Handlo, 1326), *stampania sive stampetum* (Anonymous of
Breslau, early fifteenth century).[10] These efforts on the part of the
theorists would only have complicated the question and concealed
the identity of *estampie* and *stantipes* if we did not fortunately possess
a series of dances entitled *estampies royales*,[11] the form of which corresponds more or less to the description given by Johannes de Grocheo.

These pieces are composed of a series of *puncta*, each of which is

---

[1] *Roman de Tristan* by Thomas, ed. J. Bédier (Paris, 1902), lines 843 ff.

[2] Ch. V. Langlois, *La vie en France au moyen âge*, i (Paris, 1924), p. 15.

[3] *Roman de la Violette* (*c*. 1228), ed. D. Labaree Buffum (Paris, 1928), lines 1400 ff.

[4] *Claris et Laris*, ed. J. Alton (Stuttgart, 1884), lines 9940–4.

[5] *Vie de saint Panuce*, ed. A. T. Baker. *Romania*, xxxviii (1909), lines 19–20.

[6] Richard de Fournival, *Li bestiaires*, ed. Hippeau (Paris, 1860), p. 16.

[7] See the text and German translation by Johannes Wolf in *Sammelbände der internationalen Musikgesellschaft*, i (1899–1900), p. 97, or Ernst Rohloff's revised text, *Der
Musiktraktat des Johannes de Grocheo* (Leipzig, 1943), p. 52. Cf. p. 501, n.1.

[8] *Zeitschrift für Musikwissenschaft*, ii (1920), pp. 194 ff.

[9] *Eine Weltgeschichte des Tanzes* (Berlin, 1931), p. 193.

[10] *Archiv für Musikwissenschaft*, i (1919), p. 336.

[11] *Estampies et danses royales* (Paris, 1907), published with facsimiles and transcriptions
by Pierre Aubry, from Bibl. nat., fr. 844, fos. 5 and 103ᵛ–104ᵛ.

divided up into two slightly unequal portions. These begin similarly, but the first part ends with an 'open' cadential formula (*apertum*), while the second ends on the final of the mode and, according to Grocheo, is commonly called *clausum*. The *puncta* of each dance all have in common this refrain with its double ending. According to Grocheo (though he ignores exceptions to the rule, which we sometimes meet) there are three or four *puncta* (he uses the masculine singular and neuter plural forms) in the *ductia*, six or seven in the *estampie*. As a matter of fact the fourth of the seven *estampies royales* in the collection referred to above is divided into seven *puncta*; and this manuscript is nearly contemporary with Grocheo. Here are the first *punctus* and the opening of the fifth:

Ex. 173

The clearly measured notation of these *estampies* and *danses royales* enables us to establish the fact that ternary rhythm is absolutely predominant, but that the old rhythmic modes of the *chanson* and primitive motet are becoming out of date and less rigid. It is quite possible that countries outside France were already dancing in duple time, which would explain why the documents of the fourteenth century in which English and Italian dances are preserved show many examples of duple rhythm.

We have evidence that dances of this kind could be polyphonic. In the first place many literary sources give us pictures of the performance of an *estampie* by a group of jongleurs, in one case by four *ménestrels de viole*. In scenes of a pastoral character the shepherd's pipe and tabor produce a rudimentary polyphony. But the musical documents tell us more, and tell it more precisely. Earliest in date are the three two-part dances in the Harley manuscript 978[1], already

---

[1] Facsimile in Wooldridge, *Early English Harmony*, i (1897), pls. 18–19; transcription

referred to in vol. II (pp. 337–9), simple in rhythm and regularly symmetrical. And then there is in an Oxford manuscript[1] a monophonic dance in which suddenly, towards the end, three-part writing makes its appearance (see vol. II, Ex. 182). The three-part passage may be a suggestion, a sort of pattern, showing how it would be possible and desirable to harmonize all the thematic repetitions in the course of the piece.

THE INSTRUMENTAL MOTET

In a manuscript which can be dated very shortly after 1300[2] are found together five three-part variations on the theme 'In saeculum', from the Verse 'Confitemini' of the Easter Gradual. They have no words. One of them is specifically entitled 'In saeculum viellatoris'. It has been assumed from this that the piece was played by three viols, and that it is the oldest known instrumental composition. That does not necessary follow, for it may simply be that the piece was written by a professional vielle-player. Another of the five variations is called 'In saeculum d'Amiens'. This makes the collection international if it is true that the first 'In saeculum' is by a Spaniard.[3] Be that as it may, it is legitimate to assume that these compositions, in common with many other polyphonic compositions which have no words, at least passed through a phase when they were played simply by instruments.

This last hypothesis is valid for certain groups of works which, for want of a better name, have up to now been called *clausulae* or *melismata*, or occasionally in the manuscripts by some ambiguous name such as *neuma*.[4] The *clausulae* of the school of Pérotin perhaps represent an intermediate stage between the liturgical organum and the popular motet, from which instrumentalists drew material for their repertory.[5] As for the 'St. Victor' melismata, so called from the manuscript in which they are found,[6] it is possible that we ought

by Wolf, 'Die Tänze des Mittelalters', *Archiv für Musikwissenschaft*, i (1918), pp. 19–20. Recorded in *The History of Music in Sound* (H.M.V.), ii.

[1] Bodl. Douce 139, fo. 5ᵛ; facsimiles in Wooldridge, op. cit., pl. 24, and J. F. R. and C. Stainer, *Early Bodleian Music*, i, pl. 7; transcriptions by Wolf, op. cit., p. 22, and J. Handschin, *Zeitschrift für Musikwissenschaft*, xii (1929), p. 13. See also Davison and Apel, *Historical Anthology of Music*, i, no. 40c.

[2] Bamberg Ed. IV, 6, ed. P. Aubry, *Cent motets du XIIIᵉ siècle* (Paris, 1907), nos. 104–8; cf. Montpellier manuscript, nos. 2–3.

[3] Coussemaker, *Scriptorum*, i, p. 350a; cf. Y. Rokseth, *Polyphonies du XIIIᵉ siècle*, iv (Paris, 1939), p. 55 and note 4.

[4] No. 102 of the Bamberg MS.; the same could be said of no. 103.

[5] Seventeen specimens may be found in H. Husmann, *Die 3- und 4-stimmigen Notre-Dame-Organa* (Leipzig, 1940), pp. 133–49. See also vol. II, p. 349.

[6] See vol. II, p. 349 and pl. VI; facsimiles in Gennrich, *Sankt Viktor Clausulae und ihre Motetten* (Darmstadt, 1953).

to consider them as pre-existing secular motets from which the words had been discarded in order that the music might be used in church:[1] thus transformed into absolute music, they were available as additions to the instrumental repertory.

The two-, three-, and four-part motets of the thirteenth century, sacred as well as secular, must often have been performed by instruments of different kinds or by a mixture of voices and instruments. They were regarded as a 'subtle' kind of music and were reserved for the connoisseurs, while the *rondeaux* (*rotundelli*) were considered better suited for popular merrymakings.[2] The part on which the motet was built, the tenor, could often have been entrusted to an instrument since, having no words, it was of no interest to the listeners, who were mainly preoccupied with the subject of the poems. Towards the end of the thirteenth century the tenor was often a dance-tune and was probably played on a viol. Thus we find in one collection of motets three which are marked *Chose Tassin* and one *Chose Loyset*,[3] which are certainly *puncta* of *estampies* and call for performance on an instrument.

The conductus, also, could have allowed the participation of instruments in some cases; the possible instrumental performance of the long textless vocalizations (*caudae*) has already been discussed in vol. II (see p. 334). The conducti with preludes, like the motets with preludes,[4] paved the way for the motets of the *ars nova*, some of which have wordless parts.

USES OF THE VIOL

In choosing the instrument on which any particular piece was to be played, it was necessary to exercise discernment and take into account the nature of the work. A French theorist writing in 1274[5] warns us not to imitate those ignorant singers who force their voices and try to perform passages difficult of intonation, which would be better rendered by an instrument, especially a viol. A warning such as this shows that the field of instrumental execution was wider in certain respects than that of the voice. This rather upsets the ideas hitherto held concerning the relationship between singing and playing. It appears from the works of the theorists that they gave pride of place to vocal music; in their eyes instrumental music was only a second

[1] Cf. Y. Rokseth, op. cit. iv, p. 70, note 3.
[2] Joh. de Grocheo, ed. Wolf, p. 106; ed. Rohloff, p. 56.
[3] Fos. 299, 333ᵛ, 336ᵛ, and 339ᵛ of the Montpellier MS.: cf. *Polyphonies du XIIIᵉ siècle*, nos. 270, 292, 294, and 297.
[4] Montpellier MS., nos. 300, 322, 340, 343.
[5] Elias Salomonis, in Gerbert, *Scriptores*, iii, p. 61*b*.

best, though it had the advantage in its variety of resources and in ensuring accuracy of intonation. For this reason singers were advised to practise with the help of instruments of fixed pitch: thus they could find their way through the labyrinth of modes and mutations, and solve the mysteries of *musica falsa*. The author of the *Summa musicae* extols the monochord and the *symphonia quae dicitur organistrum*, that is to say the hurdy-gurdy or *vielle à roue*, for this purpose. He also recommends the assistance of the organ:

> colat [cantor] instrumenta sonora,
> clavibus et tactis jungat concorditer ora[1]

(Let the singer use sonorous instruments: let him join his song in concord with the keys and notes.)

The viol was esteemed not only because of its ability to distinguish all the various kinds of music (*in viella tamen omnes formae musicales subtilius discernuntur*) but also because of its universality; for, said Grocheo, when he tried to classify musical forms according to the instruments best fitted to each,[2] there was no composition of any kind which could not be performed by a good viol-player.

THE ORGAN

The reputation of instrumental music was enhanced above all by the skill which some clerks displayed on the organ, enabling them to perform passages too rapid for the human voice. Their performances were looked upon as remarkable, almost miraculous.[3] When the Princess Isabella, sister of Henry III of England and affianced bride of the Emperor Frederick II, entered Cologne in 1235, she was welcomed by boats coming down the Rhine to meet her, bearing clerks playing on tuneful organs. The hearers were astounded by these novel melodies.[4] May it not have been the same strange charm which plunged Blessed Angela of Foligno (d. 1309) into ecstasy, when one day her soul was raised to the Uncreated Light while the organ was playing the *Sanctus* in the Church of St. Francis?[5]

This leads us to the question of the use of organs and other instruments in churches. Unimpeachable sources tell us that they sometimes gained admittance; but rather to add splendour to some special ceremony than to accompany regular liturgical services.[6] Thus when

---

[1] Gerbert, iii, pp. 216*b* and 217.
[2] Joh. de Grocheo, ed. Wolf, pp. 96–97; ed. Rohloff, p. 52.
[3] Arnulphus de S. Gilleno, in Gerbert, iii, p. 316*b*.
[4] Matthew Paris, *Chronica majora*, ed. Luard, iii (London, 1876), p. 322.
[5] *Théologie de la croix* (Cologne, 1696), p. 328.
[6] See also E. A. Bowles, 'Were Musical Instruments used in the Liturgical Service during the Middle Ages?', *Galpin Society Journal*, x (1956), p. 40; and further, ibid. xi, p. 85, xii, p. 89.—*Ed.*

Lambert, Abbot of Saint-Bertin, near Cambrai, was staying in England in 1118 and stopped at Winchester on the feast of the Epiphany, he was received with great pomp, *cantantibus organis et consonae musicae instrumentis*[1] ('with the sound of the organ and instruments of concordant music'). On the day of the patronal festival at the abbey of Saint-Denis, near Paris, minstrels were allowed in to make music. It also became the custom to let them play at the beginning of monastic meals.[2]

Yet it would be unwise to say that already at this time the organ enjoyed the privilege of being considered the ideal companion of sacred song. Undoubtedly there are plenty of descriptions of the feasts of the church in which tribute is paid to the *organa*. But the term is applied to the whole consort of musical instruments, and, furthermore, *organum* is often used as a name for polyphonic singing in general. As a rough rule, unless there is definite indication to the contrary, we may be fairly safe in referring the plural *organa* to the instrument, the single *organum* to vocal harmony. Nevertheless, it does seem that the great cathedrals one by one adopted the organ. In the second half of the thirteenth century it is accepted as part of the normal furniture of churches, so that we find writers including it with censers and candlesticks as an accessory of worship;[3] ecclesiastical customaries mention its presence;[4] and generous benefactors leave money to buy an organ for their church, as at Barcelona in 1259.[5] Organ-builders established themselves in the most remote regions of Europe, for example in Norway and Iceland.[6]

We can only guess at the pieces played on the organ, whether as preludes to the singing, or at the *Sanctus*, the point at which Guillaume Durand, bishop of Mende (d. 1296), tells us it was heard. (He was a contemporary of Angela of Foligno, whom we have just mentioned.) Yet it is not too much to suppose that it imitated in its own way, by adding ornaments or embroideries, music of vocal origin. It was these ornaments, which had to be played rapidly, that were the admiration of all who heard. The long notes of the chant were broken up into a number of short ones, and numerous *fioriture* were written around the essential notes. The hearer was spellbound by this torrent of notes, in which the organist displayed his skill. These are

[1] *Monumenta Germaniae Historica, SS.*, xv, pars ii (Hanover, 1888), p. 952.
[2] Archives nationales, in Paris, LL 1240, 61ᵛ, 122ᵛ, and 282.
[3] *Blacandin ou l'Orgueilleuse d'amour*, ed. Michelant (Paris, 1867), lines 3894 ff.
[4] Ulysse Chevalier, *Ordinaire et coutumier de l'église cathédrale de Bayeux* (Paris, 1902), p. 302.
[5] H. Anglès, *La Música a Catalunya fins al segle XIII* (Barcelona, 1935), p. 84.
[6] Cf. *Revue de musicologie*, xi (1930), p. 195.

the very same procedures which we still find firmly established when we come to the earliest surviving species of keyboard music, those of the fourteenth century.

INSTRUMENTS IN WAR AND SOCIAL LIFE

The foregoing remarks do not apply to the group of instruments known as *hauts* (meaning loud, not 'high' in the modern sense): trumpets, bugles (*buccinae*), and horns of every kind. Specifically musical information about them is much rarer than about the *bas* or soft instruments. Yet these open-air instruments played a considerable part in social life. In the morning, from the top of the tower, they aroused the citizens; later they summoned them to meals, for which the phrase was *corner à l'eau*—a 'call to water' (for washing).[1] Trumpets, large and small, horns, clarions, *buccinae*, and nakers (kettle-drums) announced the opening of a tournament. In war they made a hullabaloo in order to cause panic in the enemy's camp. Historians of the Crusades describe the mighty noise made by nakers and Saracen horns at the moment of assault. Richard Cœur de Lion also used this means of stirring up his troops and frightening the enemy. The chronicler would have us believe that a fanfare helped Richard to become master of Acre in 1191.[2] And as they sounded to battle, so they sounded the retreat. Horn calls were an essential accompaniment to hunting.[3] Kings and queens seldom entered town without an escort of great bands of minstrels. Every procession was accompanied by the sound of trumpets, *buisines*,[4] and nakers. But these went no farther than the gates of the palace; on entering, one saw the players on viols, harps, and flutes seated in the embrasures of the windows, ready to strike up. But frequently all types of instruments joined together for the banquet, playing near the tables or in the minstrels' gallery.

Clear evidence of the importance of minstrels in the houses of the great is provided by a source as abundant as literature and often more accurate: the mural paintings, the miniatures, and (later) the tapestries and easel-paintings, which faithfully reflect the day-by-day life. These sources of information become particularly rich in the fourteenth century, though from the thirteenth onwards there are illuminated

[1] *Doon de Nanteuil*, line 122; *Roman de l'Escoufle* by Jean Renart, lines 686 ff. These two poems go back to *c.* 1200.
[2] Chronicle of Raoul de Diceto, in *Recueil des historiens de la Gaule et de la France*, xvii, p. 640E. Cf. p. 503D concerning Henry II, in his life by Benedict of Peterborough.
[3] Guillaume de Dole, lines 416 ff.
[4] See p. 476.

manuscripts showing players of instruments in characteristic attitudes. Conspicuous among these is the Escorial manuscript of Alfonso the Learned, the *Cantigas de Santa Maria*,[1] in which are portrayed forty musicians busily playing different instruments: wind, strings (plucked or bowed), and percussion. These detailed figures[2] make it practically certain that the King's *Cantigas* called for instrumental participation, or at least instrumental ritornelli: and this conclusion may be extended to cover certain other sacred pieces of the same period.

FOURTEENTH-CENTURY DANCES

The forms of instrumental music cultivated in the thirteenth century persisted in the fourteenth. But some developed, while others deteriorated. The verse chronicle, chanted to the accompaniment of viol or *organistrum*, was in decline: it was left for blind men to declaim at street corners. On the other hand, the instrumental *estampie* was elevated to the rank of prelude. If Boccaccio is to be believed, the élite of Italian society listened with delight to dances played on lute and viol.[3] The lute was also used to accompany songs.[4] On the last Day of the Decameron an *estampie* played on the viol by an expert musician, Minuccio, equally gifted as singer and player, serves as prelude to a *canzone*.[5] So highly esteemed was the playing of the viol, which the lute had not yet dethroned, that a king and his courtiers are struck dumb, are *sospesi ad ascoltare*, when Minuccio begins to sing to his viol. Women as well as men played on all these instruments, which were an ornament and pleasure of everyday life.

It is quite possible to get a concrete idea of the kind of music which the Italians of the trecento listened to. When they played polyphonic works on their instruments they had at their disposal the immense repertoire of the *ars nova*, *cacce*, madrigals, *ballate*, many of which have come down to us.[6] No songs of a more popular kind have been discovered so far, but there are a few dances recorded in the manuscripts only in the form of a single written part. It is probable that these tunes were accompanied by percussion instruments, little drums, tambourines and bells, for which no notation was needed.

A series of such dances has been preserved in a manuscript in the

[1] See vol. II, p. 261.

[2] Escorial j–b–2; reproduced in *Cantigas de Santa Maria de Don Alfonso el Sabio* (2 vols., Madrid, 1889). Another manuscript of the *Cantigas*, Escorial T–j–l, is even more lavishly illustrated with pictures of musicians.

[3] *Decameron*, Introduction. See also p. 35.

[4] Ibid., First Evening.

[5] Ibid., *novella* 7.

[6] See Chap. II.

British Museum (Add. 29987), fos. 56ᵛ–64ᵛ. Fifteen of these have refrains like the French *estampie*, but only the first eight have a development comparable with that of the *estampie* with its separate *puncta*. Next come four dances entitled *saltarello*, and one called *trotto* (significant names, implying leaps or very animated steps). Finally come two works entitled *Lamento di Tristano* and *la Manfredina*.[1] These are peculiar in form, for after three couplets with *ouvert* and *clos* endings follows a second part, the *rotta*, which was certainly played more quickly and is a variant, though a shortened variant, of the first part.

The *saltarelli* and *trotto* differ from the *estampie* not so much in the form of their strophes—which have *ouvert* and *clos* endings—as in their relative shortness and, doubtless, in tempo. Although the manuscript gives no indication whatever of speed, they were probably played fast and perhaps even furiously.[2] The rhythm of the *saltarelli* is sometimes reminiscent of the later gigue.

While the French dances of the thirteenth century are all in triple time with binary division of smaller note-values, this series of Italian dances has a great variety of rhythms. Sometimes the rhythms implied by the modern signatures $\frac{6}{8}$ and $\frac{4}{8}$ occur successively in the same piece, sometimes within the same section. Thematic elements are often grouped in longer periods which are represented by the signatures $\frac{3}{4}$, $\frac{2}{4}$ and $\frac{6}{8}$, or $\frac{12}{8}$:

Ex. 174

In short, we find in the British Museum dances the rhythmic richness and diversity of fourteenth-century Italian polyphony. On the other hand, the melodic lines seem slightly less free and supple than

[1] All these dances have been published by Joh. Wolf, 'Die Tänze des Mittelalters', *Archiv für Musikwissenschaft*, i (1918), pp. 24–42; single examples in Davison and Apel, *Historical Anthology of Music* (Cambridge, Mass., 1942), i, p. 63; Gleason, *Examples of Music before 1400* (New York, 1946), and Schering, *Geschichte der Musik in Beispielen* (Leipzig, 1931), pp. 20–21.
[2] Cf. Curt Sachs, *World History of the Dance* (London, 1938), pp. 293–7.

those of the French *estampies*. They over-use these mechanically repeated formulae of variation, these conventional and monotonous embroideries, and these frequent leaps of fifth and fourth, repeated tirelessly up or down the scale, which become positively tedious, as in the *Istampita Isabella* (fourth section, bars 20–23):

Ex. 175

This melodic material is rather like that used in the keyboard tablature of the Robertsbridge manuscript (British Museum, Add. 28550, fo. 43ᵛ), a collection examined later on pp. 420–3:

Ex. 176

It was formerly thought that the fifteen dances in British Museum, Add. 29987,[1] were intended for the organ. It would be equally hazardous now to adopt the opposite view that they were never played on one of those *organetti* which the Italian painters of the time are so fond of depicting.[2] Some of them would sound well on the viol, and we need not rule out bagpipes and recorders. The minstrels needed only to consider how to reconcile the technique of the instrument with the style of the piece. They would also certainly choose instruments suitable for the space the sound was to fill; open-air dances were not played on chamber instruments.

INSTRUMENTS IN ENSEMBLE MUSIC

Musicians could easily change from one instrument to another, for most of them were at home on several. What was said of Landini, that he excelled on them all, could be said of many another. Not only was Landini extraordinarily skilful on the keyboard, with a keen sense of time, but although blind he had studied various stringed instruments from his childhood. He also played wind instruments and even invented an instrument. When taking part in a concert among a select group he would be at one moment a virtuoso soloist, the next he would play sweet preludes for songs or perform a love-song on his

---

[1] A. Hughes-Hughes, *Catalogue of Manuscript Music in the British Museum*, iii (London, 1909), p. 77.

[2] See, for instance, figures 8–16 reproduced by H. Hickmann, *Das Portativ* (Kassel, 1936).

portable *organetto*.[1] This celebrated blind organist, of whose secular activities we know more than we do of his work at San Lorenzo at Florence, thus became the pattern for the versatile musicians described by Italian literature round about 1400, and still numerous in the fifteenth century. It was perhaps of 'Francesco degli organi', as he was called, that Prodenzani was thinking when he portrayed in his sonnets that enchanting character, 'Il Sollazzo', who sang and played on all kinds of instruments.[2]

In France all the instruments known in the thirteenth century, now joined more and more frequently by the lute, took part in the performance of motets, ballades, *rondeaux* and *virelais*. Sometimes they even supported the singing at Mass. But their special domain seems to have been the tenor and countertenor of the isorhythmic motets. In these lower parts of the motets the extreme difficulty of the melodic line, with its curves too long for normal human breath and the awkward intonation of its intervals, seems to defy performance by voices. Everything seems to point to the use of instruments. It is possible also that the wordless sections in some motets imply instrumental performance. As has been mentioned earlier (vol. II, pp. 327–8), textless passages suggesting or strongly implying instrumental interludes are a familiar feature of the thirteenth-century *ars antiqua*. And at the opening of the fourteenth century we find some *ars nova* motets with textless passages suggesting the same method of performance. For example, the motet 'Impudenter / Virtutibus', attributed to Philippe de Vitry,[3] which ends with a long coda in hocket style, only makes use of an already established practice.

The process in the *ballades* and *rondeaux* of Machaut is not quite so clear. In some of his four-part *ballades* only one voice has words, and the same is the case with many of his three-part *ballades*. In the three-part *rondeaux* the texted part is found either above two slow wordless parts or between a quickly moving *triplum* and a slow tenor. Now the question arises whether these wordless parts are quite certainly instrumental and exclude the possibility of voices either supplying words known to the singers or vocalizing. It is not always possible to answer this question with absolute certainty. Neither the melodic

---

[1] According to the *Paradiso degli Alberti* of Giovanni da Prato (1389) ed. Wesselofsky (Bologna, 1867). See also the evidence of Villani referred to on p. 78.

[2] See p. 36. These sonnets are commented on, as regards their musical significance, by Schering, *Studien zur Musikgeschichte der Frührenaissance* (Leipzig, 1914), pp. 102–23.

[3] See the transcriptions of this piece by A. Gastoué, *Le Manuscrit d'Apt* (*Publications de la Société française de musicologie*, x) (Paris, 1936), no. 16, and Schrade, *Polyphonic Music of the Fourteenth Century*, i (Monaco, 1956), p. 91.

contour, nor the grace of the melismata, neither the complex rhythms nor the wide leaps, are the sole property of either vocal or instrumental music. Things change only with Machaut's immediate heirs, whose *ballades* written at the close of the century often look like vocal solos accompanied by instruments. However, in the course of the fifteenth century the taste for diversity of combinations did not develop nor did individual initiative tend to produce variety.

We have to be content with suppositions rather than exact knowledge about many of the practical details of fourteenth-century performance, and with that indecision which Machaut himself exhibits so blandly. Writing to Péronne of Armentières, to send her one of his *ballades*, he suggests that it can be played on the organ or the bagpipes or other instruments, and evidently thinks that sufficient indication of the method of performance. The interpretation of fourteenth-century polyphony should therefore be approached with discretion and reserve and an avoidance of absolute pronouncements. Attempted systematization in this sphere has so far produced no more than insubstantial hypotheses. It is going too far to assert that all textless examples, such as No. 80 (fo. 64ᵛ) of the Ivrea manuscript, were intended exclusively for instruments. But at least we may be sure that musicians were expert at choosing in each case the method of performance which fitted best with their own ideas and with the means at their disposal.

THE EARLIEST KEYBOARD MUSIC

Yet there are some sources, admittedly very rare, where certain indications show that the music is instrumental, and almost certainly for keyboard. The *Summa musicae*[1] informs us that other instruments had their own methods of notation, according to their several needs; instruments with fixed sounds used a different system from those which were tuned by the player. Such a system is called tablature. But it is only the few surviving fragments of keyboard music which are entitled to that name; in these the different parts are written one above the other so that they may be more easily read by a single player, instead of being separated as in the case of works for different performers.

From the fourteenth century onwards we find two kinds of keyboard notation. One appears for the first time in an English manuscript, the Robertsbridge fragment mentioned below. Here the top

---

[1] Attributed, without foundation, to the Norman Johannes de Muris (Gerbert, *Scriptores*, iii, p. 214ᵃ).

part is written on a staff, the notes of the other parts being represented by one or more series of letters. This kind of notation was soon abandoned throughout the West, except in Germany, where it survived for centuries. The other method uses a brace of staves and the usual signs of vocal music, adding only the vertical lines which are the ancestors of our modern bar-lines. This notation is found in an Italian manuscript of the end of the fourteenth century (Paris, Bibl. Nat. n.a. fr. 6771), the so-called Codex Reina,[1] containing two fragments of instrumental music. The French, English, and Italian tablatures of the sixteenth century are no more than an improvement on it. Willi Apel[2] thinks there are indications that the English tablature discussed in the next paragraph belongs to the notational system of the Italian *ars nova*, but this assertion seems inconsistent with the fact that at the end of the century the Italians had an entirely different system of writing for the keyboard.

The Robertsbridge pieces for organ or *clavicembalum*[3] in the British Museum are usually dated between 1325 and 1350;[4] they are found on two folios which remain from a manuscript which may have been much larger, bound up with an old register of the Abbey of Robertsbridge in Sussex, whence the name by which it is sometimes known: the 'Robertsbridge Fragment'. Of the six pieces it contains, the beginning of the first and the end of the last are missing. The complete items are two compositions divided into *puncta* like the *estampies*, one into four, the other into five,[5] and two arrangements of *Fauvel* motets.[6]

The chief interest lies in the lively and rapid upper melody, which is written out in full on a stave of five lines. Below these notes, but also on the staff, are the letters *a* to *g*, which give the course of the

---

[1] Cf. *supra*, pp. 46 and 143.

[2] *The Notation of Polyphonic Music, 900–1600* (Cambridge, Mass., 1942), p. 384, and in *Journal for Renaissance and Baroque Music*, i (1946), p. 244.

[3] The earliest mention of the *clavicembalum* is in 1397, when the Paduan lawyer Lambertacci speaks of an instrument 'quod nominat clavicembalum' invented by Magister Armanus de Alemania; see A. Pirro, 'Pour l'histoire de musique', *Acta musicologica*, iii (1931), p. 51. The *clavicembalum* is also mentioned in Eberhard Cersne's *Der Minne Regel* (1404). But it had ancestors, among which were the French and Italian *manicorde*, and the *eschaquier d'Engleterre* referred to by Machaut. The Duke of Burgundy had one in his chapel in 1385. See also p. 483.

[4] Add. 28550, fos. 43–44; facsimile in Wooldridge, *Early English Harmony*, i, pls. xlii–xlv.

[5] Both transcribed by J. Handschin in *Zeitschrift für Musikwissenschaft*, xii (1929), pp. 14–18. There is a partial transcription of the second *estampie* in Davison and Apel, *Historical Anthology of Music*, i, No. 58.

[6] Transcribed by Johannes Wolf, one in *Kirchenmusikalisches Jahrbuch*, xiv (1899), pp. 19–28; the other in *Geschichte der Mensural-Notation*, iii (Leipzig, 1904), no. 78. Some corrections are needed in these transcriptions.

PLATE IV

(*a*) THE EARLIEST ENGLISH KEYBOARD MUSIC

Part of a page of the Robertsbridge Codex showing the fragment reproduced as Ex. 178
(British Museum MS. Add. 28550, fo. 43)

(*b*) THE EARLIEST ENGLISH PRINTED MUSIC

Opening of the bass part of Cornysh's 'Pleasure yt ys' from *XX Songes* (1530) (see p. 348)

accompaniment but do not denote the register of the sounds. There is
thus some doubt as to the octave in which some of the alphabetical
notes are meant to be sounded. There is also uncertainty as to the
meaning of certain white or 'void' notes placed after certain important, long-held notes: Handschin transcribes them as notes
decorated with mordents, while Wolf regards them as mere repetitions of the principal note. The interpretation as mordents seems
questionable, and we may be on safer ground if we take them as
prolongations intended to make it clear from the start whether the
mode is perfect or imperfect.

The first of the two keyboard *estampies* differs in structure from
the second. Each of the four *puncta* begins with a distinctive motive:
but at a point marked by the word 'return' there is an episode common to all the strophes and including the *overt* and *clos* of the refrain.
In the second fantasia the repeat does not occur at a fixed place in the
first *punctus*, but at a variable point which has to be ascertained by
examination.

Here then is an instrumental style in which the writing presents
special features. In the vocal polyphony of the time we do not find
these consecutive fifths and octaves, the effect of which is far from
unpleasing:

Ex. 177

This writing has a grace and transparency which must have been
well brought out by the delicate sounds of the portable organ, or the
penetrating accents of the clavichord. The composer appears to be at
home with all the chromatic accidentals which, without producing
real modulation, add a sheen to such passages as this:

Ex. 178

This last fragment comes from the incomplete piece at the top of fo. 43 (see pl. IV (a)). Note the E flat, which is represented by a D sharp.

Another specifically instrumental feature is the liberty the composer allows himself of adding, from time to time, a third part to the normal two, so as to fill out the more prolonged chords. This procedure is specially noticeable in the motet transcriptions.

These transcriptions help us to fix the date of the fragments, because the vocal originals are two pieces added in France about 1314 to the *Roman de Fauvel*.[1] If the English tablature actually dates from about 1330 this confirms the fact already noted, and well established by other evidence, that the artistic relations between England and France were most active, and that new compositions quickly crossed the Channel. The date is, however, purely hypothetical, for there is no reason to suppose that the music of *Fauvel* did not retain its popularity for several decades.

All the long notes of the upper voice and some of those of the middle voice in the two vocal motets are converted into very quick figuration in the instrumental arrangement. Alternating notes and incessant ornamentation hold the listener's attention; wide leaps are filled in by fragments of scale, while the more conjunct intervals are decorated with *fioriture*. It is all rudimentary variation of a rather mechanical character, which scarcely shows anything more than the adapter's power of synthetic recollection and the agility of his fingers. We can best understand his method by comparing the end of the motet 'Tribum / Quoniam / Merito' in the *Fauvel* original[2] with the organ transcription (both shown here in the same key):

Ex. 179

Keyboard version

- us   Quam nil ha - bu - is - se se - cun - dum.

[1] See p. 5.   [2] Paris, Bibl. Nat. fr. 146, fos. 41ᵛ–42.

(Note that the F♯ in the penultimate bar of the keyboard version actually appears in the part noted by letters.)

There is already more ease and rhythmic suppleness in the two previously mentioned pieces[1] copied into the Reina manuscript at the end of the fourteenth or the beginning of the fifteenth century. The contents of this manuscript are partly Italian, partly French, but it seems to have been an Italian hand that wrote out these pieces. The first is a transcription of Francesco Landini's *ballata* 'Questa fanciulla'; the second is unfinished. Strokes regularly joining the two staves of six lines each seem to prove that we have here music for the keyboard. In 'Questa fanciulla' the arranger has ornamented the notes of the upper part. Moreover, being no doubt an Italian, he has substituted the duple rhythm preferred by the Italians for the triple beloved by the French. The change shows his skill in thinking out the whole composition anew. The opening of the piece has been published by Johannes Wolf;[2] and here we give the end, printing below it Landini's original (taken from Paris, Bibl. Nat. ital. 568):

Ex. 180

Two other *ballate* by Landini, 'Non arà mà pieta' and 'Che pena questa', similarly transformed, occur in a manuscript found at

---

[1] Bibl. Nat. nouv. acq. fr. 6771, fo. 85 ʳ⁻ᵛ. Cf. p. 420.
[2] *Handbuch der Notationskunde*, ii (Leipzig, 1913), pp. 253–5.

Ferrara and now in the Biblioteca Comunale at Faenza.[1] This codex, in the same type of notation as the Reina manuscript, is a particularly important document for the early history of keyboard music, containing transcriptions of no fewer than twenty-nine pieces, some French, some Italian, including two by Machaut, the popular 'De ce que foul pense' of Pierre des Molins, five by Jacopo da Bologna, three by Bartolino da Padova, and the two already mentioned by Landini. The first phrase of 'Non arà mà pietà' has already been quoted in original and transcribed forms on p. 80 (see Exs. 37 and 38). It will be seen that the three-part vocal original is reduced to two parts, of which only the upper one has its melody ornamented in accordance with the special technique of instrumental writing. But the piece seems more old-fashioned in style than 'Questa fanciulla': its melodic line is not so flowing, and it retains the alternating fourths so prominent in the Robertsbridge fragment. Ex. 177, above, may be compared with bars 4–8 of Ex. 38.

The Faenza manuscript also provides exceptions—a *Kyrie* and two *Kyrie-Gloria* pairs, all based on Mass IV ('Cunctipotens genitor Deus')[2]—to the rule that all the fourteenth-century fragments which can be assigned to the organ or other keyboard instrument consist of secular music. Yet it is certain that the organ had been used in churches for centuries. In particular, the characteristic custom of using the organ alternately with the voices during Mass and for verses of the *Te Deum* and *Magnificat* had already begun. In the convent of the Canonesses at Essen we read that, at an Easter ceremony, the master of ceremonies directs that the *Te Deum* shall be divided between the nuns and the clerks, unless 'what has not heretofore been done' in that conventual church be preferred, namely that the organ, canonesses, and clerks each take a verse in turn: 'quod tamen hic non vidi, organa incipient et cantabunt primum versum, conventus secundum, clerici tertium, et sic de aliis'[3] ('a fashion which I have not seen here, the organ will begin and play the first verse, the convent will sing the second and the clerks the third, and so on with the rest').

In the absence of musical evidence, we must suppose that for a long

---

[1] Faenza, Bib. Com. 117 (sometimes referred to as the Bonadies Codex). See Dragan Plamenac, 'Keyboard Music of the 14th Century in Codex Faenza 117', *Journal of the American Musicological Society*, iv (1951), pp. 180–201, and 'New Light on Codex Faenza 117', *Utrecht Kongressbericht* (Amsterdam, 1953), p. 310.

[2] Facsimile and transcription of the separate *Kyrie* in Plamenac, 'Keyboard Music', p. 192; transcription of one of the other Kyries in Plamenac, 'New Light', p. 320. In both the plainsong is played by the left hand in long notes while the right hand has a florid part.

[3] K. Young, *The Drama of the Mediaeval Church*, i (Oxford, 1933), pp. 534 ff.

time 'versets' such as these were improvised or alternatively that the organist used copies intended for vocal performance, adapting them for his instrument, according to already well-established conventions. We know from other sources that some church libraries possessed choir-books for the use of their organists.[1] These choir-books have all disappeared, just as the customaries have disappeared, worn out by constant usage, while the splendid manuscripts copied for important persons and carefully preserved in their libraries are still in existence.

FIFTEENTH-CENTURY PRACTICES

In the first half of the fifteenth century the custom of entrusting to instruments the slower voices of polyphonic works—tenor and contratenor—became even commoner in sacred and secular music alike. At the time of Dunstable and Dufay it seems to have been normal for all kinds of players and singers to collaborate; and this should be borne in mind in interpreting the music of the period.

This laxity, which tends to disappear, led composers to add directions, few and terse though they were to begin with. The introits[2] to some pieces are sometimes given specific indications, as for example the *Trumpetta introitus* attributed to Johannes Franchois.[3] We find the trumpet again in the tenor of a *Gloria* by Arnold de Lantins[4] and in the contratenor of a song by Pierre Fontaine.[5] A three-part piece from the lost Strasbourg manuscript, dating from the beginning of the fifteenth century, is entitled *Tuba gallicalis*:[6] its tenor and contratenor consist of motives based on the C major triad. A sacred song in the same manuscript, attributed to Henry of Freiburg, also uses fanfare motives, both for the voice and in the two accompanying parts.[7] On certain solemn occasions it may be that a trio of trombones replaced the singers; it was in this manner that the English prelates were received on their entry into the Council of Constance (1414–18): 'die

[1] Y. Rokseth, *La musique d'orgue au XVe siècle et au début du XVIe* (Paris, 1930), p. 173.   [2] Cf. p. 154.

[3] See pp. 156 and 235. Several of the preludes in the same manuscript are designated as *introitus*; cf. A. Pirro, 'Remarques sur l'exécution musicale de la fin du 14e au milieu du 15e siècle', *Report of the First Congress of the International Society for Musical Research* (Liège, 1930), p. 63.

[4] Oxford, Bodleian, Canonici misc. 213, fo. 64; ed. Ch. Van den Borren, *Polyphonia sacra* (London, 1932), p. 63.

[5] Ed. P. Aubry, *Sammelbände der internationalen Musikgesellschaft*, viii (1907), pp. 526–8. See also p. 234.

[6] Facsimile of Coussemaker's copy, in which alone it survives, in *Die Musik in Geschichte und Gegenwart*, ii (Kassel, 1952), col. 1757.

[7] Both pieces published by Ch. Van den Borren, *Bericht über den musikwissenschaftlichen Kongreß in Basel*, 1924 (Leipzig, 1925), pp. 92–100.

pusauner pusaunoten über einnander mit dreyen stymmen, als man sunst gewonlichen singet'[1] ('the trombonists tromboned together in three parts as one is otherwise accustomed to sing'). And combinations of singers and minstrels were to be found in the galleries of cathedrals.[2]

However, during the second half of the century a distinction between vocal and instrumental music began to be made. On the one hand the great development of imitative writing gave the different polyphonic voices parts of equal importance, which led to homogeneous, entirely vocal, performance: a method which before long came to be preferred, particularly in church, to performance by any combination of voices and instruments. On the other hand, the peculiar qualities of each instrument and the increasing number of specialized executants made for differentiation of styles. Organ and keyboard generally, and lute, each began to have its own literature. From this point onwards we shall be concerned in this chapter only with this instrumental music proper.

The organ is the only instrument for which we have a whole series of documents enabling us to follow the development of its literature from about 1430. By a strange chance practically all the fifteenth-century evidence comes from Germany, and the corresponding works of English,[3] French, Italian, and Spanish organists have disappeared. These countries have organ music in the sixteenth century for which there must have been a preparatory period, but up to now no trace has been found of the work of Abingdon, Crasbouel, or Squarcialupi, to mention three names only.

EARLY GERMAN ORGAN TABLATURES

We must therefore be content to study the collections and stray pieces of German organ music, of which the oldest seems to be that preserved at Breslau, dating from about 1425.[4] It contains interludes for the *Gloria* of the Mass. Organ versets for the Mass are also to be found in a Berlin manuscript of about 1430, in bad condition, which

---

[1] J. Handschin, *Schweizerische Musikzeitung*, lxxiv (1934), col. 459.

[2] Cf. *Revue de musicologie*, xiv (1933), pp. 206–8.

[3] Thurston Dart has printed and described an English 'Felix namque' of the early fifteenth century (in Oxford, Douce 381) in *Music & Letters*, xxxv (1954), p. 201.—*Ed.*

[4] All the fragments discovered at Breslau have been described by Fr. Feldmann, 'Mittelalterliche Musik und Musikpflege in Schlesien', *Deutsches Archiv für Landes- und Volksforschung*, ii (1937), pp. 431–6, and 'Ein Tabulaturfragment des Breslauer Dominikanerkloster aus der Zeit Paumanns', *Zeitschrift für Musikwissenschaft*, xv (1933), pp. 241–58. See Leo Schrade, 'The Organ in the Mass of the 15th century', *The Musical Quarterly*, xxviii (1942), pp. 329–36 and 467–87.

also contains an arrangement of a German song.[1] A Munich manuscript (before 1436) includes several liturgical fragments, among them
a *Magnificat* on the eighth tone.[2] Far more important than these
scraps is a tablature of 1448, copied by Adam Ileborgh, Rector of
Stendal, a little town in the Margravate of Brandenburg.[3]

Ileborgh's manuscript is a collection of preludes, some for manual
only, others for manual and pedal. There are fantasias with a range
of two octaves or more, unprecedented in their rhythmic freedom and
variety. The right hand is given the important part, and the bass
moves much more slowly, often consisting merely of long-held pairs
of notes. The earlier pieces are short and may be transposed into
various keys. The first prelude, for example, is headed: 'Sequitur
praeambulum in c et potest variari in d, f, g, a' ('Here follows a prelude in C: it can be played also in D, F, G, or A').The third prelude
can be played with pedals (if the instrument has these, still novel,
additions) or on the manual only: 'Praeambulum bonum pedale sive
manuale . . . Et nota quod omnia praeludia . . . possunt applicari
secundum varietatem ad omnes notas' ('A good prelude for pedal or
manual . . . and note that all the preludes can be transposed to any
pitch'). Here is the short second prelude, as transcribed by Apel:

Ex. 181

Praeambulum bonum super C manualiter

---

[1] Berlin, Staatsbibliothek, theol. lat. Quart. 290. Cf. L. Schrade, *Die handschriftliche
Überlieferung der ältesten Instrumentalmusik* (Lahr/Baden, 1931), pp. 87–91.

[2] Munich, Staatsbibliothek, cod. lat. 5963. Cf. Schrade, ibid., pp. 91–93.

[3] Now in the Curtis Institute of Music, Philadelphia. Cf. W. Apel, 'Die Tabulatur
des Adam Ileborgh', *Zeitschrift für Musikwissenschaft*, xvi (1934), p. 193. Facsimile
of the first two pages in Wolf, *Handbuch der Notationskunde*, ii, facing p. 10,
and of the first page in Apel, *Notation of Polyphonic Music*, p. 41; complete facsimile
and transcription by Gerhardt Most in *Atlmärkisches Museum: Jahresgabe 1954*,
pp. 43–66. Transcriptions of the first and fourth preludes are easily accessible in
Davison and Apel, *Historical Anthology of Music*, i (Cambridge, Mass., 1946), Nos.
84 *a, b.*

After the first five preludes Ileborgh gives three long pieces built on the same *canto fermo*, borrowed from a German song. This is the earliest known series of keyboard variations on a theme. The bold harmony of this collection is no less remarkable than the richness of its rhythms. There are numerous chromatic alterations. His keyboard must, moreover, have been fairly quick in action for his long and prolix rhapsodies to be played with ease. Yet in spite of the ingenuity of his patterns, many of which are attractive and lie easily under the organist's fingers, his tablature shows little more than gropings after an independent organ style. However, it is preferable in this respect to many a later collection of greater renown where invention is stifled by the didactic purpose and by the necessity of transcribing popular songs of the day.

In Ileborgh's tablature the upper voice is noted on a stave and the lower voices by letters, as in the Robertsbridge fragment, though with striking differences. In general the German tablatures retained this method of notation for a long time, but they vary in many details one from the other, both in the notation of rhythm and in the indication of chromatic alteration.

The personality of Conrad Paumann predominates in the organ books written between 1450 and 1473, the year of his death. He was born blind, at Nuremberg, about 1410. Like Landini in the previous century, he played on all kinds of instruments, but he won his fame principally as an organist. His career opened in the church of St. Sebald in his native town, whence his reputation soon spread to Italy. The princes of that country were anxious for his services, and he made several journeys to their courts. He finally settled down with Albert III, Duke of Bavaria, and died at Munich. His instruction was highly prized, and in 1452 his principles were recorded in a collection headed *Fundamentum organisandi Magistri Conradi Paumanns Ceci de Nuremberga* at the end of the *Lochamer Liederbuch*.[1]

Paumann begins with finger-exercises and practice in ornamentation. He gives his pupils basses, first progressing by seconds, then by thirds, fourths, fifths and sixths. Above these given basses the student has to put upper parts, using formulae suggested by the master, which thus constitute a table of decorative figures, a model of all the embellishments that can be applied to the various movements of counterpoint over a given theme. Learners are then taught how to

---

[1] Cf. p. 372. The whole manuscript has been published in facsimile by K. Ameln (Berlin, 1925). Paumann's *Fundamentum* has been transcribed by F. W. Arnold and H. Bellermann in *Jahrbücher für musikalische Wissenschaft*, ii (1867), pp. 177–224.

compose variations for organ no longer upon a scale or an elementary series of notes, but upon a plainsong. A model is given for the *Magnificat* on the sixth tone, and another for a verse of the 'Salve Regina' ('O clemens'). Another kind of exercise is the transcription of motets or songs with more or less conventional ornaments. One French song, one Italian song, and numerous German songs are given in this form.[1]

Having thus acquired skill and developed his imagination, the organist can proceed to the composition of original preludes. Three of these are given at the end of the *Fundamentum*. The most interesting is the first which, even at this early date, has the form and amplitude of a toccata. It begins with eleven bars of massive three-part chords. Then, the key of F major being well established, the upper part describes a long design, during which the left-hand part is reduced to a single line. The whole range of the keyboard is covered two or three times, sometimes in notes of equal value, sometimes in dotted rhythm. Then the music slows down, the note-values become longer, and the composition ends with a broad flourish.

Ex. 182

fo. 91ᵛ

Paumann or his influence reappears in several other manuscripts, some of which are only fragmentary. Among them are Hamburg, Staatsbibliothek.N D VI, M. 3225 (the latter part of which is the tablature of Wolfgang de nova domo, i.e. possibly Neuhaus in Bohemia) and Erlangen, Universitätsbibliothek, MS. 729.[2] Far more complete is the collection in the *Buxheimer Orgelbuch* (Munich, Staatsbibliothek, Cim. 352b).[3]

The Buxheim book, written between 1460 and 1470, contains more than 250 pieces of keyboard music: exercises similar to, and partly identical with, those of Paumann's *Fundamentum*, many pieces of

---

[1] One of the German songs, 'Mit ganczem Willen', is recorded in *The History of Music in Sound*, iii.

[2] These two manuscripts are described by Schrade, op. cit., pp. 94–101.

[3] Described and partly published by Eitner, *Monatshefte für Musikgeschichte* (Beilagen), xx–xxi (1887–8). Cf. H. Schnoor in *Zeitschrift für Musikwissenschaft*, iv (1921), p. 1. Complete facsimile, ed. B. A. Wallner, in the series *Documenta Musicologica* (Kassel, 1955).

church music, preludes, and transcriptions of vocal works. Compositions by the great masters of the century, Dunstable, Dufay, and Binchois, are drawn on as bases for adaptation. Vocal originals borrowed from Arnold de Lantins and Johannes Franchois de Gembloux are covered with suitable embroideries. Some of the organ arrangements are ascribed to composers bearing French names: Guillaume Legrant, Jacques Vilette, Jean Touront. But most of them were done by Germans: Johannes Goetz, Baumgartner (who was possibly the scribe), and Paumann himself, whose name predominates and whose skill stands out in contrast to the others.

An interesting feature of the *Buxheimer Orgelbuch* is the series of variations on the same theme, where the ornamentation is varied at each statement. This has been done with Binchois's *ballade* 'Je loe amours'.[1] Similarly, the German song 'Der Winter will hin weichen'[2] appears in three successive forms (nos. 5, 6, and 7) showing an attempt to vary the harmony as well as the rhythm. Paumann takes great care to introduce independent rhythms in the different voices, and employs a number of devices—albeit very ingenuous ones—to disguise the pedantic parallelism of the fauxbourdon-like chords:

Ex. 183

Whereas the *Fundamentum* of 1452 consists mainly of two-part music, the Buxheim book is mostly in three parts, which are usually distributed in such a way that the right hand plays quick mordents, ornaments, and runs, while the left hand supplies the harmony with the two other parts. Sometimes one of these has the lower notes, sometimes the other; sometimes they are marked to be played on the pedals.[3] When a liturgical *canto fermo* is used, the right hand plays a highly ornamented version of the theme while the other parts suggest it more soberly. Ex. 184 shows the beginning of the 'Salve Regina' as found in the *Buxheimer Orgelbuch*, together with the version published by Arnold Schlick in 1512. The comparison shows how the *canto fermo* technique had developed in organ music during fifty years. In Schlick's version

---

[1] See p. 232, and cf. H. Funck, 'Eine Chanson von Binchois im Buxheimer Orgel- und Lochheimer Liederbuch', *Acta musicologica*, v (1933), p. 3.   [2] Cf. p. 373.

[3] For the use of the pedals in the *Buxheimer Orgelbuch* see Schering, *Studien zur Musikgeschichte der Frührenaissance* (Leipzig, 1914), pp. 141–73.

there is no more ornamental variation; the melody is stated in a broad and uniform pattern by the tenor, the other parts surrounding it with counterpoints, often in imitation.

Ex. 184 (*b*) also shows how bar-lines appear regularly in the

Ex. 184[1]

(*a*) LITURGICAL THEME

Sal - ve re - gi - na, *etc.*

(*b*) BUXHEIMER ORGELBUCH

(*c*) SCHLICK

[1] For this version of the melody of the antiphon, used in Germany, see Paul Runge, 'Der Marienleich Heinrich Laufenbergs', *Liliencron-Festschrift* (Leipzig, 1910), p. 231.

Buxheimer Orgelbuch (Schlick does not mark them, but leaves a space where they would occur). Their function is often to prepare a strong accent after the ornamental group preceding a cadence.[1]

Most of the German tablatures—the Buxheim book, the collections of Kotter, Kleber, and other manuscripts, as well as printed works such as Schlick's—have one striking feature in common: the mixture of liturgical pieces with secular songs or dances. We may conclude that the secular and sacred repertories were more or less mixed, that songs were played on the church organ, and that a transcribed motet or part of a Mass would be performed in house or hall for the benefit of music-lovers. As for the preludes, they no doubt had a double function: in church they filled the intervals between liturgical actions, or accompanied processions, while on secular occasions they showed off the player's skill and perhaps gave singers their notes for the opening of a vocal piece.

Arnold Schlick represents the bourgeois tradition of central Germany half a century after Paumann. In 1511 he published a treatise on organ-building, the *Spiegel der Orgelmacher und Organisten*,[2] which does not concern us here, the subject of this chapter being instrumental music, not musical instruments. Schlick mentions in this work that he is organist to the Elector Palatine and has received a letter of privilege from the Emperor Maximilian. In the following year he published at Mainz a work entitled *Tabulaturen etlicher lobgesang und lidlein uff die orgeln und lauten*, the second and third parts being songs with lute and lute pieces.[3] The first part of the *Tabulaturen* is the earliest printed organ music we possess, except the two pages of tablature given as specimens by Sebastian Virdung in his *Musica getutscht*, the first work to deal with the manufacture and

---

[1] Leo Schrade is of a different opinion; see his dissertation, *Die ältesten Denkmäler der Orgelmusik als Beitrag zu einer Geschichte der Toccata* (Leipzig, 1927), pp. 43 ff.

[2] Published by R. Eitner in *Monatshefte für Musikgeschichte*, i (1869), and by E. Flade (Mainz, 1932). Cf. R. Kendall, 'Notes on Arnold Schlick', *Acta musicologica*, xi (1939), p. 136, and G. Frotscher, *Geschichte des Orgelspiels und der Orgelkomposition*, i (Berlin, 1935), pp. 86–104.

[3] New edition by Gottlieb Harms (Klecken, 1924; 2nd edition, Hamburg, 1957). Eitner had reprinted the organ pieces in *Monatshefte für Musikgeschichte*, i (1869).

technique of musical instruments, printed at Basle in 1511.[1] Schlick died, blind and fairly old, in 1517 or later.

Of the fourteen organ pieces in his tablature only one is a *chanson*. All the others are liturgical versets or (like 'Maria zart')[2] embellished sacred songs. Six of the compositions are in four parts, the rest in only three. All show the breadth of Schlick's thought. The parts freely cross and re-cross, and a part is given to the pedals when neither of the two keyboards can cope with it.

Schlick employs various methods. Some of his variations on a liturgical *canto fermo* are intended to be played alternately with the singing of the choir:[3] in the 'Salve Regina', for example, where the organ plays the odd verses and the choir sings the even. Others, such as the three variations on 'Da pacem Domine', simply present three different musical forms of the same theme, the first time with the plainsong in the highest part, the second time in the tenor, the third in the bass.[4] In some pieces short motives are echoed by different voices ('Eia ergo', 'Pete quid vis', 'Benedictus'). More often Schlick unfolds long phrases which show his mastery and his fine appreciation of the organ's peculiar resources. This last trait is clearly shown in the first verse of 'Salve Regina' the opening of which has been quoted in Ex. 184 above.[5] Schlick is not very fond of the mordents, gruppetti and *fioriture* of every kind with which the German organists of his day cluttered their works. He takes great care to see that the polyphonic parts are continuous and independent. In this verset of 'Salve Regina' the *canto fermo* moves in long and repeated note-values in the tenor, while the contrapuntal voices sing long ascending and descending lines, each having its own pattern.

Although Schlick played several times before Maximilian I, who had a great admiration for him, he did not belong to the group of Imperial court musicians. Heinrich Isaac and Paul Hofhaimer were the most prominent members of that circle, in which all forms of

[1] New edition in facsimile by Eitner, *Publikationen älterer Musikwerke*, xi (Berlin, 1882).

[2] 'Maria zart' has been published by A. G. Ritter, *Zur Geschichte des Orgelspiels* (Leipzig, 1884), no. 59, and by Davison and Apel, *Historical Anthology of Music*, i, no. 101.

[3] Cf. *supra*, p. 424.

[4] Of the eight versets on 'Gaude Dei genitrix' composed in 1520 for the coronation of Charles V, the *canto fermo* is in the tenor in the first six, in the descant in the last two; the versets are followed by two settings of 'Ascendo ad patrem meum', one in two parts, the other in ten (ed. M. S. Kastner, Barcelona, 1954).—*Ed.*

[5] Facsimile in the edition by Harms, p. 13, and in Apel, *Notation of Polyphonic Music*, p. 27; complete—but not altogether accurate—transcription in Davison and Apel, op. cit., no. 100.

music were eagerly cultivated and organ music was well to the fore. Though Isaac was born in Flanders and Hofhaimer in Salzburg, they may be considered together, as their careers were so similar.[1]

Hofhaimer, like Schlick, had a thorough knowledge of the organ, and he superintended in person the erection of large organs in the Imperial cities. Like Landini, he is said to have invented new stops; like him also, he was proficient on other instruments, notably the viol and lute. His reputation as a teacher was widespread, and his pupils —styled (by one of them) the 'Paulomimes'—spread his methods far and wide, for they had charge of the finest organs of the time: at Strasbourg (Luscinius), Trent, Vienna (Grefinger), Freiburg im Breisgau (Konrad Buchner), Freiburg in Switzerland, later Berne, (Hans Kotter), Constance (Johann Buchner), Speyer (Brumann), Passau (Schachinger), at the court of Saxony and at the monastery of St. Gall, and perhaps also at Venice and at the court of Henry VIII of England (Dionisio Memmo). Some of them compiled volumes of keyboard music, in which they took special care to give their master's works in a form suitable for the instrument.

Curiously enough, neither Isaac nor Hofhaimer seems to have taken the trouble to write down his organ compositions for posterity. It is only their vocal works that have come down to us in indisputably authentic forms. The most we have is a few pieces which Hofhaimer himself seems to have intended for instrumental performance. It seems as if the greatest masters considered instrumental music, at least that performed by a single player, a matter of improvisation; it was the less skilful organists, those unable to play without a book, who were obliged to compile the tablatures which preserve for us today the art of the 'Imperial' school. These pupils paid homage to their masters by borrowing their songs and motets, which they adapted for the keyboard with the customary ornaments. What the tablatures give us are arrangements. Furthermore, there is no doubt that the methods of 'coloration' used by the 'Paulomimes' were themselves part of their master's teaching.

Isaac, moreover, had cultivated forms specially suitable as foundations for organists' variations. His textless *chansons*,[2] which paved the way to the *ricercar*, supplied organists and lutenists with subjects for

---

[1] Cf. Chap. VIII, pp. 279 ff. and 287–8.

[2] Printed in *Denkmäler der Tonkunst in Osterreich*, xiv and xvi. The editor, Johannes Wolf, also gives various transcriptions from contemporary tablatures for organ and lute. Two of these pieces are recorded by a consort of viols in *The History of Music in Sound*, iii.

all sorts of variations. They used these models even during his life-
time, ornamenting them in accordance with current practice. There
are other collections of works which seem, like Isaac's, to have been
chosen on account of their suitability for instrumental performance.
Such, for instance, is Leipzig Univ. Bibl. 1494.[1] Players on the organ
or clavichord had only to dip into this collection, and transform the
piece in the usual way. The short compositions by Adam of Fulda or
Heinrich Finck[2] needed only the ornaments which every well-trained
performer had at his finger-tips to become organ versets. From this
source he could draw the whole round of interludes needed for the
hymns, Magnificats, Masses, and *Te Deum*. He could also get from
it a series of *fugæ* in four or five parts, for which the organ was so
specially suited.

Of the tablatures which preserve the works of Isaac and Hofhaimer
in keyboard transcription, one of the most important is that of Johan
Kotter of Strasbourg (d. 1541). Its two volumes, still in Basle University Library,[3] were assembled between 1513 and 1532 for the use of
the humanist, Boniface Amerbach of Basle, who played the pieces on
his clavichord. Kotter not only skilfully arranges music by his two
favourite masters, and works by Josquin, Pierre Moulu, Jean Rousée,
Sixtus Dietrich, and others; he gives versets of his own composition,
a number of dances by Buchner, Hans Weck, or himself, and finally
ten pieces of free construction. These, too, are his own. He styles
them *praeambulum*, *preludium*, *prooemium* or ἀναβολή, *harmonia*,
fantasia, or *carmen*, just as his fancy takes him. In these pieces he tries
to transfer to the keyboard the various procedures of polyphonic
writing, but does not quite succeed in finding a true instrumental
style. Yet the embellishments and passing-notes put life into these
pieces, which are in three parts, except the *Preludium in la* and the
Ἀναβολή *in fa*,[4] which are in four.

[1] Printed by Rudolf Gerber as *Der Mensuralkodex des Nikolaus Apel* (*Das Erbe
deutscher Musik*, xxxii–xxxiv).   [2] See p. 286.

[3] MS. F. IX. 22 is the more important; there are a few pieces in F. IX. 58. A *Fundamentbuch* dated 1515 by Oswald Holtzach (MS. F. VI. 26c) is related to Kotter's books;
see Wilhelm Merian, *Die Tabulaturen des Organisten Hans Kotter*, Diss. Basle (Leipzig,
1916), 'Drei Handschriften aus der Frühzeit des Klavierspiels', *Archiv für Musikwissenschaft*, ii (1920), pp. 22 ff., and *Der Tanz in den deutschen Tabulaturbüchern, mit
thematischen Verzeichnissen, Beispielen zur Intavolationspraxis und einer Studie über die
Anfänge des Klavierstils* (Leipzig, 1927), especially pp. 37–75, where he prints all the dances
and preludes gathered by Kotter, three complete song transcriptions, and incipits of
the rest. The 'Salve Regina' (see next page) is printed by Moser, *Frühmeister der
deutschen Orgelkunst* (Leipzig, 1930), p. 22.

[4] A facsimile of this piece is given in Apel, *The Notation of Polyphonic Music*, p. 29;
transcriptions in Davison and Apel, *Historical Anthology of Music*, i, No. 84 g, and
Apel, *Musik aus früher Zeit*, i (Mainz, n.d.), p. 7.

At the beginning of his tablature Kotter gave some explanations of rudiments for the use of beginners: first a table showing the shapes of the different notes, then the manner of marking accidentals (*semitonia*), ornaments (*mordantes*), &c. It was quite usual for organists to give little instructions of this kind. Oswald Holtzach shows the chromatic keyboard of the organ, from FF to a', with all the semitones except FF♯ and GG♯, which were not used.

Another tablature of the same school is preserved in the Library of St. Gall (MS. 530), where it was copied by Fridolin Sicher.[1] This collection contains one of the very rare specimens of Hofhaimer's organ music, a series of versets for the 'Salve Regina'[2] in which a fragment by Kotter was thought worthy of interpolation. Ex. 185 shows the opening of Hofhaimer's 'Salve', with a few bars of another 'Salve' by Kotter (from Basle, Univ. Bibl. F. IX. 22), both of which should be compared with Ex. 184. The plainsong theme is in D in the *Buxheimer Orgelbuch* and in Kotter, but is transposed to G by Schlick and Hofhaimer; Kotter and Hofhaimer use the first two notes, bracketed in Ex. 184 (*a*). The gap of fifty years separating the first from the other three makes a difference far greater than that caused by variety of school, region, or personality between the three contemporaries:

Ex. 185
  (*a*) KOTTER

¹ See W. R. Nef, 'Der St. Galler Organist Fridolin Sicher und seine Orgeltabulatur', *Schweizerisches Jahrbuch für Musikwissenschaft*, vii (1938), and Apel, *The Notation of Polyphonic Music*, pp. 31–32.

² No. 2 of the complete works, published, with a substantial study of Hofhaimer's life and surroundings, by H. J. Moser, *Paul Hofhaimer, ein Lied- und Orgelmeister des deutschen Humanismus* (Berlin, 1929). See also Moser's 'Hofhaimeriana', *Zeitschrift für Musikwissenschaft*, xv (1932), pp. 127–38, where he prints a second 'Salve Regina', and his 'Eine Trienter Orgeltabulatur aus Hofhaimers Zeit', *Festschrift für Guido Adler* (Vienna, 1930), p. 84.

(*b*) HOFHAIMER

In Hofhaimer the richness of the rhythm and the firmness of the
ornamentation call for remark: these were assuredly the qualities
which captivated princes and aroused the enthusiasm of disciples.
His passion for melody is such that at times it modifies the *canto
fermo* itself, as in bar 5 of the example above. One feels that he is
master of his material and not, like smaller men, the servant of fixed
melodic material.

Like most of the organists of his time Hofhaimer is most at his ease
when the *canto fermo* is in the tenor; but his verset 'O dulcis', with the
plainsong in the top part, is a fine piece of work. After the second bar
he breaks the rigid line of the theme into flexible curves; then he halts
it to allow the accompanying parts to speak, and they in turn prepare
the re-entry of the plainsong. Even more marked is the rhythmic
complexity of an organ arrangement of a secular song by Isaac, 'Ain
frewlich wesen', in which every voice breaks into a perfect cascade
of notes.[1]

This last work is preserved in a third tablature, collected between
1520 and 1524 by Leonhard Kleber of Goppingen in Württemberg
(*c.* 1490–1556).[2] Whether a pupil of Hofhaimer or not, his enthusiasm
for the Emperor's organist and his circle was no whit less than

---

[1] Ed. Moser, no. 4 of the secular works. There is another transcription of the same
song by Kotter: see Merian, *Der Tanz in den deutschen Tabulaturbüchern*, p. 38.

[2] Berlin, Staatsbibliothek, Mus. MS. Z 26. See Hans Löwenfeld, *Leonhard Kleber
und sein Orgeltabulaturbuch* (Diss. Berlin, 1897). This tablature was written between 1520
and 1524. A good manuscript transcription by A. G. Ritter is owned by the Library of
the Conservatoire de musique, Paris.

Kotter's and Sicher's. The same names are found in his collection, and he draws upon the same masters for the vocal originals of the pieces he adapts. If his coloraturae were pruned away one would easily lay bare the originals he borrowed from Brumel and Finck, Senfl and Josquin, Isaac, Obrecht, Agricola, and Loyset Compère. For Kleber was an eclectic and familiar with all the schools of composition. He actually demonstrates this work of 'decoloration', placing side by side in his book a four-part motet 'Decem precepta' for a pedal organ and the same piece arranged for only three voices, *non colloratum* (nos. 75 and 76). All he has done is to take out the mordents and replace the semiquaver passages by more sober movement. Tranquil, fluid lines replace agitated rhythms. The peculiar characteristics of organ music have disappeared.

The eighteen pieces of prelude type which Kleber copied out are not all his own compositions.[1] Some are actually attributed to his colleagues Buchner, Brumann, and Schapf; but the rest are probably his own, and they are the most noteworthy things in the collection. Most of them are found in the first part of the book, which contains 51 pieces to be played on manuals alone, while the 61 pieces of the second part are all headed 'pedaliter'. Kleber's free compositions are less like adaptations of songs than are Kotter's; the organ's special powers are better exploited, especially in the long scale-passages and dreamy chords which give a rhapsodical air to his fantasias (particularly the *Preambalon in re*, no. 43, and the *Praeambulum in sol b moll*, no. 55).[2] In all these characteristics Kleber's preludes belong to the Adam Ileborgh tradition. On the other hand, one finds in his work (notably in no. 1, a *Praeambulum in ut*) those contrasted rhythms which play such a large part in contemporary English organ music, especially in that of Philip ap Ryce. Kleber has therefore the distinction of being one of the German musicians most aware of international currents, as well as one whose talent took the most varied forms. He helped to create the instrumental type of motive, capable of rapid and concise developments. Admittedly the English went much farther in this direction, and revealed a quite different kind of maturity. Yet the short sections of the first prelude, repeated in different registers, are already attempts at instrumental 'conversation'. The same procedure may be observed in the *Fantasia in re*

---

[1] They were all published as a supplement to *Monatshefte für Musikgeschichte*, xix (1887). Separate ones have been printed by Apel, *Musik aus früher Zeit*, i, pp. 7–8, and Davison and Apel, *Historical Anthology*, i, nos. 84*e* and *f*.

[2] Published by A. G. Ritter, op. cit., no. 60, and Frotscher, op. cit., pp. 115–16.

published by Ritter (no. 62), and attributed in the manuscript to 'A.T.D. Card Sal.', perhaps a Salzburg cardinal.

It is not for the brilliance of his preludes that we admire another of Hofhaimer's pupils, called indifferently Hans or Johann Buchner or Hans von Constantz (where he was organist of the cathedral for a long time). The prelude by him in Kleber's tablature (no. 97) has lively and energetic rhythms, but is otherwise mediocre, like his transcriptions of songs.[1] Buchner's fame rests not on his virtuosity but on his development of the art of treating a liturgical theme as *canto fermo*. For while Schlick, Hofhaimer, and the rest were content to put a plainsong in the middle of their versets and then to surround it with ornamental figures, Buchner draws the material of his counterpoints from the theme itself; by stating it in the different parts he gives the piece a fundamental unity. The theoretical rules of this fine art, with a collection of examples, were recorded in 1551, more than ten years after his death, in a manuscript *Fundamentum* (*Fundamentum, sive ratio vera, quae docet quemvis cantum planum, sive (ut vocant) choralem redigere ad justas diversarum vocum symphonias*) copied, like Kotter's tablature, for the use of Boniface Amerbach.[2]

Buchner employed his structural method mainly in versets for the Ordinary of the Mass, and in a few introits, sequences, and hymns. It is very pleasant (*jucundissimum auditu*), he says in his precepts for beginners, to allude to the chosen theme from the beginning, in all the parts. But these fugal entries may be treated in different ways. The *canto fermo* may pass from one voice to another: this is called *permutatio*, and excludes neither imitations nor canonic entries. There is an example in the first verset of the sequence 'Victimae paschali'. There are also pieces in which treble and tenor state the plainsong in canon, while alto and bass imitate one another on another theme. In some compositions the liturgical theme appears only covered with embroideries. In others, five and six parts are handled with independence but thematic unity. Buchner takes great care to give variety to the successive versets of a *Sanctus* or *Agnus*, and to the five versets played by the organ in an alternating performance of a *Kyrie*.

His *Kyrie eleison angelicum sollemne*,[3] for instance, is constructed as follows: the first verset, in four parts, has the plainsong in the

---

[1] One of the best of these, from Sicher's tablature, is recorded in *The History of Music in Sound*, iii.

[2] Basle, Universitäts-Bibliothek, MS. F. I. 8. Another manuscript, possibly a few years older, is at Zürich, Zentralbibliothek, Cod. 284. The Basle manuscript was studied and partially published by Carl Päsler, *Vierteljahrsschrift für Musikwissenschaft*, v (1889), p. 1. Cf. E. von Werra, 'Johann Buchner', *Kirchenmusikalisches Jahrbuch*, x (1895), p. 88.　　　　　　　　　　　　　　[3] Päsler, op. cit., pp. 123–35.

tenor, *pedaliter*, though the treble has already stated the same theme in the higher octave; meanwhile the other two parts proceed with mutual imitation. In the second verset a canon in long note-values shares the plainsong between tenor and bass, while the two higher parts carry on a lively dialogue. The third verset is for three parts only; the theme is in the treble, but decorated with ornaments which are imitated by the other parts, though they become less and less rich in the lower parts. The fourth verset is for five parts, of which four are interlinked by their statements of the theme, the middle part alone running in free counterpoint; the imitations are in descending direction, treble and tenor at the interval of an octave, alto and bass respectively a fifth below them. The last *Kyrie* passes the theme from one to another of the four parts in long notes, according to the principle of *permutatio*. This fine series of versets points the way to that form of variation on a *canto fermo* which Bull, Titelouze, and Sweelinck were soon to develop simultaneously.

ITALIAN LUTE MUSIC

All the forms of keyboard music cultivated in Germany during the first third of the sixteenth century are found in other countries. Let us consider Italy first, where another popular form of solo instrumental music claims our attention.

The oldest printed collection of solo instrumental music is the *Intabulatura de Lauto: Libro primo*, containing compositions and transcriptions by Francesco Spinacino, published by the Venetian printer Petrucci in 1507. Petrucci had already in 1498 obtained from the Republic a privilege to print organ tablatures, but he seems not to have made use of it. At any rate no volume of keyboard music from his press has yet been discovered. But he published three more volumes of lute-tablatures: a *Libro secondo* the same year, a *Libro terzo* of which no copy has survived, and *Libro quarto* containing compositions by the Milanese lutenist Joanambrosio Dalza in 1508. Further, in 1509 and 1511 he issued two books of *Tenori e contrabassi intabulati col sopran in canto figurato per cantar e sonar col lauto* by Franciscus Bossinensis, containing not only *frottole* with lute accompaniment but twenty *recercari* for lute only.[1]

Recercari had already figured among the pieces by Spinacino and Dalza; there are 17 in Petrucci's *Libro primo*, 10 in the second, and 8 in the fourth. Like the German organ preludes described above,

[1] See Claudio Sartori, 'A Little-known Petrucci Publication', *The Musical Quarterly*, xxxiv (1948), p. 234. The *recercari* have been published by Benvenuto Disertori (Milan, 1954).

they are non-thematic improvisations consisting of chords and passage-work, usually short, though Körte has transcribed a longer *Recercare de tutti le toni*[1] from the first book, of which the first two sections may be quoted:

Ex. 186

In these, the earliest known *recercari*, there are only the faintest suggestions of the imitative, motet-like technique later associated with the term.[2] They are simply preludes, sometimes to specific songs or transcriptions; Spinacino has, among others, a *r. de tous biens*, that is, a prelude to Hayne's 'De tous biens plaine' (cf. Ex. 101) which Petrucci had published in 1501 in his *Odhecaton*; and Dalza indicates which *recercari* are to be used as preludes to his various transcriptions. Dalza also has four curiously titled *Tastar de corde con li soi recercar dietro*,[3] in which the *tastar de corde* (touching of the strings) is followed by a rather more shapely piece.

Except for these *recercari*, Spinacino's two books consist almost entirely of transcriptions of polyphonic pieces—religious and secular—which had appeared in Petrucci's other publications. He applies the principles of ornamentation already familiar in organ transcriptions

[1] *Laute und Lautenmusik bis zur Mitte des 16. Jahrhunderts* (Leipzig, 1901), p. 129. Other *recercari* by Spinacino have been reprinted in Schering, *Geschichte der Musik in Beispielen* (Leipzig, 1931), no. 63*b*, and Davison and Apel, op. cit., no. 99*b*.
[2] See H. H. Eggebrecht, 'Terminus *Ricercar*', *Archiv für Musikwissenschaft*, ix (1952), p. 137.
[3] An example is given in Körte, op. cit., p. 132, and Davison and Apel, op. cit., no. 99*a*. A *tastar de corde* without *recercar* is given in Wolf, *Handbuch der Notationskunde*, ii, p. 54, and *Musik aus früher Zeit*, i, p. 20; there is another example in Adler, *Handbuch der Musikgeschichte*, i (Berlin, 1930), p. 398.

and is driven by the limitations of the instrument to employ most of the devices for suggesting polyphony and sketching harmony that were to be essential features of the lute idiom for the next hundred years. His method may be shown most clearly by comparing the opening of his 'Christe de si dedero' (*Libro secondo*, 4v.) with the original, the *Christe* from Obrecht's Mass 'Si dedero' which Petrucci published a few months later in his *Missarum diversorum autorum liber primus*:[1]

Ex. 187

Spinacino gives one *bassadanza* in each of his two books. On the other hand, dances actually predominate in Dalza's collection. In addition to the *tastar de corde* and transcriptions of *frottole*, he prints *padovane diverse*, *calate a la spagnola* and *calate a la taliana*. Moreover each of his 'pavanes' is really a miniature suite, as he expressly points out: 'Note that each pavane has its saltarello and piva.' The pavane is always in $\frac{4}{4}$ or $\frac{2}{4}$ time and the piva in $\frac{3}{8}$, but the saltarello may be in $\frac{3}{4}$, $\frac{2}{4}$, or $\frac{3}{8}$. Each set is unified by key, but there is only the faintest suggestion of thematic affinity, for example:[2]

Ex. 188

[1] Schering, op. cit., nos. 62*b* and 63*a*, gives an instrumental *chanson* by Josquin from Petrucci's *Canti C cento cinquanta* (1503), followed by Spinacino's lute transcription.

[2] Körte, op. cit., pp. 148–9. Dalza also gives an alternative version of the *pavana alla venetiana*, which has been transcribed by Apel, *Musik aus früher Zeit*, i, p. 20.

Generally speaking, these lute dances are more remarkable for rhythmic verve than for melodic charm. The harmonic element is much slighter than in the *recercari* and the vocal transcriptions, but two of the *calate*—dances in common time[1]—are written for two lutes. (Spinacino also has a piece for two lutes in his *Libro secondo*.)

ITALIAN KEYBOARD MUSIC

If Petrucci neglected to publish music for keyboard instruments, despite his privilege, another Italian printer was soon prepared to do so. On 27 December 1517 Andrea Antico (Antiquo, Antiquis), a clerk born at Montona, who had been established as a music publisher at Rome since about 1510, received a similar privilege from Pope Leo X. This he used to publish the *Frottole intabulate da sonar organi*,[2] which bear the date '13 January 1517'. These two dates (that of the issue of the privilege and that of the publication) seem oddly inconsistent. But as many Italian cities still retained the custom of beginning the year on Lady Day, 25 March, it may well be that the *Frottole* were not actually issued until 13 January 1518, about a month after the grant of the privilege.[3]

The notation is clear and simple: two staves of five lines with regular bar-lines, time signatures and repeat marks, and dots above or below notes to indicate chromatic alterations, both sharp and flat. In general the notation is identical with that of the French tablatures of the same period. The phrase *da sonar organi* in the title is not meant to confine performance to the organ but rather, generically, to indicate that the music is intended for all keyboard instruments and adopts their system of tablature.

Most of the pieces here adapted for keyboard, like the voice-and-

[1] Quittard prints a *calata de stramboti* in Lavignac and la Laurencie, *Encyclopédie de la musique*, 1re partie, iii, p. 1220.

[2] The only copy extant belongs to the Marchese Polesini at Parenzo.

[3] Jeppesen offers a different explanation of the conflict between the dates: see *Die italienische Orgelmusik am Anfang des Cinquecento* (Copenhagen, 1943), p. 58, n. 4. This work contains, after a substantial introduction, six pieces from the *Frottole intabulate* (with the vocal originals) and the complete work of Marco Antonio da Bologna. Though the present writer has herself transcribed both the Antico tablature and Marco Antonio's, the examples cited here are borrowed from Jeppesen, his note-values being halved.

lute songs of Bossinensis, are borrowed from the two most famous composers of *frottole*, Bartolomeo Tromboncino and Marchetto Cara. Tromboncino alone is represented by 19 of the 26 pieces. Almost all the *frottole* for organ, no fewer than 23, are based on pieces which had appeared in the *frottola* collections published by Petrucci and Antico. With the exception of Petrarch's 'Vergine bella', which after two centuries still inspired musicians, all the titles indicate secular songs. As for the arranger, he may well, as Jeppesen suggests,[1] have been Andrea Antico himself.

The process of arrangement for the organ is carried so far that the *frottole intabulate* differ essentially from the originals. Whether the *frottola* was usually sung by several voices or (as would seem more likely) by one voice accompanied by three instruments,[2] it was almost always a homophonic composition in which the various parts moved at the same pace and in the same rhythm, so that it consisted mainly of unbroken series of concords. The organ arrangement gives independence to the parts by the ornamentations given to each in turn, and the numerous passing notes and embellishments introduce dissonances which enrich the harmony. Certain chords are filled out with an extra note which temporarily increases the number of parts to five, as in 'Non resta in questa', bars 7–8:

Ex. 189

Passages in conjunct motion are enriched with bold chromatic alterations, as may be seen from the opening of the transcription of 'Che farala, che dirala', a famous *frottola* by Michele Vicentino which was incorporated, after translation into French by Marguerite, Queen of Navarre, in the nineteenth *nouvelle* of her *Heptameron*:

Ex. 190

---

[1] Op. cit., p. 64.   [2] Cf. *supra*, p. 398.

Unprepared dissonances on strong beats of the bar are more frequent in a work that appeared five years after the *Frottole intabulate*, the collection of Marco Antonio Cavajono or Cavazono entitled *Recerchari, Motetti, Canzoni, libro primo* (1523).[1] The composer, who is also known as Marco Antonio da Bologna, after his birthplace, and Marco Antonio d'Urbino, no doubt because he lived in that town, was the father of Girolamo d'Urbino, or Cavazzoni, who himself while quite young produced in 1542 and 1543 a series of versets and *ricercari* for the organ in which he shows himself a worthy successor to his father.[2]

On the death of his employer Pope Leo X in 1521, Marco Antonio returned to an earlier patron, the noble Venetian Francesco Cornaro, at that time procurator of Saint Mark's, to whom he dedicated the *Libro primo*.[3] The privilege which he secured, however, was granted by Pope Adrian VI; it protected both the musician and his publisher, Bernard de Vercelli, whose press was in Venice. The *Libro primo*, which is his only known publication, contains two preludes called *ricercare* and six transcriptions, two of motets and four of songs, though up to now it has not been possible to trace any of the vocal originals.

As we have seen, the lutenists Spinacino, Dalza, and Franciscus Bossinensis had already published *ricercari*. But those of Marco Antonio differ entirely from the attempts of the lutenists, although these two fine preludes are not the basis of the form which was to spread with the Venetian school later in the century, and which was better anticipated by his son Girolamo. The imitative style is not predominant throughout, as it was to be in the *ricercar* of the future. Antonio combines imitation very freely with the grandeur of chordal sections and with passages which anticipate certain aspects of the

---

[1] The only copy extant is in the British Museum. See *Catalogue of Printed Music published between 1487 and 1880 now in the British Museum*, ii (London, 1912), p. 90.

[2] See vol. IV.

[3] Facsimile of the title, dedication, and two pages of the music, with complete transcription, in Jeppesen, op. cit.

toccata, and preserves the original conception of the prelude as intended primarily to establish a tonality and to loosen the fingers of the performer. In fact, the two *ricercari* are placed each before one of the two big motets, 'Salve virgo' and 'O stella maris' and serve as introductions to them. Each pair of pieces is linked by the same tonality, suggesting a comparison with the similar relationship which Bach, in the *Wohltemperiertes Klavier*, established between prelude and fugue. The similarity is heightened by the fact that Marco Antonio makes the second piece more strictly imitative than its prelude.

The *ricercari* are remarkable both for the breadth of their composition and for the density of their texture. To give more fullness to sections made up of a series of concords, the composer increases the number of voices to as many as six; but one of the parts soon frees itself from the harmonic mass to form an independent pattern, following its own path like a coloured thread in an otherwise uniform fabric. The music as a whole moves from modulation to modulation by means of remarkably clear and numerous cadences, in what appears to be a carefully thought out plan. No vocal composition before 1530 provides such a rich cycle of modulations.

Marco Antonio applied to the keyboard that method of developing short motives by rising and falling steps, of which Josquin des Prez had set the example in his vocal style, and which the French organists of the time also employed. There is an example in the *Recercare secondo*, bars 17–22:

Ex. 191

His figuration is rich and varied, fluid rhythms alternating with strongly marked chords; numerous syncopations prepare piquant dissonances by suspension, notably in the *Recercare primo*, bars 115–19:

Ex. 192

The trills at the tenth, the alternations of thirds, and the double embellishments of imperfect consonances contribute their varied charm, as in the *Recercare secondo*, bars 82–83: ·

Ex. 193

These two preludes, with their widespread melodic pattern and their clear tendency to go beyond the limits of vocal style, would seem to demand the use of pedals. Although less widespread in Italy than in Germany, Switzerland, or France, the pedal organ had been installed in the largest churches, notably in San Petronio at Bologna. But it never had more than a small pedal board.

The four songs which follow the double series of *ricercari* and motets have titles in corrupted French: 'Perdone moi sie folie', 'Madame vous aves mon cuor', 'Plus ne regres', and 'Lautre yor per un matin'. How did these songs come to be known by Marco Antonio, and why did he choose these for transcription for the organ rather than *frottole*? A possible explanation, both of his acquaintance with the titles and of his mistakes in transcribing them, is that he came to know them through Roger Saignand, a Burgundian who was organist at the cathedral of Bologna throughout Marco Antonio's childhood. In fact this Frenchman held his post at San Petronio for nearly half a century, from 1474 until 1522.[1] The young Marco Antonio must have heard him many times; perhaps he was actually his pupil. It is possible that he remembered French tunes on which Roger liked to extemporize and now in his turn tried his hand at organ versions of them. We know that Roger Saignand was prepared to give lessons to the youths of Bologna. In 1478 he agreed under contract to train a boy named Ludovico so that at the end of his course he should be able to play 'Kirie cum Gloria et Credo cum omnibus suis versibus differentibus, duos versus septimi toni, Magnificat, et sex carmina seu cantus ad voluntatem dicti Ludovico'.[2] May not French songs have been among the 'sex carmina seu cantus'? And Marco Antonio, too, may well have been trained on similar tunes.

[1] Cf. Yvonne Rokseth, *La musique d'orgue au XVᵉ siècle et au début du XVIᵉ* (Paris, 1930), pp. 117–18.

[2] L. Frati, 'Per la storia della musica in Bologna dal secolo XV al XVI', *Rivista musicale italiana*, xxiv (1917), p. 451.

It must be admitted that the four songs by no means equal the *ricercari* in interest. The original is altered by little more than long trills, sometimes lasting a whole bar, which replace the longer notes. One also comes across whole strings of thirds, sixths, and faux-bourdon-like chords; gaps filled by rising and falling scales; passing notes connecting two fragments of which the second echoes the first in a different register. These features are generally restrained and graceful, as at the beginning of 'Madame vous aves':

Ex.194

Repeated notes, so characteristic of the French *chanson* of the early sixteenth century, are plentiful. But passages containing repeated notes or chords also occur in the two *ricercari*, and Marco Antonio appears to have been the first to introduce them into keyboard music. It is true that the *frottola* also contained plenty of repeated chords. But it is noteworthy that Antico's *Frottole intabulate* of 1517 tend not to reproduce these repetitions, preferring usually to mask them with ornaments.

ATTAINGNANT'S COLLECTIONS FOR KEYBOARD

If it is true that Marco Antonio's teacher was a Frenchman, we shall not be surprised at the number of the musical idioms he shares with the Parisian school. Admittedly French keyboard music was written in a variety of forms which at the beginning of the sixteenth century were international and which we have already met in the Teutonic countries: versets for the canticles at Mass and Vespers, preludes, and transcriptions of motets, songs, and dances. But the underlying spirit of the French composers has a real affinity only with the music of Italy. Instead of exactly reproducing vocal polyphony with the addition of a few ornaments, both French and Italian keyboard composers aim rather at a synthetic reflection of it. Their ornamentation is thoroughly integrated in the musical thought, not merely applied on the surface. And the French organists, like Marco Antonio, conceive their instrumental music in terms of the keyboard and make full use of the range and power which their instruments already possessed. It is regrettable, however, that no French name can be inscribed beside Marco Antonio's in the annals of organ music, for we know the names of none of the composers whose work was issued by the Parisian publisher, Pierre Attaingnant, in the first four months of 1531.

Seven small books of music set *en la tablature des orgues, Espinettes et Manicordions* came out successively between January and April 1530 O.S., that is, in our reckoning, between January and April 1531. There must have been manuscript collections which preceded this edition. Such a clear straightforward style, represented in a simple clear notation little different from our modern symbols and, moreover, almost identical with that used in Antico's *Frottole intabulate* and Marco Antonio's *Libro primo*, could not have been developed suddenly at the first attempt.

This collection appeared in the following order:

1. January 1531: *Dixneuf chansons musicales reduictes en la tablature des Orgues, Espinettes et Manicordions, et telz semblables instrumentez.*
2. and 3. February 1531: *Vingt et cinq chansons* . . . and *Vingt et six chansons musicales reduictes.* . . .
4. About the same date: *Quatorze Gaillardes, neuf Pavennes, sept Branles et deux Basses Dances, le tout reduict de musique en la tablature.* . . .[1]
5. Probably in March 1531; *Tablature pour le jeu D'orgues, etc., sur le plain chant de Cunctipotens et Kyrie fons, Avec leurs Et in terra, Patrem, Sanctus et Agnus Dei.* . . .
6. March 1531: *Magnificat sur les huit tons avec Te deum laudamus et deux Preludes, le tout mys en la tablature.* . . .

[1] These four books have been published in facsimile by Eduard Bernoulli, *Chansons und Tänze. Pariser Tabulaturdrucke für Tasteninstrumente* (Munich, 1914), 5 vols. Up to now, no complete transcription in modern notation has appeared. One *chanson* from the first book is given in Ritter, op. cit., no. 37; one dance in Blume, *Studien zur Vorgeschichte der Orchestersuite im 15. und 16. Jahrhundert* (Leipzig, 1925), Anhang, no. 18c; twelve dances in Eitner, 'Tänze des 15. bis 17. Jhdts.', *Monatshefte für Musikgeschichte*, vii (1875), Beilage, pp. 78–88. Schering republished three, together with one *chanson*, in *Geschichte der Musik in Beispielen* (Leipzig, 1931), no. 91, Apel three in *Musik aus früher Zeit*, ii, pp. 21–22, and Davison and Apel one in *Historical Anthology*, i, no. 104.

7. April 1531: *Treze Motetz musicaulx avec ung Prelude. . . .*[1]

The seventy songs contained in the first three volumes are all the more interesting in that, being taken from the most popular composers of the day, many of them were published almost simultaneously in other forms, both instrumental and vocal. It is therefore possible to make instructive comparisons. Already in 1528 Attaingnant had begun to publish his numerous collections of *chansons à quatre parties*. In the earliest of these, the *Chansons nouvelles* of 1528, occur a score of the pieces which three years later the organists were to set in their *chansons en tablature*. The lutenists had indeed seized on them before the organists, and a volume of thirty-four songs, the majority for voice with lute accompaniment, a few for lute alone,[2] appeared in October 1529; sixteen of the songs in this collection reappear among the organ arrangements. There is no essential difference between the ways in which this common material is adapted for the lute and for keyboard instruments. Both are marked by respect for the original structure, which is decked with fragments of scales, rapid embroideries, and figures of various kinds whenever a sustained vocal note has to be replaced by a less static passage.[3] It is taken for granted that the instrument has to coin the vocal note-values into small change. Neither type of transcription diminishes the charm of the original; on the contrary, the adaptations take on a peculiar elegance from the speed and brilliance which are the attributes of instruments with struck strings (manicordion) or plucked strings (lute, spinet).

There can be no doubt that it was the spinet and its successors, not the organ, which were more often used to play the songs of the first three books. Their titles do not really mean that they were intended indifferently for organ or spinet, but that their system of notation was that used for keyboard instruments. It is also reasonable to presume that the book of dances which forms the fourth volume in Attaingnant's series is a collection of chamber music intended for the staccato sounds of the spinet rather than for the somewhat heavy-breathed organ.

Lionel de la Laurencie has noted[4] that the first examples of instrumental dances published by Attaingnant about 1530 already show

---

[1] Nos. 5 and 6 have been printed in modern notation by Y. Rokseth, *Deux livres d'orgue parus chez Pierre Attaingnant en 1531* (*Publications de la Société française de musicologie*, i) (Paris, 1925). No. 7 has been published in the same way by the same editor, *Treize motets et un prélude pour orgue* (in the same series, v) (Paris, 1930).

[2] *Tres breve et familiere introduction pour entende et apprendre . . . lutz*. The 24 *chansons* with lute accompaniment from this have been published by L. de la Laurencie, A. Mairy, and G. Thibault (*Publications de la Société française de musicologie*, iv) (Paris, 1934).

[3] Cf. Ex. 187.   [4] *Les Luthistes* (Paris, 1928), p. 53.

the ternary arrangement which was to be that of the French suite, and
that they mark the beginning of the organization of the suite by
development of elements from the first piece of each set. Friedrich
Blume[1] has proved that the *Dixhuit basses dances* for lute (1529),
the *Neuf basse dances*, &c.,[2] for four instruments (1530), and the
Quatorze Gaillardes, &c., for keyboard (1531) are the origin of the
whole development of the orchestral suite. The galliards, pavanes,
basses danses, and branles for tablature must be looked on as essays
in which are outlined the laws which in the following century were
to control the sequence and structure of the instrumental suite.

The instrumental dances published around 1530 were not intended
to be actually danced to; neither the spinet nor the chamber organ,
still less the lute, with their feeble carrying power, would have been
able to dominate the tumult of a ballroom. The rhythmical periods
which had been imposed on the music by the necessities of the dance
serve from now on only to define the purely musical structure. The
dances published by Attaingnant thus represent an intimate, pleasant,
and lighthearted art. The technique of variation already takes on an
air of learning. Thus in the dance-pairs, pavane-galliard (dances
which follow each other, the former with a walking step in duple
rhythm, the latter leaping, in triple time) one often finds that the same
theme has been used for both. Broad and in $\frac{4}{4}$ time for the pavane,
it is remodelled for the galliard:

Ex. 195
Pavane

---

[1] Op. cit., *passim.*

[2] *Neuf basse dances deux branles vingt et cinq Pauennes auec quinze Gaillardes en
musique a quatre parties.* There is a complete transcription in score by F. J. Giesbert
(Mainz, 1950), including also the six galliards and six pavanes published by Attaingnant
in his *Treze chansons musicales a quatre parties* of 1529. Some of the four-part dances
also appear in the collections for lute or keyboard.—*Ed.*

The artistic level reached by these dances is best seen by comparison with those in Kotter's collection, still so heavy and awkward. The French dances show consistently an intimate fusion of the clean incisive rhythm with the melodic motives which carry it. Hence comes an ease, a balance of periods which, without sacrificing variety, makes each of these little pieces something finished and of its kind completely satisfying.

The fifth and sixth books of the Paris collection contain liturgical versets, used when the organ alternated with the choir in the Mass, *Magnificat*, and *Te Deum*.[1] The basic principle of all these versets is the employment of the ecclesiastical chant as *canto fermo*, usually with one note of the chant for each bar of music. This rule is, however, modified by considerable variety in its application and by liberties taken in successive versets on the same theme. Thus the theme, which is usually stated first straightforwardly, is subsequently broadened, interpreted, transferred from one voice to another, cut up by interludes or replaced by ornamental figures. Thus monotony is avoided and the listener's interest stimulated.

The composer does not strive like Buchner for strictness of canonic imitation, nor like Hofhaimer for richness of ornamentation, but for the melodic smoothness of a counterpoint which otherwise would run grave risk of aridity. The ornaments, unlike many of those introduced by the German *Coloristen*, are not in the least mechanical. They are light touches, placed here and there to mark a cadence or to fill out a long note-value. The writing is sometimes content with the simplicity of two-part polyphony, a simplicity not devoid of charm and variety

[1] Cf. p. 424.

(as in the 'Benedictus', p. 26),[1] but is more often in three parts. And frequently chords are filled in so that the number of parts is momentarily increased to four. The composer usually prefers a highly melodious style in which one part after another moves in supple lines above chords in the other parts, but he also knows how to use a characteristic motive as the theme of canonic entries ('Et ex patre', p. 13; 'Benedictus', p. 16; 'Tu solus', p. 24; *Secundus versus*, p. 38; 'Tu devicto', p. 55; 'Aeterna fac', p. 56). Like Marco Antonio, he is fond of chains of 'imperfect' concords which, handled discreetly as in this opening of the *Kyrie* 'Cunctipotens' (p. 19), have a pleasing flow:

Ex. 196

Gregorian theme

He is rarely content to put a decorative flourish above the plainsong note. His counterpoint is melodious and itself forms significant themes, as may be seen in the opening of the verset 'Domine Deus rex' of the *Gloria* which follows the *Kyrie* 'Cunctipotens' (p. 23):

Ex. 197

Gregorian theme

Like Marco Antonio, but with greater skill (for they had to overcome the tyranny of an obligatory theme), the French composers knew how to work up their melody to a sort of explosion, as in the *Secundus versus* of the *Magnificat* in the sixth mode (p. 44):

[1] Page references, for the three books of sacred music, are to the modern editions.

Ex. 198

Three preludes, very different in length and form, occur in the Attaingnant collections for organ. Two of them open the volume of Magnificats, while the third is in the seventh volume of the series. One of the most characteristic features of the *Preludium* and *Prélude sur chacun ton* placed at the beginning of the sixth book is the use of syncopated suspensions to mark either a discord or an imperfect concord. This is specially frequent in the second of these pieces and gives it a special interest. The many prepared discords are handled with perfect ease, while the unprepared ones are equally a part of the plan, as in this example from the *Preludium* (bars 23–25, p. 30):

Ex. 199

But what is most noteworthy in these preludes, as in all the French organ-tablatures, is their melodic intensity. The musical phrase, usually placed in the upper part, ranges over a couple of octaves with a sustained power, an elasticity and a complete freedom from dryness, showing complete mastery of technique. The *Prélude sur chacun ton* (p. 31) demonstrates that short melodic figures, of which it offers a varied collection, can act as the scaffolding for a musical structure; they appear in turn on all degrees of the scale,[1] with results which overstep the limits of the hexachord. We are now far beyond the modal theories so stubbornly repeated by the writers of the Middle Ages: and it is quite clear that the organists of 1531 are no longer thinking in terms of hexachords, 'natural', 'hard', and 'soft'. The octave is the basis of their musical world and they generally move in a tonality little different from the modern major.

Thus these two preludes are written in a key hardly distinguishable from our F major. The opening of the *Prélude sur chacun ton*, with

[1] Bars 8–12, 18–22, 38–40, 63–67, 69–72, 74–78, 79–82.

its close full harmonies, well shows the extent to which the structure of the typical major cadence, marked by the subdominant and dominant of the key, has already established itself:

Ex. 200

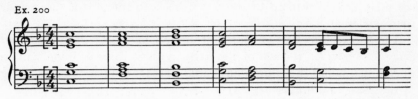

The short prelude at the end of the *Treze Motetz* simply unfolds one long melodic thought through thirteen bars without break or repetition. This tune moves almost entirely by conjunct intervals and in even notes. In spite of this simplicity it possesses an engaging charm. The final of the mode is G, with a B flat in the key-signature. It is therefore in the ecclesiastical mode of D, a mode whose reality is still fairly perceptible. The modern minor, as a matter of fact, took longer to emerge from the old modes of D than our major did to establish its independence of the F modes. While the transformation had already been completed in the case of the major at the period of these tablatures, it was still fluid in the case of the minor.[1]

Among the thirteen motets transcribed in Attaingnant's seventh volume there are some with famous works as their vocal source. Thus one of them is built on Obrecht's celebrated 'Parce Domine' and another on the 'O vos omnes' of Loyset Compère. Two of them, on the other hand, are transcriptions of anonymous Italian songs. The originals of the rest are drawn from that brilliant group of composers who fill the interval between the death of Ockeghem and the second generation of pupils of Josquin des Prez. The oldest of these musicians were probably Antoine de Févin and Antoine Brumel, the youngest Pierre de Lafage and Pierre Moulu, the most fashionable at Paris round about 1530 being Claudin de Sermisy.

The organist—or organists—who arranged this music for his instrument did his best to find a new equivalent for the vocal ensemble it replaced. Had he intended his arrangements to be played solely on the organ he could have retained the broad chord-progressions and the majestic canonic entries of the voices, which would have sounded very well. The two motets by Févin and the fifteenth-century 'Dulcis

---

[1] When I edited Attaingnant's books, I was too generous in the addition of flats and sharps. I still believe that the original editions need additional accidentals, but great caution is necessary in their restoration. In the case of this Prelude (*Treze Motetz*, p. 1), I admit that most of the added accidentals are open to objection except the flat in the bass part, bar 3.

amica' would have needed no transformation. But he must have fore-
seen that all these pieces would attract a spinet player, who would
prefer brilliant passage-work to sustained breadth; moreover, the
organist himself wanted to show that his instrument was more agile
than voices.

The successions of four-part harmonies have been respected, but
free scope is given to each of the parts in turn; three of them remain
unchanged while the fourth has rapid passages, as at the beginning
of the 'Sancta Trinitas' (p. 28):

Ex. 201

or else two voices proceed in parallel sixths or tenths within the firm
harmonic framework provided by the immobility of the other two
parts (see 'Si bona suscepimus', after Claudin de Sermisy, bars 77–
78).

When the original motet uses imitation, the arranger devises a
serpentine line to join the successive entries of the voices, so forming
a new melody which touches in turn each of the notes of the original
design. These additions are seldom in the sense of simple ornamentation, and it is this which gives these transcriptions their novel
value. The old theme is replaced by a new melody, more florid, with
more notes, but no less supple and graceful. It even happens, as at
the end of the 'Sancta Trinitas', that the organist is so carried away
that he gives his motet the sweep of a toccata (p. 35):

Ex. 202

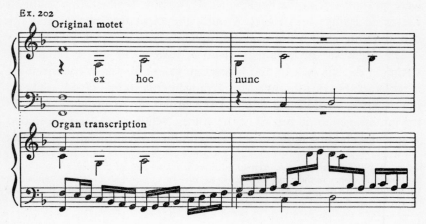

EARLY TUDOR KEYBOARD MUSIC

To complete this rapid survey of keyboard music in the first third of the sixteenth century we must turn to the English tablatures. In the present stage of our knowledge they present a problem difficult to grapple with, yet wide in range and of great importance. We still know so little about the majority of the musicians represented in these tablatures that one hardly knows which to include in the period covered by this chapter. However, it appears that the organists grouped round St. Paul's Cathedral and John Redford can in general be held to belong to the first third of the century.

We have found organ music printed in Germany (1512), Italy (1518), and France (1531), but it seems that no British printer set out to provide anything comparable. The works of the English composers who adorned the reign of King Henry VIII have come down to us only in manuscript copies dating from about 1520 to 1560. Nearly all these copies are in the British Museum; a small number are to be found at Christ Church, Oxford. The oldest manuscript, British Museum, Royal App. 58, gives, in addition to pieces for various instruments or for the lute, eleven compositions probably meant for the spinet or virginals: they are song-transcriptions and dances.[1] Only one of these pieces is signed, a 'Hornepype' (fo. 40ᵛ) bearing the name of Hugh Aston. The manuscript Royal App. 56 gives organ versets for the Mass (fo. 15 ff.) and for hymns, with other pieces, including a 'Felix namque'.

British Museum, Add. 15233 was copied round about 1530. Its first pages give some organ works by Redford: four hymns, a *Te Deum* and an Offertory. Much more important are Add. 29996[2] and Add. 30513 (the *Mulliner Book*).[3] These two tablatures give a collection, outstanding both in quantity and in quality, of English organ pieces between 1520 and 1560. The first of these reveals three stars of the first magnitude—John Redford, Thomas Preston, and Philip ap Ryce—as well as such by no means contemptible composers as Richard Wynslate, organist of Winchester, J. Thorne of York, Robert Coxsun, E. Strowger (or Strogers), and Kyrton. In the

[1] Ten of the eleven pieces have been edited by Frank Dawes in *Schott's Anthology of Early Keyboard Music*, i (London, 1951). The Aston 'Hornepype' is also printed by Wolf, *Sing- und Spielmusik aus älterer Zeit* (Leipzig, 2nd edn. 1931), no. 24, and Apel, *Musik aus früher Zeit*, ii, p. 5. See also Ch. Van den Borren, *The Origins of Keyboard Music in England* (London, 1913), pp. 22–26. 'Lady Carey's Dompe' from the same manuscript (sometimes attributed to Aston) is printed in Davison and Apel, *Historical Anthology of Music*, No. 103 and recorded in *The History of Music in Sound*, iv.
[2] Six pieces edited by Denis Stevens in *Altenglische Orgelmusik* (Kassel, 1954).
[3] Edited by D. Stevens in *Musica Britannica*, i (London, 1951).

Mulliner Book Redford reappears surrounded by younger composers: Shepherd, Tye, Tallis, Farrant, Blitheman, Allwood, and others.

It must remain an open question, in spite of the opinion of Hughes-Hughes,[1] whether or no the first fifty pieces of Add. 29996 are in Redford's handwriting and the twenty following in Preston's. If one accepts 1550 as the approximate date for the oldest part of the manuscript, Redford is excluded since it is known that he died in 1547.[2] The date of his birth is uncertain, but it seems that he was brought up at St. Paul's and became organist there about 1525, almoner in 1532, and later choirmaster. It is probable that his organ music was composed during the time he was organist, that is between 1525 and 1532. Preston and ap Ryce are held to have been his contemporaries. Leaving these questions on one side until such time as a serious study of these biographical questions has been made, we shall consider here only the more important musical characteristics of the first two sections of this manuscript.

It is evident at the start that this is a religious collection, for no secular piece occurs, and the numerous series of versets on a single theme correspond to the liturgical practice of the time and to the custom of alternating organ and choir. A dozen or more of these pieces are hymns, the majority consisting of several verses. In the same way Redford's *Te Deum* (one of several by him)[3] is divided into a number of versets according to the general custom of the time. But the division adopted is not identical with that made by contemporary French organists: from verset 8 on, Redford allots to the organ those verses which the Parisians of 1531 give to the choir. Philip ap Ryce, who also held a post at St. Paul's, as appears from this manuscript (fo. 28^v), is the author of a collection of versets for the Mass Vatican IV,[4] for he signs the last piece of the series. Since the *Kyrie* is lacking and blank pages have been left for the *Credo*, the Ordinary of this Mass is reduced to *Gloria, Sanctus, Benedictus,* and *Agnus,* together with an Offertory for the feast of the Trinity.[5]

Offertories for the organ based on the corresponding liturgical plainsongs are found at this time in England only. There are no fewer

[1] *Catalogue of Manuscript Music in the British Museum,* iii (London, 1909), p. 80.

[2] A. W. Reed, *Early Tudor Drama* (London, 1926), p. 55.

[3] Redford's complete works have been published by C. F. Pfatteicher, *John Redford* (Kassel, 1934). The majority are easily accessible in *Musica Britannica,* i. His 'O Lux on the faburden' is recorded in *The History of Music in Sound,* iii.

[4] *Graduale Romanum* (1908), p. 14, *Liber Usualis* (1950), p. 25.

[5] See further D. Stevens, 'Pre-Reformation Organ Music in England', *Proceedings of the Royal Musical Association,* lxxviii (1952), p. 7. The Mass has been edited by Stevens in *Altenglische Orgelmusik,* p. 24.

than twenty-one of these in the older part of Add. 29996. These pieces bear witness to the custom, still existing today in the Latin rite, of giving to the organ alone the music before the Preface sung by the priest. No other piece from the Proper of the Mass occurs in this manuscript,[1] except an Offertory by J. Thorne ('Exsultabunt sancti', fo. 37[v]). German, Italian, and French organists have left us no written proof that the organ was substituted for singing in this type of music. But we may suppose that antiphons or responds of the Proper were in all countries played by the organist, who would improvise on them as on other traditional themes by surrounding them with ornamental variations.

The English school develop liturgical motives in a great variety of ways. Sometimes the melody is stated straightforwardly from beginning to end, in long notes, in one of the parts (usually the highest), in which case the notes of the *canto fermo* may be repeated in triple time. As we have seen, Schlick and Kotter also use this method (see Exs. 184 and 185). But the English music, more complex and more learned, uses such a rhythm only as a pretext for subtle essays in syncopation and allusion. Thus Preston in his Offertory 'Diffusa' (fo. 49), persistently contradicts in the counterpoints the triplet rhythm of the plainsong in the highest part:

Ex. 203

Diffusa est gra - - - ti - - a

---

[1] Denis Stevens has since shown that fos. 62[v]–67[v] are a Mass Proper for Easter Sunday by Preston: see 'Further Light on *Fulgens praeclara*', *Journal of the American Musicological Society*, ix (1956), p. i.—*Ed.*

The English organists frequently quote only the first notes of the liturgical theme, using them as a springboard for a series of free canonic imitations. Robert Coxsun takes the first notes of the Offertory 'Laetamini'[1] and from them builds this scaffolding of motives:

Ex. 204

The Gregorian theme is not loaded with mordents and trills superficially, as with some Continental organists. It is transformed and given greater breadth by the remodelling of the melody according to the best English tradition since the time of Dunstable. This is shown in the following anonymous example, which show the openings of a series of three versets of the hymn 'Conditor alme siderum':

Ex. 205

---

[1] Published in Stevens, *Altenglische Orgelmusik*, p. 38.

In the same way Redford, starting from the Offertory 'Precatus est' (which he begins at the word 'Moyses') refashions it so completely that the original can be recognized only after careful examination. The ornamental motives are entirely derived from the liturgical theme without the addition of conventional, ready-made graces. Such music as this is rich because the imitations are numerous, free and full. Severe and sober, though closely knit and full of ideas, its principal qualities are continuity and persistence of design:

Ex. 206

Examples 204 and 206 show that the English used an organ keyboard with a range unusually wide at this period both in bass and in the treble. The compass of their pieces exceeds in both directions the

range for which the continental organists write. Whereas Schlick and
Buchner, like the French, use three octaves and two tones, and Marco
Antonio employs four octaves, Redford and his compatriots write for
four octaves and a fifth (from C to g''', although this top limit is only
twice reached by Redford). This wide register compels them to use
two staves with usually more lines than the French or Italian tablatures.[1] Sometimes as many as eight lines are employed. Moreover
these two staves are sometimes joined to form one of fourteen, fifteen,
or even sixteen lines. This feature is found again later in some of the
virginal books. Another feature of these tablatures is the irregularity
of the bar-lines, which are placed without regard to any constant
number of rhythmic units.

The wide compass of the keyboard, and the boldness with which
Preston and Redford in particular make use of it, saves their music
from the accusation which one would otherwise be tempted to make:
that it is vocal in style and makes hardly any use of instrumental
idioms. As a matter of fact, their melodies are often too wide in range
for the human voice. It is not infrequent for the right hand to run
through two octaves and a half in a single sweep. The manual dexterity
of these composers is most remarkable, as is the skill with which they
divide the three or four voices of the polyphony between the two
hands of the player, especially when the speed is relatively fast and
the musical line complicated. The point may be illustrated by this
example from a 'Felix namque' by Preston (fo. 46, plainsong in the
bass),[2] whose virtuosity is unique for this period and anticipates the
feats of Giles Farnaby.

Ex. 207

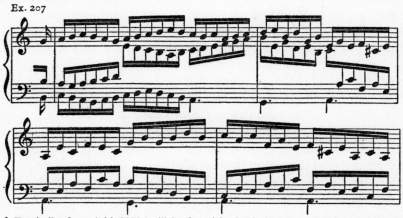

---

[1] Facsimiles from Add. 29996 will be found in Apel, *Notation of Polyphonic Music*,
pp. 11 and 13, and in *Proceedings of the Royal Musical Association*, lxxviii (1951–2),
frontispiece and facing p. 8.   [2] Printed in Stevens, *Altenglische Orgelmusik*, p. 6.

It is well known that the Offertory 'Felix namque' of the Office of
our Lady was a favourite with the English organists, although it
gradually yields its place in the course of the sixteenth and even
seventeenth centuries to the 'In nomine' and 'Miserere'. Two settings
of 'Felix namque' by Thomas Tallis occur in the *Fitzwilliam Virginal
Book*, and three, by Blitheman, Farrant, and Shelbye, in the *Mulliner
Book*. It is less well known that it was firmly rooted in the first third
of the sixteenth century. Redford, Preston, and ap Ryce all make frequent use of it. Thomas Preston makes a particularly happy use of
this theme in a set of seven variations (fo. 53ᵛ–60), in which he achieves
an astonishing diversity of treatment. The first four variations are in
four-part polyphony with the *canto fermo* (in long notes) placed in
the treble, bass, alto, and tenor in turn. The three following variations
contract and ornament the melody, which passes incessantly from
part to part. Preston makes frequent and masterly use of double canon
with the parts linked in pairs, thus applying to organ music the
thematic technique of Josquin.[1]

While the most constructive contemporary organists on the Continent, Marco Antonio and the French, were content to use hardly any
means of development other than melodic sequence and polyphonic
imitation, Preston and Redford were able to make their themes live
by shortening or expanding them, changing them gradually and giving
them a series of different shapes. They thus paved the way for the
large-scale variations of Byrd and Bull. They were also able, in their
sequences, to combine and alternate two motives. The musical figure
may preserve its rhythmical structure and change its intervals, or it
may retain its melodic outline and alter its rhythm. These are features
of style which at the end of the century the Italians were to adopt and
incorporate in the great *ricercari* from which the fugue is derived.

The qualities of the English organists about 1530 may then be
summarized as suppleness and subtlety of rhythm, clever and marked

[1] See p. 265.

use of syncopation, combination and overlapping of triple and duple rhythms, solidity of counterpoint, wealth of figuration, and interest and musicianship in thematic treatment.

MUSIC FOR INSTRUMENTS OR VOICES

To end this chapter it is necessary to repeat what was said at the beginning: that we have not yet reached a clear separation between vocal and instrumental music. There is still a vast field of mixed material, on the edges of which are to be found, on the one hand, strictly vocal polyphony, such as many Masses, and, on the other, specifically instrumental music written in tablature. Between these two poles lies a wide range of compositions which every group of amateurs performed according to taste and resources. The existence of songs unprovided with words in the song-books of 1450–1530 met the somewhat vague needs of such performers. Thus the Trent Codices contain wordless pieces which could be considered as instrumental trios.[1] The songs printed in 1501 in Petrucci's *Odhecaton* have no words except their *incipit*, and his *Canti C* of 1503 have only incomplete texts. Such collections were plainly addressed to musical circles which intended to play rather than to sing, although singing was not excluded if one of the group happened to know the words. Before long the individual parts were, for greater convenience, printed in separate books instead of opposite each other in the same volume, so that each player might have his music under his eyes. Attaingnant presented his four-part dances of 1530 in this way.

The double destination of much of the music of this period is evident also in such titles as that of Ott in 1534 (songs *lustig zu singen, vnd auff allerley Instrument dienstlich*) and of the Italian publishers (*Musica nova accomodata per cantar et sonar sopra organi et altri strumenti*, 1540).[2] Such titles abounded up to the end of the century, when this confusion was ended by the increasing development of techniques peculiar to different instruments.

[1] Benvenuto Disertori has shown that the piece on fos. 402ᵛ–403 of Codex 89 was probably intended for three viols: cf. 'L'unica composizione sicuramente strumentale nei Codici Tridentini', *Collectanea Historiae Musicae*, ii (Florence, 1957).—*Ed.*

[2] G. Benvenuti, preface to *Istituzioni e monumenti dell' arte musicale italiana*, i (Milan, 1931), p. lii.

XIII

MUSICAL INSTRUMENTS

By GERALD HAYES

INTRODUCTORY

THE musical interest in the instruments of the first fifteen hundred years of the Christian era must be given mainly to the last four or five centuries of that period. Even if we had—and we certainly have not—any clear knowledge of the instrumental resources of the Dark Ages, it would be of little value, for there is no music of that period known to be intended for them. With the later centuries it is far otherwise: as the preceding chapter shows, there is a large body of medieval and early Renaissance music in which clearly instruments were employed, while literary and artistic evidence of the same periods reveals a great wealth of varied instruments in everyday use.

INSTRUMENTS OF LATE CLASSICAL DAYS

The classical instruments were naturally carried on in the Roman world for some centuries: the lyre and the *kithara*, the organ, the reed pipes and the trumpets, the cymbals and, perhaps, the psaltery (see vol. I, pp. 406–10). Many later Roman designs show ladies playing what at first sight seems to be the lute: the body is small and rounded with a long, very broad neck, carrying a large number of strings. But there is no indication of any stopping, and it seems almost certain that this was merely a rather extravagant form of *kithara*. Some clear examples are in the Louvre, and a specially interesting relief, showing two instruments, is found on a sarcophagus in Agrigento Cathedral, though this has been sadly misdrawn in some books,[1] while numerous statuettes, usually of terra-cotta, from Tanagra, Alexandria, Myrina, and other places attest the wide use of an instrument so like the later mandora, or little lute, that it is difficult to realize that these figures are not products of fourteenth-century Europe.

These classical 'lutes' reflect their Eastern origin[2] and may have been classed as barbaric and so without the pale of respectability: certainly Persian silver-ware found in south Russia, and dated in the

[1] For a selection see Hortense Panum, *The Stringed Instruments of the Middle Ages*, English ed. revised and edited by J. Pulver (London, 1941), or Kathleen Schlesinger, *Instruments of the Modern Orchestra* (London, 1910).
[2] Cf. vol. I, pp. 423–7.

dynasty of the Sassanids, shows the large lute to perfection, even including indications of the rectangular peg box thrown sharply back. The Sassanids drove out the more civilized Arsacids in the third century A.D. and were a more Oriental race; it is significant that similar instruments are represented on fifth-century paintings found in Turkestan. If writings only were our guide we should not suspect that such instruments were used in Europe in the early Christian centuries, but there are some late Roman reliefs that prove that it must have had sufficient familiarity to be used as a normal object in the reliefs on funeral monuments. Examples are in Rome and also in the Lateran Museum,[1] but the most remarkable is from a limestone sarcophagus found near Arles.[2] This shows a side view of a full-bodied lute standing beside a normal *kithara*: fragments of the pegs remain, but hardly enough to determine the number of strings. Above the instruments a 'book' hangs from a peg and this may be a set of tablets with music, for the tomb seems most likely to have been that of a musician. A small object with an arrow-like head is usually regarded as a plectrum. In photographs of this relief the lute looks very clumsy, but this is partly because one unconsciously assumes a large piece of stone: it comes as a surprise in the Museum at Arles to find that it is really quite small and the roughness only what would be expected on that scale. It is rather strange that this exciting piece of evidence of the use of the lute in the second century A.D. in France has not aroused more inquiry among antiquarians.

It is clear that an instrument of the lute or mandora type was in use in Roman Europe, and some tradition of it, if not its actual use, may have survived through the Dark Ages.

THE EARLY PSALTERY

The psaltery of the Dark Ages has been made something of a mystery, in spite of the richness of reference in word and picture. The trouble seems to have started with Ambros, who dismissed all the illustrations as mere 'lucubrations of the imagination of the medieval monks'.[3] Panum followed his strictures even to denying the possibility of any knowledge of what the word 'psaltery' meant in that

---

[1] See C. Robert, *Die antiken Sarkophag-Reliefs* (Berlin, 1890), and *Bullettino della Commissione Archeologica communale di Roma* (1877).

[2] A most misleading engraving of this in Millin's *Monuments antiques inédits* (Paris, 1802) was unfortunately used by Panum (op. cit., p. 211), who draws unwarrantable conclusions from it in consequence. See photograph in Kinsky, *Geschichte der Musik in Bildern* (Leipzig, 1929), p. 21, fig. 1.

[3] *Geschichte der Musik*, quoted in Panum, op. cit., p. 165.

period, and claiming that the instrument to which we now apply the name was unknown in Europe until it was introduced from Oriental sources about the eleventh century.[1] The early Church writers, however, from St. Augustine[2] onwards make extensive use of the difference between the square box of the psaltery and the open frame of the *kithara* for religious and moral symbolism. There would have been no point in using these objects if they had not been familiar to their readers, yet we are asked to suppose that they were inventing something to fit into a Biblical allusion that they did not understand. The descriptions are, in fact, remarkably clear and consistent: the psaltery was made of wood (Augustine and Isidore), perhaps occasionally of brass (Eusebius), and had two forms, square[3] and triangular,[4] the square shape being the more general: it had ten strings. A typical description is

Non quod in modum citharae, sed quod in modum clypei quadrati conformetur cum chordis decem.[5]

(It should be not in the shape of a *kithara*, but in the shape of a square shield with ten strings.)

EARLY ORGANS

The use of the keyboard organ in classical times is now well attested, and the remains of a Roman hydraulic organ of the third century, very well preserved, have been found in Hungary.[6] Cassiodorus[7] and many other early writers have left descriptions of the organ that prove its wide use in early Christian centuries. It was an important ceremonial instrument at the Byzantine court, and an obelisk of the Emperor Theodosius I shows an organ with men standing on bellows to provide the wind, for the pneumatic organ was as well known to antiquity as the hydraulic.[8] There is a very circumstantial account of the gift of an organ to Pepin by the Emperor Constantine Copronymus: it arrived at Compiègne in 757 and is stated to have had leaden pipes.[9] But the making of organs remained a Byzantine secret in Charlemagne's time, until a Venetian monk made one at Aix-la-Chapelle for Louis the Pious and so restored the status of the Emperor

---

[1] Cf. vol. I, pp. 444–5.
[2] Cf. J. P. Migne, *Patrologia Latina*, xxxvi, cols. 280, 479, 671, 900; xxxvii, col. 1036.
[3] e.g. Augustine, Rabanus Maurus, pseudo-Jerome.
[4] e.g. Cassiodorus, Isidore.   [5] Migne, op. cit. cxi, col. 498.
[6] See vol. I, p. 408.   [7] Migne, op. cit. lxx, col. 1052.
[8] See E. Wellesz, *A History of Byzantine Music and Hymnography* (Oxford, 1949), p. 94.
[9] *Annales archéologiques*, iii (1846), p. 279; H. Degering, *Die Orgel, ihre Erfindung und ihre Geschichte bis zur Karolingerzeit* (Münster, 1905), p. 60.

of the West. Much earlier that most unchurchmanlike bishop, Venantius Fortunatus, writing in sixth-century France, had described the music in a church, with its organ, trumpet, cymbals, shrill shawms (*calami*), soft pipe (*fistula*), children's flute (*tibia*), and lyre.[1]

Aldhelm, in his poem in praise of the Virgin (late seventh century), refers to the thousand voices of the organ,[2] while Wulstan's panegyric of Bishop Elphege, who installed the great organ in Winchester Cathedral late in the tenth century, is too familiar for quotation.[3] True, Wulstan says of the bishop's organ, 'like thunder the iron voice batters the ear', but taken in their context his references to the volume of sound seem no more than poetic hyperboles, inserted to impress its magnificence on the reader: the spirit of high praise for Elphege, allied to the detailed description of the method of working and playing this elaborate organ, forbids any suspicion of intended ridicule. However, the Winchester organ was the last great organ to be built for several centuries as far as we know. Whether, as William of Malmesbury[4] seems to suggest, St. Dunstan first introduced the organ into England cannot be proved, but the continuous use of organs, both large and portable, throughout the first thousand years A.D. must be pictured all over western Europe: there was no break in the tradition.[5]

One important change took place in European instruments: the greater wind pressure made the rather delicate keyboard mechanism of the classical instruments ineffective, and the slider came into use. As these had to be pulled out and pushed in, the range of music was limited even with the two players so often depicted.[6] These sliders remained in use long after the keyboard was rediscovered (perhaps one should say, until a mechanism suited to the greater wind pressure was invented), and the practice of painting on or above them the letters denoting the notes of the scale ultimately led to the alphabetical organ tablature. An eleventh-century miniature shows this very clearly (pl. V*a*). Although the thirteenth-century Belvoir Psalter is the earliest representation of a keyboard in use, there is a tenth-century tract on organ construction that contains definite indications of a keyboard mechanism.

[1] *Carmina*, ii. 9.
[2] Migne, op. cit. lxxxvi, col. 240.
[3] Ibid. cxxxvii, col. 110.
[4] *De gestis pontificum*, ed. N. E. S. A. Hamilton (London, 1870), p. 407.
[5] The whole question of early organs is discussed in a scholarly article by Willi Apel in *Speculum*, xxiii (1948), pp. 191–216, in which previous accounts are amended and some fresh evidence presented, both of the instruments and of their music.
[6] For example, in the Utrecht Psalter.

The incomprehensible instruments displayed in the spurious letter of Jerome to Dardenus (*c.* 800)[1] were copied in manuscripts, especially in pictures of David, for two centuries or more: they were given fresh life in Virdung's treatise of 1511 and even found their way into Praetorius more than a hundred years later. Perhaps sufficient credit has not been given to the author's sense of humour; the whole thing may have been a hoax. The Boulogne Psalter of the tenth century shows a late version of his *bombulum*, which is here called *bunibulum*. The name sounds onomatopoeic: it may have been an attempt to describe an organ, known from hearsay only.

NEW INSTRUMENTS IN THE DARK AGES

As the Teutonic and Scandinavian races infiltrated throughout western Europe they brought new instruments with them: of these the outstanding examples were the harp and the *chrotta* or rote. Venantius Fortunatus in the sixth century records:

> Romanusque lyra plaudat tibi, barbarus harpa,
> Graecus achilliaca, chrotta Britanna canat.[2]

(Let the Roman praise you on the lyre, the barbarian on the harp, and the Greek on the *kithara*, and let the British play the *chrotta*.)

The Roman with his lyre and the Greek with the *kithara* we know: to whom did he refer as barbarians and Britons? It has long been decided that the barbarians with their harps were the Northmen whose invasions of Britain and the northern coast of western Europe had already begun.[3] The final proof turned up in the sixth-century Saxon treasure-trove at Sutton Hoo in 1939; the major portions of a harp, of superb craftsmanship, were found, and this has been reconstructed with convincing certainty (pl. V*b*).[4] Authorities regard this instrument as a funeral miniature of an original many times larger. If it is true that the *chrotta* or rote was the characteristic instrument of the Bretons and the Britons, it is rather surprising that the earliest known example, dating from about the seventh century, was found in the Black Forest in Germany.[5] There is extant a letter written in the eighth century from Cuthbert, a Northumbrian abbot, to Lullus,

---

[1] Migne, op. cit. xxx, col. 214.   [2] *Carmina*, VII. viii. 63–64.
[3] The case is well summarized in Galpin's *Old English Instruments of Music* (3rd ed., London, 1932), pp. 9–10. Sachs, on the other hand, in *The History of Musical Instruments* (New York, 1940), pp. 262 ff., argues that *harpa* = 'lyre' and *chrotta* = 'harp'.
[4] See R. L. S. Bruce-Mitford in *Archaeological News Letter*, i (1948), p. 11.
[5] Now in the Ethnographical Museum, Berlin.

Archbishop of Mainz, asking for the loan of a performer on the *chrotta* or rote, as he had an instrument but no player:

Delectat me quoque cytharistam habere, qui possit citharisare in cithara, quam nos appellamus rottae [*sic*], quia citharam habeo, et artificem non habeo.[1]

(I should like also to have a musician who could perform on the *kithara* which we call the rote, as I have an instrument and no one to play it.)

The early use of the rote in Scandinavia is attested by the discovery of an example dating only a little later than the Black Forest find.

Two things are evident: the use of the rote, if once confined to the British people, which is very doubtful, had spread rapidly over middle and north-eastern Europe: and the use of *lira* and *kithara* for the rote was getting confused. The rote continues to be one of the most frequently used names of instruments up to the fifteenth century, and its importance as a basic type can hardly be exaggerated (pl. VI). It is beyond the scope of this chapter to discuss its origins; it may have been a British or a Teutonic invention, but it is so akin to the *kithara* that it may well have derived from Roman settlers.

In the ninth century the west German monk Otfrid, in a well-known passage, mentions the organ, *lira*, harp, rote, panpipes and *fidula*.[2] This is the first time that the word *fidula*, which was to take so many forms, appears: it is derived from the late Latin *vitula*, though indirectly; but in Otfrid's time it can hardly have been a bowed instrument. Meanwhile the quadrangular harp or cruit, with a distinct front pillar, had been developed in Ireland, as a stage between the rote proper and the triangular harp that was to adopt the same name about the tenth century in that country,[3] and from there to spread, with Irish learning and culture, into Europe. Irish scholars and missionaries, both directly and indirectly, were the most important cultural influence in north-western Europe in Carolingian times. If our information is very cloudy about the nature of instrumental music in this first millennium of the Christian era, we are in no doubt about the extent and importance of it in musical life throughout Europe during that period.

EARLY CRAFTSMANSHIP

Before we enter the last third of our period[4] there are two general principles upon which too much emphasis cannot be laid. Some

[1] Migne, op. cit. xcvi, col. 839.
[2] Otfrid's *Evangelienbuch*, v. 23, 197–9; ed. P. Piper, i (Paderborn, 1878), p. 668.
[3] See Galpin, op. cit., pp. 287–8.
[4] Musical references in early religious literature may be studied in Th. Gérold, *Les*

unconscious habit of mind tends to make people think that musical instruments must have been crudely made until the famous craftsmen of the seventeenth century appeared; even musical histories, written within living memory and still standard works, contain fantastic references to instruments of times as late as 1550. There is not the slightest reason to suppose that instruments were ever anything but perfect: the craftsmanship that could solve the difficult problems of constructing prehistoric Danish *luren*, the Sutton Hoo harp, the Black Forest rote, and other early remains, did not die, and when it became allied to the elegant tradition of Roman and Greek instrument-making, it could produce only the best. Whatever faults are laid at the doors of the Dark and Middle Ages, bad craftsmanship has never been one, and the onus of proof that musical instruments were an exception to an otherwise general rule would be heavy indeed.

The second point is that when an instrument becomes available, somebody will fairly soon become a virtuoso on it. This we can see around us today in many walks of life into which no formal tuition penetrates: these players of early days would not find their way into musical textbooks of their period, but when they became professionals—for example, *jongleurs* or travelling minstrels—their techniques would certainly reach a high standard. It is necessary to emphasize this, as purely antiquarian research can lead scholars into fantastic deductions.[1]

EARLY BOWED INSTRUMENTS

The most significant event in the history of European instruments was the introduction of the bow. The origin of the bow, and how (or, indeed, if) it was brought to Europe, are still matters of debate:[2] the certain fact is that there is no record of its use earlier than a repre-

---

Pères de l'Eglise et la musique (Paris, 1931). A useful source-book for the whole period in England is F. M. Padelford, *Old English Musical Terms* (Bonn, 1899). For the later part of this period a mine of English literary references can be found in G. Schad, *Musik und Musikausdrücke in der mittelenglischen Literatur* (Frankfurt-am-Main, 1911). The explanations of instruments by both Padelford and Schad should be received with some caution. The quotations given in this chapter are mainly additional to the material collected by these two writers.

[1] e.g. Pulver's note on an eleventh-century miniature showing bowed rotes in Panum, op. cit., p. 223. He maintains that as there is no sign of a fingerboard the strings were obviously bowed open. It requires little imagination to realize that no musicians of that period would have tolerated continuous scraping on three or four open strings: if that was all that could be got out of such an instrument it would have died stillborn.

[2] Curt Sachs has advanced the theory that in its origin the bow was a mark of decadence and not advance: see his article 'Die Streichbogenfrage', *Archiv für Musikwissenschaft*, i (1918–19), p. 3.

sentation on an ivory casket assigned to the ninth century and believed to be of Byzantine design, though possibly carved in Italy. In
the eleventh century it is shown with confidence as something in
common use and, further, in use with several quite distinct instruments. How this happened we do not know; without the casket we
should not even suspect its existence before it is found in regular use.

The early history of bowed instruments has a very large literature
of conflicting theories and claims: attention here must be limited to
the barest outline of facts. When the first definite evidence—the
eleventh-century manuscript illuminations—is examined, we find that
the bow is treated as something in normal and widespread use: the
date of its general introduction therefore cannot be much later than
about 1000. From the beginning four separate types can be discerned,
which gradually became more and more clearly the four instruments
known in the fifteenth century as the viol, the crowd (or *crwth*), the
rebec, and the *lira* (*da braccio*). The first three are found in manuscripts
of the eleventh century; the fourth perhaps not until the next century.
What is remarkable is that the earliest representations of the viol show
the method of holding, bowing, and stopping almost as perfected as
that of the textbooks of the seventeenth century (see pl. V*a* and VII).
For a century and more the outline of the viols shows great variation,
from the sharp waist formed between two ovals to a waistless, almost
rectangular instrument: an example of the latter type with its bow,
and significantly placed vertically, is labelled 'viola' in a fourteenth-
century manuscript,[1] though this pattern is shown long before that
date.[2] This variety of outlines is only what one would expect in formative days when intercourse was difficult and no standard for the whole
of Europe had been evolved or accepted.

The crowd is clearly a bowed *chrotta* or rote; a fingerboard has
been inserted between the sides, joining the top bar to the sound-box,
and a bridge added to raise the strings. In its earliest representations
it has incurved sides, on the pattern of the Black Forest rote, but
rectangular instruments soon appeared and this shape later became the
standard. The very earliest examples, which date from the first half
of the eleventh century, show some players using a curious stopping
technique: the left hand is placed over the top of the instrument so
that the fingers have only a very limited movement (see pl. VI).[3] The

---

[1] Brit. Mus., Sloane 3983.

[2] See Galpin, op. cit., pl. xv, for a twelfth-century example at Barfreston Church in
Kent. In the plate it is wrongly labelled 'rybybe'.

[3] In St. Leopold's Prayer Book from Klosterneuburg (now in Vienna), also of about
this date, two players are stopping from the side in the usual way.

bowed rote or lyre seems to have been used from one extreme of Europe to the other at a very early date: there is evidence of a wide use of it in Scandinavia,[1] and it is shown on early sculptured reliefs in Ireland,[2] though precise dates are uncertain. The rectangular form became the standard and the crowd remained a very popular instrument until the end of the fourteenth century; it survived in Wales and was in sufficiently general use in 1738 to be mentioned then without comment.[3] The incurved form, often shown with a small hand-opening, may possibly have merged into the *lira*.

On the whole, the crowd must be written off as a false line of development; it provided nothing that could not be obtained better on other instruments. It was far otherwise with the rebec, to which the same dismissal has often been applied. From Spain to Scandinavia, through France, Germany, and England, we find this bowed mandora in wide use in the eleventh and twelfth centuries: whether it was an importation from the Arabs, or the bow applied to the plucked instrument surviving from classical days, we do not know.[4] The earliest Spanish evidence is a little later than that found elsewhere, but this may be accidental. At first the rebec has no separate neck, but later this develops; in the lost St. Blasius MS. of the twelfth century, reproduced by Gerbert,[5] the neck is somewhat in evidence and the instrument is labelled 'lyra'. The absence of a sound-post consequent on the rounded body and flat belly has led the rebec to be condemned as acoustically unsound, but the fact remains that it has a unique tone colour, a penetrating, almost snarling brilliance, that is not represented by any other instrument. It began to lose favour at the end of the fifteenth century and had faded away by 1700. Jerome of Moravia[6] (*c.* 1250) gives it two strings tuned in fifths, and its later three strings were invariably tuned in fifths. The name rebec does not emerge until the fifteenth century; earlier it is always called rubebe, rybybe, ribeba, or ribible (probably a diminutive), from the Arabic *rabé* or *rabāb*. A long list of instruments of the mid-fourteenth century[7] includes the *rebebe à corde terne*.

[1] See Otto Andersson, *The Bowed Harp* (London, 1930), and Panum, op. cit.

[2] St. Finian's Church, Waterville, Co. Kerry, first reported in 1927 by Dr. Sandvik; reproduced in Panum, op. cit., p. 227.

[3] Letter from Lewis Morris dated 30 December 1738: Hon. Society of Cymrodorion, xlix (1947), pt. i.

[4] Brit. Mus., Cotton Tiberius C. VI; manuscript in Leipzig University; carvings at Chartres and Montpellier; carving in Gamtofte Church, Fünen; *Cantigas de Santa Maria* (Madrid, 1889). And cf. vol. I, p. 445.

[5] *De Cantu et Musica Sacra* (St. Blaise, 1774), ii, pl. xxxii, no. 18.

[6] *Tractatus de musica*, in C. E. H. de Coussemaker, *Scriptorum de musica medii aevi nova series* (Paris, 1864–76), i, p. 152.   [7] Jean Lefèvre, *La Vielle* (Paris, 1861), p. 19.

It was mentioned above that the early viols sometimes show an almost square outline: this shape, or an oval shape, may even then denote a different instrument, for an oval instrument of distinct type, usually shown played on the shoulder, had emerged by the early thirteenth century. Records are confusing, especially those of Spanish origin, where some such instrument is shown played in all positions: but this flattish, waistless instrument with its long bow and typical head became clearly distinct from the viol. Later one or more bourdon strings were always present,[1] though not regularly before the fourteenth century.[2] This instrument, to be known soon after 1500 as the *lira da braccio*, became ubiquitous in the thirteenth and fourteenth centuries and seems to be the one to which the rather indefinite name *fiedel* (in all its various guises) was applied. Jerome of Moravia[3] gives considerable information about it; it had five strings, one of which was a bourdon while two others formed a single course in unison. But of the three methods of tuning that he prescribes one is without a bourdon and all the strings are single: this, he says, is especially useful for the professional minstrels. The fifth is the principal interval, used in combination with fourths: there is a significant affinity with the tuning of the *lira da braccio* given by Lanfranco.[4]

TRUMPETS AND HORNS

The literature about 1200 is so rich in references to and lists of musical instruments that it is impossible to believe that this was a matter of recent growth; the forms and their usage must have been going on for some centuries. The authors have an annoying habit of mentioning what is apparently the same instrument by different names in the same line or in neighbouring lines. Were there different forms that their contemporaries would recognize by these names or was it a poetic mannerism of the times? For the horn or trumpet we have beme in English as well as tromp:

> In benwyk the browgh with bemys bryght.

([They entered] in Benwyk town with shining bemys.)

> The trompettis uppon the wallis went[5]

[1] An early example is shown in Brit. Mus., Add. 28681 (thirteenth century).

[2] Panum, op. cit., pp. 376 and 379, reproduces an example from the twelfth century from the Abbey door of St. Denis (after Grillet) and a thirteenth-century example, very clear in detail, from La Maison de Musique, Rheims.

[3] Coussemaker, op. cit. i, p. 153. Jerome's information about bourdon strings is not at all clear and should be read with caution.

[4] *Scintille di Musica* (Brescia, 1533), p. 136.

[5] *Le Morte Arthur* (Early English Text Society, lxxxviii), 2707 and 2723; also Layamon's *Brut*, 24475, *Sir Beves*, 3793.

and, rather later:

> Bemes thane herde he blowe fulle lowde.[1]

In France we find *trompe, cor, buisine, graisle, moinel, cor sarrazinois,* and *araine* (this may be an adjective), e.g.:

> Cors sonent, trompes et araines[2]

The frequent early appearances of the word *buisine* or *buzine* are rather puzzling, for the true long, straight trumpet does not seem to be shown in pictures or sculpture before the mid-thirteenth century; possibly it referred to a long horn. It is almost certain that names were changed in their application between the eleventh and the four-teenth centuries. Clarion is a rather late-comer in the thirteenth century.

The horn, both short (as a bugle) and long, had been in use for many centuries: at some early date it was provided with finger holes after the manner of a vertical flute and so became the cornett. It is shown in the eleventh-century manuscript illustrated in pl. VI, and is of frequent occurrence throughout our period.[3] The word 'bugle' —presumably meaning the horn of a young bull—occurs early, e.g.:

> The kynge his bugul con blau, opon the bent bides,[4]

(The King blew his bugle, he waits on the field.)

and

> His bugulle can he blaw.[5]

Circular horns, large enough to go over the player's shoulders, were in use by the end of the fourteenth century:[6] and about that time, or very soon after, the true trumpet was folded, first in the form of a letter S,[7] then in the form still with us today. It is to this folded type of trumpet that the name 'clarion' becomes confined.

The whole question of wind instruments between 1100 and 1450 is extremely confused and the nomenclature very uncertain: it is badly in need of careful research.[8] A serious example of this need is

---

[1] *The Romance of Sir Isumbras* (c. 1400), stanza xxxvii (The Thornton Romances).
[2] *Roman de Fauvel*, 555.
[3] Another eleventh-century example is seen in a Catalan psalter (Paris, Bibl. Nat. lat. 11550, fo. 7ᵛ); it is reproduced in Th. Gérold, *Histoire de la musique des origines à la fin du XIVᵉ siècle* (Paris, 1936), pl. xv.
[4] *The Anturs of Arthur* (before 1300), stanza xxvi (London, 1842).
[5] *The Avowing of King Arthur* (before 1300), stanza vi: ibid.
[6] Shown on a carving of that date in Worcester Cathedral choir stalls.
[7] Lambeth Palace Library MS. 6 (c. 1400), reproduced in Galpin, op. cit., pl. xl.
[8] Anthony Baines kindly placed his then unfinished studies at the writer's disposal, but he must not be held responsible for the brief outline given here. [But see A. Baines, *Woodwind Instruments and their History* (London, 1957).—*Ed.*]

the date of the appearance of the sackbut or trombone: the name occurs in Lombard documents of the late fourteenth century, and a representation of a sackbut was identified with some certainty on a Burgundian chessboard now in the National Museum at Florence.[1] This ivory work, however, is now thought to show something of the nature of the *Zugtrompete* or *tromba da tirarsi*[2] of Bach's day, in which only the mouthpiece end of the tube was extended. Once the true clarion form was evolved, with the cylindrical bore and parallel tubes, the way was open for invention to give the full chromatic range: perhaps this form of clarion must be dated rather earlier in the fourteenth century. The trombone is not known with certainty until the second half of the fifteenth century:[3] Castiglione's joke about the player swallowing his trumpet[4] shows that either trombone or slide-trumpet must have been in regular use in Venice before 1507.

REED-PIPES AND SHAWMS

The reed instruments have an unbroken record from remote antiquity, but it is in examining these that we notice the only real weakness of instrumental music before the fifteenth century: there were very few bass instruments. If we omit the organ, which was available only in special circumstances, there seems to have been nothing beyond the very limited resources of the trumpet and horn in the low register, and the largest viols, which were then smaller than a modern violoncello. The large lute, larger viols, and the slide-trumpet mark the first advance, but the true tenor shawm, like the sackbut, did not appear until the fifteenth century; the full bass shawm was a century later still.

The reed pipe or *chalemel* comes out of the Dark Ages in its narrow, cylindrical form, often doubled by a second pipe parallel to the first,[5] or by divergent pipes[6] after the classical manner: even triple parallel pipes are shown.[7] It was early adapted for use with an air reservoir

---

[1] Galpin, op. cit., p. 207: in his *Textbook of European Musical Instruments* (London, 1937), p. 240, the author considerably modified his early views.

[2] See Curt Sachs, 'Chromatic Trumpets in the Renaissance', *The Musical Quarterly*, xxxvi (1950), p. 62.

[3] Cf. H. Besseler, 'Die Entstehung der Posaune', *Acta Musicologica*, xxii (1950), p. 8.

[4] *Libro del Cortigiano* (Venice, 1528): trans. by Sir Thomas Hoby (London, 1561).

[5] Paris, Bibl. Nat., lat. 1118 (eleventh century).

[6] Madrid, Bibl. Nac., Codex *Beati commentarius* (tenth century).

[7] The plates in J. Strutt, *The Sports and Pastimes of the People of England*, ed. J. C. Cox (London, 1903), provide numerous examples of all types: the references to the manuscripts from which they are taken can always be found in the text.

formed by a bladder or sack: both the bladder-pipe and its more elaborate cousin the bagpipe, originally called *chorus*, appear in the twelfth century, though the drone does not seem to have been added till the next century.[1] But the bagpipe, in principle, is an instrument of ancient times, and there is no reason to suppose that its use, in some form, had ever died out.

The shawm proper, father of our oboe but not really superseded by it, was rather late in invention: the famous carvings of musicians from the church of Santiago de Compostella (late twelfth century) show a double shawm, with divergent pipes; and a large single instrument, presumably an alto in range, is in the early thirteenth-century carvings on Rheims Cathedral. This application of the double beating reed to a conical bore with a wide bell gave a new tone colour to music and was widely used. The name appears as *schalmei*, e.g.:

> Noch phife, floyte, noch schalmey[2]

and many variations on it such as *shalmele, shalme, schalmye*: and it is probably a shawm, not a bagpipe, that is mentioned in *Sir Degrevant*:

> With trompe and with nakere
> And the scalmuse clere.[3]

It became the instrument of the waits or watchmen and received their name:

> Grete lordys were at the assent;
> Waytys blewe, to mete they went.[4]

It is not so easy to recognize in Lydgate's *Reson and Sensuallyte*:

> Lowde shallys and doucetes
> Passyng of gret melodye.[5]

The name *bombarde* is usually applied to the large tenor shawm with one key: although this word occurs in the latter part of the fourteenth century,[6] a clear representation of the instrument has not

---

[1] An excellent example, though not the earliest, is in the Gorleston Psalter (*c.* 1300) —a witty and valuable source for information on instruments (see Galpin, *Old English Instruments*, p. 176). The thirteenth-century Spanish *Cantigas de Santa María* (see p. 415, n. 2) show two forms.

[2] Eberhard Cersne von Minden, *Minneregeln* (1404), ed. F. X. Wöber (Vienna, 1861).

[3] Stanza lxviii (The Thornton Romances) (London, 1844).

[4] *Sir Eglamour of Artois*, stanza xcv: ibid.; assent = gathering.

[5] 5590–1 (Early English Text Society edn.). This poem, written soon after 1400, is a free adaptation of the earlier French poem *Les Échecs Amoureux*.

[6] Gérold, *La Musique au moyen âge* (Paris, 1932), p. 406, quotes an instance of 1391: there are others, e.g. Gower, *Confessio Amantis* (1393), mentions 'the sounde of bumbarde and of clarionne' (iii. 358). It also occurs in Lydgate's *Pilgrimage*, 14,303 (early fifteenth century).

been found dating before about 1420.[1] Earlier carvings of the plain shawm indicate an instrument almost of tenor size. In Germany *bombarde* became *pommer* and was ultimately applied to the whole family, as in Praetorius.

FLUTES

The flutes were of three types: the vertical tube, blown across the open end, the transverse flute, and the fipple flute. The first type, although examples of a single tube are shown (and were used by the ancient Egyptians), was restricted for all practical purposes to the panpipes, which go back to ancient times. Otfrid (see p. 471) in the ninth century mentions the panpipes as 'managfaltu suegala' (multiple pipe), and they are often depicted later, though the name by which they were known is uncertain. One of the most regularly listed instruments in French poetry of the twelfth to the fourteenth centuries is *frestel*, and this is usually translated as panpipes, e.g.:

> C'a dit Huyns: 'Vos dites mal, Robert,
> Ja n'i avrez fleuste ne frestel.'[2]

(Huyn said, 'You say wrongly, Robert, then you will have neither *fleuste* nor *frestel*.')

Out of 104 instrumental references collected from 184 purely pastoral poems of this period, *frestel* heads the list with twenty-four mentions. In ten passages in which it is mentioned with one or two other instruments, it appears as something distinct from *muse, musete, chalemel*, flute, *flajol*, pipe, bells, tabor, and viol, which are all well identified. These pastoral poems are highly stylized and there are only three mentions of stringed instruments—one each of viol, harp, and rote: ninety-four references are to wind instruments, the remaining seven being to bells and tabors. Shepherds have traditionally played the panpipes from classical times, and it is most probable that this was in the minds of the authors of these poems. In Provençal the word appears as *flestella*, e.g.:

> L'us estiva, l'autre flestella,[3]

(The one [played] the *estiva*, the other the *flestella*.)

and this may be an earlier formation, possibly to be linked to *flajol*. In references elsewhere, apart from long lists of instruments, it is also distinct from the *estive* (itself a doubtful quantity). Pending

---

[1] Anthony Baines has found an Italian example of this date.
[2] C. Bartsch, *Altfranzösische Romanzen und Pastorellen* (Leipzig, 1870), p. 199.
[3] *Flamenca* (c. 1250), 607; ed. Paul Meyer (Paris, 1901).

a more certain definition *frestel* may be accepted as meaning panpipes, if only as an interim measure.

The transverse flute is also an old form; it is shown with great precision in the *Hortus deliciarum* written about 1150 and in the next century it occurs again in Germany and in Spain,[1] but no certain example of its use in England has been found until about 1500.

The use of the flute in France is mentioned in early poetry, but it is very difficult to know to which instrument the various names refer: there is clear evidence for the use of the transverse flute in the mid-thirteenth century, e.g.:

Flahutes d'argent traversaines,[2]

but it would be rash to say that this was its earliest date in that country.

The case of the fipple flute, which became the three-holed 'pipe' or *galoubet*, the eight-holed recorder, and the six-holed flageolet, is also obscure: this method of exciting the air-column in a tube is old and is frequently found in primitive surroundings, so that we need not look for an invention of the principle but only for its development into serious instruments. Illustrations in England and France of the twelfth century have been said to contain reliable representations of recorders, but it is difficult to be quite certain until the twelfth century is well advanced: the probabilities are in favour of an early use of some sort of fipple flute. The three-holed flute was played with one hand while the other played on a small drum or tabor: the technique is complex but a considerable range can be obtained, and it says much for the accomplishments of lowly players that the 'pipe-and-tabor man' is shown so frequently in pictures of strolling players from the early fourteenth century onwards,[3] where the player often accompanies an acrobat or juggler.

The earliest use of the word 'recorder' seems to date from about 1400:

With fydle, recorde, and dowcemere,[4]

and we have no clear proof that it acquired the full set of eight holes until the fifteenth century. By the time Virdung wrote his treatise of 1511 the recorder (or *Blockflöte*) was well established with eight holes

[1] *Cantigas de Santa María*: see also Kinsky, *Geschichte der Musik in Bildern* (Leipzig, 1929), p. 46, no. 3.

[2] Adenès li Roi, *Li Romauns de Cléomadès* (c. 1260), 7255; ed. A. van Hasselt (Brussels, 1865).

[3] Cf. Strutt, op. cit.   [4] *The Squyre of Lowe Degre*, 1075.

PLATE V

SAXON HARP OF THE SIXTH CENTURY

Reconstructed from original found at Sutton Hoo, 1939

(*By courtesy of the Trustees of the British Museum*)

MANDORA OF THE NINTH CENTURY

(Psalter of Lothaire, British Museum, Add. 37768, fo. 5)

CHIME BELLS, SHAWM, VIOL, AND ORGAN OF THE ELEVENTH CENTURY

(Bible of St. Stephen Harding, Bibliothèque de Dijon)

as a family of four sizes, and many references attest its general use in the fifteenth century. Although the recorder, with its almost cylindrical exterior and rudiment of a bell opening, should be quite distinct from the shawm, of which the conical shape and wide bell are usually rather exaggerated, yet in many pictures it is not easy to be certain which is represented: some, usually labelled as recorders, turn out on close examination to be almost certainly reed instruments.

Two entries in Henry VII's *Privy Purse Expenses* within a few weeks of each other in 1492 suggest the use of both the recorder and the transverse flute:

To the Childe [i.e. of the Chapel Royal] that playeth on the Records
                                                                    0.20.0.
To Guillim for flotes in a case   0.70.0.

and the detailed lists of Henry VIII's instruments[1] half a century later strongly support this.

PSALTERY AND DULCIMER

Plucked instruments were many and various: the rote is seldom omitted from lists and had at least two forms: the older Teutonic type with seven or eight strings and a Spanish type with more strings.[2] But it must have been somewhat of a survival, for it is unlikely that it did anything that the harp could not do as well or better.

The psaltery was equally popular, but seems to have abandoned the old rectangular shape for the trapezoid Eastern form of the *qānūn*, though the thirteenth-century *Cantigas de Santa María* show square and even semicircular shapes. From the word *qānūn* came a variety of European equivalents: *canon* and *micanon* in France, *kanon* in German, *caño* in Spanish, with *canale* as a Latin form. The last gave *medium canale* for a small size, which frequently appears, rather disconcertingly, as *medicinale*. All these forms occur in Eberhard Cersne's *Minnereglen* (1404):

> Noch medicinale
> Noch portitif, noch psalterium
> Noch figel, sam canale;

[1] Printed in Galpin, *Old English Instruments of Music*, pp. 292–300, and Hayes, *The King's Music* (London, 1937), pp. 86–88.

[2] Cf. Lydgate, *Reson and Sensuallyte*: 'For there were Rotys of Almagne, And eke of Aragon and Spain.' Nearly two centuries earlier the Provençal poet Guiraut de Calanson, in his advice to a jongleur beginning 'Fadet joglar con potz preguar' had mentioned 'la rotta a deszest cordas garnier'.

and in an early thirteenth-century poem we have

> Vieles et sauterions,
> Harpes et gigues et canons,
>
> . . . . .
>
> Et mandoires et micanons.[1]

A form was devised in which the short strings were carried on a projection from the middle of one long side; the plain, long side was held against the breast and the arms passed behind the instrument so that the hands came from below on each side of the projection; this is shown as early as the eleventh century[2] and is so often represented that it must have been popular. Praetorius, in 1619, says that it was called in Italy *istromento di porco*, no doubt with reference to the snout-like effect of the small side: he shows the two plectra, which are often indicated in early pictures or carvings.[3]

The psaltery has never died: it was widely used in Finland as a folk-instrument under the name *kantele*,[4] and the zither, familiar in such places as the Tyrol, is first cousin to it. There seems no limit to the psaltery's powers of shape variation: many forms look like harps with a sound-box under the strings. The most important development was the change from plucking to hitting the strings with hammers, which gave the dulcimer: and from the dulcimer there evolved eventually the pianoforte. Today psaltery-players are rarely seen,[5] but the dulcimer is not unfamiliar in London streets; the dexterity of the players, who must be largely self-taught, and the remarkable range of tone and volume they produce, form eloquent testimony to the musical effects in the Middle Ages.

It is difficult to determine the date of the appearance of the dulcimer in Europe: there do not seem to be any representations in Western art before the fifteenth century,[6] though it is hard to believe that it took so long to appear. If the various forms of the word, such as *dowsemere*, mean the same thing, then it is mentioned in Spain in the fourteenth century[7] and in England by 1400 in the quotation from

---

[1] *Cléomadès*, 17273–4 and 17280.

[2] Brit. Mus., Add. 30045.

[3] *Syntagma Musicum*, ii (Wolfenbüttel, 1619), index, no. 98; pl. xxxvi, no. 3 (facsimile eds., Kassel, 1929 and 1958).

[4] Cf. Panum, op. cit., pp. 176–8. This book is especially valuable for information about early Scandinavian instruments—an important aspect of the subject that had formerly been unduly neglected.

[5] I last saw one in 1935, entertaining a theatre queue and performing prodigies of virtuosity.

[6] e.g. Manchester Cathedral.

[7] As *dulcoemel*, quoted by Galpin, op. cit., p. 62.

the *Squyr of Lowe Degre* (see p. 480): in the fifteenth century more references are found, though it is never a frequent name, like sawtry or harp. The German name was *Hackbrett*, and Praetorius, who depicts it with its hammers,[1] has to call the plain psaltery 'a *Hackbrett* played with the fingers'.[2] It is probable that the long plectra used for plucking the psaltery were also used for striking the strings, and that it only gradually became recognized as a separate instrument.

The word 'cymbal,' which was applied to a variety of instruments, from clash-pans to hurdy-gurdy,[3] meant either a psaltery or a dulcimer about the year 1400: Cersne[4] (1404) lists the psaltery as *canale, medicanale*, and *psalterium*, and he has also the line

Noch cymbel mid geclange,

which sounds more like the struck dulcimer. To German-speaking people today the word 'cymbal' suggests a *Hackbrett*.[5] On the other hand, the harpsichord was originally called *clavicymbalum*, and it is very definitely not a keyed dulcimer but a keyed psaltery.

VIRGINALS AND CLAVICHORD

The earliest history of keyboard stringed instruments is very obscure. Something emerges in the mid-fourteenth century by the name of *eschiquier*. Guillaume de Machaut (d. 1377) mentions it twice,[6] adding the words 'd'Angleterre'. In 1388 John I of Aragon wrote to the Duke of Burgundy asking for the loan of an experienced player on the *exaquier* and the 'little organ'.[7] In 1360 Edward III of England gave an *eschiquier* to King John of France, then his prisoner; and there are several other references to it in this period.[8] Pirro quotes a late use of the name (1511) in a connexion that indicates a keyboard instrument contrasted with *espinettes*.[9]

In Cersne's list of instruments, from which quotations have already been made, we find three names that were soon to become fixed to well-known types: *Schachtbrett, clavichordium*, and *clavicymbalum*. Were there three distinct instruments? He uses at least three names for

[1] Op. cit. ii, pl. xviii.
[2] Ibid., pl. xxxvi.
[3] e.g. Brit. Mus., Sloane 1326, fo. 122, and Harl. 2027, fo. 272 (both mid-seventeenth century).
[4] Op. cit.
[5] Cf. the Hungarian *zimbalon*.
[6] *Prise d'Alexandrie* and *Li temps pastour*.
[7] Gustave Reese, *Music in the Middle Ages* (New York, 1940), p. 384.
[8] See Galpin, *A Textbook of European Musical Instruments*, p. 103. The corresponding word 'chekker' is found in England in 1392–3.
[9] *Les Clavecinistes* (Paris, 1935), p. 7.

'psaltery', possibly indicating different shapes or sizes, and four names for bowed instruments—*gyge*, *videle*, *lyra*, and *rubebe*—which do not seem to fit the known forms very comfortably. Is it unlikely that clavichord changed its meaning quickly enough to have become so definite fifty or sixty years later in Germany and England? In Spain, Italy, and France that instrument was invariably manicord, never clavichord, which in Spain, at least, always meant harpsichord. If authorities are right in deriving *schachtbrett* from a north German and Netherland word *schacht*, meaning the quill end of a feather, then that instrument must have been the plucked psaltery or virginals.

One of the very numerous guesses at the origin of the word *eschiquier* (or *eschaquier*) is that it came from this word *schacht*:[1] in that case *schachtbrett*, *eschiquier*, and virginals are the same, and that type of keyboard instrument may clearly be dated from the mid-fourteenth century. On the other hand, if the word has something to do with 'check', it may be a different instrument altogether.

We are then left with *clavicymbalum*, which, by all the rules of later usage, ought to mean the virginals; but it obviously means a keyed cymbal, and Cersne's cymbal is probably the dulcimer. Neither clavichord nor virginals is a keyed dulcimer, though a modern pianoforte is a highly developed one. If Cersne is not simply duplicating names,[2] we must look for three, instead of two, different types of keyed mechanism: a slightly later treatise gives a strong clue to the solution. A Latin manuscript in the Bibliothèque Nationale in Paris, dating from about 1425,[3] gives clear descriptions of the structure of musical instruments, and among these is a special type of dulcimer (*doucemelle*) in which the strings are hit by a rebounding hammer which is jerked upwards by a checked key; in fact, in essentials, the principle of the pianoforte action is worked out. How far such an instrument was used and why it did not develop are alike unknown;[4] but it is quite possibly this instrument that is listed by Cersne as *clavicymbalum*.

Between clavichord and virginals priority cannot be assigned.

[1] Cf. Gérold, *La Musique au moyen âge*, p. 389, and Sachs, op. cit., p. 337.

[2] There is a rather earlier reference to the *clavicembalum*, see p. 420, n. 3.

[3] lat. 7295. Facsimile in *Les Traités d'Henri-Arnault de Zwolle et de divers anonymes*, with translation by G. Le Cerf and E.-R. Lebande (Paris, 1932). This action is also described in a German manuscript of the same period or possibly slightly earlier: see *Music and Letters*, xxix (1948), p. 199. For another opinion see Sachs, op. cit., pp. 343–4. See also C. Clutton, 'Arnault's MS.', *Galpin Society Journal*, v (1952), p. 3.

[4] Arnold Dolmetsch, *The Interpretation of the Music of the XVIIth and XVIIIth Centuries* (London, 1915), p. 431, records examining a pianoforte dated 1610: it had a very simple form of the Viennese action and so was considerably more elaborate than Arnault's instrument. Perhaps there had been some use and development, but no whisper of such an action is found in any treatise until the eighteenth century.

Representations of both appear for the first time in the early fifteenth century, though the references given suggest that one, at least, was in use some seventy years before. There is a supposed mention of a keyboard instrument with nineteen strings one hundred years earlier,[1] but the supposition rests on a mistranslation. Simplicity of action strongly favours the clavichord, but the first references, if *eschiquier* be read aright, indicate the virginals.

The actions of the virginals and of Arnault's keyed dulcimer both began with the same principle. A balanced key, which is checked in the arc through which it can move, is depressed at one end: the other end, in rising, jerks upward a strip of wood which falls again under its own weight when the key returns to its former position. In Arnault's instrument this strip, which is weighted with lead, hits the string from below, just as the hand-held hammer hits the dulcimer string from above. In the virginals the strip passes close to the string and, as it passes, a small plectrum in it plucks the string, as the finger or plectrum plucks the psaltery string. But the problem in the virginals is far more complex, for the strip of wood with its plectrum has to pass the string again on its return, and a second plucking is not wanted: in overcoming this the real inventive genius of its unknown originator is displayed. The plectrum is fixed to a small inset-strip hinged in the main strip so that it slips back past the string almost without sound, while a tiny spring, usually made of a bristle, brings it into position again for striking on the next upward movement.[2]

In the clavichord an entirely different principle is used. If a taut string is struck a sound emerges even if the striker continues to press against it. Obviously the whole string is not vibrating; there are, in fact, two notes, one from each portion of the string between striker and support. By damping one end of the string with cloth, the only note heard is given by the length between the striker and the un-damped end: hence a number of strikers placed at different points along one string will give a number of different notes. With a soft or blunt striker the note can hardly be heard, as when the stopping finger comes down smartly on a violin string; but if the string is free and the striker hard and sharp the note is clear, and the presence of a sound-board increases its volume. In the clavichord the balanced key has a blade-ended striker fixed vertically at one end; when the other

[1] Reese, op. cit., p. 383. See Walter Nef, 'The Polychord', *Galpin Society Journal*, iv (1951), p. 21, for the explanation.

[2] For clear diagrams and full details of the action, which is necessarily more compli-cated than here described, N. Bessaraboff, *Ancient European Musical Instruments* (Boston, 1941), is recommended, in addition to the older standard works.

end is depressed, this blade impinges on the string and is held against it while a note is heard formed by the vibrating length between striker and support (e.g. a bridge). As soon as the striker leaves the string all sound ceases, for the string, now free, is damped by the cloth at the other end. But this is not all: the pitch of the note depends not only on the length of the string but also on its tension, and as the striker is pressed harder so the pitch of the note rises. As the pressure on the key is varied while holding the blade against the string, so the pitch varies and a tremolo effect, analogous to the 'close shake' on a violin, can be obtained.

The striking-blade, usually made of brass, is called the 'tangent': a number of tangents suitably placed under a single string would enable a melody to be played. With more strings and less tangents to each, two or more notes can be sounded together. The logical finality of one string with one tangent for each note of the chromatic scale did not come till about 1700, but before the sixteenth century the keyboard had been ingeniously arranged so that only very unusual combinations were unobtainable; the earliest representations, such as that in St. Mary's at Shrewsbury, or the contemporary picture in the *Weimarer Wunderbuch*,[1] show fewer strings with more tangents on each.[2]

'SYMPHONY' AND ORGAN

The clavichord has a tiny, elfin sound, but is capable of a considerable range of volume and colour, and is specially well suited to contrapuntal music. Its origin is seen by many authorities in the impact of the loose, bladed keys on the melody string of the *organistrum* or *symphonia* (*chifonie*), later called in France the *vielle à roue*. This is a very old instrument: it consists of a melody string over a box resonator, with bourdon strings, all of which are kept in continuous sound by contact with a wheel. Odo of Cluny has left a description of the construction of this instrument, so that it must have been well established early in the tenth century.[3] At first it was large and required two players, one to turn the handle and the other to work the stops, which in the early forms were plates that turned against the strings. But by the late thirteenth century the loose, falling key had

---

[1] Reproduced in P. James, *Early Keyboard Instruments* (London, 1930), pl. xi *a*.

[2] Each 'string' was double, or even treble, in the early instruments: Virdung, *Musica getuscht* (Basle, 1511), says it was so arranged in case a string broke, and he advocates steel wires in preference to brass. Later, single strings became the invariable rule.

[3] *Quomodo organistrum construatur*, in Gerbert, *Scriptores*, i, p. 303.

been devised and the size reduced so that a single player could use it, as we see in the Belvoir Psalter of about 1270.

It is one of the instruments most frequently depicted and mentioned, and although it ultimately fell to low estate it is shown in the hands of angels until the end of the fifteenth century. In many early references it is found in company with something called *armonie* or *almonie*, e.g.:

> L'uns harpe, l'autres chifonie
> Flagol, saltere ou almonie.[1]

It is unlikely, therefore, that the two words mean the same instrument.[2]

One reason for the decline of the 'symphony' may have been the appearance in the early fourteenth century of a little organ hung from the shoulders and played with one hand while the other worked the bellows; this portative organ became extremely popular and was often used by singers, e.g.:

> Orgues i r'a bien maniables
> A une sole main portables,
> Ou il meismes souffle et touche
> Et chante avec a pleine bouche.[3]

(And there are handy organs carried on one arm, on which he plays with bellows and sings as well with a full voice.)

The famous blind organist and composer Francesco Landini (*c*. 1325–97) is shown in more than one design playing on the portative.[4] The particular interest of this little organ is that the light wind-pressure enabled a true key action to be recovered and once again the organist's fingers flew about with the agility attributed over a thousand years earlier to players of the Roman organs.[5]

MANDORA AND LUTE

The plucked instruments, with strings stopped on a fingerboard,

---

[1] Gerbert de Montrueil, *Continuation* of Chrestien's *Perceval*, 3825–6, ed. Mary Williams, i, Paris, 1922); other examples (*armonie*) can be found in Wace's *Brut* and in *Les deux bordeours ribauds*; all are of or before the early thirteenth century.

[2] Sachs, however, *Reallexikon der Musikinstrumente* (Berlin, 1913), considers them identical in meaning.

[3] *Roman de la Rose*, 21,819–22.

[4] Tomb in Basilica S. Lorenzo, Florence (see p. 79), and in the Squarcialupi manuscript.

[5] See p. 469, n. 5, for references; and Villani's biography of Landini, quoted at length by Gérold, *Histoire de la musique*, p. 378, and *Musique au moyen âge*, pp. 342 ff. and p. 421.

were the mandora, citole, gittern, and lute. The mandora is included in the earliest lists in Provençal poetry, e.g.:

L'us mandura e l'autre acorda
Lo sauteri ab manicorda,[1]

(The one [plays] the *mandura* and the other tunes the *sauteri* to the *manicorda*.)

and in another, of the early thirteenth century:

Cymbales, rotes, timpanons
Et mandoires et micanons.[2]

Since the mandora was popular in classical times, it quite possibly survived in Europe: a Psalter of the mid-ninth century (pl. V*c*) shows an instrument that may well be intended for a mandora.[3] A slightly different type appears on a tenth-century vase from Cordoba.[4] Unfortunately we know nothing of its tuning until the sixteenth century; there it is usually tuned to the same intervals as its larger brother, the lute proper.

Information about the true lute is at first scanty, and it is tempting to date its introduction rather late, perhaps not before 1300; but there are early thirteenth-century uses of the name, e.g.:

Leüs, rubebes et kitaires,[5]

and at the same period in the *Roman de la Rose*.[6] A 'luter' is included in the minstrels at the Westminster Pentecostal Feast of 1306,[7] and there are many other mentions of the word for nearly a century before a clear representation of the lute as we know it in later times is found. One of the earliest examples is a relief attributed, rather doubtfully, to Giotto but certainly not later than 1350, in the campanile of the cathedral in Florence. In this the form of the large rounded body, with three double strings and a single *chanterelle*, is shown with the typical fretted neck and sharply thrown back peg-box.

In the fourteenth century it became extremely popular,[8] and during the next 350 years it was the vehicle for the most cultivated form of

---

[1] *Flamenca*, 609–10. See *infra*, p. 493, n. 2.
[2] *Cléomadès*, 17,279–80.
[3] Brit. Mus., Add. 37768, fo. 5.
[4] See Besseler, *Musik des Mittelalters und der Renaissance* (Potsdam, 1931), p. 78.
[5] *Cléomadès*, 17,274.
[6] In the continuation by Jean de Meung, *c*. 1260.
[7] See Hayes, op. cit., pp. 30–31, for details of this list.
[8] For numerous names and references see Lionel de la Laurencie, *Les Luthistes* (Paris, 1928).

solo music. That the fourteenth century thought of the lute as a large instrument, in distinction from the older mandora, is shown by the Archpriest of Hita's reference to it as *corpudo laúd*[1] and by the line in *Les Échecs amoureux* of about 1370:

> Leüs qui sont de plus grant ton.

Although it had acquired a seventh string (or rank, of double strings) by Virdung's day, as an addition to the standard six, the system of German tablature notation proves that five ranks must have been the standard up to the second half of the fifteenth century.

CITOLE AND GITTERN

The citole[2] is a very old instrument and probably one of purely European descent; leading authorities[3] agree in seeing the citole in the hands of adoring saints in the Soissons Breviary,[4] the Latin Gospels executed for Charlemagne in the eighth century, and although it is difficult to feel absolutely certain, it is equally difficult to say what else the instrument can be. The characteristic of the citole is a round, almost circular body which is flat-backed; the neck is distinct, despite very flowing shoulders in early representations. It is plucked either with the fingers or with a plectrum. The citole is mentioned early in the thirteenth century as an instrument that young ladies should play,[5] and references are frequent in poetry from then onwards; it was always given a rather respectable setting, which was not invariably the lot of other instruments. A thirteenth-century poet says:

> Et quant je fui sus levez
> Si commenz a citoler.[6]

(And when I have got up then I begin to play the citole.)

In *Les Échecs amoureux*, its tone colour is well indicated:

> Et citoles meismement
> Qui sonnoient molt doucement

(And citoles also, which played very sweetly),

---

[1] J. Ruiz, *El Libro de Buen Amor* (*c.* 1350): see next page.
[2] In Italian *cetra*, and later, in most countries, cittern or cithren.
[3] e.g. Sachs and Galpin.
[4] See Panum, op. cit., p. 461.
[5] Guiraut de Calanson, *Clef d'amor*, 2605 ff.
[6] Bartsch, *Altfranzösische Romanzen und Pastorellen*, p. 22.

and this is more beautifully expressed in an English poem of the same date:

> Bot sytole-stryng and gyternere
> Her reken myrthe moght not retrete.[1]

(Citole and gittern could not imitate her radiant mirth.)

Two points about the citole that were essential to it from 1500 onwards cannot be defined in its early life: it invariably had wire strings and it had a tuning so curious that it is hard to believe that this was not hallowed by long usage:

These intervals are, of course, irrespective of actual pitch.

The gittern (not to be confused with cittern), to which philologists would deny the final n, was another flat-backed instrument, but with a narrow body and incurved sides. An English form, not constant but thought by Galpin to have been an early type abandoned under French influence, had a peculiar neck; this had the full depth of the body with an oval hole in it through which the hand passed. In French literature it appears variously as *kitaire, ghisterne, quinterne*, and *guiterne* from the early thirteenth century onwards, and it is included in Cersne's German list of 1404. The specially English form has the distinction of being the only wooden instrument of the fourteenth century of which a specimen has survived; this is the famous Warwick Castle gittern, stupidly turned into a violin by some misguided 're-storer':[2] the carving dates it about 1325, perhaps as early as 1280.

There was another pattern of gittern specially associated with Arab influence: this is probably the oval-bodied instrument shown, with the normal European form, in the *Cantigas de Santa María*, and it must have had a very distinct tone quality:

> Ally sale gritando la guitara morisca,
> Delas boses aguda e delos puntos arisca,
> El corpudo laúd que tyene punto ala trisca,
> La guitarra latyna con esos se aprisca.[3]

(There comes out, shouting, the *guitarra morisca* with its sharp sounds and shrill notes; the bellied lute which gives the air to a dance, the *guitarra latina* [found] in the fold with them.)

[1] *The Pearl* (c. 1375), 91–92.
[2] A replica, still as a violin, is in the Victoria and Albert Museum. Cf. Galpin, *Old English Instruments of Music*, pp. 23–24 and pl. vii.
[3] J. Ruiz, *El Libro de Buen Amor* (c. 1350), 1228–31.

Johannes de Grocheo (*c.* 1300) mentions a *quitarra sarracenica*.[1] The point is of some importance in connexion with a curious word *morache* that turns up in fourteenth-century French poems.

In 1349 a list of the musicians of the Duke of Normandy includes Jean Hautemer for the *guiterre latine* and Richart l'abbé for the *guiterre moreche*.[2] Guillaume de Machaut twice uses *morache* at about the same date:

> Viële, rubebe, guiterne,
> Leü, morache, michanon,[3]

and

> Leüs moraches et guiternes
> Dont on joue par ces tavernes.[4]

Most editors insert commas between the names, so making *morache* definitely a noun, but this, though probable, is not absolutely certain, for it might be an adjective. If it is a noun, it is thought to mean the Moorish guitar; the lute was well established at this date and it is unlikely to have needed qualification, but the possibility that it was still thought of as distinctly Moorish must not be forgotten.

BELLS AND DRUMS

Percussion instruments were many and various. Chime bells persisted from the earlier centuries[5] and appear under a great variety of names: in addition to all the obvious changes on *cloche*, some words that appear to derive from the Latin *signum* were in common use in thirteenth-century France, such as *sein*, *saine*, or *saint*, e.g.:

> A tant sonent li saint as glises,[6]
> (Then the church bells ring.)

but some words seem closer allied to the German *Glocke*:

> Fes lo tam ben qu'eis le cloquiers
> S'en meravilla el mostiers,[7]

(He played it so well that the very bell-ringer in church wondered at it.)

while *nola*, as a contraction or diminutive of *campanola*, is used by some very early writers.[8] Other forms are *eschelle*, whence *esquille* and *ache-*

---

[1] *Sammelbände der internationalen Musikgesellschaft*, i (1899–1900), p. 96, or E. Rohloff (ed.), *Der Musiktraktat des Johannes de Grocheo* (Leipzig, 1943), p. 52.

[2] Panum, op. cit., p. 456; the date is given by Gérold, *La Musique au moyen âge*, p. 380.

[3] *Le Remède de Fortune*, 3962–3; edn. E. Hœpffner (Paris, 1911).

[4] *La Prise d'Alexandrie*, 1150–1, edn. de Mas Latria (Geneva, 1877).

[5] Gregory of Tours (sixth century) mentions their use in churches.

[6] Gerbert's *Continuation* of *Perceval* (ed. Williams), 4108.   [7] *Flamenca*, 383–4.

[8] e.g. Walafrid Strabo in Migne, *Patrologia latina*, cxiv, col. 924.

lette and German *Schelle*. Bells are usually shown as suspended from a bar or strap, and struck with a hammer (see pls. V*a* and VII).

Drums played an important part in medieval music, but the word 'drum' itself, outside Germany, belongs to the sixteenth century; of the two principal forms in use the cylindrical, or sometimes waisted, with the double head, seems to be the older and was known as the tabor (from the Arabic *ṭabl*).[1] The tabor, when used alone, is usually shown in a horizontal position, with each hand playing on an end;[2] but when it was used in its most familiar company of the pipe, that is, the three-holed recorder type of flute, it is slung from the wrist in a vertical position and played with a stick. The instrument, as one would expect, is also called timpanon.[3]

The timbrel, our modern tambourine, goes back to pre-Christian days and never lost its popularity. The scene in the *Roman de la Rose*[4] of the players throwing their timbrels high in the air and never missing their catch is too familiar for quotation. Fifty or sixty years earlier Chrestien de Troyes wrote of the music at a wedding feast[5] including those who

> Sonent timbre, sonent tabor.

An early fourteenth-century illustration shows the timbrel complete with plates in the rim and a snare across the skin.[6]

The other type of drum was in a form similar to that of the kettle-drum of our modern orchestras and military bands, but much smaller: a hemispherical body, usually of metal, is covered with skin over the open top. This is always represented by a pair of instruments often suspended from the waist and played with sticks, and it was known as the nakers, from the Arabic *naqqārāt*.[7] A nakerer is included amongst the musicians of the Westminster feast of 1306. Joinville, in his *History of Saint Louis* (1309), mentions the terrifying effect of the Saracen *nacaires* and horns. In the fourteenth century the nakers became a commonplace in literary reference.

Cymbal could mean many things, as has been mentioned above, but it undoubtedly meant to some what it does to us today. In *Les Échecs amoureux* (c. 1370), music for a dance is described with

---

[1] See vol. I, pp. 438 and 442.
[2] e.g. in the Utrecht Psalter (*c*. eighth century).
[3] *Cléomadès*, 17279.
[4] 767–80.   [5] *Erec*, 2042 ff.
[6] Brit. Mus., Harl. 6563, fo. 14, reproduced in Galpin, *Old English Instruments of Music*, p. 241.
[7] See vol. I, pp. 443 and 468.

PLATE VI

INSTRUMENTS OF THE EARLY ELEVENTH CENTURY

Crowd, harp, rote, cornett, clapper, and panpipes (?)

(Psalter *c.* 1015. Cambridge University Library MS. Ff. 1. 23, fo. 4v)

details of instruments chosen 'pour le grant noise qu'ils faisoient', and among these are:

> Trompez, tabours, tymprez, naquairez,
> Cymballes (dont il n'est mes guaires)
> (. . . such as you never heard.)

The triangle was also used and is shown in miniatures and sculpture: its French name was *trepié*, while in Germany it was called *Stegreif* (stirrup):

> Noch stegereyff, noch begil.[1]

UNCERTAIN NAMES

In the long lists of instruments that form such a remarkable feature of the literature of the Middle Ages there are many names to which it is difficult to assign a particular form of instrument with any certainty, and there are several names that seem to have been introduced for special reasons, some of which are even noncewords. We cannot yet sort out all the forms implied in the many variations on *flageol*, *flehute*, and *muse*. Words so different in origin as *manicorda*[2] and *monocorde* seem to be used indifferently for the same thing, though we may be in error in this; though Theoger of Metz[3] about 1100 mentioned that in antiquity the monochord had eight strings, a century later Guiraut de Calanson instructed the jongleur to be proficient on the *manicorda ab una corda*.[4] Johannes de Muris uses the name for an instrument with nineteen strings in the first half of the fourteenth century,[5] yet it is defined with firmness as a single-string instrument by Guillaume de Machaut not long after de Muris wrote:

> Buisines, eles, monocorde
> Ou il n'a qu'une seule corde.[6]
> (. . . on which there is only one string.)

Ele in this passage is a nonce-word that has engendered much dispute; some see in it a contraction of *frestel* (panpipes), whilst others think it means a small organ, the wing-shape of the pipes suggesting

---

[1] Cersne, *Minnereglen* (1404): the meaning of *begil* is not known.

[2] e.g. *Flamenca*, loc. cit. Prescott, in an able translation (London, 1930) of this delightful story, hazards the rash guess 'Jew's harp' for *manicorda*. It is clear that in this case the *manicorda* is being used as a tuning device, and so is certainly a monochord.

[3] Gerbert, *Scriptores*, ii. 183; Reese, *Music in the Middle Ages*, p. 383; but Walter Nef, *Galpin Society Journal*, iv (1951), p. 21, considers that Theoger referred to eight notes on a single string.

[4] Bartsch, *Denkmäler der provenzalischen Literatur* (Stuttgart, 1856), p. 94.

[5] Gerbert, *Scriptores*, iii, p. 283, but cf. Nef, op. cit.

[6] *Le Remède de Fortune*, 3973–4.

the word *aile*: the panpipes equally suggest a wing-shape, and *orgues* appear earlier in the list. We are not often so fortunate as with the French word *viele*, about which Colin Muset (*c.* 1270) sets any doubts at rest in the lines:

> J'alai a li el praelet
> Atout la viele et l'archet,
> Si li ai chanté le muset
> Par grant amour.[1]

(I went to her in the little meadow with my *viele* and bow and played the *muset* for her with tender love.)

BAGPIPES

If in Germany the true viols were known as foreign *geigen* (*welhische gigen*)[2] long before Agricola and other sixteenth-century writers so defined them, French writers acknowledge many instruments from Eastern Europe:

> La chevrecte d'Esclavannie
> Et la fleuthe de Behaigne
> E la musette d'Allemaigne[3]

and

> Et le grant cornet d'Alemaigne,[4]

and players as well as instruments were acknowledged:

> Et des flauteurs de Behaigne
> Et des gigeours d'Allemaigne.[5]

Behaigne is Bohemia, and the many references to these flute-players have led to the theory that it means that the transverse flute was regarded as an importation from that part of Europe. *Chevrecte* (*chevrette*) is one of the many names for bagpipes; others are *cornemuse*, *choron*, and *muse*, though *muse* may be also the simple reedpipe, just as *chalumeau* may sometimes be the chanter of a bagpipe, as in the line 'la muze au grant challemel'.[6] The great popularity of the bagpipes for so many centuries, even today in Italy, can only be understood when associations with the modern Scottish bagpipes are

[1] *Les Chansons de Colin Muset*, ed. Joseph Bédier (Paris, 1938), p. 1.
[2] In *Apollonius de Tyr* (*c.* 1315).
[3] Jean Lefèvre, *La Vielle* (mid-fourteenth century) (Paris, 1861), p. 19.
[4] *Le Remède de Fortune*, 3970.
[5] *Cléomadès* (early thirteenth century), 2887–8.
[6] But cf. 'En la muse au grant bourdon'; perhaps it means the drone and not the chanter. See Bartsch, *Romanzen und Pastorellen*, for numerous examples in the Pastorals; in one, Jehan Erars mentions a 'muse au grant forrel'.

put aside; the smaller pipes, now so little heard, were quiet and sweet and were well suited to indoor entertainment.

Estive is very common in French and Provençal literature and is usually understood to mean some sort of bagpipes, though this has been doubted. It is mainly a thirteenth-century word. In all the Romance languages there is a word of this form meaning 'to crowd together' or 'to press'; our English 'stevedore', one who stows the cargo, belongs to this group and presumably all look back to the Latin *stibare*. In *Cléomadès*, in which the instrument *estive* is mentioned twice, there is a passage in which *estiver* is used in the sense of crowding.[1] Hence it is reasonable to assume that it indicated the arm pressing the wind-bag, or just possibly it might have been used for the type of bagpipes in which bellows are worked by the arm. It is difficult to see to what other instrument it could have been applied, but certainty is not yet attained.

One special type is very frequently specified in early French poetry, that is the *estive de Cornuaille*. In the *Roman de la Rose* it appears as a grisly sort of instrument:

> Or times he made a dismal wail
> On bagpipes loud of Cornouaille,[2]

while elsewhere it is noted for its sweetness:

> A estive de Cornoaille
> Li note I menestrex sanz faille
> Li lai Goron molt dolcement.[3]

(On an *estive de Cornoaille* a minstrel played sweetly and without fault the lays of Goron.)

Some writers have questioned whether the place-name refers to England or Brittany, but the inclusion of the *estive de Cornuaille* in the large variety of instruments carried by the team accompanying Tristram when he visits King Mark seems to be conclusive, as the passage is surrounded by references to the British kingdom spelt in exactly the same way.[4] The whole of this long episode is of considerable instrumental interest. As King Carmans, in *Cléomadès*, had an *estive de Cornouille*, this name must go back nearly to 1250; practically all the references belong to the thirteenth century.

[1] 12,940–6.
[2] 4079–80: Ellis's fairly literal translation. Chaucer, l. 4250, gives 'Hornpipes of Cornwall', but his rendering is too free for evidential use; for example, he gives 'harpe and gittern' for 'vielle et fleute'.
[3] Gérold, *La Musique au moyen âge*, p. 405, quoting *Romania*, xxxv, p. 526.
[4] Gerbert de Montreuil, *Continuation* of *Perceval*, 3828 (ed. Mary Williams).

Guillaume de Machaut has left other puzzles in his lists as well as the *ele* discussed above; it is only his supreme importance as a musician and poet that justifies reference to them:

> Douceinnes, simbals, clochettes,
> Timbre, la flaüste brehaingne.[1]

Brehaigne means sterile and is not uncommon in poetry of this period:

> Vaillant une berbis brehaigne
> Ne redoute Percheval point.[2]

(Rating [his opponent] as a barren wether Perceval had no fear.)

The only tentative solution offered is that it means a mirliton or eunuch flute,[3] though we have no evidence that such an instrument existed in fourteenth-century Europe. Before any more ink is spilt on this question, it should be ascertained whether Machaut really wrote 'brehaigne' or whether it is not simply a scribal error for 'Behaigne'.

RUSTIC INSTRUMENTS

In the same list Machaut gives *floiot de saus*, which is presumably a flute—or reed-pipe—made out of osiers. In a *chanson* of the same period by Colin Muset, the poet says:

> L'autr' ier en mai, un matinet,
> M'esveillerent li oiselet,
> S'alai cuillir un saucelet,
> Si en ai fait un flajolet.[4]

(The other day on a May morning the little birds woke me up: I went to cut a reed and have made a *flajolet* of it.)

Other rustic instruments in this list are the *muse de blez*, a reed-pipe made out of straw, familiar to Chaucer:

> Pipes made of grene corne
> As have these little Herde-groomes,[5]

and the *muse d'ausay*, a pipe, or fipple flute, made from a willow and its detachable bark: perhaps some readers may recall with the writer the thrill in country childhood of the few notes that came after cutting the holes and notch, and fixing the stopper successfully.[6]

---

[1] *Le Remède de Fortune*, 3968–9. One MS. (Bibl. Nat., fr. 9221) reads 'de bre-haingne'.   [2] Gerbert de Montreuil, op. cit., 11,188–9.

[3] Gérold, *Histoire de la musique*, p. 411.

[4] *Chanson III* in Joseph Bédier's edition (Paris, 1938). Gérold, op. cit., quotes an analogous passage from a German author, Ulrich von Lichtenstein.

[5] *House of Fame*, 1224–5.

[6] In the analogous catalogue in *La Prise d'Alexandrie* (Geneva, 1877), *muse de blé* and *flaies de saus* occur, but v. 1163 reads 'Muses d'Aussay, riches et belles'; the adjectives, with the capital letter, lend colour to Gérold's interpretation, 'muse d'Alsace'.

The *douceinne* referred to above has, so far, defied satisfactory explanation, yet it is one of the most generally mentioned instruments from the early thirteenth century onwards.[1] The word has many forms, such as *doucaine* and *doucete*, and, in Ruiz's *Libro de Buen Amor*, *dulçema*. One thing is quite clear: it had nothing to do with the *dulcian* or *dulceuse* of the sixteenth and seventeenth centuries, for that was a form of bassoon, and the bassoon principle was not evolved until nearly the middle of the sixteenth century. If it were not for the early date of some references, it would be tempting to accept the explanation frequently offered that it was the *krumhorn*: but, except for the bladder-pipe type suggested in the Spanish *Cantigas*, there is no evidence for the existence of the *krumhorn* until late in the fifteenth century, after which it enjoyed a hundred years and more of popularity. There is just a suspicion that it might have been a type of flute; this arises from an apparently adjectival use of the word in a poem, of which a contemporary translation in Low German has survived:[2]

> Chalemies, bombares,
> Muses, fleutes douchaines,
> et nacaires.

The second line appears in the German as

> Cornemusen, floyten douchainen,

but here again we are at the mercy of editorial punctuation, and one extra comma would equate this with all the other references.

That very ancient instrument, the Jew's Harp or *guimbarde*, is shown in the art of the Middle Ages[3] and appears in Virdung's book of 1511: but no name by which it is to be recognized can be identified.

MARINE TRUMPET

The monochord, regularly mentioned from the twelfth century onwards as an instrument for music distinct from its purely theoretical use, is only a name to us until the very close of our period. We do not know whether it was plucked or bowed or whether different notes were obtained by stopping with the finger or by a moveable bridge. But at the close of the fifteenth century it appears in a new guise as the 'marine trumpet' or *trumscheit*, of which the characteristic feature

---

[1] e.g. *Cléomadès, Dit de la Panthère, Les Échecs amoureux, House of Fame, Reson and Sensuallyte*, &c.

[2] *Livre des Mestiers*, ed. Michelant. Anthony Baines has kindly supplied this reference.

[3] e.g. Exeter Cathedral carvings (fourteenth century).

is the 'trembling bridge': although this constitutes an entirely novel instrument, it strongly suggests an evolution from a previous bowed state with a fixed bridge. It is possible that this, the date usually accepted, is at least fifty years too late, for a Dutch Bible illustration, dated 1425, shows two instruments suspiciously like the small *trum-scheit* depicted around 1500, though the bridges are vague.[1] The bridge, precariously balanced on one foot beneath the string, vibrates when harmonics are played and by its impact on the belly of the long box resonator, produces a remarkable tone quite genuinely resembling that of a trumpet. There is one position, and one only, in which the bridge will so act: and the string is touched, but not stopped, by the finger—later, the thumb—between the bow and the bridge. Hans Memling's (d. 1495) angel[2] holds the instrument aloft with one hand, but it is difficult to see how it could have been played held unsupported in this fashion: in the next century it became much larger and heavier. This example shows, as do some others, a shorter string, probably with an ordinary bridge, alongside the main chord.

MEDIEVAL USAGE

Fifteen hundred years of change, invention, and importation form a large canvas to cover, and many interesting details have had to be omitted: but the irresistible effect of the whole is to demonstrate the enormous importance of instrumental music in those days, most especially (but perhaps because best documented) in the period from 1100 to 1500. Not only are there the numerous lists of instruments in the poetry of European countries, but also the countless passing references that are introduced so naturally that it is impossible to regard them as mere poetic artifice. It may be doubted whether any other age can show such a widespread acceptance of instrumental music in its literature: and to this must be added the parallel richness of the representation in sculpture and painting.

It might be argued that so much attention was given precisely because this was a new element in life, but there is no evidence to support that theory and the internal evidence of the literature itself is quite opposed to it. Economic and political changes may have had their part, for life in the Dark Ages was grim indeed: yet even in the blackness of sixth-century Gaul there are occasional flashes of something almost idyllic.[3] The influences of the East, through returning

[1] Reproduced in Kinsky, *Geschichte der Musik in Bildern* (1929), p. 54, pl. 3.
[2] In the long picture of *Angels making Music* now in the Antwerp Museum.
[3] See, for example, Venantius Fortunatus, *Carmen* x. 9.

Crusaders, the new trade routes from the Adriatic, and the Moslems in Spain, have always received their full, and too often more than their full, share. Insufficient attention has been paid to the Scandinavian and Baltic influences, while it is almost forgotten how, in the mid-thirteenth century, the contact with the enlightened court at Karakorum became so freely used. Many have celebrated the gorgeous life of Frederick II, 'Stupor Mundi', but no one has written in detail of the music with which he is known to have surrounded himself; and we may be sure that his music embraced the best of everything then known in West and East.

With the instruments that survived into the succeeding period, such as the viol, lira, rebec, lute, shawm, recorder, flute, cornett, horn, trumpet, cithren, virginals, clavichord, and small organ, we are justified, at all events as an interim measure, in accepting their usage as we find it accepted at the opening of the sixteenth century, ridding the mind entirely of any thought that construction was crude and technique childish in the Middle Ages. Thus, for a large part of the field, we have at least something near to the instrumental voices of those days: but we must be careful to bear in mind limiting dates, even if these are vague enough. Bowed instruments before A.D. 1000 would be hard to justify, while, except for the organ, a keyboard instrument before the mid-fourteenth century would be improbable: nothing of the bassoon type of instrument existed before the sixteenth century was well advanced. As research proceeds, it will be possible to define usage much more precisely.

The most urgent need is for knowledge of how the instruments were used: what instruments would be best suited to a certain type of composition, and what instruments were used in combination.[1] With so much of the playing in the hands of professional groups—in the thirteenth and fourteenth centuries, each under its own 'king'— very little of the music, and none of the technique, got written down.

The theorists do not tell us much about the instruments of their period: when Jerome of Moravia (c. 1250) says that the bagpipe is above all other instruments, he is only copying something that John Cotton had written over a century earlier, with more reference to symbolism than to music.[2] But when Johannes de Grocheo (c. 1300) argues that the viol (viella) is the best, because the most completely expressive, of all stringed instruments, we feel that this is a practical opinion.[3] De Grocheo is one of the few theorists who concern

---

[1] See previous chapter, pp. 410 ff. and 417–19.
[2] Gerbert, Scriptores, i, p. 5 and ii, p. 233.   [3] See supra, p. 412.

themselves seriously with secular music, and his work is for that reason especially valuable. However, half a century later Güillaume de Machaut wrote:[1]

> Et de tous instrumens le roy
> Diray premiers, si com je croy,
> Orgues, ...

([I will tell the names of all the instruments. . . .] And of all instruments, that which I believe to be the king shall come first. Organs, [viols, etc.].)

Only very occasionally do we find any instrument specified with musical texts and these rare cases are vocal pieces. Thus, Hermann, the Monk of Salzburg (*c.* 1370), has an aubade, 'Das Nachthorn', in which a bombarde (*der pumhart*) plays the lower part, and in an ingenious *Tagelied* there are short passages for a trumpet.[2] In the well-known Bamberg manuscript, one of the three-part compositions on the *In saeculum* theme is entitled *In saeculum viellatoris*;[3] and although Jacques Handschin will not allow this to be unambiguous,[4] it obviously had something to do with viols.

LINES OF RESEARCH

A more fruitful source of information may be found in the literary references, but not in their isolated readings: there must be a long and laborious process of extracting all the useful passages from all the possible sources, followed by an even more tedious work of collating them with relation to the instruments, compositions, and social settings mentioned, with due regard to their respective periods and countries. From such an examination, it is almost certain that a great deal of information would emerge. But such examination must be not only exhaustive and critical, but undertaken with instrumental understanding and musical sympathy: undertaken as an academic exercise, it is pre-doomed to failure.

A simple example will illustrate what is possible: there is a form of composition known as the *estampie* (Italian *stampita*) that was very popular in the thirteenth and fourteenth centuries. It is almost cer-

---

[1] *La Prise d'Alexandrie*, 1146–8 (Geneva, 1877).

[2] In the *Tagelied*, a youth and a maiden converse in one part, while a watchman keeps up a running commentary in the lower part (Vienna, MS. 2856): see Arnold F. Mayer on these works in *Acta Germanica*, iii and iv (1894–6).

[3] P. Aubry, *Cent motets du XIIIe siècle*, ii, p. 226; and Gleason, *Examples of Music before 1400* (New York, 1946), p. 58.

[4] *Acta Musicologica*, x (1938), p. 29, n. 19. See also *supra*, p. 410.

PLATE VII

INSTRUMENTS OF THE LATER TWELFTH CENTURY

Chime bells, harp, rebec, panpipes, recorder, viol, handbell, psaltery, and organistrum.

(Psalter *c.* 1270, MS. 229, press-mark U. 32, Sect. 6, fo. lv in the Hunterian Library of the University of Glasgow)

tainly the same thing as the wordless ('sonus illiteratus') *stantipes* of Johannes de Grocheo.[1] When *estampies* are mentioned with instruments, the viol is nearly always present:

> Cil vieleur vielent lais,
> Cançonnetez et estampies;[2]

(The violists play *lais* on their viols, and *cançonnetez* and *estampies*.)

and again, this time possibly indicating several parts,

> IV menestreil de viele
> Ont une estampie nouviele
> Devant la dame vielee.[3]

(Four minstrels played on their viols a new *estampie* before the lady.)

Later, Boccaccio tells us that

Con una sua vivuola dolcemente sono alcuna stampita e canto appresso alcuna canzone.[4]

(He played a *stampita* sweetly on his *vivuola* and sang a song with it.)

These are three of very many that could be quoted: but when we find other instruments, such as

> Guis dou tabor au flahutel
> Leur fait ceste estampie[5]

(Guy with his *tabor* and *flahutel* plays them this *estampie*),

we see that this is a rustic fête of shepherds. Even from such a perfunctory analysis we can be fairly certain that in cultured circles the *estampies* were normally played on viols though Froissart speaks of minstrels 'piping' *estampies*, in *La Prison amoureuse*.

In *Les Échecs amoureux* the loud instruments for dancing include

---

[1] See p. 408 above. *Estampie* and its variations all look back to the Germanic *stampjan* and so indicate something with stamping (e.g. to mark the rhythm): *stantipes*, formed from the Latin, means something standing on the feet. Therefore, say the pedants, these must be two quite different things. But what happened is surely obvious: *stantipes* is practically a nonce-word and was coined by de Grocheo (who lacked our philological background) in order to make a Latin equivalent for the popular word *estampie*.

[2] *Gilles de Chin* (early thirteenth century), quoted by Gérold.

[3] Baudouin de Condé, *Messe des oiseaux* (early thirteenth century).

[4] The Tenth Day (*Novella VII*) in the *Decameron*. Boccaccio is a rich mine, yet to be worked thoroughly, for instrumental details.

[5] Jehan Erars: from Carl Bartsch, op. cit., p. 257.

trumpets, tabors, timbrels, nakers, cymbals, bagpipes, shawms, and horns. Later the author remarks

> Quant mendre noise demandoient
> Flazoz, fleütes et douchaines
> Qui sont moult douches et moult saines
> Et telz autres instrumens bas.[1]

(Since less sound was wanted *flazoz*, *fleütes*, and *douchaines*, which are soft and very pleasant, and other such quiet instruments. . . .)

Lydgate's *Reson and Sensuallyte* is a very free translation of this poem: when he mentions 'instrumentys high and lowe' we must see in this, as in the 'instrumens bas' in the above quotation, a reference to tone quality and not to pitch. Combinations of instruments would be a further step in the analysis: even on a cursory examination, the association of bowed and plucked instruments seems very general. Pictorial evidence may help here, though many additional factors would affect the conclusions to be drawn.[2]

---

[1] The poem is still unpublished, but a study of its musical aspects has been made by H. Abert, 'Die Musikästhetik der *Échecs Amoureux*', *Sammelbände der internationalen Musikgesellschaft*, vi (1905), p. 346.

[2] The evidence of pictures was examined briefly many years ago by Hugo Leichtentritt in *Sammelbände der internationalen Musikgesellschaft*, vii (1906), p. 315, and Marius Schneider, *Die Ars Nova des XIV. Jahrhunderts* (Wolfenbüttel, 1930), pp. 27–28, has tabulated the combinations shown in forty pictures.

BIBLIOGRAPHY

GENERAL

ADLER, GUIDO: *Handbuch der Musikgeschichte*. 2nd ed., 2 vols. (Berlin, 1930).

AMBROS, A. W.: *Geschichte der Musik*. 3rd ed., vol. ii (Leipzig, 1891); 2nd ed., vol. iii (Leuckart, 1893); 3rd ed., vol. v (Leuckart, 1911).

APEL, WILLI: *The Notation of Polyphonic Music, 900–1600*. 4th ed. (Cambridge, Mass., 1950).

BESSELER, HEINRICH: *Die Musik des Mittelalters und der Renaissance* (Potsdam, 1931–4).

—— 'Studien zur Musik des Mittelalters'. *Archiv für Musikwissenschaft*, vii–viii (1925–7).

CHAILLEY, JACQUES: *Histoire musicale du moyen âge* (Paris, 1950).

COMBARIEU, JULES: *Histoire de la musique*. 4th ed., vol. i (Paris, 1924).

COUSSEMAKER, C. E. H. DE: *Scriptorum de musica medii aevi nova series*. 4 vols. (Paris, 1864–76 and reprints).

DAVISON, ARCHIBALD T. and APEL, WILLI: *Historical Anthology of Music*. 2nd ed., vol. i (Cambridge, Mass., 1949).

DUFOURQ, NORBERT: *La musique des origines à nos jours* (Paris, 1946).

FERAND, ERNST: *Die Improvisation in der Musik* (Zürich, 1938).

GERBERT, MARTIN: *Scriptores ecclesiastici de musica sacra potissimum*. 3 vols. (St. Blaise, 1784 and reprints).

GÉROLD, THÉODORE: *Histoire de la musique des origines à la fin du XIVe siècle* (Paris, 1936).

—— *La Musique au moyen âge* (Paris, 1932).

GLEASON, HAROLD: *Examples of Music before 1400* (New York, 1942).

HANDSCHIN, JACQUES: *Musikgeschichte im Überblick* (Lucerne, 1948).

KINSKY, GEORG: *A History of Music in Pictures* (London, 1930).

LANG, PAUL HENRY: *Music in Western Civilization* (New York, 1941).

PARRISH, CARL: *The Notation of Medieval Music* (London, 1958).

PIRRO, ANDRÉ: *Histoire de la musique de la fin du XIVe siècle à la fin du XVIe* (Paris, 1940).

PRUNIÈRES, HENRI: *New History of Music* (London, 1943).

REESE, GUSTAVE: *Music in the Middle Ages* (New York, 1940).

—— *Music in the Renaissance* (New York, 1954).

RIEMANN, HUGO: *Geschichte der Musiktheorie im IX–XIX Jahrhundert*. 2nd ed. (Leipzig, 1921).

—— *Handbuch der Musikgeschichte*. 2nd ed., vols. i, 2 and ii, 1 (Leipzig, 1920).

SCHERING, ARNOLD: *Geschichte der Musik in Beispielen* (Leipzig, 1931).

SMIJERS, ALBERT: *Algemeene Musiekgeschiedenis* (Utrecht, 1938).

URSPRUNG, OTTO: *Die Katholische Kirchenmusik* (Potsdam, 1931).

WAGNER, PETER: *Geschichte der Messe*, vol. i (Leipzig, 1913).

WOLF, JOHANNES: *Geschichte der Mensural-Notation von 1250–1460*. 3 vols. (Leipzig, 1930).

—— *Geschichte der Musik in allgemeinverständlicher Form*. 2nd ed. (Leipzig, 1930).

—— *Handbuch der Notationskunde*. 2 vols. (Leipzig, 1913–19).

—— *Musikalische Schrifttafeln* (Bückeburg and Leipzig, 1923).

—— *Sing- und Spielmusik aus älterer Zeit* (Leipzig, 1926). Reprinted as *Music of Earlier Times* (New York, 1946).

CHAPTER I

ARS NOVA IN FRANCE

(i) *Sources*

APEL, WILLI: *French Secular Music of the Late Fourteenth Century* (Cambridge, Mass., 1950).

AUBRY, PIERRE: *Les plus anciens monuments de la musique française* (Paris, 1903).

—— *Le Roman de Fauvel* (Paris, 1907).

CHAILLEY, JACQUES: *Guillaume de Machaut: Messe Notre-Dame* (Paris, 1948).

COUSSEMAKER, C. E. H. DE: *Messe du XIIIe siècle* (Paris, 1861).

FICKER, RUDOLF VON: *Denkmäler der Tonkunst in Österreich*, xl (Vienna, 1933).

GASTOUÉ, AMÉDÉE: *Concert vocal historique . . . Ire série* (Paris, 1930).

—— *Le manuscrit de musique du Trésor d'Apt* (Paris, 1936).

GENNRICH, FRIEDRICH: *Rondeaux, Virelais und Balladen*. 2 vols. (Dresden, 1921–7).

HOEPFFNER, ERNEST: *Œuvres de Guillaume de Machaut*. 3 vols. (Paris, 1908–21).

HÜBSCH, H.: *Guillaume de Machault: La Messe de Notre Dame* (Heidelberg, 1953).

LUDWIG, FRIEDRICH: *Guillaume de Machaut: Musikalische Werke*. 4 vols. (Leipzig, 1926–9; Wiesbaden, 1954).

MACHABEY, ARMAND: *Guillaume de Machault: Messe Notre-Dame* (Liège, 1948).

SCHRADE, LEO: *Polyphonic Music of the Fourteenth Century*. Vols. i–iii (Monaco, 1956).

VAN, GUILLAUME DE: *Monuments de l'Ars Nova* (Paris, 1938).

—— *Guglielmi de Mascaudio Opera*, i. *La Messe de Nostre Dame* (Rome, 1949).

VAN DEN BORREN, CHARLES: *Missa Tornacensis* (American Institute of Musicology, 1957).

(ii) *Books and Articles*

ANGLÈS, HIGINI: 'Cantors und Ministrers in den Diensten der Könige von Katalonien-Aragonien im 14. Jahrhundert'. *Bericht über den musikwissenschaftlichen Kongress in Basel, 1924* (Leipzig, 1925).

—— 'Dos tractats medievals de musica figurada'. *Festschrift für Johannes Wolf* (Berlin, 1929).

APEL, WILLI: 'The Partial Signatures in the Sources up to 1450'. *Acta Musicologica*, x–xi (1938–9).

BESSELER, HEINRICH: 'Ars Nova'. *Die Musik in Geschichte und Gegenwart*, i (Kassel and Basle, 1949).

—— 'Studien zur Musik des Mittelalters. II. Die Motette von Franco von Köln bis Philippe von Vitry'. *Archiv für Musikwissenschaft*, viii (1926–7).

BOER, C. DE: 'Guillaume de Machaut et l'Ovide moralisé'. *Romania*, xliii (1914).

BOHN, PETER: 'Philipp von Vitry'. *Monatshefte für Musikgeschichte*, xxii (1890).

BORGHEZIO, GINO: 'Un prezioso codice musicale ignorato'. *Bolletino storico bibliografico subalpino*, xxiv (1921).

—— 'Poesie musicali latine e francese in un codice ignorato della Biblioteca capitolare d'Ivrea'. *Archivum Romanum*, v (1921).

BRAGARD, ROGER: 'Le Speculum Musicae du compilateur Jacques de Liége'. *Musica Disciplina*, vii–viii (1953–4).

BRENET, MICHEL: *Les Musiciens de la Sainte Chapelle du Palais* (Paris, 1910).

—— *Musique et musiciens de la vieille France* (Paris, 1911).

BUSH, HELEN: 'The Recognition of Chordal Formation by Early Music Theorists'. *Musical Quarterly*, xxxii (1946).

CHAILLEY, JACQUES: 'La messe de Besançon et un compositeur inconnu du XIVᵉ siècle: Jean Lambelet'. *Annales musicologiques*, ii (1954).

CHICHMAREF, VALDEMAR: *Guillaume de Machaut: Œuvres lyriques*. 2 vols. (Paris and St. Petersburg, 1909).

CLERCX-LEJEUNE, SUZANNE and COLLAER, PAUL: *Compte-rendu du Colloque International d'Ars Nova, Liège, 1955* (1956).

COUSSEMAKER, C. E. H. DE: *Les harmonistes du XIVᵉ siècle* (Paris, 1869).

COVILLE, ALEX. ALFRED: 'Philippe de Vitri'. *Romania*, lix (1933).

DAHNK, EMILIE: *L'hérésie de Fauvel* (Leipzig and Paris, 1935).

DROZ, EUGÉNIE and THIBAULT, GENEVIÈVE: 'Un Chansonnier de Philippe le Bon'. *Revue de musicologie*, x (1926).

FEDERHOFER, HELMUT: 'Denkmäler der ars nova in Vorau Cod. 380'. *Acta Musicologica*, xxii (1950).

FEININGER, L. K. J.: *Die Frühgeschichte des Kanons bis Josquin des Prez* (Emsdetten, 1937).

FICKER, RUDOLF VON: 'Beiträge zur Chromatik des 14. bis 16. Jahrhunderts'. *Studien zur Musikwissenschaft*, ii (1914).

—— 'Formprobleme der mittelalterlichen Musik'. *Zeitschrift für Musikwissenschaft*, vii (1925).

—— 'Polyphonic Music of the Gothic Period'. *Musical Quarterly*, xv (1929).

GASTOUÉ, AMÉDÉE: *Les Primitifs de la musique française* (Paris, 1922).

GENNRICH, FRIEDRICH: *Abriß der frankonischen Mensuralnotation* (Nieder-Modau, 1946).

—— *Abriß der Mensuralnotation des XIV. Jahrhunderts und der ersten Hälfte des XV. Jahrhunderts* (Nieder-Modau, 1948).

—— 'Zur Musikinstrumentenkunde der Machaut-Zeit'. *Zeitschrift für Musikwissenschaft*, ix (1927).

GEORGIADES, THRASYBOULOS: *Englische Diskanttraktate aus der ersten Hälfte des XV. Jahrhunderts* (Munich, 1937).

GILLES, A.: 'Un Témoignage inédit de l'enseignement de Philippe de Vitry'. *Musica Disciplina*, x (1956).

GLEASON, HAROLD: 'Isorhythmic Tenors in the Three-part Motets of the Roman de Fauvel'. *Bulletin of the American Musicological Society* (1943), no. 7.

GOMBOSI, OTTO: 'Machaut's Messe Notre-Dame'. *Musical Quarterly*, xxxvi (1950).

GRÖBER, GUSTAV: *Grundriß der romanischen Philologie*, ii (Strasbourg, 1902).

GRÖBER-HOFER: *Geschichte der mittel-französischen Literatur*, vol. i (Berlin and Leipzig, 1933).

GROSSMANN, WALTER: *Die einleitenden Kapitel des Speculum Musice* (Leipzig, 1924).

HANDSCHIN, JACQUES: 'Die ältesten Denkmäler mensural notierter Musik in der Schweiz'. *Archiv für Musikwissenschaft*, v (1923).

—— 'Über Voraussetzungen sowie Früh- und Hochblüte der mittelalterlichen Mehrstimmigkeit'. *Schweizerisches Jahrbuch für Musikwissenschaft*, ii (1927).

—— 'Zur Frage der melodischen Paraphrasierung im Mittelalter'. *Zeitschrift für Musikwissenschaft*, x (1928).

—— 'Zur Geschichte von Notre Dame'. *Acta Musicologica*, iv (1932).

HARDER, HANNA: 'Die Messe von Toulouse'. *Musica Disciplina*, vii (1953).

HAYDON, GLEN: *The Evolution of the Six-Four Chord* (Berkeley, Calif., 1933).

506   BIBLIOGRAPHY

HIBBERD, LLOYD: 'Musica Ficta and Instrumental Music c. 1250–1350'. *Musical Quarterly*, xxviii (1942).
—— 'On Instrumental Style in Early Melody'. *Musical Quarterly*, xxxii (1946).
HIRSCHFELD, ROBERT: 'Notizen zur mittelalterlichen Musikgeschichte (Instrumentalmusik und Musica Ficta)'. *Monatshefte für Musikgeschichte*, xvii (1885).
HOEPFFNER, ERNEST: 'Anagramme und Rätselgedichte bei Guillaume de Machaut'. *Zeitschrift für romanische Philologie*, xxx (1906).
—— 'Die Balladen des Dichters Jehan de le Mote'. *Zeitschrift für romanische Philologie*, xxxv (1911).
—— *La Prise amoureuse von Jehan Acart de Hesdin* (Dresden, 1910).
—— 'Les poésies lyriques du Dit de la Panthère de Nicole de Margival'. *Romania*, xlvi (1920).
—— 'Virelais et ballades dans le chansonnier d'Oxford (Douce 308)'. *Archivum Romanicum*, iv (1920).
HOPPIN, RICHARD H.: 'Partial Signatures and Musica Ficta in Some Early 15th-Century Sources'. *Journal of the American Musicological Society*, vi (1953).
KAMMERER, FRIEDRICH: *Die Musikstücke des Prager Kodex XI E 9* (Brno, 1931).
LÅNGFORS, ARTHUR: *Le Roman de Fauvel* (Paris, 1914–19).
LANGLOIS, CHARLES-VICTOR: 'Jean de Lescurel, poète français'. *Histoire littéraire de la France*, xxxvi (Paris, 1924).
—— *La Vie en France au moyen âge de la fin du XIIe siècle au milieu du XIVe siècle d'après les moralistes du temps*, ii (Paris, 1908).
LANGLOIS, ERNEST: *Recueil d'Arts de seconde rhétorique* (Paris, 1903).
LA FAGE, J. ADRIEN L. DE: *Essais de diphtérographie musicale* (Paris, 1864).
LOWINSKY, EDWARD E.: 'Conflicting Views on Conflicting Signatures'. *Journal of the American Musicological Society*, vii (1954).
—— 'The Functions of Conflicting Signatures in Early Polyphonic Music'. *Musical Quarterly*, xxxi (1945).
LUDWIG, FRIEDRICH: Review of J. Wolf's 'Geschichte der Mensural-Notation 1250–1460'. *Sammelbände der internationalen Musikgesellschaft*, vi (1905).
—— 'Die mehrstimmige Messe des 14. Jahrhunderts'. *Archiv für Musikwissenschaft*, vii (1925).
—— 'Die mehrstimmige Musik des 14. Jahrhunderts', *Sammelbände der intertionalen Musikgesellschaft*, iv (1902).
—— 'Musik des Mittelalters in der Badischen Kunsthalle Karlsruhe'. *Zeitschrift für Musikwissenschaft*, v (1923).
MACHABEY, ARMAND: 'Guillaume de Machault'. *Revue musicale*, xi–xii (1930–1).
—— *Guillaume de Machaut*, 2 vols. (Paris, 1955).
—— *Histoire et évolution des formules musicales* (Paris, 1928).
—— 'Notice sur Philippe de Vitry'. *Revue musicale*, x (1929).
—— 'Quelques remarques sur la polyphonie vocale du XIVe siècle'. *Polyphonie*, iii (1948).
OLSON, C. C.: 'Chaucer and Music of the Fourteenth Century'. *Speculum*, xvi (1941).
PAGÈS, AMÉDÉE: *La Poésie française en Catalogne du XIIIe à la fin du XVe siècle* (Toulouse and Paris, 1936).
PARIS, PAULIN: *Guillaume de Machaut: Le livre du Voir Dit* (Paris, 1875).
PATTERSON, WARNER FORREST: *Three Centuries of French Poetic Theory*. 2 vols. (Ann Arbor, 1935).
PERLE, GEORGE: 'Integrative Devices in the Music of Machaut'. *Musical Quarterly*, xxxiv (1948).

PIETZSCH, GERHARD: *Die Klassifikation der Musik von Boetius bis Ugolino von Orvieto* (Freiburg im Breisgau, 1929).

PIRRO, ANDRÉ: 'Musiciens allemands et auditeurs français aux temps des rois Charles V et Charles VI'. *Adler-Festschrift* (Vienna, 1930).

—— 'Remarques sur l'exécution musicale de la fin du XIVᵉ siècle au milieu du XVᵉ siècle'. *International Society for Musical Research, First Report, Liège, 1930* (Burnham, 1931).

PRESTON, RAYMOND: 'Chaucer and the "Ballades notées" of Guillaume de Machaut'. *Speculum*, xxvi (1951).

QUEUX DE SAINT-HILAIRE and RAYNAUD, GASTON: *Eustache Deschamps, Œuvres complètes*. 11 vols. (Paris, 1878–1903).

QUITTARD, HENRI: 'Notes sur Guillaume de Machaut'. *Bulletin de la société française de musicologie*, i (1918).

REANEY, GILBERT: 'A Chronology of the Ballades, Rondeaux and Virelais Set to Music by Guillaume de Machaut'. *Musica Disciplina*, vi (1952).

—— Articles 'Chanson I', 'Color', 'Egidius de Murino', 'Franciscus', 'Froissart'. *Die Musik in Geschichte und Gegenwart*, ii–iv (1951–5).

—— 'Fourteenth Century Harmony and the Ballades, Rondeaux and Virelais of Guillaume de Machaut'. *Musica Disciplina*, vii (1953).

—— 'The "Ars Nova" of Philippe de Vitry'. *Musica Disciplina*, x (1956) and xi (1957).

—— 'The Ballades, Rondeaux and Virelais of Guillaume de Machaut: Melody, Rhythm and Form'. *Acta Musicologica*, xxvii (1955).

—— 'The Lais of Guillaume de Machaut and their Background'. *Proceedings of the Royal Musical Association*, lxxxii (1955–6).

—— 'The Manuscript Chantilly, Musée Condé 1047'. *Musica Disciplina*, viii (1954) and x (1956).

—— 'Voices and Instruments in the Music of Guillaume de Machaut'. *Kongress-Bericht, Bamberg, 1953* (Kassel, 1954).

SCHERING, ARNOLD: *Studien zur Musikgeschichte der Frührenaissance* (Leipzig, 1914).

SCHNEIDER, MARIUS: *Die Ars Nova des XIV. Jahrhunderts in Frankreich und Italien* (Berlin, 1930).

SCHRADE, LEO: 'A Fourteenth Century Parody Mass'. *Acta Musicologica*, xxvii (1955).

—— 'The Mass of Toulouse'. *Revue belge de musicologie*, viii (1954).

—— 'Philippe de Vitry: Some New Discoveries'. *Musical Quarterly*, xlii (1956).

SUCHIER, HERMANN: 'Das Anagramm in Machauts Voir Dit'. *Zeitschrift für romanische Philologie*, xxi (1897).

TRAVERS, ÉMILE: *Les Instruments de musique au XIVᵉ siècle d'après Guillaume de Machaut* (Paris, 1882).

VAN DEN BORREN, CHARLES: 'Le Fragment de Gand'. *Festschrift für Johannes Wolf* (Berlin, 1929).

—— *Le manuscript musical M. 222 C. 22 de la Bibliothèque de Strasbourg* (Antwerp, 1924).

VAN, GUILLAUME DE: 'La Pédagogie musicale à la fin du moyen âge'. *Musica Disciplina*, ii (1948).

—— 'La Prolation mineure chez Guillaume de Machaut'. *Sources*, i (1943).

WOLF, JOHANNES: 'Ein anonymer Musiktraktat aus der ersten Zeit der "Ars Nova"'. *Kirchenmusikalisches Jahrbuch*, xxi (1908).

—— 'Ein Beitrag zur Diskantlehre des 14. Jahrhunderts'. *Sammelbände der internationalen Musikgesellschaft*, xv (1913).

WOLF, JOHANNES: *Geschichte der Mensuralnotation von 1250–1460 nach den theoretischen und praktischen Quellen*. 3 vols. (Leipzig, 1904).
—— 'Zur Geschichte der Orgelmusik im vierzehnten Jahrhundert'. *Kirchenmusikalisches Jahrbuch*, xiv (1899).
ZWICK, GABRIEL: 'Deux motets inédits de Philippe de Vitry et de Guillaume de Machaut'. *Revue de musicologie*, xxx (1948).

CHAPTER II

THE FOURTEENTH CENTURY IN ITALY

(i) *Sources*

BONFANTINI, MARIO: *Le sacre rappresentazioni italiane* (Milan, 1942).
CARAPETYAN, ARMEN (ed.): *Notitia del valore delle note del canto misurato* (*Corpus Scriptorum de Musica*, v) (Rome, 1957).
CARDUCCI, GIOSUÈ: *Cacce in rime dei secoli xiv e xv* (Bologna, 1896).
CELLISI, LUIGIA: 'Documenti per la storia musicale di Firenze'. *Rivista musicale italiana*, xxxiv–v (1927–8).
ELLINWOOD, LEONARD: *The works of Francesco Landini* (Cambridge, Mass., 1939).
LIUZZI, FERNANDO: *La lauda e i primordi della melodia italiana*. 2 vols. (Rome, 1935).
MARROCCO, W. THOMAS: *Fourteenth-century Italian Cacce* (Cambridge, Mass., 1942).
—— *The Music of Jacopo da Bologna* (Berkeley and Los Angeles, 1954).
PIRROTTA, NINO: *The Music of Fourteenth Century Italy*, i (*Corpus mensurabilis musicae*, viii, 1) (Amsterdam, 1954).
STAINER, JOHN, J. F. R., and C.: *Dufay and his Contemporaries* (London, 1898).
VAN, GUILLAUME DE: *Les Monuments de l'Ars Nova. Fascicule l. Morceaux liturgiques I. Œuvres italiennes* (Paris, 1938).
VAN DEN BORREN, CHARLES: *Polyphonia sacra* (Burnham, 1932).
WESSELOFSKY, A.: *Il Paradiso degli Alberti: ritrovi e ragionamenti del 1389 romanzo di Giovanni da Prato*. 3 vols. (Bologna, 1867).
WOLF, JOHANNES: *Der Squarcialupi-Codex Pal. 87 der Biblioteca Laurenziana in Florenz* (Lippstadt, 1955).

(ii) *Books and Articles*

BERTONI, GIULIO: *I trovatori in Italia* (Modena, 1915).
BONAVENTURA, ARNOLDO: 'Boccaccio e la musica'. *Rivista musicale italiana*, xxi (1914).
—— *Dante e la musica* (Leghorn, 1904).
CAFFI, F.; *Storia della musica sacra nella già cappella ducale di San Marco in Venezia dal 1318 al 1797* (Venice, 1855).
CHAYTOR, H. J.: *The Troubadours of Dante* (Oxford, 1902).
COVILLE, A.: 'Philippe de Vitri'. *Romania*, lix (1933).
CULCASI, C.: *Il Petrarcha e la musica* (Florence, 1911).
FISCHER, KURT VON: *Studien zur italienischen Musik des Trecento und frühen Quattrocento* (Berne, 1956).
—— 'The Manuscript Paris, Bibl. nat., nouv. acq. frç. 6771'. *Musica Disciplina*, xi (1957).
—— 'Trecentomusik—Trecentoprobleme', *Acta Musicologica*, xxx (1958).
—— 'Zur Entwicklung der italienischen Trecento-Notation'. *Archiv für Musikwissenschaft*, xvi (1959).
FRATI, L.: 'Il Petrarcha e la musica'. *Rivista musicale italiana*, xxxi (1924).
GHISI, FEDERICO: 'Frammenti di un nuovo codice'. *La Rinascita*, v (1942).

GHISI, FEDERICO: 'Italian Ars Nova music. The Perugia and Pistoia fragments of the Lucca musical codex'. *Journal of Renaissance and Baroque Music*, i (1947).

—— 'A Second Sienese Fragment of Italian Ars Nova'. *Musica Disciplina*, ii (1948).

GIDEL, ANTOINE CHARLES: *Les Troubadours et Petrarque* (Angers, 1857).

KÖNIGSLÖW, ANNEMARIE VON: *Die italienischen Madrigalisten des Trecento* (Würzburg, 1940).

KORTE, WERNER: *Studie zur Geschichte der Musik in Italien im ersten Viertel des 15. Jahrhunderts* (Kassel, 1933).

LI GOTTI, ETTORE: 'L' "ars nova" e il madrigale'. *Atti della Reale Accademia di scienze, lettere e arti di Palermo*, series iv, vol. 4, part ii (1945).

—— 'Poesie musicali italiane del sec. XIV'. *Atti della Reale Accademia di scienze, lettere e arti di Palermo*, series iv, vol. 4, part ii (1945).

—— and PIRROTTA, NINO: *Il Sacchetti e la tecnica musicale del trecento italiano* (Florence, 1935).

LIUZZI, FERNANDO: 'Musica e poesia del trecento nel codice Vaticano Rossiano 215'. *Atti della Pontifica Accademia Romana di Archeologia*, series III, *Rendiconti* XIII (1937).

LUCIANI, S. A.: 'Le ballate a una voce del codice Squarcialupi'. *Archivi d'Italia*, series ii, vol. 3 (1936).

LUDWIG, FRIEDRICH: 'Die mehrstimmige Messe des 14. Jahrhunderts'. *Archiv für Musikwissenschaft*, vii (1925).

—— 'Die mehrstimmigen Werke der Handschrift Engelberg 314'. *Kirchenmusikalisches Jahrbuch*, xxi (1908).

MARROCCO, W. THOMAS: 'The 14th-century Italian Cacce'. *Speculum*, xxvi (1951).

MUONI, DAMIANO: *Gli Atignati organari insigni* (Milan, 1883).

PIRROTTA, NINO: 'Marchettus de Padua and the Italian Ars Nova'. *Musica Disciplina*, ix (1955).

—— 'Paolo da Firenze in un nuovo frammento dell' ars nova', *Musica Disciplina*, x (1956).

—— 'Per l'origine e la storia della "caccia" e del "madrigale" trecentesco'. *Rivista musicale italiana*, xlviii–xlix (1946–7).

—— 'Scuole polifoniche italiane durante il sec. XIV'. *Collectanea historiae musicae*, i (Florence, 1953).

PLAMENAC, DRAGAN: 'Another Paduan Fragment of Trecento Music'. *Journal of the American Musicological Society*, viii (1955).

SARTORI, CLAUDIO: *La notazione italiana del trecento* (Florence, 1938).

SCHNEIDER, MARIUS: *Die Ars nova des XIV. Jahrhunderts in Frankreich und Italien* (Berlin, 1930).

VAN DEN BORREN, CHARLES: *Les débuts de la musique à Venise* (Brussels, 1914).

WOLF, JOHANNES: 'Die Rossi-Handschrift 215 der Vaticana und das Trecento-Madrigal'. *Jahrbuch der Musikbibliothek Peters*, xlv (1938).

—— 'Florenz in der Musikgeschichte des 14. Jahrhunderts'. *Sammelbände der internationalen Musikgesellschaft*, iii (1902).

—— 'Italian Trecento Music'. *Proceedings of the Musical Association*, lviii (1932).

CHAPTER III

ENGLISH CHURCH MUSIC IN THE FOURTEENTH CENTURY

(i) *Sources*

DICKINSON, F. H.: *Missale ad usum Insignis et Praeclarae Ecclesiae Sarum* (Burntisland, 1861–83).

FICKER, RUDOLF VON: *Denkmäler der Tonkunst in Österreich*, xl (Vienna, 1933).

FRERE, WALTER HOWARD: *Antiphonale Sarisburiense* (London, 1901–25).

—— *Graduale Sarisburiense* (London, 1894).

GENNRICH, FRIEDRICH: *Abriß der frankonischen Mensuralnotation* (Nieder-Modau, 1946).

—— *Abriß der Mensuralnotation des XIV. Jahrhunderts und der ersten Hälfte des XV. Jahrhunderts* (Nieder-Modau, 1948).

RAMSBOTHAM, A., COLLINS, H. B., and HUGHES, DOM ANSELM: *The Old Hall Manuscript*, 3 vols. (London, 1933–8).

ROKSETH, YVONNE: *Polyphonies du XIIIᵉ siècle*. 4 vols. (Paris, 1935–9).

STAINER, JOHN, J. F. R., and C.: *Early Bodleian Music*. 2 vols. (London, 1901).

(ii) *Books and Articles*

ANDREWS, H. K. and DART, T.: 'Fourteenth Century Polyphony in a Fountains Abbey MS Book'. *Music and Letters*, xxix (1958).

BUKOFZER, MANFRED F.: *Geschichte des englischen Diskants und des Faux-bourdons nach den theoretischen Quellen* (Strasbourg, 1936).

—— *Studies in Medieval and Renaissance Music* (New York, 1950).

—— 'The Gymel, the earliest Form of English Polyphony'. *Music and Letters*, xvi (1935).

GEORGIADES, T.: *Englische Diskanttraktate aus der ersten Hälfte des XV. Jahrhunderts* (Munich, 1937).

HARRISON, F. LL.: *Music in Medieval Britain* (London, 1958).

REANEY, GILBERT: 'The Manuscript Chantilly, Musée Condé 1047'. *Musica Disciplina*, viii (1951) and x (1956).

SQUIRE, W. BARCLAY: 'Notes on an undescribed Collection of English 15th-Century Music'. *Sammelbände der internationalen Musikgesellschaft*, ii (1901).

STEVENS, DENIS: 'A Recently Discovered English Source of the Fourteenth Century'. *The Musical Quarterly*, xli (1955).

—— 'The Second Fountains Fragment: a Postscript'. *Music and Letters*, xxix (1958).

CHAPTER IV

POPULAR AND SECULAR MUSIC IN ENGLAND

(i) *Sources*

ADLER, GUIDO and KOLLER, OSWALD: *Denkmäler der Tonkunst in Österreich*, vii (Vienna, 1900), xi, part i (Vienna, 1904).

BUKOFZER, MANFRED F.: *Musica Britannica*, viii. *John Dunstable, Complete Works* (London, 1953).

FULLER MAITLAND, J. A.: *English Carols of the Fifteenth Century* (London, 1891).

JEPPESEN, KNUD: *Der Kopenhagener Chansonnier* (Copenhagen and Leipzig,1937).

MARIX, JEANNE: *Les Musiciens de la cour de Bourgogne au XVᵉ siècle* (Paris, 1937).

M[YERS], S. L.: *Music, Cantilenas, Songs &c. from an early Fifteenth Century Manuscript* (London, 1906).

STAINER, JOHN, J. F. R., and C.: *Early Bodleian Music*. 2 vols. (London, 1901).

STEVENS, JOHN: *Musica Britannica, iv. Mediaeval Carols.* (London, 1952).
WOOLDRIDGE, H. E.: *Early English Harmony*, vol. i (London, 1897).

(ii) *Books and Articles*

BUKOFZER, MANFRED F.: 'An unknown Chansonnier of the Fifteenth Century (the Mellon Chansonnier)'. *Musical Quarterly*, xxviii (1942).
—— 'The First English Chanson on the Continent'. *Music and Letters*, xix (1938).
—— 'The First Motet with English Words'. *Music and Letters*, xvii (1936).
—— 'Gymel, the earliest Form of English Polyphony'. *Music and Letters*, xvi (1935).
—— 'Popular Polyphony in the Middle Ages'. *Musical Quarterly*, xxvi (1940).
—— *Studies in Medieval and Renaissance Music* (New York, 1950).
BUSH, HELEN E.: 'The Laborde Chansonnier'. *Papers of the American Musicological Society 1940* (1946).
CHAPPELL, WILLIAM: *Popular Music of the Olden Time.* 2 vols. (London, 1855–9). 2nd ed., as *Old English Popular Music*, by H. E. Wooldridge (London, 1893).
GREENE, RICHARD L.: *The Early English Carols* (London, 1935).
—— 'Two Medieval Musical Manuscripts: Egerton 3307 and some University of Chicago Fragments'. *Journal of the American Musicological Society*, vii (1954).
KENNEY, SYLVIA W.: 'Contrafacta in the Works of Walter Frye'. *Journal of the American Musicological Society*, viii (1955).
LEDERER, VICTOR: *Über Heimat und Ursprung der mehrstimmigen Tonkunst* (Leipzig, 1906).
PLAMENAC, DRAGAN: 'A Reconstruction of the French Chansonnier in the Biblioteca Colombina, Seville'. *Musical Quarterly*, xxxvii–xxxviii (1951–2).
SCHOFIELD, BERTRAM: 'A Newly-discovered Fifteenth Century Manuscript of the English Chapel Royal'. *Musical Quarterly*, xxxii (1946).

CHAPTER V

THE TRANSITION ON THE CONTINENT

(i) *Sources*

ADLER, GUIDO and KOLLER, OSWALD: *Denkmäler der Tonkunst in Österreich*, vii (Vienna, 1900); xi, part i (Vienna, 1904); xix, part i (Vienna, 1912).
APEL, WILLI: *French Secular Music of the late Fourteenth Century* (Cambridge, Mass., 1950).
CESARI, GAETANO, and FANO, FABIO: *La Cappella musicale del duomo di Milano* (Milan, 1956).
FICKER, RUDOLF VON: *Denkmäler der Tonkunst in Österreich*, xxxi (Vienna, 1924); xl (Vienna, 1933).
FICKER, RUDOLF VON and OREL, ALFRED: *Denkmäler der Tonkunst in Österreich*, xxvii, part i (Vienna, 1920).
GASTOUÉ, AMÉDÉE: *Le Manuscrit de musique du trésor d'Apt* (Paris, 1936).
KAMMERER, FRIEDRICH: *Die Musikstücke des Prager Kodex XI E 9* (Augsburg and Brno, 1931).
MARIX, JEANNE: *Les Musiciens de la cour de Bourgogne au XVe siècle* (Paris, 1937).
REANEY, GILBERT: *Early Fifteenth-Century Music* (American Institute of Musicology, 1955).

REHM, WOLFGANG: *Codex Escorial: Chansonnier* (*Documenta Musicologica*, series
II, ii) (Kassel, 1958).
STAINER, JOHN, J. F. R., and C.: *Dufay and his Contemporaries* (London, 1898).
VAN, GUILLAUME DE and BESSELER, H.: *Guillaume Dufay, Opera Omnia*.
(Rome, 1947–   ).
VAN DEN BORREN, CHARLES: *Polyphonia Sacra* (London, 1932).

(ii) *Books and Articles*

ADLER, GUIDO: 'Studien zur Geschichte der Harmonie'. *Sitzungsberichte der
philosophische-historische Klasse der Akademie der Wissenschaft in Wien*,
xcviii (Vienna, 1881).
APEL, WILLI: 'The French Secular Music of the late 14th Century'. *Acta
Musicologica*, xviii–xix (1946–7).
BESSELER, HEINRICH: *Bourdon und Fauxbourdon* (Leipzig, 1950).
—— 'Das Ergebnis der Diskussion über "Fauxbourdon".' *Acta Musicologica*,
xxix (1957).
—— 'Hat Matheus de Perusio Epoche gemacht?' *Die Musikforschung*, viii
(1955).
—— 'The manuscript Bologna Biblioteca Universitaria 2216'. *Musica Disciplina*,
vi (1952).
BORGHEZIO, G.: 'Un prezioso codice musicale ignorato'. *Bolletino storico
bibliografico subalpino*, xxiv (1921).
—— 'Poesie musicali latine e francesi in un codice ignorato della Biblioteca
capitolare d'Ivrea'. *Archivum Romanum*, v (1921).
BUKOFZER, MANFRED F.: *Geschichte des englischen Diskants und des Faux-
bourdons nach den theoretischen Quellen* (Strasbourg, 1936).
CHAILLEY, JACQUES: 'La Messe de Besançon et un compositeur inconnu du
XIVᵉ siècle: Jean Lambelet'. *Annales musicologiques*, ii (1954).
CLERCX-LEJEUNE, SUZANNE: 'Johannes Ciconia de Leodio'. *Kongreßbericht der
internationalen Gesellschaft für Musikwissenschaft in Utrecht, 1952* (Amster-
dam, 1953).
—— 'Johannes Ciconia théoricien'. *Annales musicologiques*, iii (1955).
DANNEMANN, ERNA: *Die spätgotische Musiktradition in Frankreich und Burgund
vor dem Auftreten Dufays* (Strasbourg, 1936).
FICKER, RUDOLF VON: 'Die frühen Messenkompositionen in den Trienter
Codices'. *Studien zur Musikwissenschaft*, xi (1924).
—— 'Die Kolorierungstechnik der Trienter Messen'. *Studien zur Musik-
wissenschaft*, vii (1920).
—— 'Formprobleme der mittelalterlichen Musik'. *Zeitschrift für Musik-
wissenschaft*, vii (1925).
—— 'Zur Schöpfungsgeschichte des Fauxbourdons'. *Acta Musicologica*, xxiii
(1951).
FISCHER, KURT VON: 'The Manuscript Paris, Bibl. Nat., nouv. acq. frç. 6771'.
Musica Disciplina, xi (1957).
FLASDIECK, HERMANN M.: 'Franz. "faux-bourdon" und frühneuengl. "fa-
burden"'. *Acta Musicologica*, xxv (1953).
GASTOUÉ, AMÉDÉE: 'La Musique à Avignon et dans le Comtat, du XIVᵉ au
XVIIIᵉ siècle'. *Rivista musica italiana*, xi (1904).
GEORGIADES, T.: *Englische Diskanttraktate aus der ersten Hälfte des XV. Jahr-
hunderts* (Munich, 1937).
GHISI, FEDERICO: 'Bruchstücke einer neuen Musikhandschrift der italienischen
Ars nova'. *Archiv für Musikforschung*, vii (1942).

GHISI, FEDERICO: 'Frammenti di un nuovo codice'. *La Rinascita*, v (1942).
—— 'Italian Ars Nova Music. The Perugia and Pistoia Fragments of the Lucca Musical Codex'. *Journal of Renaissance and Baroque Music*, i (1947).
—— 'L'Ordinarium missae nel XV secolo ed i primordi della parodia'. *Atti del congresso internazionale di musica sacra, 1950* (Tournai, 1952).
GURLITT, WILLIBALD: 'Burgundische Chanson- und deutsche Liedkunst des 15. Jahrhunderts'. *Bericht über den Musikwissenschaftlichen Kongress in Basel 1924* (Leipzig, 1925).
HOPPIN, RICHARD H.: 'The Cypriot-French Repertory of the Manuscript Torino Biblioteca Nazionale, J. II. 9'. *Musica Disciplina*, xi (1957).
JACKSON, ROLAND: 'Musical Interrelations between Fourteenth Century Mass movements'. *Acta Musicologica*, xxix (1957).
KENNEY, S. W.: ' "English Discant" and Discant in England'. *Musical Quarterly*, xlv (1959).
KORTE, WERNER: *Die Harmonik des frühen 15. Jahrhunderts in ihrem Zusammenhang mit der Formtechnik* (Münster, 1929).
—— *Studie zur Geschichte der Musik in Italien im ersten Viertel des 15. Jahrhunderts* (Kassel, 1933).
KROYER, THEODOR: 'Das a cappella Ideal'. *Acta Musicologica*, vi (1934).
LA FAGE, ADRIEN L. DE: *Essais de diphtérographie musicale* (Paris, 1864).
OREL, ALFRED: 'Einige Grundformen der Motettkomposition im 15. Jahrhundert'. *Studien zur Musikwissenschaft*, vii (1920).
PIRRO, ANDRÉ: *La Musique à Paris sous le règne de Charles VI* (Strasbourg, 1930).
PIRROTTA, NINO: 'Considerazioni sui primi esempi di missa parodia'. *Atti del congresso internazionale di musica sacra, 1950* (Tournai, 1952).
—— ' "Dulcedo" e "subtilitas" nella pratica polifonica franco-italiana al principio del '400'. *Revue belge de musicologie*, ii (1948).
—— 'Il codice Estense lat. 568 e la musica francese in Italia al principio del '400'. *Atti della Reale Accademia di scienze, lettere e arti di Palermo*, series iv, vol. 5, part ii (1946).
RIEMANN, HUGO: 'Das Kunstlied im 14–15. Jahrhundert'. *Sammelbände der internationalen Musikgesellschaft*, vii (1906).
SARTORI, CLAUDIO: 'Matteo da Perugia e Bertrand Feragut, i due primi Maestri di Cappella del Duomo di Milano'. *Acta Musicologica*, xxviii (1956).
SCHERING, ARNOLD: *Studien zur Musikgeschichte der Frührenaissance* (Leipzig, 1914).
SCHRADE, LEO: 'A Fourteenth Century Parody Mass'. *Acta Musicologica*, xxvii (1955).
VAN, GUILLAUME DE: 'A Recently Discovered Source of early Fifteenth Century Polyphonic Music, the Aosta Manuscript'. *Musica Disciplina*, ii (1948).
—— 'Inventory of Manuscript Bologna Liceo Musicale Q 15'. *Musica Disciplina*, ii (1948).
VAN DEN BORREN, CHARLES: *Le Manuscrit musical M. 222 C. 22 de la Bibliothèque de Strasbourg* (Antwerp, 1924).

CHAPTER VI

ENGLISH CHURCH MUSIC OF THE FIFTEENTH CENTURY

(i) *Sources*

ADLER, GUIDO and KOLLER, OSWALD: *Denkmäler der Tonkunst in Österreich*, vii (Vienna, 1900).

BUKOFZER, MANFRED F.: *Musica Britannica*, viii. *John Dunstable, Complete Works* (London, 1953).

FEININGER, LAURENCE: *Documenta Polyphoniae Liturgicae Sanctae Ecclesiae Romanae*, series i, 2. *Leonel Power, Missa Alma Redemptoris Mater* (Rome, 1947); series i, 6. *Standley, Missa ad Fugam* (Rome, 1949); series iv, 1. *Standley, Fuga reservata Quae est ista* (Rome, 1950).

FICKER, RUDOLF VON: *Denkmäler der Tonkunst in Österreich*, xxxi (Vienna, 1924), xl (Vienna, 1933).

FRERE, WALTER HOWARD: *Antiphonale Sarisburiense* (London, 1901–25).

—— *Graduale Sarisburiense* (London, 1894).

RAMSBOTHAM, A., COLLINS, H. B., and HUGHES, DOM ANSELM: *The Old Hall Manuscript*. 3 vols. (Burnham, 1933–8).

STAINER, JOHN, J. F. R., and C.: *Early Bodleian Music*. 2 vols. (London, 1901).

WOOLDRIDGE, H. E.: *Early English Harmony*, vol. i (London, 1897).

(ii) *Books and Articles*

BESSELER, HEINRICH: *Bourdon und Fauxbourdon* (Leipzig, 1950).

BUKOFZER, MANFRED F.: 'Caput redivivum'. *Journal of the American Musicological Society*, iv (1951).

—— 'Fauxbourdon revisited'. *Musical Quarterly*, xxxviii (1952).

—— *Geschichte des englischen Diskants und des Fauxbourdons nach den theoretischen Quellen* (Strasbourg, 1936).

—— 'John Dunstable and the Music of his Time'. *Proceedings of the Royal Musical Association*, lxv (1938).

—— 'John Dunstable: a Quincentenary Report'. *Musical Quarterly*, xl (1954).

—— *Studies in Medieval and Renaissance Music* (New York, 1950).

—— 'Über Leben und Werke von Dunstable'. *Acta Musicologica*, viii (1936).

FICKER, RUDOLF VON: 'Die Kolorierungstechnik der Trienter Messen'. *Studien zur Musikwissenschaft*, vii (1920).

FLOOD, W. H. GRATTAN: 'Entries relating to Music in the English Patent Rolls of the Fifteenth Century'. *Musical Antiquary*, iv (1912–13).

—— 'The Beginnings of the Chapel Royal'. *Music and Letters*, v (1924).

GEORGIADES, T.: *Englische Diskanttraktate aus der ersten Hälfte des XV. Jahrhunderts* (Munich, 1937).

GREENE, R. L.: 'Two Medieval Musical Manuscripts: Egerton 3307 and some University of Chicago Fragments'. *Journal of the American Musicological Society*, vii (1954).

KENNEY, SYLVIA W.: 'Origins and Chronology of the Brussels Manuscript 5557'. *Revue belge de musicologie*, vi (1952).

MACLEAN, CHARLES: 'The Dunstable Inscription in London'. *Sammelbände der internationalen Musikgesellschaft*, xi (1910).

MEECH, S. B.: 'Three Musical Treatises in English from a Fifteenth-century Manuscript'. *Speculum*, x (1935).

SCHOFIELD, BERTRAM and BUKOFZER, MANFRED F.: 'A Newly-discovered Fifteenth-century Manuscript of the English Chapel Royal'. *Musical Quarterly*, xxxii–xxxiii (1946–7).

SQUIRE, W. BARCLAY: 'Notes on an Undescribed Collection of English 15th-Century Music'. *Sammelbände der internationalen Musikgesellschaft*, ii (1901).

VAN, GUILLAUME DE: 'A Recently Discovered Source of early Fifteenth Century Polyphonic Music, the Aosta Manuscript'. *Musica Disciplina*, ii (1948).

—— 'Inventory of Manuscript Bologna Liceo Musicale Q 15'. *Musica Disciplina*, ii (1948).

VAN DEN BORREN, CHARLES: *Études sur le XVe siècle musical* (Antwerp, 1941).
—— 'The Genius of Dunstable'. *Proceedings of the Musical Association*, xlvii (1921).

CHAPTER VII

DUFAY AND HIS SCHOOL

(i) *Sources*

ADLER, GUIDO and KOLLER, OSWALD: *Denkmäler der Tonkunst in Österreich*, vii (Vienna, 1900); xi, part i (Vienna, 1904); xix, part i (Vienna, 1912).

BESSELER, HEINRICH: *Capella*, i. *Drei- und vierstimmige Singstücke des 15. Jahrhunderts* (Kassel and Basle, 1950).

—— *Capella*, ii. *Guillaume Dufay, Vierstimmige Messe 'Se la face ay pale'* (Kassel and Basle, 1951).

—— *Das Chorwerk*, xix. *Guillaume Dufay, Zwölf geistliche und weltliche Werke zu 3 Stimmen* (Wolfenbüttel, 1951).

FICKER, RUDOLF VON: *Denkmäler der Tonkunst in Österreich*, xxxi (Vienna, 1924); xl (Vienna, 1933).

FICKER, RUDOLF VON and OREL, ALFRED: *Denkmäler der Tonkunst in Österreich*, xxvii, part i (Vienna, 1920).

GERBER, RUDOLF: *Das Chorwerk*, xlix. *Guillaume Dufay, Sämtliche Hymnen zu 3 und 4 Stimmen* (Wolfenbüttel, 1937).

GURLITT, WILLIBALD: *Das Chorwerk*, xxii. *Gilles Binchois, Sechzehn weltliche Lieder zu 3 Stimmen* (Wolfenbüttel, 1933).

MARIX, JEANNE: *Les Musiciens de la cour de Bourgogne au XVe siècle* (Paris, 1937).

REHM, W.: *Die Chansons von Gilles de Binchois* (Mainz, 1957).

STAINER, JOHN, J. F. R. and C.: *Dufay and his Contemporaries* (London, 1898).

VAN, GUILLAUME DE and BESSELER, HEINRICH: *Guillaume Dufay. Opera Omnia* (Rome, 1947–).

VAN DEN BORREN, CHARLES: *Polyphonia Sacra* (London, 1932).

—— *Pièces polyphoniques profanes de provenance Liégeoise (XVe siècle)* (Brussels, 1950).

(ii) *Books and Articles*

AUBRY, PIERRE: *Iter Hispanicum* (Paris, 1908).

BAIX, FRANÇOIS: 'La carrière "bénéficiale" de Guillaume Dufay'. *Bulletin de l'Institut historique belge de Rome*, viii (1928).

BESSELER, HEINRICH: *Bourdon und Fauxbourdon* (Leipzig, 1950).

—— 'Dufay in Rom'. *Archiv für Musikwissenschaft*, xv (1958).

—— 'Dufay, Schöpfer des Fauxbourdons'. *Acta Musicologica*, xx (1948).

—— 'Von Dufay bis Josquin'. *Zeitschrift für Musikwissenschaft*, xi (1928).

BROWN, S. E.: 'New Evidence of Isomelic Design in Dufay's Isorhythmic Motets'. *Journal of the American Musicological Society*, x (1957).

BUKOFZER, MANFRED F.: 'Caput redivivum'. *Journal of the American Musicological Society*, iv (1951).

—— *Studies in Medieval and Renaissance Music* (New York, 1950).

—— 'An unknown Chansonnier of the Fifteenth Century (the Mellon Chansonnier)'. *Musical Quarterly*, xxviii (1942).

DÈZES, KARL: 'Das Dufay zugeschriebene "Salve regina" eine deutsche Komposition'. *Zeitschrift für Musikwissenschaft*, x (1927–8).

DOORSLAER, G. VAN: 'La Chapelle musicale de Philippe le Beau'. *Revue belge d'archéologie et d'histoire de l'art*, iv (1934).

GERBER, RUDOLF: 'Die Hymnen der Handschrift Monte Cassino 871'. *Anuario musical*, xi (1956).

GURLITT, WILLIBALD: 'Burgundische Chanson- und deutsche Liedkunst des 15. Jahrhunderts'. *Bericht über den Musikwissenschaftlichen Kongress in Basel, 1924* (Leipzig, 1925).

HABERL, FRANZ XAVER: *Bausteine für Musikgeschichte*. 3 vols. (Leipzig, 1885–8).

HARRISON, FRANK LL.: 'An English "Caput"'. *Music and Letters*, xxxiii (1952).

MARIX, JEANNE: *Histoire de la musique et des musiciens de la cour de Bourgogne sous le règne de Philippe le Bon* (Strasbourg, 1939).

OREL, ALFRED: 'Einige Grundformen der Motettkomposition im 15. Jahrhundert'. *Studien zur Musikwissenschaft*, vii (Vienna, 1920).

PLAMENAC, DRAGAN: 'A Reconstruction of the French Chansonnier in the Biblioteca Colombina, Seville'. *Musical Quarterly*, xxxvii–xxxviii (1951–2).

—— 'The "second" Chansonnier of the Biblioteca Riccardiana', *Annales musicologiques*, ii (1954).

REESER, EDUARD: 'Een isomelische mis uit den tijd van Dufay'. *Tijdschrift der Vereeniging voor Nederlandsche Muziekgeschiedenis*, xvi (1942–6).

—— 'Guillaume Dufay, "Nuper rosarum flores" 1436–1936'. *Tijdschrift der Vereeniging voor Nederlandsche Muziekgeschiedenis*, xv (1939).

VAN, GUILLAUME DE: 'A Recently Discovered Source of early Fifteenth Century Polyphonic Music, the Aosta Manuscript'. *Musica Disciplina*, ii (1948).

—— 'Inventory of Manuscript Bologna Liceo Musicale Q 15'. *Musica Disciplina*, ii (1948).

VAN DEN BORREN, CHARLES: 'A Light of the Fifteenth Century: Guillaume Dufay'. *Musical Quarterly*, xxi (1935).

—— *Études sur le XVe siècle musical* (Antwerp, 1941).

—— *Guillaume Dufay* (Brussels, 1926).

—— 'Guillaume Dufay, centre de rayonnement de la polyphonie européenne à la fin du moyen âge'. *Bulletin de l'Institut historique belge de Rome*, xx (1939).

—— 'The Codex Canonici 213 in the Bodleian Library at Oxford'. *Proceedings of the Royal Musical Association*, lxxiii (1947).

WOLFF, H. C.: *Die Musik der alten Niederländer* (Leipzig, 1956).

CHAPTER VIII

THE AGE OF OCKEGHEM AND JOSQUIN

(i) Sources

ACHLEITNER, I.: *Harmoniae poeticae Pauli Hofheimeri* (Salzburg, 1868).

ADLER, GUIDO and KOLLER, OSWALD: *Denkmäler der Tonkunst in Österreich*, vii (Vienna, 1900); xix, part i (Vienna, 1912).

ALBRECHT, HANS and GOMBOSI, OTTO: *Denkmäler deutscher Tonkunst*, lxv. *Thomas Stoltzer, Sämtliche lateinische Hymnen und Psalmen* (Leipzig, 1931).

BESSELER, HEINRICH: *Altniederländische Motetten* (Kassel, 1929).

—— *Das Chorwerk*, iv. *Johannes Ockeghem, Missa Mi-Mi* (Wolfenbüttel, 1950).

BEZECNY, EMIL B. and RABL, WALTER: *Denkmäler der Tonkunst in Österreich*, v, part i, *Heinrich Isaac, Choralis Constantinus, Part I* (Vienna, 1898).

BIRTNER, HERBERT: *Das Chorwerk*, xxxi. *Aulen, Missa* (Wolfenbüttel, 1934).

BLUME, FRIEDRICH: *Das Chorwerk*, i. *Josquin des Prés, Missa Pange Lingua* (Wolfenbüttel, 1929); xi. *Pierre de la Rue, Requiem und eine Motette* (Wolfenbüttel, 1931); xx. *Josquin des Prés, Missa Da Pacem* (Wolfenbüttel, 1950); xlii. *Josquin des Prés, Missa de Beata Virgine* (Wolfenbüttel, 1951).

CARAPETYAN, ARMEN: *Antonii Brumel Opera Omnia*, i. *Missa l'Homme armé* (Rome, 1951).

CUYLER, LOUISE: *Heinrich Isaac, Choralis Constantinus*, Part III (Ann Arbor, 1950).

—— *Heinrich Isaac, Five Polyphonic Masses* (Ann Arbor, 1957).

DROZ, EUGÉNIE and THIBAULT, GENEVIÈVE: *Trois Chansonniers français du XVe siècle*, i (Paris, 1927).

EITNER, ROBERT: *Publikation älterer praktischer und theoretischer Musikwerke*, viii. *Heinrich und Hermann Finck, Auswahl von geistlichen und weltlichen Liedern, Hymnen und Motetten* (Leipzig, 1879).

EXPERT, HENRY: *Les Maîtres musiciens de la Renaissance française*, viii. *Brumel, Missa de Beata Virgine*; *P. De la Rue, Missa Ave Maria* (Paris, 1898).

FEININGER, LAURENCE: *Monumenta Polyphoniae Liturgicae Sanctae Ecclesiae. Romanae*, series i, I, 2–10. *L'homme armé Masses by Busnois, Caron, Faugues, Regis, Ockeghem, de Orto, Basiron, Tinctoris, Vacqueras* (Rome, 1948).

—— *Documenta Polyphoniae Liturgicae Sanctae Ecclesiae Romanae*, series i B, i. *P. de la Rue, Missa Ave Sanctissima* (Rome, 1952).

FINSCHER, L.: *Das Chorwerk*, lv. *Loyset Compère, Missa Alles regrets* (Wolfenbüttel, 1956).

—— *Loyset Compere: Opera Omnia* (American Institute of Musicology, 1958–).

GERBER, RUDOLF: *Das Chorwerk*, ix. *Heinrich Finck, Acht Hymnen* (Wolfenbüttel, 1930).

—— *Das Chorwerk*, xxxii. *Heinrich Finck, Adam von Fulda, u.a., Zwölf Hymnen* (Wolfenbüttel, 1934).

—— *Der Mensuralkodex des Nikolaus Apel* (*Das Erbe deutscher Musik*, xxxii–xxxiv) (Kassel and Basle, 1956).

GOMBOSI, OTTO: *Das Chorwerk*, vi. *Thomas Stoltzer, Erzürne dich nicht* (Wolfenbüttel, 1930).

HASSE, KARL: *Das Chorwerk*, xxi. *Heinrich Finck, Missa in Summis* (Wolfenbüttel, 1932).

HEWITT, HELEN: *Harmonice Musices Odhecaton A* (Cambridge, Mass., 1942).

HEYDEN, REINHOLD: *Das Chorwerk*, vii. *Heinrich Isaac, Missa Carminum* (Wolfenbüttel, 1930).

JEPPESEN, KNUD: *Der Kopenhagener Chansonnier* (Copenhagen and Leipzig, 1927).

KAST, PAUL: *Das Chorwerk*, lxx. *Jean Mouton, Missa Alleluya* (Wolfenbüttel, 1958).

LINDENBURG, C. W. H.: *Johannes Regis Opera Omnia* (American Institute of Musicology, 1956).

MEIER, BERNHARD: *Jacobi Barbireau Opera Omnia* (American Institute of Musicology, 1954–7).

NOWAK, LEOPOLD: *Denkmäler der Tonkunst in Österreich*, xxxvii, part 2. *Das deutsche Gesellschaftlied in Österreich von 1480–1550* (Vienna, 1930).

OSTHOFF, HELMUTH: 'Das Magnificat bei Josquin Desprez'. *Archiv für Musikwissenschaft*, xvi (1959).

PLAMENAC, DRAGAN: *Johannes Ockeghem, Complete Works*. (i, Leipzig, 1927; ii, New York, 1947).

ROKSETH, YVONNE: *Treize motets et un prélude pour orgue édités par Pierre Attaingnant* (Paris, 1930).

SMIJERS, ALBERT: *Josquin des Prés, Werken.* 44 fascicles (Amsterdam, 1921–56).
—— *Jacobus Obrecht, Opera Omnia, editio altera,* I, 1. *Missae* (Amsterdam, 1953–7).
—— *Treize livres de motets parus chez Pierre Attaingnant en 1534 et 1535.* 3 vols. (Paris, 1934–8).
—— *Van Ockeghem tot Sweelinck.* 6 vols. (Amsterdam, 1939–52).
TIRABASSI, A.: *Pierre de la Rue, Liber Missarum* (Malines, 1942).
WEBERN, ANTON VON: *Denkmäler der Tonkunst in Österreich,* xvi, part i. *Heinrich Isaac, Choralis Constantinus,* Part II (Vienna, 1909).
WOLF, JOHANNES: *Jakob Obrecht, Werken.* 30 vols. (Amsterdam and Leipzig, 1912–21).

(ii) *Books and Articles*

ANTONOWYTSCH, MYROSLAW: 'Renaissance-Tendenzen in den Fortuna-desperata-Messen von Josquin und Obrecht', *Die Musikforschung,* ix (1956).
BESSELER, HEINRICH: 'Von Dufay bis Josquin, ein Literaturbericht'. *Zeitschrift für Musikwissenschaft,* xi (1929).
BOER, C. L. W.: *Het Anthonius-motet van Anthonius Busnoys* (Amsterdam, 1940).
BRIDGMAN, NANIE: 'Un Manuscrit italien du début du XVIᵉ siècle à la Bibliothèque Nationale'. *Annales Musicologiques,* i (1953) and iv (1956).
BUKOFZER, MANFRED F.: 'An unknown Chansonnier of the Fifteenth Century (the Mellon Chansonnier)'. *Musical Quarterly,* xxviii (1942).
BUSH, HELEN E.: 'The Laborde Chansonnier'. *Papers of the American Musicological Society 1940* (1946).
COCLICO, ADRIAN PETIT: *Compendium Musices* (facsimile, ed. Bukofzer) (Documenta musicologica, I, no. 9) (Kassel and Basle, 1954).
CROLL, GERHARD: 'Gaspar von Weerbeke, an Outline of his Life and Works'. *Musica Disciplina,* vi (1952).
GOMBOSI, OTTO JOHANNES: *Jacob Obrecht, eine stilkritische Studie* (Leipzig, 1925).
HABERL, FRANZ XAVER: *Bausteine für Musikgeschichte.* 3 vols. (Leipzig, 1885–8).
KAHMANN, B.: 'Antoine de Fevin'. *Musica Disciplina,* iv–v (1950–1).
KAST, PAUL: *Studien zu den Messen des Jean Mouton* (Frankfurt, 1955).
KRINGS, ALFRED: 'Zu Heinrich Isaacs Missa Virgo Prudentissima'. *Kirchenmusikalisches Jahrbuch,* xxxvi (1952).
LENAERTS, R. B.: *Het Nederlands Polifonies Lied in de 16ᵉ eeuw* (Antwerp, 1933).
—— 'The 16th-century Parody Mass in the Netherlands'. *Musical Quarterly,* xxxvi (1950).
LEVITAN, JOSEPH S.: 'Ockeghem's Clefless Compositions'. *Musical Quarterly,* xxiii (1937).
LILIENCRON, R. VON: 'Die Horazischen Metren in deutschen Kompositionen des 16. Jahrhunderts'. *Vierteljahrsschrift für Musikwissenschaft,* iii (1887).
LINDENBURG, C. W. H.: *Het leven en de werken van Johannes Regis* (Amsterdam, 1938).
LINKER, R. W., and MCPEEK, G. S.: 'The Bergerette Form in the Laborde Chansonnier'. *Journal of the American Musicological Society,* vii (1954).
LOWINSKY, EDWARD E.: *Secret Chromatic Art in the Netherlands Motet* (New York, 1946).
MEIER, BERNHARD: 'The *Musica Reservata* of Adrianus Petit Coclico and its Relationship to Josquin'. *Musica Disciplina,* x (1956).
—— 'Reservata-Probleme: ein Bericht'. *Acta musicologica,* xxx (1958).
MOSER, HANS JOACHIM: *Paul Hofhaimer: ein Lied- und Orgelmeister des deutschen Humanismus* (Stuttgart, 1929).

OSTHOFF, H.: *Die Niederländer und das deutsche Lied, 1400–1640* (Berlin, 1938).

PERLE, GEORGE: 'The Chansons of Antoine Busnois'. *Music Review*, xi (1950).

PLAMENAC, DRAGAN: 'A Postscript to Volume 2 of the Collected Works of Johannes Ockeghem'. *Journal of the American Musicological Society*, iii (1950).

—— 'A Reconstruction of the French Chansonnier in the Biblioteca Colombina, Seville'. *Musical Quarterly*, xxxvii–xxxviii (1951–2).

—— 'The "second" Chansonnier of the Biblioteca Riccardiana'. *Annales musicologiques*, ii (1954) and iv (1956).

RIGSBY, LEE: 'Elzéar Genet, a Renaissance Composer'. *Studies in Music History and Theory* (Florida State University Studies, no. 18, 1955).

ROBYNS, JOZEF: *Pierre de la Rue: een bio-bibliographische Studie* (Brussels, 1954).

RUBSAMEN, WALTER: *Pierre de la Rue als Messenkomponist* (Munich, 1937).

SAAR, JOHANNES DU: *Het leven en de composities van Jacobus Barbireau* (Utrecht, 1946).

SARTORI, CLAUDIO: *Bibliografia delle opere musicali stampate da Ottaviano Petrucci* (Florence, 1948).

—— 'Josquin des Prés, cantore del duomo di Milano'. *Annales musicologiques*, iv (1956).

SMIJERS, ALBERT: 'Josquin des Prez'. *Proceedings of the Musical Association*, liii (1927).

STEPHAN, WOLFGANG: *Die burgundisch-niederländische Motette zur Zeit Ockeghems* (Kassel, 1937).

VAN CREVEL, M.: *Adrianus Petit Coclico* (The Hague, 1940).

VAN DEN BORREN, CHARLES: *Études sur le XVe siècle musical* (Antwerp, 1941).

—— 'À propos de quelques messes de Josquin'. *Kongressbericht der internationalen Gesellschaft für Musikwissenschaft in Utrecht, 1952* (Amsterdam, 1953).

VAN DOORSLAER, GEORGES: 'La Chapelle musicale de Philippe le Beau'. *Revue belge d'archéologie et d'histoire de l'art*, iv (1934).

WAGNER, PETER: *Geschichte der Messe* (Leipzig, 1913).

WOLFF, H. C.: *Die Musik der alten Niederländer* (Leipzig, 1956).

CHAPTER IX

ENGLISH POLYPHONY (c. 1470–1540)

(i) *Sources*

COLLINS, H. B.: *Missa O quam suavis* (London, 1927).

DICKINSON, F. H.: *Missale ad usum Insignis et Praeclarae Ecclesiae Sarum* (Burntisland, 1861–83).

ELLIOTT, KENNETH: *Musica Britannica*, xv. *Music of Scotland, 1500–1700* (London, 1957).

FRERE, W. H.: *Antiphonale Sarisburiense* (London, 1901–25).

—— *Graduale Sarisburiense* (London, 1894).

HARRISON, F. LL.: *Musica Britannica*, x–xii, *The Eton Choirbook* (London, 1955–).

HUGHES, DOM ANSELM: *Robert Fayrfax, Magnificat 'Regali'* (London, 1949).

TREFUSIS, LADY MARY: *Songs, Ballads and Instrumental Pieces composed by King Henry VIII* (Oxford, 1912).

Tudor Church Music. i and iii. *John Taverner*; x. *Hugh Aston, John Marbeck, Osbert Parsley* (Oxford, 1923–9).

(ii) *Books and Articles*

BAILLIE, HUGH: 'Nicholas Ludford'. *Musical Quarterly*, xliv (1958).

BAILLIE, HUGH and OBOUSSIER, PHILIPPE: 'The York Masses'. *Music and Letters,* xxxv (1954).

COLLINS, H. B.: 'John Taverner's Masses'. *Music and Letters,* v (1924).

—— 'John Taverner—Part II'. *Music and Letters,* vi (1925).

—— 'Latin Church Music by Early English Composers'. *Proceedings of the Musical Association,* xxxix (1913), xliii (1917).

FLOOD, W. H. GRATTAN: *Early Tudor Composers* (London, 1925).

HANNAS, RUTH: 'Concerning Deletions in the Polyphonic Mass Credo'. *Journal of the American Musicological Society,* v (1952).

HARRISON, F. LL.: 'An English "Caput"'. *Music and Letters,* xxxiii (1952).

—— *Music in Medieval Britain* (London, 1958).

—— 'The Eton Choirbook'. *Annales musicologiques,* i (1953).

—— 'The Eton College Choirbook'. *Kongressbericht der internationalen Gesellschaft für Musikwissenschaft in Utrecht, 1952* (Amsterdam, 1953).

HUGHES, DOM ANSELM: 'An Introduction to Fayrfax'. *Musica Disciplina,* vi (1952).

STEVENS, JOHN: 'Rounds and Canons from an Early Tudor Song-book'. *Music and Letters,* xxxii (1951).

WARREN, EDWIN B.: 'The Life and Works of Robert Fayrfax'. *Musica Disciplina,* xi (1957).

CHAPTER X

EUROPEAN SONG (1300–1530)

(i) *Sources*

AMELN, K.: *Locheimer Liederbuch und Fundamentum organisandi des Conrad Paumann* (Berlin, 1925).

ANGLÈS, H.: *El Codex musical de Las Huelgas.* 3 vols. (Barcelona, 1931).

—— *La musica en la Corte de los Reyes Católicos,* ii. *Cancionero Musical de Palacio (Siglos XV–XVI)* (Barcelona, 1947 and 1951).

ARNOLD, F. and BELLERMANN, H.: 'Das Locheimer Liederbuch nebst der Ars organisandi von Conrad Paumann'. *Jahrbücher für musikalische Wissenschaft,* ii (1867).

BARBIERI, F.: *Cancionero musical de los siglos XV y XVI* (Madrid, 1890).

BATKA, R.: *Die Lieder Mülichs von Prag* (Prague, 1905).

BÄUMKER, W.: *Das katholische deutsche Kirchenlied.* 4 vols. (Freiburg, 1883–1911).

—— 'Niederländische geistliche Lieder nebst ihren Singweisen aus Handschriften des XV. Jahrhunderts'. *Vierteljahrsschrift für Musikwissenschaft,* iv (1888).

—— *Ein deutsches geistliches Liederbuch mit Melodien aus dem XV. Jahrhundert nach einer Handschrift des Stiftes Hohenfurt* (Leipzig, 1895).

BÖHME, F. M.: *Altdeutsches Liederbuch* (Leipzig, 1877).

DREVES, G. M.: *Analecta Hymnica,* i. *Cantiones Bohemicae* (Leipzig, 1886).

DUYSE, F. VAN: *Het oude nederlandsche Lied.* 3 vols. (Antwerp, 1903–8).

EITNER, ROBERT: *Das deutsche Lied des XV. und XVI. Jahrhunderts.* 2 vols. (Berlin, 1876–80).

—— *Publikation älterer praktischer und theoretischer Musikwerke,* viii. *Heinrich und Hermann Finck, Auswahl von geistlichen und weltlichen Liedern, Hymnen und Motetten* (Leipzig, 1879); xxix. *Georg Forster, Der Zweite Teil der kurtzweiligen guten frischen teutschen Liedlein* (Leipzig, 1905).

EITNER, ROBERT, ERK, LUDWIG and KADE, OTTO: Ibid. iv, *Einleitung, Biographieen, Melodieen und Gedichte zu Johann Ott's Liedersammlung von 1544* (Berlin, 1876).

EITNER, ROBERT and MAIER, J. J.: Ibid., ix. *Erhart Oeglin's Liederbuch, Augsburg 1512* (Leipzig, 1880).

FUNCK, H.: *Das Chorwerk*, xlv. *Deutsche Lieder des 15. Jahrhunderts aus fremden Quellen* (Wolfenbüttel, 1937).

GEERING, A. and ALTWEGG, W.: *Ludwig Senfl, Sämtliche Werke*, ii, iv. *Deutsche Lieder* (Basle, 1938–40).

GÉROLD, THÉODORE: *Le Manuscrit de Bayeux; Texte et musique d'un recueil de chansons du XVe siècle* (Paris, 1921).

GESELLSCHAFT MÜNCHENER BIBLIOPHILEN: *Peter Schöffers Liederbuch, Mainz 1513* (facsimile) (Munich, 1909).

GUDEWILL, K. and HEISKE, W.: *Das Erbe deutscher Musik, Reichsdenkmale XX. Georg Forster, Frische teutsche Liedlein (1539–56)*, i (Wolfenbüttel, 1942).

HASSE, KARL: *Das Chorwerk*, xxix. *Fünfzehn deutsche Lieder aus Peter Schöffers Liederbuch (1513)* (Wolfenbüttel, 1934).

HOLZ, G., SARAN, F. and BERNOULLI, E.: *Die Jenaer Liederhandschrift*. 2 vols. (Leipzig, 1901).

KAMMERER, FRIEDRICH: *Die Musikstücke des Prager Kodex XI E 9* (Augsburg and Brno, 1931).

KOLLER, OSWALD and SCHATZ, JOSEF: *Denkmäler der Tonkunst in Österreich*, ix, part i. *Oswald von Wolkenstein, Geistliche und weltliche Lieder* (Vienna, 1902).

LANG, M. and MÜLLER-BLATTAU, JOSEPH M.: *Zwischen Minnesang und Volkslied. Die Lieder der Berliner Handschrift Germ. Fol. 922* (Berlin, 1941).

LILIENCRON, R. VON: *Deutsches Leben im Volkslied um 1530* (Berlin, 1884).

MAYER, F. ARNOLD and RIETSCH, HERMANN: 'Die Mondsee-Wiener Liederhandschrift und der Mönch von Salzburg'. *Acta Germanica*, iii, part 4 and iv (Berlin, 1894–6).

MINCOFF-MARRIAGE, E.: *Zestiende-eeuwsche Dietsche Volksliedjes. De oorspronkelijke teksten met de in de Souterliedekens van 1540 bewaarde Melodieen* (The Hague, 1939).

MOSER, HANS JOACHIM: *Die erhaltenen Tonwerke des Alt-Strassburger Meisters Thomas Sporer* (Kassel, 1929).

—— *Gassenhawerlin und Reutterliedlein zu Franckenfurt am Meyn, bei Christian Egenolf 1535* (Augsburg, 1927).

—— 'Neun alte Volksliedweisen mit versprengten Texten'. *Jahrbuch für Volksliedforschung*, i (1928).

MOSER, HANS JOACHIM and BERNOULLI, E.: *Das Liederbuch des Arnt von Aich* (Kassel, 1930).

MOSER, HANS JOACHIM and QUELLMALZ, A.: 'Volkslieder des 15. Jahrhunderts aus St. Blasien'. *Volkskundliche Gaben* (Berlin, 1934).

MÜNZER, G.: *Das Singebuch des Adam Puschmann* (Leipzig, 1906).

NOWAK, LEOPOLD: *Denkmäler der Tonkunst in Österreich*, xxxvii, part 2. *Das deutsche Gesellschaftlied in Österreich von 1480–1550* (Vienna, 1930).

OREL, D.: *Kancionál Franusův* (Prague, 1922).

PIERSIG, F.: *Reutterische und Jegerische Liedlein durch M. Caspar Othmayr mit vier Stimmen componirt, Nürnberg 1549*. 2 vols. (Wolfenbüttel, 1928–33).

RANKE, F. and MÜLLER-BLATTAU, JOSEPH M.: *Das Rostocker Liederbuch nach den Fragmenten der Handschrift* (Halle, 1927).

REISS, J.: 'Zwei mehrstimmige Lieder aus dem 15. Jahrhundert'. *Zeitschrift für Musikwissenschaft*, v (1923).

RIETSCH, H.: *Die deutsche Liedweise; mit einem Anhang: Lieder und Bruchstücke aus einer Handschrift des 14/15. Jahrhunderts* (Vienna, 1904).

—— *Denkmäler der Tonkunst in Österreich*, xx, part 2. *Gesänge von Frauenlob, Reinmar von Sweter und Alexander* (Vienna, 1919).

RINGMANN, H. and KLAPPER, J.: *Das Erbe deutscher Musik*, iv, viii. *Das Glogauer Liederbuch*. 2 vols. (Kassel, 1936–7).

RUNGE, P.: *Die Lieder des Hugo von Montfort mit den Melodien des Burk Mangolt* (Leipzig, 1906).

—— *Die Lieder und Melodien der Geissler des Jahres 1349* (Leipzig, 1900).

—— *Die Sangweisen der Colmarer Handschrift und die Liederhandschrift Donaueschingen* (Leipzig, 1896).

SALMEN, WALTER and KOEPP, J.: *Liederbuch der Anna von Köln* (Düsseldorf, 1954).

SCHEURLEER, D.: *Een deuoot ende Profitelyck Boecxken . . . Geestelijck Liedboek met melodieen van 1539* (The Hague, 1889).

SCHMIEDER, W. and WIESSNER, E. *Denkmäler der Tonkunst in Österreich*, xxxvii, part i. *Lieder von Neidhart von Reuental* (Vienna, 1930).

SUÑOL, DOM G. M.: 'Els cants dels romeus (segle XIVe)'. *Analecta Montserratensia*, i (1917).

THOMAS, W.: *Michael Weisse, Gesangbuch der Böhmischen Brüder vom Jahre 1531* (Kassel, 1931).

WIORA, WALTER: *Europäischer Volksgesang* (Cologne, 1952).

WÖBER, F. X.: *Der Minne Regel von Eberhardus Cersne aus Minden 1404; mit einem Anhang von Liedern* (Vienna, 1861).

WOLF, JOHANNES: *Denkmäler der Tonkunst in Österreich*, xiv, 1, and xvi, 1. *Heinrich Isaac, Weltliche Werke* (Vienna, 1907–9).

ZAHN, JOHANNES: *Die Melodien der deutschen evangelischen Kirchenlieder*. 6 vols. (Gütersloh, 1889–93).

(ii) *Books and Articles*

ABERT, ANNA AMALIE: 'Das Nachleben des Minnesangs im liturgischen Spiel'. *Die Musikforschung*, i (1948).

ALBRECHT, H.: *Caspar Othmayr* (Kassel, 1950).

ANGLÈS, H.: 'Das spanische Volkslied'. *Archiv für Musikwissenschaft*, iii (1938).

—— 'Der Rhythmus der monodischen Lyrik des Mittelalters und seine Probleme'. *Bericht über den Musikwissenschaftlichen Kongress in Basel 1949* (Basle, 1951).

—— 'Die spanische Liedkunst im 15. und am Anfang des 16. Jahrhunderts'. *Theodor Kroyer-Festschrift* (Regensburg, 1933).

—— *La música en España* (Barcelona, 1944).

—— *La música en la Corte de Carlos V* (Barcelona, 1944).

—— *La música en la Corte de los Reyes Católicos*. 2 vols. (Madrid and Barcelona, 1941–7).

—— 'La música en la Corte del Rey Don Alfonso V de Aragón, el Magnánimo (años 1413–1420)'. *Spanische Forschungen der Görresgesellschaft*, viii (1940).

BAUMANN, A.: *Das deutsche Lied und seine Bearbeitung in den frühen Orgeltabulaturen* (Kassel, 1934).

BESSELER, HEINRICH: 'Das Lochamer Liederbuch aus Nürnberg'. *Die Musikforschung*, i (1948).

DUYSE, F. VAN: *De Melodie van het Nederlandsche Lied en hare rhythmische Vormen* (The Hague, 1902).

EBERTH, F.: *Die Minne- und Meistergesangweisen der Kolmarer Lieder-Handschrift* (Göttingen, 1932).

FALLERSLEBEN, A. H. HOFFMANN VON: *Geschichte des deutschen Kirchenliedes bis auf Luthers Zeit* (Hanover, 1861).

FEIFALIK, J.: 'Altčechische Leiche, Lieder und Sprüche des 14. und 15. Jahrhunderts'. *Sitzungsberichte der Akademie der Wissenschaft in Wien*, xxxix (1862).

FREDRICH, E.: *Der Ruf, eine Gattung des geistlichen Volksliedes* (Berlin, 1936).

GEERING, A.: 'Die Vokalmusik in der Schweiz zur Zeit der Reformation'. *Schweizerisches Jahrbuch für Musikwissenschaft*, vi (1933).

GEIGER, A.: 'Bausteine zur Geschichte des iberischen Vulgar-Villancico'. *Zeitschrift für Musikwissenschaft*, iv (1921).

GENNRICH, F.: 'Deutsche Rondeaux'. *Beiträge zur Geschichte der deutschen Sprache und Literatur*, lxxii (1950).

—— *Grundriß einer Formenlehre des mittelalterlichen Liedes* (Halle, 1932).

GMELCH, J.: 'Unbekannte Reimgebetkompositionen aus Rebdorfer Handschriften'. *P. Wagner-Festschrift* (Leipzig, 1926).

GURLITT, WILLIBALD: 'Burgundische Chanson- und deutsche Liedkunst des 15. Jahrhunderts'. *Bericht über den Musikwissenschaftlichen Kongress in Basel, 1924* (Leipzig, 1925).

HANDSCHIN, JACQUES: 'Die Schweiz, welche sang'. *Festschrift für Karl Nef* (Zürich and Leipzig, 1933).

—— 'Erfordensia I'. *Acta Musicologica*, vi (1934).

—— 'Peripheres'. *Mitteilungsblatt der Schweizerische musikforschende Gesellschaft*, ii (1935).

HASE, G.: *Der Minneleich Meister Alexanders und seine Stellung in der mittelalterlichen Musik* (Halle, 1921).

HÜBNER, A.: *Die deutschen Geißlerlieder* (Berlin, 1931).

KOTHE, J.: *Die deutschen Osterlieder des Mittelalters* (Breslau, 1939).

KÜHN, A.: *Rhythmik und Melodik Michel Beheims* (Bonn, 1907).

LENAERTS, R. B.: *Het Nederlands polifonies lied in de XVIᵉ eeuw* (Amsterdam, 1933).

LILIENCRON, R. VON: 'Die Chorgesänge des lateinisch-deutschen Schuldramas im XVI. Jahrhunderts'. *Vierteljahrsschrift für Musikwissenschaft*, vi (1890).

—— 'Die Horazischen Metren in deutschen Kompositionen des 16. Jahrhunderts'. *Vierteljahrsschrift für Musikwissenschaft*, iii (1887).

LINDENBURG, C.: 'Notatieproblemen van het Gruythuyzer handschrift'. *Tijdschrift voor Muziekwetenschap*, xvii (1948).

LOEWENSTEIN, O.: *Wort und Ton bei Oswald von Wolkenstein* (Königsberg, 1932).

MEY, K.: *Der Meistergesang in Geschichte und Kunst* (Leipzig, 1901).

MOSER, HANS JOACHIM: 'Das deutsche monodische Kunstlied um 1500'. *P. Wagner-Festschrift* (Leipzig, 1926).

—— 'Hans Ott's erstes Liederbuch'. *Acta Musicologica*, vii (1935).

—— *Paul Hofhaimer: ein Lied- und Orgelmeister des deutschen Humanismus* (Stuttgart, 1929).

MÜLLER-BLATTAU, JOSEPH: 'Über Instrumentalbearbeitungen spätmittelalterlicher Lieder'. *A. Schering-Festschrift* (Berlin, 1937).

—— 'Wach auff, mein hort! Studie zur deutschen Liedkunst des 15. Jahrhunderts.' *G. Adler-Festschrift* (Vienna, 1930).

—— 'Zu Form und Überlieferung der ältesten deutschen geistlichen Lieder'. *Zeitschrift für Musikwissenschaft*, xvii (1935).

NAGEL, B.: *Der deutsche Meistersang; poetische Technik, musikalische Form und Sprachgestaltung der Meistersinger* (Heidelberg, 1952).

NEJEDLÝ, Z.: 'Magister Záviše und seine Schule'. *Sammelbände der internationalen Musikgesellschaft*, vii (1905–6).

—— *Dějiny husitského zpěvu za válek husitských* (Prague, 1913).

NOWAK, LEOPOLD: 'Das deutsche Gesellschaftslied in Österreich von 1480 bis 1550'. *Studien zur Musikwissenschaft*, xvii (1930).

OREL, D.: *Hudební prvky svatováclavské* (Prague, 1937).

OSTHOFF, H.: *Die Niederländer und das deutsche Lied* (Berlin, 1938).

PEDRELL, FELIPE: 'Folk-lore musical Castillan du XVIᵉ siècle'. *Sammelbände der internationalen Musikgesellschaft*, i (1899–1900).

PFLEGER, M. C.: *Untersuchungen am deutschen geistlichen Lied des 13.–16. Jahrhunderts* (Berlin, 1937).

POPE, ISABEL: 'Musical and Metrical Form of the Villancico'. *Annales musicologiques*, ii (1954).

REINHARDT, C.: *Die Heidelberger Liedmeister des 16. Jahrhunderts* (Kassel, 1939).

ROSENBERG, H.: *Untersuchungen über die deutsche Liedweise im 15. Jahrhundert* (Wolfenbüttel, 1931).

SALMEN, WALTER: 'Das Liederbuch der Anna von Köln und seine Beziehungen zu den Niederlanden'. *Kongressbericht der internationalen Gesellschaft für Musikwissenschaft in Utrecht, 1952* (Amsterdam, 1953).

—— *Das Lochamer Liederbuch* (Leipzig, 1951).

—— 'Die altniederländischen Handschriften Berlin 8° 190 und Wien 7970 im Lichte vergleichender Melodienforschung'. *Bericht über den Musikwissenschaftlichen Kongress der deutschen Musikgesellschaft in Bamberg, 1953*.

—— *Die Schichtung der mittelalterlichen Musikkultur in der ostdeutschen Grenzlage* (Kassel, 1954).

—— 'Vermeintliches und wirkliches Volkslied im späten Mittelalter'. *Bericht über den Musikwissenschaftlichen Kongress der Gesellschaft für Musikforschung in Lüneburg, 1950*.

—— 'Werdegang und Lebensfülle des Oswald von Wolkenstein'. *Musica Disciplina*, vii (1953).

SCHMITZ, A.: 'Ein schlesische Cantional aus dem 15. Jahrhundert'. *Archiv für Musikforschung*, i (1936).

SPANKE, H.: 'Das Mosburger Graduale'. *Zeitschrift für romanische Philologie*, li (1930).

SZABOLCSI, B.: 'Die metrische Odensammlung des Johannes Honterus'. *Zeitschrift für Musikwissenschaft*, xiii (1931).

TAYLOR, A.: *A Bibliography of Meistergesang* (Bloomington, 1936).

TREND, J. B.: *The Music of Spanish History to 1600* (London, 1926).

URSPRUNG, OTTO: 'Spanisch-Katalanische Liedkunst des 14. Jahrhunderts'. *Zeitschrift für Musikwissenschaft*, iv (1921–2).

—— 'Vier Studien zur Geschichte des deutschen Lieds'. *Archiv für Musikwissenschaft*, iv–vi (1922–4).

WIORA, WALTER: 'Alpenländische Liedweisen der Frühzeit und des Mittelalters im Lichte vergleichender Forschung'. *Angebind für J. Meier* (Lahr, 1949).

—— 'Der mittelalterliche Liedkanon'. *Bericht über den Musikwissenschaftlichen Kongress der Gesellschaft für Musikforschung in Lüneburg, 1950*.

—— *Die deutsche Volksliedweise und der Osten* (Wolfenbüttel, 1940).

WIORA, WALTER and SALMEN, WALTER: 'Deutsche Tanzmusik des Mittelalters'. *Zeitschrift für Volkskunde*, 1 (1953).

WOLF, JOHANNES: 'Altflämische Lieder des XIV.–XV. Jahrhunderts und ihre rhythmische Lesung'. *Bericht über den Musikwissenschaftlichen Kongress in Basel, 1924* (Leipzig, 1925).

—— 'Deutsche Lieder des 15. Jahrhunderts'. *A. Schering-Festschrift* (Berlin, 1937).

CHAPTER XI

SECULAR VOCAL MUSIC IN ITALY (c. 1400–1530)

(i) *Sources*

BARTOLI, B.: *Composizioni vocali polifoniche* (Milan, 1917).

CESARI, G., MONTEROSSO, R., and DISERTORI, B.: *Le frottole nell' edizione principe di Ottaviano Petrucci*, i (Libri I, II, e III) (Cremona, 1954).

EINSTEIN, ALFRED: *Canzoni Sonetti Strambotti e Frottole, Libro Tertio (Andrea Antico, 1517)* (Northampton, Mass., 1941).

JEPPESEN, KNUD: *Die mehrstimmige italienische Laude um 1500* (Leipzig, 1935).

MASSON, PAUL-MARIE: *Chants de carnaval florentins* (Paris, 1913).

SCHWARTZ, R.: *Ottaviano Petrucci: Frottole I und IV* (Leipzig, 1935).

TORCHI, LUIGI: *L'arte musicale in Italia*, i (Milan, 1897).

WESTPHAL, K.: *Das Chorwerk*, xliii. *Karnevalslieder der Renaissance* (Wolfen-büttel, 1936).

(ii) *Books and Articles*

BUKOFZER, MANFRED F.: 'Three Unknown Italian Chansons of the Fifteenth Century'. *Collectanea Historiae Musicae*, ii (Florence, 1956).

CESARI, GAETANO: *Die Entstehung des Madrigals im 16. Jahrhundert* (Cremona, 1908). Reprinted and revised as ' Le origine del madrigale cinquecentesco'. *Rivista musicale italiana*, xix (1912).

CORTE, ANDREA DELLA: *Le relazioni storiche della poesia e della musica italiana* (Turin, 1937).

EINSTEIN, ALFRED: 'Das elfte Buch der Frottole'. *Zeitschrift für Musikwissenschaft*, x (1928).

—— 'Eine unbekannte Ausgabe eines Frottolen-Druckes'. *Acta Musicologica*, viii (1936).

—— 'Italian Madrigal Verse'. *Proceedings of the Musical Association*, lxiii (1937).

—— *The Italian Madrigal*. 3 vols. (Princeton, 1949).

FERAND, ERNST: 'Two unknown Frottole'. *Musical Quarterly*, xxvii (1941).

GERSON-KIWI, EDITH: *Studien zur Geschichte des italienischen Liedmadrigals im 16. Jahrhundert* (Würzburg, 1938).

GHISI, FEDERICO: *I canti carnascialeschi nelle fonti musicali del XV e XVI secoli* (Florence, 1937).

—— 'Strambotti e Laude nel travestimento spirituale della poesia musicale del Quattrocento'. *Collectanea Historiae Musicae*, i (Florence, 1953).

HELM, EVERETT: 'Heralds of the Italian Madrigal'. *Musical Quarterly*, xxvii (1941).

JEPPESEN, KNUD: 'Die neuentdeckten Bücher der Lauden des Ottaviano dei Petrucci und andere musikalische Seltenheiten der Biblioteca Colombina zu Sevilla'. *Zeitschrift für Musikwissenschaft*, xii (1929).

—— 'Über einige unbekannte Frottolenhandschriften'. *Acta Musicologica*, xi (1939).

PIRROTTA, N. and LI GOTTI, E.: 'Il codice di Lucca'. *Musica Disciplina*, iii (1949).

RUBSAMEN, WALTER: *Literary Sources of Secular Music in Italy* (Berkeley, 1943).

SCHWARTZ, R.: 'Die Frottole im 15. Jahrhundert'. *Vierteljahrsschrift für Musikwissenschaft*, ii (1886).

—— 'Zum Formproblem der Frottole Petruccis'. *Theodor Kroyer-Festschrift* (Regensburg, 1933).

CHAPTER XII

INSTRUMENTAL MUSIC OF THE MIDDLE AGES

(i) *Sources*

AMELN, K.: *Locheimer Liederbuch und Fundamentum organisandi des Conrad Paumann* (facsimile) (Berlin, 1925).

APEL, WILLI: *Musik aus früher Zeit für Klavier* (Mainz, 1934).

ARNOLD, F. and BELLERMANN, H.: 'Das Locheimer Liederbuch nebst der Ars organisandi von Conrad Paumann'. *Jahrbücher für musikalische Wissenschaft*, ii (1867).

AUBRY, PIERRE: *Cent motets du XIIIᵉ siècle* (Paris, 1907).

—— *Estampies et danses royales* (Paris, 1907).

BERNOULLI, EDUARD: *Chansons und Tänze. Pariser Tabulaturdrucke für Tasteninstrumente* (Munich, 1914).

GIESBERT, F. J.: *Pierre Attaingnant, Pariser Tanzbuch aus dem Jahre 1530* (Mainz, 1950).

GLYN, MARGARET: *Early English Organ Music* (London, 1939).

HARMS, GOTTLIEB: *Arnold Schlick, Tabulaturen etlicher Lobgesang und Lidlein* (Klecken, 1924; 2nd edition, Hamburg, 1957).

MOSER, HANS JOACHIM: *Frühmeister der deutschen Orgelkunst* (Leipzig, 1930).

MOST, GERHARD: 'Die Orgeltabulatur des Adam Ileborgh aus Stendal'. *Altmärkisches Museum: Jahresgabe 1954* (facsimile) (Stendal, *c.* 1955).

PFATTEICHER, CARL FRIEDRICH: *John Redford* (Kassel, 1934).

ROKSETH, YVONNE: *Deux Livres d'Orgue parus chez Pierre Attaingnant en 1531* (Paris, 1925).

—— *Treize motets et un prélude pour orgue* (Paris, 1930).

STEVENS, DENIS: *Altenglische Orgelmusik* (Kassel, 1954).

—— *Musica Britannica*, i. *The Mulliner Book* (London, 1951).

WALLNER, B. A.: *Das Buxheimer Orgelbuch* (facsimile) (Kassel, 1955).

WOOLDRIDGE, H. E.: *Early English Harmony*, vol. i (London, 1897).

(ii) *Books and Articles*

APEL, WILLI: 'Die Tabulatur des Adam Ileborgh'. *Zeitschrift für Musikwissenschaft*, xvi (1934).

—— 'Early German Keyboard Music'. *Musical Quarterly*, xxiii (1937).

—— 'The Early Development of the Organ Ricercar'. *Musica Disciplina*, iii (1949).

BLUME, FRIEDRICH: *Studien zur Vorgeschichte der Orchestersuite im 15. und 16. Jahrhundert* (Leipzig, 1925).

BOWLES, E. A.: 'The Role of Musical Instruments in Medieval Sacred Drama'. *Musical Quarterly*, xlv (1959).

—— 'Were Musical Instruments used in the Liturgical Service during the Middle Ages?' *Galpin Society Journal*, x (1956).

DART, THURSTON: 'A New Source of Early English Organ Music'. *Music and Letters*, xxxv (1954).

DISERTORI, BENVENUTO: 'L'unica composizione sicuramente strumentale nei codici tridentini'. *Collectanea historiae musicae*, ii (Florence, 1956).

DONINGTON, ROBERT and DART, THURSTON: 'The Origin of the English In Nomine'. *Music and Letters*, xxx (1949).

EITNER, ROBERT: 'A. Schlick, Spiegel der Orgelmacher und Organisten'. *Monatshefte für Musikgeschichte*, i (1869).

—— 'Das Buxheimer Orgelbuch'. *Monatshefte für Musikgeschichte*, xix–xx (1887–8).

EITNER, ROBERT: 'Tänze des 15. bis 17. Jahrhunderts'. *Monatshefte für Musikgeschichte*, vii (1875).

FARMER, H. G.: 'Crusading Martial Music'. *Music and Letters*, xxx (1949).

FELDMANN, F.: 'Ein Tabulaturfragment des Breslauer Dominikanerklosters aus der Zeit Paumanns'. *Zeitschrift für Musikwissenschaft*, xv (1933).

—— 'Mittelalterliche Musik und Musikpflege in Schlesien'. *Deutsches Archiv für Landes- und Volksforschung*, ii (1937).

FLADE, E.: *Arnold Schlick, Spiegel der Orgelmacher und Organisten* (Mainz, 1932).

FROTSCHER, GOTTHOLD: *Geschichte des Orgelspiels und der Orgelkomposition*, i (Berlin, 1935).

FUNCK, H.: 'Eine Chanson von Binchois im Buxheimer Orgel- und Locheimer Liederbuch'. *Acta Musicologica*, v (1933).

HANDSCHIN, JACQUES: 'Über Estampie und Sequenz'. *Zeitschrift für Musikwissenschaft*, xii–xiii (1929–30).

JACQUOT, JEAN (ed.): *La Musique instrumentale de la Renaissance* (Paris, 1955).

JEPPESEN, KNUD: *Die italienische Orgelmusik am Anfang des Cinquecento* (Copenhagen, 1943).

KENDALL, R.: 'Notes on Arnold Schlick'. *Acta Musicologica*, xi (1939).

KINKELDEY, OTTO: *Orgel und Klavier in der Musik des 16. Jahrhunderts* (Leipzig, 1910).

KÖRTE, O.: *Laute und Lautenmusik bis zur Mitte des 16. Jahrhunderts* (Leipzig, 1901).

LÖWENFELD, HANS: *Leonhard Kleber und sein Orgeltabulaturbuch* (Berlin, 1897).

LOWINSKY, E. E.: 'English Organ Music of the Renaissance'. *Musical Quarterly*, xxxix (1953).

MERIAN, WILHELM: *Der Tanz in den deutschen Tabulaturbüchern* (Leipzig, 1927).

—— *Die Tabulaturen des Organisten Hans Kotter* (Leipzig, 1916).

—— 'Drei Handschriften aus der Frühzeit des Klavierspiels'. *Archiv für Musikwissenschaft*, ii (1920).

MILLER, HUGH M.: '"Fulgens Praeclara": A Unique Keyboard Setting of a Plainsong Sequence'. *Journal of the American Musicological Society*, ii (1949).

MOSER, HANS JOACHIM: 'Das Streichinstrumentenspiel in Mittelalter', in A. Moser: *Geschichte des Violinspiels* (Berlin, 1923).

—— 'Eine Trienter Orgeltabulatur aus Hofhaimers Zeit'. *Guido Adler-Festschrift* (Vienna, 1930).

—— 'Hofhaimeriana'. *Zeitschrift für Musikwissenschaft*, xv (1932).

—— *Paul Hofhaimer, ein Lied- und Orgelmeister des deutschen Humanismus* (Berlin, 1929).

NEF, W. R.: 'Der St. Galler Organist Fridolin Sicher und seine Orgeltabulatur'. *Schweizerisches Jahrbuch für Musikwissenschaft*, vii (1938).

PÄSLER, C.: 'Fundamentbuch von Hans von Constanz'. *Vierteljahrsschrift für Musikwissenschaft*, v (1889).

PIRROTTA, NINO: 'Note su un codice di antiche musiche per tastiera' [Faenza 117]. *Rivista musicale italiana*, lvi (1954).

PLAMENAC, DRAGAN: 'Keyboard Music of the 14th Century in Codex Faenza 117'. *Journal of the American Musicological Society*, iv (1951).

—— 'New Light on Codex Faenza 117'. *Kongreßbericht Utrecht 1952* (Amsterdam, 1953).

REESE, GUSTAVE: 'The Origin of the English "In Nomine"'. *Journal of the American Musicological Society*, ii (1949).

RIEMANN, HUGO: 'Der Mensural-Kodex des Magisters Nikolaus Apel'. *Kirchenmusikalisches Jahrbuch*, xii (1897).

RITTER, A. G.: *Zur Geschichte des Orgelspiels* (Leipzig, 1884).

ROKSETH, YVONNE: *La musique d'orgue au XVe siècle et au début du XVIe* (Paris, 1930).

SACHS, CURT: 'Die Besetzung dreistimmiger Werke um das Jahr 1500'. *Zeitschrift für Musikwissenschaft*, xi (1929).

SARTORI, CLAUDIO: 'A Little-known Petrucci Publication'. *Musical Quarterly*, xxxiv (1948).

SCHERING, ARNOLD: *Aufführungspraxis alter Musik* (Leipzig, 1931).

—— *Studien zur Musikgeschichte der Frührenaissance* (Leipzig, 1914).

SCHNOOR, H.: 'Das Buxheimer Orgelbuch'. *Zeitschrift für Musikwissenschaft*, iv (1921).

SCHRADE, LEO: *Die ältesten Denkmäler der Orgelmusik* (Leipzig, 1931).

—— 'The Organ in the Mass of the 15th Century'. *Musical Quarterly*, xxviii (1942).

STEVENS, DENIS: 'A Unique Tudor Organ Mass'. *Musica Disciplina*, vi (1952).

—— 'Further Light on *Fulgens praeclara*'. *Journal of the American Musicological Society*, ix (1956).

—— 'Pre-Reformation Organ Music in England'. *Proceedings of the Royal Musical Association*, lxxviii (1952).

—— *The Mulliner Book: A Commentary* (London, 1952).

—— 'Thomas Preston's Organ Mass'. *Music and Letters*, xxxix (1958).

VAN DEN BORREN, CHARLES: 'La Musique pittoresque dans le manuscrit 222 C 22 de la Bibliothèque de Strasbourg (XVe siècle)'. *Bericht über den musikwissenschaftlichen Kongress in Basel, 1924* (Leipzig, 1925).

—— *The Sources of Keyboard Music in England* (London, 1913).

WERRA, E. VON: 'Johann Buchner'. *Kirchenmusikalisches Jahrbuch*, x (1895).

WOLF, JOHANNES: 'Die Tänze des Mittelalters'. *Archiv für Musikwissenschaft*, i (1918).

—— *Denkmäler der Tonkunst in Österreich*, xiv, 1, and xvi, 1. *Heinrich Isaac, Weltliche Werke* (Vienna, 1907–9).

—— 'Zur Geschichte der Orgelmusik im vierzehnten Jahrhundert'. *Kirchenmusikalisches Jahrbuch*, xiv (1899).

CHAPTER XIII

MUSICAL INSTRUMENTS

(i) *Sources*

EITNER, ROBERT: *Publikation älterer praktischer und theoretischer Musikwerke*, xx. *Martin Agricola, Musica instrumentalis deudsch, erste und vierte Ausgabe, Wittenberg 1528 und 1545* (Leipzig, 1896).

FLADE, E.: *Arnold Schlick, Spiegel der Orgelmacher und Organisten* (Mainz, 1932).

LE CERF, G. and LEBANDE, E.-R.: *Les Traités d'Henri-Arnault de Zwolle et de divers anonymes* (Paris, 1932).

SCHRADE, LEO: *Sebastian Virdung, Musica getutscht (Basel, 1511)* (Kassel, 1931).

(ii) *Books and Articles*

ANDERSSON, OTTO: *The Bowed Harp* (London, 1930).

ANGLÈS, HIGINI: *La Música a Catalunya fins al segle XIII* (Barcelona, 1935).

APEL, WILLI: 'Early History of the Organ'. *Speculum*, xxiii (1948).

BAINES, ANTHONY: *Woodwind Instruments and their History* (London, 1957).

BESSARABOFF, NICHOLAS: *Ancient European Musical Instruments* (Boston, 1941).

BESSELER, HEINRICH: 'Die Entstehung der Posaune'. *Acta Musicologica*, xxii (1950).

BOWLES, E. A.: 'Haut and Bas: the Grouping of Musical Instruments during the Middle Ages'. *Musica Disciplina*, viii (1954).

BUCHNER, ALEXANDER: *Musical Instruments through the Ages* (trs. Iris Urwin) (Prague, n.d.).

BUHLE, EDWARD: *Die musikalischen Instrumente in den Miniaturen des frühen Mittelalters* (Leipzig, 1903).

COSACCHI, STEPHAN: 'Musikinstrumente im mittelalterlichen Totentanz'. *Die Musikforschung*, viii (1955).

DEGERING, H.: *Die Orgel, ihre Erfindung und ihre Geschichte bis zur Karolingerzeit* (Münster, 1905).

DUFOURCQ, NORBERT: *Esquisse d'une histoire de l'orgue en France du XIIIe au XVIIIe siècle* (Paris, 1935).

FARMER, HENRY GEORGE: *Studies in Oriental Musical Instruments* (London, 1931).

GALPIN, FRANCIS W.: *A Textbook of European Musical Instruments* (London, 1937).

—— *Old English Instruments of Music* (London, 1910).

Galpin Society Journal, i– (1948–).

GEIRINGER, KARL: *Musical Instruments* (London, 1943).

GÉROLD, THÉODORE: 'Les instruments de musique au moyen âge', *Revue des Cours et Conférences*, xxix (1928). *Les Pères de l'Église et la musique* (Paris, 1931).

HAYES, GERALD: *The King's Music* (London, 1937).

HICKMANN, HANS: *Das Portativ* (Kassel, 1936).

JAMES, PHILIP: *Early Keyboard Instruments* (London, 1930).

LA LAURENCIE, LIONEL DE: *Les Luthistes* (Paris, 1928).

LEFÈVRE, JEAN: *La Vielle* (Paris, 1861).

LEICHTENTRITT, HUGO: 'Was lehren uns die Bilderwerke des 14.–17. Jahrhunderts über die Instrumentalmusik ihrer Zeit?'. *Sammelbände der internationalen Musikgesellschaft*, vii (1906).

RUSSELL, RAYMOND: *The Harpsichord and Clavichord: an Introductory Study* (London, 1959).

SACHS, CURT: 'Die Streichbogenfrage'. *Archiv für Musikwissenschaft*, i (1918–19).

—— *Handbuch der Musikinstrumentenkunde* (Leipzig, 1920).

—— *History of Musical Instruments* (London, 1940).

—— *Real-Lexikon der Musikinstrumente* (Berlin, 1913).

SCHLESINGER, KATHLEEN: *The Instruments of the Modern Orchestra and Early Records of the Precursors of the Violin Family.* 2 vols. (London, 1910).

SCHNEIDER, MARIUS: *Die Ars nova des XIV. Jahrhunderts in Frankreich und Italien* (Berlin, 1930).

SCHNEIDER, MAX F.: *Alte Musik in der bildenden Kunst Basels* (Basle, 1941).

LIST OF CONTENTS OF
THE HISTORY OF MUSIC IN SOUND
VOLUME III

The History of Music in Sound is a series of volumes of gramophone records, with explanatory booklets, designed as a companion series to the *New Oxford History of Music*. Each volume covers the same ground as the corresponding volume in the *New Oxford History of Music*, and is designed as far as possible to illustrate the music discussed therein. The records are issued in England by The Gramophone Company (H.M.V.) and in the United States by R. C. A. Victor, and the booklets are published by the Oxford University Press. The editor of Volume III of *The History of Music in Sound* is Dom Anselm Hughes.

The History of Music in Sound is available on LP and 78 r.p.m. records, and side numbers for both versions are given below.

CHANSONS OF THE 15TH CENTURY

	LP		78		
Side III	*Band* 1	*Side* 11	(*a*)	*O rosa bella* (Johannes Ciconia)
	Band 2		(*b*)	*O rosa bella* (attrib. Dunstable)

GUILLAUME DUFAY (d. 1474)

| | *Band* 3 | *Side* 12 | (*a*) | *Ave Regina coelorum* |

BURGUNDIAN CHANSONS: 15TH CENTURY

| | *Band* 4 | *Side* 13 | (*a*) | *Filles à marier* (Binchois) |
| | *Band* 5 | | (*b*) | *Pour l'amour de ma douce amye* (Dufay) |

JOHANNES OCKEGHEM (d. 1495)

| | *Band* 6 | *Side* 14 | | *Kyrie* from Mass: *Fors seulement* |

NETHERLAND CHURCH MUSIC: *c.* 1500

| | *Band* 7 | *Sides* 15 & 16 | (*a*) | *Si oblitus fuero* (Obrecht) |
| | *Band* 8 | *Side* 16 | (*b*) | *Introit* from Requiem Mass (Pierre de la Rue) |

JOSQUIN DES PREZ (d. 1521)

Side IV	*Band* 1	*Side* 17	(*a*)	*El grillo*
	Band 2		(*b*)	*Je ne me puis tenir d'aimer*
	Band 3	*Side* 18	(*a*)	*Sanctus* (opening) from Mass: *L'homme armé* (*super voces musicales*)
	Band 4		(*b*)	*Tribulatio et angustia*

ENGLISH CHURCH MUSIC: 1475–1500

| | *Band* 5 | *Side* 19 | (*a*) | *Timuerunt valde, dicentes: Vere Filius Dei* from Passion Music (Richard Davy) |
| | *Band* 6 | | (*b*) | *Gloria* from Mass: *Custodi nos* (anon.) |

ROBERT FAYRFAX (d. 1521)

| | *Band* 7 | *Side* 20 | | Verse II and *Gloria* from *Magnificat: Regali* |

JOHN TAVERNER (d. 1545)

| *Side* V | *Band* 1 | *Side* 21 | | *Benedictus* from Mass: *Gloria tibi Trinitas* |

ORGAN MUSIC: EARLY 16TH CENTURY

	Band 2	*Side* 22	(*a*)	*Mit ganczem Willen* (Paumann)
	Band 3		(*b*)	*Es gieng ein Mann* (Buchner)
	Band 4		(*c*)	*O Lux, on the faburden* (Redford)

INSTRUMENTAL ENSEMBLE: 15TH–16TH CENTURIES

	Band 5	*Side* 23	(*a*)	*Chanson* (Isaac)
	Band 6		(*b*)	*La la hö hö* (Isaac)
	Band 7		(*c*)	*Innsbruck, ich muss dich lassen* (Isaac)
	Band 8	*Side* 24	(*a*)	*Alta* (de la Torre)
	Band 9		(*b*)	*Nous sommes de l'ordre de Saint Babouin* (Compère)
	Band 10		(*c*)	*Der Bauern Schwanz* (Rubinus)

INDEX

Abert, H., 502 n[1].
Abingdon, Henry, 426.
'Abyde Y hope', 123.
Acart de Hesdin, Jehan, 14, 15; see also *Prise amoureuse*.
'A che son hormai', Demophon, 395 n[1].
'Ach hülff mich layd', Adam of Fulda, 285.
'Ach Jupiter', Adam of Fulda, 285.
Achleitner, 288 n[6].
Adam (of MS. Bodl. Can. Misc. 213), 234.
Adam de la Hale, 2, 12, 32, 84.
Adam of Fulda, 284, *285*, 435.
Adami, Andrea, 262.
'A definement / Adae finit perpete / Adae finit misere', 86.
Adenès li Roi, 480 n[2]; see also *Romauns de Cléomadès*.
'Ad honorem / Coelorum', Grenon, 147.
'Adieu m'amour', 230.
'Adieu mes amours', Cornysh, 347–8; see also Mass-settings.
Adler, Guido, 441 n[3].
'Adoretur / In ultimo / Pacem', 164 n[4].
Adrian VI, Pope, 445.
'Agincourt Carol', 122, 123; see also 'Worship of vertu'.
'Agmina', 84.
Agnus Dei, see Mass-sections.
Agricola, Alexander, 270, *277–9*, 284, 286, 291, 300, 438.
Agricola, Martin, 494.
'Agwillare habeth', 130.
Ailly, Pierre de, Bp. of Cambrai, 216.
'Ain freulich wesen', Isaac, 437.
Alanus, Johannes (= John Aleyn), 99, 100, 146, 167.
'Alas, alas is my chief song', 130, 131.
'Alas departyng', 131.
'Albane missae / Albane doctor', Ciconia, 156 n[3].
'Albanus roseo', Dunstable, 328 n[6].
'Albanus', Missa, see Mass-settings.
Albert III, D. of Bavaria, 428.
Alberti, Antonio degli, 42.
Alberti, Leon Battista, 381.
'Aleć nade mną Wenus', 300.
Alexander, Master, 360.
Aleyn, John, see Alanus, J.
'Alfonsina, La', Ghiselin, 292.
Alfonso X (= 'the Learned'), K. of Leon and Castile, 415.
Alfonso I, D. of Ferrara, 292.
'Alleluia', Isaac, 282.

'Alleluia ad Rorate', Sebastjan z Felsztyna, 301.
'Alleluia Nativitas' [or 'Solemnitas'], see 'Hoquetus David'.
'Alleluia, Veni electa', Taverner, 339, 341.
'Alles regrets', see Mass-settings.
Allwood, Richard, 459.
'Alma redemptoris', Dunstable, 188; Forest, 194; Ockeghem, 258–9; *Credo* (Anglicanus), 204; see also Mass-settings.
'A l'ombre d'un buissonnet', Isaac, 280; see also Mass-settings.
'Alone I lyve', 132.
'Alpha vibrans / Coetus', 146.
Altdeutsches Liederbuch, Böhme, 353.
'Altissimi potentia', Cornysh, 318 n[2].
Ambros, August W., 247 n[1], 256 n[1], 266, 286 n[2], 288 n[5], 289 n[3], 297 n[1], 299 n[1], 467.
Ameln, Konrad, 353 n[2], 372 n[3], 428 n[1].
Amerbach, Boniface, 435, 439.
'Amis tout dous vis', Pierre des Molins, 29.
'Amor che sospirar', Agricola, 279.
'Amor mi far cantar', 37, 38.
'Am Sabath früh Marien drei', Herman, 358.
'Amours par qui', 59.
Andersson, Otto, 474 n[1].
Andrea dei Servi (? = A. Stefani), 33, 34, 46, 70, 80–81.
Andreas, 81.
Andrews, Hilda, 105 n[3].
Andrieu, Franciscus (= Magister Franciscus), 27, 140, 141 n[1].
Angela of Foligno, Blessed, 412, 413.
Angelico, Fra (= Guido di Pietri), 381.
'Angelorum psallat', 141.
'Angelus ad virginem', 115–17.
Anglès, Higini, 32, 83 n[6], 84 nn[1, 2], 130 n[4], 349 n[2], 352 n[1], 354 n[2], 377 nn[1–3], 379, 413 n[5].
'Anglia tibi turbidas', 124.
'Anglicanus' (of Trent Codex), see Souleby, H.
'Anima mea liquefacta est', Forest, 194–5; Power, 175–6.
'Anna mater matris', Plummer, 198–201.
Anne de Lusignan, 144.
Anne of Brittany, Q. of France (consort of Louis XII), 298.
'Anni novi novitas', 369.
Anonymous of Breslau, 408.